SHAKESPEARE
and the Culture of Christianity
in Early Modern England

STUDIES IN RELIGION AND LITERATURE
John L. Mahoney, Series Editor

1. John L. Mahoney, ed. *Seeing into the Life of Things: Essays on Religion and Literature.*
2. David Leigh, S.J. *Circuitous Journeys: Modern Spiritual Autobiographies.*
3. J. Robert Barth, S.J. *The Symbolic Imagination: Coleridge and the Romantic Tradition.*
4. Beth Hawkins. *Reluctant Theologians: Franz Kafka, Paul Celan, Edmond Jabes.*
5. J. Robert Barth, S.J., ed. *The Fountain Light: Studies in Romanticism and Religion. Essays in Honor of John L. Mahoney.*

SHAKESPEARE
and the Culture of Christianity in Early Modern England

edited by
DENNIS TAYLOR
and
DAVID BEAUREGARD

Fordham University Press
New York
2003

Studies in Religion and Literature, No. 6
ISSN 1096–6692

Library of Congress Cataloging-in-Publication Data

Shakespeare and the culture of Christianity in early modern England/edited by Dennis Taylor and David Beauregard.—1st ed.
p. cm.—(Studies in religion and literature, ISSN 1096-6692; no. 6)
ISBN 0-8232-2283-7 (alk. paper)—ISBN 0-8232-2284-5 (pbk. : alk. paper)
1. Shakespeare, William, 1564–1616—Religion. 2. Christianity and literature—England—History—16th century. 3. Christianity and literature—England—History—17th century. 4. Christian drama, English—History and criticism. 5. Catholics—England—History—16th century. 6. Catholics—England—History—17th century. 7. Drama—Religious aspects—Christianity. 8. England—Church history—16th century. 9. England—Church history—17th century. I. Taylor, Dennis, 1940– II. Beauregard, David N., 1937– III. Studies in religion and literature (Fordham University Press); no. 6.
PR3011.S34 2003
822.3'3—dc21   2003012072

Printed in the United States of America
07 06 05 04 03   5 4 3 2 1
First edition

To
Peter Milward, S.J.

CONTENTS

Introduction: Shakespeare and the Reformation   1
    Dennis Taylor

1. *The Comedy of Errors* and *The Calumny of Apelles*:
    An Exercise in Source Study   26
    Richard Dutton

2. "Obsequious Laments": Mourning and Communal
    Memory in Shakespeare's *Richard III*   44
    Katharine Goodland

3. Oxford University and *Love's Labour's Lost*   80
    Clare Asquith

4. Shakespeare's Religious Background Revisited:
    Richard II in a New Context   103
    Jean-Christophe Mayer

5. Sacral and Sacramental Kingship in the
    Lancastrian Tetralogy   121
    Timothy Rosendale

6. Mocking Oldcastle: Notes Toward Exploring a Possible
    Catholic Presence in Shakespeare's Henriad   141
    Gary D. Hamilton

7. Shakespeare's Fairy Dance with Religio-Political
    Controversy in *The Merry Wives of Windsor*   159
    Regina M. Buccola

8. Catholic and Protestant, Jesuit and Jew: Historical
    Religion in *The Merchant of Venice*   180
    John Klause

9. This Side of Purgatory: Ghostly Fathers and the Recusant
Legacy in *Hamlet*   222
John Freeman

10. Wittenberg and Melancholic Allegory: The Reformation
and Its Discontents in *Hamlet*   260
Jennifer Rust

11. The Accent and Gait of Christians: Hamlet's Puritan Style   285
R. Chris Hassel Jr.

12. Shakespeare on Monastic Life: Nuns and Friars in
Measure for Measure   311
David Beauregard

13. Helena and the Reformation Problem of Merit in *All's
Well That Ends Well*   336
Maurice Hunt

14. Paris Is Worth a Mass: *All's Well That Ends Well* and
the Wars of Religion   369
Lisa Hopkins

15. Blasphemous Preacher: Iago and the Reformation   382
Richard Mallette

16. Love and Lies: Marital Truth-Telling, Catholic Casuistry,
and *Othello*   415
Paula McQuade

Notes on Contributors   439

Index   443

Introduction: Shakespeare and the Reformation

by Dennis Taylor

THE PLAYS discussed in this volume are bounded by two defining moments in Shakespeare's lifetime: the execution of Mary Queen of Scots, and the Gunpowder Plot. Both were death knells for English Catholicism, an entity that took a long time dying, and indeed was never entirely extinguished. The premise of this collection of essays is that the Reformation was the defining event of Shakespeare's background. Such a contention might seem banal, except that it has traditionally been ignored, and is only recently coming into view. The implication of such a background for the study of Shakespeare is enormous, and for that reason, perhaps, has long been resisted.

Richard Dutton's essay, "*The Comedy of Errors* and *The Calumny of Apelles:* An Exercise in Source Study," begins with a deceptively modest task: showing Shakespeare's indebtedness to a classical source, Lucian's essay, "On not believing rashly in slander," describing a painting on the theme of slander by Apelles. By the time Dutton's essay is concluded, a whole world of Elizabethan division has been portrayed. *The Comedy of Errors* (dated 1592–94 in Evans and Tobin 1997) puts us in a world of slander creating havoc in human relationships, with brothers, wives, servants at each other's throats. Such characters continually misunderstand and thus calumniate each other. What is the ultimate referent of this world of slander? Dutton suggests that it is Shakespeare's England, whose religious unity has long been riven asunder by the slander heaped by one side on the other. The papal bull slanders Elizabeth, the Elizabethan decrees slander the Catholics. Images of slander, in painting and bookplates, are used to slander each side. The slander has been especially painful for the oppressed Catholic population, which tries to defend its loyalty to the English government and argues that it is consistent with its outlawed religion.

Dutton notes that the play was written about the time of the French religious war from which Henri of Navarre emerged as Henri IV— alluded to in 3.2.122–23: "France . . . arm'd and reverted, making war against her heir." Henri was later notorious for "converting" from Huguenot Protestantism to Catholicism ("Paris is well worth a mass"), a move excoriated by Elizabeth, but reflecting a long tradition of French Academy irenicism.

Does Shakespeare see any way out of the nest of misunderstandings in *The Comedy of Errors* and, correspondingly, out of the deep divide in a religiously riven Elizabethan England? In the play, and in the world alluded to, is there a "truth" that would emerge from calumny over the course of time? (Such truth emergent is the subject of paintings based on Apelles's lost portrait of "Calumny.") Shakespeare's solution takes romantic comedy form: the play moves toward a reconstruction of family unity, which also implies a reconstruction of national unity. "The fact that this process is conducted under the aegis of the Abbess/Mother, so redolent of the Virgin Mary in Ephesus, perhaps points us toward the Catholic faith as the vehicle of redemption." In any event, "the pressures of the play are toward inclusiveness rather than vindictive exclusion." I have here, as below, too quickly summarized a nuanced account.

Dutton's basic assumption is that the religious division of England, specifically the Catholic/Protestant split, provides the ultimate social context for the divisions in Shakespeare's plays, much as, say, the "paranoid 1950s Cold War, with its nights of the living dead" (Dutton's words) motivated Arthur Miller's *The Crucible* (though Dutton does not cite this example). How this background is reflected in Shakespeare is the question of questions. Do plays simply reflect the general atmosphere of the times? A different analogy than Miller might be *Antigone* as performed in occupied France in the early 1940s. (Goodland, in the next essay, cites the analogy of Antigone and Lady Anne in *Richard III*.) *Antigone* was seen by its audience to reflect the tyranny of the times, but the play itself was innocent of this intent, except when made pointed by the director. And so, the Nazi authorities did not take offense. Was Shakespeare similarly innocent of what might be made of his plays? Or are his allusions to his times deliberate, amounting to allegory and topicality? We cannot simply dismiss the possibility of allegory out of distaste for the religious topic, as was done by mainstream Shakespearean criticism in earlier sectarian days. Happily, cultural studies has taken the edge and bitterness out of the religious contexts.

Katharine Goodland's essay, "'Obsequious Laments': Mourning and Communal Memory in Shakespeare's *Richard III*," draws the knot a little tighter. She finds in *Richard III* (dated 1592–93) an emphasis on royal women mourning the dead. Shakespeare traces an enormous current of mourning directed at the loss of the old medieval Catholic order and conveyed in a form of ritual that illustrates that order: a mourning ritual full of grief at the souls embarked, it is prayed, to Purgatory. This is the theme recently discussed by Stephen Greenblatt in *Hamlet in Purgatory* (2001). It was this lament, among other rituals, that Protestants strove to eliminate because it threatened to keep the old Catholic culture intact within the Protestant Reform. Protestants by contrast transformed funeral rituals into acts of personal recollection by the living ("never send to know for whom the bell tolls; it tolls for thee," as Donne said). In the lamenters' success in urging Richard's overthrow, the play reawakens the power of medieval mystery plays, with, for example, the queens paralleling the three weeping Marys in the Resurrection plays. (In 1592, Southwell was arrested; his *Marie Magdalens Funeral Teares* represented Counter-Reformation culture in England.) Also vindicated—indirectly—by Richard's women, called "pew-fellow[s]," are the prayers for the dead at the Catholic mass, with an attendant horror at the maimed rites promoted by the reformers. Here Richard reminds us of a later perpetrator of maimed rites, Claudius. (Interestingly, Richard, halting the funeral rites, swears "by Saint Paul," evoking Lutheran theology.) Goodland's application of the pietà image to Lady's Anne's lament for her son looks forward to a great pietà scene at the end of *King Lear.*

In Goodland's account of *Richard III,* we enter more deeply into the difference between the two mindsets, Catholic and Protestant. On the Catholic side, we find communalism, continuity with the dead, sacred ritual, Purgatory, intercessory prayer, tradition, mystery, emotionalism, superstition, and ancient Church authority. On the Protestant side, we find "inwardness and individuality," separation and atomism, biblical primacy, hermeneutical suspiciousness, a new communalism in "national identity," and the state, which Protestant heraldic funerals (like Sidney's) celebrate. Shakespeare would seem to tip the balance

toward the Catholic pole in making Richard III a villain who embodies Protestant individualism turned to Machiavellianism and
Marlovian villainy; the heraldic funeral he sponsors is "an empty ceremony while . . . lamentation . . . [is] a communal ritual that possesses
profound emotional and rhetorical power."

But the issue is not so easily settled in Shakespeare. When
Richmond, the future Henry VII, comes in at the play's conclusion to
end the War of the Roses, and seemingly reconciles the Yorks and the
Lancastrians (Goodland especially associates Catholic mourning rituals with those recorded in Lancaster), what is that reconciliation about?
The Tudor apologists saw it as a celebration of Tudor order, climaxing
in Henry VIII and Queen Elizabeth. It is questionable that Shakespeare
saw it this simply, given his images of mourning for the lost order; but
reconciliation implies a compromise between two sides. How does
Shakespeare integrate the Catholic and Protestant dimensions of his
beloved England, "[t]his blessed plot," famous for resisting the "envy
of less happier lands," and also famous for the "true chivalry" of
Catholic crusades?

For Dutton, *The Comedy of Errors* registers Shakespeare's response
to the painful religious division of his country, and his attempt at fictional resolution. This early play sets up a pattern for the comedies to
come. For Goodland, *Richard III* shows Shakespeare's powerful nostalgia for some characteristics of the old religion, characteristics integrated into the new order established at the end of the play. *Richard III*
concludes the first tetralogy and sets up a pattern of integration for the
history plays to follow, as we shall see.

Clare Asquith's "Oxford University and *Love's Labour's Lost*" is the
most controversial of the essays so far and for some draws the knot
unacceptably tight, arguing topical allusions in the play (dated
1594–95, revised 1597). The play was perhaps performed at Oxford
and argues, Asquith claims, for a return to a liberal Catholic humanism
at the university, with the relevant contemporary figures captured in
the play's characters. Peter Milward is preeminent in arguing this kind
of topical Catholicism, with Mary Queen of Scots, Lord Burghley, and
others embodied in Shakespeare characters (1973). The Catholic case
should not rise or fall on such topical allusions; but given the kind of
general context and background argued by Dutton and Goodland, I see
no reason to disallow tentative arguments about topical parallels. The

same might be done with *The Crucible* and, for that matter, with *Antigone,* with Creon seen as the quisling mayor. Here, much is in the eye of the beholder.

So for Asquith, the oath taken by those joining the academy is an oath well forsworn because it evokes the Oath of Supremacy required for admission to Oxford. And Shakespeare urges Elizabeth to behave like the Princess who would lead the men out of their restrictive existence into the wide open neoplatonic spaces of love connected with learning, in the style of Erasmus and the early Thomas More. Some delightful possibilities are explored, like the parallel between "Armado" and Antonio de Corro, the Oxford tutor whose students included John Donne (thus "Moth"). Admittedly, *credam ut intelligam* is necessary here. But why not? Larger principles, as in Dutton and Goodland, are also at stake. Asquith's conclusion has to be considered: "Unlike the many commentaries which align the plot with the philosophic Renaissance academies of Italy or the politics of the court of Navarre, this analysis assumes that Shakespeare's English audience, accustomed to coded dramatizations of the 'matter of England,' would be likely to relate the play to matters closer to home." We may in fact prefer Francis Yates, but the principle is the same. Furthermore, the ultimate object of *Love's Labor's Lost* is as ambitious as any charted for *The Comedy of Errors* and *Richard III*: an appeal to reinstate a certain kind of intellectual and religious life in England.

With Jean-Christophe Mayer's "Shakespeare's Religious Background Revisited: *Richard II* in a New Context," we enter an area of less speculative topical allusion, one amounting to overt historical reference. The reference is to Essex, a reference made overt in the prologue of *Henry V* (dated 1599), the last play of the second historical tetralogy, which begins with *Richard II* (dated 1595). With Mayer, the historical context of Shakespeare's plays becomes articulated into something as treacherous as anything associated with the counter-intelligence world of Christopher Marlowe. The religious context is still determining, but now it is a context occupied by warring Catholic factions, with Essex and Southampton, and thus Shakespeare, at the center of a controversial case. The controversy concerns the patriotism of English Catholics and their efforts to distinguish themselves from pro-Spanish rebels, called "Puritan papist[s]" by Lord Northumberland. Essex is the hope of patriotic

Catholics (and other marginal groups) attempting to influence the course of government through parliamentary and other means, an attempt supported by a performance of *Richard II* with its portrait of Bolingbroke (an ancestor of Essex) invoking Parliament in his overthrow of Richard. When Queen Elizabeth said, "I am Richard II. Know ye not that," Shakespeare was as close to trouble as he ever was. And Robert Persons (Parsons), S.J., attempted, in Mayer's view, to crash Essex's boat by congratulating him for his parliamentarism and dedicating to him the anti-Elizabeth *Conference About the Next Succession* (1594). Persons did not want his radical Jesuitical challenge circumvented by Essex's support of toleration. But the reconciliatory Shakespeare that we have seen in Dutton's *Comedy of Errors* supported Essex, until the disaster of Essex's execution and Shakespeare's own near escape from prosecution. What was Shakespeare's position? This remains the great question. Mayer concludes that Shakespeare "had, without realizing it, agreed to cross the line that separated political support from potential treason."

Here we touch again on an issue that haunts the whole Shakespeare and Reformation case. Is Shakespeare aware of the implications drawn by our essayists, but covering his tracks? Or is he simply the dramatist (a popular view) making hay with contemporary themes, and meaning nothing by them? Is he simply stupid, trespassing "without realizing it" on contemporary concerns? Is he so wise that he is simply above the fray, evading all new historicist nets? This collection of essays, if we can summarize so many, argues that the contemporary resonances, the patterns of implication, and the repetition and depth of historical allusions are so intense in the plays that they must be understood as Shakespeare's careful and seasoned responses to the most important characteristic of Elizabethan England—namely, its religious Reformation and all that attended it.

Timothy Rosendale's "Sacral and Sacramental Kingship in the Lancastrian Tetralogy" entirely reverses the field of play. Here Shakespeare is not a closet Catholic, nor fellow traveler, nor even Catholic sympathizer; his second tetralogy represents the new Protestant order of figurality and fictiveness. The old Catholic order, hierarchical, magical, univocal in its use of signifiers and signifieds, is happily replaced by a post-medieval sophistication that sees signs as artificially constructing identities; the identity implied in the eucharistic formula

("This is my body") replaced by a symbolic relationship. Henry IV and V replace Richard II; theater replaces liturgy; statecraft replaces magic. There were signs of post-Catholic trouble in the earlier essays: Goodland, for example, acknowledges that there is some doubt about the supernatural efficacy of Catholic mourning in *Richard III*. Though recent revisionist critics have connected Shakespeare with his Catholic roots, what about the Protestant Renaissance Shakespeare who has traditionally defined English identity? Rosendale reminds us that the question is complicated, and heavily charged, and that Shakespeare stands at a crossroads of Catholic and Protestant culture in England. Clearly, Shakespeare shares in both worlds. Interestingly, toward the end of his triumphal essay, Rosendale starts stressing the "loss," the "tremendous, if necessary, price" involved in movement out of the old order. We recall that Peter Milward, the godfather of Catholic critics, has claimed for (some forty plus) years that the defining angst in Shakespeare is "the lamentable division" (1990).

My point is not to side with Rosendale or his predecessors, but simply to claim that the issue needs to be discussed in much more depth. One Shakespearean topic that has been lacking is discussion of his relation to Catholic and Protestant psychologies, such as those that Rosendale defines. The issue is pressing, important, and slippery—slippery because the two sides tend to infiltrate each other. For example, Catholicism was not characterized by naive representationalism and brute authority—look at Erasmus, the early More, the liberal Catholic academy tradition alluded to by Asquith, the French Catholicism of Rabelais and Montaigne. And Protestants had not given up on authority directing consciences; the church was replaced by the state, which decreed (in Rosendale's proto-Foucauldian reading) what figural readings would be enforced. It is tempting to give up the whole Catholic/Protestant game and simply look for degrees of each cutting across church lines, left, middle, right, like Puritan, Anglican, Catholic. But I think it is important to maintain the Protestant/Papistical distinction as fundamental (and always to remember that the Anglican via media emerged very slowly). (Such is the revisionist historical thesis of Collinson and others cited by Hamilton in his essay.) The primal distinction was certainly fundamental for Cranmer, who was burned, and Southwell, who was hanged, drawn, and quartered. There is also in Shakespeare's play a drumbeat of allusions to contemporary executions, such as the Finsbury Fields execution cited by Dutton and the Oxford execution cited by Asquith.

It would seem that Falstaff in *1 Henry IV* (dated 1596–97) proves Shakespeare's anti-Puritanism, if not anti-Protestantism. Gary D. Hamilton's "Mocking Oldcastle: Notes Toward Exploring a Possible Catholic Presence in Shakespeare's Henriad" builds up a case that Falstaff stands in for Elizabeth's corrupt counselors as portrayed in Catholic satire, and that Henry, in rejecting Falstaff, represents the Catholic fantasy that the successor to Elizabeth might reject Protestantism and all its nasty works. (Here, again, I am condensing a nuanced argument.) One problem with this view, and with the long-standing view that Falstaff is the butt of anti-Puritan (at least) satire, is that Falstaff is not the object of satire, but the cause of satire, "the cause that wit is in other men." Admittedly, the anti-Lollard thesis would help the Catholic case. But I do not see Falstaff as a foul-mouthed dissolute Puritan (if Shakespeare wants to satirize Puritans, he does so more clearly in Angelo and Malvolio), but as a foul-mouthed dissolute Catholic drunk; not a "stage puritan," but a stage Irishman *avant la lettre*. Robbing those Canterbury pilgrims, he seems more Chaucerian than Verstegen, more Simon Dedalus than John Foxe. He is a papist in Oldcastle's pants. I don't pretend ability to defend this view here (Harold Bloom has listed several Falstaff parallels that unwittingly happen to be from Catholic cultures: wife of Bath, Panurge, Sancho Panza, Montaigne's Socrates, the Joycean, a character out of Oscar Wilde, the "reverend vice" of the morality plays, and old John Shakespeare himself), but simply to say that the satire in Shakespeare, especially in Falstaff, spins in centrifugal directions. Does this support Rosendale's view of the Protestant Henry, ridding himself of dissolute Catholicism (another Catholic dissolute is Richard II), against Hamilton's view of a papist Henry, ridding himself of Lollards and their Elizabethan equivalents? I don't think necessarily so because Henry, like Bolingbroke, might be moving away from a corrupted Catholicism into a reformed, or counter-reformed, kind. In other words, Shakespeare's Catholic sympathies, if that's what they are, need not be taking him toward a return to the old papism, but toward some kind of synthesis of Catholicism and Protestantism, some synthesis of the Catholic values of the sacred, the sacramental (pace Rosendale's usage), the ritual, the communal, with Protestant values of the individual, the critical mind, the subjective, and the nation. Shakespeare was not the first to write a utopia; and if the "teleology" (Rosendale's term) of the Henriad points at such a utopia, that would be something worth discussing.

The problem with Falstaff, excusing my O'Neillian interpretation, is that of the portrayal of minorities in Elizabethan drama. A marginalized Puritan has many parallels with a marginalized papist, and, for that matter, with a marginalized Jew (and, for that matter, a marginalized Moor). Which is an allegory of which? In a world of inconsistent but dangerous censorship, the pointer spins wildly. Nevertheless, it is the function of the critic to attempt some ordered view. All we can do is make our case; this anthology argues that the case must include the religious issues of the Reformation.

Regina M. Buccola's "Shakespeare's Fairy Dance with Religio-Political Controversy in *The Merry Wives of Windsor*" considers the "liminal zone" of a wood "on the margins of the Windsor community" haunted by fairies deeply connected with the old Catholic culture (in this play dated 1597, revised c. 1600–01). At a time when a Puritan reformer was executed for demanding that the queen reform the superstitions of Wales, Shakespeare presents a Welsh parson participating happily in a fairy masque. Buccola reminds us what a consistent tissue of things was connected in the old culture: fairies, superstition, Catholicism were common objects for the Protestant reformer. It was not enough for Henry VIII to dismantle papal authority; he and his successors eventually had to dismantle the whole web—monks, nuns, holy days, Friday fasts, pilgrimages, cults of the saints, shrines, Purgatory, prayers for the dead, indulgences, confession, chantries, relics, rosaries, images, processions, altars, transubstantiation, the mass, Marian devotions, some of the sacraments, holy water, pyxes, adoration of the host, holy things, mystery, miracle and morality plays, penance, works, and so on—a cascade of cultural destruction lasting the sixty-three Protestant years of Henry (despite his late turn against radical Protestantism), Edward, and Elizabeth. This sheer length of time explains how "policy and police" could succeed at such cultural dismantling. Catholicism, from a bird's eye view, tended to be all of piece, from pope to penance, and its sense of the sacred often allied itself in popular culture with a sense of the magical and of Faeryland. (Spenser is an odd mixture of faerie elements and Elizabethan Protestantism.)

We have in *Merry Wives* the familiar question: if Shakespeare was drawn to the old Catholic culture—and his plays are full of the Catholic objects listed in the previous paragraph—what is the significance of that attraction? Did it constitute belief, or simply nostalgia, or fodder for good drama? Complicating the question is the fact that Catholicism was different in the 1590s from what it had been in pre-Reformation times, and even in Marian times. What was it like to be a Catholic living in a post-Catholic English world? Was Catholicism becoming a ghost of itself like the ghost of old King Hamlet? Buccola notes that interest in the spirit world, in James I and the others, was becoming self-conscious and acute just at the time when the old world of magic was declining, to use Keith Thomas's terms (1971). What is the nature of supernaturalism and the sacred and the superstitious in Shakespeare? This should be a hotly debated and nondismissable question. To further complicate this question, historical distortion is compounded by the distortion produced by the need to evade the censors. Buccola argues that the tribute to the fairy queen in the play is Shakespeare covering his tracks. No wonder Shakespeare is hard to discern. ("If we knew he was a Catholic, we would never have heard of him," runs the old joke.) But such difficulty of discernment should be the beginning, not the end, of criticism. What's more, we should be cautious in making undiscernability the answer by deciding that there was nothing religious to discern in Shakespeare.

John Klause, in "Catholic and Protestant, Jesuit and Jew: Historical Religion in *The Merchant of Venice,*" brings us to a new level of complexity in this religio-political "allegoresis" (for this play, dated 1596–97). Klause reminds us there are various ways of situating Shakespeare in relation to his religious contexts. Those contexts may be biblical, in a generic Christian sense, resulting in great amounts of scholarship on Shakespeare's relation to Christianity. One shadow on these traditional studies is that Christianity in Elizabethan England was sectarianly inflected; there were Protestant Christianity, Catholic Christianity, and various adaptions of these—not generic Christianity, except perhaps in the irenical minimalist vision of the more ecumenical Elizabethans. So Shakespeare's use of Christian allusions is charged, but charged in which direction? A second way of situating Shakespeare is to take a sort of cultural studies approach, simply to note the various Catholic things that populate his plays, from shrines to shriving. These may be simply consistent with the Italian settings as in *The Merchant of Venice,* but the problem is that there is an excess of such things, especially at points of thematic importance, as when Portia describes herself as visiting a monastery and, accompanied by a holy hermit, "By holy crosses, where she kneels and prays." What is the meaning of this excess? Is Shakespeare consciously constructing a Catholic culture as a norm by which things are measured? Is he unconsciously reflecting the culture in which he was raised?

The remainder of Klause's essay shows how Robert Southwell's phrases and images seeped into Shakespeare's imagination. So many are these that the recent (1595) martyr's words must have deeply embedded themselves in his mind. This adds complexity to Shakespeare's joking use of allusion to contemporary rackings and torture, as when Bassanio says that, as a lover, "he lives upon the rack." These light allusions exist throughout Shakespeare; what do we make of them? Is Shakespeare sketching a shadow behind the jollity? This leads to the next way of situating Shakespeare, as intervening somehow in the political/religious disputes of the Elizabethan era, an intervention necessarily conducted with great caution and indirection. Let the play capture the conscience of the Virgin Queen. This is at once the most controversial and promising dimension of recent studies, turning some readers off this charged topicality, and yet promising to lead others into the heart of Shakespeare's time and its deepest conflicts.

So the religious pressure on *The Merchant of Venice* is there, but what is the result? In *Merchant,* the conflict between Jew and Christian is emphasized—but why, Klause speculates, except to signify some deeper more relevant conflict, that "of a divided Christendom—a problem more broadly and immediately critical to Elizabethans than was their 'Jewish question'"? But who in the play parallels what in Elizabethan England? Is Shylock a Jew, a Puritan, a Protestant law enforcer, or some other thing? Is he the oppressed minority or the established government, backed by law and police, ready to inflict its ultimate penalty on its victim? In this case his victim, Antonio, could be the ensnared Catholic victim. But Antonio is here part of the majority order that persecutes Shylock, in this case putting him back into the victimized minority category. The object and perpetrator of persecution keeps reversing. Klause's solution is that Shylock is the Puritan Protestant facing two Southwells: one is the martyr-like Antonio, on whom Shylock would inflict some of what was done to Southwell on the executioner's block; the other is Portia, the liberal continental Southwell, who would teach mercy to both sides in the controversy. "What you do unto others shall be done unto you" becomes a principle playing all over the civil scene, like a loose cannon spraying all sides.

Adding complexity to the problem of who is up, who is down, is the fact that Essex was responsible for the prosecution and execution of Dr. Lopez, the queen's Jewish physician. Shakespeare probably had deep ambivalence about Essex's stunt, done for political reasons; and this ambivalence is reflected in the play's question about who should show mercy to whom.

John Freeman, "This Side of Purgatory: Ghostly Fathers and the Recusant Legacy in *Hamlet*," brings us to the center of any case for the religious dimension in Shakespeare. It reminds us of the fundamental premise on which this collection of essays is based: that the ghost of the old Catholicism haunts Shakespeare and his Elizabethan world. It should not be so difficult to see *Hamlet* (dated 1600–01) as registering the most important transition of the Elizabethan spiritual landscape (Freeman notes Margareta De Grazia's point that the Ghost as mole moving under the earth simulates this seismic shift). Traditionally, *Hamlet* has been seen as embodying the problems of post-Renaissance Western consciousness. Freeman reminds us that this problem occurs at the break line between the old and new religious orders. Freeman describes how "the ambidextrous religious life" (Walsham's phrase) of a divided recusant, marginalized and fearful, the antic disguises, the terrible divisions of mind, the self-protective disguises, and the necessity for a hidden inner life echo in the play. "Hamlet's 'antic disposition' evokes the recusant strategy of disguising one's inner thoughts and even one's identity as a protective measure against danger and persecution." The Ghost's Purgatorial dungeon also reflects the in-between world of Elizabethan recusants groping in prisons and hideouts, essentially fugitive.

Freeman's essay is in one respect like traditional "Catholic Shakespeare" essays in taking seriously John Shakespeare's apparent recusancy, his supposed "Spiritual Testament" found in the rafters of the Stratford house, Shakespeare's possible sojourn in Lancaster as "William Shakeshafte" in the Catholic household of the Hoghtons, and so forth. We have heard much of the two smoking guns that have rejuvenated the Catholic Shakespeare case in recent years (though the discoveries themselves took place in the first half of the twentieth century): the discovery of the Cardinal Borromeo template, which provided the model for John Shakespeare's testament, and the discovery that one of Shakespeare's Stratford teachers had connections with Hoghton Castle, where the lord of the castle left a legacy to "William Shakeshafte." It is important to emphasize that such things are interesting, potentially important, but secondary to the basic issue of the way Catholicism haunts Shakespeare's plays. Freeman calls it the "return of the repressed," and employs the Torok/Abraham theory of social haunting by unnamed ghosts of the past.

But then Freeman adds his own twist: the play *Hamlet* represents not a recovered Catholic world, but a distorted Catholic world that has been driven into hiding and disguises, and has ended as a grotesque phantom of its former self. The Ghost is like "a holographic image created from interference patterns," the twelfth century mounted on the sixteenth century when Purgatorial ghostliness was outlawed. The air of distortion is particularly represented by the Ghost and its controversial status as Senecan and Catholic, as Purgatorial soul and demon. The grotesque distortion of some old religious order haunts the stable Elizabethan world of Claudius and Gertrude, resulting in unresurrected bodies and maimed rites, the latter illustrated by Claudius's confession, Ophelia's prayers and burial, Hamlet playing confessor with his mother, and the Black Mass at the end with the poisoned chalice.

This leads to the question: exactly how does Catholicism appear in Shakespeare's plays, in what strange and perhaps distorted forms? And this, in turn, leads to the question of questions for Western culture: how does Catholicism appear in the Protestant and then secular consciousness that has defined Englishness since Shakespeare? Shakespeare is often considered the definer of English identity, and for this reason the definition of Shakespeare is a hotly contested issue. As Shakespeare goes, so goes the nation. The question of the ghost of Catholicism in Shakespeare is an important subset of the question of the ghost of Catholicism in English consciousness, where Catholicism goes through various metamorphoses—as anti-Christ, whore of Babylon, anti-Enlightenment bigotry, marginal sect, Scottish romance, Gothic past, medievalism, Italian art, Anglican underpinning, home of lost causes, charming decadence, *Brideshead Revisited,* and so on. But the

ghost of Catholicism defining itself as the "other" within Protestantism
and to a lesser degree secularism is like the Punch-and-Judy effigy of
Guy Fawkes; it does not go away. (It has also become the subject of
some very interesting recent books by Jenny Franchot [1994], Paul
Giles [1992], on the American scene, with English scholarship recently joining the discussion.)

We suggested earlier that Shakespeare's utopian project for his history plays is to move toward some reconsideration of Catholic/
Protestant relations. Traditionally, this theme has been considered sectarian and narrowing. But what we are suggesting here is that it is the
biggest theme of all, an engagement with the fundamental long-lasting
schism in Western consciousness: the Reformation.

Jennifer Rust's "Wittenberg and Melancholic Allegory: The
Reformation and Its Discontents in *Hamlet*" turns the mirror in the
opposite direction to Freeman: Hamlet is not the image of recusant
restlessness, but the image of Protestant anxiety. The allusions to
Wittenberg underscore the importance of Hamlet's post-Reformation
Protestant consciousness. In *Hamlet,* Shakespeare portrays the plight
of the new consciousness of an interiority unleashed from old sacred
shared sources and launched onto a sea of interpretative chaos. In a
world where interiority depends on an original unguided relation with
the printed Bible, the relation between inner and outer, between interi-
or spirit and outer letter, is no longer secure. The signs that Hamlet
must read are the distorted ghostly signs of his own subjectivity. Where
he had earlier attempted clear distinctions in the "know not seems"
speech, the Ghost arrives and deranges "the boundaries between interior transcendence and the external world." In this uprooted world,
inside and outside become strangely distorted like the ghost of King
Hamlet, who is an ultimate grotesque, a spirit layered with a leprous
crust. Hamlet tries one mode after another of finding an external form
for a "secure, transcendent interiority." In the end, he follows "a course
of 'indiscretion' [that] supersedes any concern with an inner state." He
enters into a "drastic externality," gives himself up to "rashness," and
embraces "his own guilty participation in a radically immanent world."

Victorian scholars may think of Carlylean action, of the hero of
"Locksley Hall" who goes a-warring as a way to defeat melancholy.
My argument is that Shakespeare's engagement with Catholic/
Protestant issues returns us to the point where "modern" consciousness

begins. Hamlet can only leave his tale to (in Rust's words) be "told 'in pain,' persisting in the disquiet of the deadly letter rather than the serenity of the living Spirit." Like the Ghost, he is "another spirit embedded in the opaque materiality of language." Our modern consciousness is the heir of the furious anti-idolatrous impulse of the Protestant, an anti-idolatry that questions all forms, all expressions, leaving the self endlessly refashioning existence into one tentative allegory after another. Such is the melancholy of endless inauthenticity charted by Walter Benjamin. Shakespeare invites us to reflect on the cost and gains of this turning point, the Reformation. We are asked to view again transformation of Catholic sacrality into Protestant idolatry and thence into the critical consciousness that has elaborated itself in manifold ways ever since.

After Freeman and Rust, the question remains: are we dealing with a Catholic or a Protestant nightmare? This question may be too simple because, in a post-Catholic world, both recusant and reformer enter a universe where appearances are radically separated from realities, where interiority is unleashed like a wandering soul among the shreds and patches of a once allegorical world.

R. Chris Hassel Jr.'s "The Accent and Gait of Christians: Hamlet's Puritan Style" follows Rust in coming at the chameleon Hamlet from a Protestant direction, but suggests to us how closely intertwined are the Protestant and Catholic paradigms. He begins by showing how the problems of Puritan spirituality are embedded in Hamlet, who uses, and sometimes parodies, Puritan moral and vocational formulas. (Falstaff is a comic version of this Puritan vesting.) What for Freeman is caused by an ambivalent recusant trying to stay true to his Catholic father's injunctions, is for Hassel a conflicted Puritan trying to stay true to an elected conscience. What are we to do with a Protestant from Wittenberg carrying out a Purgatorial ghost's commands? Does the energy of resistance to a corrupt government derive from Catholic or Protestant sources? Hamlet struggles within these varying paradigms, resisting them, mocking them, and being shaped by them, and to what ultimate end? Hassel reminds us how embedded Protestant and Catholic paradigms are within each other, how each religion struggles with similar paradoxes of work and faith, form and sincerity, mercy and scrupulousness; and how each religion is the counter-complement of the other. Hamlet may attempt to restore the ancient religion (as in some accounts), but in doing so, he is netted in by his contemporary Protestant culture. In attacking it, he would seem to be attacking himself. Thus the religious war is deeply tied in with the complexities of a post-medieval interiority and self-questioning. The play *Hamlet* tempts us to speak most personally of Shakespeare, of his deep anguish and bewilderment at his own participation in the split religious culture of his time.

I have discussed these essays in roughly chronological order, with some exceptions for thematic grouping, as though Shakespeare's life and works represented an unfolding story. (David Bevington [1997] suggests somewhat different date ranges for the plays discussed earlier: 1589–94 for *The Comedy of Errors,* 1592–94 for *Richard III,* 1588–97 for *Love's Labor's Lost,* 1603–4 for *Measure for Measure,* 1601–5 for *All's Well That Ends Well,* 1603–4 for *Othello,* and so forth; in fact, determining dates needs close integration with the kind of thematic concerns explored in this volume.) When we arrive at *Hamlet,* it would seem that Shakespeare's confrontation with Reformation issues is at its most acute. The idea of a Shakespeare story has been in disrepute at least since Lytton Strachey (1922) attacked the story-making of Edward Dowden and the tradition of bildungsroman as applied to Shakespeare. But Strachey was not attacking the idea of a story; he attacked Dowden's story in favor of another story that he, Strachey, preferred. Only in postmodern times has the very idea of a story, "narrative," been called into question.

But *Shakespeare and the Culture of Christianity in Early Modern England* calls for reconsideration of the unfolding story of Shakespeare. How did he respond to the changing events of the Reformation in the 1590s and thereafter? The death of Essex and the hopes he aroused, and the apparently sempiternal existence of Elizabeth, may have led Shakespeare into the darker intensities of *Hamlet.* Or something else may have; but the question is worth considering. The advent of James, son of Mary Queen of Scots, caused a false fire of hope to run through Catholic circles. Did this result in the brief period of problem comedies, with their strained re-entertainment of the possibilities of English religious reconciliation? Our collection proceeds to two plays that may be from this period, *Measure for Measure* and *All's Well That Ends Well.*

David Beauregard's "Shakespeare on Monastic Life: Nuns and Friars in *Measure for Measure*" argues that throughout Shakespeare's plays, and in this one (dated 1604), Shakespeare shows a respect for Catholic religious life and moral values (such as chastity and celibacy) that is surprising for an Elizabethan culture. The play presents a conflict between a Puritan governance such as Angelo's and a Catholic one such as that of the Duke disguised as a friar. Three interesting problems present themselves: the problem of simulating a cleric to the point of administering the sacrament of confession, the problem of Isabella's silence at the end of the play when the Duke proposes marriage to her, and the problem of mercy. Beauregard is right, I believe, in denying that the Duke's simulation implies a mocking demystification of the priesthood. Nor does it demonstrate a Shakespeare interested only in theatricalization. But the simulation of a confessing friar, like Paulina's simulation of a Catholic miracle at the end of *The Winter's Tale,* is an interesting development of Elizabethan Catholicism. We have seen its grotesque distortion in the Purgatorial ghost. Here we see Catholicism at some strange remove, something detached from actual practice (in real life, simulating sacramental confession would be a serious blasphemy), entertained in the mind's eye. The peculiar mode of this detachment needs more discussion.

With regard to Isabella's silence, Beauregard observes that it satisfies and equally dissatisfies both Protestant and Catholic audiences, the former wanting marriage to replace celibate religious life, the latter wanting to maintain the ideal of "single blessedness" (as in the important quotation from *A Midsummer Night's Dream*). Isabella's silence represents an aporia in Elizabethan drama, a place where these competing values are being fought out, with no clear outcome, yet historically clear.

The most stunning aspect of *Measure for Measure* is the act of mercy accomplished by Isabella and orchestrated by the Duke. That mercy reconciles two orders: the Puritan order of Angelo, and the Catholic order of the Duke's earlier reign. Again we see that Shakespeare's reconciliation has important consequences for Reformation politics. Yet the artificed nature of the play reflects perhaps the hectic but unrealistic hope entertained in those first Jacobean moments before the new oath of allegiance was imposed, followed by the Gunpowder Plot.

Maurice Hunt, "Helena and the Reformation Problem of Merit in *All's Well That Ends Well,*" brings us to Shakespeare's perhaps most

Catholic heroine (in this play dated 1602–3), with her association with miracles, Marian intercession, and pilgrimages to St. James. Hunt's topic is how Shakespeare makes play with the theological disputes of the day, disputes made into jokes or into platitudes where it is almost impossible to determine which theological view Shakespeare himself holds. This indeterminacy reflects the actual confusions of the disputes. These disputes seem to follow clear divisions and clear terminological differences, such as Catholic salvation earned by merit versus Protestant salvation gained by faith, or infused versus imputed sanctification. But in the real spiritual life of Christians, these distinctions were often impossible to maintain. The Christian struggle is fundamentally paradoxical, requiring absolute submission to God as well as intense effort on the human side (if only the effort to submit). Theologians can at various times weigh more heavily one or the other side of the paradox; and at various times in history, one or the other side is dangerously overemphasized. The tragedy of the Reformation was that theological differences, which ideally are leavened into an ongoing dialectic and piggybacked onto the political power struggle, resulted in a split within the once universal (Western) church. Whether this tragedy was in fact providential and necessary is a good subject for debate.

Hunt is not sanguine about reconciliation in *All's Well That Ends Well,* but sees the play as a "deliberate forcing together of radically incompatible accounts" (in Greenblatt's words), one in accord with the Catholic belief in the efficaciousness of merit, the other in accord with Protestant rejection of merit in favor of faith. So are Helena's good deeds and tricks seen as the "merit" that earns her the Prince; or does her marriage with the Prince occur almost in despite of these things? How meritorious is her merit?

Hunt begins with the Princess's joke, in *Love's Labor's Lost,* a joke that can stand for the difficulty of determining Shakespeare's position on merit versus faith, and indeed for the difficulty of really sorting out this distinction in the spiritual life of the individual Christian. The Princess gives her forester a tip and gains from him a compliment to her beauty. She responds:

> See, see, my beauty will be sav'd by merit.
> O heresy in fair, fit for these days!
> A giving hand, though foul, shall have fair praise.

Supposedly, this illustrates the Protestant critique of merit, as does Falstaff's "O, if men were to be sav'd by merit, what hole in hell were hot enough for him" (1.2.107). But the jokes are complicated and spin in different directions. Falstaff says, in effect, "If there is a heaven that can be earned by merit, Poins has no chance at it." Falstaff's intent is not to satirize the theology of merit, but to satirize Poins as totally devoid of merit. The joke glances at the merit/faith controversy, and, it might be argued, holds out the benevolent possibility of faith ("fortunately for you Poins you will in fact not need merit to get into heaven"). But the intent is to insult Poins as meritless; if the joke calls anything into question, it is the existence of heaven and hell themselves, however they are to be gained. Similarly, the Princess's joke glances at the theological controversy and makes it spin in opposite directions. Though she is foul (a sinner), she can buy a compliment (salvation) by a bribe (merit); such is the French heresy of Catholicism. But who calls this heresy? Whom is she quoting? In fact she is beautiful and in fact she gets the compliment—so the heresy works, and if it works, who dare call it heresy? And why is it "fit for these days" (days characterized in Shakespeare's sonnets as foul)? Fit because this is how Protestants label the efficacy of merit? Fit because contemporary sinners refuse to change their disbelief, and so try to buy their way by merit into heaven, as Protestants complain? Fit because contemporary good people (like the Princess, a Catholic princess) are libeled and need to buy back their good reputations?

These jokes illustrate the complexity of Shakespeare's engagement with the theological differences of the two major sides, as he inhabits each side depending on what makes for the best joke. Indeed in the Princess's joke, the theology of merit ends up sounding like the theology of imputed justification: a foul hand gaining undeserved praise. More important, Shakespeare sees the whole subject as the occasion for making jokes. Thus in ecumenical style, the Clown in *All's Well* asserts: "young Chairbonne the puritan and old Poisson the papist, howsome'er their hearts are severed in religion, their heads are both one: they may jowl horns together like any deer i'th' herd" (1.3.52–55). Whatever our theologies, we all end up cuckolds. And Hamlet takes away with one Catholic hand what he has just given with a Protestant one: "Use every man after his desert, and who shall scape whipping? . . . the less they deserve, the more merit is in your bounty"

(2.2.529–32). This is not to say that the Catholic/Protestant split is not fundamental for Shakespeare; but it is perhaps more fundamental as a familial and cultural and liturgical division than as a theological one (though interesting work in sacramental and virtue theology has been done). Shakespeare's plays are full of the culture of Catholicism mixed in with elements of the new culture of Protestantism. It is between these two mindsets that he is negotiating, trying to imagine how the Protestant horse can be put back into the Catholic barn, or conversely, how English Catholics can ride into a Protestant future.

Lisa Hopkins, "Paris Is Worth a Mass: *All's Well That Ends Well* and the Wars of Religion," sees "all's well" as pointing toward some ultimate reconciliation of the religious wars. The play evokes a classical and Christian past shared by both England and France—Protestant and Catholic countries—and through the veil of pastoral and magic suggests a "healing" of this division. "The splitting of Christendom effected by schism can only by healed (the healing here being imaged by the marriage) by reversion to a much older, quasi-magical mode of thought and worship that preceded the splitting of the faiths and the theological controversies that consequently ensued." *All's Well*, like *The Comedy of Errors* and *Love's Labor's Lost*, evokes the recent French religious wars, but then suggests that these troubles can be transcended "by reference to a past still further back, in ways that will allow hope for the future." Hopkins does not comment on the Clown's statement that "his answer is as fit . . . as the nun's lip to the friar's mouth." But part of the "reversion" is reversion to a time when such satire was Chaucerian, Erasmian, not yet characterized by the reformers' wrath. And with the reversion comes a return to another time, another place, where classical and Christian study was conducted harmoniously by humanists within an undivided Christendom. Some of this had been evoked in Richard Dutton's Ephesus where Diana is conflated with the Virgin Mary, or in Katharine Goodland's London where Hecuba's mourning is compared with Catholic mourning rites, or in Regina Buccola's Windsor where priestesses and nuns are interchangeable. The reversion is indeed quasi-magical, a term that characterizes the utopian fantasy in these problematic comedies written in this deceptive halcyon period at the beginning of James's reign. When Shakespeare first began writing comedies, they had this romantic quality, as Dutton notes about *The Comedy of Errors:* "The errors of the play are wanderings, literal, theological, and slanderous; the comedy lies in a magical regression to a state where they no longer exist." In the late romances, this romantic quality will become romance itself. Tim Rosendale spoke about the problem of the "teleological readings of the history plays." Here we are ambitiously tracing a story projecting a teleological reading of Shakespeare's career out of the Elizabethan comedies and history plays, through the interruption of *Hamlet,* into the false dawn of these problem plays, and on to the high tragedies and late romances.

The original call from the journal *Religion and the Arts* for this collection of refereed essays on "Shakespeare and the Reformation" read:

> Essays might respond to the current revisionist debate about the Reformation, and new approaches to the religious culture of Shakespeare's plays. The following might be considered: the nuances of religious divisions in Shakespeare's time, their reflection in Shakespeare or Shakespeare's close contemporaries, the subsequent history of such issues. Among other themes might be theatricality, censorship, cultural politics, iconoclasm, national definition, hidden trauma, hegemony, reader response. But any topic concerned with Shakespeare's religious contexts will be welcome. Much has been said about Shakespeare's Catholic connections in recent years, but *Religion and the Arts* would like to move the conversation to the next level.

Interestingly, the offerings that were accepted did not include essays on the late romances, which are often grist to Catholic readings, or, with the exception of two on *Othello,* essays on the Jacobean tragedies, which are most resistant. There is no place to discuss the tragedies' responses to the darkest moment in early modern English Catholicism, or how James's allegiance oath, his stricter prosecution of recusants, and the finale of the Gunpowder Plot and trial prepared the way for the deepest Catholic despair about the possibilities of reconciliation.

In Richard Mallette's "Blasphemous Preacher: Iago and the Reformation" about *Othello* (dated 1604), Iago is the deepest and darkest picture so far in Shakespeare of the demonic version of a Protestant preacher, one who parodies the language of the Homilies and prayerbook to ensnare Othello in agonies of faith and doubt, until Othello turns against the most precious thing in his life and becomes

> one whose hand,
> Like the base Indian, threw a pearl away
> Richer than all his tribe . . .

In Mallette's words, "The situation between the two principals diabolically mimes the relationship of a godly divine to a member of his
flock." The play ends with a kind of return to Catholic rhetoric, but
now a "residual and officially outmoded Roman Catholic discourse"
under the glare created by Iago's Puritanism. Desdemona, "blessed"
and instinctively Catholic in her language, is taught to mime awkward-
ly Iago's Puritan idiom. Even Othello reverts to the older Catholic language ("confess freely of thy sin"), but that language is now possessed
by Iago's satanic mimicry. We have the sense that opposites, and opposite kinds of religious language, turn into each other, to destructive
effect. In Othello's words, "Chaos is come again." The play enacts the
process by which a new Puritan rhetoric invaded the Catholic landscape and dispossessed it.

What is the significance of Othello's role as a black man, a Moor,
with perhaps an allusion to the Moroccan ambassador to England in
1600? Here we need to return to Richard Dutton's essay. Dutton notes
that one Elizabethan "slander" often compared Catholics to the Turks
and other anti-Christ groups. *The Comedy of Errors* takes place in
Ephesus, a famous Christian location associated with the Virgin Mary,
but now under the control of the Turks—alluded to in the name
"Solinus," Duke of Ephesus, reflecting Suleiman the Turk. England's
relation to the Turk was complicated: on the one hand, she identified
with the Christian victory over the Turks at Lepanto; on the other hand,
she allied herself at times with the Turks against the continental
Catholics. The Turk was an image of the in-between figure, the enemy
of my enemy and thus my friend, but still the anti-Christ. Thus in *The
Comedy of Errors,* the final reconciliation of Ephesus with Syracuse
stands for the resolution of this complicated conflicted circle of Turk,
Catholic, and Protestant. But the comic resolution has long since faded
by the time of *Othello* and will only be resuscitated behind the veils of
romance in the last plays.

Othello is a figure of contradiction, a fulfillment of the implicit
irreconcilability that Maurice Hunt argued for in *All's Well That Ends
Well.* He is the Turk and he is the Christian hero who defeated the
Turks. He is the hero of Lepanto and also its conquered subject. Where
is this strange minority, this black man, stranger in his alienness than
Shylock, or Caliban, or the outlawed exiles in the other plays, to be
placed in the religio-political world of Shakespeare? At the end,

Othello plays the Catholic hero striking the Turk, or the Protestant hero striking the anti-Christ. But the person is he is striking is himself:

> Set you down this;
> And say besides, that in Aleppo once,
> Where a malignant and a turban'd Turk
> Beat a Venetian and traduced the state,
> I took by the throat the circumcised dog
> And smote him, thus. . . .

It is not them against us. It is us against us. The Reformation did not come from outside England; it came from inside—within counties, within towns, within families, within individuals. This historical trauma, the great division within England, haunts Shakespeare in play after play.

The historical overlay conditions our reading of individual lines. An example is Desdemona's "I say, it is not lost"—her lie to Othello about the handkerchief. This is the subject of the final essay of our collection, Paula McQuade's "Love and Lies: Marital Truth-Telling, Catholic Casuistry, and *Othello.*" The essay demonstrates that for the interpretation of single lines, a sorting out of the Catholic and Protestant dimensions of Shakespeare is often necessary. McQuade's argument is that *Othello* assumes a Protestant notion of companionate marriage characterizing the marital relation of Othello and Desdemona. But there is a hidden disability in the companionate notion, a blindness to the structural inequality of men and women. This inequality forces women into a position where they may feel obliged to use equivocation, or outright lies, to protect themselves. If we admire the initial companionate love of Othello and Desdemona, we sympathize with her need to equivocate about the loss of the handkerchief. This double reaction reflects the religious points of view, for while the Protestants provided the most articulate defense of companionate marriage, the Catholics provided the most rationalized justification for equivocation, a fact exploited in the Gunpowder Plot trial, and alluded to in *Macbeth.*

In *Othello,* this nod toward Catholic casuistry (consistent with other "Catholic" characteristics of Desdemona) suggests a competing Catholic culture, more seasoned and urbane, more worldly and traditional, than the idealistic and demanding Protestant culture. Shakespeare again seems to be negotiating between two mindsets: the Protestant companionate ideal needing the compassion and realism of the Catholic casuistry. This negotiation is complicated by the political

realities within which Shakespeare is writing. The parallel of the casuistry used by wives, and the casuistry used by Catholic missionaries,
points to a common oppression by the official culture, the Reformation
imposed from above with often-fatal consequences. The fact that we
both admire their love, and yet have compassion for Desdemona and
her equivocation suggests that we also, as readers and viewers, share
mentally in the Protestant/Catholic split that is the coded subject of
much of Shakespeare's work.

On or about 1985, the landscape of Shakespeare and religion studies began to change. In that year, Ernst Honigmann and Gary Taylor,
representing mainline Shakespeare criticism, argued for the continuing
influence of Shakespeare's Catholic background on his plays. Since
1985, there has been a flood of criticism reconsidering Shakespeare's
relation to his Catholic contexts. This criticism has been liberated from
the old sectarian agendas—Protestant, secular, Catholic—which, prior
to 1985, made the religious issue almost impossible to view in a disinterested light. What we have seen since 1985 is the widespread acceptance of the importance of Shakespeare's Catholic background on both
his mother's and father's side, so much so that Honigmann and
Taylor's 1985 work—and Peter Milward's *Shakespeare's Religion
Background* (1973)—are now routinely cited, with various qualifica-
tion, in standard editions and biographies of Shakespeare.

This collection of essays attempts to move the conversation "to the
next level," to a point where we can more maturely estimate the presence of Catholic, Protestant, and secular strands in Shakespeare. In
taking this next step, we do not intend to dilute the excitement that has
accompanied the great number of recent discoveries made about
Shakespeare's Catholic contexts and influences. (John Klause on
Southwell, in this collection, is a preeminent example of such discovery.) But we need to begin to digest these findings. It may be that we
will end with the traditional Shakespeare of English national Protestant
consciousness. Or it may be that we will find a Shakespeare who poses
a new and surprising view of the English Catholic heritage and of the
Reformation agon. Whatever our final position, it will be a position
arrived at not in traditional ignorance of Shakespeare's Reformation
contexts, but in full acknowledgment of them.

This book is dedicated to Peter Milward, S.J., to honor his pioneering work in Shakespeare and religion, work that began with a 1960

article entitled "Shakespeare no Higeki" and that now consists of some 200 books and articles, most recent among them *Shakespeare's Meta-drama—Hamlet and Macbeth* (2003).

Works Cited

Benjamin, Walter. *The Origin of German Tragic Drama.* Trans. John Osborne. London: Verso, 1998.

Bevington, David. "Canon, Dates, and Early Texts." In *Complete Works of Shakespeare,* 4th ed. New York: Longman, 1997.

Evans, G. Blakemore, and J. J. M. Tobin. "Chronology and Sources." In *The Riverside Shakespeare,* 2d ed., ed. G. Blakemore Evans et al. Boston, Mass.: Houghton Mifflin, 1997.

Franchot, Jenny. *Roads to Rome: The Antebellum Protestant Encounter with Catholicism.* Berkeley, Calif.: University of California Press, 1994.

Giles, Paul. *American Catholic Arts and Fictions: Culture, Ideology, Aesthetics.* Cambridge, England: Cambridge University Press, 1992.

Greenblatt, Stephen. *Hamlet in Purgatory.* Princeton, N.J., and Oxford: Princeton University Press, 2001.

Milward, Peter, S. J. "The Homiletic Tradition in Shakespeare's Plays with Special Reference to Hamlet" (1967). In *The Mediaeval Dimension in Shakespeare's Plays.* Lewiston, Maine: E. Mellen Press, 1990.

_____. "Shakespeare no Higeki" (Shakespeare's Tragedies). *Seiki* (Sophia University) 119 (April 1960): 40–50.

_____. *Shakespeare's Meta-drama—Hamlet and Macbeth.* Tokyo: Renaissance Institute, Sophia University, 2003.

_____. *Shakespeare's Religious Background,* 2d ed. (no changes). Chicago, Ill: Loyola University Press, 1985.

Persons (Parsons), Robert. *A Conference abovt the next Svccession to the Crowne of Ingland.* Antwerp, 1594. STC 19398.

Strachey, Lytton. "Shakespeare's Final Period." In *Books and Characters.* New York: Harcourt, 1922.

Thomas, Keith. *Religion and the Decline of Magic.* London: Weidenfield and Nicholson, 1971.

1

The Comedy of Errors and The Calumny of Apelles: An Exercise in Source Study

by Richard Dutton

Lancaster University, Lancaster, England

THE MAIN SOURCES of *The Comedy of Errors* are familiar friends, possibly too familiar to receive the attention they warrant: Shakespeare drew the main plot of twins separated at birth from the *Menaechmi* of Plautus (possibly consulted in part in William Warner's translation); further material, including the addition of a second set of twins, from the same playwright's *Amphitruo;* and lesser details from such works as George Gascoigne's *Supposes,* John Lyly's *Mother Bombie,* and John Gower's *Confessio Amantis.* The usual narrative of all this is of Shakespeare fleshing out, humanizing, and Christianizing these disparate materials. That is what we find, for example, in T. W. Baldwin's repeated attentions to the play, including his exhaustive *On the Compositional Genetics of "The Comedy of Errors"* (1965), or more succinctly in R. A. Foakes's Arden edition (1962).[1]

Christianizing is an important element in the process, associated with Shakespeare's translation of the action from Epidamnus, in Plautus, to Ephesus. The hint for this may have come from the tale of Apollonius of Tyre in Gower, but if so, the dramatist built extensively on this to incorporate most of the biblical resonances of Ephesus (mainly associated with St. Paul in the *Acts of the Apostles* and his *Epistle to the Ephesians*) into his story.[2] So much so that, as Joseph Candido puts it in one of the shrewder and more imaginative studies of Shakespeare's use of his sources, "one could easily argue that Shakespeare's play is at least as much Pauline as it is

Plautine" (Candido 1990, 221). As Donna Hamilton succinctly summarizes, "Ephesians includes statements on the need to maintain a hierarchical relationship between master and servant and husband and wife, and instructions to 'Put on the whole armour of God that ye may be able to stand against the assaults of the devill'; in Acts, Ephesus is a place where evil spirits abound" (Hamilton 1992, 64).[3] It will be readily apparent how much these themes inform the play that Shakespeare wrote. So Glyn Austen, in an explicitly Christian reading of the play, has no difficulty in suggesting that "Shakespeare's primary reason for shifting the setting from the Epidamnum of his Plautine source to Ephesus would have been to capitalize on the proverbial quality of the latter as a disordered society" (Austen 1987, 58).

So far so good. But traditional accounts both of the sources and of the change of location leave a good deal that is not explained about the play and its origins late in the 1580s or early in the 1590s.[4] Donna Hamilton's is the one attempt to relate these matters fully to the religious tensions of the immediate period, taking the play to be an allegory of church politics at a time when the Church of England was reacting intemperately to criticism from nonconformists (Hamilton 1992, 59–85). I want to propose a different context, however; one suggested by a hitherto overlooked source that carries with it a considerable freight of Reformation baggage. In adapting Plautus, Shakespeare changed the name of the principal twins from Menaechmus (admittedly a mouthful in English) to Antipholus—or "Antipholis" as it appears twice in the First Folio text, the only early witness. What does the name mean, and where did Shakespeare find it? It is instructive here to follow T. W. Baldwin's exhaustive labors on this, as on so many other features of the play, since he came very close to the answer but failed to recognize it because (I suggest) it did not square with what he wanted or expected to find.

Unable to identify a specific source for Antipholus, Baldwin examined a variety of options, concluding that it is the type-name of a lover, deriving from the Greek feminine Αντιφιλα (Antiphila: "worthy of devotion"). In arguing this, Baldwin considered—only to reject—Henry Cunningham's suggestion that Shakespeare's usage parallels that of Philip Sidney and William Camden, who both use the name "Antiphilus":[5]

Quite evidently also, Shakespeare did not get Antipholis, Antipholus from the correct Latin transliteration Antiphilus of Sidney, as Cunningham suggested. In the *Arcadia*, *"Erona* irreligious gainst Loue, must loue the base *Antiphilus"* as punishment, since this Antiphilus lived a "false-harted life, which had planted no strong thought in him, but that he could be vnkind." This Antiphilus is "vnkinde," anti-love.

Also Camden dubs Ralph Brooke, who had attacked him, Antiphilus, "mihi iugulum petit iste Antiphilus"; this here cutthroat Antiphilus! Brooke had been "anti," against or in opposition to "philus," a calumniator, as Camden repeats. These Antiphili of Sidney and Camden certainly do not represent Shakespeare's idea; they are anti, whether it be in Antiphilus. Antipho, etc. (Baldwin 1965, 100–101)[6]

And this line of thought has largely been adopted by recent editions, though R. A. Foakes is properly circumspect: "Antipholus appears to stem from the Greek 'Antiphilos,' listed as a proper name for a lover in H. Estienne (Stephanus), *Thesaurus Graecae Linguae* (1572), but we do not know where Shakespeare found it" (2, n. 1).[7] This is very reasonable if we assume that the play is essentially a romantic comedy. But in fact romantic love, though considerably more prominent an issue than it is in Plautus, remains a secondary theme in the play. Whatever warmth there ever was between Antipholus of Ephesus and his wife, Adriana, has cooled a good deal by the time of the play. And though Antipholus of Syracuse seems attracted for a time to Adriana's sister, Luciana, Shakespeare cannot be bothered even to confirm if this leads to a marriage at the end of the play. It is the same-but-not-the-same pairing of the two sets of twins that is at the heart of the play, not their romantic attachments—they serve only as catalysts to the main action.

In this blinkered conviction that Shakespeare was really concerned with romantic comedy, Baldwin failed to appreciate that Antipholus in fact derived from what in the Renaissance was one of the most famous essays of classical antiquity:[8] Lucian's περι του μη ραιδιωσ πιστευιεν διαβοληι, best known by its name in Latin translation, *Calumnia non temere credendum,* "On not believing rashly [or, being too quick to put faith] in slander." This was evidently where Sidney and Camden also found the name, though as we shall see, there are reasons for supposing that Shakespeare found it directly in Lucian. There were several translations of the essay in the fifteenth and sixteenth centuries, both into Latin and into various European vernaculars. Though there was, apparently, no complete translation into English, it was widely drawn on, notably by Sir Thomas Elyot in his influential *Book of the Governor* (1531), which contains a chapter, "Of Detraction and the ymage therof made by the painter Apelles." Most famously, the humanist scholar, biographer, and friend of Martin Luther, Philip Melanchthon, translated it into Latin in 1518. This version was reprinted many times, often collected together with other translations of Lucian by Erasmus and Sir Thomas More—by far the best-selling of all their works throughout the sixteenth century.

The essay *Calumnia* was particularly famous, as Elyot's title indicates, because it contained a detailed description of a painting on the theme of slander by Apelles, the greatest artist of classical antiquity. The painting had long been lost, but during the Renaissance a number of artists, including Botticelli, Raphael, Mantegna, Dürer, Breugel, and Rubens, attempted to recreate Apelles's masterpiece from Lucian's account.[9] Of particular interest from our perspective is the section of the essay that explains how Apelles came to paint his masterpiece, spurred on by the experience of being slandered himself:

> I should say, however, that Apelles of Ephesus long ago preempted this subject for a picture; and with good reason, for he himself had been slandered to Ptolemy on the ground that he had taken part with Theodotas in the conspiracy in Tyre, although Apelles had never set eyes on Tyre and did not know who Theodotas was. . . . Nevertheless, one of his rivals named Antiphilus, through envy of his favour at court and professional jealousy, maligned him by telling Ptolemy that he had taken part in the whole enterprise, and that someone had seen him dining with Theodotas in Phoenicia. (Lucian 1913–67, 363)

Apelles was born in Colophon, but spent part of his working life in Ephesus, and this is where Lucian locates him. This passage thus appears to be the only instance outside of Shakespeare that brings together the town of Ephesus with the name "Antiphilus" (Αντιφιλοσ in the original Greek). This in itself—given Shakespeare's adoption of Ephesus as his setting, in defiance of his other sources—creates a strong prima facie case for its having been where he found it. But there are, as we shall see, other aspects of the essay that also relate closely to the play, and they suggest why Shakespeare might have found it so apposite for his purposes.

Slander

There are features of the story as Lucian tells it that show that it cannot be true in its entirety: the ruler to whom Apelles is said to have been slandered was not even born before the painter died. Moreover, this Antiphilus is otherwise unknown: his name, which may well therefore be fictional, is a cognomen in the essay for a slanderer, "'vnkinde,' anti love," as in the forms Baldwin cites from Sidney and Camden. It would be ironic to the point of sarcasm if it were also to be understood "as a proper name for a lover." There are, rather, compelling grounds for supposing that Shakespeare associated "Antipholus" with slander in this way. One of the primary consequences of the presence of Antipholus of Syracuse in Ephesus is the inadvertent chain of slanders that he unleashes on his brother, his brother's wife, and his brother's creditors. Shakespeare draws attention to it by making it the subject of a sustained passage by the merchant Balthasar warning Antipholus of Ephesus against actions that will all too easily destroy reputations:

> Herein you war against your reputation,
> And draw within the compass of suspect
> Th'unviolated honour of your wife. . . .
> If by strong hand you offer to break in
> Now in the stirring passage of the day,
> A vulgar comment will be made of it;
> And that supposed by the common rout
> Against your yet ungalled estimation,
> That may with foul intrusion enter in,
> And dwell upon your grave when you are dead;
> For slander lives upon succession,
> For e'er hous'd where it gets possession.
>   (3.1.86–106)

This offers a disinterested perspective on a concern with honor and reputation that is common to all the principal characters. The issue is never simply whether they are honorable or virtuous, but whether they are thought to be so, whether public gossip accounts them so: the power of words alone to rob them of something that is intimately part of their own identity. So Adriana berates a bemused Antipholus of Syracuse, believing him to be her husband (and so, in a Pauline sense, her flesh, herself):

> How dearly would it touch thee to the quick,
> Shouldst thou but hear I were licentious?
> And that this body, consecrate to thee,
> By ruffian lust should be contaminate?
>
> (2.2.130–33)

Similarly, doubts about financial probity challenge reputation as closely as do imputations of sexual impropriety, as we see in Antipholus of Ephesus's quarrel about the chain of gold:

ANTIPHOLUS OF EPHESUS: You gave me none; you wrong me much to say so.
ANGELO: You wrong me more, sir, in denying it.
Consider how much it stands upon my credit. . . .
This touches me in reputation.

> (4.1.66–72)

Later Angelo acknowledges the reputation Antipholus has enjoyed hitherto, in words that pointedly conflate money and public estimation:

> Of very reverend reputation, sir,
> Of credit infinite, highly belov'd,
> Second to none that lives here in the city;
> His word might bear my wealth at any time.
>
> (5.1.5–8)

If the text never quite rises to the eloquence of Cassio's lament in *Othello* for his reputation, it is nevertheless shot through with the same concern.

Adriana unwittingly compounds her husband's loss of reputation simply by telling (as she thinks) the truth:

> O husband, God doth know you din'd at home,
> Where would you had remained until this time,
> Free from these slanders and this open shame.
>
> (4.4.63–65)

And Angelo similarly takes him (or, in fact, his brother of Syracuse) to task for so endangering both of their reputations:

> Signior Antipholus, I wonder much
> That you should put me to this shame and trouble,
> And not without some scandal to yourself. . . .
>
> (5.1.13–15)

Scandal and slander are etymologically and conceptually cognate (see *OED* under "Slander"), different public manifestations of ruined reputation, of lost honor. These are among the deepest concerns of the play.

The Comedy of Errors is a play about identities and selfhoods: the collision of two long-separated pairs of identical twins undermines the comfortable, conventional certainties the four of them have enjoyed about themselves and their places in the world. For the twins are not only physically indistinguishable, they also share the same names— socially, the signifiers by which identity and individuality are primarily conferred. The uneasy farce that this generates may be understood as figuring forth a number of deepseated psychological insecurities, which in this play are to be resolved in the reconstruction of the lost nuclear family—unlike the action of most of Shakespeare's Elizabethan comedies, where resolution at least notionally lies in the construction of new families by marriage.[10] As part of this *regressive* process there is an important sense in which the two Antipholuses (like the two Dromios) *are* the same person, are undifferentiated versions of the same selfhood. Or, as the Duke puts it: "One of these men is *genius* to the other" (5.1.332).

In that identity lie the seeds of slander and scandal: in simply existing as they do, *they* as it were slander *him*self. By being in the same place, and being the-same-but-not-the-same, Antipholus of Syracuse repeatedly (if unwittingly) slanders Antipholus of Ephesus, giving rise to a scandal in which his brother denies receipt of a precious object and fails to pay his debts. At the same time, he compounds a sexual slander that Antipholus of Ephesus has largely brought upon himself, with some assistance from Adriana's jealousy: that he is shunning her and being unfaithful. Adriana puts the worst construction on her husband's tardiness, which Antipholus of Syracuse tends to confirm by denying her and lavishing his attentions on Luciana. Conversely, Adriana's refusal to admit her true husband for lunch prompts him to imagine *her* cuckolding *him,* so giving rise to a mirror image of the scandal in which she had supposed *him* unfaithful to *her.* Even worse, Antipholus of Ephesus takes this as grounds for misbehaving himself, supping with the courtesan at the Porcupine and taking her ring (easily construed by slander as a sexual favor), promising the gold chain or carcanet commissioned for his wife in return. When the courtesan believes that he will neither give her the chain nor return her ring, she resolves to get even by forging the only *deliberate* slander in the play:

> My way is now to hie home to his house,
> And tell his wife that, being lunatic,
> He rush'd into my house and took perforce
> My ring away.
>
> (4.3.89–92)

It is a moot point whether Adriana would have preferred her husband proved a lunatic or an adulterer. In all of this, slander has the force of nightmare, giving life and credibility ("credit") to the deepest fears and insecurities about social, financial, mental, and sexual integrity, before it is banished by truth in the form of the abbess/mother.

Although the theme of slander (as instigated by an Antiphilus in Ephesus) is what most compellingly links Shakespeare's play with Lucian's essay, there are other suggestive details. One is the repeated likening of both Dromios to asses, culminating in this exchange:

ANTIPHOLUS OF EPHESUS: Thou art sensible in nothing but blows, and so is an ass.
DROMIO OF EPHESUS: I am an ass indeed; you may prove it by my long ears.

> (4.4.25–28; see also 2.2.199, 3.1.15)

Of course, the Dromios are the butts of much of the comedy, and the likening of fools to asses is commonplace, even proverbial. Yet a prominent feature of Lucian's account of Apelles's picture, and its many Renaissance imitations, is that the man who hears the slander (commonly referred to in translations as a judge or prince) has an ass's ears: "On the right of it sits a man with very large ears, almost like those of Midas, extending his hand to Slander while she is still at some distance from him" (Lucian, 365). By the same token, the choice of Luciana as the name of a character for whom there is no parallel in Plautus is intriguing in the context of the debt I suppose to Lucian. The name clearly has associations with the Latin *lux,* light, and its tradition-al Christian associations with truth, so this may be coincidental. But both in Lucian and in the visual tradition, Truth herself is the antithe-sis of Slander, counterbalancing on one side of the composition the man with the large ears on the other. For someone alert to the parallels, the play repeatedly seems to recall features of the famous essay.

RELIGION

Outside the confines of Plautine farce, where is slander—and most particularly *self*-slander—a pressing issue? In the context of the play Shakespeare crafted, it is in matters of religion: the whole dimension opened up by the translation of the action to Ephesus. The slander of Antiphilus against Apelles, according to Lucian, was political—that he had conspired against the ruler, Ptolemy. But in Counter-Reformation England, there could be no distinction between what Queen Elizabeth herself linked as "matters of religion or of the governaunce of the estate of the common weale."[11] "In the preface to the Latin versions, dedicated to Frederick III, Elector of Saxony, Melanchthon spoke of the elegance of Lucian's style, the vividness of the account of Calumny found in it, and the seriousness of the moral prescriptions Lucian set down. Calumny is a pestilential vice, so he wrote, one so pervasive that even a wise prince like Frederick would be well advised to be on constant guard against its workings" (Cast 1981, 95). The interest of Melanchthon, Elyot, and other humanists in Lucian's essay was partly stylistic, but more urgently a matter of its moral teaching, which readily translated into the religious/political sphere.

In a pioneering study that shows how this theme relates both to the integrity of the humanist artist and to religious controversy, Fritz Saxl (1936) traced the subject through various pictorial representations in the early sixteenth century, and most particularly in a woodcut adopted by Marcolini da Forti as a trademark for his publishing house in Venice, eventually known as the *Bottega della Verità*. This "shows Truth rising from an abyss towards Heaven, while Saturn in the person of an old man with an hour-glass takes her by the arm to save her from the danger of falling back into the pit and at the same time from the onslaught of a creature with a dragon's tail who pulls her tail and beats her with snakes" (199). This combines "the Greek idea that Truth must be brought up from the depths, and the Latin that Saturn is the father of Truth," while the dragonly creature can be identified as:

> *Calumnia*. This extension of the basic theme, that Truth is the child of Time, brings it into association with one of the most celebrated of the Renaissance allegories, the traditional Calumny of Apelles. The design is, in fact, essentially a modified *Calumnia Apellis*. According to Lucian, Calumny drags her victim by the hair into the presence of the

Unwise Judge, and Truth stands in the background, raising her eyes towards Heaven. In Marcolino's *impresa* there is no Judge. Of all the base figures of Lucian's account, only Calumny remains; and it is no mere mortal, but Truth herself, who is the object of attack. Time comes to her aid in her affliction. (200)

Saxl suggests that Marcolino's associate Pietro Aretino particularly espoused the theme: "For him old Lucian's fable was no mere antique tale, the sport of fashionable erudition. It [that is, the vindication of truth] was, on the contrary, an essential canon of his creed; and the basic theme of the classical account—that the courts of princes are the seats of Calumny, where to speak honestly is to invite indignity, and truth and repentance follow slowly—is in no small degree a factor in the literary life of Aretino" (201).[12] For Aretino and other such humanist commentators, "Time conquers Calumny; Time is the deliverer of Truth from persecution and oppression, and in the end brings honour and reputation" (201).

But Marcolino's *impresa* clearly also relates to religious themes. It bears the motto *Veritas filia Temporis* (Truth, the daughter of Time), and Saxl shows that this entered Renaissance circulation in association with a parallel woodcut in "William Marshall's *Goodly Prymer of Englyshe,* issued just at the time of Henry VIII's breach with Rome . . . The drawing stands for the liberation of Christian Truth (as seen by Protestant reformers) from her captivity under the monster of Roman hypocrisy" (203). The whole motif became deeply embedded in Reformation controversy, and employed by Protestants and Catholics alike, as in the case of Hieronymus Lauretus, who, in his compilation of the *Forest of Allegories* (1570), considers heretics as slanderers whose false accusations are their dogmas. This almost certainly explains why Philip Melanchthon should have been drawn to translate Lucian's essay: few texts would more convincingly marry his classical erudition (he became a professor of Greek at the age of eighteen) with his Lutheran convictions. As Jean Michel Massing relates:

En 1538 Eoban Hess commence son apology de Melanchthon, un long poème écrit à la demande du réformateur, par une description de la peinture d'Apelle; dans son analyse, il conclut que la calomnie est le pire des maux, surtout dans les controverses religieuses. Hess attaque viollement les bulles papales contre Luther mais la finalité du poème est de défendre Melanchthon de ses détracteurs qui l'avaient accusé de compromission. (Massing 1990, 146)[13]

Massing also shows how the theme of the overthrow of slander/heresy can be read into the way emblemists like Hadrianus Junius and Geoffrey Whitney skillfully brought together pictures and texts on the theme of truth: "Quelques emblèmes présentent les figures de la Calomnie integrées dans une scène plus complex. Junius et Whitney les on reprises dans leur allégories du Temps révélant la Vérité (*Veritas filia temporis*). Ce motif et cette maxime . . . ont été influents pendant tout le XVIe siècle, surtout dans les controverses religieuses et la propagande politique anglaise" (99–100).[14]

Once we understand that the *Calumny of Apelles* is a text/motif that was readily understood as a metaphor for religious heresy, we are better placed to comprehend the nature of the multiple "slanders" that Shakespeare locates in Ephesus. Yet these are only fully intelligible in relation to that specific location and its resonances. Some of these we have already noted, all deriving ultimately from the Bible: demons and witchcraft (the Greek for slander is διαβολη, whence "diabolic"), disorder, the proper relationship between husbands and wives (Kinney 1988). But we need also to consider post-biblical resonances that attached to Ephesus, specifically those that associated the town with the Virgin Mary, and the town's significance in Shakespeare's own day.

The links of Ephesus with the Virgin Mary were particularly strong because many believed she went to live there with St. John after the death of Christ, and that she died (or, as some would say, was received into heaven) there: "Jerusalem's claim to Mary's grave was disputed. Other scholars assert that the Virgin died at Ephesus, where the Council of 431 proclaimed her *Theotokos,* and where she lived in John's care after the Crucifixion. The tradition of John's stay in Ephesus is very strong, and Jesus' recommendation of Mary to his keeping offers weighty support for the argument that she lived with him" (Warner 1976, 87–88). There was a compelling theological sequence to this account in that in pagan antiquity, Ephesus was closely associated with the virgin goddess, Diana, whose temple there was (and is) famous. As Anne E. Mather puts it: "fervor for the local Diana of the Epheisans gave way very quickly to equally deep devotion to Mary" (Mather 1992, 91; qtd. in Markidou 1999, 86). Marina Warner glosses this further: "There could be, therefore, a chain of descent from Hippolyte to Diana to the Virgin, for one tradition holds that Mary was assumed into heaven from Ephesus, where she spent the last years of her life, and where St. Thomas, according to the legend, received her heavenly girdle as proof" (Warner 1976, 280).[15]

It is difficult to believe that Shakespeare's original audiences did not associate the Diana/Virgin traditions of Ephesus with the abbess and the priory, which are the focal point of the play's resolution. This seems all the more likely when we also consider the contemporary associations of the place, which made any such Christian presences highly unlikely. By the late sixteenth century, Ephesus was one of the ancient and revered Christian sites that had fallen to the Ottoman Turks, a shame that was felt across divided Christendom, as we see, for example, in John Foxe's *Book of Martyrs,* which carefully lists such losses (Foxe 1583, 760).[16] The Plautine and biblical derivations of the play inevitably focus our attention on the classical past, as if the action takes place (if we have to date it at all) up to fifteen hundred years before Shakespeare wrote.

But there are good reasons for supposing that it would have been received as a contemporary tale. When Dromio of Syracuse is "find[ing] out countries" in the servant, Luce/Nell, his master asks him, "Where America, the Indies?" (3.2.112/13, 131)—the only direct reference in the whole of Shakespeare to the continent unknown in classical times. Yet the name of the Duke of Ephesus, Solinus (only voiced in the opening line), possibly reminded audiences either of Suleiman the Magnificent or of his successor Selim or Selimus II, Sultan of Turkey until his death in 1574.[17] Inasmuch as Shakespeare allows us to be specific at all, we are in modern times, in a land probably ruled by the Moslem Turks, and this gives substance to the otherwise inexplicable enmity between Christian Syracuse (cf. Antipholus of Syracuse avers "as I am a Christian," 1.2.77) and Ephesus, which is so strong as to condemn Egeus to death simply for being in the wrong place and requires Antipholus and Dromio of Syracuse to keep secret their origins.[18] In such a context, it is all the more surprising that the resolution of the play should hinge on the discovery of a palpably Christian abbess and priory.

We should beware, however, of being too simplistic in our understanding of how the Turk registered on the Elizabethan consciousness. While the whole of Christendom feared the westward progress of the Ottoman Empire, not effectively blocked until the sea battle of Lepanto in 1570 (the context in which *Othello* is situated), England actually cultivated diplomatic and trading links with Constantinople, primarily to counterbalance the growing sway across Europe and the Mediterranean of the Catholic Hapsburg powers.

Indeed, if we examine the very context in Foxe's *Book of Martyrs,* where the loss of Ephesus to the Turks is recorded, we find some interesting equations being drawn. A running header for the account in the 1583 edition is "Prophesies of the Turke and the Pope, which of them is the greater Antichrist" (765–66). Foxe tries to suggest a link between the adoption of the doctrine of Transubstantiation in 1215 and the rise of the Ottoman Turks shortly thereafter (Foxe's side note reads, "The tyme of Transubstantiation. The tyme of the Turkes," 768); and there is a developed comparison between the Turks and the Pope:

> Now in comparing the Turke with the pope, if a question be asked whether of them is the truer or greater Antichrist, it were easy to see and judge, that the Turke is the more open and manifest enemye against Christe and hys Church. But if it be asked, whether of them two hath bene the more bloudy and pernitious adversary to Christe and his members: or whether of them hath consumed and spilt more Christian bloud, he with sword, or this with fire and sword together, neither is it a light matter to discerne, neither is it my part here to discusse, which doe onely write the history, and the Actes of them both. (773)

But we can reach our own conclusions! From a zealous Protestant perspective, Roman Catholicism and Turkish Islam both constitute aggressively alien and implicitly similar "others."

The similarities are such, in fact, that it is commonly possible for Catholic and Turk to be interchangeable signifiers in the early modern period, and that, I suggest, is what is at work in *The Comedy of Errors.* Ephesus is both the modern town under the Turkish yoke and the town traditionally associated with the Virgin Mary, so central to Roman Catholic Christianity. So the Syracuse/Ephesus divide in the play is not only that between Christian and Turk; it is also that between Protestant and Catholic. Once that discourse is activated, the allegory of two sets of identical and identically named twins slandering each other simply by being in the same place is easily decoded. In that Counter-Reformation world, identities and allegiances depended as never before on inscrutable inner faith, in a way that generated suspicion, mistrust, and false understandings. Antipholus slandered his brother Antipholus, perhaps unwittingly, to the ass-eared Dromio, while Repentance and Truth lagged far behind. The parallels with the often-paranoid 1950s

Cold War, with its nights of the living dead, give modern generations some idea of what it must have been like. It is particularly chilling in this context to remember T. W. Baldwin's suggestion (so much more compelling than his explanation of "Antipholus") that the sentence of death hanging over Egeon throughout the play would have reminded theatergoers at the Curtain or Theatre of the execution of William Hartley, a seminary priest, hard by in Finsbury Fields in 1588 (Baldwin 1931). Egeon is only ever so named at the end of the text. Solinus first addresses him as "Merchant of Syracusa" (1.1.3), and in the First Folio speech-prefixes invariably identify him as "Merchant" (in a play full of merchants) or "Father": "merchant" was the code term, as the authorities well knew, by which the Jesuits at large in England referred to each other. The "merchant" under threat of death is a potent reminder throughout the play of the utterly malign force of religious slander.

This is not the place to speculate about what, if anything, this tells us about Shakespeare's own faith. It is not immediately apparent that people from Syracuse are more admirable than those from Ephesus, or vice versa. On the contrary, the pressures of the play are toward inclusiveness rather than vindictive exclusion. In particular, they move toward the reconstruction of the original nuclear family of Egeon and Emilia, their sons, and their servants; the differences located in the relationships of the Antipholi with the sisters Adriana and Luciana are doubtless important, but they are secondary in the context of that life-saving regression to the primary unit. The fact that this process is conducted under the aegis of the abbess/mother, so redolent of the Virgin Mary in Ephesus, perhaps points us toward the Catholic faith as the vehicle of redemption. But it is more psychologically compelling in this context that the Catholic was the Old Faith, the faith of an undivided Christendom, where brother did not slander brother just by what he believed, or was thought to believe, or where he lived. The errors of the play are wanderings, literal, theological, and slanderous; the comedy lies in a magical regression to a state where they no longer exist.

NOTES

1. Baldwin also addressed these matters in his edition of the play for Heath's American Arden Shakespeare and *Small Latine & Lesse Greeke* (1944). See Foakes's edition, "The Sources" (1962, xxiv–xxxiv). All references to the text,

unless otherwise noted, are to this edition. An earlier form of the present essay was published in *Religion and the Arts* 7.1/2 (2003).

2. Foakes reproduces the key biblical passages in an appendix (1962, 113–15).

3. Hamilton reads the play as a parodic commentary on contemporary ecclesiology, the "errors" or wanderings of the Church of England between the Catholicism of Rome and the ever more extreme Protestantism of the Puritans, largely on the associations of Ephesus as the place where Paul had appointed Timothy to a position in the church (1 Timothy 3 ff.): whether that position was as a bishop, as traditional Episcopalians claimed, or as an evangelist preacher, as Presbyterians and other Puritans claimed, was matter of fierce debate in the late sixteenth century.

4. The terminal dates for the play are usually taken to be 1589 and 1594, the period of the French civil war from which Henri of Navarre emerged as Henry IV, which seems to be alluded to at 3.2.120–22.

5. Between Greek, Latin, and English forms, any of these names—Antipholus, Antipholis, Antiphilos, and Antiphilis—might well be interchangeable in sixteenth-century usage.

6. Baldwin is here citing Cunningham, (1907, xxix); Philip Sidney's *Arcadia* (1590, 159r, 231v); and William Camden, *Britannia* (1600), *Ad Lectorem,* at end, 4.

7. Foakes, publishing a few years before *Compositional Genetics,* here follows Baldwin's version of things in *Shakespere's Five-Act Structure* (1947, 695–96). They cover similar territory. A more recent but improbably random suggestion about the derivation of Antipholus is that of Elizabeth Truax: "Shakespeare created the name Antipholus by combining the name Pholus, a centaur mentioned by Ovid in *Metamorphoses* XII. 306, with 'anti,' the antipathy between Syracuse and Ephesus which is so important to the intrigue of the play" (1992, 35). Quoted in Markidou (1999, 70).

8. I am happy to acknowledge that it was in the course of reading Michael Frayn's splendid novel, *Headlong* (1999), that I first came across the associations between Lucian, Apelles, Antipholus, Ephesus, and slander. Some of the work for this essay was done during a month's fellowship at the Huntington Library in 2001, travel for which was paid by the British Academy: I am extremely grateful to both institutions.

9. The tale of the Renaissance rediscovery and transmission of Lucian's essay, and the paintings it inspired, has been told in detail by Cast (1991) and Massing (1990).

10. For different psychoanalytic readings of the play see MacCary (1978) and Freedman (1980).

11. Proclamation of May 16, 1559, to mayors and other local officials on the licensing of plays; cited in Chambers (1923, 4: 263).

12. Repentance, a haggard old woman, stands between Calumny and Truth in Lucian's essay and paintings based on it.

13. "In 1538 Eoban Hess begins his apology for Melanchthon, a long poem written at the request of the reformer, with a description of the Apelles's painting; in his analysis, he concludes that slander is the worst of evils, above all in religious controversies. Hess violently attacks the papal bulls against Luther, but the ending of the poem is concerned to defend Melanchthon from his detractors, who had accused him of compromising himself" (*my translation*).

14. "Several emblems present figures of Calumny integrated in a more complex scene. Junius and Whitney reprised them in their allegories of Time revealing Truth (*Truth the Daughter of Time*). This motif and this maxim . . . were influential throughout the whole of the sixteenth century, above all in the religious controversies and English political propaganda."

15. Even accounts of the Virgin Mary's death in Jerusalem often want to preserve the link with Ephesus. For example, "Now it happened that John was preaching in Ephesus when suddenly there was a clap of thunder, and a shining cloud picked him up and whisked him to Mary's door" (De Voragine 1993, 78).

16. Ephesus (Efez) is, of course, still in modern Turkey.

17. Solinus is actually the name of a third-century Roman geographer, and it is far from clear why Shakespeare used it except that his book, commonly known as *Polyhistor,* dealt with the Eastern Mediterranean; chapter 52 refers specifically to "Ephesus."

18. I am indebted to Vassiliki Markidou's unpublished doctoral thesis, "Shakespeare's Greek Plays" (1999), for this perspective on the sixteenth-century associations of Ephesus.

Works Cited

Austen, Glyn. "Ephesus Restored: Sacramentalism and Redemption in *The Comedy of Errors.*" *Literature and Theology* 1 (1987): 54–69.

Baldwin, T. W., ed. *The Comedy of Errors.* Boston: Heath, 1928.

_____. *On the Compositional Genetics of "The Comedy of Errors."* Urbana, Ill.: University of Illinois Press, 1965.

_____. *Shakespere's Five-Act Structure.* Urbana, Ill: University of Illinois Press, 1947.

_____. *William Shakespeare Adapts a Hanging.* Princeton, N.J.: Princeton University Press, 1931.

_____. *William Shakespere's Small Latine & Lesse Greeke*. 2 vols. Urbana, Ill.: University of Illinois Press, 1944.

Candido, Joseph. "Dining Out in Ephesus: Food in *The Comedy of Errors*." *SEL* 30 (1990): 217–41.

Cast, David. *The Calumny of Apelles: A Study in the Humanist Tradition*. New Haven, Conn., and London: Yale University Press, 1981.

Chambers, E. K. *The Elizabethan Stage*. 4 vols. Oxford, England: Clarendon Press, 1923.

Cunningham, Henry, ed. *The Comedy of Errors*. The Arden Shakespeare. London: Methuen, 1907.

De Voragine, Jacobus. "The Assumption of the Virgin." In *The Golden Legend: Readings on the Saints*. Trans. William G. Ryan. 2 vols. Vol. 2: 77–97. Princeton, N.J.: Princeton University Press, 1993.

Foakes, R. A., ed. *The Comedy of Errors*. The Arden Shakespeare. London: Methuen, 1962.

Foxe, John. *The ecclesiasticall histories, conteining the acts and monuments of martyrs . . . Newly recognised and inlarged by the author*. London: John Day, 1583.

Frayn, Michael. *Headlong*. London: Faber, 1999.

Freedman, Barbara. "Egeon's Debt, Self-Division, and Self-Redemption in *The Comedy of Errors*." *ELR* 10 (1980): 360–83.

Hamilton, Donna B. *Shakespeare and the Politics of Protestant England*. Hemel Hempstead, England: Harvester Wheatsheaf, 1992.

Kinney, Arthur. "Shakespeare's *Comedy of Errors* and the Nature of Kinds." *Studies in Philology* 85 (1988): 25–52.

Lucian. "Slander." In *Lucian,* ed. and trans. A. M. Harmon. Loeb edition. 8 vols. Vol. I. 359–93. Cambridge, Mass.: Harvard University Press, 1913–67.

MacCary, W. Thomas. "*The Comedy of Errors:* A Different Kind of Comedy." *New Literary History* 11 (1978): 525–36.

Markidou, Vassiliki. "Shakespeare's Greek Plays." Unpublished doctoral thesis, Lancaster University, 1999.

Massing, Jean Michel. *Du Texte à L'Image: La Calomnie d'Apelle et Son Iconographie*. Strasbourg, France: Presses Universitaires de Strasbourg, 1990.

Mather, Anne E. "The Virgin Mary: A Goddess." In *The Book of the Goddess. Past and Present: An Introduction to Her Religion,* ed. Carl Olson. 80–96. New York: Crossroad, 1992.

Saxl, F. "Veritas filia Temporis." In *Philosophy and History: Essays Presented to Ernst Cassirer,* ed. Raymond Klibansky and H. J. Paton. 197–222. Oxford, England: Clarendon Press, 1936.

Truax, Elizabeth. *Metamorphosis in Shakespeare's plays: A Pageant of Heroes, Gods, Maids, and Monsters.* Lewiston, Maine: Edwin Mellen Press, 1992.

Warner, Marina. *Alone of All Her Sex.* London: Weidenfeld and Nicolson Ltd., 1976.

2

"Obsequious Laments": Mourning and Communal Memory in Shakespeare's *Richard III*

College of Staten Island, City University of New York

In 1590, outraged reformers in Lancaster documented "enormities and abuses" and "manifold popish superstition used in the burial of the dead" by the local community:

> And when the corpse is ready to be put into the grave, some by kissing the dead corpse, others by wailing the dead with more than heathenish outcries, others with open invocations for the dead, and another sort with jangling the bells, so disturb the whole action, that the minister is oft compelled to let pass that part of the service and to withdraw himself from their tumultuous assembly. (Raines 1875, 57)[1]

The Elizabethan prelates decry the practice of "wailing the dead" as a lawless abomination that undermines civil authority and impedes the progress of the reformed church. In Shakespeare's *Richard III,* Gloucester and Buckingham similarly view lamentation as a threat. They worry that their furtive execution of Hastings will cause the citizens to revolt, and they imagine that rebellion taking the form of wailing the dead. Buckingham asks the mayor to justify their assassination to the citizens because he fears they "haply may / Misconstrue us in him and wail his death" (3.5.60–61).[2] Buckingham's words directly link politics and lamentation: he implies that the citizens will "wail" for Hastings not as a matter of course, but as a deliberate means of protest.

The citizens do not rebel against Richard, but the women do, staging their rebellion in the same manner that is denounced both within the world of the play and without. In act 4, scene 4, which Nicole Loraux dubs "the scene of mothers" (1998, 1), the Duchess of York, Queen Elizabeth, and Old Queen Margaret congregate outside the Tower and "wail" their dead. They invoke the spirits of their dead sons and husbands with "heathenish" cursing and chanting. Earlier in the play, Lady Anne performs a similar ritual over King Henry VI's corpse, invoking his ghost, weeping over his body, and calling down curses on his murderer.

Scholars often refer to the ritualistic nature of the women's laments in *Richard III*. However, no one has yet recognized that these scenes evoke actual mourning practices that were viewed as increasingly problematic after the Reformation. In this essay, I explore Shakespeare's tragic history of an England divided against itself in the context of Elizabethan tensions over mourning and burial ritual. As I hope to show, the reintegration of the fragmented kingdom depends not upon the proud elegies of the men in power, but instead upon the woeful laments of the disenfranchised women. My approach qualifies Stephen Greenblatt's recent reading of *Richard III*, in which he argues that the ghosts in the play "function as the memory of the murdered, a memory registered not only in Richard's troubled psyche . . . but also in the collective consciousness of the kingdom . . . [and] as the agents of a restored health and wholeness to the damaged community" (2001, 180). I propose that it is the women, not the ghosts, who articulate the communal consciousness and catalyze the healing of the kingdom. For the appearance of the ghosts and Richard's troubled dreams are poetically and dramatically linked to the ritual laments of the widowed queens. *Richard III* thus probes the relationship between funeral ritual and communal consciousness, registering a sense of loss for the medieval structure of communal mourning and remembrance that was dismantled by the Reformation.

I

Shakespeare wrote *Richard III* "about 1592" (Baker 1974, 708), within two years of the riotous ceremony recorded in Lancaster. It is a striking coincidence that he stages a similar Lancastrian uprising with his weeping widowed queens. Whether or not he knew about this particular event, the conjunction of drama and ecclesiastical record suggests, however, that "wailing for the dead" was a matter of some concern in late sixteenth-century England.

What is it about "wailing for the dead" that threatens those seeking political power, as in the case of Shakespeare's *Richard III*, or ecclesiastical control, as in the case of the Lancastrian visitation record? For Buckingham and Gloucester, it represents not only public grief, but also civic grievance: a communal commemorative ritual that would call them to account for their crimes. For the Elizabethan reformers, the practice demonstrates the tenacity of indigenous mourning customs despite an extensive official program to eliminate them.[3] These instances embody different anxieties, but both demonstrate the power of funerary rites to perform and suppress communal memory.[4]

In ideal circumstances, as anthropologists and social historians have shown, burial rituals accomplish the cultural work of upholding and reintegrating communities when they are faced with death.[5] Death rites perform, in order to contain, the "disintegrating impulses" that "threaten the very cohesion and solidarity of the group" (Malinowski 1926, 47–50). In the broadest sense, funeral ritual resolves the social and psychic disruption caused by death through the symbolic enactment of continuity—in the immediate family, in the larger kin groups, and in the wider community. However, in post-Reformation England, funerals were often sites of discord, sources of angst rather than solace as tensions surrounding the practice of wailing the dead suggest.[6]

This unrest arose from the eradication of the doctrine of Purgatory, which, as recent studies show, was one of the most unsettling aspects of the Reformation in England.[7] It changed, almost overnight, the raison d'être of ceremonies for the dead. The consequent alterations to funeral ritual were often subtle yet profound. On the one hand, many practices, such as heraldic processions and bell-ringing, retained their external shapes with only minor modifications. On the other hand, these seemingly slight alterations transformed the meaning of the ritual.

Most changes were designed to efface all traces of the doctrine of Purgatory, effectively cutting off communion with the dead and curtailing the acceptable period of public mourning for the bereaved. Richard L. Greaves describes the "delicate problem" of the Elizabethan Protestants: "They wanted to curtail ceremonies and symbols associated with such Catholic doctrines as satisfaction and purgatory, but they needed to retain the traditional pomp as an underpinning of the social order; they had to avoid so alienating the common folk that Protestantism was repudiated" (1981, 695). The banners of the Catholic saints were removed from the processions of heraldic funerals and the tolling bell was given a new meaning. John Donne's memorable line, "never send to know for whom the bell tolls; it tolls for thee" succinctly encapsulates this revised message ("XVII Meditation" 344). The ringing bell, a relic of the Middle Ages, still signals the death knell, but to a different end: those who hear it are exhorted to turn inward, to contemplate their own fates, and not concern themselves with the souls of others for whom they now can do nothing. The outward sign remains, but its new message of inwardness and individuality is remote from its functional origin, which was to alert the entire community, even farmers tilling their fields, to join in intercessory, shared prayers for the souls of the dying. The emphasis of funeral practices thus shifted from the communal and spiritual focus of intercession to the more personal and secular focus of commemoration. As Keith Thomas explains, the transformation in the discourse of the afterlife not only altered the relationship between the living and the dead, but also changed the communities of the living:

> Protestant doctrine meant that each generation could be indifferent to the spiritual fate of its predecessor. Every individual was now to keep his own balance-sheet, and a man could no longer atone for his sins by the prayers of his descendants. This implied an altogether more atomistic conception of the relationship in which members of society stood to each other. No longer would they allocate so much of their resources to the performance of rituals primarily intended for the spiritual welfare of their dead ancestors. (1971, 603)

In contrast to the medieval discourse that emphasized continuity and reciprocity between the living and the dead, the post-Reformation construction of death made the ultimate end final, with no possibility for mitigation or alteration. The bereaved had no hope of helping their loved ones through compassionate intercessory prayer or weeping. As Michael Neill puts it, intercession was a "liturgy of remembrance," irrevocably silenced by the Reformation: the living could no longer "intervene on behalf of the dead; each man's death had become . . . a private Apocalypse, whose awful Judgment could never be reversed. The dead might still call upon the duty, love, and pity of the living, but the new theology rendered all such emotion painfully ineffectual"

(1985, 180). This separation between the living and the dead, Eamon Duffy points out, is evident in the revised funeral service: "it is not too much to say that the oddest feature of the 1552 burial rite is the disappearance of the corpse from it" (1996, 475). The banishment of the body from the burial rite suggests early Protestantism's deep anxiety over any hint of a communicative link between the world of the dead and the community of the living.

To many Protestants, the change meant a gain in godliness, a cleansing of the church from corrupt, pagan-inspired practices, and a nascent sense of national identity.[8] But to many others, it was disturbing, not only on the personal level, but also in terms of the larger society. The Catholic system of intercessory prayer, despite religious corruption, had served important psychological and communal functions in England. It had kept the memory of the deceased alive in the community and given the living a sense of spiritual agency in the heavenly destiny of their loved ones, thus providing a legitimate, cyclical pattern of cathartic ritual for the bereaved. The concept of Purgatory had evolved over a millennium, embracing preexisting practices, and encompassing a vast, mutually supporting community that had become deeply ingrained in English culture.[9]

The complexity of this evolution is evident in the reformers' account of the Lancastrian funeral. For they refer to such ritual gestures as kissing the corpse, and openly invoking and wailing for the dead as both "popish" and "heathenish." These actions were perhaps tolerated, but never officially sanctioned by the medieval Catholic Church. Such accommodation was possible because, on a deep level, both intercessory prayer and wailing for the dead are grounded in similar ideas about the afterlife. Moreover, there is a strong affinity between weeping and prayer. Margery Kempe, who wept for hours on end to assuage the suffering of souls in Purgatory, is the best-known example of the medieval idea that tears, like prayers, could be offered for the dead.[10] Wailing the dead thus seems to be an earlier practice that was partially acculturated to Christian doctrine.

Because wailing the dead was an oral practice rather than a literary genre, the evidence for its existence as an indigenous English custom rests primarily in two types of sources: official denunciations of the practice in church records and sermons, and the popular Corpus Christi cycle plays. Scholars have long recognized medieval English drama as a collaborative cultural ritual designed to reconcile local customs with Christian doctrine and biblical history. Using recent research on the genre of archaic lament, Peter Dronke argues that the women's laments in medieval drama "draw upon archaic kinds of women's lament" (1988, 111). Anyone familiar with the representation of Mary in the medieval English cycles, especially the N-Town cycle, knows that she is hardly the stoic Mary of the Gospel accounts. The N-Town Mary mourns violently for her son, tearing her hair, throwing herself on the ground, and interrogating even God himself as to why her son must suffer and die. In the N-Town *Lazarus* episode, Martha and Mary Magdalene perform similar gestures at their brother's tomb. Dronke's sensitive study of these representations focuses on how similar their vernacular poetics are to archaic lament. He notes the love for life invested in motifs in which Mary laments the decay of Christ's physical beauty; the frequent use of direct address, a prominent rhetorical feature of archaic lament; and Mary's "unredeemable grief" that prevails over the Christian promise of salvation (1988).

The women's laments in medieval drama evoke the archaic genre of lamentation for the dead in other striking ways. In the N-Town *Burial* and *Lazarus* plays, the women's gestures recall those of the ancient practice. Mary cradles Jesus's body and mourns over him. Martha and Mary, prevented from kissing their brother's corpse, kiss the ground instead. They also attempt to remain at the gravesite, but are reprimanded by their consolers. Their laments embody all the rhetorical features of archaic lament: apostrophe, cursing, and gestures of self-mutilation, such as tearing the hair and throwing themselves on the ground. These moments, in a communal drama designed for and produced by a diverse community, I propose, provide glimpses into popular medieval mourning and burial practices that had been tenuously embraced by the Christian construction of death.

Official denunciations of wailing the dead, such as that found in the Lancastrian record, extend to the end of the sixteenth century and provide further evidence of its existence as an ethnic cultural practice. The post-Reformation suppression of purgatorial practices resulted in the loss of ritual justification for mourning and ignited concern over the appropriate demonstration of grief, ever an area of social scrutiny. On the one hand, sorrow was considered natural, an expected, even obligatory response to the loss of a loved one. On the other hand, sorrow could be excessive, self-indulgent, and construed as contrary to faith because it was believed to stem from doubt about the Resurrection. Especially during the early years of the Reformation, parishioners were exhorted to refrain from wailing the dead.

Two sermons delivered by high-ranking prelates within sixteen years of each other frame the period in which the Reformation gained its first foothold in England, and demonstrate this significant change in the official policy on public displays of grief. In 1535, John Longland, Bishop of Lincoln and staunch upholder of the royal supremacy of his king, Henry VIII, delivered a sermon in which he encouraged his congregation to empathize with the three Marys, joining them to weep over Christ's body:

> Yonder it lyes, yonder is hys bodye, in yonder tombe, in yonder sepulchre. Lett us goo thidre, lett us wepe with these Maryes, lett us turne and wynde thys bodye of Christe, lett us turne it thys wayes and that wayes, to and froo, and pytussely beholde hit. And what shall we fynde. We shall fynde a bloody bodye, a body full of plages and woundes. Not that hit nowe is fuul of woundes and plages, or nowe deede: but y[e]t thowe oughtest nowe as the tyme of the yere falleth, with the churche to remembere this body. Howe it was for the broken, howe it was for the rente and torn, howe bloody it was, howe full of plages, and howe it was wounded. And in recollection and remembrance therof, wepe and lament, for it was doon for the. (1535, sig. R4)

In Longland's sermon, the three Marys perform their traditional role of mourning for the dead. His imagery suggests that they are shrouding the body in its winding sheet while they weep. He exhorts his parishioners to join the three mourning women, weeping and winding the body in their minds, picturing it as wounded and bleeding. At the very moment in his sermon that this conception of death seems to contradict Christian doctrine, Longland reminds the faithful that the body is not now dead or full of wounds. Their tears are instead commemorative and empathetic: they lead to compunction for sin, a penitential act appropriate to Lent. As Eamon Duffy explains, the phrase "pytussely beholde" is "the technical term for meditation on the Passion . . . the liturgy is being used here as a trigger for penitential meditation" (1996, 37). The weeping of the three Marys for Christ provides the emotional link between mourning and memory, guiding the appropriate response of all Christians, whose sins were the cause of Christ's painful suffering and death. This sermon delineates the pedagogical function of the tears of the Virgin as well. As Duffy explains, the Virgin's grief was "not an end in itself, but . . . a means of arousing and focusing sympathetic suffering in the heart of the onlooker. In this literal compassion, this identification, with the sufferings of Christ by sharing the grief of his Mother, lay salvation" (259).

Less than two decades after Longland urged his parishioners to identify with a sorrow that was identified as feminine and weep over Christ's death in public communion, Matthew Parker, who would eventually become the Archbishop of Canterbury, chastised his congregation to reform their attitudes toward the dead. In his 1551 funeral sermon for Martin Bucer, he exhorts his listeners, "it agreeth not with the rules of faith, for a christian man to bewayle the dead. For who can deny that to be against faith, which is flatly forbidden by the scriptures?" (1587). He refers to the practice as "wommanish wayling, and childish infirmite" admonishing his congregation to renounce mourning altogether, for:

> it is both unseemly and wicked to use any howling or blubbering for him, unlesse we desire to be accounted creatures rather with beastly nature then furnished with the use of reason: to be deemed Heathen people rather then true christians: envious caitives then wel meaning friends: void of hope and faith, not understanding our happy estate, and persons doubtful and uncertain of their salvation, rather then constant beleevers undoubtedly embracing and crediting the infallible worde of God, therby as by a rule directing all and every our actions, thoughts and affections, and valiantly subduing and entirely triumphing over our imbecillity and weaknes. (1587)[11]

The two sermons do not differ significantly in their underlying Christian doctrine. Both affirm the promise of the Resurrection. What has changed is their respective tolerance for grief. Whereas Longland's sermon encourages weeping, Parker's completely denounces grief. As G. W. Pigman points out, "Parker has done nothing but equate grief with impiety and unmanliness," he has no "sympathy for the plight of the bereaved" (1985, 30). Indeed, in the second part of the sermon, as Pigman points out, Parker idealizes Martin Bucer and blames the living for his death: "Bucer's death is a sign of God's wrath, and we must confess our wicked and detestable lives, repent, beg pardon, and amend them. The allowance of grief for ourselves quickly becomes grief for the wickedness which caused Bucer's death. . . . Bereavement is a form of punishment" (31). Tears for the dead are guilty tears.

In late sixteenth-century England, these guilty tears are inextricably associated with women, and especially with the Virgin Mary, the embodiment of Catholic piety. Matthew Parker's sermon typifies what G. W. Pigman calls "rigorism," characteristic of the prevailing attitude toward grief in the early years of the Reformation. Rigorism, as Pigman notes, prohibits and condemns all grief for those who have died virtuously and are therefore (presumably) in heaven (1985, 27). Others, like Hugh Latimer, Miles Coverdale, and John Jewel argue that grief is permissible, but should be moderate. What constituted "moderate" mourning, however, was highly subjective. As Pigman points out, "unrestricted mourning never finds a theological champion, but some advocates of moderation insist upon mourning as a necessary expression of humanity" (27). Almost without exception, however, "excessive" mourning is synonymous with femininity and popery.[12] Two "sample" consolatory letters, seventy-four years apart and both addressed to men, demonstrate that, although what constituted "moderate" mourning varied widely, *immoderate* mourning (however defined) was always gendered female. Georgius Macropedius's *Methodus de conscribendis epistolis* (1543), a religious treatise that reached a wide audience in England, includes a section on consolation, in which he provides a sample letter to a grieving man. The letter shames the man, telling him that he behaves like a woman:

> you do your father no good, you do yourself harm, and you disturb your wife, your children, and all who love you; you cause everyone to grieve. You must cease weeping, if you desire us all, who bewail you more justly than you bewail your father, to control our tears. Don't, I pray, let us be exposed to the ridicule of ill-wishers who laugh at your tears, which have flown like a woman's.[13]

Several generations later, Gervase Markham's *Hobsons Horse-Load of Letters* (1617) includes a sample consolatory letter that is much more sympathetic to the emotions of the bereaved; nevertheless, excessive mourning is still pejoratively identified with female sorrow:

> Though you may seeme (vertuous) to have a worthy cause of much lamentation and teares, having lost such a Sonne, of whom al men conceived great hope, and his own towardnesses promised with an assurance

they should not be decieved; yet, if with judgement and truth taking away the veile of passion which blindeth our reason, we looke never [sic: for "neaer"] into it, there will small or no cause appeare of such immoderate grieving: a few drops are timely and well becomming a friendly Hearse; but, continuall languishment, as if you would dissolve into tears, like Niobe, shew either much weaknesse of man in you, or else bewray feare and ielousie, of you Sonnes undoubted and happie deliveries from this earthly prison, into a place of everlasting joy and delight.[14]

Though the established church under Elizabeth compromised, retaining vestiges of earlier ritual, it invalidated the underlying structure of shared empathy and remembrance, especially in the first decades after the Reformation. Open expressions of grief were viewed as effeminate, "heathenish," and "popish," because such mourning suggested communicative links with the dead, as well as with Rome and the medieval Catholic past. Although sermons and letters from the last decades of the sixteenth century indicate a more tolerant attitude toward grief, the communal structure that had given it legitimacy had been dismantled. The dramatic power embodied in Shakespeare's weeping, widowed queens is especially intriguing in the context of this cultural ambivalence over mourning for the dead. For in *Richard III,* Gloucester carries the forward-looking, atomistic post-Reformation attitude toward death to the extreme, while the mourning women repeatedly obstruct his progress with their vigils for the dead.[15] The body that was banished from the church funeral ritual takes the stage in *Richard III* in the form of the deceased King Henry VI, becoming the literal emblem of this conflict.

The lamentations of the widowed queens are strikingly similar to those of the holy women in medieval English drama. But Shakespeare's characterization of them also weaves together allusions to classical drama, the Easter liturgy, Celtic mythology, and, as the Lancastrian visitation record shows, actual mourning practice. This complex and subtly layered representation of mourning mothers suggests that Shakespeare seems to be concerned not with the loss of a particular religious doctrine, but with the loss of public mourning as a communal form of memorialization. *Richard III* explores the ramifications of this change. As the play suggests, the ability to mourn as a community—to acknowledge the political and moral consequences of the past, not simply in the form of private compunction, but also in a public forum that allows the expression of intense grief—is essential to the functioning and continuity of a cohesive society.

Certainly, intercessory prayer and weeping over the dead were not the only forms of public memorialization in England. Even as Elizabethan officials descended upon the countryside to investigate abuses of mourning ritual, the queen supported ever more grand funeral pageants for her aristocrats. The funerals of Sir Philip Sidney and Mary Queen of Scots are perhaps the most well-known examples of how she deployed these pageants to manipulate communal memory. As Ronald Strickland observes, "aristocratic funeral practices served as an important form of propaganda in support of the dominant aristocratic ideology and the existing social hierarchy" (1990, 19). Although Elizabeth's reign was ostensibly a time of "smooth-fac'd peace" (*Richard III* 5.5.33), civil and religious strife simmered just beneath the surface and around the edges of the kingdom. Elizabeth executed her Catholic cousin, Mary Queen of Scots, in February 1587. Sir Philip Sidney died fighting in the Low Countries for the Protestant cause only four months earlier. Though the timing of the funeral pageant depended partly upon a lack of funds, it was also politically motivated. Sidney was mourned as a Protestant champion eight days after Elizabeth dispatched her Catholic rival. As Dennis Kay suggests, Sidney's funeral "seems to have been arranged at least in part to help maintain public order in the midst of the controversy surrounding the execution of Mary Queen of Scots" (1990, 69). Sir Philip Sidney's funeral included an elaborate procession with hundreds of black-clad mourners (Strickland 1990, 31). Sidney's procession through the streets of London from outside of Aldgate to St. Paul's Cathedral seems consciously designed to promote the legitimacy of the secular ruler.

Although all funeral practices are acts of remembrance, different types of ceremonies articulate distinct personal and social needs. In early modern England, the primary purpose of the heraldic funeral was to demonstrate the continuity and solidarity of the aristocracy. The most publicly visible event of the heraldic funeral was the grand procession in which the embalmed body of the deceased was carried through the streets. The canopied hearse was at the heart of the cortege, with relatives, townsfolk, nobleman, governmental and religious officials, and the poor organized according to rank from front to rear. Aristocratic funeral pageants thus reinforced the status quo, representing the existing social hierarchy in processional form. The hooded black-crepe robes worn by all in the procession were referred to as "mourning." But, as Jennifer Woodward notes, this was a public performance and not a vehicle for the channeling of grief: "the primary purpose of the heraldic funeral was social and concerned with the public persona of the dead nobleman, rather than the burial of his private body. The church ceremony was about the transfer of the undying title, not taking leave of the dead" (1997, 35). It is not surprising, then, that in the majority of aristocratic funerals, mourners were rarely present at the interment. Thus England was left with a highly politicized ceremony that left little room for the articulation and channeling of complex emotions as a legitimate public activity.

In *Richard III*, Shakespeare illuminates and interrogates the difference between these two forms of communal memorialization by exposing the heraldic funeral as an empty ceremony while portraying lamentation as a communal ritual that possesses profound emotional and rhetorical power.

II

The opening scene of the First Tetralogy draws attention to the contrasting funeral rituals that frame the dramatic action, establishing a gendered opposition between politically sanctioned funeral pageantry and the unlawful pre-Reformation custom of wailing the dead. Gesturing toward the proscenium, Bedford begins his elegy for Henry V: "Hung be the heavens with black" (1.1.1). Poetically, his words imply a cosmic sense of loss, "importing change of time and states" (1.1.2). Literally, they point to Elizabethan stage convention for the performance of tragedies (Bevington 1988, 17 n.1). The roof projecting over the stage would have been shrouded in black, giving the theater the ambiance of a funeral church (Neill 1997, 281–83). As he stands over the corpse of Henry V, Bedford prophesies:

> Posterity, await for wretched years,
> When at their mothers' moist'ned eyes babes shall suck,
> Our isle be made a nourish of salt tears,
> And none but women left to wail the dead
> (*1 Henry VI* 1.1.48–51)

To warlike Bedford, women's laments denote impotence and defeat. But the concluding play of the tetralogy presents a very different picture of wailing women.

From the perspective of burial rites, the concluding play of the tetralogy encompasses a struggle between Richard's will to forget the dead, to effect political amnesia by a perpetual orientation toward the future, and the mourning women who embody the past, the insistence and intrusion of memory upon human action. Significantly, the women's communal lament in act 4 is the only uninterrupted mourning ritual in the entire tetralogy.

Richard imagines a world where the dead are beyond the reach of the living, and the living are thus released from the claims of the past; he thinks that the world is free for him to "bustle in" (1.1.152). In his opening soliloquy, he confidently declares that because his Lancastrian foes are dead, they cannot affect him: "And all the clouds that lowr'd upon our house / In the deep bosom of the ocean buried" (1.1.3–4). But in the very next scene, Lady Anne proves him wrong, confronting him with Henry VI's corpse, the literal embodiment of the Lancastrian dead. Richard makes much of his success in wooing her, but the scene also shows that he cannot escape or dismiss the presence of the dead. For the entire play, even as he cuts his path to power, the women impede his progress with the memory of the dead and the wrongs of the past. Margaret materializes from the other side of the channel; the women stage a mourning ritual outside the Tower of London; and the dead rise up to curse Richard in his sleep on the eve of the Battle of Bosworth. The wailing women and the world of the dead embody a moral force that prevents Richard from severing himself from the past, a past that ultimately overwhelms and destroys him.

1 Henry VI and *Richard III,* the opening and concluding plays of the First Tetralogy, deploy funeral ritual as embedded metaphors for the state of the kingdom and hence the dramatic action (Neill 1985, 168). Aristocratic funeral pageants reinforced the status quo, representing the existing social hierarchy in processional form (Strickland 1990, 19). As Huntington and Metcalf explain, royal funeral procession promoted the political ideology of the king's two bodies: "the funeral has a three-part diachronic structure that relates to the sociological/political issue of succession. And this rite of passage progression is animated by a synchronic opposition between the immortal dignity (*dignitas*) of the kingship and the mortal remains of the king; an opposition that is radical at first, ambiguous during the procession, and resolved at burial" (1979, 172). The stability of the kingdom is most precarious during the procession, when the *dignitas,* the political and social body of the king, is in a transitional state (162–65). The elaborate funeral march for Henry V, led by the powerful Duke of Bedford, which inaugurates the tetralogy, contrasts with the maimed rites for Henry VI, led by the murdered King's disenfranchised daughter-in-law, heralding the tetralogy's imminent conclusion. Shakespeare's departure from his sources emphasizes this contrast, for the real Anne Neville was nowhere near the funeral of Henry VI (Bullough 1962, 146; Saccio 1977, 166 n.).

Contrasting rhetorical rites accompany the contrasting funeral processions. In *1 Henry VI,* the Duke of Bedford delivers a eulogy for warlike Harry, whereas in *Richard III,* Lady Anne performs an obsequious lament for his son, the saintly Henry VI. Bedford's elegy mimics Tudor political funeral pageantry, while Ann's pietà-like lament summons the Catholic images and rituals of England's medieval heritage. Evoking the Blessed Virgin weeping over Christ's tortured body, she "pour[s] the helpless balm of [her] poor eyes" into his wounds (1.2.13). These processions differ in form, but they are alike in their lack of completion. Both processions are interrupted, leaving the status of the *dignitas* unresolved and the state of the kingdom in turmoil. Neill argues that in *1 Henry VI,* "Henry V's funeral . . . memorialize[s] a heroic past and . . . enact[s] the forms of political order that the subsequent action will shatter," while in *Richard III,* the maimed royal rites for Henry VI perform "a ritual display of humiliation . . . which announces an already shattered frame of order" (1985, 170–71). But in *1 Henry VI,* the Bishop of Winchester and the Duke of Gloucester bicker throughout Henry V's funeral ceremony, exposing this heraldic pageant as a veneer for an already fragmented kingdom. A messenger further disrupts the dirge, heralding incipient chaos with his news of "Sad tidings . . . out of France" (1.1.58). He informs them that "Guienne, Champagne, Rheims, Orleance / Paris, Guysors, Poitiers, are all quite lost" (1.1.60–61). The messenger's dispatch undermines Henry V's heroic stature and renders suspect Bedford's elegiac hyperbole, for it suggests how precarious is the achievement of a man whose "deeds exceed all speech," who "ne'er lift up his hand but conquered" (1.1.15–16).

In the opening scene of *1 Henry VI,* the funeral procession that pur-portedly enacts continuity, the survival and immortality of the *dignitas,* instead manifests discontinuity and discord. It divulges the petty quar-rels of the nobles and subverts the notion that Henry V has subdued France during the very ceremony designed to memorialize that con-quest. Furthermore, the twice-arrested procession never reaches its destination, and therefore the ambiguity of the King's estate and the succession of the throne are never resolved.

The interruptions of Henry V's funeral pageant thus undermine the dignity and accuracy of Bedford's elegy. Lady Anne's obsequious lament for Henry VI, in contrast, is not as meek as it might first appear. It is true, as Phyllis Rackin observes, that none of the female charac-ters in *Richard III* appears on stage in battle dress, as do Joan and Margaret in the *Henry VI* plays (1993, 60). Nevertheless, Anne's role in Henry VI's funeral procession is not a simple domestic stereotype. On the one hand, like Seneca's Megara, to whom she is compared by Harold Brooks, she is a grieving widow (728). Unlike Megara, howev-er, she does not weep at an altar in an enclosed space. Shakespeare puts her in motion across the stage, which also represents civic space, the open streets of London. He makes her the chief mourner, in command of the armed halberds guarding Henry VI's funeral cortege. Anne leads a military procession, however attenuated, and she therefore recalls the female antagonists of the earlier plays (Grubb 1987, 120).

"Lady Anne transgresses the customary class and gender rules of heraldic funerals which held that mourners should be the same sex, and near in degree to the deceased" (Woodward 1997, 17). Her position as chief mourner denotes her royal lineage and claim to the throne, under-scoring the illegitimacy of Edward's reign. Her funeral procession sig-nifies that the rites of lawful succession remain unresolved because the true King (Henry VI) remains unburied. Halting twice to lament "Th'untimely fall of virtuous Lancaster" (1.2.4), Anne further delays Henry VI's burial. Violating the strictures of political funeral pageantry, Anne, like Antigone before her, stages her grief in the pub-lic sphere, directly engaging and subverting a potent political form. The opening words of her thirty-two line lament question the ethos of the heraldic funeral, which attempts to justify death in the name of an abstract principle: "Set down, set down your honourable load / If hon-our may be shrouded in a hearse" (1.2.1–2). Her mourning includes all of the characteristic features of the genre of ritual lamentation for the dead: the direct address of the corpse, the establishment of kinship, the narrative of the death, and the call for vengeance. The iconography of the scene evokes both the mourning Magdalene and the pietà. In contemporary poetic renditions of Mary Magdalene's sorrow, she weeps for a knight whose wounds bleed, just as Anne weeps over Henry VI's wounds (Grubb 1987, 124–26). Anne addresses the corpse with colloquial epithets suggestive of indigenous custom. She refers to the King as "key-cold" (1.2.5) and "Pale ashes" (1.2.6). She self-consciously refers to the illegitimate nature of her ritual: "Be it lawful that I invocate thy ghost / To hear the lamentations of poor Anne" (1.2.8–9). Her apostrophe implies the belief that the deceased King will hear and answer her cries.

After the characteristic opening invocations, Lady Anne establishes her relationship to the dead King and recounts his murder. She defines her kinship with the King, referring to herself as "Wife to thy Edward, to thy slaughter'd son, / Stabb'd by the selfsame hand that made these wounds" (1.2.9–11). As she pours "the helpless balm of [her] poor eyes" into Henry VI's seeping wounds, she curses "the hand that made these holes" and the "heart that had the heart to do it" (1.2.14–15), wishing a worse fate to Richard than "to adders, spiders, toads, / Or any creeping venom'd thing that lives" (1.2.19–20). Anne self-consciously refers to her tears as ineffectual, but her Magdalene-like compassion and compunction resonate throughout the remainder of the play, effecting a change in Queen Elizabeth. Moreover, several characters in the play view oaths as speech-acts and fear their power. Anne herself later believes she has "prov'd the subject of [her] own soul's curse" (4.1.80), while Margaret's curses make Buckingham's hair stand on end (1.3.303). These fears are linked to the ancient belief that women's laments invoke otherworldly reciprocal vengeance, a belief that is reinforced when Richard appears. The moment evokes classical tragedy while also resonating with lingering popular beliefs. In Aeschylus's *Libation Bearers,* when "the dead man is lamented, the punisher appears" (Seaford 1995, 92). Similarly, in Shakespeare's *Richard III,* Lady Anne's laments for the dead King conjure the "punisher," Richard, Duke of Gloucester. Richard is both scourge and scapegoat for the civil strife that has torn the Plantagenet clan for generations.[16] More significant than the implication of the supernatural or magical power of Lady Anne's lament, however, is the suggestion that her mourning ritual is related to communal memory and therefore the political will of the society.

As though conjured by Anne's curses, Richard interrupts her ritual, commanding the Halberds to set down the corpse in a manner that parallels the opening of the scene: "Stay, you that bear the corse, and set it down" (1.2.33). The action teeters on violence as Richard threatens the resisting Halberds with death: "Villains, set down the corse, or, by Saint Paul, / I'll make a corse of him that disobeys" (1.2.36–37). A single halberdier continues to resist: "My lord, stand back and let the coffin pass" (1.2.38). Richard intensifies his threats:

> Unmanner'd dog, [stand] thou when I command.
> Advance thy halberd higher than my breast,
> Or by Saint Paul I'll strike thee to my foot,
> And spurn upon thee, beggar, for thy boldness
> (1.2.39–42)

The threat of violence in the encounter between Anne and Richard recalls the violence of the medieval *Herod* plays. Just as the women in the *Herod* plays curse the soldiers, so Anne curses Richard and chastises her Halberds, implicitly pointing to her superior moral courage:

> What, do you tremble? Are you all afraid?
> Alas, I blame you not, for you are mortal,
> And mortal eyes cannot endure the devil.
> (1.2.43–45)

Just as the mothers of the *Herod* plays denounce the soldiers, so Lady Anne condemns Richard:

> Avaunt, thou dreadful minister of hell!
> Thou hadst but power over his mortal body,
> His soul thou canst not have; Therefore be gone
> (1.2.46–48)

Whereas Richard succeeds in obtaining the corpse by the end of the scene, Anne's curses prove true by the end of the play, when the King's soul haunts Richard in his sleep.

Anne uses her onstage audience as witnesses to her appeal to justice. She pulls the shroud from the corpse, forcing Richard to "Behold this pattern of [his] butcheries" (1.2.54), and come face to face with death. The saintly King Henry's wounds bleed in the sight of his murderer:

> O gentlemen, see, see dead Henry's wounds
> Open their congeal'd mouths and bleed afresh!
> Blush, blush, thou lump of foul deformity,
> For 'tis thy presence that exhales this blood
> From cold and empty veins where no bloods dwells.
> Thy deeds inhuman and unnatural
> Provokes this deluge most unnatural.
>
> (1.2.55–61)

Traditionally, corpses were believed to bleed in the sight of their murderers (Brooks 1980, 728). Anne's words thus hold Richard accountable for his deed, and the onstage and theater audiences witness her indictment.

Unmoved by the bodily rage of the bleeding corpse, Richard turns Anne's lament into a game of courtship. He tries a number of different arguments to win her, but their debate does not shift until he appeals to their mutual Plantagenet descent. This shift in his favor is signaled by thirty-three lines of uninterrupted speech, which counterbalance and exceed Anne's opening soliloquy of thirty-two lines. Once again, Richard's courtship of Anne forces him into the past. In order to win her sympathy, he recounts the deaths of his own father and brother. He uses Anne's compassionate nature against her, telling her that even in "that sad time [when his father and brother were murdered] / [his] manly eyes did scorn an humble tear" (1.2.163–64). Her beauty, however, has "made them blind with weeping" (1.2.166). Richard then forces her into a false dilemma by implying that a refusal to slay him will mean that she desires him: "Take up the sword again, or take up me" (1.2.183). She attempts to evade him, replying, "Arise, dissembler! Though I wish thy death, / I will not be thy executioner" (1.2.184–85). By feigning contrition and implying a movement toward compassion and reintegration of the kingdom, Richard successfully uses Anne's best traits against her. At the end of the scene, he asks her to leave her "sad designs / To him that hath most cause to be a mourner" (1.2.210–11). She releases the corpse to him, expressing her belief that his tears have been sincere: "With all my heart, and much it joys me too, / To see you are become so penitent" (1.2.219–20). Though Richard gloats over his conquest, his apparent victory over Anne costs him. In order to convince her of his sincerity, he assumes responsibility for the body and plays along with her ritual, assuring her that he will "wet [King Henry's] grave with [his] repentant tears" (1.2.215). On the one hand, Anne symbolically transfers power to Richard when she relinquishes the body to him: the remains of the legitimate King embody the immortal *ethos* of the kingdom, which is now in Richard's power. On the other hand, this transfer shows that even Richard cannot ignore the ritual and literal presence of the dead.

III

From the moment Anne confronts Richard with the literal embodiment of the Lancastrian dead, the past begins to consume the stage. In the next two scenes, the ocean of Richard's opening soliloquy continues to yield up the "secrets of the deep" (1.4.35). As if in response to Anne's capitulation and Richard's maltreatment of her husband's corpse, Margaret emerges mysteriously from the other side of the channel, hovering around the edges of the action like a ghost caught between the realms of the living and the dead. Bringing the weight of the dead with her, she ignites memories of past wrongs. She materializes amid the wrangling of the royal family, as Richard attempts to accuse Elizabeth of securing Clarence's and Hastings's imprisonment. Like Richard, Margaret addresses the audience in theatrical asides, inserting her perspective between the other characters' lines and drawing the audience into collusion with her. From the moment she appears on the stage, she influences the action.

When she appears, the dispute between Richard and Elizabeth shifts from an argument about the present to a debate about the past. In her asides, Margaret resumes where Anne ceased, cursing Richard as a "devil" for killing her "husband Henry in the Tower, / And Edward, [her] poor son, at Tewksbury" (1.3.118–19). Before she manifests herself to the Yorks, she seems to enter their consciousness, as Richard reminds Elizabeth that her first husband was slain "In Margaret's battle at Saint Albons" (1.3.129). Richard and Elizabeth take turns decrying each other's hypocrisy, causing Elizabeth to bemoan her fate as England's queen.

Elizabeth's self-pity compels Margaret forward. When she hears Elizabeth sigh, "A little joy enjoys the queen thereof, / For I am she, and altogether joyless" (1.3.154–55), she exclaims, "I can no longer hold me patient" (1.2.156). She indicts them all:

> "Hear me, you wrangling pirates, that fall out
> In sharing that which you have pill'd from me!
> Which of you trembles not that looks on me?
> If not, that I am queen, you bow like subjects,
> Yet that, by you depos'd, you quake like rebels?"
>
> (1.3.157–61)

Margaret finds no ally in the family. They unite against her, bringing up her own evil acts that ended in the destruction of her family. She, in turn, accuses them of hypocrisy:

> What? were you snarling all before I came,
> Ready to catch each other by the throat,
> And turn you all your hatred now on me?"
>
> (1.3.187–89)

In her isolation, she queries the universe, "Can curses pierce the clouds and enter heaven?" (1.3.194). Having no other recourse, she curses each of them in turn. Buckingham is of two minds about her curses. He tells her "curses never pass / The lips of those that breathe them in the air" (1.3.284–85), but moments later, after she exits, he confesses, "My hair doth stand on end to hear her curses" (1.3.303).

The scene recalls the efficacious curses of the mothers in the medieval *Herod* plays. However, Shakespeare's play embodies ambivalence concerning the supernatural power of the mourning women's curses. Many, but not all, of Margaret's imprecations are fulfilled. The dialogue interrogates the economy of supernatural justice, while suggesting that communal mourning may still serve an important social function. Everyone in the room has been publicly held responsible for their past actions. Nothing is resolved in this scene, but Margaret, like Anne before her, has called both the living and the dead to account. Margaret herself has been held accountable for her past deeds as well. The overall movement of the play suggests that the collective social conscience, however painful and volatile, possesses an objective agency that plays an important role in human morality.

In the next scene, Clarence's dream reflects the influence of Margaret's uncanny presence. The English Channel and the "melancholy flood . . . which poets write of" (1.4.45–46) merge in his purgatorial nightmare. In his dream, he imagines drowning and being unable to "yield [his] ghost" (1.4.37). He awakens, tormented by visions of those he wronged during the "wars of York and Lancaster" (1.4.15), memories that are structurally related to Margaret's emergence in the previous scene. Filled with remorse, he confesses to the keeper as though to a priest: "Ah, Keeper, Keeper, I have done these things / (That now give evidence against my soul)" (1.4.66–67). When Brackenbury enters, he attributes Clarence's apparitions to the disorienting effects of mourning, which interfere with the forward chronological movement of time: "Sorrow breaks seasons and reposing hours, / Makes the night morning and the noontide night" (1.4.76–77). In *Richard III,* the women's laments embody the objective moral force that disrupts the forward, linear movement of history figured in Richard and in the political funeral procession that inaugurates the tetralogy. Clarence's purgatorial dream of drowning in the channel and suffering torment in the "envious flood" (1.4.37) foreshadows both his and Gloucester's deaths, events that are engendered by the women's mourning voices. Their words are made flesh when the bodies of the dead rise and overtake the stage on the eve of the Battle of Bosworth.

IV

Lady Anne's public confrontation with Richard, and Margaret's public assault on the Yorkist court, point to the inextricable connection between mourning and politics. A complementary sequence of private scenes of sorrow demonstrates the symbiotic relationship between family and state. The lack of compassion among the members of the royal household is thus the ethical analogue for the shattered kingdom.

In act 1, scene 3, Queen Elizabeth, in private conference with her brother and older sons, laments her growing awareness that her husband's failing health endangers her family. Rivers, Dorset, and Grey attempt to console her, naively observing that the only harm that will ensue is her sorrow at the loss of such a lord (1.3.7). But Elizabeth accurately perceives otherwise: "The loss of such a lord includes all harms" (1.3.8). Elizabeth knows that Richard, now the Lord Protector-elect, "loves not [her]" (1.3.13). Because the personal is political, she knows that she will lose her political protection if her husband dies. Her entire family, and the heirs to the throne in particular, will be vulnerable to Gloucester's devouring ambition. Though this scene foreshadows the future, it also yields important insights into Elizabeth's political acumen. When her husband's death leaves her a widow, her apprehensions are proven correct. In act 2, scene 4, she learns that her brother and eldest son "[a]re sent to Pomfret" (42) as Gloucester's political prisoners. Her sighs employ not domestic, but political and military imagery:

> Ay, me! I see the ruin of my house:
> The tiger now hath seiz'd the gentle hind;
> Insulting tyranny begins to jut
> Upon the innocent and aweless throne.
> Welcome destruction, blood, and massacre!
> I see (as in a map) the end of all
>
> (2.4.49–54)

Elizabeth's exclaims are not inarticulate sobs, but an accurate assessment of the precarious and violent world of politics. Far from being a passive, suffering victim, Elizabeth, like the Duchess of York and Queen Margaret, is not duped by Richard's theatrical manipulations. Though Richard succeeds in wooing Lady Anne with crocodile tears, significantly, he never attempts such tactics with these women.

Elizabeth is politically astute, but she lacks Lady Anne's and the Duchess of York's compassion. In the early stages of the play, Elizabeth is indifferent to the plight of others. When Margaret first appears, Elizabeth feels no pity for the aged queen's suffering because she feels the events do not concern her: "I never did her any [wrong] to my knowledge" (1.3.308). She ignores the fact that she has "all the vantage of [Margaret's] wrong" (1.3.309), as Richard correctly points out. In the course of the play, Elizabeth learns compassion for others through her own experience of grief. Because she is the most politically astute of all the characters, save Richard, the reintegration of the kingdom depends upon her movement from selfish indifference to empathetic participation in the human community. This development manifests itself clearly in act 2, scene 2, and the opening scene of act 4.

In act 2, scene 2, the Duchess of York, Clarence's children, and
Queen Elizabeth grieve over the tragic fulfillment of Elizabeth's
prophecy. Richard has circumvented the King's stay of execution,
resulting in Clarence's murder. Clarence's unlooked-for death has
caused King Edward to die of fear and remorse. The ensuing scene
of grief does more than evoke pathos for Richard's victims: it
reveals the lack of compassion among the York family members. It
opens with Clarence's children asking their "grandam" why she
"weep[s] so oft, and beat[s] her breast" (2.2.3), and concludes with
Elizabeth, the children, and the Duchess dowager bewailing their
losses in unison. Elizabeth enters in extreme distress, "her hair about
her ears," crying to the Duchess, "Edward, my lord, thy son, our
King is dead!" (2.2.40). Clarence's children tell Elizabeth they do
not pity her: "Ah, aunt! you wept not for our father's death. . . . Your
widow-dolor likewise be unwept" (2.2.62–65). By the end of the
scene, the Duchess's maternal mourning subsumes and unites their
sorrow in her ancient grief:

> Alas! you three on me, threefold distress'd,
> Pour all your tears. I am your sorrow's nurse,
> And I will pamper it with lamentation
>   (2.2.86–88)

The Duchess's words evoke medieval English lyrics and images of the
Virgin's Compassion. She is characterized as the embodiment of
maternal mourning, a sorrow that possesses healing power. She will
nurse their sorrows in two interrelated ways: she nourishes them so
that they have full expression, and she cures them by allowing them
that expression. This moment connects to the underlying cultural concern of the play—anxiety over the repression of this form of communal mourning in English society.

When Lady Anne, the Duchess of York, and Queen Elizabeth meet
in the opening scene of act 4 and attempt to see the princes in the Tower,
they are further united in shared sorrow. The scene hearkens back to the
medieval Resurrection plays when the three Marys unite in their search
for Jesus' body. Just as Mary Magdalene wanders toward Christ's sepulchre when she meets Mary Salome and Mary Jacobi, so, in the
Duchess's words, Lady Anne "wander[s] to the Tower, / On pure heart's
love, to greet the tender Prince" (4.1.3–4). When the women ask to see

the heirs to the throne, a reluctant Brackenbury prevents their entry, and with a slip of the tongue he betrays what the future holds:

> By your patience,
> I may not suffer you to visit them,
> The King hath strictly charg'd the contrary
> (4.1.15–17)

He corrects himself, "I mean the Lord Protector" (4.1.19), and Queen Elizabeth retorts:

> The Lord protect him from that kingly title!
> Hath he set bounds between their love and me?
> I am their mother; who shall bar me from them?"
> (4.1.19–21)

Just as the mourning mothers of medieval drama embody what the plays construe as both natural and divine justice, so the weeping queens in *Richard III* appeal to an early modern idea of a natural, familial sense of justice and morality. The Duchess insists, "I am their father's mother, I will see them" (4.1.22).

When Queen Elizabeth and the Duchess fail to persuade, Lady Anne attempts to use her position in the royal family to gain entry:

> Their aunt I am in law, in love their mother;
> Then bring me to their sights. I'll bear thy blame,
> And take thy office from thee on my peril
> (4.1.23–25)

The mothers' arguments further recall the mourning of the three Marys at the sepulchre. Queen Elizabeth, the Duchess, and Lady Anne each establish their familial relationship to the princes: mother, grandmother, and aunt. In the N-Town *Announcement to the Three Maries,* the holy women authorize their laments for Christ by announcing, in hierarchical succession, their kinship with him. This rhetorical structure is a recognized feature of archaic lament. The shared empathy among the medieval Marys at Christ's tomb informs the scene in *Richard III* outside the Tower of London. For the women's shared suffering unites them for the first time in the play.

Unlike Elizabeth, who felt no pity for Clarence's orphaned nephews, Anne loves Elizabeth's sons as if she were their mother. The scene establishes the difference between Anne and Elizabeth before uniting them in a shared empathy that contrasts with the bitterness and indifference exchanged earlier between Margaret and Elizabeth. Stanley enters to announce that Anne "must straight to Westminster, / There to be crowned Richard's royal queen" (4.1.31–32). Lady Anne assumes the blame for abetting Richard's rise to power, aware of the tragic irony that she has "prov'd the subject of [her] own soul's curse" (4.4.80). Elizabeth, for the first time, discovers sympathy for the plight of another, even this woman who will soon supplant her as queen. She tells Anne, "Poor heart, adieu, I pity thy complaining" (4.1.87). Anne replies, "No more than with my soul I mourn for yours" (4.1.88). This scene suggests that communal mourning has the power to unite and heal the kingdom as the women begin to share the burden of their sorrows.

Elizabeth knows that Stanley's news means the death of her sons, who are already entombed in the Tower:

> "Ah, cut my lace asunder,
> That my pent heart may have some scope to beat,
> Or else I swoon with this dead-killing news"
> (4.1.33–35)

Even in the extremity of her anguish, however, she remains lucid. She insists that Dorset, her eldest son, "outstrip death" (4.1.41), by crossing the sea to "live with Richmond, from the reach of hell" (4.1.42). Her advice saves her son's life, and prevents her from dying "the thrall of Margaret's curse, / Nor mother, wife, nor England's counted queen" (4.1.45–46). Lord Stanley calls Elizabeth's counsel "Full of wise care" (4.1.47), implying a link between compassion and knowledge. In the same moment that the women come together in empathy, Stanley begins to design the military strategy that will eventually defeat Richard. He tells Dorset:

> Take all the swift advantage of the hours.
> You shall have letters from me to my son
> In your behalf, to meet you on the way.
> Be not ta'en tardy by unwise delay
> (4.1.48–51)

Instead of clouding Elizabeth's judgment, her grief clarifies her decisions and catalyzes the actions of the men against Richard.

V

Like Lady Anne's "obsequious laments," the scene of mothers in act 4, scene 4, resonates with culturally charged iconography that derives from the genre of lamentation. The widowed Duchess has only her wicked son Richard left, whereas Margaret has lost everything: her crown, her husband, and her son. Queen Elizabeth's sons have been murdered in the Tower, and her husband Edward is dead. She has her daughter, Elizabeth, whose royal blood makes her vulnerable, just as Anne Neville had once been vulnerable. Her son Dorset, from her first marriage, is marshalling Richmond's forces against Richard. The women lament outside the Tower of London, the tomb for Elizabeth's slaughtered sons and her brother-in-law, Clarence, and King Henry VI. It is thus a repository of memory reminiscent of the sepulcher of medieval Easter ritual, as well as the tombs that continued to crowd the interior of English churches during Shakespeare's day. Sepulchres, once the central ceremonial objects of the English Corpus Christi festivals and plays, remained popular stage properties in sixteenth-century England. As Glynne Wickham points out, "Henslowe could still find enough use for it to buy two in 1598" (1959, 38–39). The iconography of the scene conjures layered images of England's cultural inheritance. As three mourning women at a sepulchre, Old Queen Margaret, the Duchess of York, and Queen Elizabeth simultaneously evoke the triple goddesses of Celtic legend and the three Maries of medieval cycle drama and the Easter liturgy (Grubb 1987, 124–26). The play reverberates with echoes of the Easter service, the church season in which the *Herod* plays were traditionally performed.

Scholars have traced many sources for the scene, from Seneca's *Troades* and the *Quem Queritis* trope, to the holy women of medieval drama. The common element of these sources is their representation of the cultural practice of publicly wailing the dead. Sitting on the ground as though encircling a grave, the weeping queens "Tell over [their] woes" (4.4.39) in the same manner that women in England for centuries lamented their dead. Elizabeth invokes her "tender babes" to "Hover about [her] with [their] aery wings / And hear . . . [her] lamentation" (4.4.9–14). Like Euripides's Hecuba in *The Daughters of Troy,* who must rise from the dust to fulfill her obligation to lament, the Duchess sighs with world weariness: "So many miseries have craz'd my voice / That my woe-wearied tongue is still and mute" (4.4.17–18).

Despite her fatigue, she begins her lament with the distinctive opening address to the dead: "Edward Plantagenet, why art thou dead?" (4.4.19). Margaret hovers in the background, inserting her vengeful comments, and creating the characteristic antiphonal exchange and stichomythic rhythm of communal lamentation. Elizabeth challenges God's justice and mercy:

> Wilt thou, O God, fly from such gentle lambs,
> And throw then in the entrails of the wolf?
> When didst thou sleep when such a deed was done?
>
> (4.4.22–24)

The women's cries confront the most searching questions of what it means to be human: the nature of evil, the problem of faith, the desire for justice, and the immense sense of loss and suffering in the face of death.

The Duchess develops these paradoxes through antithetical thought as she refers to herself as a living ghost, aligning herself with Margaret:

> Dead life, blind sight, poor mortal living ghost,
> Woe's scene, world's shame, grave's due by life usurp'd,
> Brief abstract and record of tedious days,
> Rest thy unrest on England's lawful earth,
> Unlawfully made drunk with innocent blood!
>
> (4.4.26–30)

As she sits down, Elizabeth joins her, wishing for death:

> Ah, that thou wouldst as soon afford a grave
> As thou canst yield a melancholy seat!
> Then would I hide my bones, not rest them here
> Ah, who hath any cause to mourn but we?
>
> (4.4.31–34)

This moment, when Duchess and Queen sit upon England's soil, signals an important dramatic shift. Their gesture of communion with the forces of the universe brings Margaret forward to join them:

> If ancient sorrow be most reverent,
> Give mine the benefit of segniory,
> And let my griefs frown on the upper hand.
> If sorrow can admit society,
> Tell over your woes again by viewing mine
>
> (4.4.35–39)

Margaret's plea articulates the communal purpose of ritual lament. As each mourner in turn recalls her sorrows, everyone present meditates on their own woes. In a moment that echoes the reading of the obits during the Catholic mass for the dead, the women begin naming the seemingly endless list of names of their lost husbands and sons: the generations of Edwards and Richards and Rutlands and Henrys, who died killing one another in England's long civil war.

Margaret identifies the Duchess as the source of England's misery: "From forth the kennel of thy womb hath crept / A hell-hound that doth hunt us all to death" (4.4.47–48). She relishes the sight of the aggrieved Duchess:

> O upright, just, and true-disposing God,
> How do I thank thee, that this carnal cur
> Preys on the issue of his mother's body,
> And makes her pew-fellow with others' moan!
> (4.4.55–58)

Although Margaret is gloating, her words, especially the reference to them as "pew-fellows," emphasize that the women are sharing each other's burdens as though they were mourning together in church. This gesture toward commiseration is reinforced when the eighty-year-old Duchess, whose life extends back to the end of Henry V's reign, reminds Margaret of their common Plantagenet family ties: "O Harry's wife, triumph not in my woes! / God witness with me, I have wept for thine" (4.4.59–60). Whereas Margaret married into the Plantagenet clan, the Duchess, like Lady Anne, is of Plantagenet descent. Both she and Lady Anne were born into the house of Lancaster and married into the house of York. At the same time that the Duchess expresses empathy for Margaret, she also asserts the seniority of her grief. Her words of sorrow effect a subtle change in Margaret, who now asks the women to "Bear with [her]" hunger for revenge (4.4.61).

Although she threatens revenge, what Queen Margaret seems to desire most is a sympathetic audience to witness her rage and grief. She recounts her sorrows and points out that Elizabeth, who "didst usurp [her] place" now "[u]surp[s] the just proportion of [her] sorrow" (4.4.109–10). Having unburdened herself, Margaret begins to leave for France, but Elizabeth calls her back: "O thou well skill'd in curses, stay awhile, / And teach me how to curse mine enemies!" (4.4.116–17). Margaret's response is filled with painful irony:

"Forbear to sleep the [nights], and fast the [days];
Compare dead happiness with living woe;
Think that thy babes were sweeter than they were,
And he that slew them fouler than he is.
Bett'ring thy loss makes the bad causer worse;
Revolving this will teach thee how to curse
                                                (4.4.118–23)

Elizabeth implores her not to leave: "My words are dull, / O, quicken them with thine!" (4.4.124). As she exits the stage, Margaret acknowledges at last their shared suffering with her final line: "Thy woes will make them sharp and pierce like mine" (4.4.125).

The only uninterrupted burial rite in the entire First Tetralogy, the scene of ritual lamentation completes the action of mourning that until now has remained unresolved, altering the ethos of the conflict and effecting the turning point in the play. The moral force that empowers Richmond and cripples Richard derives from their laments. Like Aeschylus's Electra, whose cries summon and empower Orestes to avenge his father's death, so Shakespeare's wailing women seem to summon Richmond to seize the throne of England. As the observations of several critics indicate, this is a powerfully ritualistic moment. The women's voices, in the words of Joan Parks, "retell the history of the War of the Roses as accumulation and repetition" (1997, 6). They rise to a crescendo in which "the names return, but the identities they stand for vanish in a blur of sound. We feel surrounded by the dead" (Leggatt 1988, 46). The women's chanting elicits what Dennis Kay describes as the sonorous effect of the Catholic reading of the obits, with its seemingly endless naming of names (1990, 2). Critics have decried these communal laments as "mere monotones of complaint" (Hammond 1997, 110), and an "undifferentiated chorus of ritual lamentation, curse, and prophecy" (Rackin and Howard 1997, 116), but the women's cries illuminate rather than efface their differing natures and contrasting worldviews (Grubb 1987, 127).

The Duchess and the Queen are skeptical about the cosmic efficacy of cursing and lamentation, but nevertheless recognize its rhetorical and emotional power. The Duchess asks Elizabeth, "Why should calamity be full of words?" (4.4.126). Elizabeth explains with a legal metaphor, that words are:

> Windy attorneys to their client's woes,
> Aery succeeders of [intestate] joys,
> Poor breathing orators of miseries,
> Let them have scope! though what they will impart
> Help nothing else, yet do they ease the heart
> (4.4.127–31)

Elizabeth's statement suggests that mourning serves the important function of "easing the heart." She is skeptical of its supernatural power, but finds that it nevertheless serves an important function: it eases the heart. The overall movement of the play suggests that the easing of the heart encompasses both personal and communal moral agency. Recognizing that if laments can ease the heart, curses can trouble the soul, the Duchess commands,

> If so then, be not tongue-tied; go with me
> And in the breath of bitter words let's smother
> My damned son that thy two sweet sons smother'd
> The trumpet sounds, be copious in exclaims
> (4.4.132–35)

Empowered by their grief, the Duchess and the Queen successfully disrupt Richard's military procession.

Structural dramatic symmetry underscores that the women's sorrow makes them formidable opponents to Richard. Just as Richard had interrupted Anne's mourning ritual, so the Duchess and the Queen now succeed in halting Richard's procession. Richard acknowledges that they have impeded his progress: "Who intercepts me in my expedition?" (4.4.136). Richard again pays tribute to the rhetorical force of the women's voices when he tries to drown them out with his trumpets and drums:

> A flourish, trumpets! strike alarum, drums!
> Let not the heavens hear these tell-tale women
> Rail on the Lord's anointed. Strike, I say!
> (4.4.149–51)

His almost comical attempts to silence the women end with him being silenced by his mother. When she tells him she will never speak to him again, the best response he can conjure is "So!" (184). His weakening eloquence signifies another important shift in the play, for he is momentarily stifled by his mother's rage and grief. He stands mute as she curses him: "Bloody thou art; bloody will be thy end. / Shame serves thy life and doth thy death attend" (4.4.195–96).

These are the Duchess's final words to her son. After she exits, Elizabeth "say[s] Amen to her" (4.4.198–99). Shakespeare again employs structural symmetry to illuminate the transfer in dramatic agency from Richard to the women. The remainder of the scene between Richard and Elizabeth hearkens back to the "keen encounter of . . . wits" (1.2.115) between Richard and Anne. In contrast to the earlier scene, however, Richard never gains the upper hand. Elizabeth repudiates each of his arguments. Richard attempts to swear by "the time to come!" (4.4.387), but Elizabeth points out that he has "wronged [that] in the time o'erpast" (4.4.388). Like the melancholy flood that drowned Clarence, the past overwhelms Richard. The "babbling dreams" that "affright" his soul (5.3.308) on the eve of battle seem to be engendered by the women's "copious exclaims." Like their laments, his

> conscience hath a thousand several tongues,
> And every tongue brings in a several tale,
> and every tale condemns [him] for a villain
> (5.3.193–95)

As the Duchess prophesied, her sorrowful prayers fight on the adverse party and his end is bloody.

The placement of the women's lamentations prior to the appearance of the ghosts suggests that they have awakened the spirits from their otherworldly slumber to "sit heavy on [Richard's] soul" (5.3.131), while bringing to Richmond the "sweetest sleep and fairest-boding dreams / That ever ent'red in a drowsy head" (5.3.227–28). Just before he goes into battle, Richard notices that "the sky doth frown and lour upon [his] army," dropping "dewy tears" upon him (5.3.283–84). The clouds he thought were buried in the opening scene have been with him all along.

Richard's psychomachic nightmare hovers between two world views: a residual archaic belief that wailing the dead provokes divine justice, and an emergent early modern appeal to conscience as the cause of haunted sleep. Because the nightmare is represented rather than narrated, these opposed visions of the afterlife blend ambiguously on the stage. The audience watches as Richard dreams, but also experiences firsthand the visitation of the dead. Spanning both realms, the rhetorical power of the women's laments exhausts Richard. Their cries break his will to forget the dead and disorient his perpetual drive toward the future. For they embody the memory of the dead—the collective consciousness of the kingdom—which insists and intrudes upon the political and moral spheres of human action.

NOTES

1. Cited in Cressy (1997) 401. An earlier form of the present essay was published in *Religion and the Arts* 7.1/2 (2003).

2. All citations of *Richard III* are from Shakespeare, *The Riverside Shakespeare,* ed. Evans (1974).

3. See especially the works by Cressy (1997), Duffy (1996), Greaves (1981), Haigh (1987), and Scarisbruck (1984).

4. I am indebted to Michael Neill for this concept and phrasing. In his recent book, *Issues of Death,* Neill observes: "The rites of funeral . . . are perhaps the most conspicuous form through which memory is performed (or suppressed) in the *Hamlet* world" (1997, 261).

5. See Huntington and Metcalf (1979), Seaford (1995, esp. xi–xvi), and Alexiou (1974).

6. Greaves explains: "Controversy and uncertainty surrounded burial practices in the Elizabethan period, when anxiety was probably already intensified by repudiation of extreme unction, purgatory, and satisfactory masses" (1981, 698). Greaves's observation suggests that the controversy over ritual was separate from the repudiation of Purgatory. However, most of the disputes over the forms of funeral rites focused upon whether or not the rite articulated, either implicitly or explicitly, a conception of Purgatory. In other words, opposed conceptions of the afterlife are the source of most of the disputes over ritual.

7. See Cressy (1997), Duffy (1996), Gittings (1988), Greaves (1981), Haigh (1987), Houlbrooke (1998), Scarisbruck (1984), and Thomas (1971).

8. There have been a number of books on nationalism and England. See especially Helgerson (1992) and Gregerson (1995).

9. See Geary (1994), Greenblatt (2001), and LeGoff (1986).

10. For the ten years that her "gift of tears" consumed her, Kempe wept every year on Good Friday, "five er six owyrs togedyr" for "the sowles in Purgatory" (57.3320; 57.3326).

11. Cited in Pigman (1985) 30.

12. I am indebted to Patricia Phillippy for this observation, which forms one of the main lines of argument in her recently published book, *Women, Death, and Literature in Post-Reformation England.* Professor Phillippy shared with me her unpublished manuscript.

13. Pigman's translation (1985, 133 n. 12).

14. Sig. Ks, cited in Pigman (1985, 134 n. 13).

15. For a study of how Richard of Gloucester echoes reformist pieties, see Richmond (1984).

16. As Leggatt observes, "When we see the action [of *Richard III*] in its broadest perspective we realize that [Richard] is not just its creator but its instrument. He is also its victim" (1988, 41).

WORKS CITED

Alexiou, Margaret. *The Ritual Lament in Greek Tradition.* Cambridge, England: Cambridge University Press, 1974.

Baker, Herschel. Introduction to *Richard III.* In *The Riverside Shakespeare,* ed. G. Blakemore Evans. Boston: Houghton Mifflin, 1974.

Bevington. David, ed. *Henry VI: Parts One, Two and Three.* Toronto, Canada: Bantam, 1988.

Brooks, Harold F. "*Richard III,* Unhistorical Amplifications: The Women's Scenes and Seneca." *Modern Language Review* 75 (1980): 721–37.

Bullough, Geoffrey. *Narrative and Dramatic Sources of Shakespeare.* Volume V. London: Routledge and Kegan Paul, 1962.

Cressy, David. *Birth, Marriage, and Death: Ritual, Religion, and the Life-Cycle in Tudor and Stuart England.* Oxford, England: Oxford University Press, 1997.

Donne, John. "XVII Meditation." In *John Donne,* ed. John Carey. The Oxford Authors. 344–45. Oxford, England: Oxford University Press, 1990.

Dronke, Peter. "Laments of the Maries: From the Beginnings to the Mystery Plays." In *Idee, Gestalt, Geschicte: Festschrift Klaus Von See.* Studien zur *europäischen* Kulturtradition, ed. Gerd Wolfgang Weber. 89–116. Odense, Denmark: Odense University Press, 1988.

Duffy, Eamon. *The Stripping of the Altars: Traditional Religion in England, 1400–1580.* New Haven, Conn.: Yale University Press, 1996.

Geary, Patrick J. *Living with the Dead in the Middle Ages.* Ithaca, N.Y., and London: Cornell University Press, 1994.

Gittings, Clare. *Death, Burial and the Individual in Early Modern England* (1984). London: Routledge, 1988.

Greaves, Richard L. *Society and Religion in Elizabethan England.* Minneapolis, Minn.: University of Minnesota Press, 1981.

Greenblatt, Stephen. *Hamlet in Purgatory.* Princeton, N.J., and Oxford: Princeton University Press, 2001.

Gregerson, Linda. *The Reformation of the Subject: Spenser, Milton and the English Protestant Epic.* Cambridge, England: Cambridge University Press, 1995.

Grubb, Shirley Carr. "Women, Rhetoric, and Power: The Women of Shakespeare's Richard III as Collective Antagonist." Dissertation, University of Colorado. Ann Arbor, MI: UMI, 1987. 8716253.

Haigh, Christopher, ed. *The English Reformation Revised.* Cambridge, England: Cambridge University Press, 1987.

Hammond, Antony. Introduction to *King Richard III.* The Arden Shakespeare. 1–119. Walton-on-Thames, Surrey, England: Thomas Nelson and Sons, 1997.

Helgerson, Richard. *Forms of Nationhood: The Elizabethan Writing of England.* Chicago: University of Chicago Press, 1992.

Houlbrooke, Ralph. *Death, Ritual, and Bereavement. Death, Religion, and the Family in England, 1485–1750.* Oxford, England: Oxford University Press, 1998.

————. "Death Church, and Family in England between the Late Fifteenth and Early Eighteenth Centuries." In *Death, Ritual, and Bereavement,* ed. Ralph Houlbrooke. London: Routledge, 1989.

Huntington, Richard, and Peter Metcalf. *Celebrations of Death: The Anthropology of Mortuary Ritual.* Cambridge, England: Cambridge University Press, 1979.

Kay, Dennis. *Melodious Tears: The English Funeral Elegy from Spenser to Milton.* Oxford, England: Clarendon Press, 1990.

Kempe, Margery. *The Book of Margery Kempe.* Ed. Lynn Staley. Middle English Texts. Kalamazoo, Mich.: Medieval Institute Publications, 1996.

Leggatt, Alexander. *Shakespeare's Political Drama.* London and New York: Routledge, 1988.

LeGoff, Jacques. *The Birth of Purgatory.* Trans. Arthur Goldhammer. Chicago: University of Chicago Press, 1986.

Longland, John. *A Sermon made before the kynge.* 1535. RSTC 16795.

Loraux, Nicole. *Mothers in Mourning.* Trans. Corrine Pache. Ithaca, N.Y., and London: Cornell University Press, 1998.

Malinowski, B. *Magic, Science and Religion.* London: Sheldon Press, 1926.

Neill, Michael. "'Exeunt with a Dead March': Funeral Pageantry on the Shakespearean Stage." In *Pageantry in the Shakespearean Theater,* ed. David M. Bergeron. 153–93. Athens, Ga.: University of Georgia Press, 1985.

———. *Issues of Death: Mortality and Identity in English Renaissance Tragedy.* Oxford, England: Oxford University Press, 1997.

Parker, Matthew. *A Funerall Sermon . . . Preached at S. Maries in Cambridge, Anno 1551, at the buriall of . . . Martin Bucer.* Trans. Thomas Newton. London, 1587.

Parks, Joan. "Inconclusive Histories: The Lamenting Queens of *Richard III.*" Unpublished essay. Shakespeare Association of America, 1997.

Phillippy, Patricia. *Women, Death, and Literature in Post-Reformation England.* Cambridge, England: Cambridge University Press, 2002.

Pigman, G. W. *Grief and the English Renaissance Elegy.* Cambridge, England: Cambridge University Press, 1985.

Rackin, Phyllis. "Engendering the Tragic Audience: The Case of *Richard III.*" *Studies in the Literary Imagination* 26 (1993): 47–65.

Rackin, Phyllis, and Jean Howard. *Engendering a Nation: A Feminist Account of Shakespeare's English Histories.* London: Routledge, 1997.

Raines, F. R., ed. *A Description of the State, Civil and Ecclesiastical, of the County of Lancaster, about the year 1590.* Manchester, England: Chetham Society, 1875.

Richmond, Hugh M. "*Richard III* and the Reformation." *JEGP* 83 (1984): 509–21.

Saccio, Peter. *Shakespeare's English Kings.* Oxford, England: Oxford University Press, 1977.

Scarisbruck, J. J. *The Reformation and the English People.* Oxford, England: Basil Blackwell, 1984.

Seaford, Richard. *Reciprocity and Ritual: Homer and Tragedy in the Developing City-State.* Oxford, England: Clarendon Press, 1995.

Shakespeare, William. *The Tragedy of Richard III.* In *The Riverside Shakespeare,* ed. G. Blakemore Evans. Boston: Houghton Mifflin, 1974.

Strickland, Ronald. "Pageantry and Poetry as Discourse: The Production of Subjectivity in Sir Philip Sidney's Funeral." *ELH* 57 (1990): 19–36.

Thomas, Keith. *Religion and the Decline of Magic.* London: Weidenfeld and Nicholson, 1971.

Wickham, Glynne. *Early English Stages, 1300 to 1660.* London: Routledge, 1959.

Woodward, Jennifer. *The Theatre of Death: The Ritual Management of Royal Funerals in Renaissance England, 1570–1624.* Suffolk, England, and Rochester N.Y.: The Boydell Press, 1997.

3

Oxford University and
Love's Labour's Lost

by Clare Asquith

St. Anne's College, Oxford

AMONG THE MANY IMAGINATIVE PROPOSALS for dealing with "obstinate papists" put forward in 1584 by Lord Burghley was a plan to take their children as hostages "under colour of education."[1] Given the problems of enforcing the scheme in a country where so many of the population were Catholic, it is not surprising that the idea was dropped; but it is one indication of Burghley's shrewd grasp of the importance of education in uprooting the old religion and silencing opposition to the new. Many other measures had already been taken to ensure that by the time Shakespeare was beginning to write, it was almost impossible to be educated as a Catholic in England. Catholic teachers were banned from schools; there were stringent fines for employing private Catholic tutors; the families of those studying in Catholic colleges and schools abroad were fined, and the estates of exiles sequestered. Nonetheless, until a child reached the age of sixteen, when he was old enough to take the Oath of Supremacy, Catholic families managed to bring up their children in their own faith at home. For many, the moment of truth arrived with the question of secondary education, for by the 1580s, the universities and the Inns of Court were also slipping out of the reach of those who did not conform to the state religion.

This national issue could well be the missing element required to make sense of one of Shakespeare's earliest and most puzzling plays: *Love's Labour's Lost*. It is clearly full of topical allusions—but what is the topic? Scholars have been unable to agree on this, and no convincing frame of reference has ever been found. But it looks as if Shakespeare, like Burghley, was well aware of the key importance of learning in the struggle for England's conscience; read in the light of this debate, the play becomes a witty yet passionate appeal for humanity and enlightenment in England's universities. All the allusions converge on Oxford University, where the Oath of Supremacy had recently become so invasive that entry for conscientious Catholics and Puritans was next to impossible. The more one looks at the circumstances there, the more possible it becomes that Shakespeare and his patron were using the occasion of the queen's 1592 visit to Oxford to present the case for toleration under the guise of a sophisticated, courtly entertainment.[2]

Before turning to the play itself, we need to look at the position of Oxford in the early 1590s, when *Love's Labour's Lost* is thought to have been written. Both Oxford and Cambridge had suffered badly in the upheavals that followed the Reformation. In 1559, the Protestant bishop and apologist John Jewel was appalled at the damage: "You would scarcely believe so much desolation could have been effected in so short a time," he wrote.[3] Nicholas Sander, a Catholic, described the effect in similar terms: "The very flower of the two universities . . . was carried away, as it were, by a storm, and scattered in foreign lands."[4] But of the two, Oxford had fared worse. On the eve of the Reformation, it had been in the forefront of the movement for enlightened, humanist reform within the existing church, whereas Cambridge was already one of the centers of the new religion. Oxford, therefore, was a particular target for iconoclasts during Edward's reign. Duke Humphrey's collection of books and manuscripts was gutted and sold,[5] religious treasures were defaced or removed, and strict Protestant conformity was imposed on resentful halls and colleges. Although exiled Catholic scholars returned briefly during the reign of Queen Mary, on Elizabeth's accession, over a hundred Oxford fellows lost their posts. Oxford's obdurate sympathy with the old religion became an increasing irritant to the government, and particularly to the queen, who had hoped Oxford might provide moderate, scholarly churchmen to counteract the often ignorant Puritanism endemic in the new church. An ideal candidate caught her eye when when she visited the university in 1566: the brilliant and personable young scholar Edmund Campion, whom she singled out for patronage. But in 1573, Campion abandoned a distinguished and promising career to join the hemorrhage of Oxford men to Catholic colleges and seminaries abroad—and, like many others, returned as a priest to continue the old religion underground.

A particularly unfortunate aspect of Oxford's situation was the long chancellorship of the Earl of Leicester, which lasted twenty-four years—from 1564, when he was nominally in sympathy with the Catholic cause, to 1588, by which time he was leader of the Puritan faction. An anonymous Catholic attack on him, *Leicester's Commonwealth,* accused him of farming the university for his own benefit and that of his increasingly doctrinaire Puritan proteges; small wonder, it claims, that unlike Cambridge, Oxford produced few successful professional men—instead, its graduates were mainly exiles, dissidents, and recusants. Wood, the Oxford historian, highlights the negligence and "mischief" that characterized Leicester's office (Wood 1691). During his time, a narrow-minded administration gradually gained control, presiding over the covert and stubborn resistance of the more liberal scholars and masters.

One of Leicester's most damaging moves as chancellor was to intensify the already constricting effect on the university of the Oath of Supremacy.[6] The Oath was required on graduation by both universities and it presented Catholic students in particular with a dilemma. By ignoring all distinction between spiritual and temporal loyalty, the Oath was deliberately drafted in terms impossible for a Catholic to accept—and it is estimated that until the Armada, and the persecution that followed in 1589, at least two-thirds of the country was still Catholic in sympathy (Magee 1938, 36). A far smaller number, belonging to Puritan sects, also had difficulties with the Oath and the Thirty-Nine Articles. Thomas Cartwright, for instance, a leading Cambridge Puritan, took a bold stand against the Oath in the 1560s. But for those who lacked the courage of men like Cartwright and Campion, there were ways of avoiding the Oath and still getting through university. One was simply to leave without taking a degree—it is instructive to skim through the biographies of Shakespeare's contemporaries and see just how many did this. Another was to take advantage of a legal loophole. The Oath could not be imposed on anyone under the age of sixteen. Thus Catholic students would often begin their university course at an unusually early age—John Donne, for instance, was only twelve. Well aware of this subterfuge, Leicester introduced new Statutes of Matriculation in 1581, requiring subscription to the Oath of Supremacy and the Thirty-Nine Articles on arrival at Oxford, not merely on graduation. Suddenly, even Cambridge, which required the

Oath only on graduation, looked a more liberal option. There were only two universities, the "eyes" of England—and one of them was now effectively barred to anyone who could not agree to the strict imposition of the new state religion.

Leicester's death in 1588 brought no relief. The Statutes remained in place, and a year later, the particularly barbaric execution of Thomas Belson—a well-known graduate of good family—took place in Oxford. Belson and three other men—the two priests he had been assisting, and a servant from the Catharine Wheel Inn, where they had been arrested—were hanged, drawn, and quartered at a gallows between Longwall Street and St. Cross Road, and their heads were stuck on the walls of Oxford Castle, "by which place the Puritan Ministers passed and gashed with knives [their] faces." The motive behind this event was, in the words of Sir Francis Knollys, the member of the Privy Council who oversaw the execution, "the daunting of all papists, that before this proceeding here did proudly advance themselves."[7]

The shadow over Oxford looked as if it might lift four years later, with the inauguration of a new chancellor, Sir Thomas Sackville, Lord Buckhurst. Sir Thomas was a humane, civilized, learned man, in his younger days a notable poet and dramatist. *Gorboduc,* which he co-wrote, is celebrated as the first English tragedy, one of the influences on *King Lear*—a measured, somber play addressed to his cousin, the queen, on the dangers of a divided kingdom. The queen reinforced his appointment with a royal visit to the university in the same year, 1592—a year in which Lord Strange's men, with whom Shakespeare was at the time associated, also visited Oxford, no doubt to contribute to the many entertainments, including plays, that the university laid on for the queen.[8] She delivered an unusual speech, going well beyond her university theme, which usually consisted of a graceful and scholarly apology for her lack of learning and poor Latin. It begins with thanks for the expressions of love with which she has been entertained—is there a touch of irony in the way she refers to exactly the kind of hyperbolic expressions of love so constantly addressed to her? It is a love, she says, "that has never been heard of nor written nor known in the memory of man"; it exceeds the passion of lovers or the loyalty of friends. "It is such that neither persuasions nor threats nor curses can destroy. On the contrary, time has no power over it—time that eats away iron . . . of such a kind that I would think [it] . . . to be everlasting if I were also eternal." Turning from flattery, she gets down to business. She needs none of their "goads" to look to the affairs of Oxford—the problem is not her indifference but their own subversiveness and disobedience. They must learn to worship God in unity, observing "what the divine law commands and ours compels . . . not in the matter of the opinion of all nor according to over-curious and too-searching wits." Scruples of conscience can be left to their prince, for "shall I abandon the care of your souls? God forbid!" They must obey the laws laid down by their superiors, "not disputing whether better ones could be prescribed."[9] The university was left in no doubt that, though at last it had a learned chancellor, there would be no relaxation in the restrictions. It seems clear from this speech that the queen is rejecting arguments for mitigating the Oxford Statutes along the lines of a later appeal by a Catholic exile Nicholas Fitzherbert, who called on the university to attend to the "great matter" on which she had unaccountably turned her back—the uprooting of truth, tradition, and the ancient religion in the storm of the Reformation.

It is in this light—a plea for a return to a more liberal approach to learning, for release from an oath that made entry to university, and indeed life in England, prohibitive for so many, for a relaxation in the increasingly rigorous enforcement of conscience in England in the 1590s—that this essay will examine *Love's Labour's Lost,* written in the same language and idiom as the queen's 1592 speech at Oxford.

Nominally set in the court of the King of Navarre, *Love's Labour's Lost* is a deliberately dazzling play, performed, as the quarto tells us, before the court, and densely packed with allusions and layers of meaning. The queen was clearly invited to identify herself with the wise and beautiful Princess surrounded by irresistible ladies in waiting. The centerpiece of the play, a hunt in a deer park where she mounts a stand to make the fairest shot, mirrors the royal hunts elaborately staged at Windsor, Cowdray, and elsewhere; while the role of a princess, whose beauty makes men break vows for her sake, and who, after much witty flirtation dispatches them on distant and exacting tasks, was exactly the role in which Elizabeth liked to see herself. The smitten King's elaborate imagery of water attracted by the moon, though mocked by Berowne, must have provided a reminder of Ralegh's conceits of the ocean (Elizabeth's nickname for him was "Water") drawn by love of Cynthia, the Queen.[10] As for her councillors and courtiers, they would have been intrigued by the setting, for many of them had visited the court of Henry of Navarre and knew him personally. Henry's Protestantism made him one of their few real allies, and in the early 1590s, he received enthusiastic military and diplomatic support from England. But in 1593, with the famous words "Paris is worth a Mass," Henry became a Catholic in order to accede to the throne.

Once isolated, however, from the complex layers of political protocol and decorative courtly compliment, it becomes evident that the plot itself is not only very simple, but that it is a clear echo of the almost unique situation at Oxford University, which demanded the Oath as a prerequisite to three years' study. Whether the play was performed at Oxford or Windsor or in Shakespeare's theater at Holywell, many members of the audience, who had imperiled their souls, they believed, by taking the Oath of Supremacy, or compromised their careers by avoiding or even refusing it, must have been painfully reminded of their own predicament. The first speech would have alerted them to the veiled context. Four young men lightheartedly embark on a three-year course of study. As with most university degrees, fame rather than learning is the immediate goal—the students want to make a name for themselves. As at Oxford, certain "statutes" must be observed—the word a reminder of the Statutes of Matriculation. These go beyond the usual formal promises of good behavior—they include a deep oath to forswear love, an oath enforced by barbaric punishment. The oath is so momentous that the most reflective of the students, Berowne, only signs it after long debate, against his better judgment, and under intense peer pressure. Entertaining though it is, the terms of this scene echo the terms in which the morality of taking the Oath of Supremacy was exhaustively analyzed by Catholic apologists in their attempts to justify outward conformity as the persecution tightened. At length, Berowne takes the oath, his excuse being that the ferocious punishments are so unworkable that the oath will become a standing joke—and indeed, as so often happened at Catholic colleges, and in the case of the draconian penal laws against Catholics in the country at large, a blind eye is turned to the first offense in the play.

As we shall see, the play goes on to investigate from all angles the morality of taking and renouncing an unbearably restrictive oath. However, before Shakespeare develops this central theme, he introduces two comic characters who clearly indicate that this is a play about Oxford. In exactly the manner of plays performed by the Inns of Court, Armado and Moth appear to be based on two figures who would have been recognizable to contemporaries associated with the university, and indeed to London contemporaries who would also have known them. Both were men who suffered for their convictions at the hands of the new ideology: the first, a liberal-minded Protestant ahead of his time, the second, a Catholic forced into conformity for the sake of a career—a writer whose long struggle with his conscience was to produce some of the best poetry of his time.

The first is now a forgotten figure, but was then well known, indeed notorious.[11] His biography makes him an ideal prototype for Adriano de Armado, the play's fantastical Spaniard, who joins the scholars to amuse them in their "little academe." Antonio de Corro was born in Seville in 1527, became a monk, but at the age of thirty, left the monastery and embraced the new religion.[12] On Calvin's recommendation he became tutor in Spanish to Henry of Navarre; and in 1567, at the age of forty, came to England, where he was warmly welcomed by Burghley as a Spanish Protestant refugee and promoted among the London Spanish community by Grindal, later the Archbishop of Canterbury. But Corro quickly became a thorn in the side of the Protestant establishment. His views were controversial—he did not believe in predestination or the Trinity, and he advocated toleration for Catholics, defending his position with a "hot accusing spirit." In 1571, he was transferred to Oxford, where, in spite of Leicester's patronage, he again incurred strong Puritan opposition. The university authorities refused to endorse Leicester's appointment of Corro as one of the new politically correct "lectori catechismi" until he cleared himself of heresy—but they were overruled by the chancellor, and although Corro was willing, indeed eager, to defend himself, specific charges were never brought. He proved a godsend of course to Catholic halls and colleges like St. John's, Oriel, and Hart Hall, which were quick to select the maverick Corro as their obligatory teacher of the Protestant catechism. One of his pupils would have been Thomas Belson, who was at Oriel, another John Donne, at Hart Hall. Corro remained a controversial, unrepentant, and presumably colorful figure at the university until his retirement to a prebendal stall at St. Paul's in 1586.

In 1590, a year before his death, Corro brought out a short French-Spanish grammar, even now a clear and useful introduction to both languages (del Corro 1590). The tone of the book is at once grand and intimate: Corro is the authorial "we," the reader the "stranger" or "novice." Each point is made simply but with stately care, in what Corro himself calls the "broad and leisurely" Spanish style:

> The nouns instrumental, by which we denote some work, and by which as it were a thing is done, we sometimes put the same in the nominative case, with his article joined to it. . . . sometimes they be pronounced possessively, betokening possession, sometimes relatively, betokening relation. (de Corro 1590, 27)

He enjoys resonant synonyms like "exaggerating and magnifying" or "concurrans or mating together" (de Corro 1590, 21). He also uses precise and unusual grammatical terms: "Here I must advertise such as would attain to good knowledge of the Spanish tongue that they learn how to apply their . . ." (21). A favorite theme is the inability of foreigners to pronounce the Spanish "ch" sound; perhaps after long experience with Henry of Navarre he has given up hope of the French ("they will always say 'shickens for chickens'"), but there is hope, he thinks, for the English provided they "*exercise* themselves in the pronouncing of this letter ch" (4). Even in this small handbook, religion is never far from Corro's mind: his grammatical examples appear to be especially chosen to illustrate the loving mercy of God, while at one point the language of transubstantiation strays incongruously into advice on Spanish nouns and adjectives that "agree with the order of nature which first and chiefly doth respect the substance and afterward the accidence."

I have quoted at length from Corro's book because the reaction of anyone who knows the play might well be that of Boyet, the Princess's courtier: "I am much deceived but I remember the style." The diction of Don Armado could have been lifted straight from this book of grammar. The only time Shakespeare uses the word "epitheton" is on Armado's entry when he calls his page, Moth, a "congruent epitheton" (1.2.13). Armado, too, is fond of synonyms: "thou wert immured, restrained, captivated, bound" (3.1.126). Just as Corro's passion for his religion overflows into his grammatical examples, Armado's love for Jacquenetta mixes incongruously with grammatical terms: "I do affect the very ground, which is base, where her shoe, which is baser, guided by her foot, which is basest, doth tread" (1.2.157). On his entry in act 5, Armado even appears to be exercising Moth in "the pronouncing of

this letter ch," to the puzzlement of Holofernes: Armado: "Chirrah!'"
Holofernes: "Quare 'chirrah,' not 'sirrah'?" Many commentators have
queried this exchange, but it would have entertained anyone familiar
with Corro's linguistic fixations.

It is not only his style of speech that links Armado to Corro. There
is a reminder of Corro's objections to the Trinity in the way Moth
repeatedly teases Armado over the number three, a word Armado at
first can't bring himself to utter, preferring either to round it up to four
or to call it "one more than two" (47). Armado is a particular butt of
the Puritans in the play, who criticize him, as Corro was criticized, for
being "vain and ridiculous," "affected, odd." The way Armado boasts
of his intimacy with the King of Navarre, who would sometimes "lean
upon my poor shoulder and with his royal finger thus dally with my
excrement, with my mustachio" (5.1.110), may have recalled to
amused ex-pupils Corro's own anecdotes of the time when he was tutor
to the future king, Henry of Navarre. A final prompt to those who knew
Corro may lie in the fact that in his opening letter Armado is the only
character to mention the constable by his name, Antony Dull, recalling
one of the many variants of Corro's own name: Antony del, rather than
Antonio de Corro.

But I believe it was the comical association between the vain, stately, middle-aged Corro and the brilliantly precocious, irreverent, and
mercurial thirteen-year-old student, John Donne, who arrived at Hart
Hall in 1584, that would have made the most memorable impression
on those who were at Oxford at the time. There are two reasons for
assuming that Donne was Corro's pupil. As we have seen, Corro was
the obligatory "lector catechismi" for Hart Hall while Donne was
there; and the subjects Donne studied are thought to have included
Spanish and the Spanish mystics. If they were indeed associated in this
way, then the appearance of Moth and Armado on stage would instant-
ly have recalled this oddly assorted master and pupil, and indicates that
Shakespeare meant them to be more than a comic double act—for they
are also made to represent the two main intellectual positions officially excluded by the narrowly doctrinaire Oxford authorities.

Donne's family was not only staunchly Catholic, related to the saint
and martyr Thomas More, but two of his uncles were Jesuits. One of
them, Jasper Heywood, became head of the Jesuit order in England.
Some years later, his younger brother Henry, who came up to Oxford

with him, was to die in jail for sheltering a Catholic priest. Up to the age of twelve, the Donne boys were educated privately, presumably on Jesuit principles, which would have included rigorous training in logic and rhetoric. Isaac Walton gives us a portrait of Donne on his arrival at the university. He had a good command of Latin and French and extraordinary natural brilliance, "another Picus de Mirandola . . . rather born than made wise by study" (Walton n.d., 17). Donne describes himself as having had a "hydroptic immoderate desire of humane learning and languages," certainly the kind of "well-educated infant" able to outclass many of his tutors (Donne 1967, 456).[13] All these aspects are, of course, strongly present in Moth—whose youth and small size are also constantly emphasized. Furthermore, we know that the highly sexed Donne reacted against the early rigor of his education with a period of extreme licentiousness—and Moth's precocity includes relentless puns on the word "horn," as well as surprisingly adult advice to Armado on how to seduce women. But Donne also has a strong claim on Moth's title, stressed three times on his first appearance, as a "tender Juvenal." This could well refer to Donne's early fame as the writer of the first formal satires in English. By 1591, when Donne was seventeen, these highly original poems were circulating in manuscript and established Donne in literary circles as an English Juvenal. When *Love's Labour's Lost* was written, his daring satires and elegies were of considerable topical interest—indeed there are points where the play actually appears to refer to them.

One such reference is the name "Moth." In a prophetic passage in his *Elegy VI,* "Recusancy," Donne compares the lure of worldly advancement, which forces Catholics into oaths that betray their religion, to the way "the taper's beamie eye Amorously twinkling, beckons the giddy fly, Yet burns his wings." This elegy, which includes a vivid passage describing the Reformation in terms of a flash flood that bursts and overflows the river banks, leaving the dry bed behind, is notable for its nervous, original style and daring content: if these poems were as celebrated as scholars believe, the name Donne would have been associated at the time with the unusual image of the recusant fly, or moth, attracted to the worldly candle.

But one of the neatest ways of referring to a particular character was by means of the contemporary passion for cryptic or heraldic emblems. The Donne family crest was a sheaf of snakes. In *Love's Labour's Lost,*

Shakespeare goes to great lengths to associate Moth with this heraldic device. One of the jokes in the play is that the Puritan pedant, Holofernes, is so ignorant that although he puts on a performance of the Nine Worthies, he cannot even remember who they all are, and wrongly includes Hercules among them, compounding his mistake by giving the part to the tiny Moth. But he overrules the cast's objections by hastily explaining that Moth will of course be the *infant* Hercules, who strangled snakes in his cradle. Moth, whose every word is usually a pun, welcomes the idea with a word suggesting heraldry: "An excellent *device!*" (5.1.118). When the Worthies at last perform, they identify themselves by means of emblems on canvas boards or shields. Holofernes explains the picture on Moth's: "Thus did he strangle serpents with his manus" (5.2.584). So by a series of apparent comic accidents, Shakespeare has worked Moth into a position in which he actually stands on the stage bearing Donne's own heraldic device.[14]

A third character who has attracted much interest from allusion hunters is Holofernes, the Puritan pedant who has been identified with, among others, Gabriel Harvey and John Florio. Whoever he is based on, Holofernes is clearly meant to represent the ascendency of the narrow, ill-educated aspect of the new regime. Moreover, he has a sinister side to him. The name Holoferenes is taken from a story in the Apocrypha, much quoted at the time as an example of heretical enforcement of conscience. According to this story, the Jewish resistance heroine Judith, invited at night to Holofernes's tent, cut off the head of the tyrant who was attempting to force her people to eat food forbidden by their religion. References to this event in literature and art were commonplace throughout the Reformation, and appear in the writings of English Catholic apologists.[15] The name implies that Shakespeare's pedant is not simply sectarian, but that he is in some sense an enforcer of conscience.

This implication is strengthened during one of the only passages in *Love's Labour's Lost* when the good-humored tone momentarily slips. This is when Holofernes stars in the pageant in the role of Judas Maccabeus. He was originally cast as Alexander, but his appearance as Judas gives the audience a chance to identify him, for whatever reason, with Judas Iscariot. And here the barracking takes an unpleasant turn. When Holofernes indicates the presumably clumsy portrait of Maccabeus on his shield, the audience almost falls over itself in eagerness to supply witty conceits that revolve around severed heads, carving, and knives. These have nothing to do with Maccabeus; they obviously refer to the fate of the original Holofernes; but they could also have awakened memories among Thomas Belson's contemporaries of the heads stuck on the walls of Oxford Castle, gashed with the knives of passing Puritan ministers.

A more precise link between Holofernes and Oxford Castle in fact lies in the much-studied exchange between him and Armado:

> ARMADO: Do you not educate youth at the charge-house on the top of the mountain?
> HOLOFERNES: Or mons, the hill.
> ARMADO: At your sweet pleasure, for the mountain.
> HOLOFERNES: I do, sans question. (5.1.69–72)

The castle, then still used as a prison, would have been one of the most forbidding monuments in Oxford in Shakespeare's time. Situated in the central Westgate precinct, it originally stood on rising ground defending the southwest city walls; next to it loomed the impressive, sixty-four-foot defensive Castle Mound, which survives to this day though almost overwhelmed by modern development—its steep, conical shape lending it the appearance of a miniature mountain. In medieval times, the castle buildings included St. George's church, and a small college for poor scholars, run by a warden from Osney Abbey; it also was where the university confined its "rebellious scholars." By the sixteenth century, it contained an Assize Court and had become one of the prisons where recusants were held—Thomas Belson and his servant among them. Prison space was at a premium in the 1590s—new prison camps were overflowing with recusants in York, Ely, and Wisbech. It is likely that every inch of space was used in the castle, including a secure hexagonal twelve-foot chamber dug in to the top of the mound, originally a well-house but, on the evidence of ancient cannonballs found in the well-shaft, used at some point as a magazine for ammunition, or, to use the *OED* definition, a "charge-house." Here we have a connection between Holofernes and the young recusants interned both in the castle itself, and in the charge-house on the mound. It was standard practice for such prisoners to be subjected to constant catechising or, in Armado's phrase, "educating" from Puritan ministers; there is a record of one of the priests imprisoned with Belson routing them in argument.

Possibly this was one of the tasks of the original Holofernes—he may also have had some official function at the castle, for one of the shafts directed at him during the pageant connects him with St. George, patron of the church there.

As one might expect, sectarian sparks fly on Moth's first encounter with Holofernes. This, to us, is a mystifying exchange, yet Armado and Costard are clearly convulsed with laughter at Moth's "quick venue of wit":

> MOTH: . . . he teaches boys the hornbook. What is a, b, spelt backward with the horn on his head?
> HOL: Ba, puerita, with a horn added.
> MOTH: Ba, most silly sheep with a horn. (5.1.41–44)

One of the six commissioners chosen to enforce the 1553 reforms was the energetic and ubiquitous Robert Horne, Bishop of Winchester, responsible for much of the destruction at Winchester and Durham cathedrals, and ruthless scourge of both universities. At Oxford, his fanaticism left a trail of wreckage behind it. In the colleges that fell under his influence, he ensured the annihilation or removal of every-thing connected with popish superstition; at New College, for instance, the rich tabernacle work covering the east end of the chapel was smashed in pieces. According to the DNB, "his enemies played upon his name as indicative of his character . . . hard in nature and crooked in conditions." It looks as if Moth is doing just this, identifying Holofernes as a disciple of the infamous Horne. The schoolboy's "hornbook" could well refer to the contentious Book of Advertisements that Horne helped to draw up. It was published with-out the queen's consent in 1564, and set out hardline rubrics for the new Prayerbook service. Then, by making Holofernes baa, Moth is able to deride him as one of Horne's flock—a "silly sheep."

These three characters supply what I believe many contemporaries would have recognized as a clear Oxford context for the central theme of the play—the theme of the oath. Returning to the plot, then, we can follow it in the way they would have done, with this underlying theme in mind.

No sooner have the four students subscribed to their oath to forswear the love of women for three years than practical reasons force them to break it. "Necessity will make us all forsworn" (1.1.150) comments one of them grimly. But this first lapse merely takes the form of a meeting with the visiting Princess and her ladies; worse is to follow, as one by one they all fall in love. Too ashamed to confess it, each one soliloquizes alone, equating true knowledge with this deep love—they now realize learning in its real sense has nothing to do with "continual plodding," but is inspired by the apprehension of the divine—the very thing they have denied themselves by taking the oath. This elaborate argument uses the language and framework in which Erasmus and other Christian humanists discussed the nature of learning, relating it to the deep yearning of the human soul for God. Instead of the narrow, scripture-based scholarship of the new regime, this pre-Reformation Christian humanist learning was all-embracing—for, as Erasmus argues, to the enlightened mind everything was a potential image of the divine. Love, in particular, was a kind of ladder to the divine, human love in its highest form leading on to God. This background penetrates Renaissance iconography where Venus and Cupid, for instance, both take separate forms, representing both physical and divine love, depending on their attributes. The lovers in the play stray constantly and wittily from the human to the divine, calling on "Saint Cupid" as their patron.

Another writer might have left the allegory there—beneath the scenes of courtly love, an eloquent evocation of the way a narrow ideology was stifling the soul of a university that had once been a bastion of humanist learning. But Shakespeare can be distinguished from many other allegorists by the depth and subtlety of his hidden meaning. For the lovers do not all love the same thing. Once they have admitted to their hidden passions, Berowne becomes particularly defensive about the merits of his dark lady, aggravating the others by comparing their fair women unfavorably to his Rosaline. Though all agree on the importance of their subversive love, it already looks as though it means something different to each of them. Looking closely at the language, and comparing it to the great theological debate raging at the time, I believe the love that Berowne, Armado, Dumaine, and Longaville agonize over is not the forbidden love of women, but forbidden routes to the divine—forbidden religions. Reformer though Erasmus was, all his work, like that of More, was rooted in what we would now call a medieval piety—movingly expressed at the end of *In Praise of Folly,* his most popular work, dedicated to Thomas More. For him humanism and Catholicism went hand in hand. At the other end of the spectrum, we have seen that

Corro, the model for Armado, was persecuted for maintaining beliefs very close to those of the Protestant humanist scholar Michael Servetus, executed by fellow Protestants for heresy.

For us it may seem somehow ludicrous to suggest that Armado's irreverent, promiscuous Jacquenetta could represent Corro's liberal Protestantism, or that Rosaline, Katharine, and Maria also represent forbidden lines of thought and belief. For those who recoil from the idea that Shakespeare could use such natural, vivid characters allegorically it is worth remembering that Renaissance allegory did not always come as heavily labeled as Spenser's or Durer's—and especially not in England, where most dissident writers were too prudent to risk immediate interpretation. Nonetheless, under a rich overlay of deceptive realism, many of them still used the stock in trade images of Renaissance allegory to address dangerous issues—in particular, figures of women, who stood for England, Geneva, Truth, Free Will, Virtue, Catholicism. John Donne was one of these writers. Conveniently for us, he left his allegories boldly labeled when it came to publication. His third satire, for instance, contains the famous image of Truth as a woman seated on a hill—"And he that will/Reach her about must and about must go." But it also contains a less familiar passage in which he personifies as pairs of lovers the three choices of religion that lay before him. The first lover is Mirreus. His "unhous'd" beloved has, he believes, fled to Rome, where he adores her rags as if they were robes of state—clearly, banished Catholicism. Crantz's beloved is at Geneva: she is "plain, simple, sullen, young, contemptuous yet unhandsome"—an equally clear picture of Lutheranism. The third option, foisted on an unwilling Graius, remains at home—she is the English reformed religion, described in contemptuous terms and summed up as a bride forced on a ward by his guardian. The Earl of Southampton and William Herbert both suffered literally in this way at the hands of Lord Burghley, who made a fortune out of his position as Master of the Court of Wards—both men had to pay a considerable fine for refusing Protestant wives from Burghley's own family—Herbert went on to marry a Catholic. But metaphorically, a disagreeable arranged marriage is a graphic image of the way dissidents saw the new religion.

It is likely then that contemporaries would have had no difficulty in identifying Berowne's Rosaline, like Crantz's plain young contemptuous Lutheran, with the Genevan religion. She is not "my lady," but plain unadorned "Joan." She is like "a German clock ... never going aright"—here again, Shakespeare characteristically uses the calendar difference between Catholic and Protestant countries as a neat identification. Protestant countries, which refused to adopt the new Gregorian calendar, were always unpredictably out of step with Catholic ones, necessitating constant recourse to almanacs—hence "ever out of frame" and "being watched, that it may still go right" (3.1.192).[16]

Berowne uses another typical contemporary distinction between the old and new religion in the opposition of beauty (more specifically, "fair" beauty) with plainness (correspondingly "dark"). Echoing Protestant polemicists, Berowne condemns artificial beauty, painting, wigs. Rosaline, he boasts, is not ashamed of her own unfashionable black hair; with typical allegorical subtlety, Shakespeare implies that she has even set her own fashion in black, forcing women to conceal their natural beauty in order to match hers—another reference to the Protestant enforcement of conscience in England. Berowne goes even further—too far, in fact:

> Her favour turns the fashion of the days
> And therefore is she born to make black fair,
> For native blood is counted painting now
> And therefore red that would avoid dispraise
> Paints itself black, to imitate her brow.
>   (4.3.257–62)

The thought is compressed, but the topical gist would have struck a familiar chord with the audience, and it evidently preoccupied Shakespeare as the idea recurs in almost exactly the same involved terms in a number of his sonnets (most notably, sonnet 127). Rosaline's lovers, Berowne complacently suggests, scorn not merely the ornaments of her rivals' beauty but their natural beauty as well—for he observes that even the "native blood" of naturally rosy cheeks is now dismissed as artifice in the light of Rosaline's dark beauty. In the same way, Puritans deplored not merely the accretions but the very essence, the intrinsic beauty, of the native English religion—the mass itself.

Not surprisingly, this infuriates Dumaine and Longaville, for, though the Princess is allegorically neutral, their women have Catholic attributes. The white-clad Katharine, in particular, is fair as opposed to dark, and unlike Rosaline, her beauty, like that of Maria and the Princess, is obvious—for Catholics and for all Christian humanists beauty was a means, not a bar, to the divine. A brisk exchange with Rosaline endows Katharine with more detailed attributes. Her sister died on the "shrewd unhappy gallows" of love (5.1.12); like "Love's Tyburn, that hangs up simplicity" (4.3.54), this phrase is a reminder that the play was written at the time of the executions of Catholics following the Armada. Katharine contrasts her sister's melancholy with Rosaline's "light, nimble stirring spirit" (4.1.16)—a description that Rosaline suspiciously interprets as superficial, opportunist, and factious; Catholic criticisms of the new religion. She flashes back, "Look what you do, you do it still in the dark" (24)—a hit at the catacomb world of the recusants. Rosaline's dark looks are next associated with the black ink of a copy book, which gives Rosaline the chance to link Katharine's more obvious charms with red and golden letters. This is a sly reference to a forgotten sectarian dispute, furiously debated at the time—the reformers were determined to print the new calendar, even the vital domenical letter, entirely in black; while "golden" illuminated letters were a feature so much associated with the old practices that the early reformers in Oxford automatically burned any books that contained them. Katharine's face, too, is full of "O's"—a catty hint at smallpox scars, but also, continuing the theme of books, a reference to the illuminated "O's" that began so many prayers in the old missals—the Advent sequence, for instance, is still known as "the Great O's." This reading of the quarrel between Rosaline and Katharine might explain the Princess's admiring comment—"a set of wit well played." On a literal level it is almost meaningless. In the light of the allegorical significance of their women, no wonder Dumaine and Longaville respond to Berowne's "dark lady" rhapsody with a mocking parody.

Nonetheless, like the sincere English Catholics and Puritans whose spirituality made them joint victims of the government insistence on uniformity, they sink their differences, for "Are we not all in love?" There follows the great speech in praise of love (4.3.285–361), a speech that does not quite work as love poetry, but which, once the neoplatonist idea of the "eyes of the mind" is associated with the phrase "women's eyes," captures the essence of the all-embracing humanism of pre-Reformation Oxford, of the enlightened learning and spirituality of Erasmus and Colet. This divinely inspired thirst for learning, Berowne suggests, cannot be regulated—it is uniquely experienced by every individual: "Learning is but an adjunct to ourself And where we are our learning likewise is." The speech ends with an unequivocal identification of love with the divine, "for Love's sake, a word that loves all men," and the argument concludes with the Catholic reasons for refusing the Oath of Supremacy, associating it with the gospel warning not to seek the world at the expense of your soul:

> Let us once lose our oaths to find ourselves
> Or else we lose ourselves to keep our oaths
> It is religion to be thus forsworn
> For charity itself fulfills the law
> And who can sever love from charity?
>
> (4.3.357–61)

Once they have decided to renounce the oath, the lovers in the play, now interestingly described as "traitors" by Costard, enter a world of subterfuge. On the level of the plot, this takes the form of ridiculous schemes to make love to their women in masks and disguises. On the deeper level, the charge of subversiveness was leveled at both dissident Puritans and the easygoing "church papists," typical of the early part of Elizabeth's reign, who reconciled their consciences by attending both communions, the Catholic one in secret. By the 1590s, the choice had become starker; lip service to the new regime would no longer do. This hard line is reflected in the play. The women refuse to take their equivocating, duplicitous lovers seriously. However much they protest, the women are adamant—for all their lyrical love poetry, the words of men who have already perjured themselves by going back on their word are not enough; only action will prove their sincerity. This follows precisely the line of argument that drove so many into exile. Each lover in turn is given his sentence—a year of austerity, a year in a hermitage, a period of penance. The tone of the play darkens as the implications of their new commitment begin to sink in. They leave to begin their period of trial. It seems an unsatisfactory ending for a romantic comedy—there is no hint of what is to happen at the end of the penitential year. But on the allegorical level, the ending is historically right. Robert Southwell, one of the idealistic young Catholic exiles who later returned like Campion as a missionary priest, describes the difficulties involved in the decision to "abandon our country, friends and all such comforts as naturally all men seek and find in their native soil; we must relinquish all possibilities of favour, riches and credit; we must limit our minds to the restrained and severe course of the Society of Jesus, or the seminaries, where the place is in exile, the rules strict, the government austere, our wills broken, the least faults chastised and an absolute virtue exacted" (Southwell 1953, 7.20–27).

The whole movement of the play from ivory tower to love and lastly to the harsh realities involved in real commitment is concentrated in the famous final song in which a courtly, pastoral spring "when shepherds pipe on oaten straws" is succeeded by an ordinary English winter in which "milk comes frozen home in pail," "when blood is nipped and ways be foul," and "Marian's nose looks red and raw." The first verse ends with the song of the deceitful cuckoo, suggesting that outward conformity (including its literature) is built on falsehood; the second ends with the wise owl, for though the new life is one of deprivation, poverty, and winter, the note of the owl is "merry." The spiritual richness of the sacrifice is accentuated further in Armado's cryptic farewell, a coda gracefully recalling the learned neoplatonist language of the lovers: "The words of Mercury are harsh after the songs of Apollo." In traditional Christian alchemical wisdom, mercury was the essential catalyst for the journey of the soul.

An interesting detail, and one which at first sight fits neither the historical nor the literal level of the play, is the rather different fate of the spokesman for the lovers, Berowne. Instead of austerity and exile, he is condemned to another kind of servitude. To cure his flippancy, Rosaline commands him, "with all the fierce endeavour of your wit" (5.1.841), to entertain "groaning wretches" (840) and the "speechless sick" (839). He must "enforce the pained impotent to smile" (842) and entertain those "deaf'd with the clamour of their own dear groans" (852). The incredulous Berowne has difficulty in accepting: it is impossible, he says, to "move wild laughter in the throat of death" (843)—but ruefully agrees that only this will bring about a true "reformation" (857) in his character. There are few records of university men entertaining the sick in hospitals; but a number of them did become London playwrights. This passage may conceivably refer to the nature of the audience they found there. John Donne's biographer, John Carey, describes the level of persecution in the early 1590s as "a terror," and though "pained impotent" may sound excessive to us, it was exactly how Catholics described their own condition at the time. Before long, several of the London University Wits did indeed change their tune and began to write what might now be called protest literature, a number of them responding to the influential poetry of Robert Southwell, and some, like Lodge and Constable, eventually converting openly and leaving the country. There may even be an element of autobiography here, for the language of Berowne's "dark lady" love poetry has close affinities with a number of Shakespeare's sonnets—perhaps he, too, was altered by his encounter with a London audience at a point when persecution was at its height.

Shakespeare scholars often lament the lack of information about the way contemporary audiences reacted to his plays. There is, however, one intriguing record at the end of *Alba,* a long and melancholy lover's lament by Robert Tofte, published in 1598. He did not enjoy *Love's Labour's Lost,* he says: it reminded him painfully of his own situation. His mistress, Alba, has abandoned him; in spite of his misgivings he was forced to attend the play with his "froward dame," a woman whom he elsewhere describes as an "envious Stepdame," embodiment of a "Froward Will." This is the language Catholic dissidents used for the usurping queen and her "wilful" government, a breakaway from the authority of the Universal Church. The cruel mistress is the mother church that appeared to have abandoned them—here the name Alba associates her with Albion, for they saw Catholicism as England's native religion. The picture is of a covertly Catholic courtier reluctantly attending the play with the queen, whom he describes as stony and unmoved; he himself is deeply affected.

Another member of that audience—perhaps even the man behind the production—would have been the company's patron, Ferdinand, Lord Strange. The King of Navarre is called Ferdinando, not Henry, and there is wordplay throughout on Strange's name and motto, "sans changer." Strange was an enigmatic figure: one of the large Catholic Stanley clan, based in Lancashire, he was soon to become the Earl of Derby, and his strong claim to the throne was eagerly supported by many English Catholics. Prudently, he kept his religious beliefs to himself, but was always under suspicion: his death in 1594, immediately after a plot to put him on the throne, was thought at the time to be the result of poison. The play, which diplomatically gives his name to a Protestant prince, may have held a special resonance for him. In 1573, at the age of fourteen, he was summoned from Oxford, where he had been studying for only a year, to the court at Windsor. No post awaited him there; but in that year St. John's College, Oxford, must have been, in the eyes of Lord Burghley, a particularly dangerous place for a boy in Strange's position, for it was then that Edmund Campion, along with seven other men from St. John's, left England for Douai. If Strange was removed for this reason, the defection of Campion would have left a deep impression; many of the arguments traced in the play may well have been familiar to him; and so would the contrast in the play between the cloistered, male retreat and the queenly hunt outside. There may even have been a delicate compliment to the queen in the choice of plot, for it would have been a reminder that their patron, like the play's King of Navarre, also abandoned his studies for the court of a beautiful princess.

In relating the strands of *Love's Labour's Lost* to the different elements and concerns of an audience that ranged from Elizabeth's court to the theater at Holywell, this reading suggests that Shakespeare's intention was unusually ambitious—it was to appeal to the many layers of a deeply divided England and to plead the particular case of one of them. Unlike the many commentaries that align the plot with the philosophic Renaissance academies of Italy or the politics of the court of Navarre, this analysis assumes that Shakespeare's English audience, accustomed to coded dramatizations of the "matter of England," would be likely to relate the play to matters closer to home. The mere association of the three concepts of an oath, learning, and religion would have been enough to alert most people to the fact that this was more than a romantic comedy—it was at the same time an exploration of one of the major issues of the day. For those familiar with Oxford—and this included most of the Catholic faction at court—the inclusion of topical references and well-known academic characters would not only have made the play still funnier, it would have sharpened the impact of its theme, the appeal for a rebirth of true learning in a benighted Oxford, and by extension, a rebirth of true religion in England.

Notes

1. See Burghley's *Memorial of 1584* in Devlin (1956) 330.

2. Although most modern editors have accepted 1594–95 for the play's composition, Bevington and others have also considered a wider range, 1588–97; see Bevington (1997, A2).

3. Letter to Henry Bullinger, 1559, quoted by Caraman (1960, 14).

4. Nicolas Sander, quoted in Caraman (1960, 140).

5. See Waugh (1935, 15). According to the Duke Humphreys's collection librarian, William Hodgetts, only nineteen of the original books have since been recovered.

6. The 1588 Oath of Supremacy required recognition that the queen "has and ought to have all superiority, jurisdiction, preeminence and authority over all persons both ecclesiastical and secular in England and Ireland." The loyal subject was required to "pursue unto death all those who in any way attempt to . . . in the smallest way infringe her rights within her dominion." (The text of the Oath is quoted in Caraman (1964, 75–76). Thus the terms of the Oath did not distinguish between the temporal powers of the Church—negotiable for many Catholics—and its universal spiritual authority.

7. *Breve Relation,* Rome, 1590, quoted in Kelly (1987, 100).

8. A contemporary observer, Philip Stringer, gives a full account of the entertainments, though he omits the titles of plays and the names of actors. See Plummer (1887).

9. Queen Elizabeth's Latin speech to the Heads of Oxford University, 28 September 1592, 327–28.

10. See Sir Walter Ralegh, "The 21th: and last booke of the Ocean to Cynthia" and "Praysed be Dianaes faire and harmelesse light," in *Poems* (4, 48).

11. There is a long tradition of speculation about the identifications of Armado and Moth, which include most commonly Ralegh and Chapman, or Harvey and Nashe.

12. For accounts of Corro's life, see Dent (1983), Collinson (1979), and also DNB.

13. From a letter to Henry Goodyere, 1608.

14. One of Donne's most impenetrable poems, "The Undertaking," begins and ends with the lines:

> I have done one braver thing
> Than all the Worthies did.

It is possible that in associating himself with the Worthies, and in the references to his concealment from the prophane of a secret love, which is yet not romance ("forget the Hee and She"), there is a connection with Shakespeare's play.

15. In 1578, William Carter was executed for printing Gregory Martin's *Treatise of Schism,* which included the story of Judith and Holofernes, thought to encourage regicide.

16. Shakespeare's subtle use of the two calendars is explored by Sohmer (1999).

WORKS CITED

Bevington, David. "Canon, Dates, and Early Texts." In *The Complete Works of Shakespeare,* ed. David Bevington. Updated 4th ed. A1–A21. New York: Longman, 1997.

Caraman, Philip. *Henry Garnet, 1555–1606, and the Gunpowder Plot.* London: Longmans, 1964.

_____. *The Other Face.* London: Longmans, 1960.

Collinson, Patrick. *Archbishop Grindal, The Struggle for a Reformed Church.* London: Jonathon Cape, 1979.

de Corro, Antonio. *The Spanish Grammar.* With dictionary added by John Thorius. London: John Wolfe, 1590.

Dent, C. M. *Protestant Reformers in Elizabethan Oxford.* Oxford, England: Oxford University Press, 1983.

Devlin, Christopher. *The Life of Robert Southwell.* London: Longmans, 1956.

Donne, John. *Complete Poetry and Selected Prose.* Ed. John Hayward. London: Nonesuch, 1967.

Elizabeth I, Collected Works. Ed. Marcus and Rose Mueller. Chicago, Ill: University of Chicago Press, 2000.

Kelly, Christine. *Blessed Thomas Belson.* London: Colin Smythe, 1987.

Magee, Brian. *The English Recusants.* London: Burns Oates, 1938.

Plummer, Charles, ed. *Elizabethan Oxford.* Oxford, England: Oxford Historical Society at the Clarendon Press, 1887.

Ralegh, Sir Walter. *The Poems of Sir Walter Ralegh.* Ed. Michael Rudick. Tempe, Ariz.: Renaissance English Text Society, 1999.

Shakespeare, William. *The Complete Works.* Ed. Stanley Wells and Gary Taylor. Oxford, England: Clarendon Press, 1986.

Sohmer, Steve. *Shakespeare's Mystery Play.* Manchester, England: Manchester University Press, 1999.

Southwell, Robert. *An Humble Supplication to her Majestie* (1595). Ed. R. C. Bald. Cambridge, England: Cambridge University Press, 1953.

Walton, Isaak. *Izaak Walton's Lives.* London: T. Nelson & Sons, n.d.

Waugh, Evelyn. *Edmund Campion.* London: Longmans, Green, 1935.

Wood, Anthony. *Athenae Oxonienses* (1691). Ed. P. Bliss. London: Rivington, 1813–20.

4

Shakespeare's Religious Background Revisited: *Richard II* in a New Context

by Jean-Christophe Mayer

University of Montpellier, France

WHEN SHAKESPEARE completed *Richard II* in 1595, he was writing in a period that historians have ceased to regard as congenial.[1] Those "nasty nineties," as Patrick Collinson observed, were certainly not a period of stabilization, routinization, or secularization: this was not "a decade of sweetness and light, of incipient puritan piety and mellowing Anglicanism, but a rather ugly decade, when the going got tough and unpleasant for all parties" (Collinson 1995, 153). It was in this context that Shakespeare launched a sequence of four plays on the Lancastrian period of English history with the story of the deposition of the Plantagenet King Richard II.[2]

By the mid-1590s, the story and the allusions to the reign of Richard II had already been used by historians and law specialists to discuss the terms by which a king might be deposed. The theme was appropriated also by malcontents to point to the moral of the story, in ways that repeatedly challenged what some critics would still like to call "the Elizabethan status quo."[3] In other words, allusions to Richard II had become commonplace when commenting on the realm of politics.

The aim of this essay is not, therefore, to affirm that Shakespeare was the first to seize upon the theme (even if the dramatist's contribution to it is of course unique), but it does make a claim to put Shakespeare's play in a context that has so far been overlooked—a context showing that theater, politics, and polemic sometimes wrestled with the same specific issues. To throw a detailed light on this context, it is useful to focus on events surrounding two major dates: 1595 and 1601. Both dates, as we shall see, involve the same play—Shakespeare's *Richard II*—and the same protagonists: the players of Shakespeare's acting company, Robert Devereux, Earl of Essex, and the English Jesuit and political activist Robert Parsons.

Much attention has been given to the links between the publication of John Hayward's *The First Part of the Life and Raigne of King Henrie the IIII* (1599) and Shakespeare's play.[4] Despite its title, Hayward's book was mostly concerned with the last years of Richard II's reign. The unsettling elements in Hayward's work were its many invented speeches. The Archbishop of Canterbury, for instance, was made to address a totally fabricated speech of encouragement to Henry Bolingbroke as he was contemplating the deposition of Richard II.[5] The dramatization of history was something the authorities regarded with suspicion, especially in the work of an historian. It must be noted, however, that Hayward's politically controversial historical account was written in 1599. Shakespeare could not have consulted Hayward's manuscript to write *Richard II*, as the dates of Shakespeare's play cannot be made to match the historian's.[6] We will thus turn to another work, which—as we shall try to argue—has greater topical relevance.

This work, published the same year as Shakespeare's *Richard II*, has attracted considerably less attention, even though Robert Parsons's *Conference About the Next Succession to the Crown of England* (1594) was dedicated to someone who, in many ways (and especially because of his popularity) resembled Henry Bolingbroke—Robert Devereux, Earl of Essex. As its title indicates, the treatise was concerned with the very pressing and very dangerous issue of Elizabeth's succession, and it also contained several passages on what the Jesuit father clearly regarded as the *lawful* deposition of Richard II.

The context in which this work appeared and the considerable interest it stirred is the story this essay aims to recount with a view that Shakespeare's *Richard II* may appear in a different light—one that reveals the very complexity of the relationship between religion and politics in Elizabethan England. But prior to these considerations, it is necessary to picture a world in which the ideological polarization of discourse produced an outwardly oppositional view of society—one that probably still misleads us today into thinking that these oppositions actually existed. "In early modern England the relation between Englishness and Christianness was important, contested, and uncertain" (Taylor 1994, 288). Because so much was at stake politically in these ideological and religious debates, those who entered the polemic often created an imaginary opposition so as to give more weight to their arguments. Catholics, Protestants, Puritans had thus very little in common according to their most radical defenders. For the sake of argumentation, polemicists tended to ignore the very different and multiple *shades* of belief. Those who sought to cross boundaries, or simply chose to disregard the artificial polarities generated by Elizabethan society, risked their career and sometimes their life, as they could easily be called "traitors" to several causes.

What the ideological circumstances surrounding and following the writing of *Richard II* may reveal is precisely the imaginary constructions of opposition and the interchangeability of some of the poles of opposition. In this way, I would like to suggest that Patrick Collinson's analysis of the historical validity of the term "Puritan" could be extended to other polarized terms of opposition in Elizabethan society, such as "Catholic," "recusant," or "heretic." Collinson writes indeed that:

> ... the term "puritan" is indicative not so much of an entity and a state, puritanism, as of a situation with at least two sides to it, and of a dynamic, unstable and stressful process: a particular example of the cultural phenomenon of definition and reification through stigmatization, indicative of polarity and contributory to polarity. (Collinson 195, 155)

There are many concrete proofs of the instability of such terms. Among these, I have recently come upon a somewhat calculated use of the term "Puritan papist" by Henry Earl of Northumberland in a letter to Elizabeth's future successor, James VI of Scotland. Regarding the possible support that might be given to a Catholic opponent of James, Henry of Northumberland writes: " ... this man is committed to prison, and I assure your Maiesty condemned by all of them, ore the most pairt, that are Catholiklye affected, vnles it be by some of them that are puritane papistes that thirst after a spanish tytle" (Bruce 1861, 74). Clearly, the purpose in creating the term "Puritan papist" was to make a practical distinction—a distinction that blurred the all-too-frequently polarized picture of English Catholicism and created another pole of opposition within the opposition itself. Northumberland sought simply to distinguish between the "hardliners," as he saw them, those who looked toward Spain, and those whose loyalty deserved respect and perhaps toleration from the future sovereign. There is reason to believe, as I shall now try to show, that Shakespeare, in his handling of the themes of loyalty and betrayal in *Richard II,* was also aware of the many shades that these highly charged terms could comprise.

I. ESSEX, PARSONS, AND SHAKESPEARE—
TOPICAL ALLUSIONS AND HIGH POLITICS

But now behold,
In the quick forge and working-house of thought,
How London doth pour out her citizens.
The Mayor and all his brethren, in best sort,
Like to the senators of th'antique Rome
With the plebeians swarming at their heels,
Go forth and fetch their conqu'ring Caesar in—
As, by a lower but high-loving likelihood,
Were now the General of our gracious Empress
   —As in good time he may—from Ireland coming,
Bringing rebellion broachèd on his sword,
How many would the peaceful city quit
To welcome him!
                              (*Henry V,* 5.2.22–34)[7]

Shakespeare knew of Robert Devereux and was no doubt aware of the political importance of the Earl of Essex, as this prologue from *Henry V* amply testifies. The martial hero, seemingly so close in the eyes of Shakespeare to a king (Henry V) or to an emperor (Caesar), is through the paradox of "lower but high-loving" put back into a place that was more hierarchical and thus a trifle less threatening for Elizabeth—that of "General of our gracious Empress." Shakespeare's *Henry V,* which dates back to 1599, has apparently captured the topical mood of a moment in history and frozen a picture of the earl that was to be quickly challenged in the ensuing two years leading to his demise, trial, and execution for treason.[8]

But it may well be that Shakespeare had captured an earlier topical mood in his *Richard II*—one that also contained elements that could be deemed dangerous for the Elizabethan régime. *Richard II* begins, strangely enough, with accusations of treachery and a trial. In the subtle world of the play's high politics, it is not quite clear who the traitor is. There is, however, much talk of "high blood" on the part of Bolingbroke in an atmosphere that is very ritualized and outwardly imbued with chivalric ideals: "By that and all the rites of knighthood else / Will I make good against thee, arm to arm," says Bolingbroke to his rival Thomas Mowbray (1.1.75–76).[9]

In his dedication to the Earl of Essex in the *Conference About the Next Succession,* the Jesuit Robert Parsons is keen to insist upon the earl's lineage, "your noble ancestors," as he calls them, pointing out that all this is "recorded by our Inglish histories" (Parsons 1594, 2–3). By insisting on the earl's lineage, Parsons thus manages through his argumentation to place Robert Devereux at the heart of the succession struggle, creating (artificially) a nearness to the queen that reminds us of Bolingbroke's dangerous closeness to power in Shakespeare's play:

> ... no man is in more high & eminent place or dignitie at this day in our realme, then your selfe, whether we respect your nobilitie, or calling, or fauour with your prince, or high liking of the people, & consequently no man like to haue a greater part or sway in deciding of this great affaire ... then your honour, and those that will assist you & are likest to follow your fame and fortune. (Parsons 1594, 2)

The "high liking of the people" associated to Essex's person is redolent in some ways of Bolingbroke's own popularity that comes back to haunt Richard time and time again: "As were our England in reversion his, / And he our subjects' next degree in hope" (1.4.36)—in other words, as if Bolingbroke was the next person in line for the throne. It is a strange coincidence also that Hereford was a name borne by Bolingbroke *and* by the Essex family, as Walter Devereux—Robert's father—was elevated by Elizabeth from Viscount Hereford to Earl of Essex in 1572.[10] But it is the antiquary and historian William Camden who unwittingly reveals the associations between Bolingbroke—the defender of his murdered uncle, Woodstock—and Robert Earl of Essex. In the eyes of some of the Catholics, recalls Camden in his history of the reign of Elizabeth I, Essex had antecedents for the crown and these Catholics "cast their eyes upon the Earle of Essex, ... feigning a Title from *Thomas of Woodstock,* King Edward the third's sonne, from whom hee derived his Pedigree" (Camden 1630, 4:57).[11]

It is clear that Shakespeare's *Richard II* weaves a web of associations that may not be entirely fortuitous for a playwright caught up in a system of patronage that implied a measure of dialogue with the ruling classes, and sometimes necessitated some fine tuning and subtle positioning. To take the measure of this positioning, one must turn to the fast-moving environment in which the dramatist had to operate.

II. Essex and the "Rites of Knighthood" (1595)

But why did Robert Parsons, under the name of Doleman, dedicate his *Conference* to Robert Earl of Essex? The meaning of this dedication is perhaps found in the events surrounding the writing of Shakespeare's *Richard II* and Parsons's treatise.

On Sunday, February 25, 1593, Robert Earl of Essex took the Oath of Supremacy and the oath of a privy councillor. In the early 1590s, the queen's Privy Council had become an aging body and was in great need of new blood. At twenty-seven, Essex was then seen as definitely on the rise; he was recognized as one of the queen's chief advisers in matters of state and particularly in the domain of foreign affairs. Essex's martial prowess turned him into an ideal courtier in the slightly surreal and artificial atmosphere of chivalry that the queen sought to create around her. But he was someone also who had an impressive intelligence network in England and abroad—which was a great asset for the queen and her other councillors. In the ensuing years he was to develop this network even further.

This policy opened diplomatic doors for Essex in Europe and set him off at home against other men of state such as William Cecil, Lord Burghley, who had become synonymous with bloody repression in the eyes of the Catholic community. In many ways, Essex was also anticipating without realizing it the policy of Robert Cecil, who would later have the same underhand involvement with Catholic circles. For the more militant Catholics, however, Essex's policy of toleration could be seen as a threat and as something that could stall plans for the restoration of the old Catholic order in England by the force of arms. There was indeed an element of political calculation in Essex that helped him to enter many circles of power, including oppositional circles. Publicly he displayed the reassuring image of a staunch Protestant, but behind the scenes he engineered quite a different policy (Hammer 1999, 174). In the early 1590s, he had already started to send positive signs to those members of the English Catholic community who were loyal to the government and who considered themselves anti-Spanish. In 1593, he was instrumental in securing the brief release from prison of the well-known recusant Sir Thomas Tresham; and during the Cadiz expedition of 1596, he also sought to appear more like an anti-Spanish agent than an anti-Catholic one (Hammer, 175).

This was certainly what worried the author of the *Conference About the Next Succession.* Whereas Essex saw his dealings as subtle and discreet, the Dedication sought to expose him in order to destabilize him. First, by openly associating him with the Catholic community, Parsons turned him into a potential collaborator and double agent: "First then I saye," writes Parsons, "that my particular obligation towards your honours person, riseth partly of good turnes and benefites receaued by some frendes of myne at your Lordships handes . . ." (Parsons 1594, 2). Then, by linking him to the burning issue of the succession, the Jesuit father was probably trying to alienate him from the queen— Essex was suddenly exposed as a conniving agent provocateur—a Bolingbroke whose dealings were dubious and who was invited through the repeated allusions to Richard II in the treatise to take appropriate action. Parsons's book thus complicated matters in a political climate that was already extremely tense.

Some of the correspondence exchanged by the courtiers at the time shows how serious a threat Parsons's treatise represented, and also how many people had heard of it, had read it, or were wanting to read it. On September 25, 1595, Robert Beale writes the following to Sir Robert Sidney:

> Our irresoluteness at home, and the little estimation of us abroad make me fear we shall receive some blow. . . .
>
> I hear of late a vile book has been printed in English in Antwerp touching the succession of the Crown, and deriving a strange pretence from John of Gaunt upon the King of Spain. If you could procure me one of the books, I should be beholden. I hear it is dedicated to the Earl of Essex, of intent surely to bring him in jealousy and disgrace. (Kingsford 1934, 2:165)

On November 3, 1595, Parsons's *Conference* comes into the hands of the queen, who then shows it to Essex (Spedding 1861–74, 1.374). Two days later, on November 5, Rowland Whyte, this time, shares the latest gossip from the court with Sire Robert Sidney in a letter:

Vpon *Monday* last, 1500 [Queen *Eliz.*] shewed 1000 [Earl of *Essex*] a printed Book of *t—t,* Title to *a*—a: In yt their is, as I here, daungerous Praises of 1000 of his Valour and Worthines, which doth hym harme here. At his comming from Court he was obserued to looke wan and pale, being exceedinglie troubled at his great Piece of Villanie donne vnto hym; he is Sick, and continewes very ill. *1500* visited hym Yesterday in Thafternoone. He is mightelie crossed in all Things. . . .

Whyte's postscript to the same letter shows the true impact of Parsons's controversial book: "The Book I spake of is dedicated to my Lord *Essex,* and printed beyond Sea [sic], and tis thought to be Treason to haue it. To wryte of these Things are dangerous in so perillous a Tyme . . ." (Collins 1746, 1:357–58).

On November 12, 1595, another letter by Rowland Whyte addressed to Sir Robert Sidney announces that Essex is back in favor and that the storm is momentarily over. Essex is again at the helm of the queen's foreign affairs: "My Lord of *Essex* hath put off the Melancholy he fell vnto, by a printed Booke deliuered to the Queen; wherein the Harme was meant hym, by her Majesties gracious Fauor and Wisdom, is turned to his good, and strengthens her Loue vnto hym; for I heare, that within these 4 Days, many Letters sent to her self, from forren Countries, were deliuered only to my Lord of *Essex,* and he answered them . . ." (Collins 1746, 1:360).

Later that same month, Essex's adviser Francis Bacon was to try and heal the wounds between the earl and the queen during the Accession Day tilt—an occasion for a celebration of the Elizabethan régime through the somewhat allegorical rites of a neomedieval chivalric ethos. Bacon thus composed for his patron a masque of "Love and Self-love" that was to accompany the highly ritualized Accession Day tournaments. The occasion was supposed to reinforce the bond between Essex and the queen through a form of neomedieval pageantry that could serve as a powerful means of mediation in times of doubt or crisis. But in this case, what the spectators of the masque witnessed was a breakdown of "the rites of knighthood," to quote Shakespeare's Bolingbroke (1.1.75). In the same way that Shakespeare's Richard II puts a premature end to a form of ritual that could serve traditionally to resolve conflicts (1.3.124 onward), the queen, who could see (like Richard) only too clearly through the so-called ritual and allegory of Bacon's Masque, simply stormed off, thus ending abruptly the allegorical dialogue of reconciliation initiated by Bacon. Rowland Whyte reports again in his correspondence that the queen got up all of a sudden and said, "that if she had thought their had bene so much said of her, she wold not haue been their that Night, and soe went to Bed" (qtd. in McCoy 1989, 86).

Shakespeare's *Richard II* depicts a world in which it is clear from the start that the rites of chivalry are no longer capable of reconciling opposites. It becomes gradually obvious that other means of mediation have to be used, rediscovered, or reinvented. Despite the failure of Bacon's masque, 1595 was the year when Essex's influence over the queen had reached its height. In July 1596, however, the newly appointed Secretary of State Robert Cecil—Lord Burghley's son—was to become suddenly a fierce competitor. Opposition within the queen's Privy Council was even more deeply entrenched. Mediation had to be sought, and it was to be sought in already existing bodies or offices that suddenly acquired a new value. One of these bodies was Parliament, while the office that was to turn Essex into an overambitious courtier in the eyes of some of his contemporaries was the ancient office of Earl Marshal and Constable, to which he was appointed in 1597.

With his insistence on the powers of Parliament, Robert Parsons had turned an existing political body into something more dangerous—an institution that had the power to step in if and when the monarchy was in crisis. As Cyndia Susan Clegg points out, "Not until Parsons argued that the Spanish Infanta's succession to the crown of England was legitimate *because* Parliament deposed Richard II did Parliament's powers become incorporated into oppositional discourse. Parsons' book thus created in the mid-1590s an issue where one had not existed before" (Clegg 1997, 445). It therefore becomes more understandable that the Parliament or deposition scene in *Richard II* (4.1.154–317) did not appear in print until 1608 (when the succession issue was over), as (from the point of view of the censors dealing with printed books) its implications were unacceptable as long as the issue was not settled. For the censors of play texts, however, this was a less burning issue, and it is likely that the play continued to be performed with the deposition scene as it most certainly was in 1601 when the supporters of the Essex rising paid the Chamberlain's Men (the Bard's own acting company) to perform a play that in all likelihood was Shakespeare's *Richard II*.[12]

In Shakespeare's play, the role of Parliament became immediately *visible* to the audience, and it is the very staging of the deposition that, in the eyes of Bolingbroke, guarantees the legitimacy of the whole process:

> Fetch hither Richard, that in common view
> He may surrender. So we shall proceed
> Without suspicion.
>
> (4.1.155–57)

Parsons himself had presented both the Privy Council and Parliament as safeguards against tyranny. In his *Conference,* Parliament is seen as the almost ultimate guarantee that succession crises are resolved in a satisfactory manner (God's will in these matters is consciously played down by Parsons). For the Jesuit activist, the deposition of Richard II:

> ... could not be executed in better nor more conuenient order. First for that it vvas done by the choice and inuitation of al the realme or greater and better parte thereof as hath bin said. Secondly for that the king vvas deposed by act of parlament, and himself coniunced of his vnworthy gouerment, and brought to confesse that he vvas vvorthely depriued. ...
> (Parsons 1594, 67)

That the *Conference* was dedicated to the Earl of Essex may not be fortuitous either, because Parsons may have been aware that the earl had a will to find constitutional solutions that would help curtail the whims of royal authority. When Essex was appointed Earl Marshal in 1597, he became immediately interested in reviving the ancient powers of this highest surviving feudal office and commissioned researchers to look into the status and privileges of the office. The findings themselves were potentially seditious in that they reinstated an authority that partly endangered the concept of royal sovereignty. In this sense, as Richard C. McCoy points out in a seminal study, "The research initiated by Essex is . . . another 'missing link' between earlier medieval and Tudor theories of mixed government and the parliamentary opposition of the seventeenth century" (McCoy 1989, 94).

III. Rebellion and the Polarization of Discourse

Essex's ambitions were to be thwarted, nonetheless, both by the man who had become his rival and by his military ventures, which caused his estrangement from the circles of power, and, as a consequence, encouraged him to take desperate measures to regain his lost influence.

The end of the 1590s saw many of the familiar hauntings of the decade reemerge. Parsons's defense of the rights of the Infanta of Spain to the throne of England had not been forgotten, and the topic itself kept rearing its head in the correspondence addressed to the Secretary of State, Robert Cecil. In a letter dated June 27, 1599, Sir Henry Neville even proposed to use the Infanta as a means of testing the loyalty of potential suspects:

> ... whether yt be not convenient, that suche *Preists* or notorious Recusants as shall be hereafter apprehended, be *severely examined,* whether they have not *sollicited others, or bin sollicited themselves, to subscribe to that Title of the Infanta.* And lastly, whether yt will not be fit, when you shall come to treat with the *Archduke,* to insist upon an *Article,* of the *Infanta's Resignation of any pretended Title.* (Sawyer 1725, 1:52)

The whole issue of the succession as well as its religious and political implications had become a means of tracking down opponents, of creating an opposition. Be that as it may, the secretary himself played a game very similar to that of Essex, who sometimes got dangerously involved with some of the members of the Catholic community in England or abroad. It even appears that Cecil could have been secretly interested in potential negotiations with the Infanta. A series of letters addressed to him by one Filippo Corsini seems to point in that direction. Starting, as far as the evidence shows, at the beginning of August 1599, these letters give news of the whereabouts of the Infanta and of the Archduke her husband, and they also reveal that Cecil requested that a portrait of the couple be sent to him in all secrecy. Corsini writes to him on September 3, 1599: "I have received your letter and seen your wish to have the picture, and on Saturday when the courier starts I will write as from myself and to a friend of mine, who will see that you have it as soon as possible, in the manner you ordered, and with all secrecy and speed" (*Calendar of the Manuscripts* 1883–1976, 9:345). On November 14, the paintings arrived, and Corsini promised to continue to treat the whole matter with the uttermost secrecy: "I have received from Antwerp the portraits of the Infanta and the Archduke Albert her husband. I send them to you by my friend the bearer. They are present to me and I humbly beg you to accept of them from me. You may be assured that this affair has been carried out in all secrecy" (9:391).

On Sunday, February 8, 1601, the supporters of the Earl of Essex staged their ill-fated coup. The day before, a play that probably was Shakespeare's *Richard II* had been performed by the playwright's own company. Sir Gilly Meyrick—Essex's faithful attendant—had even given the players an extra forty shillings: "So earnest hee was to satisfie his eyes with the sight of that Tragedie, which hee thought soone after his Lord should bring from the Stage to the State. . . ." (Bacon 1601, sig. K3). The earl's supporters were soon arrested and the trial began. On February 18, some of the evidence was brought before the Privy Council:

> Your letters of the 17th of this present touching the seditious and pro-voking speeches uttered by the Earl [of Essex] to stir the people to adhere unto him in his rebellious actions, we receive in the evening about eight o'clock; and according to the straitness of the time, we have examined divers that did hear the Earl publish and intimate to the peo-ple those seditious and provoking speeches that the crown of England was sold or betrayed to the Infanta of Spain, and to that effect: whose examinations we have taken in writing, upon their oaths, and do send them to you inclosed herein.[13]

Essex's indignant outcry in the streets of London foreshadows the accusations directed against him during his trial and points to the same process of outward and artificial polarization that we outlined at the beginning of this essay. Essex is executed on February 25, 1601. A few days later (on March 4), Monsieur de Boisisse, the French ambassador in England, recalls the accusations against Essex:

> . . . *qu'il estoit papiste; qu'il retinoit les Jesuits en sa Maison; qu'il vouloit usurper la Couronne;* qu'il avoit de grandes Intelligences en Escosse, & *en* Irelande *avec le Conte* de Tyrone. *Bref, qu'il avoit vendu la Ville de* Londres *al* Infante, & *qu'il en avoit reçeu quelque Argent. Voila ce que generallement ilz luy objecterent.* (Sawyer 1725, 1.298)[14]

The ambassador then tells of Essex's desperate ploy. Indeed, during the trial the earl had also attempted to incriminate Robert Cecil, accus-ing him of conniving with the opposition:

> . . . *ilz font venir* le Secretaire, *comme personne interposeé* [sic] *en leur tragedie. Lequel ayant plus de deux ans passé, bien songé à ce qu'il avoit à dire, tonnà une quantité de paroles contre le Conte* d'Essex.

Lequel n'eut faute de responce de moyens pour maintenir au Secretaire, qu'il avoit eu Intelligence avec le feu Roy d'espagne l'année de la Grande Flotte. Ce que picqua si fort le Secretaire, (pour en estre paraventure quelque chose) qu'il se prit à crier tout/hault, qu'il ne feroit jamais service à sa Majesté, si on ne luy ostoit la teste comme à un Traistre. (Sawyer 1725, 1:298)[15]

All through the trial other commonplace accusations resurfaced, among them, allusions to *Richard II*—the play that Essex's supporters had actually used on the day of the rebellion to further their cause. Extracts of the hearing show how much the whole issue of the deposition of *Richard II* was present in the minds of the accused, but also in those of the accusers, especially in this dialogue between Southampton and the Attorney-General:

SOUTHAMPTON: Good Mr Attorney, let me ask you what, in your conscience, you think we would have done to her Majesty if we gained the Court?

ATTORNEY-GENERAL: I protest upon my soul, and in my conscience, I do believe she should not have lived long after she had been in your power. Note but the precedent of former ages: how long lived King Richard the Second after he was surprised in the same manner. The pretence there was also to remove certain councillors; but it shortly after cost the King his life. Such is the unquenchable thirst of ambition, never satisfied so long as any greatness is unachieved. But I know this for certain, that to surprise the Court or take the Tower by way of defence from private enemies, is plain treason. (Jardine 1832, 1:337)

Another accusation dealt with what had disappeared in the published quartos of Shakespeare's play (until 1608), that is to say, the whole issue of the powers of Parliament. On February 26, 1601, the day that followed Essex's execution, Robert Cecil, writing to Lord Deputy Mountjoy, painted a picture of what—according to him—Essex had envisaged politically: " . . . and then, having her [the queen] in their possessions, to have used the shadow of her authority for *removing of all they misliked, and for* change of the Government; and so to have called a Parliament, and have condemned all those that should have been scandalized to have misgoverned the State" (*Calendar of State Papers* 1860–1912, 1:199).

Beyond the artificial polarization of discourse, all the accusations of betrayal, of supporting the cause of Spain, of conniving with Catholics, this was probably the crucial issue that cost the earl his head—the parliamentary issue, one that had also forced the publishers of Shakespeare's early quartos to cut the so-called "woeful pageant" (4.1. 320) of Richard II's parliamentary demise. The reappearance in 1601 of *Richard II*—Shakespeare's "old play," as the actors themselves referred to it—is a proof of the play's enduring topical nature. It may also suggest that its strong contextual associations both at the time of its writing and after open a new field of interpretation—one that points to the very incompleteness of thematic readings and that also "challenge[s] the assumption that a progression narrative is a suitable model for the construction of Shakespeare's career" (Hamilton 1992, xii).

In the extremely tense political context of February 1601 (the Earl of Essex felt much maligned), the agreement to stage a play on the deposition of Richard II could surely not be motivated by commercial reasons alone—such a decision was no doubt a statement of support to the disgraced earl.[16] Shakespeare had toyed with ideas of rebellion in *Richard II*—ideas that Robert Parsons had also used to destabilize the Elizabethan state—but whereas Parsons prayed that his arguments would one day force change to happen, it is unlikely that Shakespeare and his fellow actors were aware that their play was just a rehearsal of an open rebellion taking place the next day. Nevertheless, they had, without realizing it, agreed to cross the line that separated political support from potential treason.

NOTES

1. I follow Gurr's conclusions regarding the date of the play (Shakespeare 1990, 1).

2. See Shakespeare, *King Richard II* (1990, 1).

3. For non-Shakespearean uses of the theme, see Campbell (1964, 191).

4. This question is well documented, thanks to a string of articles by Albright (1927) and Heffner (1930, 1932) in *PMLA*. A recent article by Dutton (1993) is also extremely useful.

5. " . . . our auncestors liued in the highest pitch and perfection of libertie, but we of servilitie, being in the nature, not of subiectes, but of abiectes, and flat slaues; not to one intractable Prince onely, but to many proude & disdainefull fauorites; . . . And therefore we are now compelled to shake off our shoulders this importable yoke, and submit our selues to the soueraigntie of some

more moderate and worthy person." (Hayward 1599, sig. I4). The work also bore a lavish dedication in Latin to the Earl of Essex.

6. See Heffner (1930, 767).

7. See Shakespeare, *Henry V* (1986, 592–93).

8. On the evidence that the prologue (or chorus) scenes are absent from the 1600 quarto edition of *Henry V* (Q1), it has been argued that these scenes are a later addition, and that the allusion to "the General of our gracious Empress" actually refers to Charles Blount, Lord Mountjoy, who was Queen Elizabeth's (more successful) general and lord deputy in Ireland from 1600 to 1603 (see Smith 1954). Taylor, in his edition of the play, demonstrates convincingly that this is unlikely (Shakespeare 1994, 4–7). Taylor also emphasizes the topicality of the play: "The date of *Henry V* can thus not only be established with—for Shakespeare—extraordinary precision; it is also of extraordinary importance. Reflections of contemporary history have been suspected in many of Shakespeare's plays, but the allusion to the Irish expedition in 5.0.29–34 is the only explicit, extra-dramatic, incontestable reference to a contemporary event anywhere in the canon" (7).

9. All references to the play are taken from Shakespeare, *King Richard II,* ed. Gurr (1990).

10. See Hammer (1999, 18–19).

11. Also quoted in Campbell 180. More accurately, according to Shakespeare, Thomas was Edward's sixth son, and the third son was Lionel, Duke of Clarence (see *2 Henry VI* 2.2.10 ff.).

12. For this distinction between the two types of censorship, see Shakespeare, *King Richard II* (1990, 9). That it *was* Shakespeare's play is a logical supposition. As Schoenbaum pointed out, no real contradictory elements have been discovered to demonstrate that the play was *not* Shakespeare's (1975, 7).

13. February 18, 1601, Sir Edward Wotton, Sir Henry Brouncker, and Mr Recorder Croke to the Council (*Calendar of the Manuscripts* 1883–1976, 11:66–67.

14. " . . . that he was a papist, that he had Jesuits to stay at his house, that he wanted to usurp the Crown; that he had secret intelligence with men in Scotland and with the Earl of Tyrone in Ireland. In short, that he had sold the city of London to the Infanta and that he had received money in exchange. These were the main accusations."

15. March 4, 1601, London, "Copy of a Letter from Monsieur *de Boisisse* (the *French* Ambassador then residing in *England*) to Monsieur *de Rohan*": " . . . they bring in the Secretary [of State] to play the middle man in their tragedy. He had had time during the last two years to think about what he wanted to say and he thus vented all his anger against the Earl of Essex. The

Earl was quick to retort that the Secretary had had secret intelligence with the late King of Spain in the year of the Armada. The Secretary was so stung by this (which suggests that this may have been truthful), that he cried out that he would leave the service of her Majesty if the traitor was not beheaded."

16. As Thomson writes, "The agreement to stage the play on Saturday 7 February was an open statement by a company of players that they supported the maligned Earl of Essex. When, on Sunday 8 February, Essex's discontent broke out into rebellion, such support was no longer easily distinguishable from treason" (1992, 139).

WORKS CITED

Albright, Evelyn May. "Shakespeare's *Richard II* and the Essex Conspiracy." *PMLA* 42 (1927): 686–720.

Bacon, Francis, Viscount St. Albans. "A declaration of the practices & treasons committed by Robert late Earle of Essex." 1601. *STC* 1133.

Bruce, John, ed. *Correspondence of James VI of Scotland with Sir Robert Cecil and Others in England, During the Reign of Queen Elizabeth.* London: Camden Society, 1861.

Calendar of State Papers Relating to Ireland, of the Reign of Elizabeth. Ed. H. C. Hamilton, E. G. Atkinson et al. 11 vols. London: 1860–1912.

A Calendar of the Manuscripts of the Most Hon. the marquis of Salisbury, KG, &c, preserved at Hatfield House, Hertfordshire. 24 vols. London: 1883–1976.

Camden, William. "The historie of the most renowned and victorious princesse Elizabeth" 1630. *STC* 4500.5.

Campbell, L. B. *Shakespeare's "Histories," Mirrors of Elizabethan Policy.* London: Methuen, 1964.

Clegg, Cyndia Susan. "'By the choise and inuitation of al the realme': *Richard II* and Elizabethan Press Censorship." *Shakespeare Quarterly* 48 (1997): 432–48.

Collins, Arthur, ed. *Letters and Memorials of State . . . from the originals at Penthurst Place in Kent.* 2 vols. London: 1746.

Collinson, Patrick. "Religious Satire and the Invention of Puritanism." In *The Reign of Elizabeth I, Court and Culture in the Last Decade,* ed. John Guy. Cambridge, England: Cambridge University Press, 1995.

Dutton, Richard. "Buggeswords: Samuel Harsnett and the Licensing, Suppression and Afterlife of Dr. John Hayward's *The first part of the life and reign of King Henry IV.*" *Criticism* 35 (1993): 307–20.

Hamilton, Donna B. *Shakespeare and the Politics of Protestant England.* Lexington, Ky.: University Press of Kentucky, 1992.

Hammer, Paul E. J. *The Polarisation of Elizabethan Politics, The Political Career of Robert Devereux, 2nd Earl of Essex, 1585–1597.* Cambridge, England: Cambridge University Press, 1999.

Hayward, John. *The First Part of the Life and Raigne of King Henrie the III.* London, 1599.

Heffner, Ray. "Shakespeare, Hayward, and Essex." *PMLA* 45 (1930): 754–80.

———. "Shakespeare, Hayward, and Essex Again." PMLA 47 (1932): 898.

Jardine, David. *Criminal Trials.* London: Lily, Wait, Lolman, Holden, 1832.

Kingsford, C. L., ed. *Report on the Manuscripts of Lord De L'Isle & Dudley Preserved at Penshurst Place.* 6 vols. Historical Manuscripts Commission. London: HM's Stationery Office, 1934.

McCoy, Richard C. *The Rites of Knighthood, The Literature and Politics of Elizabethan Chivalry.* Berkeley and Los Angeles, Calif., and London: University of California Press, 1989.

Parsons (Persons), Robert. "A Conference about the next Succession to the Crowne of Ingland." Antwerp, 1594. *STC* 193–98.

Sawyer, Edmund, ed. *Memorials of Affairs of State in the Reigns of Q. Elizabeth and K. James I Collected (chiefly) from the Original Papers of the Right Honourable Sir Ralph Winwood, Kt. Sometime One of the Principal Secretaries of State.* 3 vols. London: T. Ward, 1725.

Schoenbaum, Samuel. "'Richard II' and the Realities of Power." *Shakespeare Survey* 28 (1975): 1–13.

Shakespeare, William. *Henry V.* The Complete Works. Ed. Stanley Wells and Gary Taylor. Oxford, England: Clarendon Press, 1986.

———. *Henry V.* Ed. Gary Taylor. World's Classics. Oxford, England, and New York: Oxford University Press, 1994.

———. *King Richard II.* Ed. Andrew Gurr. New Cambridge Shakespeare. Cambridge, England: Cambridge University Press, 1990.

Smith, W. D. "The *Henry V* Choruses in the First Folio." *Journal of English and Germanic Philology* 53 (1954): 38–57.

Spedding, James, ed. *The Letters and the Life of Francis Bacon.* 7 vols. London: Longman, 1861–74.

Taylor, Gary. "Forms of Opposition: Shakespeare and Middleton." *English Literary Renaissance* 24 (1994): 283–314.

Thomson, Peter. *Shakespeare's Professional Career.* Cambridge, England: Cambridge University Press, 1992.

5

Sacral and Sacramental Kingship in the Lancastrian Tetralogy

by Timothy Rosendale

Southern Methodist University, Dallas, Texas

ARCHBISHOP THOMAS CRANMER'S 1554 disputation at Oxford—one of the set pieces of a prosecution occasioned in large part by his espousal of Reformed doctrine and his authorship of the *Book of Common Prayer* (*BCP*)—reads predominantly like a hermeneutic squabble. A main focus of contention between Cranmer and his Marian opponents was the proper interpretation of Christ's words at the Last Supper (*hoc est enim corpus meum*—"this is indeed my body"). Cranmer's Catholic interrogators, hostile to any destabilizing reading that might challenge the doctrine of transubstantiation, insist repeatedly on a strictly literal interpretation, and emphatically reject figural understandings as inherently deceptive. In response, Cranmer doggedly upholds a figural reading, maintaining the Reformed understanding that the dominical words (and the sacramental elements to which they referred) were to be understood figuratively or "sacramentally." When at one point the prolocutor asserts flatly that, "whosoever saith that Christ spake by figures, saith that he did lie," Cranmer responds in puzzlement:

> ... who say it is
> necessary that he which useth to speak by tropes and figures should lie
> in so doing?
>
> OGLETHORPE:—Your judgment is disagreeing with all churches.
> CRANMER:—Nay, I disagree with the papistical church. (Cranmer 1844, 401)

Despite its varied and extraordinarily rich medieval interpretive tradition, the Roman Catholic Church under Reformed pressure reverts here to a dogmatic and uncompromising literalism, a hermeneutically reactionary rejection of figurality in general. The Reformed challenge, which undercut the institutional power of transubstantiation by circumventing it with a figural reading—and thus reorienting both doctrine and sacrament away from institution and elements and toward the individual—polarizes the Reformation debate around questions of representation and hermeneutics.[1]

Central to the Reformed understanding of the Eucharist—as well as to the Protestant emphasis on individual Bible reading—was an affirmation of the transformative power of representations. Although Catholic doctrine located the divine efficacy of the sacrament in the transformation of the elements themselves into the very literal body and blood of Christ, Reformed theology reconceived the elements as sacramental signs, tropes, texts, which *represented* the new covenant of Christ's sacrifice; divine power and grace resulted from a proper internalization of God's promises through faith (Tyndale, for example, strikingly describes Christ's institution of the Last Supper as an act of authorship, and its reception as an act of reading).[2] A belief in the actual physical presence of God was replaced in the Prayerbook by a principle of sacred representation and interpretation through which divine grace was transmitted—a transition whose foundational cultural importance is difficult to overestimate (indeed, from our perspective, difficult not to underestimate). In short, the Reformed sacrament transformed the participant, not through physical divine immanence, but through what representations could accomplish in a context of subjective and hermeneutically aware faith.

At the same time, this discursive field of representation was equally important to the constitution of communal (and specifically national) identity. Evangelical theology, in all its representationality, had been established as orthodoxy by a state seeking to free itself from the overarching authority of papal Rome; this theology was thus both a tool and a hallmark of the consolidating English nation-state. And the official liturgy instituted by this state, holding in tension as it did the principles of Protestant individualism and a hierarchical early modern national sovereignty, set the grounds of this tension's negotiation around the pivotal locus of multivalent representation. In the

Prayerbook, the balance and relationship of individual and communal identity were perpetually worked out on a field defined in terms of representation and hermeneutics.[3]

This crucial Reformation dynamic can, I think, shed a provocative and useful new light on subsequent literature (specifically here on Shakespeare's Lancastrian plays). Although the *BCP* has frequently been recognized over the centuries for its aesthetic power, its peculiar felicities of language and style, and its subsequent influence on the English language, the radically and emphatically representational logic it embodies may provide a deeper and more concrete cultural link to the literary flowering of the English Renaissance. The long history of conflict surrounding the Prayerbook, as well as the profound tensions it embodied from the start, center around both the fragility and the enormously enhanced cultural potential of representation itself. Might there not be some essential and positive link between the Reformation's redistribution of authority, its recasting of representation as a mode of profound transformative and unifying potential, and the subsequent explosion of literary representation (much of it notably self-reflexive) later in the century? For there is in later-century literature a vision of representational power strikingly analogous to that advanced, in a theological context, in the Prayerbook.

My intention is not to assert a direct causal relationship between the Prayerbook and the works I address here; though the legal requirement of liturgical uniformity makes it virtually certain that Shakespeare was familiar with the *BCP* and steeped in its expression, he never explicitly engages its form, content, or cultural logic. Rather, my aim is to trace a subtler and deeper route of cultural consequence from Reformation to Renaissance, from liturgy and theology to political theory and literary practice. The English Reformation (and especially the *BCP*) had replaced the immanent presence of God himself with a newly stressed faith in the power of representations and their faithful interpretation to define, express, and transform our relation to the divine; at the same time, representation became the active field of negotiation between the identity and authority of both the individual and the collective sociopolitical order. This distinctive overlapping of representation, religion, individual autonomy, and national identity—a tense and productive concatenation made uniquely possible by the English Reformation—is clearly visible in the plays I am about to examine. In the process, my analysis will articulate some important links between early modern political, religious, and literary culture in England.

These Reformation concerns play a subtly important role in the English histories of Shakespeare, where questions of representation repeatedly intersect with questions of authority, identity, order, and religion. I will argue that Shakespeare's Lancastrian tetralogy is a potent political manifestation of the post-Reformation emphasis on the power of signs. These plays trace, after the devastating nihilism of the Yorkist plays, a rehabilitation of political representation into a constructive and unifying cultural process; eventually, the ideal monarch is characterized as much by fictivity (recognized—and contributed to—as such by his subjects) as by good faith. Much critical capital has been made in recent years of Shakespeare's "subversive" exposure and interrogation of the role of theatricality in the construction of monarchical power. I'd like to suggest that Shakespeare ultimately presents this political theatricality as a positive thing: in these royal representations—much as in the Prayerbook—the divisions between sovereign and subjects, church and state, and collective and individual authority are bridged and reworked into productive new syntheses that are distinctively English and Protestant. *Richard II* portrays the collapse of what I will call a sacral model of kingship, the authority of which derives from the asserted presence and immanence of the divine in the person of the King; *Henry V* replaces this failed system with a sacramental[4] model of kingship—one in which royal authority is constituted and sustained through the interpretive cooperation of its subjects. This political movement from divine immanence to participatory representation has significant hermeneutic and theatrical implications, and mirrors the earlier theological shift from Roman Catholic transubstantiation to Reformed eucharistic remembrance.

In the critical reaction of recent decades to the former hegemony of idealized Christian readings of Shakespeare, considerations of the relationship between Shakespeare's theater and contemporary Christianity have generally followed two main paths. One has focused on the opposition between the two, especially as it involved the iconoclastic Puritan hostility to "idolatrous" representation of all kinds.[5] The other, exemplified in the work of Louis Montrose and Stephen Greenblatt,[6] argues that the success of the theater was in substantial part due to its restoration of cultural ritual to a populace hungering for its lost Catholic ceremonies;

theatrical representation thus becomes a form of compensation for the supposed bareness of Reformed worship. In both cases, the relationship between drama and the adolescent English Protestantism is figured as a negative one of opposition and antagonism.

Recently, however, a few critics have taken seriously Foxe's "triple bulwark" of "players, printers, and preachers" (1877, 6.57) and begun to argue that the relationship of Protestantism and literary/theatrical practice was more constructive and positive than has heretofore been thought. Huston Diehl, for example, has contended that:

> [o]bserving (celebrating) the Lord's Supper and observing (watching) the Lord Chamberlain's men are . . . related cultural activities that help to structure the way Elizabethans and Jacobeans know and understand their world. . . . [Both] insist on the figurative power of the visible sign, inculcating a new mode of seeing that, while it requires people to be skeptical about what they see and self-reflexive about their own looking, also encourages them to be receptive to the capacity of signs, in conjunction with spoken words, to move, persuade, and transform. (Diehl 1991, 150–51)[7]

Even more significantly, Robert Weimann has undertaken a sweeping historical theorization of "the culturally potent links between the crisis of authority and the simultaneous expansion of representational form and function in the Reformation and Renaissance" (1993, 168).[8] He argues that in the wake of the Reformation's dismantling of traditional, unitary structures of authority, representation and discourse became the grounds and sources of a recognizably modern cultural concept of authority. The following reading of Shakespeare's Lancastrian plays situates itself generally with this latter critical grouping, and reads them in the light of the representational dynamics of the *BCP.* Ultimately, I will argue, the political discourse of these history plays is a recognizable heir to the English Reformation's reconfiguration of representation, authority, and national identity in the cultural matrix.

The tetralogy begins with a complex and ambiguous play. The tragic hero of *Richard II* is, of course, the irresponsible poet-King, and Henry Bullingbrook is the able and pragmatic usurper; this tension of providential inheritance versus Machiavellian effectiveness constitutes a traditional critical axis of the play, and centuries of debate have revolved around who is in fact the hero, which is the ascendant political philosophy. How are we to regard Richard's deposition and

Bullingbrook's rise? As tragic necessities, or as crimes against a divinely appointed political order? Queen Elizabeth herself, in famously identifying herself with Richard, seems to have agreed with the supporters of Essex who paid to have the play performed the night before his rebellion: *Richard II,* though appalled at the prospect, dangerously endorses the deposition of a divine-right monarch in favor of a more popular and able claimant. Many other readers—and here I would include any supporters of teleological readings of the histories, in which the tumults of the fifteenth century are a direct punishment for this crime—regard the play as Richard's, and see Bullingbrook as a grasping Machiavel little better than Richard III.

The long duration of these controversies, I think, bears witness to the determined ambiguity of the play itself. Richard is unquestionably a bad king who has forfeited any conditional right to authority (acts 1 and 2 are an exhaustive demonstration of this point); yet his assertions of indefeasible right are seriously questioned only by the actual course of events. Bullingbrook is undeniably a usurper, yet no judgment rains down on him from heaven for his deeds—certainly not in this play, and arguably not in any other. The play's presentation of the simultaneous fall and rise is horrified by the one, fascinated by the other, and characterized by a profound ambivalence: it is impossible to decisively evaluate Bullingbrook's claims, Richard's divine connections (or his role in his own downfall), or the play's position on their intersection. The key scenes of transfer (3.3, 4.1) are so ambiguous, so vague regarding clear agency or motive or action, that readers are left without a clear sense of moral direction. Consequently, most partisan readings of the play seem to end up saying more about the reader's politics than about those of the play. If we can say with any confidence what *Richard II* is politically "about," perhaps it is simply about this difficulty, about the complexity and intractability of this clash of two diametrically opposed political philosophies—one which envisions authority as flowing unconditionally downward from heaven through a hierarchical society, and another which sees it welling up contingently from below (that is, in which performance criteria and popular as well as aristocratic assent can play a significant role).

But, one might think, there *must* be a way out of this dilemma; surely the play cannot ultimately be about the impossibility of political decision or of the establishment of stable sociopolitical authority. I'd like to suggest that there is a constructive solution proposed, but that it lies out-side the boundaries of this play. *Richard II* presents us with a conflict, much like that addressed by the *BCP*, between two sociopolitical visions: one is based on a divinely ordained vertical order and the immanent presence of divine authority in the person of the King (this is what I have called a sacral model of kingship); the other on the more pragmatic claims of contingency and dispersed authority. In the tetralo-gy, this struggle is not resolved until Henry V, the "mirror of all Christian kings" (*Henry V* 2.Cho.6), is able to effectively bridge the gap and unite the claims of both. My readings of these plays will argue that, as in the case of the Prayerbook, this synthesis depends on the function of representation itself in the construction of a new and stable polity.

The two central characters of *Richard II* do more than present us with two competing political philosophies; there is something about their respective approaches to signification itself that is worth thinking about. Richard is not only a divine-right absolutist (and a bad and tyrannical one), he's also a poet and something of a literalist, and these terms are related. When confronted with a problem or crisis, his char-acteristic response is to convert it wholly into language, metaphorizing it, exploring and explicating these metaphors, wrapping himself in folds of gorgeous eloquence. For Richard, a meditation on kingship becomes an eloquent speech on a crown (3.2.160–70), itself further metaphorized as a theater in which he plays; a threat of deposition is figured less as a politically consequential event than as a personal exchange of accouterments and signs.

> I'll give my jewels for a set of beads,
> My gorgeous palace for a hermitage,
> My gay apparel for an almsman's gown,
> My figur'd goblets for a dish of wood,
> My sceptre for a palmer's walking-staff,
> My subjects for a pair of carved saints. . . .
>   (3.3.147–52)

In the deposition scene (4.1), Richard figures himself as a betrayed Christ (170–71, 239–42), a tear-filled bucket (184–89), a "mockery king of snow" (260) to Bullingbrook's sun; his lost authority is only fully realized and grasped when it becomes a smashed mirror. Even at Pomfret, Richard continues in his complex and involuted soliloquy to "people this little world" with "still-breeding thoughts" (5.5.9, 8) and metaphors.

Richard, in short, exists, both poetically and politically, at the level of the signifier, in what Thomas M. Greene has described as "a kind of formalist heresy" (1991, 193). In his world of symbols, signs are directly equivalent to their referents: the crown *is* kingly authority; his name *is* a standing army. There is no sense of slippage or potential dissociation between signifier and signified (in this respect, of course, the poet-King is a rather poor poet indeed, perhaps even an antipoet). And in this respect, this hermeneutic is strikingly reminiscent of medieval Catholic theology, in which the sacramental elements were dogmatically not signs that pointed to some external referent, but precisely *were* that referent; in the Reformed account, this collapsed hermeneutic led not only to authority but to tyranny. In Richard's case as well, this absorption is symbolically and thematically related to his political philosophy, which hinges on a similarly irrefragable and unproblematic identity of person, authority, and office: for him, kingship is not conditional, but immutable and divinely ordained, and his authority as king is absolute (and absolutely contained in his person). He preserves his conviction that "Not all the water in the rough rude sea / Can wash the balm off from an anointed king" (3.2.54–55)—and his solipsistic engrossment in the world of signs—in the only way possible: by washing it off himself ("With mine own tears I wash away my balm" [4.1.207]). Richard's corrupt and failed absolutism manifests itself in his systematic hermeneutic collapsing of sign and referent, and vice versa. He is lost in his own mastery of signification, as he is in his personal rule, unmoored from any stable referential reality, and unaware that he's adrift.

Richard's rival is conspicuously free of this weakness. Bullingbrook is keenly aware of the dissociability of person and office—as a usurper, he has to be—and this sensibility is closely related to his semiotic awareness. His political ascent is enabled and precipitated by Richard's disastrous absorption in the signifiers of words and the crown, and the systematic abuses that stemmed from it across England; Henry's pragmatic ability to manipulate signs and their attendant uncertainties in the service of the realities of power establishes him, despite the tragedy of the deposition, as a better and more effective ruler who saves England from Richard's abusive misrule. Bullingbrook realizes, as Richard doesn't, that the relation of king to kinghood is as contingent as that of signifier and signified. Bullingbrook's hermeneutic sophistication, his grasp of the limits of language and imagination, insists on the distance between representation and reality. But rather than being restricted by this boundary, he remakes it into a condition of his power.[9] Richard ignores the signifying gap in a systematic, solipsistic, and self-destructive way; Bullingbrook proceeds to *occupy* it as a constructive site of effective and ultimately positive and unifying (though this will take several plays) authority. He is perhaps, in all his opacity, ambivalence, opportunism, and plausible deniability, Shakespeare's ultimate politician.

These qualities have contributed in large part (out of critical frustration, one suspects) to the historical tendency to view him and his son as unscrupulous Machiavels whose successors got what was coming to them. But this reductive view is not supported by the plays. *Richard II* would not be such an ambiguous and historically contentious play if the two central characters didn't present competing philosophical claims to power of at least roughly equal viability (divine, inheritory authority on Richard's behalf, pragmatism and ability and support from below on Bullingbrook's). Furthermore, if we think of Richard's absolutism as part of his hermeneutics (that is, that there is no possibility of slippage in the irrecusable and unconditional link between— actually, identity of—royal person and monarchy), and if we think of Bullingbrook's conditionalism as part of his (that is, that the monarch essentially represents a set of responsibilities and standards, upon which his status as monarch is contingent), the latter system is clearly portrayed as the one that yields better results. Richard's ideology produces abuses; Bullingbrook's, even in its most limited claims, upholds traditional legal and property rights, and as king, he is noteworthy for his magnanimity toward Mowbray, Carlisle, and Aumerle, as well as for his broad popularity (5.2) and the strict discipline endorsed in the garden scene (3.4).

This is, admittedly, a notoriously difficult point, with a contested critical genealogy as old as the play itself: the Lancastrians' methods are certainly not untroubling ethically—Hotspur's description of Bullingbrook as a "vile politician" (*1 Henry IV* 1.3.241) has proven for many readers remarkably easy to sympathize with—and the loss of divine authority with Richard reverberates as a genuinely tragic and epochal moment of history (a similar sense of disillusionment and loss, I should note, also animates a great deal of Catholic and revisionist historiography of the English Reformation). But I'd like to suggest what

I think Shakespeare does: Bullingbrook's representational approach can also serve as a preventive and corrective to the tyrannous abuse of power. Implicit in Richard's literalist and absolutist ideology is a belief that the monarch can do no wrong (none, at any rate, that legitimizes political consequences from below). The Lancastrians' greater hermeneutic and political flexibility allows the belief that the monarch is accountable to external standards, and that power is conditional on this reckoning. Representational thinking may have its downside politically, particularly in its decidedly unattractive pragmatism, but it also serves here as a means of justice and the pursuit of certain ideals, a site of potential resistance to excessively concentrated power.

In the play that bears his name, Henry V, the "mirror of all Christian kings" (2.Cho.6), brings the English monarchy to its zenith in a land newly free of the discord that had racked it in all the previous histories. Internal strife has been relocated across the Channel, as domestic unrest and civil war give way to international conquest. No English lords vie with Henry for our attention, let alone for the crown. Questions of legitimacy and authority, so central to the preceding plays, all but vanish, replaced by a unified focus on the King's glorious exploits. And though these exploits are often manipulative, self-serving, and morally questionable, this play concentrates on unification and heroic success, produced in large part by Henry's potently constructive combination of successive legitimacy and pragmatic ability—the latter largely constituted by his long apprenticeship to signification and representation in the intervening *Henry IV* plays. In this play, the meditations of Hal and Shakespeare come to their fulfillment, as the theatrical representations of both king and play construct a new sociopolitical order characterized primarily by expansiveness, inclusivity, and unity.

At the very beginning of *Henry V,* we are presented with a significantly new church-state polity. The nervous consultation of the bishops in act 1, scene 1, and their self-interested support of the King's French expedition in the following scene, do little to convince us of their Christian piety or moral authority, but they do indicate something important: in Henry V's world, the interests of the church are thoroughly bound up with, and subordinated to, the interests of the crown. The Roman origins of the bishops' power are entirely irrelevant, and, in contrast to Shakespeare's early histories, they never attempt to use this power to oppose the King. In other words, although we don't see Henry making doctrinal pronouncements à la Henry VIII, the political order of this play is recognizably post-Reformation in nature. After this point is made, the bishops vanish completely from the play, digested into the unified national pursuits of the King.

The specifically Reformed nature of this order has been further pre-emphasized in the closing words of *2 Henry IV*, where the epilogue insists that Falstaff is not the historical Sir John Oldcastle. This is usually attributed to pressure exerted on Shakespeare or his associates by one of Oldcastle's descendants, but there is a further reason why the distinction is important. The Lollard Oldcastle, burned for heresy in 1417, had become transformed by the historiographic lens of the Reformation into a proto-Protestant martyr; Shakespeare goes out of his way to remove the taint of Catholic persecution from his hero-King. Though historically, of course, Henry V was a loyal son of the Universal Church, Shakespeare's version of him is a nonpartisan Christian who rules an anachronistically Reformed English polity.

Within this polity, Henry carries on further efforts at unification along class and regional axes. His modification of Henry IV's strategic absence into strategic presence enables him to use not only the traditional rhetoric of martial valor with his soldiers, but also the more inclusive and class-transcending rhetoric of brotherhood that he had learned in Eastcheap. "There is none of you so mean and base," he tells his troops at Harfleur (3.1.29–30), "that hath not noble lustre in your eyes." And in his famous speech before Agincourt, he refers to the assembled host as:

> We few, we happy few, we band of brothers;
> For he to-day that sheds his blood with me
> Shall be my brother; be he ne'er so vile,
> This day shall gentle his condition;
> And gentlemen in England, now a-bed,
> Shall think themselves accurs'd they were not here;
> And hold their manhoods cheap whiles any speaks
> That fought with us upon Saint Crispin's day.
>
> (4.3.60–67)

The shared experience of this battle, Henry assures his enormously extended family, promises to elevate the "vile" (with whom he has participated all his life) over the comfortable gentry back home in manhood.

This sense of brotherhood is, of course, a trope, a rhetorical tool, designed to inspire his troops into the performance of their lives. And it works in part because everyone recognizes and participates in it as such; whereas Richard II, addressing the earth on his return from Ireland, found it necessary to exhort his friends to "mock not my senseless conjuration" (3.2.23), Henry's speech elicits no sign of puzzlement or misunderstanding. And this, I think, is because, in a figural but nonetheless genuine sense, Henry himself seems to believe in this brotherhood. His night vigil in 4.1, though a disguised exercise of power, of course, concludes with him alone on stage, lamenting the insomnia that seems to run in his family. His meditation on ceremony is something of a thematic culmination of the previous plays.

> And what have kings, that privates have not too,
> Save ceremony, save general ceremony?
> And what art thou, thou idol Ceremony? . . .
> Art thou aught else but place, degree, and form,
> Creating awe and fear in other men? . . .
> Canst thou, when thou command'st the beggar's knee,
> Command the health of it? No, thou proud dream,
> That play'st so subtilly with a king's repose.
> I am a king that finds thee; and I know
> 'Tis not the balm, the sceptre, and the ball,
> The sword, the mace, the crown imperial,
> The intertissued robe of gold and pearl,
> The farced title running 'fore the king,
> The throne he sits on, nor the tide of pomp
> That beats upon the high shore of this world—
> No, not all these, thrice-gorgeous ceremony,
> Not all these, laid in bed majestical,
> Can sleep so soundly as the wretched slave. . . .
>   (4.1.238–40, 246–47, 256–68)

Henry's speech seems to echo two primary sources in the previous plays: Falstaff's subversive catechism on the mystified ideal of "honor" (*1 Henry IV* 5.1.127–41), and Henry IV's tortured apostrophe to sleep (*2 Henry IV* 3.1.5–31). Insofar as it partakes of the latter, it participates in the care-worn mystique of monarchy, which suggests that the sleep enjoyed by the lowly is preferable to the power wielded by the great. But to the extent that it echoes the former, it depicts a skeptical but now ultimately constructive view of royal authority. To

Hal, the "ceremony" that distinguishes king from subjects is primarily a convergence of signs ("place, degree, and form" as well as the itemized catalogue he proceeds to give). And though this symbolic order of difference has no inherent power—a recognition unimaginable for Richard II—it unmistakably does matter, creating not only "awe and fear," but also, in turn, royal authority and the entire sociopolitical order. Hal's soliloquy simultaneously recognizes both his genuine commonality with all his subjects and the genuine difference made by the representational order of power. Richard felt his mortality only out of despair; Henry V reworks it into an enabling condition of his power.

This expansive and class-inclusive sense of unity among ruler and ruled also transcends the geographic differences that figured so heavily in the previous plays. In *Richard II,* the Irish are unruly outsiders, and the Welsh are unreliable allies; in *Henry IV,* both the Welsh and the Scots are rebellious enemies of the crown. But in *Henry V,* English, Welsh, Irish, and Scottish soldiers fight side by side, putting aside their petty squabbles to focus on their common allegiance to Henry. The King particularly encourages his Welsh connections, embracing the symbolic leek as a "memorable honor" (4.7.104). And two scenes later, this leek becomes the emblem of a decisively new order of merit and unity: in the comic action of act 5, scene 1, Pistol, the last surviving member of the formerly vigorous tavern world, is forced by Fluellen to eat it, after which he slinks off forever. Henry's good subject becomes his agent, reproducing the symbolic order and extinguishing the last embers of a subversive subculture that has no place left under Henry's rule.

The hero-King's authority, like the Reformed Eucharist, is thus constructed fundamentally on an inclusive and unifying sense of signification, and on the communal participation of subjects in these representations (this self-consciously figural, cooperative, interpretive model is what I mean by "sacramental" kingship). But this dynamic also radiates outward in (and beyond) the play. *Henry V* highlights, to an exceptional degree, its own status as a theatrical work of literary representation, and explicitly enjoins its audience to imaginatively compensate for its limitations as such. The chorus that opens each act repeatedly acknowledges the inherent inadequacy of its own representation, its inability to be that to which it refers. At the same time, it insists that participative interpretation can effectively transcend these limits, making the performative text into something that is real and powerful both despite and precisely because of its fictivity.

> O for a Muse of fire, that would ascend
> The brightest heaven of invention!
> A kingdom for a stage, princes to act,
> And monarchs to behold the swelling scene! . . .
> But pardon, gentles all,
> The flat unraised spirits that hath dar'd
> On this unworthy scaffold to bring forth
> So great an object. Can this cockpit hold
> The vasty fields of France? Or may we cram
> Within this wooden O the very casques
> Which did affright the air at Agincourt?
> O, pardon! since a crooked figure may
> Attest in little place a million,
> And let us, ciphers in this great accompt,
> On your imaginary forces work. . . .
> Piece out our imperfections with your thoughts. . . .
> (1.Cho.1–4, 8–18, 23)

The subsequent prologues continue to exhort the audience to compensate for the limits of the stage (which, significantly, I just mistyped as "state"), to traverse and transform space, time, and event (both real and staged) with their imaginations: "Linger your patience on, and we'll digest / Th' abuse of distance; force a play" (2.Cho.31–32); "Still be kind, / And eche out our performance with your mind" (3.Cho.34–35);

> we shall much disgrace
> With four or five most ragged foils
> (Right ill dispos'd, in brawl ridiculous)
> The name of Agincourt. Yet sit and see,
> Minding true things by what their mock'ries be
> (4.Cho.49–53)

> admit th' excuse
> Of time, of numbers, and due course of things,
> Which cannot in their huge and proper life
> Be here presented
> (5.Cho.3–6)

Henry V, in short, does as a play exactly what its hero does as a king: it relies on its representationality, and the cooperation of its audience, to achieve a final effect that exceeds the potential of any other mode— even the "real" or the immanent divine. Although the pious King is careful to attribute his victory to God, the success of his performance is due at least as much to the interpretive participation of both subjects and audience. Lancastrian power, I've argued, is built on a hermeneutic and political awareness of representational difference, and the enormous possibilities that essentially fictive signs hold when read by cooperative interpreters. This final play not only shows us this constructive ability in the hands of a virtuoso, it also draws us into the circuit of participation: by imaginatively treating the player as a king, we ultimately contribute to the dazzling theatrical power of the player-King himself. The wicked transparency of Richard III (whose role-playing coexists uncomfortably with its theatrical setting) creates the possibility of watching and even enjoying his exploits without interpretively supporting them; in *Henry V,* the representational practices of king and theater are so intimately and persuasively connected that such distance may not be possible. Surely this is a play and a tetralogy that, as Stephen Greenblatt has argued in a brilliant and influential essay, lays bare the modes of power "even as they draw their audience irresistibly toward the celebration of that power" (1985, 20). But whereas Greenblatt sees this as part of a complex dynamic of subversive exposure and power-enhancing containment, in which the generation of doubt paradoxically undergirds faith, I'm suggesting a different way of looking at these plays. In them, I contend, Shakespeare demonstrates the constructive political potential of a recognizably Reformed sense of representation, in which ruler and subjects, actor and audience participate self-consciously in a positive and redemptive system of signs.[10]

This, I would argue, owes something to the Reformation's reconstruction, effected in large part by the *BCP,* of the cultural status and potential of representation itself. The Prayerbook had theologically refounded English Christianity (and the reconfigured church-state polity) on a new conception of the Eucharist as, essentially, an interpretive phenomenon; the sacramental elements were recast as a signifying text, and the divine grace they promised was realizable only if they were internalized, in faith, as representational signs. This instituted the competent, autonomous, interpreting Reformed individual in official liturgical discourse, which had traditionally stressed the necessary mediation of the institutional church in brokering the restricted contact between the human and the immanent divine. At the same time, it established representation itself as the ground of negotiation between this individual and the larger polity of the early modern nation (in which, after the Reformation, the sociopolitical and the ecclesiastical were coterminous). The identity and authority of order and individual thus became, in this post-Reformation English context—as I've argued they are in *Henry V*—representationally and mutually constituting; subject and structure are simultaneously and perpetually constructed through hermeneutically aware engagement in systems of signs.

If, then, the divinely energized sign became the locus of these profound cultural transactions, it is less than surprising that the status and significance of representation began to grow exponentially in all directions. Thirty years after the introduction of the Prayerbook (and scarcely twenty after the end of its Marian hiatus), Philip Sidney translated the logic of sacramental representation to the worldly sphere of the literary. His *Defence of Poetry* posits a particularly close relationship between figurality and truth, and positions poetic representation as a peculiarly sensitive site of synthetic access and constructive negotiation between real and ideal, mundane and transcendent, earth and heaven. Ultimately, the Sidneian engagement with fictive signs offers nothing less than a worldly version of the transforming grace available to the faithful participant in the Reformed sacrament.

Shakespeare takes this in a different direction. His history plays trace the rehabilitation of the uncertainty and fictivity of representation into a means of *national* salvation from sociopolitical chaos (this arc is even clearer when the preceding Yorkist plays are taken into account). And though the Lancastrian plays keenly register the costs of the loss of divine immanence, they also suggest the necessity of a more consciously figural alternative. In this world of intertwined political and hermeneutic questions, self-conscious representation ultimately emerges as a potential force for justice, authority, and a unified and inclusive national order. The status of the "mirror of all Christian kings" depends on his ability to understand and manipulate signs, and equally on communal participation in them as signs. Order and subjects, no less in *Henry V* than in the *BCP*, reciprocally constitute one another around a fulcrum of hermeneutically aware representation. For Hal as for Cranmer, the construction of the "godly order" is a cooperative and interpretive—and ongoing—venture.

Of course, given the profound contradictions they sought to address, none of these attempted resolutions proved to be completely successful;

the conflicts and tensions inherent in each continue to the present day. The Prayerbook failed to prevent the emergence of discord and revolution within England and its church, and controversy over its status and significance has played a major role in English history and identity through the end of the twentieth century. Sidney's salvific trust in literature has borne dubious historical fruit, and the antihumanist thrust of much recent criticism has seriously questioned the very possibility of disinterested and morally elevating literature. Furthermore, Shakespeare's presentation of the Lancastrian solution is shot through with conflict and ambivalence (which my analysis has attempted to acknowledge even as it works its way through a particular reading), forming a field of vigorous contestation for centuries of critical discourse; as the ominous final epilogue warns, this stability will be fragile and short-lived, and will end in national catastrophe. But in each of these sixteenth-century instances, questions of authority and identity, religion and politics, and order and individual intersect in distinctive and similar ways, and their provisional answers are forged out of a culturally potent hope in representation. And their pervasive, and perhaps deliberate, ambiguities suggest and demand that we act as interpretive partners in this process of perpetual reconstitution.

NOTES

1. This particular set of alignments sits rather curiously beside both Protestant literalism and Roman Catholic allegorism—though I think both of these tensions can ultimately be explained in terms of political and hermeneutic exigencies. And it is essential to understand that in the Catholic sacrament, the relation of sign and referent (in this case, accidents and substance) is emphatically *not* a figural one, as it explicitly *is* in the Reformed.

2. "Christ wrote the covenant of his body and blood in bread and wine; giving them that name, that ought to keep the covenant in remembrance. And hereof ye see, that our sacraments are bodies of stories only . . ." (Tyndale 1848, 357–58).

3. This tension offers some insight, I think, into the perennial historiographical debate over the English Reformation. Rather than seeing the Reformation as either a top-down political exercise or a bottom-up groundswell of evangelical sentiment, I think that the *BCP* shows us that we need to understand it as *both*—an ideologically conflicted, and perpetually renegotiated, synthesis of two contrary cultural imperatives.

4. I, like Cranmer (1844), am using this term in its specifically Reformed sense—something akin to "figural" or "representational." That is, in contrast to the sacral immanence of Richard's authority, which parallels the claims of the transubstantiatory mass, Henry's political model resembles the Reformed sacrament as a representational and communally participatory phenomenon *through which* authority is constituted.

5. See, for example, Howard (1994, 28): "anti-Catholic and antitheatrical polemics converge in this period because in a strongly Protestant discourse, . . . the theater, like the Catholic Church, is constructed as committing its patrons to the worship of hollow idols: outward signs, not inward essences, things of the flesh, not of the spirit." See also Barish (1981, ch. 4, ch. 6) and Herman (1996), who looks beyond the theater to find a general antipoetic bias in Protestantism. My objection to such accounts is not that there is no truth in them—there were, of course, evangelicals who opposed literary/theatrical representation for religious reasons—but that the model of a *necessary* antagonism is a distorting oversimplification (one that indicates various critical biases of its own, and which excludes from the outset important angles of insight into the Renaissance and its literature). For corrective accounts, see not only the present study and those cited later in this essay, but also Lewalski (1979), as well as Butler, who demonstrates "how false it is to conceive of puritan feeling as being in a state of intransigent hostility towards the theatres in the 1630's" (1984, 94).

6. See, for example, Montrose (1980) and Greenblatt (1988).

7. See also Diehl's *Staging Reform, Reforming the Stage* (1997) for a lengthier exposition of these insights.

8. See also Weimann's "Discourse, ideology and the crisis of authority" (1987) and his book-length collection of essays, *Authority and Representation in Early Modern Discourse* (1996).

9. The two parts of *Henry IV,* which I don't have the space to discuss at length here, are essentially an extended exposition of how this is done (and passed on to Hal, who will remake these principles into astonishing new configurations).

10. This reading also opposes Rackin's assertions that monarchic and theatrical representation are "severely qualified" and "deeply compromised" by their interdependence (1990, 61, 80)—though I am, of course, not contending that all tensions are resolved, all questions answered, all politics redeemed; indeed, a tremendous, if necessary, price has been paid in the transition from the politics of divinity to the politics of modernity, and the conflicted interpretive history of these plays bears witness to the residual tensions in the post-Reformation yoking of structure and subject. Norman Rabkin, in a seminal 1977 essay, argued that the mutually exclusive readings this play has tended

to produce are extensions of the radical ambivalence between the two parts of *Henry IV* (which embody, respectively, "our deepest hopes and fears about the world of political action" [296]).

WORKS CITED

Barish, Jonas. *The Antitheatrical Prejudice.* Berkeley, Calif.: University of California Press, 1981.

Butler, Martin. *Theatre and Crisis, 1632–1642.* London: Cambridge University Press, 1984.

Cranmer, Thomas. *Writings and Disputations of Thomas Cranmer . . . Relative to the Sacrament of the Lord's Supper.* Ed. J. E. Cox. Cambridge, England: Parker Society, 1844.

Diehl, Huston. "Observing the Lord's Supper and the Lord Chamberlain's Men: The Visual Rhetoric of Ritual and Play in Early Modern England." *Renaissance Drama* 22 (1991): 147–74.

_____. *Staging Reform, Reforming the Stage.* Ithaca, N.Y.: Cornell University Press, 1997.

Foxe, John. *The Acts and Monuments.* Ed. Josiah Pratt. 8 vols. London: Religious Tract Society, 1877.

Greenblatt, Stephen. "Invisible bullets: Renaissance authority and its subversion, *Henry IV* and *Henry V.*" In *Political Shakespeare,* ed. Dollimore and Sinfield. 18–47. Ithaca, N.Y.: Cornell University Press, 1985.

_____. "Shakespeare and the Exorcists." In *Shakespearean Negotiations: The Circulation of Social Energy in Renaissance England.* 94–128. Berkeley, Calif.: University of California Press, 1988.

Greene, Thomas M. "Ritual and Text in the Renaissance." *Canadian Review of Comparative Literature* 18:2–3 (June/September 1991): 179–97.

Herman, Peter C. *Squitter-wits and Muse-haters: Sidney, Spenser, Milton, and Renaissance Antipoetic Sentiment.* Detroit, Mich.: Wayne State University Press, 1996.

Howard, Jean E. *The Stage and Social Struggle in Early Modern England.* London: Routledge, 1994.

Lewalski, Barbara Kiefer. *Protestant Poetics and the Seventeenth-Century Religious Lyric.* Princeton, N.J.: Princeton University Press, 1979.

Montrose, Louis A. "The Purpose of Playing: Reflections on a Shakespearean Anthropology." *Helios* 7 (1980): 51–74.

Rabkin, Norman. "Rabbits, Ducks, and *Henry V.*" *Shakespeare Quarterly* 28 (1977): 279–96.

Rackin, Phyllis. *Stages of History.* Ithaca, N.Y.: Cornell University Press, 1990.

Shakespeare, William. *The Riverside Shakespeare.* Ed. G. Blakemore Evans. Boston: Houghton Mifflin, 1974.

Tyndale, William. *Doctrinal Treatises.* Ed. Henry Walter. Cambridge, England: Parker Society, 1848.

Weimann, Robert. *Authority and Representation in Early Modern Discourse.* Baltimore, Md.: Johns Hopkins University Press, 1996.

_____. "'Bifold Authority' in Reformation Discourse: Authorization, Representation, and Early Modern 'Meaning.'" In *Historical Criticism and the Challenge of Theory,* ed. Janet Levarie Smarr. 167–82. Urbana, Ill.: University of Illinois Press, 1993.

_____. *"Discourse, ideology, and the crisis of authority." REAL: Yearbook of Research in English and American Literature* 5 (1987): 109–40.

6

Mocking Oldcastle:
Notes Toward Exploring a
Possible Catholic Presence
in Shakespeare's Henriad

by Gary D. Hamilton

University of Maryland, College Park, Maryland

IN DEDICATING HIS 1565 TRANSLATION of Bede's *Ecclesiastical History of England* to "Elizabeth . . . Defendour of the Faith," Thomas Stapleton counseled his Queen that monarchs, as defenders of the faith, were to seek to unite Christendom, as the worthiest of those past "Princes of every singular province in Christendom" had attempted to do after they were no longer "one empire" (Stapleton 1565, >1r). Prominent among the named actions for Elizabeth to imitate was the "extirping of the heresies of John Wicleff and the Bohems," and prominent among the actors to emulate was England's own Henry V, who postponed fulfilling his private political goals until he had acted to promote the cause of Christian unity:

> In the history of Polidore we read of that Noble Prince . . . that having called a Parlement, and decreed therein a voyage in to Fraunce for recovery of his right . . . yet the generall Councell of Constance then beinge appointed, he staied his privat quarrel for Gods cause, directed his legats unto the Councell . . . and in the meane while appeased the rebellion of John Oldecastle labouring by force and disobedience against his Souverain (as the new Wicleffs do presently in Fraunce and Scotland) to maintaine the heresy of Wicleff, and pronounced traitours all the adherents of that wicked secte. By this speedy diligence of that gratious Prince, bothe that heresy was then quailed in your highnes dominions, and (as Polidore noteth) the Noble victories of that valiaunt prince

> ensued: God undoubtedly prospering his affaires, who had preferred the quarrell of him, before his own prepared viage. (Stapleton 1565, >2r)

In the preface to the reader, Stapleton revealed how closely the course of action he proposed to Elizabeth in the dedication—to act as a Catholic prince—approximated the task that Stapleton imagined himself to be performing in publishing Bede's work. In the dedication, Stapleton urged Elizabeth to defend what Bede had shown to be "the first and true Christen faith planted in your Graces dominions . . . the pretended faith of protestants to be but a bastard slippe proceding of an other stocke (as partly of old renewed heresies, partly of new forged interpretations upon the written text of Gods word)." Removal of this plant was necessary lest "left in time . . . it overgrowe the true branches of the naturall tree, consume the spring of all Christianitie, and sucke out the ioye of al right religion" (Stapleton 1594, >2v–3r). Then, addressing the reader, Stapleton declared that his translation of Venerable Bede, whom he regarded as the equal to any valued historian "in any respect either off lerning, honesty or truthe" (A4v) would replace the "lewde lies and malicious surmises upon the lives of holy men" (A3v) by "upstert sectaries" (C1r).

Foremost among Stapleton's targets for replacement were the lies of John Foxe. When defending Bede in the area where his account might seem most questionable, namely, his relation of miraculous occurrences, Stapleton argued that if one condemns Bede's miracles, then one must do the same for "the Acts and Monuments of M. Fox," a work that relates "miserable miracles to sette forth the glory of their stinking Martyrs" (C1r). Foxe was an unnamed presence in the dedication to Elizabeth as well, for in urging Elizabeth to act as Henry V by acting against Wycliffe's spiritual descendants, Stapleton was in effect turning Foxe's heroes back into traitors, as Catholic writers had depicted them. Appearing around the time of Nicholas Harpsfield's attack on Foxe's portrait of Oldcastle—an attack that Foxe answered in his 1570 edition (1.Nn2v–Pp2v)—Stapleton's singling out of Oldcastle as the arch Protestant might be viewed as a poignant reinforcement from the same Catholic arsenal of weapons that Harpsfield's mocking portrayal was drawn.

Awareness of the centrality of the Oldcastle controversy in sixteenth-century religious polemics inevitably moves us to name the significance of Shakespeare's version of Oldcastle/Falstaff, forcing us to measure the extent to which we might reasonably resist suspicions held in the seventeenth century (by John Speed and Richard Davies) and today (by Gary Taylor and others) that the dramatist was showing himself to be "a papist" (Taylor 1985, 99–100). A serious pursuit of this matter involves being attuned both to similarities and differences between Shakespeare's portrayals and indisputably pro-Catholic ones. In Shakespeare, as in Stapleton, the focus is not only on Oldcastle's actions, but also on the actions of the Prince, whose rejection of this tarnished figure is what is necessary to attain his future exemplary status. Thus the Catholic question, too, must be phrased accordingly. If Shakespeare presented, as he surely did, a distinctly anti-Foxean Oldcastle / Falstaff, did he also present his rejecter as a distinctly Catholic monarch? In contemporary terms, the question seems worth pursuing not only because Catholics like Stapleton and Robert Parsons praised Henry V highly for his loyalty to Rome,[1] but also because Foxe, too, singled out this subservience while criticizing it and lamenting its consequences.

If one adopts David Womersley's reading of Shakespeare's Henriad, the relevant issues seem to reach their maximum complexity, for according to Womersley, Shakespeare took the lead of the Protestant historian Edward Hall in fashioning Henry V as a forerunner to Henry VIII. According to Hall, Henry V was a reforming monarch; he turned away from the corruption that surrounded him. Especially significant in Womersley's reading is that Shakespeare presents, in *Henry V,* act 4, scene 1, this monarch's appreciation, "apparently . . . for the first time, [of] a characteristic Protestant belief in the inefficacy of intercessory prayer and good works to atone for sin," a moment that "follows Henry's account of the way in which he has up to now allowed these identifiably Catholic practices and institutions, derived from the doctrine of purgatory—building chantries, buying prayer, and masses—to shape his conduct" (Womersley 1996, 19). Thus, Henry says:

> O, not to-day, think not upon the fault
> My father made in compassing the crown!
> I Richard's body have interred new,
> And on it have bestowed more contrite tears
> Than from it issued forced drops of blood;
> Five hundred poor I have in yearly pay,
> Who twice a day their wither'd hands hold up

> Toward heaven, to pardon blood; and I have built
> Two chantries, where the sad and solemn priests
> Sing still for Richard's soul. More will I do;
> Though all that I can do is nothing worth,
> Since that my penitence comes after all,
> Imploring pardon.
>
> (4.1.310–22)

Though this particular character development resolves for Womersley the problem of Shakespeare's previous apparent "mocking [of] the complex historiographic traditions of reformed religion" (21), can we really leave unexplained the strange choice of tactics by which the dramatist changed this Catholic prince into a Protestant one? At the center of this reading is the puzzling irony that Henry's growing into a Protestant monarch entails separating from a prominent Protestant martyr/hero. Is it any wonder that Shakespeare changed Oldcastle's name?

There are, of course, a number of other ways of dissolving this irony, some of which involve us deeply in problems of historical understanding and of relating that understanding to a Shakespearean text. One possibility is that Womersley misconstrued the significance of the reforming monarch because he conceived of the idea of reformation too exclusively as a Protestant one; and that, moreover, he took his understanding of Catholicism from Protestant caricatures of Catholic doctrines and practices. An example of the latter problem might readily be located in Womersley's interpretation of Henry's supposedly climactic "Protestant" declaration, "More will I do, / Though all that I can do is nothing worth" (4.1.284–85). In privileging the Protestant disdain of justification by works and celebration of justification by faith as the proper context in which to understand this utterance, Womersley effectively isolates Henry's words from those of a host of sixteenth-century Catholic writers who, as Lucy Wooding has recently shown, frequently defined the role of works as subsidiary.[2] Just as the denial of the efficacy of works without faith was an element in sixteenth-century Catholic doctrine, so was the idea of a reforming monarch a potent element in Catholic rhetoric of the period, and especially in the 1590s. If, as Womersley suggests, the image of the reforming monarch could invoke for Protestants the accomplishments of the father of the queen who now ruled England, it might well invoke among Catholics in the final decade of the century their hopes for a better monarch soon to replace her.

Though we will have occasion to pursue the contours of this particular Catholic concern later, some of its implications for Womersley's argument are obvious. Because the linguistic evidence used to support this Protestant reading is not in fact the exclusive property of Protestants, the case for Shakespeare's having transformed Henry V into a Protestant must remain inconclusive. It is possible—perhaps even likely—using precisely the kinds of pro-faith, anti-idolatry linguistic evidence that Womersley cites, that a Protestant contemporary of Shakespeare would have been inclined to adopt such a reading. But it is just as likely that a Catholic in the 1590s would have adopted a different reading of this monarchical transformation. So where is Shakespeare the papist in this presentation of a transformed monarch? If he does exist somewhere in this portrayal, he remains sufficiently hidden, it would appear, so that we might never be certain that we have found him there. Does the key to exposing him, if he does exist, thus lie in the anti-Foxean portrayal of Oldcastle after all? Here, too, we must begin and end with the problem of our historical understanding.

Is there any historically plausible way of imagining that Shakespeare's anti-Foxean adaptation of Oldcastle could have elicited Protestant approval? The answer is simple if one moves ahead to the 1630s and proceeds to follow the career of Peter Heylyn into the 1660s. Heylyn, who began by assisting his employer, Archbishop Laud, in articulating his anti-Calvinist and pro-clericalist agendas, devoted many pages of his writings after Laud's downfall to attacking Foxe's endorsement of the Lollards, whom Heylyn discerned to be unsavory, heretical schismatics. In his ambitious *Ecclesia Restaurata,* he systematically replaced Foxe's martyrs with his own account of those suffering clergy who had to endure poverty and dishonor when rapine and sacrilege were given full reign in the land under Edward VI (Heylyn 1661, 1:94–95, 131–35). For our purposes, the most interesting part of that long work might well be its dedication, addressed in 1660 to Charles II. Just as Stapleton advised Elizabeth to follow the example of Henry V, so Heylyn advised his monarch to follow the example of Elizabeth, who acted firmly and decisively against nonconformity in order to protect both church and state. For Heylyn, Elizabeth truly was the ideal Protestant monarch for whom Henry V might have been the shadowy type.[3]

But can the Heylyn model of response be plausibly transported from a sharply divided 1630s-style Protestant state of affairs under the control of a decidedly anti-Calvinist Laudian clericalism back into the 1590s, and can we then imagine Shakespeare's Oldcastle portrait functioning in the service of these clericalist interests?[4] As for the transportation problem, we do well to heed the warnings of Patrick Collinson and others who have argued that, though their concept of the "puritan" may have been invented in the 1590s, much of what Laudians (and later historians) associated with the term was to a certain extent mainstream Protestantism in the 1590s.[5] Rather than transporting and working with a later response model, we would surely do better to develop one from the period. And here the question arises: was there an articulated anti-Foxean sentiment among some Protestants in the 1590s? It is not difficult to imagine that Richard Bancroft, with his intense clericalist interests, might have been as upset by Foxe's celebration of the Wycliffites as Heylyn professed to be. But was Foxe fair game for even a hostile Protestant clergyman to attack, or was he so much a part of an accepted Protestant identity that staging an attack on his martyrs would be seen as crossing the Protestant line?[6] Such was ever the case with Heylyn in the seventeenth century, for example, as his critics persisted in attacking the non-Protestant character of his writings, attacks fueled not only by his rejection of Calvin but his attacks on Wycliffe and thus the Protestant tradition as defined by Foxe.[7] No doubt the line marking what a Protestant could not say without losing his Protestant identity was fluid and constantly moving in the 1590s, a shifting that surely makes speculating on the cultural work that Shakespeare's Oldcastle/Falstaff performed more interesting (if also less likely to arrive at certitude) than were that line firmly fixed.

Much attention has been given in recent years to the importance of the Marprelate controversy, with Collinson proclaiming it the point at which Puritanism was reinvented, an invention that had little to do, he suggests, with the everyday lives and practices of many of those Protestants whom later generations designated by that name (1995, 156–70). Kristen Poole has mined the controversy for the origins of Shakespeare's Oldcastle/Falstaff, finding in this character both a transference of Martin's attractive energy and the attributes that anti-Martinist writings loved to ridicule. Placing Shakespeare's portrayal of this character in the company of other "stage puritans," Poole lists among the relevant Puritan attributes the use of Calvinist language concerning election and vocation (1995, 63–67). Because such language was surely commonplace among the mainstream Protestants of the day, one is inevitably left to ponder how, and the extent to which, this particular kind of (presumably Protestant) mocking of a Puritan might differ from a Catholic mocking of a 1590s-style mainstream Protestant? Not much, perhaps. The question that Poole's analysis prompts me to ask is really no different from the one that the Marprelate controversy itself elicits. Although the flurry of anti-Martinist literature appeared at the instigation of Whitgift and the church hierarchy and was clearly perceived to serve their needs, was it only their interests that it served? Is it possible that the suppression of the anti-Martinists, along with Martin, might itself be evidence that the bishops recognized interests at work besides their own? As Poole notes, when "the cavalier Pasquill . . . reappeared briefly in the summer of 1590 . . . to offer *Pasquills Apologie,*" he "defends himself against the backlash toward the anti-Martinists, his overzealous attacks on puritanism having earned him accusations of being a Catholic" (62). Even if we should choose to take such accusations lightly, we would do well to raise some questions about the origins of the anti-Martinist voice. Might they possibly be found among the writings of those Catholics who mocked Bale's and Foxe's "stinking martyrs" and railed against the anti-Catholic aspects of Elizabethan policies? Clearly the habits and perspectives of the Catholic libel need to be considered here.

To bring this segment of our excursion to rest, whether or not the bishops' hired guns had Catholic sympathies, there need be little doubt that the anti-Martinist tracts contributed, at least marginally, to the Catholic cause as well as to that of the bishops. The same probably also needs to be said of Shakespeare's portrayal of Oldcastle/Falstaff. Catholics could savor yet another mocking of one of Foxe's martyrs as the bishops witnessed the neutralizing of a prominent representative of the Wycliffite anticlericalist legacy. To recall how readily the Oldcastle story could be put to use against the bishops' interests, we need only consult a contemporary work that answered Shakespeare's portrayal, the play *Sir John Oldcastle, Part 1* (by Munday, Drayton, Hathway, and Wilson). In this work (as in Weever's *The Mirror of Martyrs*), the corruption that Shakespeare (following *Famous Victories* and a Catholic historical tradition) placed within Oldcastle is instead located within the clergy, who succeeded in convincing the King that one of his noble and loyal servants was a traitor. By dramatizing the dishonesty and self-interestedness of the persecuting clergy, and by emphasizing that Oldcastle's religious views and his political loyalty were two separate issues, the authors of *Oldcastle, Part 1* effectively served the cause of England's ever-threatened nonconformists. In the interest of doing justice to the complexity of this political reality, we need further to acknowledge that the nonconformist communities, well served by depicting a wronged loyal nonconformist, would, of course, have been Catholic as well as Protestant. Furthermore, if a Catholic interest was (at least marginally) served in *Oldcastle, Part 1*—and it is difficult to think otherwise—we must further observe that the choice of the celebration of a Foxean martyr to serve that interest is indeed deliciously ironic.

The pleasures to be savored from Shakespeare's Oldcastle portrait move us in quite a different direction, however. They can be more fully appreciated when we move that portrait out of the isolation of a Foxean hagiographical tradition and view it in combination with another facet of contemporary religious warfare, the Catholic libel that focused on the relationships between the Queen and her corrupt counselors. If it is the hilarity of Oldcastle/Falstaff's biblical language that keeps the (Catholic) anti-Foxean presence alive in the Henry plays, it is the sharp and persistent focus on the need for Prince Henry to remove himself from Oldcastle/Falstaff's corrupt influence that can allow this vein of Catholic libeling to be felt as a presence in these plays. As has often been noted, it is not only Oldcastle/Falstaff that is an object of satire but the Prince's reluctance to detach himself from the fat thief's company as well. In turning to another brand of Catholic polemics to explore this double-edged critique, I shall revisit and reformulate issues that have already been addressed in slightly different terms, but in doing so, I touch briefly on two as-yet-unaddressed topics, namely, the matter of the Lords Cobham (the contemporary Oldcastles often held responsible for Shakespeare's renaming of his Oldcastle), and the question of the succession, a topic that Richard Dutton's recent essay on the Duchy of Lancaster provocatively introduces into the mix.

In describing the brand of Catholic polemics that featured Elizabeth's corrupt counselors, I confine myself to two core works where the strategies that inform this kind of writing are as visible as the anxieties that produced them are palpable. One of these works appeared in 1592 with the title, *Advertisement to a secretarie of my L. Treasurers;* Richard Verstegan wrote it using the pseudonym John Philopatris. The other work, which provides a model for Verstegan's piece, is John Leslie's *A Treatise of Treasons against Q. Elizabeth, and the Croune of England;* it appeared anonymously in 1572.[8] The relationship of these two works to a third Catholic book, Robert Parsons's *A conference about the next succession to the Crowne of Ingland* (1594), will become self-evident. Positing their relationship to Shakespeare's plays is more problematic, of course. As was the case with the anti-Foxean element, the positing of a Catholic presence on the basis of a structure found in Catholic polemics is complicated by the likelihood that such a structure was useful for many reasons and to more than one interest group.

Like Prince Hal in *Famous Victories* and in Shakespeare's Henriad, Elizabeth as represented in Leslie's *A Treatise of Treasons* and in Verstegan's *Advertisement* was a monarch who had surrounded herself with thieves. *A Treatise of Treasons* focused exclusively on the Queen's two powerful advisors, Nicholas Bacon and William Cecil, who are depicted rather like Vice figures whose anti-Catholicism was guided not by genuine religious conviction, but by their desire to control the succession and continue to reap the profits attained from ruling over the land. Verstegan added to their company three other advisors who had come and gone. One of them, Christopher Hatton, received from Verstegan the least unfavorable treatment because, despite his bitter public speeches, he had "upon sundrie occasions protested . . . in secret . . . That his hand had never subscribed to the death of any one catholique" (1592, A7r). But for the others, Verstegan had only condemnation. Singling out Francis Walsingham for his espionage activities and cruelty against Catholics, Verstegan made a causal link between that cruelty and his unfortunate end, a rhetorical move analogous to the language in Foxe's accounts of Catholic persecutors. According to Verstegan, Walsingham "died in debt . . . and strooken in the secret partes of his body, as Eusebius reporteth of Maximus the Tyrant" (A7r). Leicester too had a "miserable death," poison having eaten "great holes" through his stomach—a fit ending for a life consumed with "adulteries, murders, and rapines." Upon hearing of his demise, people "rejoysed, that so wicked a monster was dead" (D3r). None was deemed more worthy of condemnation, however, than those two despicable targets of *A Treatise of Treason,* Bacon and Cecil, and here Verstegan adhered closely to the modes of attack used by Leslie.

"Exceeding gross-bodied" Nicholas Bacon—about whose great girth everyone from Camden to Elizabeth to Bacon himself made comment, and whom one scholar has suggested was the original of Shakespeare's Falstaff—was a target for Catholic libels because of the responsibility he assumed for handling church affairs in the early part of her reign. His dismissal of French Catholics from England in 1572, after the St. Bartholomew's massacre, provoked a flurry of such libels, resulting in Elizabeth's 1573 Proclamation against libels, an edict in which Bacon was singled out for praise.[9] Not only had Bacon's personal wealth increased enormously from the large tracts of confiscated church lands that he had acquired, but it was further alleged that he had added to it greatly through his office-holding. Verstegan stated that when Bacon "came to be lord keeper," he "shewed himselfe so corrupt and partiall for bribery, as never man before, or since in that place" and reported an "alleged . . . protestation also of Plowden the famous lawier, made at the Chauncery . . . that he woulde never returne thither so long as so corrupte a judge should sitt in that place" (1592, A6r).

More dangerous than any of these four figures, however, was Cecil, Lord Burghley, the Lord Treasurer of England, whom Verstegan targeted in his title and covered "more largely then of any of the reste, for that he yet liveth, and for that . . . he more then all the reste together, hath and doeth in deede seeke the destruction of the Catholiques by covert means" (1592, A7v). In developing his case against the Lord Treasurer, Verstegan relied heavily on *A Treatise of Treasons.* While castigating Burghley at every turn for his treatment of Catholics and sinister manipulations of Elizabeth's foreign policy, Verstegan (like Leslie) focused his ridicule on three closely related aspects: the Lord Treasurer's mean birth, his political ambitions, and his corrupt nature. Verstegan repeated the material that Leslie had presented on Cecil's humble origins, claiming that though he had spent his life trying to rule over the nobility, and even claiming he "is descended of the very old Princes of Wales themselves" (Verstegan 1592, C3v), he was really the grandson of an innkeeper. Moreover, this innkeeper had started out as "an Ostler in that Inn and after to have maried the hostesse" (C4v). The tragedy for the realm was that Cecil had isolated Elizabeth from her true friends, the old Catholic nobility, including the Duke of Norfolk, whose tragic execution Leslie was contemplating when he emphasized this point. The effect of the Queen's isolation was to strengthen Cecil's power, a goal that Cecil (in Leslie's words) did "daily contrive" to achieve by "the wresting and diverting of your Crowne from that course, race and line, in which the Lawes of your Countrey . . . have established and settled it" (Leslie 1572, L4v).

On the point of Cecil's political ambitions, Verstegan reiterated and updated the kinds of concerns that Leslie had expressed two decades earlier. For Leslie, Bacon and Cecil had two main strategies. One of them involved "the making of them selves might an strong in money, plate, Jewels, Armour, an other shorte treasures, by their long Bribery, corruption, and sale of Justice" (Leslie 1572, O1v). The other strategy entailed arranging marriages for their children: "with wily wit and wealth together, they winde in your other noblest houses unto them that are least . . . in credit and countenance" (O1v). But the marriages about which Leslie was most incensed involved the matter of succession. Noting that Bacon and Cecil had, "by their own mariages, allied alrady to the house of Suffolke of the Bloud Roiall, and by consequence thereof to the house of Hartfoord" (M8v), he maintained that it had been part of their master plan to assure that Elizabeth remained unmarried, that the line of Margaret be extinguished (Mary now being held prisoner and her infant son unlikely to survive to maturity), and that the house of Suffolk be on the throne.

In 1592, with Mary's execution in the past and the succession yet unsettled, but with James waiting in the wings to take revenge—as some Catholics hoped—on the Protestants who had killed his mother, Verstegan presented the Lord Treasurer as busy not only plotting to obtain important government positions for his sons, but also to marry his grandson to Lady Arabella Stuart and thereby to control the succession. One who might have been looking at English politics through this same Catholic lens five years later could have found much in recent events that fit Leslie's interpretive model. For our purposes, the career of Burghley's son Robert Cecil might be of interest. Having married Elizabeth Brooke, daughter of William, Lord Cobham (and brother of Henry, successor to that title in March 1597 upon her father's death), Robert created the familial link to the contemporary Oldcastle. In August 1597, the Queen (against Essex's expressed wishes) finally appointed Robert the Chancellor of the Duchy of Lancaster, a position for which he had lobbied for two years.[10]

If the "mean" births of Bacon and Cecil were not enough indication of their corrupt natures, their desires to improve themselves and the means by which they succeeded provided more proof for Leslie and Verstegan of the monstrous depravity of these royal counselors. But there was another, almost as strong, indication of their corruption, one directly related to their being Protestants. Two slightly different but closely linked issues emerge here, presenting us with possibilities relevant perhaps to the task of imagining what there might be in a Catholic libel that could suggest to readers of anti-Martinist satires that these satires, too, had been produced by Catholics. On the one hand, the wrongness of these counselors' religion is not so much the issue, for according to Leslie and Verstegan, the counselors do not believe in it anyway. At one point, Leslie speaks of Cecil as a "Sinon" engaged in bringing down the Trojan nation. A "principal worker of al the Treason," he possessed "a shamelesse face, no honour, litle honestie, and lesse conscience . . . pretending great devotion to the Goddesse Pallas, he covered his hypocrisie" (Leslie 1572, E4v–E5r). But the point is not exactly what we might expect. It is not merely that Bacon and Cecil were pretending to be Protestant; more precisely, their very pretending confirmed their Protestantism. Extending his Sinon/Trojan War analogy to clarify that point, Leslie identified "the Protestant" with the "falsehood, and lewed propertie of the Greekish Nation" at war with the "modestie and conscience of the Catholike partie" (E6r). Leslie meant exactly what Stapleton wrote when asking the Queen to eradicate "the pretended faith of protestants." When Leslie called Bacon and Cecil "Churche-robbers," for example, he understood them to be doing what Protestants do, a point that Verstegan built on when he noted that Cecil, by encouraging thousands of foreign Protestants to come to live in England, had encouraged an influx of "theeves, murderers, Churche-robbers" (Verstegan 1592, N8r). Verstegan also expanded on Leslie's point about the demeanor of Catholics when he addressed Cecil's elaborate efforts to detect the "many hundreds" of students returning from English Catholic colleges on the continent and now living "in common attire of other men" (C6r). The best way to know "a papist or Catholique yonge man" is "to note his modestie, his silence, his gravitie, his composition of body and countenance" (C6v). A Protestant, on the other hand, is one who "they know . . . to be a good felow . . . that is to wit, that he will eate, and drincke and tosse potts with any man, that he will fight, and brawle, sweare and . . . cutt and hack, and take a purse when opportunitie is offered. . . . no purseuvante in Ingland would ever lay handes on such a man for a recusant" (C6v).

To return to the central question at hand. At one point Verstegan facetiously suggested that Burghley's recusant-hunters might have had more success in ferreting out their prey had they focused less on mere habits of prayer, fasting, and alms (1592, C6v) and more on obvious, essential distinguishing marks. In the case of Shakespeare, what appears to some to be a fairly obvious distinguishing mark of Catholic sympathies—the Oldcastle/Falstaff depiction—seems far less so to others. Indeed, the argument could be made that Shakespeare drained away any potential religious significance by presenting Henry's rejection of his robber companions in the "common attire" of mere moral transformation. In Shakespeare's Henriad as in *Famous Victories,* the Prince's action signifies his attainment of princely virtues needed for just rule. So why should we see a papist in this rejection? Though common sense might tell us that there is nothing of Stapleton's religious emphasis here, our brief examination of Leslie and Verstegan suggests that our "common sense" reading might bear little resemblance to a reading produced by way of such a Catholic lens as theirs.

In drawing any connections between Verstegan's libel and Shakespeare's plays, we simplify our task, therefore, by acknowledging our goal to be not that of solving the case of a dramatist's true identity, but of exploring the contours of a plausible Catholic response to the plays, an exploration that would involve speculation on which aspects of these plays might be viewed as supporting Catholic interests, and at what points the support would seem to be blocked.

In looking at the play through the Bale-and-Foxe-loathing, Elizabethan-court-bashing lens of a Catholic libel, Oldcastle/Falstaff looks more like the Catholic's monstrous Protestant, of course, than merely that monstrous anti-prelatical wing of Protestantism that the bishops wanted other English Protestants to learn to hate. Indeed, because every inch of his fat, lying, partying, Bible-quoting, conscience-less, dishonorable, lecherous, thieving self matches the details about the Protestant that Verstegan and others had depicted, it is not difficult to see in the Prince's rejection a dismissal of the diseased Elizabethan Protestantism that had fragmented the country and perverted its administration of justice. In looking through these lenses, we might savor many details that might seem less noteworthy to other lens-wearers. For example, Oldcastle/Falstaff and his companions are not ordinary purse-takers, but the kind in which Protestants were seen to specialize. In targeting "pilgrims going to Canterbury with rich offerings," they show themselves being true to their Protestantism as church robbers, guilty of committing sacrilege. And speaking of being true to one's nature, Catholic viewers might also savor the moment when the monstrous Protestant lover takes to bed the diseased whore, Doll Common, a worthy rejoinder to those Protestant polemicists who featured Catholics in bed with a Romish (Babylonian) whore. As for the extent to which our privileged viewers might imagine court satire as well as Protestant satire in this portrait, we can probably be confident that any admirers of Leslie and Verstegan would take special pleasure in the tavern/innkeeper setting for the Prince's waywardness. It is just such a setting, we will recall, in which these libelers persistently anchored their attacks on innkeeper William Cecil, on whose company Elizabeth, too, unwholesomely relied. But Cecil was never really viewed in isolation by these writers. To the extent that Oldcastle/Falstaff appeared to these viewers as a full-blown Protestant portrait, he could, therefore, easily be taken as a composite of all of Elizabeth's counselors; for if it was the monstrosity of Protestantism that was their legacy to England, it was out of the monstrous image of "the Protestant" that their portrait deserved to be cast.

From a Catholic point of view such as this one, the Elizabethan problem was, however, never simply Elizabeth's Protestant counselors; it was the shaky legal grounds on which the reign was supported. And quite simply, the former problem greatly exacerbated the latter. If Catholic writers like Stapleton had once looked to the past for examples by which to warn and guide the monarch, they now looked mainly to the future, imagining the moment when Elizabeth's successor would make things right again. The problems and possibilities of the succession permeate the Prince Henry plays. A Catholic-oriented summary of what Shakespeare accomplished might begin by noting that in these plays, the two different (but closely related) problems plaguing Elizabeth's disastrous reign are handled by two different (but closely related) historical figures. In each case, contemporary parallels cannot be exact, but are close enough to be brought in line with

Catholic scenarios of the future. The first problem—the corrupt Protestant counselor—plays itself out around the matter of the Prince's rejection of Oldcastle/Falstaff. The resolution of the problem occurs by way of a transformation within the Prince himself and technically not by the death of one ruler and the transfer of power to a better one. But because the effects of this transformation were to be realized mainly in this prince's own ascension to the throne, the scenario by which many Catholics envisioned a better future (through a new monarch sympathetic to Catholic interests) might be seen to be given a powerful representation here.

The other Elizabethan problem—that of a questionable succession that had produced a much fragmented nation—has a more indirect if no less relevant representation of Catholic concerns, all centering in this case, somewhat ironically, around an old and guilt-ridden, albeit Catholic, monarch in need of penance for political and personal sins. Like Elizabeth's world as represented by Catholic detractors, the world of Shakespeare's Henry IV is diseased, unstable, and preoccupied by talk of rebellion. A not insignificant dimension of Shakespeare's handling of the problem would seem to be the sympathetic representation of the rebel's cause, especially the (Catholic) archbishop's encouragement of their actions. Because there is evidence of censorship of the archbishop's encouraging sentiments, speculation has arisen that the Elizabethan (Protestant) church hierarchy might have objected to seeing churchmen so displayed (Clare 1999, 89–90). No doubt Catholics could have come up with a different explanation, the perceived need to silence defenses of rebellion of the kind that Robert Parsons and other Catholics had produced. In Shakespeare's Henriad, the rebels come to a bad end, of course, but not without our knowing that the reasons for their rebellion went back to the monarch himself. If death in battle or on the gallows provides one way of ending rebellion, the succession provides another. Whereas the old ruler only succeeds in uniting his political enemies against him, the new King unites all of Britain—a welcome change indeed. If King Henry V's accomplishment of British unity in Shakespeare's version is not really the same version that Stapleton held up to Elizabeth when he encouraged the fostering of Christian unity, at least there is the renewed possibility that justice might again prevail in the land and thus that the reasons for rebellion might cease.

NOTES

1. Parsons, *An answere to the fifth part of [Cooke's] reportes* (1606), mentions Henry V's "reverence to the spiritual authority of the Bishop of Rome" (314).

2. See Wooding (2000, 98–99, 154–66).

3. *Ecclesia Restaurata,* "To the Reader," praises Elizabeth's "Severity" in keeping a "Constant Hand in the Course of Her Government, She held so great a Curb on the Puritan Faction, that neither Her Parliaments, nor Her Courts of Justice, were from thence forth much troubled with them, in the rest of her Reign" (Heylyn 1661).

4. On the range of Protestant efforts both to endorse the Foxean version of Wycliffe and to put distance between it and Anglicanism, see Dobbins, who persuasively argues that "to a remarkable extent Protestant thought during the sixteenth and seventeenth centuries paralleled the history of the various attacks and refutations of attacks upon this one phrase of Foxe's work" (1955, 63).

5. See Collinson, "Ecclesiastical vitriol: religious satire in the 1590s and the invention of puritanism" (1995, 155, 150–70), and Collinson, *The Religion of protestants: The Church in English Society, 1559–1625* (1982).

6. It is significant that, unlike Heylyn, Richard Bancroft avoided any mention of the Wycliffe legacy in both his famous *Sermon at St. Paul's Cross* (1588) and in *Dangerous Positions* (1593), in both of which he instead used Scotland as his point of reference, accusing contemporary Protestant trouble-makers of "English Scottizing" for having succumbed to John Knox's poisonous influence.

7. In *A Review of the Certamen Episolare* (1659), and in *Plus Ultra: or Englands Reformation* (1661), Henry Hickman focuses on the "popish" character of Heylyn's writings, with considerable emphasis on his disparagement of Wycliffe and rejection of the Foxean perspective on the English Reformation.

8. I am indebted to Donna B. Hamilton for guiding me to this material and for making available to me her extensive research on and knowledge of Catholic writings of this period.

9. See "Nicholas Bacon," *DNB,* and *Notes and Queries* (3rd series: iii, 83, 105).

10. For a relevant discussion of relationships between the Cecil/Brooke and the Essex court factions in this period, see Hammer (1995).

WORKS CITED

Bancroft, Richard. *Dangerous positions and proceedings, published and practised within this Iland of Brytaine, under pretence of Reformation, and for the Presbiteriall discipline.* London: Wolfe, 1593.

_____. *A sermon preached at Paules Cross the 9. of Februarie: being the first Sunday in the Parleament anno. 1588.* London: Gregorie Seton, 1588.

Clare, Janet. *'Art made tongue-tied by authority': Elizabethan and Jacobean Dramatic Censorship.* 2d ed. Manchester, England: Manchester University Press, 1999.

Collinson, Patrick. "Ecclesiastical vitriol: religious satire in the 1590s and the invention of puritanism." In *The Reign of Elizabeth: Court and culture in the last decade,* ed. John Guy. Cambridge, England: Cambridge University Press, 1995.

_____. *The Religion of protestants: The Church in English Society, 1559–1625.* Oxford, England: Clarendon Press, 1982.

Dobbins, Austin C. "Foxe, Wicliff, and the Church of England." *Review and Expositor* 52 (1955): 63–83.

Dutton, Richard. "Shakespeare and Lancaster." *Shakespeare Quarterly* 49 (1998): 1–21.

Foxe, John. *Acts and Monuments of these latter and perilous dayes, touching matters of the Church.* 2 vols. 1570.

Hammer, Paul. "Patronage at Court, faction and the earl of Essex." In *The reign of Elizabeth I: Court and culture in the last decade,* ed. John Guy. 65–86. Cambridge, England: Cambridge University Press, 1995.

Heylyn, Peter. *Ecclesia Restaurata; or the History of the Reformation.* 2 vols. London: 1661.

Hickman, Henry. *A Review of the* Certamen episolare *betwixt Pet. Heylin D.D. and Hen. Hickman B.D.* London: Adams, 1659.

_____. *Plus Ultra: or Englands Reformation.* London: 1661.

Leslie, John. *A Treatise of Treasons against Q. Elizabeth, and the Croune of England.* London: Fowler, 1572.

Munday, Anthony, et al. *A Critical Edition of Sir John Oldcastle.* Ed. Jonathan Rittenhouse. New York: Garland Pub., 1984.

Parsons (Persons), Robert. *An answere to the fifth part of reportes lately set forth by Syr Edward Cooke*. Saint-Omer, 1606.

———. *A conference about the next succession to the Crowne of Ingland* (1594). Menston: Scholar Press, 1972.

Poole, Kristen. "Saints Alive! Falstaff, Martin Marprelate, and the Staging of Puritanism." *Shakespeare Quarterly* 46 (1995): 47–75.

Stapleton, Thomas, trans. *Bede . . . The History of the Church of England*. Antwerp: John Laet, 1565.

Taylor, Gary. "The Fortunes of Oldcastle." *Shakespeare Survey* 38 (1985): 85–100.

Verstegan, Richard. *An aduertisement written to a secretarie of my L. Treasurers of Ingland, by an Inglishe intelligencer as he passed throughe Germanie towards Italie*. Antwerp: 1592.

Weever, John. *The Mirror of Martyrs, or The life and death of . . . Sir John Oldcastle*. London: William Wood, 1601.

Womersley, David. "Why is Falstaff Fat?" *Review of English Studies* (new series) 47 (1996): 1–22.

Wooding, Lucy E. C. *Rethinking Catholicism in Reformation England*. Oxford, England: Clarendon Press, 2000.

7

Shakespeare's Fairy Dance with Religio-Political Controversy in *The Merry Wives of Windsor*

by Regina M. Buccola

Roosevelt University, Chicago, Illinois

Fairies "much affect the papacie."

Robert Herrick, "The Fairie Temple," from *The Complete Poetry of Robert Herrick*

DESPITE SEVERAL RECENT ATTEMPTS to begin redressing the disparity,[1] fairy tradition has lost out in the critical conversation about early modern drama to the ideologies of Christianity and classical Greece and Rome. However, the fairy tradition is every bit as significant to our critical attempts to situate early modern plays in their historical contexts as the struggles associated with state-mandated religious beliefs, and the delineation of classical literary influences are widely agreed to be. Fairy beliefs were much more than rural superstitions in sixteenth- and seventeenth-century Britain. When fairies appeared in popular plays and were invoked in public debates in London and its environs, their airy bodies were made to resonate with a political and religious import that extended far beyond folklore.

Fairies were imaginative responses to the stresses of life in a rapidly changing world. The sixteenth and seventeenth centuries in Britain witnessed significant social changes, including religious reforms with immense socio-political implications, and a widening gap between urban, mercantile culture and rural, agrarian life. The powers and characteristics popularly attributed to fairies serve as a measure of early modern socio-cultural anxieties in the face of these changes.[2] Early modern writers ranging from Reginald Scot (*The Discoverie of Witchcraft*, 1584) to James I (*Daemonologie*, 1597) to Robert Burton (*The Anatomy of Melancholy*, 1621) published attacks on fairy belief, which, paradoxically, served to preserve and perpetuate the traditions. During the early modern period of religious reform, fairy belief came to be reviled as the antithesis of Christianity by Reform Christian sects, particularly Puritans. Religious reformers equated Catholic worship of the Virgin Mary, the prominence of the saints, and the lavish ceremony of the Catholic mass with the polytheistic pagan tradition and, often, with pagan-linked fairy belief.

The early modern conception of fairies figured them as utterly liminal figures. They at times acted in ways similar to pagan gods or witches and their demonic familiars, yet they were something other than gods or demons. In their status as something other than divine or demonic, fairies occupied an ambiguous spiritual zone that gave no clear sense of their moral stature or the effect that interaction with them might be likely to have on a human's spiritual account. Popular culture provided at least two distinct accounts of the origin of the fairies and their realm, which were steeped in Christian mythology. The first of these myths of origin cast a taint of darkness over both fairies and fairyland, positing that fairies were companions of the angels that fell from paradise with Satan and, therefore, subject to the torments of hell at the Last Judgment. Other theories about the nature of fairies aligned fairyland in some way with Purgatory, the Catholic-conceived intermediary zone between heaven and hell. One theory, explicitly aligned with religious conceptions of Purgatory, maintained that fairyland was a space reserved for the souls of those dead who as yet belonged neither in heaven nor hell, suspended between the poles of eternal salvation and damnation until Last Judgment. Nineteenth-century antiquarian Andrew Lang notes that people abducted into fairyland reported meeting recently deceased relatives who cautioned them not to eat the food, lest they be trapped there forever, as in "the pre-Christian Hades" (1895, xxii). Belief in Purgatory was one of the teachings that came to distinguish "popery" from Protestantism.

In *Letters on Demonology and Witchcraft* (1970), Sir Walter Scott attributes the loss of popular belief in the validity of witchcraft accusations over the course of the late seventeenth and early eighteenth centuries to a preceding loss of faith in fairy belief. He asserts that "in the time of Queen Elizabeth the unceasing labour of many and popular preachers, who declaimed against the 'splendid miracles' of the Church of Rome, produced also its natural effect upon the other stock of superstitions" (148). It is ironic that the decline of belief in fairies is traceable to the period of the very monarch so intimately associated with them. But what is most significant about Scott's observation is the fact that, over the course of the Reformation, fairy lore was conflated with Catholicism, and Protestants of various stripes wrote off both belief systems as vain, pagan superstitions. This is also the period in which Shakespeare achieved popular and royal acclaim on the London stage.

Scott had numerous early modern authorities to draw upon in linking Catholicism's fall from grace in Britain to the loss of fairy faith. In his *Daemonologie,* James I dismissively compares the fairy capacity to "contract a solide bodie within so little roome" to the Catholic belief in transubstantion: "I thinke it is so contrarie to the qualitie of a naturall bodie, and so like to the little transubstantiat god in the *Papistes Masse,* that I can neuer beleeue it" (1969, 40). Such conflation of fairy belief with Catholic doctrine became a Reform Protestant strategy for attacking rural superstition and Catholicism, both of which were perceived as ideological threats to the primacy of Protestantism.

John Webster similarly dismisses fairy belief, explicitly linking fairies to Catholicism. He writes: "In a few ages past when Popish ignorance did abound, there was no discourse more common (which yet is continued amongst the vulgar people) than of the apparition of certain Creatures which they called Fayries, that were of very little stature, and being seen would soon vanish and disappear" (1677, 283). In several important witchcraft trials of the sixteenth and seventeenth centuries,[3] fairies are mentioned in conjunction with priests, bishops, saints, the Virgin Mary, or "popery" outright. Protestants distanced themselves from all of these aspects of Catholicism in the process of distinguishing their religion from the tradition against which they had rebelled. Once they had been linked to the trappings of Catholicism, it became necessary to reject fairies and the lore associated with them, too.

SHAKESPEARE, FAIRIES, AND RELIGIOUS CONTROVERSY

A profound silence shrouds William Shakespeare's religious sympathies. He was both friend and rival to the erstwhile Catholic Ben

Jonson,[4] and circumstantial evidence exists linking his father, John Shakespeare, to the recusant Catholic community (Greenblatt 1997, 43). As with most aspects of his personal life, however, the question of whether or not Shakespeare himself shared such sympathies remains a mystery. Like many of the playwrights with whom he lived and worked, Shakespeare typically took pains to avoid raising religious issues in anything like a definitive way in his scripts. This circumspection extends to his treatment of fairy lore and its religious implications in the period as well, with one notable exception. Although *The Merry Wives of Windsor* is often regarded as lightweight fare when set off against the Henry IV tetralogy that supplies some of its characters, the comedy contains some rather weighty references to contemporary religious controversy.[5]

The majority of Shakespeare's plays that invoke fairy lore and/or fairy characters skirt the implications of the relationship fairy beliefs came to bear to the political and religious debates surrounding Reform Christianity in the sixteenth and seventeenth centuries. *The Tempest* and *Romeo and Juliet* are both either set in or linked to Italy, the seat of the Catholicism with which fairy lore came increasingly to be linked over the course of the Reformation. The Italian settings invoked in these plays mitigate the potential religious import of the fairy figures who appear in them, since the presumptive Catholicism of the plays' Italian characters can account for any nascent "popery" that might appear in the text.

The Tempest, for example, oscillates in its superabundant exposition between two politically and religiously significant locales:

1. an obscure island inhabited by the orphaned son of a devil and a witch—along with a sylph[6]—lorded over by a deposed, shipwrecked Italian magus; and

2. the corrupted duchy of Milan from whence Prospero was exiled after his studies, including magic, diverted him from his rule.

For early modern theologians—including the monarch for whom this play was likely written, James I—there was nothing to choose between them. Devil was to sylph as Catholicism was to black magic. The radical otherness of these locales and characters served as a convenient smokescreen for any subversive religio-political ideas that might emerge from a play in which the hero, Prospero, proves less human(e) than his servant-sprite, Ariel, who is compelled to chastise his master into morality. Prospero learns Christian pity and forgiveness from the sylph, who tells him that he knows his heart would melt at the sight of his enemies in the throes of exquisite psychological torture on the grounds that "Mine would, sir, were I human" (5.1.20). The credulity-straining romance plot involving a band of Italians stranded on an unidentified island somewhere between the African continent and Italy sufficiently detaches it from the Protestant confines of the British Isles to alleviate any pressure the playwright might otherwise have faced for the implications of such scenarios. Given the dubious distinctions drawn between demons and fairies on the one hand, and pagan superstitions associated with fairies and the ritual excesses of Catholicism on the other, a Prospero who must learn forgiveness from an air spirit might otherwise have raised questions about the playwright's religious sensibilities.

In *A Midsummer Night's Dream* and *Cymbeline,* on the other hand, Shakespeare dodges the religious controversies encoded in the plays' fairy lore foundations by explicitly setting them in pre-Christian Athens and Britain, respectively. In *A Midsummer Night's Dream,* Hermia is threatened with a choice between entering the sisterhood or being executed, before she is saved from either fate by a proactively sought-out sojourn in the fairy wood. There is a decidedly Catholic savor, that sounds remarkably like the Catholic sisterhood, to Theseus's menacing order that the intractable Hermia adopt a life of chastity if she continues to defy her father's wish that she marry Demetrius. He cautions her to consider well:

> Whether, if you yield not to your father's choice,
> You can endure the livery of a nun,
> For aye in shady cloister mewed,
> To live a barren sister all your life,
> Chanting hymns to the cold fruitless moon.
>
> (1.1.69–73)

Pagan goddesses had devotees who lived out their lives in worship just as priests, monks, and nuns did in the Christian tradition. However, the terminology that Theseus uses has pointed Catholic reference.

Theseus says that Hermia will be held hostage in a "cloister" as a "barren sister." The earliest cloisters date from medieval times, and the female attendants of pagan shrines are referred to as votaresses or priestesses, but not typically addressed as "sister." In keeping with the play's pre-Christian setting, the "hymns" that Hermia will spend her time chanting will be to the moon and not a Catholic saint, but the terminological links to Roman Catholicism here are still strong. Significantly, although Catholic doctrine is glanced at, it appears as a threat: "Either to die the death or to abjure / Forever the society of men" (1.1.65–66). Living as a "barren sister" is presented as at least equal to immediate death. This scene, therefore, offers no particular indication of Shakespeare's religious biases, but does encapsulate some key doctrinal distinctions at issue during the Reformation. The Catholic resonances in the play hardly end here, however, since Hermia's own boldness and daring as it is seconded by the fairies will save her from the barren sisterhood.[7] Were anyone to take issue with the play's mischievous dance with Catholicism, the ready response available is anachronism. *A Midsummer Night's Dream* is ostensibly set in pre-Christian Athens, and the play was staged in Reform Christian Britain, where convents and monasteries had been largely shut down.[8]

There are no fairy characters in *Cymbeline,* but fairies are referenced at pivotal moments in the experience of some of the play's central characters, including Imogen, Belarius, Guiderius, and Posthumus. The play is triangulated by references to fairies at key plot points that also involve various levels of social role pretense: the Italian Iachimo's midnight invasion of Imogen's chamber and person, the initial meeting between Imogen and her brothers in the wilds of Wales, and the pagan burial of Imogen in the tomb with Cloten's corpse. In the first of these textual moments, the evil Iachimo waits, having secreted himself in a trunk stowed in Imogen's room, while she reads in bed. When Imogen asks the time just before going to sleep, her maid tells her it is "Almost midnight, madam" (2.2.2)—the fairy time, the witching hour. When she puts the book aside, Imogen prays:

> To your protection I commend me, gods.
> From *fairies* and the tempters of the night
> Guard me, beseech ye
>
> (my italics 2.2.8–10)

Immediately thereafter, Iachimo emerges to gather furtively the evidence he needs to convince Imogen's banished husband, Posthumus, that she has been unfaithful. During this fact-finding mission, he discovers that she has, significantly, gone to bed reading the tale of Tereus' rape of Philomel.

Once she realizes that her husband considers her an adulterer and wants her dead, Imogen flees the court in search of him. She happens upon her long-lost brothers in Wales, where she lives disguised as a boy until, Sleeping Beauty fashion, she is accidentally drugged into a deathlike stupor. During a pagan celebration of fairy-inflected last rites, her eldest brother issues the peculiar benediction: "With female fairies will his tomb be haunted" (4.2.219), before accompanying her other brother in an antiphonal elegy that consigns her body to no other fate than turning to dust.

Finally, Imogen's estranged husband, Posthumus, is treated to a dream vision of all of his dead family members and the god Jupiter, who promises that he will be restored to his wife and prestige in the British court. Walking ghosts, as discussed in the introduction of this essay, were associated with Purgatory and/or fairyland by early modern Britons. They need not have made this connection on their own, however, since Posthumus awakes from his dream and asks in amazement: "What fairies haunt this ground?" (5.4.133).

With its emphasis on disguise, deception, and role-playing, *Cymbeline* explores the ways in which both class and gender roles are artificial, and thereby ideologically intersects with the early modern fray over the artifice of the theater. The antitheatricalists used Reform Christian doctrine as ammunition in their assaults on the blasphemous excesses of the stage, which were perceived as threats to national stability on all fronts: political, religious, and social. Fairies were implicated in the moralistic debate over the ethics of performance since they were renowned for their abilities to impersonate anything they chose, animate or not. Yet, the theatricality of fairies was the least of the religious reformers' concerns about continued belief in them. They were far more uneasy about the potential challenge fairy belief posed to the primacy of the Christian tradition. Many reformers perceived continued devotion to fairies and their erratic conduct as a threat to the propagation of Protestantism in all of its own varied permutations.[9] Shakespeare dodged the religious implications of *Cymbeline*'s fairy elements by virtue of the play's setting in a pre-Christian and, therefore, forgivably pagan world. Indeed, paganism is explicitly invoked in each of the scenes in which fairies are referenced: the mythological Philomel, a burial rite void of the possibility of resurrection, and the god Jupiter. Were this the extent of the Shakespeare fairy corpus, there would be a limited foundation on which to build theories of fairy-inflected religious subversion. There is, however, one more play in this ethereal body of work.

"Trib, Trib, Fairies. Come and Remember Your Parts"

Unique among the Shakespearean plays that involve fairies is *The Merry Wives of Windsor*.[10] Unlike his other fairy plays, *Merry Wives* is set in an England that—despite the interpolation of characters such as Falstaff from the Henriad—seems noticeably Elizabethan.[11] The title locale sets the play's events in the Protestant Queen's own backyard, and the faux fairies conjured by the clever Windsor wives open their ceremonies by praising Queen and court. Finally, this play features a cleric, Parson Hugh Evans, who takes an inordinate interest in the fairy antics that the Windsor community gets up to in seeking vengeance upon the lecherous fat knight, Falstaff.

At the play's opening, Falstaff, ever in need of funds to fuel his sack-and-sherris habit, has hit upon the idea of pursuing a superficial sexual intrigue with either Mistress Page or Mistress Ford (or both), with the real purpose of getting at their husbands' money. Mistress Ford's husband, already suspicious of her every move, becomes mani-acally jealous when he discovers the knight's intentions. After putting the entire town into an uproar under the suspicion that his wife is a whore, Ford realizes the error of his ways and contritely agrees to par-ticipate in a fairy play within the play,[12] staged by the wives with the intent of publicly punishing Falstaff and mending Mistress Ford's domestic coils with her jealous spouse.

The final act depicts the wives' planning and execution of this fairy play in which Falstaff is publicly humiliated at the hands of Windsor's "fairies"; the Pages' daughter, Anne, elopes under cover of a fairy dis-guise; and Ford's jealousy, Falstaff's lechery, and Anne's insurgency are communally addressed by Windsorites still costumed as fairies. The Fords reconcile at home, but the public celebration of this recon-ciliation occurs in the fairy realm; the plan adopted is, moreover, the imaginative creation of the Mistresses Page and Ford. As Diane Purkiss notes, "It is this female power to invent and stage supernatu-ral stories which constitutes their principal weapon against their importunate suitors and suspicious husbands" (1996, 195). Fairy lore offered early modern women supernatural alibis for everything from extended absences from home and husband (that is, tales of fairy abduction of people believed to be dead until their abrupt, unexpected return) to mistreatment of children (that is, the cruel "tests" to confirm the presence of a changeling). Making the most of local superstition, the Windsor wives elude inappropriate sexual advances and clear themselves of accusations of sexual impropriety via fairy subterfuge. As in *A Midsummer Night's Dream,* the fairy space in which the wives' ultimate triumph unfolds is a liminal zone: a wood on the margins of the Windsor community, delineating the space between ruler and ruled.

The fairy elements invoked in *Merry Wives* are the product of theatrical inventiveness on the part of the Windsor wives. The Windsor parson, Sir Hugh Evans, opens the scene that includes the formulation of the fairy plot with the approving observation, "'Tis one of the best discretions of a 'oman as / ever I did look upon" (4.4.1–2). Evans offers his enthusiastic support of the wives' plan and links himself—as they do in dreaming the plan up—to the fairies, promising:

> I will teach the children their behaviors, and I
> will be like a jackanapes also, to burn the knight with
> my taber

$$(4.4.66–68)$$

In an era in a country in which religion was dictated by the state, it is significant that the Windsor Parson supports the wives' fairy plan to punish an overbearing lecher and an overjealous husband as no less a participant than the ringleader of the fake fairy band.

John Penry, a Welsh Anglican educated at Oxford and Cambridge, fought hard in the late sixteenth-century British Parliament to persuade the Queen and her councilors to look to the religious education of Wales. In his view, the Welsh clergy were so poorly schooled in official Protestant doctrine that they were risking the salvation of all of their parishioners. In particular, Penry took umbrage at the persistent loyalty of the Welsh clergy to beliefs both pagan and Catholic, construed as pagan because they could be linked to Catholicism. The "astonishing reuerence of the fairies" that such irresponsible pseudo-divines had reputedly lodged "into the harts of our silly people" came under Penry's particular censure (Penry 1960, 32–33).[13] Central among the "silly people" Penry figures as susceptible to and prime advocates of fairy belief are women. Thus, the Welsh Hugh Evans, sporting on the green with the women and children of Windsor, teaching them the ways of the ephemeral fairies, cut a figure with powerful religio-political resonance by the time *Merry Wives* was written and performed (probably not later than 1601).[14]

Penry appealed repeatedly to Queen Elizabeth I and her Parliament to intervene into the spiritual health of Wales, which was his homeland. An Oxbridge man, Penry feared for the heretical ignorance of his countrymen, marked by a persistent superstition perpetuated particularly by women starved of the saving grace of scripture because they spoke Welsh and did not understand the English *Book of Common Prayer.* On February 28, 1587, Edward Dunn Lee and Job Throckmorton presented a petition of Penry's to Parliament begging that the gospel be openly preached in Wales in the vernacular, and that lay theologians be permitted to lead worship, since the English bishops in Wales were so hopelessly corrupt. Lee and Throckmorton got into deep trouble for their pains. They, along with Penry, were ultimately accused in the Martin Marprelate controversy, and Lee was removed from his parliamentary commission for presenting the petition (Penry 1960, xiv–xv). Penry fared far worse: he was executed.

I am going to quote a lengthy passage from Penry's work that demonstrates the sixteenth-century perception of the connection between fairy belief (and its promulgation) and women—in particular, women who assert authority in a self-evidently unruly manner—and between fairy belief and persistent Catholicism (or outright ungodliness). The full title of the treatise in question is *A treatise containing the aeqvity of an hvmble svpplication which is to be exhibited vnto hir Gracious Maiesty and this high Court of Parliament in the behalfe of the Countrey of Wales, that some order may be taken for the preaching of the Gospell among those people* (1587). In the midst of a passionate passage devoted to his observation that there are no truly godly men in Wales except for those who have had the great good fortune to encounter Anglican doctrine in England, or through their own private religious studies, Penry attacks the abundant superstition in Wales. He writes:

> The rest of our people are either such as neuer think of anie religion true or false, plainely meere Atheists or stark blinded with superstition. The later are of 2 sorts. The first crue is obstinate idolaters that would fain be

again in execrable Rome, & so hold for good diuinity whatsoeuer hath bin hatched in that sacrilegious nest. But these may doe what they wil with vs: for nether ciuil magistrat nor Bishop wil controul them ... Hence flow our swarmes of southsaiers, and enchanters, such as will not stick openly, to professe that they walke, on Tuesdaies, and Thursdaies at nights, with the fairies, of whom they brag themselues to haue their knowledge. These sonnes of Belial, who shuld die the death, Leuit. 20.6. haue stroken such an astonishing reuerence of the fairies, into the harts of our silly people, that they dare not name them, without honor. We cal them *bendith û mamme,* that is, such as haue deserued their mothers blessing. Now our people, wil neuer vtter, *bendith û mamme,* but they wil saie, *bendith û mamme û dhûn,* that is, their mothers blessing (which they account the greatest felicity that any creature can be capable of) light vpon them, as though they were not to be named without reuerence. Hence proceed open defending of Purgatory & the Real presence, praying vnto images &c. with other infinit monsters. (1960, 32–33)

Protestantism cannot take root in a Welsh soil polluted with superstitious belief in the fairies. This superstitious belief persists because "silly people" refuse to replace the maternal blessing associated with fairy beliefs with the patriarchal benedictions privileged in Christian doctrine. Instead, they continue to credit feminine blessings suggestive of Catholic worship of the Virgin Mary, or the image worship associated by Reform Christians with prayers, to the likewise Catholic saints or, worse still, pagan idols. Mother's blessings and Catholic dogma such as belief in transubstantiation should be of little import to good Protestants.

One of the ways in which Reform Christians attacked Catholicism in early modern England was to feminize it. Protestants did away with the Catholic significance attached to Mary, the saints (many of whom were women), the religious sisterhood, and scoffed at the elaborate ostentation of the Catholic mass (with its emphasis on ritual ornamentation and display). In relegating all of these female figures or elements such as costuming and "decoration," which were negatively linked to women in the culture at large, to Catholicism, Reform Christians in effect feminized the entire religion. The connection forged between fairy belief and Catholicism simply reinforced this trend, as fairies were associated with women, their domestic work, and stereotyped images of their physique and moral vicissitudes.

A number of elements converge by the last act of *Merry Wives* to feminize Hugh Evans. He is the only adult male who participates in the actual fairy subterfuge that brings about the play's comic resolution. While everyone is amenable to the wives' fairy plot, he takes a particularly active role in it, and is therefore closely aligned with them by the final scene. Like the wrongfully abused Mistress Ford, Evans is paid little heed by the central male characters in the play, who identify him as an outsider by virtue of his Welsh origins, and poke malicious fun at his inability to handle that phallic token of masculine bravery, a sword.[15] However, something odd happens at the conclusion of the play. Evans's fairy antics breed no ill will toward him. In fact, his success as the leader of the cast of fairy actors serves to incorporate him into the Windsor community with a level of acceptance that he has failed to attain in the performance of his role as a religious leader.

Juliette Wood observes that, "Englishmen and Scots who lived in Wales were thought to be fairies" (1992, 62). Given the emphasis placed on Evans's Welsh nationality throughout the play and his subsequent role as the leader of a band of child actors impersonating fairies, one might be moved to wonder if this assumption did not also work in the opposite direction: were Welshmen living in England thought to be fairies? Evans's marginal status within the Windsor community is underscored throughout the play by Shakespeare's decision to write his lines in an approximation of Welsh dialect that aims at every opportunity for crude puns. It seems likely that the popular belief in foreigners as fairies stemmed from their differences—in language, in diet, in dress—from those of the community into which they had migrated. Differences in speech, food, and physical appearance served as fairy identifiers[16]—a fact evinced by the costumes the wives plan for their fairy band and by Falstaff's response to his fairy tormentors.

Surrounded by Sir Hugh and his band of child-fairies, Falstaff combines his perception of the outsider status of Welsh and fairy and locates the respective bases of these positions in linguistic and dietary differences. Falstaff's initial response to the army of faux fairies that sets upon him in the Windsor woods focuses on the power granted fairy language: "He that speaks to them shall die" (5.5.46). He then combines his detection of Evans's Welsh accent through the parson's fairy disguise with his fear of the metamorphic capabilities of fairies and popular ethnic slurs about the Welsh love of cheese: "Heavens defend me from that Welsh fairy, / lest he transform me to a piece of cheese!" (5.5.81–82). In fairy disguise or in his parson's weeds, Evans is ever the outsider to the male world of Windsor. In his alignment with the wives of Windsor, however, Evans finally gets the upper hand of the jeering Falstaff in a way that he never has at any other point in the play. Explicitly linking the fairies with the moral highroad, Evans confronts Falstaff once the fairy deception has been revealed: "Sir John Falstaff, serve Got, and leave your desires, and fairies will not pinse you" (5.5.128–29).[17] Falstaff replies, "You have the start of me. I am dejected. I am not able to answer the Welsh flannel" (5.5.159–62). This is the first time in the play that Falstaff is not able to "answer" Evans.[18]

According to Jeanne Addison Roberts, there is some evidence suggesting that *The Merry Wives of Windsor* is a Halloween play. Halloween, the pagan holiday that immediately precedes the Christian celebration of All Saint's Day, marks the transition from autumn to winter and, in early modern England, was believed to be "a night on which witches, fairies, and hobgoblins were thought to roam freely . . . Having had their fling, the goblins and elves [we]re prepared to be saints on the morrow" (1975, 108–9). Though acceptance of *Merry Wives* as a Halloween play is not necessary to the points I wish to make about it, an October 31 date for the play would add another element to the play's theological ambiguities. Since the wives stage their fairy playlet to purge themselves, their families, and all of Windsor of Falstaff's licentious and corrupt influence, it would be significant to stage this purgation process at midnight on October 31, the threshold between mischievous license and saintly conduct. Such a date for the play's action also adds additional resonance to Parson Evans's prominent role as leader of the fairies and their punishments, since it temporarily casts the community's ostensibly Christian, spiritual leader as the head of a band of rambunctious spirits unleashed in a woodland pagan space. Chaos reigns in fairyland all year long, but fairy chaos invades the mortal realm in a pervasive way at only a few points in the year, and All Hallow's Eve is one of these times.

Shakespeare potentially invokes a triple-headed hydra of religious controversies in depicting a Welsh parson as the stage manager of a troop of child-actor fairies. Wales, the theater, and fairyland were three locales that had proved resistant to conquest by Reform Christianity at the time of his writing. Shakespeare scholars have devoted a great deal of attention in recent years to the spectacle likely created by cross-dressed heroines (re)united with their male lovers on the stage while still dressed as boys. In *The Merry Wives of Windsor*, Shakespeare offers the equally odd spectacle of a religious leader hailing from the seat of suspect Protestantism, Wales, dressed as a fairy and dispensing theological wisdom that links adherence to God to avoidance of fairy punishment. This would have been a holy horror to a theologian of Penry's ilk. The public nature of the Martin Marprelate controversy and the subsequent convictions rendered equally widespread Penry's concerns about the theological integrity of Welsh parsons and the threat posed to the success of religious reform in Wales by persistent belief in fairies. This final scene likely had an effect on Shakespeare's audience that is lost on scholars today who choose to join Theseus's party and dismiss the fairies as "airy nothing" (5.1.16).

Staging in Hugh Evans an explicit example of Penry's fears would have been, at best, a dangerous enterprise for Shakespeare since Penry himself was executed for the blasphemy and sedition, which were seen to inhere in his charges of Anglican theological infirmity in Wales and his recommended treatments for it. It is more likely that Shakespeare is spoofing Penry's concerns in the figure of Evans, who dispenses more theatrical direction and fairy lore than he does Christian doctrine over the course of the play. As with his ambiguous references to the sisterhood in *A Midsummer Night's Dream*, Shakespeare leaves a loophole for himself should any government censors have questioned his portrayal of Hugh Evans by keeping open the possibility that the parson inhabits fifteenth-century Catholic Windsor and not late sixteenth-century Protestant Windsor. Theatergoers initially met Falstaff as a companion of the heir to King Henry IV's crown—in other words, under a monarchy still loyal to the Roman Church. His presence in this play, ambiguously placed in a fictive Windsor, offers the possibility that the play looks back to a time when Catholicism was the custom of the country. Given the Elizabethan topicality of much else in the play, however, this would have been a tenuous explanation at best.

Perhaps the ultimate pardon for any religious indiscretions that might have been perceived in this play lies in the link forged between Windsor's fairy queen and the reigning "fairy queen" at the time, Elizabeth I. Suggesting the Spenserian connection between Elizabeth, Queen of England, and Gloriana, Queen of Faery, the fairy queen whom the wives conjure is intimately interested in Windsor Castle and its welfare, a concern which leads her to purge her court of Falstaff's lechery just as the wives have sought to drive it from their community. Mistress Quickly's speech as the fairy monarch directs her spritely minions:

> About, about!
> Search Windsor Castle, elves, within and out.
> Strew good luck, aufs, on every sacred room,
> That it may stand till the perpetual doom
> In state as wholesome as in state 'tis fit,
> Worthy the owner and the owner it.
>
> (5.5.54–59)[19]

When the marshall of her fairy troops, Evans, announces, "I smell a man of middle-earth" (5.5.80), Quickly instructs them to perform a chastity test on Falstaff by touching a taper to his finger end (5.5.84–87). He fails, of course, and the fairy queen orders her band to pinch him.

The cultural association of Queen Elizabeth with the fairy queen, combined with this fairy queen's keen interest in Windsor Castle, implicitly invoke Elizabeth's "benediction" on the plays' action. Lest there be any doubt about what has transpired, "Our radiant Queen" who "hates sluts and sluttery" (5.5.45) appears to sanction it. The invocation of Elizabeth's own fairy alter ego, crafted in the poetry of Edmund Spenser, mitigates the potential subversiveness of a Welsh parson who takes on the task of teaching a band of child actors to play the part of fairies. If, in fact, Evans is a parodic portrait of the pagan hybrid of Protestantism that Penry so feared in Wales, it makes sense to invoke Elizabeth for the play's fairy dénouement, since it was her administration that executed Penry for impudently presuming to tell her how to practice religious governance in Wales.[20] Sir Hugh Evans does double duty as both a parody of what Penry feared for Wales and a means of lampooning actual clerical shortcomings. Through this complex though comic character, Shakespeare grapples more directly in *Merry Wives* than in his other fairy plays with the religious debates of the day, which relied on fairy lore to make points about sectarian reform. Like the fairies themselves, best seen between one eyeblink and the next, Shakespeare's religious and political ideologies emerge only in glimpses.

Notes

1. The most notable efforts have been in the area of Victorian literature, including Silver (1999) and Auerbach and Knoepfl-Macher (1992). For a full history of fairies in British literature and culture, see Purkiss, *At the Bottom of the Garden* (2000).

2. Silver makes a similar point, but grounds it specifically in the rapid industrialization of the Victorian era (1999, 57). Focusing on the way in which fairy poetry served as a monitor of seventeenth-century socioeconomic development, Swann contends: "Rather than mindless frivolity, the miniaturized fairies of Jacobean and Caroline literature bespeak writers' unsettled perspective on their rapidly changing society, and on their artistic role within that society" (2000, 470).

3. These cases include: The Examination of John Walsh before Maister Thomas Williams, Commissary to the Reverend father in God William bishop of Exeter, upon certayne Interrogatories touchyng Wytchcrafte and Sorcerye, in the presence of divers gentlemen and others (London: John Awdely, 1566), available on microfilm and reprinted in Rosen (1969, 64–71); the case of Bessie Dunlop in Pitcairn (1833, 1:2, 49–58); and the case of Alesoun Peirsoun in Pitcairn (1:3.161–65).

4. Jonson became "a professed Catholic" in 1599 or 1600, according to Herford and Simpson (1925, 104).

5. Poole, for example, argues that Falstaff's bombastic biblical rhetoric in the first two parts of the Henriad parodies late sixteenth-century Lollardy. However, Poole finds the Falstaff of *Merry Wives* "emptied of his religious associations" (2000, 201 n. 73). As the ensuing argument will make clear, I think that Shakespeare has simply redirected the religious commentary in *Merry Wives,* relying on the characterization of the Welsh parson, Sir Hugh Evans, to satirize Elizabethan religio-political conflicts.

6. A sylph is a kind of fairy—specifically, an air spirit.

7. Sagar refers specifically to the punishment that Theseus offers Hermia for refusing to marry Demetrius as "to become a nun" (1995, 38). He contends that this barren, unappealing form of spirituality is set off against the vibrant fertility of the play's other sort of spirits, the fairies, who oversee the play's marriages (39).

8. Henry VIII ordered the dissolution of the monasteries (including convents) in 1536 and 1539 (Crawford 1993, 22).

9. Such reformers included King James I and John Penry, whose views are discussed more fully elsewhere in this chapter.

10. All quotations are from Shakespeare, *The Merry Wives of Windsor,* in *The Complete Works of Shakespeare,* ed. Bevington (1992). The heading is from 5.4.1.

11. Neely identifies *Merry Wives* as "the only play set in contemporary England and the only comedy that deals with the middle class and in which wives are protagonists" (1989, 217). For his part, Carroll considers *The Merry Wives of Windsor* a continuation of William Shakespeare's "comic exploration of marriage, monsters, and metamorphosis" in plays such as *A Midsummer Night's Dream* rather than of the Henriad (1985, 141).

12. Carroll makes much the same point, noting: "The merry wives are the most accomplished tricksters. In conducting their deceptions, they three times resort to play-acting and theatrical imagery so openly that their performances may fairly be termed plays-within-the-play" (1977, 206).

13. This passage is quoted in full in the following section.

14. Although *Merry Wives* was likely written at least a decade after the Martin Marprelate controversy, Poole notes that the legacy of the furious religious debate "continued to thrive long after the silencing of the tracts and sensational stage manfestations" as the figure of Martin himself "remained a vivid cultural figure for the next fifty years" (2000, 32).

15. In 2.3 and 3.1 of the play, the Host of the Garter Inn deceives both the Welsh Evans and his counterpart in marginality, the French physician, Dr. Caius, by setting them up to a duel that each thinks is being held in a different location.

16. Fairies are usually imagined to wear the sort of attire in which Mistress Page costumes her fairy cast—clothing of red, white, or green (Bovet 1684, 208). Fairy food was believed to trap anyone who ate it forever in fairyland. If any human who had been living in fairyland chanced to return to the mortal realm, they often languished and died because human food could no longer nourish them. By contrast, humans offered fairy food outside of the fairy community were often granted near-miraculous abilities to sustain life without nourishment. Fairy language was frequently construed to be incomprehensible to humans unless the fairies chose to make it so. For all of these beliefs, see the general discussions of fairy lore in Keightley (1968), Briggs (1959), Narváez (1991), and Latham (1972).

17. Though Evans links the fairies with the moral and the godly, Roberts makes a rather compelling case that Sir Hugh, the "coach" for the young fairy actors, appears sporting horns of ambiguous import in the final fairy scene:

Hugh Evans, the Welsh priest, presides over Falstaff's humiliation, and the indications are strong that the man who sets out to "dis-horn the spirit" is himself wearing horns. He has said originally that he will come "like a Jacke-an-Apes" (4.4.67[2193]), but the stage direction of Q says that he enters "as a Satyr." Mistress Ford refers to the "Welch-Devill Hugh" (5.3.12[2459]) . . . Gently but surely Shakespeare is reminding us once again of the infinite ambiguity of human behavior. (1979, 116–17)

Regardless of whether Evans's horns savor of the demonic or not, Roberts's reference to the ambiguity of human behavior here is instructive—especially since, in this play, the ambiguity of human behavior is rendered most visible when the humans disguise and conduct themselves as those paragons of ambiguity, fairies.

18. But see Rees's "Shakespeare's Welshmen," where she contends that, though Evans is ultimately absorbed into his community, it is "without honour, dignity, or even language, save for a ridiculous version of the tongue of his masters" (1991, 38).

19. These direct references to Windsor Castle do not appear in the quarto text (Roberts 1979, 10).

20. For clear examples of Elizabeth's intense and public displeasure with the Martin Marprelate tracts, see Poole (2000, 31).

WORKS CITED

Auerbach, Nina, and U. C. Knoepfl-Macher, eds. *Forbidden Journeys: Fairy Tales and Fantasies by Victorian Women Writers*. Chicago, Ill.: University of Chicago Press, 1992.

Bevington, David, ed. *The Complete Works of Shakespeare*. 4th ed. New York: Harper Collins Publishers, 1992.

Bovet, Richard. *Pandaemonium, or the Devil's Cloyster, being a further blow to modern Sadduceism, proving the existence of witches and spirits*. London: Thomas Malthus, 1684.

Briggs, Katharine. *The Anatomy of Puck: An Examination of Fairy Beliefs Among Shakespeare's Contemporaries and Successors*. London: Routledge, 1959.

_____. *Fairies in Tradition and Literature*. London: Routledge and Kegan Paul, 1967.

Burton, Robert. *The Anatomy of Melancholy* (1621). Ed. Floyd Dell and Paul Jordan-Smith. New York: Tudor Publishing Company, 1941.

Carroll, William C. *The Metamorphoses of Shakespearean Comedy.* Princeton, N.J.: Princeton University Press, 1985.

————. "'A Received Belief': Imagination in *The Merry Wives of Windsor.*" *Studies in Philology* 74 (1977): 186–215.

Crawford, Patricia. *Women and Religion in England, 1500–1720.* New York: Routledge, 1993.

Greenblatt, Stephen. "Shakespeare's Family." General Introduction. 42–43. *The Norton Shakespeare.* New York: W. W. Norton & Co., 1997.

Herford, C. H., and Percy Simpson, eds. *Ben Jonson.* 2 vols. New York: Oxford University Press, 1925.

Herrick, Robert. *The Complete Poetry of Robert Herrick.* The Stuart Editions. Ed. J. Max Patrick. New York: New York University Press, 1963.

James I. *Daemonologie* (1597). The English Experience: Its Record in Early Printed Books Published in Facsimile. No. 94. New York: Da Capo Press, Theatrum Orbis Terrarum Ltd., 1969.

Keightley, Thomas. *The Fairy Mythology: Illustrative of the Romance and Superstition of Various Countries.* New York: Haskell House Publishers, 1968.

Lang, Andrew. *My Own Fairy Book.* London: Simpkin, Marshall, Hamilton, Kent & Company Ltd., 1895.

Latham, Minor White. *The Elizabethan Fairies: The Fairies of Folklore and the Fairies of Shakespeare.* New York: Octagon Books, 1972.

Narváez, Peter, ed. *The Good People: New Fairylore Essays.* New York: Garland Press, 1991.

Neely, Carol Thomas. "Constructing Female Sexuality in the Renaissance: Stratford, London, Windsor, Vienna." In *Feminism and Psychoanalysis,* ed. Richard Feldstein and Judith Roof. 209–29. Ithaca, N.Y.: Cornell University Press, 1989.

Penry, John. *A Treatise Concerning the Aequity of an Humble Supplication.* In *Three Treatises Concerning Wales,* ed. David Williams. 1–45. Cardiff, Wales: University of Wales Press, 1960.

Pitcairn, R. *Ancient Criminal Trials in Scotland.* 3 vols. Edinburgh: 1833.

Poole, Kristen. *Radical Religion from Shakespeare to Milton: Figures of Nonconformity in Early Modern England.* New York: Cambridge University Press, 2000.

Purkiss, Diane. *At the Bottom of the Garden: A Dark History of Fairies, Hobgoblins, and Other Troublesome Things.* New York: New York University Press, 2000.

_____. *The Witch in History: Early Modern and Twentieth-Century Representations.* New York: Routledge, 1996.

Rees, Joan. "Shakespeare's Welshmen." In *Literature and Nationalism,* ed. Vincent Newey and Ann Thompson. Liverpool, England: Liverpool University Press, 1991.

Roberts, Jeanne Addison. "'The Merry Wives of Windsor' as a Hallowe'en Play." *Shakespeare Survey* 25 (1975): 107–12.

_____. *Shakespeare's English Comedy:* The Merry Wives of Windsor *in Context.* Lincoln: University of Nebraska Press, 1979.

Rosen, Barbara. *Witchcraft in England, 1558–1618.* Amherst, Mass.: University of Massachusetts Press, 1969.

Sagar, Keith. "*A Midsummer Night's Dream:* A Marriage of Heaven and Hell." *Critical Survey* 7.1 (1995): 34–43.

Scot, Reginald. *The Discoverie of Witchcraft* (1584). Ed. Brinsley Nicolson. London: Elliot Stock, 1886.

Scott, Sir Walter. *Letters on Demonology and Witchcraft.* 2d ed. New York: The Citadel Press, 1970.

Shakespeare, William. *Cymbeline.* In *The Complete Works of Shakespeare,* ed. David Bevington, 1434–83.

_____. *Cymbeline.* In *The Arden Edition of the Works of William Shakespeare,* ed. J. M. Nosworthy. London: Methuen and Co., Ltd., 1955.

_____. *The Merry Wives of Windsor.* In *The Complete Works of Shakespeare,* ed. David Bevington, 252–87.

_____. *The Merry Wives of Windsor.* Ed. G. R. Hibbard. New York: Penguin Books, 1973.

_____. *The Merry Wives of Windsor 1602.* Shakespeare Quarto Facsimiles no.3. Ed. W. W. Greg. London: The Shakespeare Association and Sidgwick and Jackson, Limited, 1939.

_____. *A Midsummer Night's Dream.* In *The Complete Works of Shakespeare,* ed. David Bevington, 150–77.

_____. *The Tempest.* In *The Complete Works of Shakespeare,* ed. David Bevington, 1526–58.

Silver, Carole G. *Strange and Secret Peoples: Fairies and Victorian Consciousness.* New York: Oxford University Press, 1999.

Swann, Marjorie. "The Politics of Fairylore in Early Modern English Literature." *Renaissance Quarterly* 2 (Summer 2000): 449–73.

Webster, John. *The Displaying of Supposed Witchcraft.* London: J.M., 1677.

Wood, Juliette. "Fairy Bride Tradition in Wales." *Folklore* 103.1 (1992): 56–72.

8

Catholic and Protestant, Jesuit and Jew: Historical Religion in *The Merchant of Venice*

by *John Klause*

Hofstra University, Hempstead, New York

WHEN OVER A CENTURY AGO George Santayana wrote apodictically about "the absence of religion in Shakespeare," he meant that the poet's "positivism" allowed him no recourse to the explanatory power of religious abstraction (1957, 152–53). This secular perspective was in the philosopher's mind a matter for regret. Many readers and audiences, however, have experienced Shakespeare differently, finding his works informed, if not by piety, at least by an ethic that is in some sense religious, and for that very reason momentous. Then again, other interpreters have considered the search for religious meaning in Shakespeare's works regrettable, either because they believe that this exegetical process tends to reduce criticism to thematics, or because they find that ideological pressures often force upon a play or poem an allegorical dimension untrue to the text's complexities.[1]

To inquire into the "religion" of *The Merchant of Venice* is to face the problem of abstraction in an especially acute form. We may feel, on the one hand, that an appeal to the severely conceptual is the only way to rescue the play from the burden of anti-Semitism, with which history would otherwise oppress it. If, as G. K. Hunter and others have suggested, we should consider Shylock from a "theological" rather than a "racialist" perspective (Hunter 1978, 66), or, as Barbara Lewalski has done, we should read the work as an allegory dramatizing biblical themes, we might feel (as Lewalski says) that we have "in part transcended the controversies arising out of the literal story" (1962, 327). Because the play contains a large number of biblical allusions that can be made to fit into an ideational framework (Lewalski; Holmer 1995), such an approach may be legitimate. It is as justifiable as the "historical criticism" of Walter Cohen, which, in its primary attention to economics, attempts a "demystification of allegorical meaning" (1982, 778), but relies on allegoresis to establish its main points.[2] On the other hand, the theological tradition *adversus Judaeos* is in itself neither religiously nor ethically benign, and not obviously free from racialist purposes; and there are many recalcitrant details in the play that continue to encourage readings "against the grain of . . . allegory" (Marx 2000, 110; Gross 1992). In examining *The Merchant of Venice* it is probably best, in the words of Browning's Fra Lippo, to "count it crime / To let a truth slip," even if the work's many abstract and concrete "truths" come into conflict, cannot be perfectly harmonized, and remain a source of discomfort or even scandal.

One certain truth about the *Merchant* is that Shakespeare took special pains to introduce religion into his story where it had been for the most part absent from his literary sources.[3] It is a religious play, although its fairy-tale romance presents wealth and virtue as unproblematically compatible, and the Rialto and manor house seem larger realties than church or synagogue. There are in fact three kinds of religion with which Shakespeare is concerned.

Biblical religion, that of sacred story and example, in the first place provides characters in the play with antecedents against whom they may be measured: Shylock the "father," for example, is a descendant of "father Abram" (1.3.160), and Shylock the entrepreneur (as he believes), of "Jacob" (1.3.77); Old Gobbo and his son Launcelot are comic versions of Tobit and Tobiah;[4] Portia is "A Daniel come to judgment" (4.1.223–24); in their various kinds of prodigality, the Venetian Christians are related to the Gospel's Prodigal Son (1.1.129; 2.5.15; 2.6.14, 17; 3.1.45; cf. Lk 15:11–32).[5] The Bible also establishes theological issues that the play explores for their paradoxes: justice and mercy, law and grace, sacrifice and gain, loss and redemption, principled enmity and love. It is often suggested that "Old Testament" law and rigor, represented by Shylock, are made, in Portia's triumph, to yield to "New Testament" liberty and mercy. But Shakespeare's Christian scripture was not so neatly divided in its theology, and Portia's disquisition on the "quality of mercy" takes more language from the Old Testament than from the New (Shaheen 1999, 180–82). In any case, allusions to the Bible in the *Merchant,* whether clear or cloudy, ingenuous or ironical, seem more substantive than ornamental.[6]

A second kind of religion, that of piety and devotion, might seem mere local color in a world so intent upon the pursuit of money and well-made marriage; yet reference to religious custom and practice may invite an audience to consider the less mundane issues underlying actions of "golden" men and women who understand the value of "lead." In Catholic Italy, the language of "saint," "shrine," and "pilgrimage," or talk of "shriv[ing]" and "prayer-books" in the "pocket" and "grace" before meals, or mention of "Black Monday" and "Ash Wednesday" might be expected as a matter of course (though none of this is found in *Il Pecorone,* the chief source of Shakespeare's story, in which neither hero nor heroine is devout, nor even conventionally moral).[7] But Portia's pretending to visit a "monastery" (rather than the health spa of the Italian tale) to engage in "prayer and contemplation" as an excuse for her absence from Belmont (3.4.27–32) does not mean that her religion is shallow or negligible. In the last act, no longer needing to dissemble, she returns from Venice accompanied by a "holy hermit" and straying along the way "By holy crosses, where she kneels and prays / For happy wedlock hours" (5.1.30–33). In one sense Portia is aptly named after the daughter of Cato Uticensis, who, like her father, was famous for her stoic renunciations—the most notable of which Shakespeare reported in *Julius Caesar.* When the mistress of Belmont declares, "I stand for sacrifice" (3.2.57), she refers to herself as a sacrificial victim; but it is the role she has *chosen,* in obedience to her father's will. She stands for, witnesses to, the value of sacrifice, as Shylock "stand[s] for judgment . . . for law" (4.1.103, 142). She chooses finally not as a stoic, but as one who believes in (though she does not always relish) the biblical "cross" as the preeminent symbol of love. The lead casket's message that a worthy lover "must give and hazard all he hath" (2.7.16) could in theory be a secular as well as a religious maxim; but Portia's prayers in the shadow of wayside crosses reveal *her* assumption that the most compelling of love's models is divine. Although none of her Christian acquaintances is as overtly pious as she, their attitudes must be judged in the light of hers, as well as by the play's large store of biblical illustration and prescription. This is not to say that in the fictitious world of Belmont and Venice, Portia is a saint. Devotion and sanctity are not synonymous, and many critics have complained of Portia's "imperfections"—a haughty gentility, a not wholly attractive cunning, a color prejudice (1.2.129–31) about which she is somewhat disingenuous (2.1.13–14); but in a dramatic world universally flawed, her faults seem less injurious to her virtues than the shortcomings of other characters are to theirs.

The third type of religion in *The Merchant of Venice,* the kind that vexed as much as consoled Shakespeare's original audiences—even as it troubles modern ones—is credal and political: the "faith" that divides orthodox from heterodox and makes them enemies, demands exclusive allegiance, and insists that only the truth can save.[8] In Shakespeare's Venice, the religious division is between Christian and Jew, a hostility that had been only a superficial feature of *Il Pecorone.* Marlowe's *Jew of Malta,* which left a considerable mark on the *Merchant,* had made the conflict a central theme, the author cynically portraying Christian, Jew, and Turk as villains all, but only the Jew Barabas as "heroic" in his wickedness. It is generally recognized that Shakespeare created Jews and Christians of greater human depth than Marlowe's, and it is the complex humanity of Antonio and Shylock, arch-upholders of the ancient religious feud, that has since the days of the nineteenth-century stage-Shylocks Edmund Kean and Henry Irving interested readers and playgoers more than have ideological causes of the conflict. But Shakespeare, it seems, made a special effort to include doctrinal passion (distinct from but not unrelated to racial prejudice) as a significant part of the energy that gave his characters life.

The mutual hatred of Christian merchant and Jewish moneylender is of course no simple matter. Shylock, however, is not far wrong in succinctly identifying its causes:

> I hate him for he is a Christian;
> But more, for that in low simplicity
> He lends out money gratis, and brings down
> The rate of usance here with us in Venice.
> If I can catch him once upon the hip,
> I will feed fat the ancient grudge I bear him.
> He hates our sacred nation, and he rails
> Even there where merchants most do congregate
> On me, my bargains, and my well-won thrift,
> Which he calls interest.
>
> (1.3.42–51)

What one man considers "thrift" the other deems predation, and the anger of each at the other's practice, rooted in a long and intricate economic history,[9] and sanctioned for each by antagonistic moral principles, is hardly to be assuaged. The animosity is also nourished by an irrational "grudge," perhaps more of an ethnic than an ethical phenomenon.[10] This fact helps to explain why of all the miscreants in Venice, it is in Antonio's mind only Shylock who deserves to be kicked like a dog and spat upon (1.3.117–19, 130–31), and whose heart is understandably hard because it is "Jewish" (4.1.80); why in Shylock's mind the Christians are "fools" and prodigals to "feed upon" (2.5.33, 14), worse to have as kin than the thief and murderer Barabbas (4.1.296–97), and enemies to detest: "I hate him for he is a Christian. . . . / He hates our sacred nation. . . ." Finally, one should assume that the reasons for this stark antipathy go beyond those that have led to a personal feud and lie in the general history of prejudice, malice, and persecution bequeathed to Christians and Jews through the centuries. Belonging to this historical reality is an *odium religiosum,* a hatred inspired, if not licensed, by faith. Shakespeare makes it prominent in his play.

In Christian eyes, a Jew is an "infidel" (3.2.218; 4.1.334). As such, he or she might be considered in league with the devil, and therefore in fact "a kind of devil" (2.2.24), doomed in this state to damnation. In his clownish way, Launcelot assures Jessica that as a Jew she cannot be saved (3.5.5–6); but the issue is a serious one, and Jessica has been taught how to counter the bad news of the Gospel's "good news": "I shall be sav'd by my husband, he hath made me a Christian!" (3.5.19–20; cf. 1 Cor 7.14). If infidelity is to be detested, the infidel who refuses to abandon his unbelief may be despised for his obstinate refusal to be converted to the truth. This is surely Antonio's view, who condemns Shylock as a "misbeliever" (1.3.111). Shylock's religious exclusivism is little different. When asked to dine with Christians, he speaks scornfully of their "prophet" (a conjurer from insignificant Nazareth), of the unclean practices of his followers, and of his religion, whose prayers he will not share. To eat with Bassanio and his friend is "to smell pork, to eat of the habitation which your prophet the Nazarite conjur'd the devil into. I will buy with you, sell with you, talk with you, walk with you, and so following; but I will not eat with you, drink with you, nor pray with you"

(1.3.33–38). When his daughter runs away to marry a Christian, Shylock is as certain that she is "damn'd" (3.1.31) as the Christians are that she may be redeemed.

It is not difficult to imagine why Shakespeare would introduce biblical themes and allusions into his play, or why he would have Catholic Italians speaking and acting like Catholics. One must continue to wonder, however, why he would develop, far beyond what was suggested in his literary sources, the enmity between Christian and Jew. Perhaps, as some scholars have proposed, his motives were primarily mercenary, arising out of his sense of a moment made economically promising by the notorious case of Ruy Lopez, the Jewish physician of the Queen who was executed in 1594 on the charge that he had tried to poison her. Financial opportunity may have been suggested by the successful revival of Marlowe's *Jew of Malta* in the same year and then again in 1596. The basis for this theory has rightly or wrongly been judged "insecure" (Brown 1959, xxiv),[11] but in any case the conjecture does nothing to explain the moral vision of *The Merchant of Venice,* which is in some ways as idealistic as the ethos of Marlowe's play is cynical. If Shakespeare was moved by anti-Semitism to create the villainous Shylock (and who can be certain that he was not?), his bias was probably, as one commentator on "Shakespeare and Semitism" has suggested, "abstract and traditional" (Halio 1993, 13) and consequently an inadequate inspiration of the play's monumental religious conflict. Some have denied that for Shakespeare there was anything so compelling as a "Jewish Question," for in Elizabethan England "there were hardly any Jews," and indeed outside of Shakespeare and Marlowe's works, little serious interest in portraying Jewish characters on the Elizabethan stage (Greenblatt 1978, 291; Danson 1978, 58–59). James Shapiro has offered the opposing view that the small number of Jews in Shakespeare's England ("probably never more than a couple of hundred at any given time . . . in a population of roughly four million") belied their cultural importance (1996, 76, 88). Whatever the truth of this matter, Shapiro's insinuation that the status of the Jew as "the Other of Others" in the Renaissance somehow culturally predetermined Shakespeare's subject matter is less convincing than Lawrence Danson's insistence that the playwright's deliberate choice of his subject was not at all predictable, but surprising and "extraordinary" (Shapiro, 86; Danson, 58–60).

The surprise is somewhat diminished when it is recognized that the unholy war between the Venetians and Shylock, though hardly unimportant in itself, has an additional dimension. When considered through a genetic analysis of the play, the antagonism can be seen as a "trope."[12] That is, in *The Merchant of Venice,* the enmity between Christian and Jew can serve as a figure for the conflicted state of a divided Christendom—a problem more broadly and immediately critical to Elizabethans than was their "Jewish Question." To think of the play in this way is not arbitrarily to divert attention from its troubling and unwholesome features (trouble will not in fact be avoided); it is to give necessary recognition to a neglected truth, that in writing the *Merchant,* Shakespeare was intensely conscious not only of literary lore and legend, of contemporary realities of economics and race, of biblical codes and commandments, but of the politics of religion as it existed in his time and place. Among his many purposes was to suggest, for those especially sensitive to religious topicality, dramatic analogues to characters and attitudes prominent in the late sixteenth-century wars of truth. He rendered these resemblances only imperfectly allegorical, so that they would not seem crudely ideological and subversive. Nevertheless, his play both reveals and invites deep dissatisfaction with current political solutions to doctrinal strife, whether their advocacy stemmed from the cruel if pure idealism of an inflexible faith or from a determined pragmatism that appealed to faith in the enforcement of secular will. In order to appreciate how this may be so, it will be necessary to consider the extent to which *The Merchant of Venice* relies on the writings and example of a man whose definition of issues on one side of the Christian divide Shakespeare thought it essential to know. This Catholic was the Jesuit missionary and martyr Robert Southwell.

Claims that Shakespeare was familiar with Southwell's poetry, prose, and person have been advanced since the nineteenth century but have not won wide assent. New evidence, however, has been developed in recent years to make assertions about the Jesuit's influence on Shakespeare increasingly plausible.[13] The signs of Southwell's contribution to *The Merchant of Venice* are not, then, isolated witnesses; they are connected to testimony that becomes weightier as it grows. Since much of the evidence consists of verbal parallels in several texts, it is inevitable that some instances will seem less probative than others. But in a demonstration that relies on the convergence of probabilities, more tentative examples of influence gain in plausibility from their association with more certain ones.[14]

In the play, many of the reminiscences of Southwell's writing are brief and scattered. Some are proverbs or maxims, whose sharing might be merely coincidental if there were only one or two; but there are enough of them shared to arouse suspicion that one author's commonplaces may be unconsciously inspired by the other's. Lines and phrases in the *Merchant* echo expressions from a range of Southwell's controversial, poetical, and devotional work:[15]

SHAKESPEARE: Thus hath the candle sing'd the moth (2.9.79)
SOUTHWELL: So long the flie doth dallie with the flame,
Untill his singed winges doe force his fall (*Poems* 1967, "Lewd Love is Losse," 31–32)

SHAKESPEARE: to do a great right, do a little wrong (4.1.216)
SOUTHWELL: seeke not so greate a good by evill (*EC* 1974, 53^r)

SHAKESPEARE: If to do were as easy as to know what were good to do
. . . , poor men's
cottages [were] princes' palaces (1.2.12–14)
SOUTHWELL: the Princes presence honoreth the basest cottage (*EC* 103^r)

SHAKESPEARE: When the moon shone we did not see the candle . . . So doth the greater glory dim the less (5.1.92–93)
SOUTHWELL: seeking the sunne it is . . . booteles to borrowe the light of a candle (*MMFT* 1974, 14^v–15^r).

The play also contains an expression that the *OED* marks as Shakespeare's coinage, but which Southwell had used before him. Shylock's "a wilderness of monkeys" (subsequent to "a wilderness of Tigers" in *Titus*) could well have been derived from "a wilderness of serpents" in Southwell's *Epistle unto his Father*.[16] And there are many other miscellaneous parallels, from which the following may serve as examples:

SOUTHWELL	SHAKESPEARE
Nolite me considerare, quia fusca sum. Regard you not how blacke I am (*EC* 1974 151ᵛ; Canticles 1.5, which continues, in the Vulgate: *Quia decoloravit me sol* [because the sun hath discolored me])	Mislike me not for my complexion The shadowed livery of the burnish'd sun (2.1.1–2)
Hornets I hyve . . . Poore Agar her child . . . (*Poems* 1967, *SPC* 485, 529–31)	Hagar's offspring . . . . Drones hive not with me (2.5.44–48)
the shipp, while it is uppon the maigne sea . . . , having all the the sayles hoysed upp, and swolne with the wynde, and the banners displayed . . . , daunceth upon the waves, and allureth everye eye. . . . But when it is comen into the haven, it is strayte ransacked. . . . (*EC* 7ᵛ)	How like a younger or a prodigal[17] The scarfed bark puts from her native bay, Hugg'd and embrac'd by the strumpet wind! How like the prodigal doth she return With . . . ragged sails, Lean, rent, and beggar'd (2.6.14–19)
kisse . . . mortal, shrined, breath, saints (*MMFT* 61, 57ᵛ, 59ʳ, 62ʳ); Though wisdome wooe me to the saint, Yet sense would win me to the shrine (*Poems* 1967, "Mans civill warre," 15–16)	To kiss this shrine, this mortal breathing saint (2.7.40).
he hath often sent us embassyes of love (*EC* 18ʳ)	an embassador of love (2.9.92)
Thou wouldest happely make sale thy living, and seek him by ransome. But it is not likely they would sell him to be honoured that bought him to be murdered. If price would not serve, thou wouldest fall to praier. But how can praier soften such flint hearts? (*MMFT* 37ʳ)	pluck commiseration . . . From rough hearts of flints [spoken to Shylock after attempts to ransom Antonio have failed] (4.1.30–31)
You bleating ewes that waile this wolvish spoile Of sucking lambs (*SPC* 565–66)	You may as well use question with the wolf Why he hath made the ewe bleak for the lamb (4.1.73–74)

heavenlye Hierusalem . . . , whose porters Angels, whose streetes paved with golde, and interlaced (*EC* 189ʳ)	the floor of heaven Is thick inlaid with patens of bright gold. . . . .
angelicall harmonye (*EC* 191ᵛ)	. . . an angel sings, ...
we beinge ruled by sense . . . conceave not spirituall matters (*EC* 189ʳ)	Such harmony is in immortal souls, But whilst this muddy vesture of decay Doth grossly close it in, we cannot hear it (5.1.58–65)[18]
Well might a cocke correct me with a crow: Whom hennish cackling first did overthrow (*SPC* 275–76)	The crow doth sing . . . . every goose is cackling (5.1.102–5)

Southwell's texts appear to have "seeped" into Shakespeare's in a way suggesting the playwright has so come under the spell of the Jesuit's writings that traces of them are liable to appear piecemeal, randomly but persistently, in every part of *The Merchant of Venice*.

In several passages of the play, however, Southwell's influence can be seen as especially concentrated. The first of these, the third scene of act 1, opens with Shylock acknowledging to Bassanio, who has sought him out for a loan on Antonio's credit, the merchant's sufficiency as a credit risk:

> his means are in supposition: he hath an argosy bound to Tripolis, another to the Indies . . . he hath a third at Mexico, a fourth for England, and other ventures he hath . . . But ships are but boards, sailors but men; there be land-rats and water-rats, water-thieves and land-thieves, I mean pirates, and then there is the peril of waters, winds, and rocks. The man is notwithstanding sufficient. (17–26)

The four argosies here mentioned (later, counting the "other ventures" there will be six), which will all by false report eventually be given up for lost, have analogues in Southwell's *Epistle of Comfort*: "In the Ocean sea, of fower shippes not one doth miscarrye, and in the Sea of this worlde, of many fowers, not one is saved"—the sea with its "perilles" of "rockes," "stormes," and "waters," (1974, 112ᵛ–13ʳ, 114ᵛ–15ʳ). Shakespeare recalled these words in conjunction with matter on earlier pages (fols. 10–67), which furnished a large store of words and images to the scene. On Southwell's oceans are the "Pirates" seeking the merchandise on ships (10ᵛ); the ships that are but planks easily destroyed ("the shippes melted, and the bordes scorched" [67ᵛ]; cf. the wrecked ship's "plancke" [115ʳ]); the sailors whose vessel may have "a thousand tymes crossed the seas with great advantage of the shipmen, [but] in the end justled with a blast, is shattered in peeces" (51ʳ). By itself this vocabulary of shipwreck would mean little; but it sits in Southwell's *Epistle* in the midst of language that helps to construct the scene in its essentials. On one page are the pirates, on the preceding one "Laban" and "Jacob," then soon thereafter "Abraham" (10ᵛ, 10ʳ, 13ʳ; cf. Shylock's lines, "When Jacob graz'd his uncle Laban's sheep— / This Jacob from our holy Abram was . . . / The third possessor" [1.3.71–74]). Shylock thinks Antonio looks like a "fawning publican" (41); Southwell imagines that the devil (mentioned by Shylock in line 34) "fawn[s]" upon his enemies to win them over (10ʳ).[19] "I hate him for he is a Christian," says the Jew to himself (42), using words that appear in a single line of the *Epistle:* "we did hate him. O Christian . . ." (38ᵛ). Shylock is convinced that Antonio "hates our sacred nation" (48); Southwell, too, finds in the Jews a "nation" of special consecration, hated by others, as he quotes the author of Second Maccabees: "God dealeth not with us, as with other nations" (15ʳ). Before speaking to Antonio, Shylock resolves, "Cursed be my tribe / If I forgive him!" (51–52). The "tribe of Juda," perhaps, as referred to in the *Epistle* (29ᵛ)?[20] It could even be said that in writing of a "true Israelite" and soon thereafter of "gentils" (11ᵛ, 13ᵛ), Southwell provoked the pun to which Shakespeare resorts when Antonio finally addresses Shylock as a "gentle Jew," seeing (or pretending to see) evidence that "The Hebrew will turn Christian" (177–78; cf. *EC* 90ᵛ: "Jewes . . . Gentils").

The conversation between merchant and moneylender leads to the latter's understandable and justly notorious exasperation:

> Signior Antonio, many a time and oft
> In the Rialto you have rated me
> About my moneys and my usances.
> Still have I borne it with a patient shrug
> (For suff'rance is the badge of all our tribe).
> You call me misbeliever, cut-throat dog,
> And spet upon my Jewish gaberdine,

And all for use of that which is mine own.
Well then, it now appears you need my help.
Go to then, you come to me, and you say,
"Shylock, we would have moneys," you say so—
You, that did void your rheum upon my beard
And foot me as you spurn a stranger cur
Over your threshold; moneys is your suit.
What should I say to you? Should I not say,
"Hath a dog money? Is it possible
A cur can lend three thousand ducats?" Or
Shall I bend low and in a bondman's key,
With bated breath and whisp'ring humbleness,
Say this:
"Fair sir, you spet on me on Wednesday last,
You spurn'd me such a day, another time
You call'd me dog; and for these courtesies
I'll lend you thus much moneys"?

(1.3.106–29)

From the pages of Southwell's *Epistle,* one should especially note in comparison: "money"; "patient sufferance" and "patient sufferance . . . tribe"; martyrs' scars as "badges of Christianity"; "Misbeliefe"; "cut our throates"; "dogges . . . spurne"; "dogges . . . strangers . . . footing"; "with bondage . . . bendinge"; "breathing . . . abate."[21] These words and expressions, when added to others from *Saint Peters Complaint,* account for much of the language of Shylock's anger. It is the remorseful Peter himself who recalls his betrayal of his master, whose Jewish beard he had in a way spat upon:

[My] speeches *voyded* spight . . .
. . . .
Were all the *Jewish* tyrannies too few, . . .
. . . .
That thou more hatefull tyrannies must shew: . . .
And *spit* thy poyson in thy makers face?

(122–30, emphasis added)

Despite his resentment, or as many believe, because of it, Shylock lends Antonio "thus much moneys;" but he does so in a "merry sport" (145), demanding no interest as such,[22] asking as collateral a pound of the merchant's flesh.

When again, in act 3, Shylock denounces Antonio for treating him disgracefully, for the "reason" that, as he says, "I am a Jew," his words again echo Southwell's—and with an irony that only Shakespeare himself could have, in his own time, fully appreciated:

> Hath not a Jew eyes? Hath not a Jew hands, organs, dimensions, senses, affections, passions; fed with the same food, hurt with the same weapons, subject to the same diseases, heal'd by the same means, warm'd and cool'd by the same winter and summer, as a Christian is? If you prick us do we not bleed? If you tickle us, do we not laugh? If you poison us, do we not die? And if you wrong us, shall we not revenge? If we are like you in the rest, we will resemble you in that. (3.1.59–68)

In appealing to the humanity he shares with everyone else, Shylock in fact makes use of language that the Jesuit had used to describe the suffering body of Christ, the Jew in whose name generations of Jews had been "hurt" and made to "bleed." Verbal stimulus for the entire speech seems to have come from part of the *Epistle of Comfort* that had already left its mark on act 1, first from a passage in which Southwell details aspects of Christ's passion: in "his side . . . , his armes . . . , his head . . . , his eyes . . . , his handes," his "bleeding woundes" that are signs of his "affection"—but that his Christian followers are as ready to ignore as did the "stifnecked Jewes" who rejected him (*EC* 1974, 18ᵛ). Near these excerpts are expressions further reminiscent of Shylock's:

SOUTHWELL	SHAKESPEARE
full of provision . . . to feede uppon (*EC* 17ʳ)	fed with the same food (3.1.61)
speares . . . to wound (18ᵛ)	hurt with the same weapons (3.1.61)
kyll [with] poison (20ʳ)	If you poison us, do we not die? (3.1.65–66)
purposeth to heale (21ᵛ)	heal'd by the same means (3.1.62)
pricking (23ʳ)	If you prick us (3.1.64)

Southwell considers here Christ's "passions" (*EC* 1974, 22ʳ), and somewhat later, in reflecting on afflictions that are the common lot of humanity, writes "organe" and "senses" (42ᵛ, 43ʳ), "laughing" and "tickle" (43ᵛ, 46ᵛ), "our body . . . subject to . . . diseases" (45ᵛ), "resemble" and "juste revenge" (33ʳ, 28ᵛ).

Shylock's defense of his revengeful "passions" is situated in the middle of act 3, scene 1. Preceding it is the rumor, voiced by Salerio, that one of Antonio's ships has been wrecked in the Goodwin Sands: "a very dangerous flat, and fatal, where the carcasses of many a tall ship lie buried" (3.1.5–6). Southwell had written of "shallow places . . . hidden rockes . . . [by which] shippes [were] drawne to their owne ruine" (*EC* 82^v), and of fragments of a "broaken shippe" whose wreck had "lefte a multitude of dead carcases to the waters rage" (*EC* 115^r). Hearing the news of his daughter's elopement as well of Antonio's losses, Shylock in his fury warns Salerio that the "prodigal" Antonio should look to his "bond" (45, 50) (cf. *EC*'s "prodigall" [36^r, 43^r] and "bond" [58^r]); and when he is asked what mere "flesh" is worth to a moneylender, replies, "To bait fish withal—if it will feed nothing else, it will feed my revenge" (52–54) (cf. *EC* 17^v: "you see the fishe . . . catch the bayte"; 16^r: "feede on"; 15^r: "revenges"). The speech about a "Jew's" humanity follows (its parallels with *EC* 18^v succeeding rather closely those just noted). Shylock's friend Tubal then enters to report his daughter Jessica's extravagant spending—driving the outraged father to exclaim, "Would she were hears'd at my foot, and the ducats in her coffin!" (89–90). His words may remind one of Southwell's description of a benumbed Marie Magdalen: "her bodie seemed but the hearse of her dead heart, and her heart the cophin of her unliving soule" (*MMFT* 58^r). Jessica has exchanged her father's "turkis" ring for a monkey; the gem was a keepsake from her mother, which Shylock would not have given "for a wilderness of monkeys" (118–23)—a menagerie inspired, as earlier suggested, by Southwell's "wilderness of serpents" (*Two Letters* 1973, *EF* 17). Controlling his frenzy, Shylock asks Tubal to meet him at their "synagogue," where (it is often assumed) he will swear upon the "holy Sabaoth" to "have the due and forfeit" of his fatal bond (4.1.36–37). Southwell has much to say about the "Sinagoge," and his meaning will be considered in due course.

The scene then shifts from the turbulence of Venetian streets to the tense and therefore deceptive quiet of Portia's stately house in Belmont, where Bassanio is about to make his choice of caskets and find whether love will have its way. The proper casket is neither gold nor silver, but the leaden one with its message that a lover "must give and hazard all he hath" (2.7.9). Shakespeare's source for the casket story, *Gesta Romanorum,* had given a different "scripture" to the "vesselle . . . of leed": *"Thei that chese me, shulle fynde [in] me that God hathe disposid"* (Bullough 1957, 1:514). The change is made in accordance with the play's major theme of love as giving and sacrificial, a taking of risks even on a "prodigal" scale. When Portia tells Bassanio that he must "hazard" and "venture" for her (3.2.2, 10) (he has vowed never to marry another should he fail the test), she speaks words that occur, one or the other, eighteen times in the play. They associate Antonio's mercantile "ventures" (1.1.42), which become pledges unto death for his friend, with those of the hero of love, that same friend Bassanio, who stakes his future on the symbolic choice of absolute renunciation (a lover must "give and hazard *all* he hath," italics added) Shylock, who as a usurer was thought in Shakespeare's time to take no risks, his gain "ensured by bonds and pawns" (Holmer 1995, 35–36, 161), speaks with contempt of Antonio's "ventures," which he views as "squandered," the foolish speculations of a "prodigal" (1.3.21; 3.1.45). Antonio in return despises the moneylender, who refuses to "venture" yet still wishes to compare himself with Jacob, whose strenuous labors in the household of Laban and whose unsecured trust in the providential "hand of heaven" refute the analogy (1.3.91–94). Insofar as Shylock is scornful of risk, the play suggests he is an enemy of love, and blind to the value of mercy, which originates in love and puts justice at "hazard"—sometimes prodigally so. Again, one can see that for the sake of his theme, Shakespeare altered his source *Il Pecorone* in making a mere lender of money a usurer as well.

The ideas of risk-taking and prodigality are not absent from the stories on which Shakespeare relied in composing *The Merchant of Venice;* but they are a special feature of Southwell's thought, in which they belong, as in Shakespeare's play, to the substance of love. The words "hazard" and "venture" are everywhere in the Jesuit's writings (nearly thirty times in *The Epistle of Comfort* alone), used to define the selfless giving of the martyr. And those writings have deeply colored the second scene of Shakespeare's act 3, in which Portia must be won through "hazard" and "venture" (2, 10). To venture . . . to hazard: the association of the closely related concepts is formulaic in Southwell: "adventure the hazard" (*EF* 17); "soe venterouslie to presse . . . and hazard" (*HS* 12); "rather venture his life . . . then hazard his Conscience" (*HS* 35); "to so open hazarde, ventured them selves" (*EC*

34^r). Although such formulas are hardly unique to Southwell, there are several parts of the scene that suggest that his were those that lingered in the playwright's imagination as he fashioned it.

In *Marie Magdalens Funeral Teares,* the Saint is of a mind to "venture [her] life" for her Lord (*MMFT* 42^r) believing that love is "no love, unlesse it be as liberall of that it is, as of that it hath" (31^v). This dramatic meditation furnishes a suggestive series of parallels with the wording of act 3, scene 2, of the play:

SOUTHWELL	SHAKESPEARE
eie streams (*MMFT* 26^r)	my eye shall be the stream (46)
Thy eies were to wel acquainted with the trueth, to accept a supplie of shaddowes (29^r);	her eyes— . . . . so far this shadow
no shadow should be more priviledged then the body (36^r)	Doth limp behind the substance (123–29)
Hee was my Lord to command me, my maister to instruct mee. . . . He was mine because his love was mine, and when he gave me his love hee gave me himselfe. . . . if he be thine by being given thee once, thou art his by as many gifts, as daies, and therefore hee being absolute owner of thee, is likewise full owner of whatsoever is thine, and consequently because he is thine, hee is also his owne (31^v–32^v) defeating mee of my right (32^r)	One half of me is yours, the other half yours— Mine own, I would say; but if mine, then yours, And so all yours. . . . (16–18) her gentle spirit Commits itself to yours to be directed, As from her lord, her governor, her king. Myself, and what is mine, to you and yours is now converted (163–67) Put bars between the owners and their rights (19)
sicke with a surfet of sodaine joy (59^r)	In measure rain thy joy . . . . For fear I surfeit (112–14)

The music provided for Bassanio as he ponders his momentous choice of the caskets warns him of the unreliability of fancy:

> Tell me where is fancy bred,
> Or in the heart or in the head?
> How begot, how nourished?
> ....
> It is engend'red in the eyes,
> With gazing fed, and fancy dies
> In the cradle where it lies.
> Let us all ring fancy's knell.
>   (3.2.63–70)

The song is based, of course, on clichés, but words and phrases from the poem *Saint Peters Complaint* perhaps helped to evoke them: "Tell hartes . . . heades . . . fancies" (lines 23–33); "Nurcing . . . begat" (70); "Their lookes, by seeing oft, conceived love" (308); "eyes . . . my hungrie wishes fed" (344–45); "remisnes . . . in the cradle . . . dying"; (205–7); "fansies . . . bred" (731–35); "knill" (750). In making his decision, determining to choose "meagre lead" over more "beauteous" gold or silver, Bassanio concludes that "beauty," if it is to be the ground of love, is "purchas'd by the weight" (3.2.89–90). This insight may be founded on an Augustinian maxim, which Southwell quotes from the *Confessions:* "*Amor meus pondus meum*" ("My love is my weight") (*EC* 36ᵛ).

Also in scene 2, the language of torture and the rack may perhaps owe something to Southwell's discussions of religious persecution. An exchange between Bassanio and Portia recalls a passage in the *Humble Supplication,* which culminates in the language of venturing and hazarding:

SHAKESPEARE

BASS: . . . as I am, I live upon the rack.
....
POR: Ay, but I fear you speak upon the rack,
Where men enforced do speak anything. (3.2.25–33)

SOUTHWELL

What unsufferable Agonies we have bene put to upon the Rack. . . . [One so tortured] is apt to utter anything to abridge the sharpnes and severity of paine. [Yet even an] unskillful Lay man . . . [would] rather venture his life by saying too much, then hazard his Conscience in not answering sufficient. (*HS* 1953, 34–35)

After receiving the letter that informs him of Antonio's losses and Shylock's determination to have nothing but what is "nominated" in his bond, Bassanio imagines the "paper as the body of [his] friend, / And every word in it a gaping wound" (3.2.264–65). Southwell had already compared the wounded and ephemeral flesh of martyrs to paper: "when [our executioners] thinke to have geven us and our cause the greatest wounde . . . , they stryppe us of slyght and paper harnesse" (*EC* 1974, 137^r).[23]

The trial scene (4.1), true to convention, brings together the play's major characters and offers in this case a problematic resolution to conflict. Shylock insists on the letter of the law, on the perverse "justice" that will allow him legally to murder his enemy. Through the tangled proceedings of "stage justice" (not the kind to be found in a real court), which the disguised Portia manipulates masterfully, the moneylender is forced to deny his "bond" and himself to ask for the mercy that he had refused freely to grant Antonio. Opinion has been notoriously divided on whether the Christian "mercy" shown to Shylock is as noble a gesture, as divine a gift as Portia had described. That her eloquent speech shows traces of Southwell's discussion of mercy may not affect one side or other of the critical argument that it has provoked; but Southwell wrote of mercy as a compelling issue in a complex tangle of historical circumstances. Shakespeare's recollection of the Jesuit's words suggests that mercy's "qualities" had for the playwright more than a theoretical significance.

The influence on the play of folios 10–67 of the *Epistle of Comfort* has already been remarked upon. Near the end of these pages, Southwell asks his readers, who may be repining at their persecution for the faith, to consider that their burdens might, with justice, be heavier. They should "call unto mynde," he says, "how God mighte justly have delte with us, what he might have layde uppon us, and yett not only not exceeded, the bond of his justice, but have still shewed himselfe of infinite mercye" (*EC* 58^{r-v}). Even a merciful God, in other words, may punish exceedingly and still be distinguished for his gratuitous and loving kindness. This is surely not Portia's point, yet Shakespeare has given to her (4.1.182–205) much of the language in and around Southwell's discussions:

SOUTHWELL	SHAKESPEARE
Jewes (61ᵛ); mercifull (55ʳ)	POR: Then must the Jew be merciful
compulsion (61ᵛ)	SHY: On what compulsion must I? Tell me that?
qualitye . . . mercye; (60ʳ) strayne (30ʳ); constrayned (45ᵛ)	POR: The quality of mercy is not strain'd,
dropp [of grace] (48ᵛ); gentle (69ᵛ); rayne (65ʳ); heaven (61ʳ) place (62ʳ); underneth (58ᵛ)	It droppeth as the gentle rain from heaven
twise (37ʳ); blessed (55ᵛ)	Upon the place beneath. It is twice blest:
blessed (55ᵛ); take . . . and geve (36ʳ)	It blesseth him that gives and him that takes.
Mightye (51ʳ)	'Tis mightiest in the mightiest, it becomes
throne (31ᵛ); Prince . . . crowne (38ʳ)	The throned monarch better than his crown.
forcible . . . shewed (58ʳ) temporall (59ʳ); power (56ʳ)	His sceptre shows the force of temporal power,
majestye (58ᵛ); dreadfull (57ᵛ)	The attribute to awe and majesty,
feares (59ʳ); Emperour (50ʳ)	Wherein doth sit the dread and fear of kings;
mercye (60ʳ); swaye (51ᵛ)	But mercy is above this sceptred sway,
in a . . . throne (31ᵛ); hartes (51ᵛ) Emperour (50ʳ)	It is enthroned in the hearts of kings,
God . . . shewed himself of infint mercye (58ʳ⁻ᵛ)	It is an attribute to God himself;
power . . . earthlye (51ᵛ)	And earthly power doth then show likest
Gods . . . shewed (58ʳ)	God's
mercye (58ᵛ); seasoned (30ʳ)	When mercy seasons justice. Therefore,
justice (58ʳ); Jewes (61ᵛ)	Jew,
justice (58ʳ); pleadeth at the barr (48ʳ) consider (59ᵛ)	Though justice be thy plea, consider this,

SOUTHWELL	SHAKESPEARE
course . . . justice (41ᵛ)	That, in the course of justice, none of us
salvation (48ᵛ-48ʳ)	Should see salvation. We do pray for mercy
prayinge . . . mercye (40ʳ⁻ᵛ) prayinge (40ʳ); teach (53ᵛ)	And that same prayer doth teach us all to render
render (33ʳ) deeds (36ʳ); mercye (40ᵛ); speake (45ᵛ);	The deeds of mercy. I have spoke thus much
mitigate (48ᵛ); justice (40ᵛ) pleadeth at the barr (48ʳ)	To mitigate the justice of thy plea,
followinge (39ᵛ); strayte . . . Judge . . . verdicte . . . rigorous; (49ʳ)	Which if thou follow, this strict court of Venice
sentence (48ʳ)	Must needs give sentence . . .

The biblical and classical resonances in this text cannot be denied.[24] Yet its individual words are mostly Southwell's, and from a rather compact set of small quarto pages that had already left a significant residue of language in earlier scenes.

The case for Southwell's influence is strengthened by the appearance in the same scene of other signs of it. Bassanio, for example, pleads with Shylock to take ten times the loan's principal instead of the bond's pound of flesh, or else, if "this will not suffice, it must appear / That malice bears down truth" (213–14). In the *Humble Supplication,* Southwell declares to the Queen (as Portia does to Shylock) that, "a Prince . . . resembling . . . All-mighty god . . . should [not] beare down justice, nor [exclude] any meanenesse . . . from mercye" (*HS* 1). Turning to the Duke, Bassanio then beseeches him, "Wrest once the law to your authority; / To do a great right, do a little wrong" (215–16), echoing sentences from the *Epistle of Comfort:* "the authorityes and sayinges of Gods worde [are] wrested" and "seeke not so greate a good by evill (*EC* 82ᵛ, 53ʳ). Later, Bassanio declares his utmost devotion to Antonio by announcing his willingness to "sacrifice" all he has and is for his friend's sake:

> Antonio, I am married to a wife
> Which is as dear to me as life itself,
> But life itself, my wife, and all the world,
> Are not with me esteem'd above thy life.
> I would lose all, ay, sacrifice them all
> Here to this devil, to deliver you.
>
> (282–87)

Such radical devotion has biblical overtones, as in a passage conflated by Southwell from passages in Matthew's Gospel: "Whosoever loveth father mother, wyfe, children, house or livinges more then me, is not worthye of me and he that taketh not upp his crosse (and that) every daye can not be my disciple" (*EC* 31^r; Mt 10.37–38; 19.29; and cf. *HS* 27: "sacrifice to the Divell"). Elsewhere in the scene one might compare words of Shylock and Southwell (all of the latter's from the "usual" pages of the *Epistle of Comfort*):

SOUTHWELL	SHAKESPEARE
stunge by venemous serpents (*EC* 54^v)	What, wouldst thou have a serpent sting me twice? (4.1.69)
My conscience accuseth me of nothinge and yet in this am I not justified (*EC* 47^r; also 75^v and 1 Cor. 4:4 [Vulgate])	What judgment shall I dread, doing no wrong? (4.1.89)
viand ... seasoned ... (*EC* 30^r), in the delicacye of a gorgeous bed ... burden (*EC* 31^v), sweate (32^v)	Why sweat they under burthens? Let their beds Be made as soft as yours, and let their palates Be season'd with viands (4.1.95–97)
Southwell writes the usual "execrable" after having mentioned "dogges" (*EC* 57^v, 54^v).[25]	Gratiano is the only character in Shakespeare to use the word "inexecrable" (calling Shylock an "inexecrable dog" [4.1.128])

Some of the most important evidence that Shakespeare was thinking of Southwell as he wrote this scene comes from the Jesuit's *Epistle unto his Father* as well as from the *Epistle of Comfort*. It has long been recognized that Portia's assumption of the identity of "Balthazar," and her comparison by both Shylock and Gratiano to the prophet Daniel, may have been inspired by biblical stories concerning the young man who prophesied the end of the kingdom of Belshazzar and, on another occasion, triumphed over the elders who had falsely accused Susannah of adultery.[26] Belshazzar (also called "Baltassar" in some sixteenth-century versions of the Bible) is (wrongly) described in the Book of Daniel as the last of the kings of Babylon before its conquest by the Persians. Daniel is a Jewish youth of the exile, renamed by the Babylonians "Belteshazar" or, in some versions, "Balthasar" (Dan 1:7). At a feast hosted by Belshazzar, mysterious words are written on the wall by a phantom hand, a message that Daniel boldly interprets to mean that the king is "weighed in the balance, and [is] found too light" (5:27). The same Daniel, in the tale of Susannah, proves the lady's innocence by convicting her accusers "by their owne mouth" (v. 61). These details seem to have served well Shakespeare's purposes in *The Merchant of Venice*. The play's trial develops as it had proceeded in *Il Pecorone*; but it is the playwright alone who gives his heroine the biblical names, and who introduces into the scene the "balance" (4.1.255) that Shylock has ready to weigh the pound of flesh before he is himself weighed and found wanting—trapped in his own words, like the disgraced elders, by Balthazar, "A Daniel come to judgment" (4.1.223). The Bible, then, encroaches here as in so many other places in the *Merchant*; it is the Bible, however, recalled for Shakespeare by Southwell.

In the *Epistle of Comfort,* Southwell refers a half-dozen times to Daniel—even, as Shakespeare does, to the prophet as a type: "a Daniel" (11^v; and cf. 16^v: "come before the Judge"). In the *Epistle* he wrote to his father to reclaim him from schism,[27] the priest even compares himself to the young prophet:

> Despise not, good sir, the youth of your son, neither deem that God measureth his endowments by number of years. Hoary senses are often couched under green locks. . . . Not the most aged person, but Daniel, the most innocent infant, delivered Susanna from the iniquity of the judges. (*EF* 5)

His words are much like those in Bellario's letter that recommends Balthazar to the Venetian Duke: "I beseech you let his lack of years be no impediment to let him lack a reverend estimation, for I never knew so young a body with so old a head" (4.1.161–64).[28] Referring to the fifth chapter of the Book of Daniel and the circumstances of Belshazzar's feast, Southwell provides all the reminders that

Shakespeare needed of the scriptural names and the image of the "balance" that were to become part of his scene:

> seriously consider the terms you stand in and weigh yourself in a Christian balance, taking for our counterpoise the judgments of God. Take heed in time that the word *Thecel,* written of old against Baltazar and interptreted by Daniel (Daniel the fifth), be not verified in you, whose exposition was, "You have been poised in the scale and found of too light weight." (*EF* 7)

Portia's mentor Bellario also has an interesting name, one that introduces the possibility that the play may cover some personal references under its fictions. "Bellario" is very close to the surname of Roberto Bellarmino (in Engish, Bellarmine), the famous Jesuit controversialist—and Southwell's teacher in Rome—who is mentioned in the *Epistle of Comfort* as the author of the *Controversiae* (86ʳ).[29] Shakespeare's Bellario is also expert in "controversy" (4.1.155). He resides in Padua, famous for its school of law, but also a city in which Bellarmine had lived, preached, studied at the university, and initially made his reputation (Brodrick, 21–22). In *Il Pecorone,* Bellario has no counterpart; Shakespeare created the character, begetting the highly improbable coincidence that Portia should receive a commission from the very man whom the Duke had consulted to resolve his dilemma. The woman "lawyer" in Shakespeare's source did not present herself as anyone's emissary; and she claimed to come from Bologna, not, as did Balthazar, from Rome.[30] In much of the play, Shakespeare seems indifferent to strict canons of plausibility; here he sacrifices realism so that he may have Bellario send a learned young doctor from Rome to defeat a religious adversary in "controversy," and to plead that mercy, which "becomes / The throned monarch better than his crown" and is an "attribute to God himself," should overcome the harsh strictures of the law. So Bellarmine prepared his protégé Southwell to depart from Rome for the intellectual work of his mission in England, where the young priest would (in his *Humble Supplication*) say to a heretical Queen, whose laws required the butchering of Catholic-Christian flesh, that a Prince "supplying the place" of God should resemble him in "mercy" (4.1.188–89, 195; *HS* 1).

Another Jesuit may be alluded to much earlier in the play, and with some derision. When Portia speaks scornfully of the "Neapolitan prince" who would sue for her affections, she facetiously expresses the fear that "my lady his mother play'd false with a smith" (1.2.43–44). Such was the scurrilous rumor that was spread about Father Robert Persons, the missionary turned political activist. He was a source of conflict among Catholics themselves, some of whom were not hesitant to defame him. Persons was in fact the son of a blacksmith, and rumors of his bastardy arose as early as 1574, when he was expelled from Oxford.[31] Southwell in the *Humble Supplication* defended his colleague from the charge of "base" birth (*HS* 6); but Shakespeare seems to have considered Persons a profitable object of mirth.[32] Could the playwright have known that this Jesuit "prince" was living in Naples in the early part of 1598? (Edwards 1995, 220).[33]

A more significant possibility, however, is that Southwell himself, a partial model for "the young doctor of Rome," Balthazar, also lent something of his character to the merchant Antonio,

> one in whom
> The ancient Roman honor more appears
> Than any that draws breath in Italy
> (3.2.294–96)

Like Antonio, Southwell was by his own description a "merchant," an identity he and other missionaries assumed in their correspondence.[34] Both merchants revealed an animus against Jews. Antonio was, like Southwell, a celibate. He considered himself a "wether of the flock" (a castrated ram), "Meetest for death" (4.1.114–15)—as Southwell was a "eunuch" for the kingdom of heaven (Mt 19.12; "*eunuch[us]*" in the Vulgate), a bellwether of his "litle flocke" (*EC* 210^v), and "meet" by faith and training for the martyrdom he suffered. Antonio's status as an outsider, even when at the end of the play he is welcomed into the circle of love created by the joys of marriage and family, might be seen as irreducible. He is, like the self-abnegating priest, separated by a fundamental distinction from his lay and earthly congregation. There is a passion for the absolute in Antonio's soul (as there was in Southwell's), showing itself in his conscientious hatred of usurious practice and practitioners,[35] and in his willingness to hazard everything for the happiness of his friend. He wishes Bassanio to appreciate that the most authentic love, his own, is supremely sacrificial; and he proudly challenges his competitor in love, Portia, with his devotion unto death: "Commend me to your honorable wife," he tells his friend,

> Tell her the process of Antonio's end,
> Say how I loved you, speak me fair in death;
> And when the tale is told, bid her be judge
> Whether Bassanio had not once a love.
>
> (4.1.273–77)

"*Maiorem charitatem nemo habet, quam ut animam suam ponat quis, pro amicis suis*" ("Greater love than this no one hath, than that one lay down his life for his friends")—so Southwell quotes Christ's message for the martyr from John 15 (*EC* 137^v–38^r), a maxim that surely figures in the Venetian merchant's sense of his own love's nobility. Finally, Antonio, although he has an animus against Shylock and considers his religion vain, believes that it is mercy to convert him, to baptize him into the faith that can save his soul. In this respect, too, Antonio brings Southwell to mind, for the Jesuit had much to say about the Jews, not only in themselves, but as allegorical representatives of his true enemies, the Protestant "heretics" of his own day, whose conversion he prayed for and would have rejoiced to see.

It is not difficult to find in writings of Southwell (as it is not in those of another devout poet, George Herbert) the common "theological" anti-Semitism that was the product of Christian centuries. Southwell's poems speak of the "furious rage of Jewish ire" and the "Jewish tyrannies" that led to the death of Christ ("Christs sleeping friends," 20; *SPC* 127). In the *Epistle of Comfort,* where the Jews are portrayed as "stifnecked" and full of "malice," he remarks that the destruction of Jerusalem by the Romans was the "tragicall & straunge vengeance [that] God [did] shew unto the Jewes, for their horrible sinne in murdering Christ" (18^v, 9^v, 61^v). He blames the people as a whole for not recognizing Jesus as the Messiah, and criticizes some of them for defending "fables of theyre Talmud," in which he sees "many ridiculous things" (84^v, 184^v). He compliments the Jews for having once become "of all other [people] most famous, strong, and glorious," but laments that because of their sins, they should have incurred God's "shameful and opprobrious" punishment (63^v). Not all of Southwell's stereotypes are theologically inspired, however. He notes that at the fall of Jerusalem, the inordinate attachment of Jews to their wealth increased their sufferings at the hands of the Romans (63^r). And in *Marie Magdalens Funeral Teares* he makes use of the image of the Jews as kidnappers and mutilators, a conception that Shapiro reports had a certain currency in sixteenth-century Europe

(89–111). The absence of the dead Christ's body from his tomb suggests to Mary that it was

> the spite of some malicious Pharisee or bloudy Scribe, that not content-
> ed with those torments, that he suffred in life (of which every one to any
> other would have bin a tirannicall death) hath now stollen away his dead
> body, to practise uppon it some savage cruelty, and to glutte their piti-
> lesse eies, and brutish heart with the unnaturall usage of his helples
> corps. (22^{r-v})

This passage seems to incorporate cultural prejudice into religious devotion and theological doctrine; but it should be understood that Southwell's main purpose was not to vent his own hostile feelings toward Jews. Rather, it was to use, in this work and elsewhere, the figure of the hateful Jew to further his anti-Protestant polemic.[36] The polemical cast of the *Funeral Teares* is not difficult to discern if one considers its origins.

Because of its dedication, "To the worshipfull and vertuous Gentlewoman, Mistres D. A.," the *Funeral Teares* has been described as written for Dorothy Arundell, a member of the Arundell family of Cornwall, not related to the Philip Howard, earl of Arundell, who was Southwell's friend and fellow prisoner (Janelle 1935, 59). There is no evidence, however, that Southwell ever knew or was in touch with Dorothy Arundell. That this young woman proffered him the "vertuous request" that became his "commandement" to write the work (*MMFT* A3) is pure speculation.[37] If one is to guess the identity of the dedicatee, a more plausible candidate is Anne Dacres, suitably disguised with her title changed and initials reversed (perhaps like Henry Wriothesley's in the dedication of Shakespeare's Sonnets), who was the wife of Philip Howard, and Southwell's protector in London for most of his missionary career.[38] The *Funeral Teares* (based on a medieval homily attributed to Origen)[39] dramatizes the plight and the meditations of a Mary Magdalen who suffers almost to distraction from the loss of her Lord and best beloved. Her faith is sorely tried and is rewarded after Christ's resurrection with an incomplete reunion; for Jesus appears to her, but tells her, "noli me tangere" ("touch me not"), having assumed the remoteness of the glorified Christ, soon to escape his earthly habitation. Southwell may have thought that Mary's example, which revealed that hope and the acceptance of loss were necessary for a Christian, could help the countess deal with the loss of her own "lord" or husband. The earl, after his conversion to Catholicism and his attempts to reach Catholic leaders on the Continent, had been taken away from his wife by his religious enemies and made dead to her by his entombment in the Tower, from which he would emerge only by his own death and resurrection. Southwell emphasizes that it was "the Jewes" who had taken Jesus "prisoner" (*MMFT* 46^{r-v}). It is clear from other contexts, especially in the *Epistle of Comfort,* that when he speaks of persecutive Jews, he is often thinking of militant Protestants—like those who had imprisoned Anne Dacres's husband and who could at any time, because of Howard's conviction for treason, decide to commit the standard outrages on his body.

Southwell exhorts those suffering for their Catholic faith to "make the same account of the obliquyes of our adversaries, that [St. Steven] did of the malice of the Jewes." The church of Luther and Calvin he calls "the sinagoge of antichrist"; the church buildings of Protestants, "polluted Sinagoge[s]." "How terrible," he imagines, will the wounds of Catholic martyrs be "to the Sinagoge" on the day of judgment when the persecutors shall, like the Jews responsible for Jesus' death, "looke on him whom they have persed" and be held responsible for the murder. Southwell hopes that the Protestant, "aduoulterous Sinagogue" may still be converted: "Beleeve you and lyve you, and though you now persecute us here for a tyme: yet rejoyce with us for ever" (*EC* 9^v, 77^r, 168^r, 193^v, 209^r). He does not raise the issue of forced conversion, though he may have believed in the coercion of heretics, if not of infidels.[40]

Southwell was not unique in speaking of the synagogue in this way. The Duke of Guise in Marlowe's *The Massacre at Paris* (1968) spoke similarly of Protestants as Jews:

> There are a hundred Huguenots and more
> Which in the woods do hold their synagogue
> And daily meet about this time of day. . . .
> (11.20–22)[41]

And although English Protestants could be found referring to Catholics as Jews who blindly relied on "works" for salvation, the association of Puritans with Judaism (as in the person of Ben Jonson's Puritan "Rabbi," Zeal-of-the-land Busy) seems to have been at least as prevalent.[42] Shylock's practice of usury, his "sober house" and disdain for the "shallow fopp'ry" of "fools" at their carnival (2.5.33–36), his religious exclusivism—"I will not eat with you, drink with you, nor pray with you" (1.3.36–37)—all contribute to his "Puritan" image.[43] Catholics, of course, could be puritanical as well, and in the same respects. Southwell himself was something of a Jesuit-Puritan. But in Shakespeare's England, it was Protestants, Puritan and otherwise, who wielded the knife against the missionary "merchants" whose religion they hated. And Shylock, though belonging to a minority population and not personally a power in the state of Venice, had the "law" on his side as he looked to "have the heart" of Antonio (3.1.127), like the executioner who, in compliance with the law and without hindrance (a year or so before the play was written), had sliced through Southwell's ribcage to extract the still-beating organ.[44] When at the beginning of Antonio's trial the Duke expressed his hope that Shylock had led the "fashion" of his "malice / To the last hour of act" only to show mercy at the last minute (4.1.18–19), he echoed the words of Southwell as he stood on the cart waiting for hanging: "I am come hither to play out the last act of this poor life" (Devlin 1956, 321). In Shakespeare's fantasy of wish-fulfillment, the merchant of Venice is saved. But outside that world of imagination, in Elizabeth's London, the merchant of Rome had fallen a casualty in wars of state, which could not or would not at the time be separated from the wars of religion.

Shylock too is "saved," but through a conversion that is virtually compelled. Abhorrent to the modern mind, such forcing of "conviction" seemed even to some of Shakespeare's contemporaries a sinful outrage. Indeed, Southwell's predecessor on the English mission, Robert Persons (the same Jesuit probably alluded to, as noted, in *The Merchant of Venice*), wrote that as he was then "minded" (in 1580), he "wold not for ten thousand worldes, compell a Jewe to sweare that theire weare a blessed Trinity."[45] The conscience of a Jew who has "in no way received the faith" (as Aquinas put it) ought "by no means be coerced to receive it."[46] Following Aquinas, however, Persons was sure that though the beliefs of infidels and Jews might be tolerated, those of heretics should not be; for abandoning the faith once received was the sin of apostasy, a matter of perverse will and thus a violation of conscience rather than a privileged, protected compliance with its imperatives; and, though Persons late in his life came to adopt a more positive attitude to the toleration even of heretics (Clancy 1964, 158),[47] he contended, in the days when Southwell would have known and no doubt shared his views, that the obstinate will of an apostate might legitimately be constrained.[48] Persons must have been aware of Augustine's observation, quoted by Aquinas, that "Christ at first compelled Paul and afterwards taught him."[49]

If then under Shylock's "Jewish gaberdine" Shakespeare hid a militant Protestant, and if he stealthily traced a Roman collar around Antonio's neck, the conflict between the two characters, played out as it is, must reveal something of the playwright's response to the issues of persecution and intolerance as they were dramatized in the religious politics of his day. It seems to have been (and this can hardly be a surprise) a complex and ambiguous reaction. Shakespeare has Shylock insist on his humanity, even with words that Southwell had used to describe the suffering humanity of Christ; but then Shylock justifies on the basis of what he has in common with those he hates his passion for vengeance against them: "If you prick us, do we not bleed . . . ? And if you wrong us, shall we not revenge? If we are like you in the rest, we will resemble you in that" (3.1.64–68). We must sympathize with Shylock for the contempt he endures and the pain he suffers; but we cannot forget that he is a hypocrite and a would-be murderer, whose religion has not commanded bloodshed, but has served him as an excuse for seeking it. In this last respect he is like Southwell's Protestant "Jews," and Shakespeare's judgment of him is severe. Antonio, on the other hand, as a man prodigal with his life and means, as a martyr in mind and almost in the flesh, is meant to elicit some admiration and pity. But the "ancient Roman honor" that he embodies and upholds leads him at first to deny charity to a usurer whom he hates for his lack of charity. That Antonio detests the "heart" of the enemy who would kill him is understandable; but that he considers this heart "Jewish" in its wickedness (4.1.80) is culpably, wickedly irrational, as the play's many ironies suggest. Portia must teach Antonio the quality of mercy, which he badly needs to learn. Now the pardon that the Christians grant to the Jew is not as radical as many modern readers would like to see; and perhaps Shakespeare himself believed it should have been less "strain'd."[50] The Christians (Catholics?) themselves, none of whom is faultless, do not realize their own need for forgiveness. But Shylock, like the vengeful Protestant who has found in the law an opportunity for blood and intends to take it, receives more kindness than he was willing to give; and Shakespeare has made his clear-eyed villainy weigh more heavily on the scales of obliquity than

Antonio's prejudice, "righteous" hatred, and otherwise complacent high-mindedness. The playwright elsewhere deals with the Catholic persecutory spirit (Klause 1999); and in musing deeply on the sectarian conflict of his time he must have anticipated, we can imagine, the reflection of Jonathan Swift about the universal problem of sinister animosities dubiously sanctified by religious faith: "We have just enough religion to make us hate, but not enough to make us love one another" (*Thoughts on Various Subjects* in Davis 1939–68, 1:241). The stories of both the Marian and the Elizabethan martyrs illustrated this sad fact. *The Merchant of Venice,* however, was written in 1596 or 1597, a year or so after the death of Robert Southwell, an outlaw-priest with whose ideas and character Shakespeare seems to have developed, perilously, a special acquaintance.[51] If we can perceive in Antonio something of what Shakespeare came to believe about Southwell, we can hardly judge that response unequivocal. A martyr may be admired, pitied, feared, and scorned; he may be heeded, questioned, and resisted. Shakespeare invites all such reactions to Antonio, and perhaps to a figure like Southwell. But he makes one point clear and simple: ideals are not to be suppressed by killing the idealist (an ethical prohibition applicable to enemies on either side). Thus the quality of tolerance, at least, *is* constrained: the essence is defined and the practice required by moral principle. In a fairy tale, the martyr may be saved from himself and his adversary. Outside it, the law and the knife often exact the pound of flesh, leaving little room for public protest—except, perhaps, in a fiction, a play.

The Southwell-like Antonio has of course more than one opponent. A great anomaly of this historical reading of the *Merchant* is that Southwell has lent something of his image to both Antonio and Portia, who are in crucial respects at odds. The "clerical" merchant, celibate, self-abnegating, absolutist (though like a flexible casuist he agrees to seek a usurious loan out of love for his friend), reminds one of the Counter-Reformation missionary, martyr, and hater of heretics. Portia in her lawyer's disguise resembles the scholar and religious controversialist who struggles with the law and its upholders to turn them merciful. This pacific side of Southwell is thus attributed in the play to the "lay" Catholic (she is not *truly* the professional colleague of Bellario) who instructs the "wether of the flock" in mercy, and who also teaches him a lesson in the complexity of obligation.[52] Her point of view, then, which enjoys a certain privilege in the play, is like that of the English Catholic lay aristocracy represented by the family of Shakespeare's patron Southampton. The earl's mother, for example, "maintained a determined piety along with undiminished worldliness." In the tradition of her family, she secretly sheltered priests, but in the interests of peace she did not scruple to attend Protestant services (Devlin 1956, 218; Stopes 1922, 10). Her father kept his faith while seeking principled means of accommodation with a government of heretics to which he deferred in ways that some part of the Catholic clerical elite found unsatisfactory.[53]

Antonio's love for his friend is so generous that he would offer up his life's blood in its name; but his eagerness to use his sacrifice to simplify his friend's loyalties and draw them primarily to himself is checked. It is comically right that in the competition between Antonio and Portia for Bassanio she should win, and appropriate that the triumph should be revealed in the mundane but symbolically important trick of the ring. The heroic Antonio, who holds "the world but as the world" and assumes his role in it to be "a sad one" (1.1.77–79), stands for sacrifice. But so does the worldly Portia, from whom the world demands a special kind of "hazard" and "venture," and whose impresa contains a leaden casket. From the perspective of radical religion, her prayers at the "wayside crosses" (to obtain happiness, it should be noted) would seem a comfortable aristocrat's tepid accommodation to the tragic good. The play, however, though acknowledging this perspective does not assume it. Whatever sacrifices have been or may be required by Portia's love, she need not surrender Belmont, a golden home to a race of variously ideal and imperfect loves and lovers, the site of conjugal joys and rivalries and bawdy jokes—all the pure and impure flames of a "naughty world" (5.1.91)—where the earthly ties and ventures of husband and wife are stronger than the powerful influence of a martyr's loving claims on the friend for whom he was willing to lay down his life. A visitor to Belmont, Antonio in his singlemindedness is at once too grand and too small to be at home there, although it was his generosity that allowed it to become a place of celebration. The estate, after all, belongs to Portia (even after her marriage she seems to rule it), the lady who is victorious over two extremes, determined to save life rather than see it lost either to self-interested hatred or self-ruinous love.[54]

"Who chooseth me must give and hazard all he hath." This is a fierce ideal, which comedy finds a way to temper. Moderation is the comic value that the playwright allows to prevail, while he recognizes the paradox that it is not entirely happy or harmless. In this fairy tale, wishes are fulfilled, but not through an alchemy in which lead is turned to gold. Lead is first chosen instead of gold and is never entirely replaced; base metal (not only love's exhilarating sacrifice but the dull pain of submission and loss, Shylock's as well as Antonio's) remains in the precious element (Belmont's happiness) as residue (dross?) and alloy. Triumph lives on defeat—at least, it does so in history if not in fantasy. This complexity may be inferred, perhaps anachronistically, from the play's designation on the title page of its first quarto edition as "The most excellent Historie of the Merchant of Venice."

NOTES

1. See Rabkin (1981, 12–27), Vickers (1993, 372–84), but cf. Danson (1978, 13–14 n.). An earlier form of the present essay was published in *Religion and the Arts* 7.1/2 (2003).

2. See, for example, Cohen (1982, 772): "The concluding tripartite unity of Antonio, Bassanio, and Portia enacts precisely [the] interclass harmony between aristocratic landed wealth and mercantile capital, with the former dominant."

3. The story of the choice of "vessels" in *Gesta Romanorum* does have an explicit religious dimension. See Bullough (1957, 1:513–14).

4. The boy was "the very staff of my age," laments the old man (2.2.66–67; cf. Tobit 5:23 [Bishops' bible], in which the young Tobiah's mother speaks these words). Old Gobbo and Launcelot remind one also of Isaac and Jacob when the boy asks his blind father for his "blessing" (2.2.74–87; Genesis 27:19–24).

5. Shakespeare's text is cited throughout from *The Riverside Shakespeare,* 2d edition (1997). Scriptural references are to the Geneva Bible, unless they are translated within another text.

6. For a discussion of the different purposes of biblical allusion in *The Merchant of Venice,* see Marx (2000, 103–24).

7. 2.7.40; 1.1.120; 1.2.131; 2.2.192–93, 2.5.25–26. Ser Giovanni Fiorentino's tale is given in translation in Bullough (1957, 1:463–76). Unlike Portia and Bassanio, the lovers in *Il Pecorone* blithely commit fornication before their marriage.

8. In this sense, Bassanio speaks of "religion":

> In religion,
> What damned error but some sober brow
> Will bless it, and approve it with a text,
> Hiding the grossness with fair ornament? (3.2.77–80)

9. See the historical studies of Noonan (1957) and Jones (1989).

10. The distinction is made too cleanly in Smith's "Shakespeare and Shylock" (1964).

11. See also Danson (1978, 59).

12. See Greenblatt (1978, 293 n.). And see note 36.

13. For recent theories about Shakespeare's Catholic connections in general, see, for example, Honigmann (1985) and Taylor (1994). On Southwell and Shakespeare, see Grosart (1872, lxxxix–xci), Devlin (1956, 257–73), Milward (1973, 54–59), Brownlow (1987, 27, and 1996, 94–96), Klause (1999, 219–40; 2002, 218–21; and 2001, 401–27).

14. See Brooks's essay, "Two Principles in Source-Study" (1987), the argument of which I would qualify somewhat.

15. Southwell's works are abbreviated as follows: *EC* for *An Epistle of Comfort; EF* for *An Epistle unto His Father; MMFT* for *Marie Magdalens Funeral Teares; SPC* for *Saint Peters Complaint; HS* for *An Humble Supplication to Her Majestie.* They are cited from the editions listed in Works Cited.

16. See *OED,* s.v. "wilderness," 4: "A mangled, confused, or vast collection or assemblage of persons or things"; *MV* 3.1.122–23; *Titus* 3.1.54; *EF* 17. Southwell's *Epistle* to his father was written in 1588 or 1589.

17. Southwell uses the substantive "yongers" in "Upon the Image of Death" (33), and the adjective "prodigal" frequently throughout his writings, the parable of the Prodigal Son being one of his favorites (see, for example, *EC* 36^r, 43^r, 133^v).

18. Here, as often in Shakespeare, may be an instance of an over-determined text. See Tobin (1999), and notes 19 and 20.

19. The "fawning publican" probably owes something also to *The Jew of Malta* 2.3.20, and perhaps to Nashe's *Saffron Walden* (see Tobin 1992, 313).

20. Compare the supposedly unforgiving "tribe of Levi" in *The Jew of Malta* 2.3.18.

21. (1974, 39^r, 55^r and 28^v-29^v, 155^r). The word "badge" occurs five other times in the *Epistle,* usually associated with suffering: 76^v, 96^r, 9^r-11^r, 54^v, 51^v, 66^v-68^v.

22. Holmer proposes, in the light of late sixteenth-century English treatments of usury, that Shylock actually seeks a "covert usury" in striking the

deal with Antonio. Usurious gain, she argues, need not be money; and the financial gain that would accrue to the usurer with Antonio removed from the scene could in fact be usurious in the extreme (1995, 168–73).

23. Among other possible traces of Southwell in 3.2 are:

SOUTHWELL	SHAKESPEARE
her doore deceite, And slipperie hope her staires . . . kills the hart . . . sow not the sands (*Poems* 1967, "Loves servile lot," 61–73)	hearts as false as stairs of sands (84)
our very hairs, which are but . . . excrements (*EF* 17)	beards . . . but valor's excrement (87)
was ever any, that . . . bought so deare, the love of anye creature (*EC* 37v)	Since you are dear bought, I will love you dear (313)

24. See Shaheen (1999, 180–82), and Seneca's *De Clementia* 1.19, as suggested by Brown and others (1959, 111 n.; Furness 1888, 211–12). One of the most important of the biblical analogues is Deuteronomy 32:2, which Southwell quotes in the *Epistle of Comfort* 157^r.

25. Cf. also:

SOUTHWELL	SHAKESPEARE *MV* 4.1
paynes . . . if you continewe still in this rigorous course (*EC* 208^v–9^r)	great pains to qualify His rigorous course (4.1.7–8)
suffer . . . quietlye . . . rage (*EC* 152^r)	suffer, with a quietness of spirit, The . . . rage (4.1.12–13)
necessarye . . . dogges (*EC* 84^r)	necessary cat (4.1.55)
of so harsh and currish a humor (*EF* 5)	Thy currish spirit (4.1.133)
manifest . . . proceeded (*EC* 81^r)	manifest proceeding (4.1.358)
imperfections, wher-withal they are here coped (*EC* 188$^{r–v}$)	We freely cope your courteous pains withal (4.1.412)

26. See Nathan (1957, 334–35), and, for a more detailed application of biblical incidents to the play, Holmer (1995, 194–96).

27. This work, after long circulation in manuscript, was clandestinely printed in 1596–97, at about the time Shakespeare was writing the *Merchant*. See Southwell, *Two Letters and Short Rules of a Good Life,* ed. Brown (1973, xxiii, xlvi–xlviii).

28. And cf. *EC* 127^v: "children, that in their prowes surmounting their age, have in their childish bodye, shewed hoarye . . . mindes. . . ."

29. The first volume of the *Controversies* had been published in 1586; the second and third volumes were to appear in 1588 and 1593. See Brodrick (1961, 62–63).

30. Cf. Bullough (1957, 1: 72) and *Merchant* 4.1.153.

31. See Southwell, *Humble Supplication,* ed. Bald (1953, 6–7 n.).

32. See *Love's Labor's Lost* 4.2.83, 149–50 and Phelps (1915). Phelps does not consider the by now more usual speculation that Thomas Nashe, in addition to or instead of Southwell, might be alluded to in the first of these passages.

33. *The Merchant of Venice* was entered into the *Stationers' Register* on July 22, 1598, and not published until 1600. Reference to the "Neapolitan prince" may have been a late addition to the play. Hasty revision would help to explain why the Servingman in 1.2 refers to four suitors about to take their leave after Nerissa has mentioned six.

34. See Southwell's coded letter to Robert Persons (Pollen 1908, 301–3), in which he speaks of a fellow merchant (Edmund Campion), who, having "loaded his vessel with English wares . . . has successfully returned to the desired port" ("ha caricato la sua navicella di quelle mercantie Inglesi e si è tornato con felice successo al desiderato porto").

35. A Jesuit who had preceded Southwell on the English mission, Jasper Heywood (John Donne's uncle), fervently condemned even the 5 percent interest charged on loans in Bavaria (Flynn 1985, 48). Southwell himself did not write against the usury in ordinary financial transactions, but he denounced those who "change the kingdome of heaven for monye," who practice the perverse "usurye" of putting out their money "to such, as can not so muche as restore the principall." He had primarily in mind Catholics who betrayed their faith for the sake of material comfort, offering themselves as "detters" to the deadly sins, and for the "usury and lone of [their] wealth" could count on "presente evils, and future punishments" (*EC* 175^v–76^r). As Moisan points out, some Elizabethans considered usury a kind of "heresy" (1987, 194).

36. In his essay "Marlowe, Marx, and Anti-Semitism," Greenblatt states forcefully that "Anti-Semitism . . . is never merely a trope to be adopted or discarded by an author as he might choose to employ zeugma or eschew personification. It is charged from the start with irrationality and bad faith and only partly rationalized as a rhetorical strategy" (293 n.). One can understand

today that Southwell's "use" of the Jews as part of an argumentative tactic is hardly innocent and innocuous. It is the argument of this essay on *The Merchant of Venice* that Shakespeare follows Southwell's lead, and therefore to some extent shares his blame, although he realizes more than Southwell does the insanity as well as the oxymoronic absurdity of "religious hatred."

37. It was once thought that Southwell had preached a sermon on Mary Magdalen in the Marshalsea Prison to an audience that included Dorothy Arundell (see Devlin 1956, 117–18). Brownlow has shown, however, that someone else must have preached the sermon, for Southwell indicates in a letter that he was in Buckinghamshire on July 22, the date of the sermon (1996, 35; see Pollen 1908, 308).

38. According to one seventeenth-century report, Southwell wrote his *A Short Rule of a Good Life* for the Countess. See Brownlow (1996, 59).

39. See Brownlow (1996, 35).

40. See discussion below.

41. Quoted from the edition of H. J. Oliver. Protestants, in turn, referred to the "Romane synagogues," no doubt alluding to the same biblical phrase that Catholics had in mind: the "Synagogue of Satan" (Revelation 2.9). See the *OED* s.v. "synagogue" (2) and Mayo's *The Popes Parliament* (1591, Aiii).

42. Danson (1978, 78–80) and Cohen (1982, 769) have imagined a Catholic Shylock. On Shylock the Puritan, see Siegel (1968, 237–54), Milward (1973, 158–61), and Barroll (1974, 150).

43. In Elizabethan England, Puritans were hardly a unique usurious "class," but they were vilified by some of their enemies as among the most "open" practitioners of the "sin of usury" (see Milward 1973, 159). Richard Bancroft characterized their religious exclusivism in rhetoric that prefigures Shylock's: "Seeing our church, our government, our ministry, our service, our sacraments, are thus and thus . . . therefore they will not pray with us, they will not communicate with us . . . , they will have nothing to do with us" (*Survey of the Pretended Holy Discipline* [1593], qtd. in Milward 160; cf. *Merchant* 1.3.35–38).

44. See Devlin (1956, 324). An illustration of the executioner's butchery, his knife cutting its way to a victim's heart, was published by Richard Verstegan in his *Theatrum Crudelitatum* (Antwerp, 1587); it is reprinted in McGrath, *Papists and Puritans Under Elizabeth I* (1967, opposite p. 294).

45. *A Briefe Discours contayning certayne Reasons why Catholiques refuse to goe to Church* 5ᵛ; quoted in Clancy (1964, 146). See also Holmer (1995, 222).

46. *Summa Theologiae* 2a 2ae, q. 10, art. 8, ad 2: "Iudaei, si nullo modo susceperunt fidem, non sunt cogendi ad fidem."

47. Persons endorsed a limited kind of religious toleration in a work written in 1596 and widely circulated in manuscript: *A Memorial for the Reformation of England.*

48. Persons, *Reasons why Catholiques refuse to goe to Church* ‡‡ iiii. In the *Epistle of Comfort,* Southwell mentions, without the least doubt of its propriety, the execution, "not many yeares since," of a "Renegate Christian" who had converted to Judaism and "was burnt for this fonde doctrine" (1974, 185r).

49. *Summa Theologiae,* 2a 2ae, q. 10, art. 8, ad 2.: "Agnoscant in Paulo prius cogentem Christum et postea docentem."

50. On Shakespeare's impatience with constricted orthodoxies concerning forgiveness, see Sehrt (1952). Shakespeare's audience might have considered the Venetians magnanimous in sparing the life of a man who had attempted murder; in restoring to him, in spite of the law's harsh penalties, half of his estate; the other half in trust to Antonio, who would invest it for Shylock's daughter and son-in-law and prevent Shylock from lending it out at usurious rates. Even Shylock's forced baptism might have seemed to many of them a mercy, a potentially redemptive punishment. Perhaps Protestants and Catholics both would have missed the irony that the "Puritan" Shylock was virtually compelled to the Christian font as English law was forcing Catholics to the Protestant one, and as Roman baptizers were hoping to reverse the practice. Shakespeare's views, however, can never with certainty be reduced to those of his audience. Especially on the issue of forgiveness, he is forever confounding the conventional views of the time (Klause 1988); and on the matter of "compulsion," he often seems of a mind with Falstaff (*1 Henry IV* 2.4.236–40).

51. Of Southwell's works mentioned in this study, one, the *Humble Supplication,* and possibly a second, the *Epistle* to his father (composed in 1589 or earlier and secretly printed in 1596–97) would have been available to Shakespeare only in manuscripts circulated in the Catholic underground. The *Epistle of Comfort,* illegally published and officially suppressed, would have been dangerous to possess.

52. Shakespeare gave to Portia, it should be remembered, the apparently satiric allusion to Robert Persons, who labored intensely to direct the religious and political allegiance of all Englishmen to Rome (see discussion above). In his *Memorial for the Reformation of England* (see note 47), Persons had stressed, in opposition to Protestant tendencies, the superiority of clergy to laity (1580, 191–202). He had discussed as well other issues pertinent to the *Merchant*: alternatives to "intolerable Usury" (95) and the legitimacy and illegitimacy of forced religious conversion (32–45).

53. Southampton's grandfather, Anthony Browne, Lord Montagu, was a staunch Catholic and, at some risk to himself, a protector of Catholics. He spoke openly in Parliament against the Acts of Uniformity and Supremacy. Yet he retained the trust of Elizabeth, remained in the House of Lords, and was conspicuously loyal to the Crown in the face of the Spanish threat (*DNB;* Devlin

1956, 15, 108; Stopes 1922, 498). He seemed open to the idea that his grandson should marry Lord Burghley's grandaughter (Akrigg 1968, 32). Montagu occasionally attended Protestant services—until in his later years he was severely reproached by a priest for his error. He had as a chaplain Alban Langdale who, according to some historians, was one of the foremost Catholic opponents of the idea that recusancy was an essential sign of loyalty to the Catholic Church and faith. Robert Persons felt impelled to refute Langdale's written arguments, which had concluded that recusancy was a counsel of perfection rather than an obligation (Manning 1969, 160; Holmes 1982, 90–94; Walsham 1993, 50–54). The attitudes of the English Catholic laity toward the martyrdom their clerical leaders had sometimes asked them to face were complex, and of course not always entirely compliant. It is also true, however, that Southampton's father, the second earl, suffered much for his Catholicism. A kinsman, Thomas Pounde of (another) Belmont, in Hampshire, endured thirty years of almost continuous imprisonment for his religious beliefs, and was admitted into the Society of Jesus while in prison (Akrigg 6–15; Devlin 14; Bassett 1968, 17–18).

54. Before Bassanio's "choosing," Portia insists that she will not "teach" him "How to choose right," for to do so would make her "forsworn" (3.2.2–11). Yet she finds a way to avoid immolation to an abstract principle by offering to him clues that a "true" lover would not miss—such as, her assertion that she stands "for sacrifice" (57); the words in the song that rhyme with "lead" (63–65); the denigration in the song of "fancy" born of appearances (63–70). Bassanio seems to receive the message: "So may the outward shows be least themselves" (73). Portia, then, in her casuistical cunning, may be said to save herself as well as Antonio from martyrdom. Many critics find it impossible to believe that she should be at once so conscientious and so devious; but many devout souls in Shakespeare's Europe asserted the validity of such a paradox. See Zagorin (1990).

WORKS CITED

Akrigg, G. P. V. *Shakespeare and the Earl of Southampton.* London: Hamish Hamilton, 1968.

Aquinas, Thomas. *Summa Theologiae.* Ed. Brothers of the Dominican Order. Madrid: La Editorial Catolica, 1961.

Barroll, J. Leeds. *Artificial Persons.* Columbia, S.C.: University of South Carolina Press, 1974.

Bassett, Bernard. *The English Jesuits: From Campion to Martindale.* New York: Herder and Herder, 1968.

Brodrick, James. *Robert Bellarmine: Saint and Scholar.* Westminster, Md.: Newman Press, 1961.

Brooks, Harold F. "Two Principles in Source-Study." In *KM 80: A Birthday Album for Kenneth Muir,* by Philip Edwards et al., 25–26. Liverpool, England: Liverpool University Press, 1987.

Brown, John Russell, ed. *The Merchant of Venice,* by William Shakespeare. London: Methuen, 1959.

Brownlow, F. W. *Robert Southwell.* New York: Twayne, 1996.

———. "Shakespeare and Southwell." *KM 80: A Birthday Album for Kenneth Muir,* by Philip Edwards et al. Liverpool, England: Liverpool University Press, 1987.

———. *Shakespeare, Harsnett, and the Devils of Denham.* Newark, Del.: University of Delaware Press.

Bullough, Geoffrey, ed. *Narrative and Dramatic Sources of Shakespeare.* 8 vols. London: Routledge and Kegan Paul; New York: Columbia University Press, 1957–1975.

Clancy, Thomas H. *Papist Pamphleteers: The Allen-Persons Party and the Political Thought of the Counter-Reformation in England, 1572–1615.* Chicago, Ill.: Loyola University Press, 1964.

Cohen, Walter. "*The Merchant of Venice* and the Possibilities of Historical Criticism." *ELH* 49 (1982): 765–89.

Danson, Lawrence. *The Harmonies of the Merchant of Venice.* New Haven, Conn., and London: Yale University Press, 1978.

Davis, Herbert, ed. *The Prose Writings of Jonathan Swift.* 14 vols. Oxford, England: Basil Blackwell, 1939–68.

Devlin, Christopher. *The Life of Robert Southwell.* London: Longmans, Green, 1956.

Edwards, Francis. *Robert Persons: The Biography of an Elizabethan Jesuit, 1546–1610.* St. Louis, Mo.: The Institute of Jesuit Sources, 1995.

Flynn, Dennis. "The English Mission of Jasper Heywood, S.J." *Archivum Historicum Societatis Jesu* 54 (1985): 45–76.

Furness, H. H., ed. *The Merchant of Venice. A New Variorum Edition of Shakespeare.* Philadelphia, Pa.: J. B. Lippincott, 1888.

Greenblatt, Stephen J. "Marlowe, Marx, and Anti-Semitism." *Critical Inquiry* 5 (1978): 291–307.

Grosart, Rev. Alexander B., ed. *The Complete Poems of Robert Southwell, S.J.* London: Robson and Sons, 1872.

Gross, John. *Shylock: A Legend and Its Legacy*. New York: Simon and Schuster, 1992.

Halio, Jay, ed. *The Merchant of Venice*, by William Shakespeare. Oxford and New York: Oxford University Press, 1993.

Holmer, Joan Ozark. *The Merchant of Venice: Choice, Hazard, and Consequence*. New York: St. Martin's Press, 1995.

Holmes, Peter. *Resistance and Compromise: The Political Thought of the Elizabethan Catholics*. Cambridge, England: Cambridge University Press, 1982.

Honigmann, E. A. J. *Shakespeare: The "Lost Years."* Manchester, England: Manchester University Press, 1985.

Hunter, G. K. "The Theology of Marlowe's *Jew of Malta*." In *Dramatic Identities and Cultural Tradition: Studies in Shakespeare and His Contemporaries*, by G. K. Hunter. New York: Barnes & Noble, 1978.

Janelle, Pierre. *Robert Southwell the Writer: A Study in Religious Inspiration*. New York: Sheed & Ward, 1935.

Jones, Norman L. *God and the Moneylenders: Usury and Law in Early Modern England*. Oxford, England: Basil Blackwell, 1989.

Klause, John. "New Sources of Shakespeare's *King John*: The Writings of Robert Southwell." *Studies in Philology* 98 (2001): 401–27.

———. "Politics, Heresy, and Martyrdom in Shakespeare's Sonnet 124 and *Titus Andronicus*." In *Shakespeare's Sonnets: Critical Essays*, ed. James Schiffer. 219–40. New York and London: Garland, 1999.

———. "*The Phoenix and Turtle* in Its Time." In *In the Company of Shakespeare: Essays on English Renaissance Literature in Honor of G. Blakemore Evans*, ed. Douglas Bruster and Thomas Moisan. 206–30. Rutherford, N.J.: Fairleigh Dickinson University Press, 2002.

———. "*Venus and Adonis*: Can We Forgive Them?" *Studies in Philology* 85 (1988): 353–77.

Lewalski, Barbara. "Biblical Allusion and Allegory in *The Merchant of Venice*." *Shakespeare Quarterly* 13 (1962): 327–43.

Manning, Roger B. *Religion and Society in Elizabethan Sussex: A Study of the Enforcement of the Elizabethan Settlement, 1558–1603*. Leicester, England: Leicester University Press, 1969.

Marlowe, Christopher. *Dido Queen of Carthage and the Massacre at Paris.* Ed. H. J. Oliver. Cambridge, Mass.: Harvard University Press, 1968.

———. *The Jew of Malta.* Ed. N. W. Bawcutt. Manchester, England: Manchester University Press, 1978.

Marx, Steven. *Shakespeare and the Bible.* Oxford, England: Oxford University Press, 2000.

Mayo, John K. *The Popes Parliament.* London: Richard Field, 1591.

McGrath, Patrick. *Papists and Puritans Under Elizabeth I.* New York: Walker, 1967.

Milward, Peter. *Shakespeare's Religious Background.* Bloomington, Ind.: Indiana University Press, 1973.

Moisan, Thomas. "'Which is the merchant here? and which the Jew?': Subversion and Recuperation in *The Merchant of Venice.*" In *Shakespeare Reproduced: The Text in History and Ideology,* ed. Jean E. Howard and Marion F. O'Connor. 188–206. New York and London: Methuen, 1987.

Nathan, Norman. "Balthasar, Daniel, and Portia." *Notes and Queries* 202 (1957): 334–35.

Noonan, John T. Jr. *The Scholastic Analysis of Usury.* Cambridge, Mass.: Harvard University Press, 1957.

Persons, Robert. *A Brief Discours contayning certayne Reasons why Catholiques refuse to goe to Church* (1580).

———. *A Memorial for the Reformation of England* (1596). Reprinted in Edward Gee, *The Jesuit's Memorial.* London: Chiswel, 1690.

Phelps, John. "Father Parsons in Shakespeare." *Archiv für das Studium der Neueren Sprachen und Literaturen* 133 (1915): 66–86.

Pollen, John Hungerford, ed. *Documents Relating to the English Martyrs.* London: Publications of the Catholic Record Society, 1908.

Rabkin, Norman. *Shakespeare and the Problem of Meaning.* Chicago, Ill., and London: University of Chicago Press, 1981.

Santayana, George. "The Absence of Religion in Shakespeare." *Interpretations of Poetry and Religion.* New York: Harper & Brothers, 1957.

Sehrt, Ernst Theodor. *Vergebung und Gnade bei Shakespeare.* Stuttgart, Germany: Koehler, 1952.

Shaheen, Naseeb. *Biblical References in Shakespeare's Plays.* Newark, Del.: University of Delaware Press, 1999.

Shakespeare, William. *The Riverside Shakespeare*. Ed. G. Blakemore Evans et al. 2d ed. Boston: Houghton Mifflin, 1997.

Shapiro, James. *Shakespeare and the Jews*. New York: Columbia University Press, 1996.

Siegel, Paul N. *Shakespeare in His Time and Ours*. South Bend, Ind.: University of Notre Dame Press, 1968.

Smith, Warren D. "Shakespeare and Shylock." *Shakespeare Quarterly* 15 (1964): 193–99.

Southwell, Robert. *An Epistle of Comfort*. English Recusant Literature, 1558–1640. Vol. 211. Ilkley, Yorkshire: The Scolar Press, 1974.

_____. *Marie Magdalens Funeral Teares*. Ed. Vincent B. Leitch. Delmar, N.Y.: Scholars' Fasimiles and Reprints, 1974.

_____. *An Humble Supplication to Her Maiestie*. Ed. R. C. Bald. Cambridge, England: Cambridge University Press, 1953.

_____. *The Poems of Robert Southwell, S.J.* Ed. James H. McDonald and Nancy Pollard Brown. Oxford, England: Clarendon Press, 1967.

_____. *Two Letters and Short Rules of a Good Life*. Ed. Nancy Pollard Brown. Charlottesville, Va.: Published for Folger Shakespeare Library [by] University Press of Virginia, 1973.

Stopes, Charlotte Carmichael. *The Life of Henry, Third Earl of Southampton, Shakespeare's Patron*. Cambridge, England: Cambridge University Press, 1922.

Taylor, Gary. "Forms of Opposition: Shakespeare and Middleton." *English Literary Renaissance* 24 (1994): 283–314.

Tobin, J. J. M. "Justice for Fleay." *Notes and Queries* 244 (1999): 230–31.

_____. "Nashe and Shakespeare: Some Further Borrowings." *Notes and Queries* 237 (1992): 309–20.

Vickers, Brian. *Appropriating Shakespeare: Contemporary Critical Quarrels*. New Haven, Conn., and London: Yale University Press, 1993.

Walsham, Alexandra. *Church Papists: Catholicism, Conformity and Confessional Polemic in Early Modern England*. Woodbridge, Suffolk: Boydell Press, for the Royal Historical Society, 1993.

Zagorin, Perez. *Ways of Lying: Dissimulation, Persecution, and Conformity in Early Modern Europe*. Cambridge, Mass.: Harvard University Press, 1990.

9

This Side of Purgatory: Ghostly Fathers and the Recusant Legacy in *Hamlet*

by *John Freeman*

University of Detroit Mercy, Detroit, Michigan

HAMLET: *Hic et ubique?* Then we'll shift our ground.
Come hither, gentlemen,
And lay your hands again upon my sword.
Swear by my sword
Never to speak of this that you have heard.
GHOST: [*Beneath*] Swear by his sword.
HAMLET: Well said, old mole, canst work i' th' earth so fast?
A worthy pioner!

Hamlet (1.5.157–64)[1]

I was hardly tucked away when the pursuivants broke down the door and burst in. They fanned out through the house, making a great racket. The first thing they did was to shut up the mistress of the house in her own room with her daughters, then they locked up the Catholic servants in different places in the same part of the house. This done, they took possession of the place (it was a large house) and began to search everywhere, even lifting up the tiles of the roof to expose underneath them and using candles in the dark corners. When they found nothing, they started knocking down suspicious-looking places. They measured the walls with long rods and if the measurements did not tally they pulled down the section that they could not account for. They tapped every wall and floor for hollow spots; and on sounding anything hollow they smashed it in.

Fr. John Gerard, S.J., *The Autobiography of a Hunted Priest* (1952, 85–86)

Item, I, John Shakespear, do in like manner pray and beseech all my dear friends, parents, and kinfolks, by the bowels of our Saviour Jesus Christ, that since it is uncertain what lot will befall me, for fear notwithstanding lest by reason of my sins I be to pass and stay a long while in Purgatory, they will vouchsafe to assist and succour me with their holy prayers and satisfactory works. . . .

"The Spiritual Last Will and Testament of John Shakespeare"
(Schoenbaum 1987, 47)

AMONG SHAKESPEARE BIOGRAPHERS and critics, the question of his family's recusant nature has taken on over the years a spectral manifestation all of its own: visible to some, denied by others—fitfully sighted and cited between long periods of dormancy. The spectral quality of these recusant sightings is such that we find them surfacing in the investigations of Baker (1937) and Chambers (1923), disappearing for decades, and then resurfacing in the excited "discoveries" of biographical sleuths like Richard Wilson (1993). No doubt, ghostly fathers, real and fictional, inhabit the life and work of Shakespeare. Summoned forth by a Catholic profession of faith found in the rafters of his Stratford home, John Shakespeare has cast a figure as enigmatic and plaintive as Hamlet's own ghostly father stirring under the floorboards of the London stage.

Although Marcellus exclaims to Horatio regarding Hamlet's ghostly father, "Thou art a scholar, speak to it" (1.1.42), communing with these ghostly fathers is no easy enterprise for modern scholars. As Alexandra Walsham notes, the reconstruction of the recusant legacy is a work of remembering, for domestic Catholic recusant writers have until recently suffered an enforced obscurity (1993, 16). Moreover, modern scholars seeking to recover the recusant legacy have had to deal with individual recusant's own protective conspiracy of silence during what Walsham describes as "the unsettled half-century that followed the theological upheavals of the mid-1500's" (2). As Christopher Haigh argues, we witness in this period "the transfiguration of a Church into a sect" (1975, 26). Faced with legal and social penalties for the slightest expression of their Catholic identity, recusants were driven underground, into a Purgatorial half-life signified by the mocking labels of "church papists," "schismaticks," "demi-catholicks," and "temporizers." Under the Reformation, many English Catholics found it difficult if not impossible to live the Horatian *integer vitae,* thus contributing to the many competing versions among biographical accounts concerning John Shakespeare's religious beliefs and what role they played in the formation of William Shakespeare's character. This confusion carries over into *Hamlet,* where critics have trouble deciding whether Hamlet's own ghostly father is a Catholic spirit from Purgatory or a demonic imposter. Indeed, inadequate biographies of Shakespeare and inadequate analyses of *Hamlet* share one trait: they fail to take into account the recusant legacy lying just behind the false walls and hidden recesses of the play. The inheritor of that legacy, Hamlet reenacts the historical situation of the many recusants forced into a strangely fashioned, secularized existence, what amounted to a Purgatory on earth.

I. GHOSTLY FATHERS AND JOHN SHAKESPEARE'S WILL

Certainly, there are many hollow spots and inconsistencies in the biographical record of the Shakespeare family. The inconsistencies of John Shakespeare's private beliefs and public practice as well as the "lost years" for which we cannot account for young William's whereabouts are notable instances. In Shakespeare's personal background, the "ghostly father" we seek to engage assumes the form of John Shakespeare, a recusant who secretly signed his own profession of faith, in effect an insurance policy on his soul in perilous times. Schoenbaum describes its discovery during a renovation of the Shakespeare home:

> In April 1757 the then owner, Thomas Hart, fifth lineal descendant of the poet's sister Joan, was employing labourers to retile his roof. On the 29th Joseph Moseley, a master bricklayer described as of "very honest, sober, industrious character," found, while working with his men, a small paper-book between the rafters and the tiling. This book, or (more properly) booklet, consisted of six leaves stitched together. A Catholic profession of faith in fourteen articles, it has come to be known as the Spiritual Last Will and Testament of John Shakespeare. (1987, 45)

Asking for assistance in "so dangerous a voyage," the testator desires to "pass out of this life with the last sacrament of extreme unction" and to have anointment of his "senses both internal and external with the sacred oil of His infinite mercy" (46). A plea to be remembered by relatives in prayers after his death is also entered, in the event that "by reason of my sins I be to pass and stay a long while in Purgatory" (47). The anxious quality of this testament mirrors that felt by many recusants, who are advised by John Gerard's companion, Dr. Perne, not to give themselves up to the temporary comforts of conformity: "If you wish, you can *live* in the religion which the Queen and the whole kingdom profess—you will have a good life, you will have none of the vexations which Catholics have to suffer. But don't *die* in it" (Gerard 1952, 44–45).

Although the document seems to offer strong but circumstantial evidence concerning John Shakespeare's faith, biographers have tended either to overvalue or discount it as evidence. Those who tend to overvalue the document are best reflected by Eric Sams. Quite plausibly, Sams views this profession of faith as a heroic private gesture meant to make up for a life of many compromises that had placed the testator's soul at risk of eternal damnation. For Sams, the fact that John Shakespeare kept his Catholic testament of faith in his home in spite of the ardent persecution of recusants offers compelling evidence of the strength of his conviction at least to die a Catholic if he could not fully live as one. Arguing that the mere possession of such a document was a clear and present danger to the testator and to his family, Sams describes it as "a doubly powerful testimony to John Shakespeare's faith. It could easily have been burnt, and so could he" (1995, 34).

Unfortunately, in his later assertions, Sams sometimes goes where even angels would fear to tread. An ardent proponent of John Shakespeare's recusancy, Sams links Shakespeare's father to Hamlet's own ghostly father. He wryly observes, "The ghost of Hamlet's father, a pagan monarch in all that play's sources, is not only a good Catholic but actually quotes from the Catholic will of Shakespeare's father" (1995, 14). Sams cites the occurrence in both texts of the phrase "cut off in the blossomes of my sins" (34). In the first leaf of the document supplied by Jordan to Malone, the testator expresses a similarly worded anxiety about being "cut off in the blossom of my sins." Unfortunately, Sams does not take into account that Malone questioned the authenticity of this first leaf, an authenticity Schoenbaum rejects on the basis of a comparison with a much later formulary distributed to English recusants, St. Charles Borromeo's *The Contract and Testimony of the Soul* (Schoenbaum 1987, 51). Risking all by taking the entire document at face value, Sams argues William Shakespeare's invoking of the phrase years later authenticates his father's recusancy. Speculating that young Shakespeare may have been the trusted amanuensis who copied this testament for his father, Sams goes so far as to view the play itself as a haunting extension of the father's spiritual last will and testament in the son's own hand (33).

Neglecting to address the questionable authenticity of the first leaf of this document, Sams risks disabling his own argument. Certainly, the content of the remaining unchallenged articles of the document is echoed in *Hamlet,* as when the testator renders "infinite thanks" to God for not taking him out of this life "when I least thought of it, yea even then, when I was plunged in the dirty puddle of my sins" (1995, 47). Still, if Jordan planted the phrase "cut off in the blossom of my sins" in the document by a forged process, then the direct link from *Hamlet* to John Shakespeare's testament is broken. Had Sams pursued the matter with more patient and thorough scholarship, he might very well have been able to make his intuition about the play's connection to recusancy and the Purgatorial context into a more compelling argument.

Other biographers of John Shakespeare's life find the document relatively valueless, its professions controverted by the known activities of John Shakespeare as a Stratford official. For example, playing the role of the "non-sectarian biographer," Schoenbaum rummages for arguments against John Shakespeare's recusancy, citing instances where Shakespeare's father served on a council whose "forays into Protestantization" included the defacing of Catholic images and the demolition of a rood loft (1987, 54). Russell Fraser informs us that in 1559, John Shakespeare had voted with others to oust the Catholic curate of Holy Trinity, Robert Dyos, the man who only a year before had baptized his first son (1988, 49). These hardly seem the actions of a man confirmed in his Catholic beliefs. Indeed, the figure who emerges from a dispassionate scrutiny of council records is at odds with the desperate testator seeking to secure for himself the benefits of sacraments interdicted by the English state. Acknowledging the probable authenticity of the original testament and its importance as a possible indicator of Shakespeare's religious upbringing, Schoenbaum nevertheless opts for a "secular agnosticism" in washing his hands of a judgment on John Shakespeare's religious standing. Failing to reconcile these contradictions, Schoenbaum simply withdraws from the fray.

Contrary to Schoenbaum but not as audacious as Sams, I would argue it is the very presence of these inconsistencies in John Shakespeare's life that ought to lead investigators to recusancy as an explanatory context. Though this context cannot put to rest the important question of John Shakespeare's religious beliefs, it can provide a rationale for the divided character that he presents to the investigator. For example, what Schoenbaum overlooks in noting John Shakespeare's incongruous actions is how characteristic they were of the internal divisions endured by Catholics holding public office in a Protestant state bent on the desecration and erasure of England's Catholic heritage. In this vein, the recusant proselytizer William Allen describes in 1581 the "extreme miserie" found in England, a situation in which "the greatest part of the Countrie should be Catholikes in their hartes, and in their mouths and actions, Protestants" (1971, 27). John Shakespeare's conflicting biographical records strongly suggest he belonged to that class of "many individuals" whom Walsham describes as ambiguously straddling the boundaries between official and unofficial religion, who practiced, in Haigh's evocative phrase, an "'ambidextrous religious life'" (qtd. in Walsham 1993, 97). Allen catalogues how the enforcement of such a life on its practitioners caused internal schism. He complains of

> the prejudice and partialities of the present condition and sway of time, which by authoritie, force, and feare of lawes, favour of the Prince, domestical education, plausible preaching and persuasion of profite, peace, and pleasure, doth sometimes alter and infect the very judgement and reason of the inward man, and much oftener doth byas and pervert the external actions of many worldings even against their owne natural inclination, knowledge, and conscience: of which sort there be no doubt in our Countrie innumerable, not onely of those whose constrainte is evident, but even of such as seeme principal promoters of the one part and persecutors of the other. Who because they be wise can not be Protestants 23 yeres, that is to say, any long time together: but yet because they be also worldly, can not or wil not confess their former fall to their dis[ad]vantage in this life, which they prefere before eternal glorie. (1971, 4)

If to be a recusant involved being a "principal promoter" of one part and a persecutor of the other, then a man who kept a recusant document hidden in his roof tiles and yet participated in the defacing of Catholic images certainly would qualify as one of these "innumerable" worldlings whose external actions flatly contradicted their internal convictions. The public persona in this regard would constitute a false wall; indeed, like the knowing pursuivants who sought out such figures, we should measure the walls dividing the public and the private and, where the measurements do not tally, pull down the sections we cannot account for to find out what might lie behind them.

Such mismeasurements or hollow spots abound in the biographical information concerning John Shakespeare, and yet too seldom is the recusant hypothesis invoked to explain them. Without acknowledging the ambidextrous nature of recusants, biographers tend to tell one or the other side of John Shakespeare's life's story. For example, they are too quick to take at face value the standard excuse for John Shakespeare's absence from the Church of England service. Recusants would often argue fear of being apprehended by creditors as a reason for staying away from services. Categorizing the divided nature of the private and public religious self in Shakespeare's England, Walsham classifies Shakespeare's father with the "more timid [recusants who] concealed their motives for avoiding church service by pleading embarrassment and fear of arrest as debtors" (1993, 86). Arguing "John Shakespeare's fall from grace centered on money" (1991, 25), Garry O'Connor "excuses" him from recusancy with a line of reasoning that any sixteenth-century recusant would have welcomed as a convenient dodge from persecution:

> Although temperamentally a supporter of the old faith, it is unlikely that John Shakespeare was a Catholic recusant. Later, during the reign of Elizabeth, he was once so named in a Privy Council-inspired list of those who did not attend church monthly, as required by law, but no action was taken against him; one suspects that Stratford's rising clique of Puritans hated him, even tried to denounce him as a Catholic, in the hope of being rewarded with his land. (18–19)

In a more recent biography of Shakespeare, however, Park Honan argues that John Shakespeare's "long avoidance of halls may not be wholly attributable to a fear of debt," but was also motivated in part by a fear of "questions about his beliefs and background" (1999, 40).

Honan argues that his position on the Court of Record would have made him easily available to the solicitations of any creditor (39). Contextualizing these lists for us, F. W. Brownlow reveals that compilers of such lists were often sympathetic to their endangered friends and neighbors, adding the escape clause of fear of debtors as a means of protecting them from "the coercive power of the Tudor state" (1989, 188). But one does not need to follow a cold trail in these determinations. In this regard, Robert Persons informs us that just as "the bush of the taverne, is a signe of wyne" and the yellow bonnet and yellow turban denote respectively Jew and Turk: "Even soe, seing the whole world, at this day, doth take the absteyning from protestantes Churches, to be the only external signe of a trew Catholike" (*Brief Discours* 1973, 17).

Given the extraordinary conflicts that recusants faced, it is small wonder that they often present two contradictory sides to the biographical investigator. Walsham notes it was "often the qualified conformity of the paterfamilias" that allowed "the very establishment of an internal recusant regime" (1993, 81). Concentrating "on protecting the family's resources and reputation," the husband might make a public show of sacrificing his principles in order to ensure the continuance of such a regime. Walsham informs us: "Lancashire authorities registered their concern in 1584, requesting official guidance on the correction of men who 'go to church, but have mass at home with their wives'" (79). What differentiates John Shakespeare from more timid recusants in this regard is that, in spite of being called up before the Court of Queen's Bench in 1580 for the "uncivil" and "disloyal" breach of failing to attend services regularly, he persisted in such behavior, his name appearing on a Stratford recusant list in 1592 (Smart 1928, 72). On Shakespeare's maternal side, there were certainly many reasons to suspect an internal recusant regime in the household. Sams lists several "Ardens hanged or burnt for alleged complicity" with recusants, including the head of the clan, Edward Arden (1995, 33).

Those biographers who downplay the historical recusant context surrounding young Shakespeare's formative years risk leaving us with a contextually sanitized William Shakespeare. Certainly, such a figure would not have chosen to inject politically dangerous and anachronistic representations of Catholic beliefs, rituals, and practices into his source story. More likely, an older Shakespeare was dredging up very vivid memories of his own experiences of intensely real people very close to him leading an underground existence in perilous times. Caught in a constantly shifting middle ground, such recusants found pressures to conform were countered by pressures to resist conformity. Counter-Reformation proselytizers like Allen knew that one powerful pressure on recusants to conform lay in their fear of losing their children's patrimony. Speaking on behalf of these children, in a rather idealistic mode, Allen has these children "ask" their parents

> not to damne them selves upon pretence of saving their lands and goods to the profite of them, their children and posterities: desiring no other inheritance then their salvation and companie in heaven, the lacke whereof should be to them more then al mortal sorowes. (*Apologie* 1971, 27)

Persons, too, speaks of innocent children put at risk because of their parents' conformity, having them declare "we have felt our own parents to be murderers unto us" by denying them the benefits of their faith (*Brief Discours* 1973, 11). Recusants of any means thus found themselves having to choose between publicly declaring their faith and, in effect, disinheriting their children or conforming and putting their very souls and those of their children at risk of damnation.

Recusant manuals and devotional texts circulating privately from household to household in Shakespeare's day provide further reason to presume that many families practiced a forbidden religion behind the false walls of a seeming conformity. For example, in *A Short Rule of Good Life,* Robert Southwell advises parents to teach children their prayers, their ten commandments, "and the points of faith, specially those that heretickes deny" (1971, 61). Bedtime stories in perilous times will provide exercises in the remembrance of the children's Catholic heritage: "I must tell them often of the abbeis and the vertew of the olde Munkes & Friers, & other Priestes & religious men & women, & of the truth and honesty of the olde time, & the iniquity of ours" (*Short Rule,* 74). Tireless recusant proselytizers like Southwell refused to believe the long Catholic tradition in England would simply fade away, even in the face of persecution. Thus, in *An Epistle of a Religious Priest unto his Father: Exhorting him to the Perfect Forsaking of the World,* Southwell advises his audience that belief "by descent and petegree is in maner hereditary" (1971, 3). Although John

Shakespeare did not emboss his family's recusancy on a coat of arms, evidence of the truth of Southwell's assertion can be found in the Shakespeare family's transgenerational recusancy. O'Connor notes that Shakespeare's daughter Susanna was reported for not receiving the sacrament at Easter in 1606. In their own turn, Hamnet and Judith Sadler were also cited (241). Such public flouting of rules governing conformity by William Shakespeare's daughter and son's namesake friend suggests that an internal recusant regime may very well have carried over from one generation to another in the Shakespeare line.

Though we cannot know what took place in the Shakespeare household, connections we can trace suggest that the recusant hypothesis is more than mere conjecture. Certainly, a father who wished to avoid tarring his son William with recusant associations and exposing him to their influences might have chosen a more appropriate schoolmaster for him than Simon Hunt, a future Jesuit who would die in Rome, or John Cottom, whose brother, a Jesuit, would stand in martyrdom with Edmund Campion. As O'Connor points out, the influence of so many Catholics in Shakespeare's education demonstrates "the underlying religious identity and sympathies of Stratford, but not the public official face" (1991, 22). Paying too much attention to this public official face has caused biographers to downplay or overlook formative elements of recusancy in Shakespeare's background.

What we can surmise of John Shakespeare is that in the long run he seems to have found the ambidextrous life of the public official and the closet recusant unsustainable. The emerging profile of the man as defined by his testament and his sudden departure from office more closely fits that of the recusant struggling unsuccessfully to balance his role as a public figure with his private religious beliefs. Required to be a principal promoter of one part and a persecutor of the other, he may very well have found that the wear and tear of such contradictory biases ran against his "owne natural inclination, knowledge, and conscience." His frequent absences from council meetings, leading ultimately to his dismissal, bear witness to such an interpretation.

Reformation and Counter-Reformation forces contributed a great deal to the enigmatic and contradictory record that John Shakespeare has bequeathed to the modern investigator; and such divisive forces have not ceased to play a role in these investigations. Opportunities and risks go hand in hand whenever the question of the Shakespeare family's religious identity surfaces. Those who make the presumption of recusancy have provided us with a plausible framework for organizing young Shakespeare's "lost years." The argument here is that in the face of his complete withdrawal from public service in 1576 and his mounting economic setbacks, John Shakespeare placed William Shakespeare with the ardently Catholic Hoghton family. His signing of the profession of faith in the early 1580s suggests a deepening commitment to Catholicism during this period. A father increasingly out of favor due to his religious beliefs might be assumed to have used his Catholic connections to find a safe haven for his son. The increased persecution of recusants in this period provided a further reason for him to remove his son from possible harm.

O'Connor contends that the young Shakespeare may have spent his formative years at Hoghton Tower, "the princely and comely Lancashire seat of Thomas Hoghton," where Shakespeare "joined the family as an unlicensed schoolmaster in an area which the governing Protestant authorities had condemned both as full of unqualified schoolmasters and children trained up as papists" (1991, 27, 29). Following Honigmann's lead (1985), Richard Wilson (1993) claims that the young Shakespeare was enrolled in the household under the name of "Shakeshafte," it being "common for all the young Catholics there to revert to the names of grandparents as a kind of purifying, or stripping away, and Shakespeare's grandfather was known as Shakeshafte" (Barnes). Biographically, the young Shakeshafte's sojourn at the Hoghton Manor as an unlicensed schoolmaster would be a logical extension of his own tutelage under Catholic masters. Honigmann cites "one crucial factor" that makes Shakespeare's association with the Hoghtons more probable: "the discovery that John Cottom, the Stratford schoolmaster, was also linked with the Hoghton family" (127).

If Shakespeare indeed spent his lost years in the Hoghton household, his sojourn there would anticipate his reappearance later as an actor and playwright. In this respect, Alexander Hoghton, the family patriarch, refers in his will to a young scholar by the name of William Shakeshafte, directing a neighboring Catholic family to take him into its care should the necessity arise. Hoghton leaves to his brother Thomas "all my Instrumentes belonginge to mewsychkes & all manner of playe clothes yf he be minded to keepe & doe keppe players." If not, Hoghton assigns them to another Catholic recusant, Thomas Heskethe, directing him "to be ffrendlyye unto ffoke Gyllome & William Shakeshafte" by either taking them into his service or finding some other good master for them (Honigmann 1985, 27). Linking this Shakeshafte to the accouterments of drama, Hoghton's will suggests that the young Shakespeare—if he is indeed Shakeshafte—honed his skills in drama during the unaccounted for time before he reappeared as an actor and playwright.

Though the Lancashire hypothesis might stand as a plausible conjecture worth maintaining in case new evidence presents itself, there are risks in overstating the case. The restoration of the Hoghton Manor as a playhouse highlighting Shakespeare's recusant background demonstrates just what kind of ideological contentions are stirred up when one party or another tries to lay claim to the playwright's religious identity. Apparently, nothing less than an English national treasure is at stake, so much so that partisanship on one side or the other leads to speculative and even, in Jordan's case, possibly fabricated claims. There are risks as well in understating the importance of the recusant background for the play. We have already witnessed how taking that background into account can explain seeming inconsistencies in John Shakespeare's biography and at least provide a worthwhile hypothesis concerning young Shakespeare's disappearance.

Focusing on recusant sources and contexts can also provide a necessary corrective to criticism, past and present, that has undervalued them in its inquiries. For example, in Stephen Greenblatt's very informative recent study, *Hamlet in Purgatory,* one finds a tendency to gloss over recusant contexts in favor of sources that discount the play's Catholic elements. In his chapter on *Hamlet* in particular, one finds him opening with citations from a contemporary Protestant diatribe against Purgatory and closing with a rather scurrilous account of Jesuits using the concept to dupe the unsuspecting. In spite of his reliance on sources that place the concept of Purgatory and Catholicism generally in a bad light, however, the author does at least acknowledge "the playwright was probably brought up in a Roman Catholic household in a time of official suspicion and persecution of recusancy" (2001, 249). Still, Greenblatt's project of "speaking with the dead" (1988, 20), particularly the "perturbed" spirits that haunt Shakespeare's life and his most signal work, can never be completed unless we seek them out among their own circumstances. For too long, they have been relegated to the "dim light" of heresy, only heard as a confusion of tongues.

II. "Thou Art a Scholar, Speak to It"

Perhaps the most compelling reason to associate the Ghost with Shakespeare's own father is that scholarly interrogations of this spectral figure point to the same ambiguities observed in attempts to determine John Shakespeare's religious affiliation. False walls and hollow spots abound in their efforts to place this spirit. Denying or discounting the ghost's Purgatorial provenance, some fail to see him at all while others make him out in curious half-lights. Eleanor Prosser argues that the ghost does not appear as a penitent soul, confessing its sins, but gives Hamlet a command that clearly "violates Christian teaching" (1994, 388). Prosser cites the Ghost's movements as a "mole" down in the stage's cellarage as an argument for its provenance as more likely a hellish than a Purgatorial one. She argues that the Ghost is a demonic spirit laying a trap for Hamlet, his claim to be coming from Purgatory part of the trap. H. D. F. Kitto cites the fact that the Ghost must depart at the cock's crow, like a "guilty thing," as a sure sign that "We are in the presence of evil" (1959, 255). W. J. Birch finds the scene in which Hamlet tries to locate the "old mole" under the boards as "the most profanely ridiculous exhibition imaginable" (1972, 147).

Those who acknowledge the Ghost's provenance as Purgatorial have trouble explaining why this figure is so displaced and distorted in *Hamlet.* Like a Dantesque spirit, denied a present but allowed to extend into the past or forward into the present, the Ghost proves very difficult for these critics to place. Roy Battenhouse views Shakespeare as having moralized a story in which the Ghost's un-Christian behavior can be excused by framing it in a twelfth-century warrior context, a context John Updike admirably recreates in his *Gertrude and Claudius* (2000). Anthony Low observes that Shakespeare "obscures" the time of the play, so that we are not sure if the action of *Hamlet* takes place before or after the Reformation (1999, 453). While the original source, Saxo Grammaticus, places the action before the Conquest, we find incongruously in the play "the noise of cannons, instruments of modernity" (454). Here, Shakespeare frames the play's action to contemporary events; in this case, the imminent threat of Fortinbras's planned invasion of a country feverishly preparing for war suggests English apprehensions about a Spanish attack through the 1580s, a threat that led to the increased persecution of recusants.

The dislocated and jumbled time frames in the play's temporal schemas sometimes lead critics astray, particularly when they fail to note the mismeasurements implicit in the play's mingling of historical periods. Mark Matheson, for example, indicates that references to denied sacraments introduce "a language that is unambiguously Roman Catholic." He focuses on the distance such references mark between "the world of old Hamlet and the official ideology of contemporary England" (1995, 384, 385). Like Matheson, Low distances the play from its Catholic elements, arguing that Hamlet and the younger generation in the play have simply forgotten the idea of Purgatory: "As was the case in England, so in Hamlet's Denmark. Purgatory is not just abolished but effectively forgotten, as if it never were" (1999, 459). Low's argument that references to Purgatory are by and large muted in the play, partly to avoid offending its Protestant audience, is suspect here. The audience is at least as far removed from the point of Purgatory's abolition as Low argues the characters of the play are. What offense would be taken if their memory were so limited? Even Matheson, who views allusions to Purgatory as outdated at the time of the play's performance, indicates that Shakespeare "shows a certain daring in establishing the context of the Ghost so plainly" (385).

Ostensibly, the question of Purgatory's relative value in the play should not be a problem at all. As Greenblatt observes: "Of course, within the play's fiction, Hamlet does not know that Purgatory is a fiction, as the state-sanctioned church of Shakespeare's time had declared it to be" (2001, 253). Shakespeare, however, guarantees the Ghost's temporal ubiquity through this overlaying of time frames. Like a holographic image created from interference patterns, the Ghost owes its ubiquity to the fact that the twelfth-century context is referenced against the context of the sixteenth century, wherein both Purgatory and the very existence of such spectral visitors have been outlawed. The relatively faithful Hamlet sees it; the faithless Gertrude does not. Injecting the contemporary context into his original source, Shakespeare makes it difficult for commentators such as Matheson and

Low to put this restless spirit to sleep, for they must work within a temporal framework wherein the play time more or less corresponds to historical time, following the English Reformation by some fifty years or so. From that perspective, what Greenblatt labels the "fifty-year effect," the memory the Ghost invokes is simply too recent and too insistent to be forgotten. This displaced Ghost becomes the focal point of the play's temporal dislocations. Otherwise capable critics who discount the role of Purgatory here risk divorcing the play from the deep psychic resonance implicit in the ambient historical context.

After so many contradictory sightings of the Ghost, it is understandable that a critic as discerning as Greenblatt would wish to warn us away from the "long-standing critical game" of determining whether the Ghost is Catholic or Protestant (2001, 239). Nonetheless, critics who discount or explain away Purgatorial references in the play on the basis of incongruities in the Ghost's story leave off their interrogations at the most telling point. As any recusant hunter would know, such contradictions are dead giveaways of the suppressed Catholicism lying just behind or below. Thus, the Ghost's predicament of being denied the sacraments recalls that of many crypto-Catholics in Shakespeare's day, those who suffered what Allen describes as "The universal lacke then of the soveraine Sacrifice and Sacraments catholikely ministred, without which the soule of man dieth, as the body doth without foode" (*Apologie* 1971, 11–12). The author of *Hamlet* underscores this Catholic connection by dispensing with references to the pagan deities that other playwrights used as a means of avoiding religious controversy on either side (Low 1999, 451). Indeed, the hellish quality of the Ghost's predicament lies precisely in the fact that, for Shakespeare's audience, it comes from an interdicted place where no amount of suffering will be able to relieve its tortures. If the Ghost's movements in the cellarage seem hellish, it is because the earthly state and the Purgatorial state have become indistinguishable, as witnessed by Father Gerard's equating of his unincarcerated state with Purgatory and his entry into the Clink as a paradise in his being united with the community of believers: "Though I was locked up, I looked on this change to the Clink as a translation from Purgatory to Paradise. I no longer heard obscene and bawdy songs, but, instead, I had Catholics praying in the next cell" (1952, 105). In his *Purgatories Triumph Over Hell,* John Floyd warns his "countersnarling" debater Sir Edward Hoby not to "butt against Purgatories walls with your horned arguments" lest he "also break open the gates of Hell, that the damned may come out" (1973, 117). Prosser and Kitto's arguments may have been misplaced, but their intuitions were more correct than they realized. This is a hellish spirit, historically speaking.

Speaking for a whole class of recusants, Hamlet's ghostly father connects the plight of evicted Purgatorial spirits to the despair of another class of "damned souls," the recusants of England. Low mentions Theo Brown's documentation of "a great popular outburst of superstitious ghost lore among the common people beginning at mid-century," an outburst Brown links to "the sudden abolition of Purgatory" (qtd. in Low 1999, 455). Apparently, Purgatory's abolition left no room at all for these post-Reformation spirits. In a shifting worthy of Foucauldian investigation, however, a new Purgatorial concept erupts on the cultural landscape. This new, secularized Purgatory hearkens to the early Augustinian concept of "holes or dungeon cells" (Geary 1994, 116).[2] It stands as an inversion of the Catholic concept, its flesh and blood inmates imprisoned for their defense of Catholicism and doomed to suffer for an indeterminate period. In such times of restriction and confinement, Allen is justified in noting that "Your prisons are the onely schooles now of true consolation" (*Apologie* 1971, 120). Southwell also equates the traditional punishments of the Purgatorial realm with those suffered by recusants in the earthly realm: "It is not possible to keep any reckoning of the ordinary punishments of Bridewell, now made the Common Purgatory of Priests and Catholiques, as grinding in the Mill, being beaten like slaves, and other outrageous usages" (1953, 34). The Purgatorial state has now become one in which "purification" is administered by earthly authorities; it has become a physical place of torment occasioning a state of mind in which consolation and transcendence are achieved by self-denial and, in some cases, martyrdom. The Ghost, "forbid / To tell the secrets of my prison-house" (1.5.14–15), must surely have frighted with more than false fire many in the contemporary audience who had some inkling of what was going on in these closely guarded "purgatories." Writing, in 1582, to a foreign friend of the outrages occurring in the Tower of London, Persons notes that though these tortures "be manie and verie grevous":

Yet can they not easily come to oure knowleige, by reason of that close
and straite warde, wherein the sound of all speche, and mourninge of the
afflicted is shutt upp frome the eares of them that are abroade. Nay, our
adversaries bestowe no small diligence in this point: that the aflictions
and torments whiche are there practiced withein doores, be not browght
to the knowleige of them that are witheoute: but buried rather in dark-
nesse, and cleane hyd in blynde and obscure dungeons. . . . (*Epistle*
1973, 87)

The ambiguous middle ground occupied by recusants and fugitive
priests is explored by Julian Yates in his "Parasitic Geographies:
Manifesting Catholic Identity in Early Modern England." Here, Yates
portrays Catholics and their ministering fugitive priests as "parasites"
in the sense that they inhabited the "threshold between two worlds."
Such spaces constituted for recusants "the 'elsewhere' that made life
possible" (1999, 68). Citing the growing number of legislative moves
against Catholics, Yates notes: "In each case, every move made to
drive Catholics beyond the bounds of the realm was met by a commen-
surate move further underground" (70). The presence of such "refusing" subjects constituted a scandal for the Tudor state, for "there were
subjects who held themselves apart, who sought to maintain both a
mental and physical space that lay beyond the reach of the state but
within the borders of its authority" (71). The priest-holes found in the
houses of recusant sympathizers, hidden spaces wherein priests "fled
to the margins of the house," represent for Yates "their symbolic exclusion from the realm in both statute and proclamation" (70). As Allen
defiantly asserts, "If houses must not receive us, dennes and deserts,
and grottes shal be our harbour . . . we will not be ashamed to be, or so
to be called of our Adversaries, vagarant persons" (*Apologie* 1971, 86).
Indeed, the priests' vagrancy bears a strong resemblance to the "spectral vagrancy" of Purgatorial spirits whose reputed appearances caused
suspicious investigators to assign men "to search every inch of the
house (including the roof tiles)" (1970, 108). What is remarkable about
John Shakespeare's Spiritual Last Will and Testament is that it clearly
marks him as a marginalized figure, inhabiting a middle ground similar to that occupied by fugitive priests and spirits, caught up as they all
were in the contradictions of living both within the state and outside of
its authority. Once one locates this hidden space, literally and
metaphorically by means of mismeasurements or light breaking

through chinks in a wall, then apparent distortions or contradictions start to be reconciled. The figure is flushed out.

The critical *hic et ubique* surrounding the nature of the Ghost is not some manufactured controversy; rather, it reflects how much the figure of the Ghost is driven between Protestant and Catholic ideologies. Greenblatt is instructive here, for he links the Ghost's movements and Hamlet's Latin invocation with Purgatorial rites. In this regard, Greenblatt cites Thomas Rogers, who ridicules the Catholic custom of praying for the dead with the *Horae Beatissimae Virginis Mariae*. As petitioners moved through the graveyard, their prayer began, "Avete, omnes animae fideles, quarum corpora hic et ubique requiescent in pulvere" ("Hail all faithful souls, whose bodies here and everywhere do rest in the dust") (2001, 235). Referring to "a certain placelessness" (234) on the part of the Ghost, this phrase and that movement recall the banishment from public space and the incursions upon private space suffered by recusants. Speaking of a particularly complex set of "hides" and "double-hides" found at Harvington Hall in Worcestershire, Yates notes that here "the Jesuit finally becomes no more than the 'para' in parasite, the sum of all directions, 'turnings' and 'interturnings.' He becomes a dislocation in space. . . ." (1971, 71). The Ghost is a fugitive spirit, indeed. Like these recusants and priests, it must keep moving in its placelessness.

Other seeming contradictions found in the play find a resolution if we first situate them in the middle ground of the recusant context. For example, Greenblatt is struck by Hamlet's "spectacular" forgetting of what the Ghost has revealed about an apparent afterlife: "Hamlet receives the most vivid confirmation of the afterlife, with its 'sulph'rous and tormenting flames" (1.5.3), but then, in a spectacular and mysterious act of forgetting, speaks of death as the "undiscovered country from whose bourn / No traveller returns" (3.1.81–82). Given that the Purgatorial state has now become an earthly condition, the Ghost comes not from an afterlife but from *this side of Purgatory,* the recusant side, where the "sulph'rous and tormenting flames" reflect the banishments and martyrdoms of recusants. With no spiritual middle ground left for the repose of departed souls, Hamlet can speak without contradiction of an "undiscovered country from whose bourn / No traveller returns." The sense of "weirdness" that Greenblatt identifies in this whole setup arises not only from the

Ghost's estrangement from a once extant but currently outlawed institution, but also from the distortions involved in the resituating of Purgatory in the earthly realm.

Signaling the return of the repressed in the national consciousness, Shakespeare's portrayal of Purgatory opens up the play as a site of contestation between Catholic and Protestant ideologies. We can hear behind the Ghost's laments his desire to be remembered, the tortured supplications of the "poor prisoners of God," as described by Thomas More in his defense of Purgatory in the *Supplycacyon of Soulys*. If the Ghost behaves more like an earthly than a Purgatorial being, it is a reflection of its fallen and desperate status. The living can no longer be counted on to remember the dead, for the rituals have been banned and the observances have been stricken from the calendar. Hamlet's lament for his quickly forgotten father only points toward the impossibility of reconstructing any memory of him in the face of the dismantling of intercessory institutions:

> O heavens, die two months ago, and not forgotten yet? Then there's hope a great man's memory may outlive his life half a year, but, by'r lady, 'a must build churches then, or else shall 'a suffer, not thinking on. . . . (3.2.122–25)

Obviously referring to intercessory institutions and rituals here, Hamlet's slipping into the colloquial *'a* in speaking of the necessity of such churches seems to connect to those "deep psychic resonances among the common people" that the loss of Purgatory occasioned. Invoking Purgatory as the tiring house of the Ghost's entrances and exits, Shakespeare violates the customary neutrality of his contemporaries, putting himself at odds with Protestant theologians and aligning himself more with Catholic recusant writers who vigorously defended the concept of Purgatory.

Coming at a time of high suspicions against domestic Catholics, the Ghost serves as a spectral manifestation not only of Catholic persecution, but also of Protestant anxieties, what Walsham labels their "uneasy apprehensions about the birth of a secularized society" (1993, 106–7). The suppressed priesthood, either exiled or driven underground, elicited a collective neurosis, a paranoia, among its pursuers out of proportion to its actual numbers. Burghley aptly expressed this paranoia when he thundered:

> Let these persons be termed as they list . . . scholars, school masters, bookmen, seminarists, priests, Jesuits, friars, beedmen, romanists, pardoners, or what else you will, neither their titles nor their apparel hath made them traitors, but their traitorous secret motions and practices. . . . (qtd. in Walsham, 34–35)

A "pioner" in the truest sense of one who goes underground to undermine a foundation, the Ghost reminds its audience of the suppressed elements of recusancy, the religious persecution unresolved by the Elizabethan Settlement. It haunts England with its own past, appearing at a time Southwell describes as "this foggye night of heresie, and the confusion of tongues" (*Epistle* A5). The Ghost's appearance evokes in Horatio's mind a recollection of a time when "The graves stood [tenantless] and the sheeted dead / Did squeak and gibber in the Roman streets" (1.2.115–16). For Shakespeare's audience, such untenanted spirits as the Ghost might very well call to mind a more recent period of upheavals and spectral disturbances.

With only about 300 priests to minister to 40,000 English Catholics by the late sixteenth century, and "never more than about ten Jesuits working simultaneously in Britain before the end of the century" (Sullivan 1995, 25), many of these secret motions and practices involved disguised priests like Father Gerard roaming countryside and city in an effort to feed the flock during a time that Southwell describes as being plagued with "This generall famine of all true and Christian food" (*Epistle,* 8). Without such "ghostly fathers," the exercise of sacraments such as confession and communion became hollow rituals, offering no means for obtaining grace for the communicant. Like those in a Purgatorial state, these communicants could only go through the motions of seeking grace, with only a distant hope of an intercessor. In *A Short Rule,* Southwell sets forth the limitations on those who would practice the faith during this time of spiritual famine:

> I must notwithstanding at my usuall times prepare my selfe, & to almighty God make even in wordes the same confession that I would to my ghostly father: for though it be not a Sacramente without absolution of a trew Priest, yet is it a godly thing and good to keepe me in ure, & my conscience in awe. (1971, 61)

Unfortunately, without a priestly intercessor, the practice of the sacraments involved merely going through the motions, hoping for grace in some indeterminate future. Thus, we witness the need for spiritual testaments as insurance policies. Hamlet's ghostly father, coming from an interdicted place, also reflects the recusant predicament. The Ghost must bear its burden in relative silence, with no recourse to the sacraments. It would share in Allen's lament that "of sinne there is no way of repentaunce" (1970, 18).

Uncovering the hidden or discounted recusant and Purgatorial sources in *Hamlet* demonstrates just how much the abolition of the Catholic Church and its institutions drives the play's operations. As Geary asserts, the Catholic Church had long been "an essential third party in the exchange between the living and the dead" (1994, 78). He demonstrates how the pre-Reformation Catholic Church in England and elsewhere had taken on an increasingly proprietary role as a mediator between the living and the dead. Invoking the recusant legacy in the specter of the Ghost, *Hamlet* brings back a haunting image of an earlier time when the efficacy of Catholic sacraments was attacked and both the temporal and spiritual powers of the Church were undermined. Given this fatalistic background, it is little wonder that Hamlet's ghostly father functions as the persona or "larva" of vision literature in prefiguring the destruction of the family (Geary, 61). Blood and indiscriminate killing seem to be the only possible offerings at this point. Death and mourning in *Hamlet* occasion no consolatory sentiment, no sense of a transcending connection between the dead and those who should carry on their legacy. This loss of generational cohesion is in sharp contrast to Geary's description of the Catholic Church's maintenance of "a continuous cult in which the dead might be included . . . [making the Church] an ideal component in the family strategy for overcoming death" (91).

Shakespeare's incorporation of Purgatorial references in the play reinvokes the lost connection to the dead. For Hamlet as well as Fortinbras, the death of the father occasions a family crisis centering on obligation to the dead and inheritance. Fortinbras is willing to sacrifice 2,000 souls to regain an apparently worthless plot of land that the captain would not give five ducats to farm. Such lands, however, often symbolized past familial disgrace in terms of loss of hereditary rights for the vanquished; also, they could be used by the victors for bragging rights. Of course, the land that Fortinbras seeks to recover is just "a little patch of ground" (4.4.18). It will hardly appease his own father;

indeed, gaining it at the loss of so many lives will cause further inequalities and disturbance between the realm of the living and the dead, for the land under debate "is not tomb enough and continent / To hide the slain" (4.4.64–65). We can assume that the dead will be buried, like Polonius, "hugger-mugger," with little time for proper burial rituals to be performed. Hamlet's ghostly father is restless because the very ground on which Purgatory was based, the Church's holdings through donations, has been foreclosed upon and repossessed by the English state. Restless and untenanted, the dead cannot be appeased. Shortly after the unleashing of Purgatorial spirits to prey upon the popular imagination, Edmund Campion warned his executioners about the transgenerational consequences of their persecution: "In condemning us you condemn all your own ancestors, all the ancient bishops and kings, all that was once the glory of England" (Fraser 1988, 48). As Nicholas Rand observes, the dead, with their own lives' "unfinished business," can haunt the living: "laying the dead to rest and cultivating our ancestors implies uncovering their shameful secrets, understanding their nameless and undisclosed suffering . . . unsuspected, the dead continue to lead a devastating half-life in us" (1994, 167).

Linking the Ghost to the recusant situation of John Shakespeare advances the Horatian project of interrogating the dead and finding out how their "unfinished business" lays its claims upon the living. One can argue, of course, that John Shakespeare's profession of faith is more a signed formulary than a personal statement on his part. What evidence, after all, is there that he had not lived a fulfilled life or that he left behind for his son some "unfinished business"? The answers here are historically available to us. That John Shakespeare's economic failure and his loss of position made a lasting impression on William Shakespeare can be inferred from the playwright's efforts decades later to repair the family name by acquiring a coat of arms for his father. I would argue further that a few other noteworthy occurrences in the playwright's life suggest that he might have been seeking to recuperate more than an economic loss in regards to his family name.

Hamlet itself is implicated in the lives of four generations of Shakespeares. Its invocational force is so great that it not only calls forth Shakespeare's father but also his son, again in a Purgatorial context. In this respect, the play is situated between two very signal events that reflect intergenerational connections turned tragic in the playwright's life. On August 11, 1596, Shakespeare's only son Hamnet was buried; in 1601, Shakespeare's father died. Although he does not address the issue of recusancy, Richard P. Wheeler establishes a link between Hamnet's death and Shakespeare's efforts to restore his father's name, both occurring in 1596. Shakespeare's father apparently had sought unsuccessfully in 1576 to gain a coat of arms. The young Shakespeare was about Hamnet's age (twelve years or so) when this first attempt was made. Wheeler finds it likely

> that the great release of tragic energy into this play about a failed inheritance would have brought with it traces of the dramatist's incapacity to repair the loss of heritage inflicted by Hamnet's death. In the year of his son's death, Shakespeare had restored dignity and brought new honor to his own socially and financially humiliated father by securing the coat of arms that made them both gentlemen. In the year of his father's death, Shakespeare explores a tragic failure of father-to-son inheritance that is at once beyond all repair and yet ennobling, gathering up all manner of brutal, disturbing, and potentially humiliating materials into a life that finally comes to rest in tragic dignity. (2000, 152)

A play haunted by sons striving to carry out the wills of their fathers against formidable odds, *Hamlet* points beyond the celebrated but troubled psyche of its protagonist toward what Rand describes as "a collective psychology comprised of several generations, so that the analyst must listen for the voices of one generation in the unconscious of another" (1994, 166). The transposition from Hamnet to Hamlet barely disguises the connection between two ill-fated personages. Just as the Ghost summons forth the father, so the figuration of Hamlet recalls the son. Describing names as "a form of immaterial inheritance," Geary cites Otto Gerhard Oexle's claim that in naming the dead even the pronunciation of their names "was more than simply recollection: it was the means by which the dead were made present" (qtd. in Geary 1994, 87). The name-shifting that invests the memory of his son in the tragic protagonist leads O'Connor to view Hamlet as "an emergency self, a provisional persona" for the playwright (1991, 202). Such name-shifting also recalls Shakespeare's own adolescence, when another life-altering experience may have forced the young Shakespeare to take on a new identity as a means of preserving the traditions of the past and escaping the retributions of the present. Of course, the young Shakespeare disappears at the very moment when we might have been able to confirm O'Connor's thesis, leaving behind a few tantalizing clues under an "assumed" name.

III. *HAMLET'S* RECUSANT STANCE

In her *Catholicism, Controversy and the Catholic Literary Imagination, 1558–1660,* Alison Shell casts a rather jaundiced eye upon recent efforts "to say something new about canonical favorites," in particular, speculations about "the permanent, temporary or possible Catholicism" of a number of English writers, most recurringly Shakespeare (1999, 2). As she wisely asserts, "to identify Catholic elements in a writer's biography is one thing, and to use them to formulate a Catholic aesthetic, quite another" (2–3). No doubt, mere biographical speculations do have their limitations. Thus, whether or not a "William Shakeshafte" associated with "Instrumentes," "mewsychkes & all manner of playe clothes" lived out his "lost years" at the Hoghton Manor, and was one and the same with Shakespeare, inconclusive biographical information must cede in importance to identifying a Catholic aesthetic in *Hamlet* itself.

There is little doubt that the stage was a place where such an aesthetic could be formulated and played out. Hamlet's "antic disposition" evokes the recusant strategy of disguising one's inner thoughts and even one's identity as a protective measure against danger and persecution. In this sense, an "antic" is not only a madman but also an actor. In his attack on plays, for example, Henry Crosse urges that patrons should "leave off to maintain those Anticks, and Puppets, that speake out of their mouthes" (qtd. in Chambers 1923, 4:247). Indeed, recusants had found acting to be a survival skill in their travels through the English countryside. In this vein, William T. Costello points out that Persons had become legendary for his resourcefulness and courage in evading the "swarming" pursuivants. Outfitted in

> a very fit suit of captain's apparel . . . which of buff laid with gold and with hat and feather suited to the same," Persons disembarked at Dover on the morning of June 16, 1580, and so successfully played his part as a swaggering captain in his borrowed finery that the searcher commissioned to examine him "found no cause of doubt in him, but let him with all favour, procuring him both horse and all things necessary for his journey to Gravesend. (1957, vi)

So successful was his disguise, Persons even secured similar safe passage for Campion, who himself entered the country disguised as a merchant.

In such dangerous times, the prying and prolix Polonius's association with Lord Burghley, the chief persecutor of recusants in Elizabeth's time, underscores Hamlet's connection to the recusant context. Like recusants, Hamlet bore watching. Hamlet's own protective "antic disposition" associates his theatrical strategy with that practiced by more circumspect recusants in a state that carefully monitored their movements. Protestant invective against plays and players reveals anxieties about their seditious and subversive influences on the general populace. Phillip Stubbes's derisive labeling of actors as "doble dealing ambodexters" expresses a general distrust, especially among Protestant authorities, of those engaged in the manipulation of appearance and reality. In the growing litany of complaints about the stage, there is some evidence that the stage was viewed as a potential focal point and locale for Counter-Reformation sympathies. Around 1572, William Harrison labels these "common plaies" "semenaries of impiety" (qtd. in Chambers 1923, 4:269). Stubbes voices a commonly heard complaint in describing how plays "draw the people from hering the word of God . . . for you shall have them flocke thither, thick & threefould, when the church of God shalbe bare & emptie" (1972, n.p.). The author of an anonymously written missive to Francis Walsingham in 1587 complains of the "daylie abuse of Stage Playes": "so that when the belles tole to the Lectorer, the trumpetts sound to the Stages, whereat the wicked faction of Rome lawgheth for joy, while the godly weepe for sorrowe" (qtd. in Chambers, 4:304). If the "spilt religion" of a later period would result in Romanticism, the spilt Catholicism of Reformation England would find its lost pomp in stage productions, its forbidden rituals translated into the secularized spectacle of drama. As Sams observes, "The Mass itself may be seen as dramatic ritual, cognate with the stage masque" (1995, 11). *Hamlet* is the play *sine qua non* of such enactments.

Justifying such Protestant anxieties about the stage, the plot of *Hamlet* demonstrates just how much the play is situated in issues that formed the recusant character. Hamlet's ghostly father forces upon its audience a revisitation of divisive issues separating Catholics and

Protestants in the last half of the century. Much of what goes amiss in *Hamlet* reflects the suppression of Catholic beliefs and practices in Shakespeare's England. Indeed, the play restages a half-century of religious controversy in a very thinly veiled manner. Thus, the Catholic opposition to Henry's marriage and its defense of Purgatory are reenacted by the Ghost and its call to vengeance. Hamlet frames his own opposition along Catholic lines. Mistakenly killing Polonius instead of the King, Hamlet later informs Claudius that "a certain convocation of politic worms" is already feasting on the counselor. Hamlet's later allusion to kings going on a progress through the guts of a beggar links both Claudius and Polonius with the Diet of Worms, the Catholic Church's famous inquisition into Protestant activities. Although Greenblatt wonders why Shakespeare has "given the Protestant position to his arch-villain in *Hamlet*" (2001, 247–48), it makes perfect sense that the Ghost as representative of a fugitive church and its banned rites should find its antagonist and antithesis in Claudius. Indeed, King Hamlet's chief complaint, his wife's overhasty speeding to "incestuous sheets" to marry her dead husband's brother, plays uncomfortably close to concerns about Henry VIII's own marriage to his dead brother's widow.

Hamlet's conscientious refusal to sanction such a marriage has suggestive links to the marriage question, the fulminating source of the recusant dilemma. Allen, for example, faults Protestants for their "often divorcyes and newe mariagies in theyre wieves lyefe" (1970, 12–13). Hamlet's dilemma becomes one in which he must pledge allegiance to the memory of his father and suffer through his alienation from his mother. Expressed in familial terms, this dilemma offers parallels to the crisis of conscience faced by conforming Catholics. Southwell thunders against conformists, warning, "He cannot have God for his father, that refuseth to profess the Catholicke Church for his mother, neither can he atchive to the Church triumphant in heaven, that is not a member of the Church militant here in earth" (*Epistle,* 46). Gertrude's falling off from Hamlet's father is associated with materialist and hedonistic impulses. She stands for those who willingly chose to divorce themselves from that tradition, who chose a more comfortable compliance with the powers-that-be. As Walsham observes, recusant writers portrayed conforming Catholics as having chosen materialism over spirituality:

Such hedonism inexorably bred spiritual lethargy and moral insensibility. Minds overgrown with "the rancke weedes of Carnalitye" were incapable of transcending the base impulses of their bodies and rising to higher contemplations: there was "noe difference betwixte them, and a brute bullocke." (Walsham 1993, 42; *Brief Discours* 1973, 50)

Hamlet's disillusion with the world is expressed in similar terms:

> 'tis an unweeded garden
> That grows to seed, things rank and gross in nature
> Possess it merely
>
> (1.2.135–37)

His charge against his mother, living "In the rank sweat of an enseamed bed, / Stew'd in corruption, honeying and making love / Over the nasty sty!" (1.2.91–93), also equates her denial of her husband's memory with a spiritual decline. At a level with "a brute bullocke," Gertrude is unfavorably compared with "a beast that wants discourse of reason," which "Would have mourn'd longer" (1.2.150–51). Janet Adelman views "the covert drama of reformation" vying with "the overt drama of revenge" in *Hamlet*:

> Despite his ostensible agenda of revenge, the main psychological task that Hamlet seems to set himself is not to avenge his father's death but to remake his mother: to remake her in the image of the Virgin Mother who could guarantee his father's purity, and his own, repairing the boundaries of selfhood. (1992, 275)

Given the historical backdrop, such an elevation is far too Catholic to be possible. Interestingly enough, though, Gertrude's personal salvation can only come with a recognition of her fall from grace in which she must "Confess yourself to heaven" (3.4.149). Only a restoration of the penitent in true sacramental devotion can heal her divided self.

Enter Hamlet. With his "inky cloak," "customary suits of solemn black," and mourning cowl, Hamlet cuts the figure of a priest manqué. Battenhouse describes Hamlet as having chosen "a private and 'antic' form of priesthood" (1994, 397). The fact that Hamlet must serve as the "priest" of her redemption—"O step between her and her fighting soul"—further emphasizes the invocation of Catholic elements in the play as a means of addressing various characters' needs for the restorative force of the sacraments. Indeed, in working to purge his mother's soul, Hamlet may well be more Catholic than the Ghost, who had earlier advised him to "leave her to heaven." In a play where so many of the Catholic rituals prove inefficacious, Hamlet's effort to redeem his mother, to spare her some of the retributions of the next life, meets with comparative success. Of course, her redemption can only be had at the expense of a Purgatorial-style suffering and agony. Thus, she exclaims to Hamlet:

> Thou turn'st mine eyes into my very soul,
> And there I see such black and grained spots
> As will not leave their tinct
>
> (3.4: 91–93)

Hamlet's purging of Gertrude's soul calls to mind Greenblatt's portrayal of the Purgatorial process "as a kind of ghastly stain-removal, as if the souls were being fed into an enormous washing machine, complete with caustic cleansing solutions and alternating cycles of heat and cold" (2001, 65). The consolation of going through such a soulful sudsing process this side of Purgatory is that one pays the price of repentance before arriving at the entrance and being turned away.

Given the tenor of the times, however, what *Hamlet* more often than not stages is the inefficacy of various Catholic sacramental rites. Gertrude and Claudius's marriage and King Hamlet's hasty funeral result in an unholy mixing of the realm of the living and the realm of the dead. This unholy mixing is signified in Hamlet's response to Horatio's concession that his mother's marriage followed hard upon his father's funeral: "Thrift, thrift, Horatio, the funeral bak'd meats / Did coldly furnish forth the marriage tables" (1.2.180–81). If the abolition of Purgatory has caused evicted spirits to restlessly wander the world, at least in the popular imagination, the denial of Catholic sacraments haunts *Hamlet* in the form not only of dead bodies but also bodies that no longer seem capable of any resurrection in an afterlife. What James V. Holleran argues about funeral ritual in *Hamlet* can be equally applied to the whole range of Catholic rituals and beliefs presented in the play: prohibition causes "distorted forms of the proper ritual [to] arise and substitute for it" (1989, 67). These distortions take on various forms throughout the play: Ophelia's false devotions and maimed rites, Claudius's impotent confession, the "Black Mass" that Battenhouse maintains is celebrated by Hamlet and Claudius at the play's end. From a recusant perspective, in poisoning the cup Claudius reenacts not only his murder of King Hamlet but, in a more general sense, the pollution of the Catholic sacrament. Indeed, Thomas Wright warns "Catholique-lyke Protestantes" not to participate in the Protestant communion: "The Communion, a poisoned cupp, better it weare for you to eate so much ratsbane, then that polluted breade, & to drinke so much dragons gall, or vipers blood, then that sacrilegious wyne" (1971, n.p.). The consequences of Christ's body and blood no longer being present in the host that cannot be elevated during the mass are played out in this secularized spectacle.

As the plot of the play enacts many of the situations and themes of the recusant context, the characterization of Hamlet provides us with a study in the recusant temperament, as well as the stance recusants had to take in the face of so much persecution. Certainly, Hamlet's temperament and character are even more revealing of a recusant aesthetic than is his physical appearance. Having "that within which passes show," Hamlet constantly reminds those around him of his nonconformity, his unwillingness to bend his own mind and thoughts to the bidding of the royal prerogative. In Hamlet's efforts to maintain the integrity of his conscience, we can see glimmerings of the recusant argument that conscience was "internall, invisible, and not in the power of the greatest monarch in the world, in no lymittes to be straightened, in no bondes to be conteyned" (Walsham 1993, 12).[3] Hamlet's divided conscience calls to mind the "schismatick" mental state of recusants, the "externall protestantes, and internall catholikes" who populated Shakespeare's England at the time the play was written (as catalogued by Wright in his *The Disposition or Garnishmente of the Soule,* A3; qtd. in Walsham, 9). Walsham describes the Elizabethan feeling that schism was "a species of spiritual suicide, a ghastly form of living death." She cites Southwell's "gloomy caveat" to temporizers in this regard: "you cary aboute you your owne funeral . . . your body is a filthy tombe of a more filthy soule, not only dead, but almoste rotten in sinne" (*Epistle,* 176). Hamlet's isolation, inner divisions, and his loathing of the body recall the recusant predicament. Called back from Wittenberg, the seat of Protestant learning, Hamlet struggles with the demands of a Catholic past pressed upon him by his phantasmal father. Maria Torok comments on the phantom as a psychic inheritance from the parent that, in its "unexorcised" or unanalyzed manifestations, can block off the individual's life process (1994, 181). We witness this emotional and spiritual paralysis in Hamlet in his desire for this "too,

too solid flesh" to melt and in his wish to end his life. The Ghost's demands upon Hamlet echo those of proselytizers urging temporizing recusants to outright resistance even to the point of martyrdom.

We can look to recusant writings as providing the emotional, spiritual, and aesthetic background to Hamlet's situation and characterization. Allen's listing of all the ills of the "present condition . . . that doth sometimes alter and infect the very judgement and reason of the inward man" (*Apologie* 1971, 4) reads like a thematic subtext for Hamlet's "To be, or not to be" soliloquy. The recusant proselytizer complains that such a condition "doth byas and pervert the external actions of many worldings" (*Apologie* 1971, 4). Hamlet's transformation, whereby "nor th'exterior nor the inward man / Resembles what it was" (2.2. 6–7), is situated in the very gap that for many recusants opened up between their private practices and beliefs and their public roles and expressions. Hamlet would be a readily recognizable type to Persons, whose *Directorie* not only announced its author's intention to guide men to eternal salvation but also "to layeth down the motives to resolution . . . and removeth the impediments." Unfortunately for the temporizing Hamlet, "the native hue of resoluton / Is sicklied o'er with the pale cast of thought" (3.1. 85–86). Though Persons felt that the earlier edition of his work had inspired many faltering recusants to persevere in "the same pretious course and resolution," he knew that many others needed help in spite of "the strong knocking of Christ at their consciences" (1982, A3).

Working against such bias, Southwell tries to move recusants—who evidence many of Hamlet's symptomologies—back into balance, into a straight and determined course of committed action. David's *Psalms* seems to have motivated both Shakespeare and Southwell, as the former speaks of "a sea of troubles" and the latter of the "*many waters* of worldlye afflictions" (*Epistle,* 115). Southwellian imagery and phrasings abound in Shakespeare, suggesting perhaps a more than coincidental influence on the playwright. Thus, Southwell speaks of the body's mortality and "the generall scourges of plagues, warre, a thousand hazardes and calamityes: Finally all other incombrances, that in any respect ar incident into this lyfe. . . ." (*Epistle,* 59). Hamlet laments "the thousand natural shocks / That flesh is heir to" (3.1.63–64). Southwell asks his wavering recusant constituency to "Consider the displeasure of superiours, the malice and enmitye of our equalles, the contempt, ignominy, and reproach, we receyve of our inferiours, the fraude and trecherye of all sortes and degrees. . . ." (*Epistle,* 59). In a similar litany, Hamlet asks himself:

> For who would bear the whips and scorns of time,
> The oppressor's wrong, the proud man's contumely,
> The pangs of despis'd love, the law's delay,
> The insolence of office, and the spurns
> That patient merit of th'unworthy takes,
> When he himself might his quietus make
> With a bare bodkin?
>
> (3.1.71–77)

Providing recusants a motive and cue for action, Southwell notes, "if we pondered our thoughts and memory enough we would rather wishe by losing of lyfe to cutt of, then by avoyding death to continue" (*Epistle,* 118). Of course, for Hamlet, the temporizer, this is the rub, "the respect / That makes calamity of so long life" (3.1.69–70). Reading the recusant text against *Hamlet,* we can pursue both to the very brink of resolution, as in the above passage, as well as in the following: "Who therefore would not rejoice quickly to dye; seing that death is the passage from this worlde to the nexte, from all the presente agreevances, to all possible happynesse" (*Epistle,* 113). Where the two texts part ways, however, is in Hamlet's irresolution. Southwell's lack of patience with this type of temporizing recusant could very well serve as a marginal gloss to Hamlet's pathetic soliloquy. Citing St. Cyprian, Southwell exclaims: "You are unwilling to suffer in the worlde, lothe to depart out of the worlde, what should I doe un to you?" (*Epistle,* 122). "Crawling between earth and heaven" (3.1.127). Hamlet struggles to find an answer.

Hamlet's frequent soliloquizing underscores his isolation, his inability or unwillingness to communicate what is going on inside him. Like Hamlet, recusants had only "Words, words, words" to express themselves, having lost, in their persecution or banishment, what Richard Bristow describes as "that viva vox word of mouth [which] hath incomparably more force, then the dead pen, whether it be to edifie or destroy" (qtd. in Sullivan 1995, 14).[4] The recusant text operated as a "silent preacher" in one English translator's description, its rhetoric directed at a "dismembered" audience that could only very seldom receive sacraments or hear sermons from a depleted and fugitive priesthood. Religious rhetoric in Elizabethan England thus became an "anxious business," an undertaking seriously limited in its operations (Sullivan, 14). Against this backdrop, Hamlet's soliloquies represent anxious confessional moments that cannot be mediated by any ghostly father other than the tortured one who appears to him sporadically. As in Tom Stoppard's comic portrayal of him, our tragic protagonist can only talk to himself, by himself (1967, 51–52). Whatever "private and 'antic' form of priesthood" Hamlet seeks to enact can only be celebrated in the secular confines of the stage, a solipsistic rite in search of an audience as well as transcendence.

Hamlet's spiritual crisis is exacerbated by the lack of any ghostly counselor to allay his troubles. An image pattern of poisoned, blasted, mildewed, and cut-off ears signals but one more interdicted sacrament haunting this play: that of auricular confession. In his moments of introspection, Hamlet bears witness to Tyndale's fiery criticism of the sacrament of confession: "how sore a burden, how cruel a hangman, how grievous a torment, yea, and how painful a hell, is this ear-confession unto men's consciences" (qtd. in Marshall 1994, 9). Turned inward, such a confessional mode would provide the foundation for modern subjectivity. As Margareta De Grazia remarks, Hamlet's interiority separates and distinguishes him from Sophocles' Oedipus, for whom the focus is on what he does, "whereas Shakespeare's [focus] lights on what Hamlet knows and wills" (1999, 255). De Grazia views the "Old Mole" as a harbinger of epistemological shifts, a view that accords well with Low's linking of Purgatory to the birth of modern consciousness. Recusancy, the forge out of which the modern sense of conscience was formed, defines the terms from which this anguished interiority was fashioned.

Barred from public discourse, recusants had to engage in equivocations, reserving their true thoughts and opinions to what Garnet labels a "speech of the mynde" understood by God alone (Sullivan 1995, 140). Hamlet's defensive verbal posturing calls to mind such strategies. The soliloquy, for instance, constitutes what Sullivan describes as the recusants' auditing of the self. Like recusant authors, he engages in what Sullivan calls "self-persuasive orations" used by the orator "to sway his own will" (142). Hamlet employs the technique of recusants of "arousing affections by use of language" (20). He is his own audience, trying to move his will. Moreover, his soliloquies, like recusants'

prayers, operate as "a rhetorical assault on self" that Sullivan identifies
as typical of recusant methods. Citing Cicero, Wright points out in *The
Passions of the Minde in Generall* that "it is almost impossible for an
Orator to stirre up a Passion in his auditors, except he bee first affected with the same Passion himselfe" (1971, 172). Little wonder that the
actor playing Pyrrhus sparks such a self-derisive response in Hamlet,
who marvels at such a player who "Could force his soul so to his own
conceit" as to drive himself into a passion (2.2.553). Striving to vali-
date the Ghost and its command, Hamlet takes a stance not unlike that
of recusants who were aided by manuals such as Bristow's advising the
wavering faithful by "diverse plaine and sure wayes to finde out the
truth in this doubtfull and dangerous time of heresie." The infrequent
spectral visits of his ghostly father to whet his "blunted purpose" come
like the distant calls from Rome to encourage recusants in a desperate
cause. His efforts to fashion himself and move himself forward mirror
the efforts of recusant writers to rally their troops by insisting on the
integrity of conscience against external threats and internal pusillanim-
ity. Walsham identifies such tracts as "Representative of Counter-
Reformation literature designed to cultivate rigorous habits of moral
scrutiny and inculcate an interiorized piety" (1993, 30). Isolated and
endangered, Hamlet can only fall back on his own inner resources.

A study of recusant writings reveals what those resources were,
allowing us to reestablish the play's historical and biographical contexts. Writing near the end of an aging Elizabeth's reign, with his own
personal losses heavy on his heart, Shakespeare found himself the
medium through which a half-century of religious conflict and turmoil
would speak. A close consideration of recusant writers recovers a
whole class of dispossessed people who find their predicament reenacted in that of Hamlet's ghostly father. Their Purgatorial state is now
defined in earthly terms, and they can only express themselves in what
Southwell describes as "my Catholic, though broken, speeches"
(*Epistle,* 4). Interrogating these spirits can shed light on the play as a
"family strategy for overcoming death," as when Greenblatt sums up
the play's situation vis-à-vis the playwright's biographical situation:
"in 1601 the Protestant playwright was haunted by the spirit of his
Catholic father pleading for suffrages to relieve his soul from the pains
of Purgatory" (2001, 249). On a larger scale, however, these half-told
tales of ghostly fathers uttered in Catholic but broken speeches should

move us to listen for the restless spirits found beneath the roof tiles of John Shakespeare's Stratford home and under the floorboards of the London stage. Only then can we understand how *Hamlet* brings home to Shakespeare's audience the past and present and, for Catholics, a foreclosed-upon future.

NOTES

1. All quotations from *Hamlet* are from Shakespeare, *The Riverside Shakespeare*, ed. Evans (1997).

2. Also see Oexle (1983).

3. Walsham quotes from Edward Aglionby, "in a speech delivered in response to a proposed bill in 1571 'for coming to comon prayer and for receavinge of the communion'" (Hartley 1981, 240–41).

4. Richard Bristow. *A Briefe Treatise of Diverse Plaine and Sure Wayes to Finde Out the Truth* (1574; Antwerp [England], 1599, T8 v).

WORKS CITED

Adelman, Janet. *Suffocating Mothers: Fantasies of Maternal Origin in Shakespeare's Plays,* Hamlet *to* The Tempest. New York: Routledge, 1992.

Allen, William. *An Apologie and True Declaration of the Institution of and Endevours of the Two English Colleges. . . .* 1581. Vol. 67 of *English Recusant Literature: 1558–1640.* Ed. D. M. Rogers. Yorkshire, England: The Scolar Press, 1971.

_____. *A Defense and Declaration of the Catholike Churchies Doctrine, Touching Purgatory, and Prayers for the Soules Departed.* Vol. 18 of *English Recusant Literature: 1558–1640.* Ed. D. M. Rogers. 1565. Yorkshire, England: The Scolar Press, 1970.

_____. *A True, Sincere and Modest Defence of English Catholiques.* 1584. Vol. 68 of *English Recusant Literature: 1558–1640.* Ed. D. M. Rogers. Yorkshire, England: The Scolar Press, 1971.

Baker, Oliver. *In Shakespeare's Warwickshire and the Unknown Years.* London: Simpson Marshall, 1937.

Barnes, Paulinus. "Catholic or Not Catholic? That Is the Question about Shakespeare." *The Guardian.* August 12, 1999.

Battenhouse, Roy. "Hamlet's Evasion and Inversions." In *Shakespeare's Christian Dimension: An Anthology of Commentary,* ed. Roy Battenhouse. 395–405. Bloomington, Ind.: Indiana University Press, 1994.

Birch, W. J. *An Inquiry into the Philosophy and Religion of Shakespeare.* New York: Haskell House Publishers, 1972.

Bristow, Richard. *Briefe Treatise of Diverse Plaine and Sure Wayes to Finde Out the Truth in this Doubtfull and Dangerous Time of Heresie.* Microfilm. Ann Arbor, Mich.: UMI, 1982.

Brownlow, F. W. "John Shakespeare's Recusancy: New Light on an Old Document." *Shakespeare Quarterly* 46 (1989): 186–91.

Chambers, E. K. *The Elizabethan Stage.* 4 vols. Oxford, England: Oxford University Press, 1923.

Costello, S.J., William T. Introduction to *The Judgment of a Catholicke English-Man Living in Banishment for his Religion.* 1608. Gainesville, Fla.: Scholars' Facsimiles & Reprints, 1957.

De Grazia, Margareta. "Teleology, Delay, and the 'Old Mole.'" *Shakespeare Quarterly* 50 (1999): 251–68.

Floyd, John. *Purgatories Triumph Over Hell, Maugre The Barking of Cerberus in Syr Edward Hobyes Counter-snarle.* 1613. Vol. 143 of *English Recusant Literature: 1558–1640.* Ed. D. M. Rogers. Yorkshire, England: The Scolar Press, 1973.

Fraser, Russell. *Young Shakespeare.* New York: Columbia University Press, 1988.

Geary, Patrick. *Living with the Dead in the Middle Ages.* Ithaca, N.Y.: Cornell University Press, 1994.

Gerard, John. *The Autobiography of a Hunted Priest.* Trans. Philip Caraman, S.J. New York: Doubleday, 1952.

Greenblatt, Stephen. *Hamlet in Purgatory.* Princeton, N.J.: Princeton University Press, 2001.

———. *Shakespearean Negotiations: The Circulation of Social Energy in Renaissance England.* Berkeley, Calif.: University of California Press, 1988.

Haigh, Christopher. *Reformation and Resistance in Tudor Lancashire.* London: Cambridge University Press, 1975.

Hartley, T. E. *Proceedings in the Parliaments of Elizabeth I.* Leicester: Leicester University Press, 1981.

Holleran, James V. Introduction to *A Jesuit Challenge: Edmund Campion's Debates at the Tower of London in 1581.* New York: Fordham University Press, 1999.

———. "Maimed Funeral Rites in *Hamlet.*" *English Literary Renaissance* 19 (1989): 65–93.

Honan, Park. *Shakespeare: A Life.* Oxford, England: Oxford University Press, 1999.

Honigmann, E. A. J. *Shakespeare: The "Lost Years."* Manchester, England: Manchester University Press, 1985.

Kitto, H[umphrey] D[avy] F[indley]. *Form and Meaning in Drama.* New York: Barnes and Noble, 1959.

Le Goff, Jacques. *The Birth of Purgatory.* Trans. Arthur Goldhammer. Chicago, Ill.: University of Chicago Press, 1984.

Low, Anthony. "*Hamlet* and the Ghost of Purgatory: Intimations of Killing the Father." *English Literary Renaissance* 29 (1999): 443–67.

Marshall, Peter. *The Catholic Priesthood and the English Reformation.* Oxford, England: Clarendon Press, 1994.

Matheson, Mark. "*Hamlet* and 'A Matter Tender and Dangerous.'" *Shakespeare Quarterly* 46 (1995): 383–97.

O'Connor, Garry. *William Shakespeare: A Life.* London: Hodder & Stoughton, 1991.

Oexle, Otto Gerhard. "Die Gegenwart der Toten." In *Death in the Middle Ages,* eds. Herman Braet and Werner Verbeke. 19–77. Louvain, Belgium: Medievalia Lovaniensia 1983.

Persons, Robert. *A Brief Discours Contayning Certayne Reasons Why Catholiques Refuse to Goe to Church.* 1580. Vol. 84 of *English Recusant Literature: 1558–1640.* Ed. D. M. Rogers. Yorkshire, England: The Scolar Press, 1973.

———. *A Christian Directorie.* Microfilm. Ann Arbor, Mich.: UMI, 1982.

———. *An Epistle of the Persecution of Catholickes in Englande.* 1582. Vol. 125 of *English Recusant Literature: 1558–1640.* Ed. D. M. Rogers. Yorkshire, England: The Scolar Press, 1973.

———. *The Judgment of a Catholicke English-Man Living in Banishment for his Religion.* 1608. Gainesville, Fla.: Scholars' Facsimiles & Reprints, 1957.

Prosser, Eleanor. "Spirit of Health or Goblin Damned?" In *Shakespeare's Christian Dimension: An Anthology of Commentary*, ed. Roy Battenhouse. Bloomington, Ind.: Indiana University Press, 1994.

Rand, Nicholas T. "Secrets and Posterity: The Theory of the Transgenerational Phantom." Vol. 1 of *The Shell and the Kernel: Renewals of Psychoanalysis*. Ed. and trans. Nicholas T. Rand. 165–69. Chicago, Ill.: University of Chicago Press, 1994.

Sams, Eric. *The Real Shakespeare: Retrieving the Early Years, 1564–1594*. New Haven, Conn.: Yale University Press, 1995.

Schoenbaum, Samuel. *William Shakespeare: A Compact Documentary Life*. Oxford, England: Oxford University Press, 1987.

Shakespeare, William. *Hamlet*. In *The Riverside Shakespeare*, 2d ed., ed. G. Blakemore Evans with the assistance of J. J. M. Tobin. Boston: Houghton Mifflin, 1997.

Shell, Alison. *Catholicism, Controversy, and the Catholic Literary Imagination, 1558–1660*. Cambridge, England: Cambridge University Press, 1999.

Smart, John. *Shakespeare: Truth and Tradition*. London: Edward Arnold & Co., 1928.

Southwell, Robert. *An Epistle of a Religious Priest unto his Father: Exhorting him to the Perfect Forsaking of the World 22nd October 1589*. Vol. 78 of *English Recusant Literature: 1558–1640*. Ed. D. M. Rogers. Yorkshire, England: The Scolar Press, 1971.

———. *An Epistle of Comfort*. 1587–88. Vol. 222 of *English Recusant Literature: 1558–1640*. Ed. D. M. Rogers. Yorkshire, England: The Scolar Press, 1974.

———. *An Humble Supplication to Her Majestie*. Ed. R. C. Bald. Cambridge, England: Cambridge University Press, 1953.

———. *A Short Rule of Good Life*. 1596–97. Vol. 78 of *English Recusant Literature: 1558–1640*. Ed. D. M. Rogers. Yorkshire, England: The Scolar Press, 1971.

Stoppard, Tom. *Rosencrantz and Guildenstern Are Dead*. New York: Grove Press, 1967.

Stubbes, Phillip. "Of Stage-playes and Enterluds." In *The Anatomie of Abuses*. 1583. New York: Da Capo Press, 1972.

Sullivan, Ceri. *Dismembered Rhetoric: English Recusant Writing, 1580–1603*. Madison, N.J.: Farleigh Dickinson University Press, 1995.

Torok, Maria. "Story of Fear: The Symptoms of Phobia—the Return of the Repressed or the Return of the Phantom?" Vol. 1 of *The Shell and the Kernel: Renewals of Psychoanalysis.* Ed. and trans. Nicholas T. Rand. 177–86. Chicago, Ill.: University of Chicago Press, 1994.

Updike, John. *Gertrude and Claudius.* New York: Knopf, 2000.

Walsham, Alexandra. *Church Papists: Catholicism, Conformity and Confessional Polemic in Early Modern England.* Oxford, England: The Boydell Press, 1993.

Wheeler, Richard P. "Deaths in the Family: The Loss of a Son and the Rise of Shakespearean Comedy." *Shakespeare Quarterly* 51 (2000): 127–53.

Wilson, Richard. *Will Power: Essays on Shakespearean Authority.* Detroit, Mich.: Wayne State University Press, 1993.

Wright, Thomas. *The Passions of the Minde in Generall.* 1604. Chicago, Ill.: University of Illinois Press, 1971.

Yates, Julian. "Parasitic Geographies: Manifesting Catholic Identity in Early Modern England." In *Catholicism and Anti-Catholicism in Early Modern Texts,* ed. Arthur F. Marotti. 63–84. New York: St. Martin's, 1999.

10

Wittenberg and Melancholic Allegory: The Reformation and Its Discontents in *Hamlet*

by Jennifer Rust

University of California, Irvine

ALTHOUGH there is a general consensus in recent Shakespearean criticism that *Hamlet,* of all the great tragedies, has some special connection to the Reformation, it is notoriously difficult to identify any consistent theological position in either the play itself or its title character, despite his prominent education at Wittenberg. This difficulty is exemplified by one of the few palpable references to the turmoil of the Reformation in the play, Hamlet's conflation of the historical Diet of Worms with the decaying body of Polonius:

> KING: At supper? Where?
> HAMLET: Not where he eats, but where 'a is eaten. A certain convocation of politic worms are e'en at him. Your worm is your only emperor for diet. We fat all creatures else to fat us, and we fat ourselves for maggots. Your fat king and your lean beggar is but variable service— two dishes, but to one table. That's the end. (4.3.18–25)[1]

Aside from reemphasizing Hamlet's connection to the birthplace and bastion of Lutheranism, this cryptic reference evokes a series of supplementary associations that do not necessarily resolve themselves into a recognizable orthodoxy. Insofar as Hamlet confronts Claudius as a political rival, he places him in the position of Luther's chief persecutor, Holy Roman Emperor Charles V. As they proceed to undermine the basis of his authority by inverting or flattening conventional hierarchies (worm/emperor, king/beggar), the lines reinforce Hamlet's earlier dissolution of the King's Two Bodies ("The body is with the King, but the King is not with the body. The King is a thing . . . Of nothing" [4.2.27–30]). As it dismantles the sacramental edifice of Claudius's sovereignty by collapsing the "mystical" and natural bodies of the King, Hamlet's rhetoric also echoes Luther's denial of the sacramental authority of the Roman Church at the Diet of Worms.[2]

The primary sacrament at issue here, as at Worms, seems to be the Eucharist. Yet the utter debasement of the ritual in the image of maggots as communicants, ingesting the mingled body of the beggar/king at the common "table" of the grave appears to go beyond Luther's more nuanced doctrine of "real presence," which reduces but does not completely eliminate the sacral value of the actual bread and wine.[3] Such a vision seems particularly suited to the de-sacramentalized, thoroughly fallen, post-Wittenberg milieu of *Hamlet,* in which Hamlet's degradation of the Eucharist seems merely the expression of a commonplace. However, as Stephen Greenblatt observes, Hamlet's antic wordplay does recall a more radical strain of Reformation propaganda insofar as it draws on paradoxical attempts to rescue the true spirit of the Eucharist "from the taint of the body" by emphasizing the "material contamination" of the Catholic ritual (2001, 241–42).[4] Although such caricatures are ultimately rooted in a tendency to oppose absolutely the reality of spiritual transcendence and the realm of material existence, the invisible, immaterial substance of God is nonetheless affirmed through a discourse that burrows, like the "old mole" himself, into the depths of earthly corruption. Nonetheless, any affirmation of such transcendence seems more distant than ever in Hamlet's bleak conclusion: "That's the end." The monstrous parody of the Eucharist culminates in an apocalypse without resurrection, a progressive degradation that has lost any connection to redemption. Hamlet's conclusion emulates not the conviction of committed Protestant propagandists so much as the despair of a particularly Protestant spiritual crisis. More precisely, the riddle underscores the instability of any opposition between these two positions.

This instability is rooted in a fundamental tension within Protestant spirituality that can be illustrated through another possible point of reference for Hamlet's scrambled allusion to Worms. Alongside Luther, Hamlet's pun may also call to mind the figure of early Protestant martyr William Tyndale, who, in 1527, began producing print editions of his groundbreaking English translation of the New Testament in

Worms.[5] Tyndale's work exemplifies not only the initial shock wave of
Protestant revolt against the authority of the Roman Church, but also
the tension, embedded in this revolt at its very origins, that continues
to haunt the Reformation subtext of *Hamlet.* In *Renaissance Self-
Fashioning,* Greenblatt gestures toward a crucial source of this tension
by linking Tyndale's Protestant emphasis on the degenerate, idolatrous
character of Catholic ritual to the paradoxical effects of the
Reformation's peculiar "fetishism of Scripture" (1980, 94). Though the
manuscripts of the old church (and, by extension, its larger apparatus
of devotional rituals) possess an "aura" of intimate spiritual experience, a connection with "ritual function, or, at least, to a particular, specific human community," the Reformation takes its cue from the
"depersonalization" of the printed volume, the "absoluteness" and
"integrity" of the Word revealed in the new medium (86).[6] It is precisely through its "very lack of aura" that the depersonalized book
becomes an effective instrument of spiritual transformation; the
"*abstractness* of the early Protestant printed book" grants it "an intensity, a shaping power, an element of compulsion" foreign to the ritual
authority of the medieval church (86). The printed book maintains
such a compelling force because it is intended to be "absorbed" by its
readers. In the work of Tyndale, "words are not carried out into the
light but are destined for the opposite process: they will be studied,
absorbed, internalized . . ." (86). The artificial substantiality of the
newly printed word has a profound impact on the subjectivity of the
reader; its very exteriority to the human, its alienness, enables it to pen-
etrate and assimilate human experience; its "apparently impersonal
rhetoric" comes to determine "readers' most intimate sense of themselves" (87).

Tyndale's distillation of the Scriptures into vernacular printed texts
exemplifies David Wills's suggestion that the Protestant Reformation
is linked to a certain "prosthetic effect," a perspective that emphasizes
"the idea of *reformation* as artificial reconstruction" (1995, 219). From
this point of view, the Reformation must be thought of in the context
of the larger process of "prostheticization" unfolding throughout early
modern Europe in the wake of the advent of print technologies, in
which traditional forms of knowledge are "broken apart and artificially reconstructed" (219). In his chapter on Tyndale, Greenblatt offers an
account of one significant manifestation of this phenomenon: the

Reformation's production of a subjectivity profoundly shaped by the exigencies of the printed text (1980). Despite its evident modernity, this process generates certain side effects that undermine the supposed opposition between the Reformation's dependence on the text and the auratic rituals and objects so demonized in Reformist polemics. Elizabeth Eisenstein also draws attention to this contradiction: "Indeed, however much they attacked 'mechanical devotions,' Protestants relied much more than did papists on the services of 'mechanick printers'" (1983, 166–67). According to Wills, because the Reformation finds "its condition of possibility" in the innovation of the printed work, it becomes entangled in a paradox that threatens its iconoclastic ambitions. In its very artificiality, its dissemination of rhetorical figures and figurative images, the book "risks repeating the fallen structure of the Roman Church." In the work of Protestant rhetoricians such as Thomas Wilson, Wills detects "more than a hint of guilt by association between the idol and the book" (230–31), insofar as both are "fallen" in the sense that they substitute a "specific form of materiality" for the "immateriality" of spiritual presence (232).

Yet a certain awareness of this paradox lies at the heart of Lutheran hermeneutics, intimately connected to the doctrine of the fallen world. According to Luther, because God escapes all representation and rational comprehension, he can only become manifest via "contrary" appearances: "God wears the mask of the devil, and the devil wears the mask of God; God wants to be recognized under the mask of the devil, and He wants the devil to be condemned under the mask of God" (1955, 43). The images and rituals of the Catholic Church are idolatrous because they confuse God with his masks; Luther avoids this trap not by abandoning these "masks"—an impossibility insofar as humanity, mired in its fallen state, can only encounter God through some form of mediation—but rather by shifting their figures. God is most absent where He appears most pleasing and most present where He appears most distant and horrifying. Only the eye of faith can discern the merciful God under his demonic mask. This perspective comes to terms with the inevitability of figuration through an inversion that privileges the most foreboding, impersonal representations and emphasizes their very artificiality. Such a theology is well adapted to the "depersonalization" and heightened "abstractness" of the printed Scriptures, for it seeks God wherever He seems most alien and remote.

This principle is central to Luther's hermeneutic practice; it is especially evident in his directives on the appropriate way to "absorb" the
scriptural text. Luther hailed the advent of the printed word: "God's
highest and extremest act of grace, whereby the business of the Gospel
is driven forward" (qtd. in Eisenstein 1983, 147). Yet this "act of
grace" is not necessarily an unmitigated good. Luther adapts the
Pauline distinction between "letter" and "Spirit" to the exigencies of a
Christianity transformed by the printed scriptural text. The scriptural
word of grace is also, simultaneously, the deadly "letter" of the law of
a wrathful God. Absorbed without faith, the letter is deadly, sinful; yet
without the letter, it is impossible to attain true grace, since Luther
insists that the external letter is the necessary correlate of the spiritual
Word: "God gives no one his Spirit or his grace except through or with
the outward word which precedes it" (qtd. in Ebeling 1970, 109).
Nonetheless, the "letter" participates in the fallen world insofar as it is
"alien, remote, external" whereas the Spirit is the "good word . . . the
word of grace." Since this Spirit only ever arrives "concealed in the letter"; in interpreting the Scriptures, "the Spirit must be drawn out of the
letter" in order to become "something alive in the heart, which takes
possession of man" (Ebeling, 98–99). However, such a transmutation
can only take place through an absolute faith that is always precarious
in the "evil world." As Ebeling explains, for Luther, the struggle to
maintain a faithful understanding of Scripture takes the form of an endless dialectic: "For there is a constant threat that an understanding once
achieved will cease to be Spirit, and return to being the mere letter,
unless it is constantly attained anew and made one's own . . . The
Spirit turns into the letter, but the letter must in its turn constantly
become the Spirit once again" (99). Without the exercise of faith, this
dialectic becomes paralyzed and the soul, exiled from grace, becomes
ossified according to the rigid strictures of the fatal letter. Instead of
reinforcing spiritual well-being, the constant study of Scripture
becomes a kind of mechanical repetition that continually alienates the
individual from the possibility of salvation.

For Luther, the loss of faith poses the threat of a sheerly prostheti-
cized existence in which the individual is inhabited and determined by
the "dead letter" of Scripture as law, not Spirit. In the midst of this failure, the soul, unable to emerge from its immersion in fallenness, undergoes a total lapse into the inauthentic. With the collapse of a proper

mediation between God and humanity, men become captive to the machinery of a depraved medium. Luther's account of this captivity undergoes a further evolution in later Reformation discourses in which the symbiotic relation between the immateriality of the Spirit and the materiality of the printed letter becomes even more pronounced. According to Calvin's doctrine of predestination, authentic faith can only be "written," "imprinted," or "engraven" in the soul by God—the mark of election is frequently figured as an invisible, interior text "impressed on the heart" (1989, I.ix.3). Whereas Luther is reluctant to acknowledge any truly valid representation of Spirit, Calvin insists on the figure of Spirit as an immaterial text, the ideal form of the material printed text. In contrast to Luther's dialectic of letter and Spirit, the letter does not metamorphosize into the Spirit; rather, the invisible inner text of Spirit must be aligned with the outer visible text of the gospels, an alignment that requires the presence of a spiritual inscription "ingrafted" on the soul at its creation. Without this inner inscription, Scripture can only be "the dead and deadly letter"—instead of offering eternal salvation, "the law of the Lord kills its readers" (I.ix.3). The influence of this Calvinist conception is discernible in the English preacher William Perkins's contention that the encounter with the visible Scriptures will be depraved unless this outward reading is supplemented by an inner spiritual writing; the promise of salvation must be "written in my heart" such that "inward experience" becomes a "commentary" on the printed gospels (1970, 377). Perkins describes the perverse effects of Scripture on those who remain ignorant of their "ingrafting into Christ": as a result of their blindness, the Scriptures "become a maze unto them in which they wander as in a mist (as we say) led by Robin Goodfellow . . . They read them as men do tales of Robin Hood, as riddles, or, as old priests their Ladies' matins" (377–78). For those deficient in grace, Scripture becomes a mechanism of enchantment; at best, a mere game, at worst, a form of idolatry akin to the papist rosary.

Idolatry, faithlessly worshipping the "masks" of God as if they were the Thing Itself, is only one possible outcome of this misalignment between Scripture and soul. The symptoms described by Perkins are echoed in Robert Burton's *Anatomy of Melancholy,* which devotes an entire section to manifestations of "religious melancholy" stemming from a weakness in faith. To the religious melancholic "the Scripture is false, rude, harsh, unmethodical: Heaven, hell, resurrection mere toys and fables ... impossible, absurd, vain, ill-contrived" (1979, 113). When the individual is unable to overcome the aura of a spiritual experience tainted with inauthenticity, he is in danger of succumbing to a melancholia that colors his perception of the world at large. As Burton demonstrates, an association between melancholy and rigors of Reformation spirituality was current in the popular imagination of early modern England. Though the struggle with such melancholy was not necessarily foreign to English Protestantism, it was often more strongly associated with the spiritual struggle of the foundational figures in the Wittenberg Reformation. Raymond Waddington observes that there was "something of a cult of melancholy in the ambiance of Lutheran Germany" in this era, influenced not only by treatments of melancholic themes by followers such as Dürer and Melanchthon, but also Luther's own reputed melancholic episodes (1989, 34–35). In *Henry VIII,* the only Shakespearean play to deal explicitly with the initial events of the English Reformation, Wolsey characterizes Anne Boleyn, as a "spleeny Lutheran" (3.2.98–99; cited in Waddington, 34), identifying Elizabeth's mother with the stereotypical melancholic adherent of Wittenberg. Perhaps in the theater of a predominantly Calvinist England (in both *Hamlet* and its dramatic precursor, Marlowe's *Doctor Faustus*), Lutheran Wittenberg became the scene of an *other* Protestantism, the anti-type of Geneva, the continental center that exerted a far more profound impact on the shape of English Protestantism by the end of the sixteenth century. For such an audience, Wittenberg may have functioned as a screen, an alternate or more archaic version of Protestantism onto which lingering anxieties engendered by the upheaval of the English Reformation could be projected without directly challenging either the official Anglican church or its numerous Puritan critics.[7] Though Wittenberg may have been particularly redolent of spiritual melancholy, the condition itself was clearly a source of concern in Calvinist England as well.

In *The Origin of German Tragic Drama,* Walter Benjamin locates an undercurrent of both "the philosophy of Wittenberg and the protest against it" in Hamlet's musings on the radical immanence of human existence (1998, 139), linking Shakespeare's play to the melancholic allegory of seventeenth-century German baroque drama. According to Benjamin, the melancholic impulse arises in response to the "empty world" generated by the reformers' denial of any transcendent value in earthly works and emphasis on salvation through faith alone, a perspective that leads the most sensitive, those who cannot sustain the requisite faith, to view "the scene of their existence as a rubbish heap of partial, inauthentic actions" (139). Although the melancholic world view represents the rebellion of "life itself" against its devaluation by faith, this rebellion does not take the form of a return to an unfallen nature or a revitalization of the *aura* of sacramental objects and rituals; rather, the melancholic *mourns* the loss of transcendence, a "state of mind in which feeling revives the empty world in the form of a mask" (139). The melancholic vision of the world as "mask" is no longer informed by the experience of faith, but neither is it naively idolatrous. The mask is recognized as mask, as "artificial reconstruction," but the Spirit it conceals has become elusive; the struggle to read the world through faith undergoes a mutation, becoming the purely subjective quest for access to occult wisdom. The ultimate refuge of the melancholic is the "book as an *arcanum*" (141); this same book provides the paradigmatic structure for his allegorical reconstruction of the world. Despite its alienation from faith, this apparatus of mourning remains fundamentally tied to the Reformation; insofar as both rely upon the authority of the textualizing gesture, both are contingent on the absorption of the printed book.[8] The "depersonalization" associated with the printed word contaminates every aspect of the melancholic's lived experience. Without the consolation of faith, mourning becomes "the pathological state in which the most simple object appears to be a symbol of some enigmatic reason because it lacks any natural, creative relationship to us" (140). The attitude of mourning both devalues and overvalues this "depersonalized" world. Deprived of a coherent "natural" significance, even ordinary objects are invested with mysterious, occult meaning at the same time they continually testify to the lost connection between spiritual and earthly existence.

In Shakespeare's play, the Ghost of Old Hamlet is not merely the object of mourning; it also exemplifies the structure of "depersonalization" that Benjamin associates with Reformation melancholia, and Greenblatt identifies with Tyndale's textual work. Though it is the embodiment of the mourning of Hamlet's ideal paternal image, the Ghost is also constantly referred to as an "it," a "thing" that may ultimately consist of "nothing," as Hamlet later implies ("the King is a

thing . . . of nothing"). As Greenblatt has observed, the base materialism that characterizes Hamlet's grotesque image of the Eucharistic
Worms extends to this "distinctly Catholic" Purgatorial spirit, who possesses a "strange quasi-carnality" emphasized by Hamlet's description
of a father murdered "grossly, full of bread, / With all his crimes broad
blown, as flush as May" (3.3.80–81; 2001, 243). The immanence of the
Ghost is repeatedly emphasized in details such as its antic performance
as the "old mole," its armored body, and its poisoning by "leperous distillment." But whether it is ultimately a satanic demon, a pagan spirit,
or a soul from the fires of Purgatory, the Ghost is not merely another
sign of the desacramentalized world of the play.[9] More importantly, the
Ghost vividly figures the dynamic of melancholic allegory that ensnares
Hamlet for the remainder of the play. The inaccessible essence of the
Ghost is enclosed in a "questionable shape" that encourages endless
speculation, a "pleasing shape" for the allegorical imagination of the
melancholic. The Ghost's narration of the murder of Old Hamlet alle-
gorizes the transmutation of pure nature into its own corrupt simu-
lacrum, a transmutation that takes place as a disorientation of the proper
relationship between interiority and exteriority. The Protestant absorption of and by the book has at least a structural similarity to the absorption of the "leperous distillment" described by the Ghost insofar as both
involve the internalization of a patently unnatural substance (the poison,
the printed word) that restructures both inner and outer being, reorder-
ing the very nature of the relation between these spheres.

    Although the Ghost appears to be an ethereal entity, no longer sub-
ject to the constraints of the physical world ("it is as the air, invulner-
able" [1.1.145]), it nonetheless appears arrayed "from head to toe" in
seemingly superfluous armor, encased in "complete steel" (1.4.52).
This armor, which invites the spectator to imagine a more essential
phantasmic body, visually prefigures the "vile and loathsome crust"
that covers the dying King's "smooth body" in the Ghost's account of
the murder (1.5.72–73). This "crust" is, of course, the product of one
of the crucial "ear" scenes in *Hamlet*:

> Upon my secure hour thy uncle stole
> With juice of cursed hebona in a vial,
> And in the porches of mine ear did pour
> the leperous distillment . . .
>
> (1.5.61–64)[10]

Here, the ear is the organ through which the body is penetrated not by linguistic sounds, but rather by the poisonous "distillment," the "juice of cursed hebona in a vial" concocted by the intriguing Claudius. The narrative dwells on the unnatural quality of the poison, continuously setting it in opposition to the "natural gates and alleys of the body" through which it runs "swift as quicksilver" (1.5.66–67), a figure that distances the poison further from any biological associations. The synthesized substance "holds such enmity with blood of man" (1.5.65) that it causes this "thin and wholesome blood" to congeal, "posset and curd" (1.5.68–69), eventually bursting forth into the "most instant tetter" (1.5.71) that encompasses the King's corpse.

This "tetter" or scab is the by-product of the infiltration of the inner chambers of the natural body by the insidious "distillment," the biological reaction to penetration by an artificial substance, an amalgamation of natural interior and unnatural exterior into grotesque exoskeleton. The Ghost's narration of this exoskeleton engendered by the mingling of "thin and wholesome blood" with "quicksilver" has several different functions. Not only does it proleptically figure the enigmatic armor of the Ghost (the "quicksilver" metaphorically hardening into the "complete steel" of the apparition), but it also reenacts the "scene of the primal fall" through details, such as the garden and the "serpent"-brother, that allude to the biblical account in Genesis (Kaula 1984, 246–47). The armor-tetter exoskeleton of the Ghost tropes the fallenness of human existence as the assimilation of "wholesome" nature to the contrivance of the "leperous distillment," an internalization that turns the natural body inside out. Once interiorized, the virulent mechanism insists on re-exteriorizing itself, marking its contamination through a series of monstrous encrustations, a layering that entices the vulnerable to speculate that it possesses a more authentic concealed truth. This layering interferes with any attempt to assign a particular referential significance to the Ghost; it cannot become an object of knowledge, although it does continually tempt one to believe that such knowledge could be achieved. Although the Ghost does seem to refer to a Purgatorial condition, it ultimately declines to provide any true metaphysical revelations about its actual status:

> But that I am forbid
> To tell the secrets of my prison house,
> I could a tale unfold whose lightest word
> Would harrow up they soul . . ."
>   (1.5.13–16)

The Ghost teases Hamlet by raising the possibility of these "secrets," yet, at the same time, it thwarts the very curiosity it raises, setting the stage, so to speak, for Hamlet's subsequent attempts to determine its true ethical status through the device of "The Mousetrap."

The Ghost's account of the old King's poisoning functions as an allegory of allegorization itself, with Claudius the intriguer taking the role of the allegorist who hollows out the "smooth" natural body by means of an unnatural contrivance that freezes this body into a monstrous caricature of itself. According to Benjamin, once the textualization of experience becomes allegorical, no longer redeemed by faith in an unrepresentable God, it becomes the instrument of a perverse, absolutist will to power. The world itself is reproduced *as* a guilty text when the allegorizing imagination transmutes the "things and works" of the fallen world "into a stirring writing" (1998, 176) endowing them with a referential significance that replaces the lost meaning of the fallen world with a new subjectively determined mode of signification. To the melancholic, the allegorized object "becomes a key to a hidden realm of knowledge; and he reveres it as an emblem of this. It is a schema . . . and an object of knowledge . . . at one and the same time a fixed image and fixing sign" (184). In imposing this grid upon the natural world, the allegorist creates the illusion of a referential reality beyond the profusion of empty signs, a secret truth accessible to human knowledge. But this knowledge ultimately refers only to the subjective impulses of the allegorist himself. In the course of its "fixation," the object is deprived of "any meaning or significance of its own; such significance as it has, it acquires from the allegorist" (184). The allegorized object is hollowed out and transformed into an arbitrary figure, a "hieroglyph" permeated with a seemingly mysterious meaning. In a similar way, the exoskeleton, the "loathsome crust" that evolves into the cryptic suit of armor, endows the figure of the dead King with heightened aura of mystery, an impression the Ghost itself exacerbates with its refusal to "tell the secrets of my prison house." If these lines contain a veiled reference to Purgatory, they also reconfigure this remnant of a discarded faith into a site of forbidden knowledge; the older spiritual significance of Purgatory is demoted to the status of an enigmatic cipher woven into the figurative texture of the "steeled" Ghost.

Purgatory itself may be trivialized, transformed into a mere trapping or ornament designed to reinforce the occult significance of the apparition, but the overall impact of the Ghost on young Hamlet is, of course, not trivial at all. Its allegorical narrative also replicates the structural dynamic through which the Ghost itself comes to disrupt young Hamlet's supposedly inward-oriented subjectivity. In terms of both its visible manifestation and its own self-description, the Ghost emblematizes the trajectory of the trauma that Hamlet undergoes at the beginning of the play: the passage from the illusion of impregnable interiority to the disclosure of the corruption of this interiority by an insidious exterior substance, the exposure of an interpenetration of interiority and exteriority. It is the arrival of the Ghost that first troubles the possibility of drawing the clear-cut distinction between material body and transcendent soul that Hamlet yearns for in his initial claim to "have that within which passes show" (1.2.85) and his desire to dissolve a "too too sullied [solid] flesh" (1.2.129). Indeed, the moment in which Horatio announces the arrival of the Ghost to Hamlet is structured to make the Prince's earlier appeals to a notion of transcendent interiority seem curiously ridiculous:

> HAMLET: My father, methinks I see my father.
> HORATIO: Where, my lord?
> HAMLET: In my mind's eye, Horatio.
> HORATIO: I saw him once. A was a goodly king.
> HAMLET: A was a man, take him for all in all,
> I shall not look upon his like again.
> HORATIO: My lord, I think I saw him yesternight.
> HAMLET: Saw? Who?
> HORATIO: My lord, the King your father.
> HAMLET: The King my father? (1.2.183–92)

In this darkly comic exchange, a certain disorientation ensues when Horatio literalizes Hamlet's ostentatious rhetoric of mourning ("Where, my lord?"). The initial dilemma that the Ghost poses for young Hamlet is framed as an ironic derangement of the boundaries between interior transcendence and the external world that he had attempted to delineate clearly in his earlier claim to "know not seems." In Horatio's announcement, Hamlet discovers that what he had assumed remained contained "within" his inviolate "mind's eye"—the idealized image of the unique "goodly king"—has already exteriorized itself by visibly stalking the battlements of Elsinore nightly, available to the outer, physical eyes of all onlookers. In his encounter with the Ghost, Hamlet confronts a supernatural entity, intimately connected to his own sense of identity, who *descends* rather than transcends, compelling Hamlet's companions to "swear" a holy oath of secrecy from beneath the earth ("Well said, old mole! Canst work i' the earth so fast? A worthy pioner" [1.5.162–63]). If the exchange with Horatio reveals that the Ghost *is* Hamlet's interiority, then Hamlet's subsequent encounter suggests that both this "image" and the interiority it inhabits are bound to a condition of radical immanence.

The profound shock that accompanies the jarring exteriorization of the internal image that Hamlet had claimed to hold sacrosanct is amplified not only by the perversity of the apparition and its story but also by its final injunction, "Remember me" (1.5.91), which demands that Hamlet re-interiorize this grotesque "shape" and its cry for revenge. After the Ghost issues its parting command, Hamlet cannot at first respond in a coherent manner. He struggles to maintain a stable frame of reference for comprehending the import of the Ghost's visitation:

> O all you host of heaven! O earth! What else?
> Shall I couple hell? O fie! Hold, hold my heart,
> And you, my sinews, grow not instant old,
> But bear me stiffly up
>
> (92–95)

In his struggle to regain composure, Hamlet flashes through all the possible points of origin for the Ghost, unable to settle on a provisional answer that would quell his physical and mental turmoil. The sexual innuendo in Hamlet's question "Shall I couple hell?" reinforces the association of the Ghost with a kind of intimate contamination that, in turn, threatens physical paralysis ("my sinews, grow not instant old"). Upon repeating the Ghost's parting phrase ("Remember thee?"), Hamlet restores a measure of coherence by embarking on a new strategy to cope with the shock of the Ghost and its demands:

Yea, from the table of my memory
I'll wipe away all trivial fond records,
All saws of books, all forms, all pressures past
That youth and observation copied there,
And thy commandment all alone shall live
Within the book and volume of my brain,
Unmixed with baser matter.

(97–104)

Previous critics have observed that Hamlet's speech, accompanied by a pantomimed or actual act of writing ("My tables—meet it is I set it down" [107]), contains an implicit reference to Old Testament Scripture—the sequence from the Book of Exodus in which God bequeaths the "tablets" containing the Ten Commandments to Moses.[11] The underlying allusion refers to a scriptural moment in which the transcendent will of God and its material inscription simultaneously appear in a unified form. The allusion adds a special layer of irony to Hamlet's behavior here, since the Ghost who issues these "commandments," marked by numerous signs of immanence, is only quasi-transcendental at best. Hamlet's frenzied "play" of writing parodies the biblical account insofar as the written "commandment" is infused with the dead life or living death of the spectre, rather than the pure presence of a living God. In this regard, the "commandment" most resembles Paul's characterization of the Ten Commandments as the "old law," the "deadly letter" that must be superseded by "Spirit" of the new covenant of the Christian gospels, the crucial distinction that Luther and Calvin so carefully tailored to the needs of the print culture of the Reformation.[12]

The new covenant that Hamlet seeks to record on his inner "tablets" cannot be purified of the "baser matter" of the Spirit itself, in spite of his best efforts. This charade of writing is an inverted image of the earlier scene in which Horatio interrupts Hamlet's interior idealized tableau of mourning with news of the Ghost's phenomenal manifestation. Insofar as he figures his "brain" as a "book and volume" that must be erased and replaced with a new document, Hamlet's impulse to rewrite the Ghost's message into a falsified "scripture" enacts a twisted version of the Calvinist logic of inner and outer writing. Because the figure of the Ghost and the story that it tells seriously disrupt the coherence of his inner script, Hamlet is compelled to write an external text

that would reassert this lost coherence. In this case, Hamlet seeks to
forestall any contamination by the apparition by exteriorizing the com-
muniqué that he has been ordered to internalize, effacing its most perplexing and disturbing elements in order to re-interiorize the "revised
text" without seriously compromising the integrity of his soul.
Hamlet's return to the illusion of a secure, transcendent interiority is
predicated on the generation of an exterior text to supplement an inner
deficiency. This distorted re-inscription allows Hamlet to regain a certain stability because it reconfigures the meta-allegory of the Ghost
into a pseudo-scriptural document that conforms to his previously
established views; in effect, Hamlet re-allegorizes the Ghost by fixing
it within his own predetermined frame of reference. However, this
effort remains only a parodic gesture. In writing the "commandments"
of the Ghost, Hamlet empties them of any meaningful content, reduc-
ing this complex and contradictory discourse to a few hollow, moralistic banalities—Gertrude becomes the archetypal faithless woman and
Claudius a hypocritical Vice figure ("O most pernicious woman! / O
villain, villain, smiling, damnèd villain!" [105–6])—and virtually erasing the all-important order to revenge.

Though this play of writing may briefly stabilize Hamlet's relation
to the Ghost, explicit doubts about the Ghost suddenly return at the end
of act 2, this time to be confronted by the writing of a play. As he formulates the rationale for "The Mousetrap," Hamlet connects his suspicion of the Ghost to a suspicion of his own inherent flaws:

> The spirit that I have seen
> May be a devil, and the devil hath power
> T'assume a pleasing shape, yea, and perhaps
> Out of my weakness and my melancholy,
> As he is very potent with such spirits,
> Abuses me to damn me. I'll have grounds
> More relative than this. The play's the thing
> Wherein I'll catch the conscience of the King.
>   (2.2.610–17)

Hamlet is most perturbed by the Ghost's potential to exploit his inner
weakness. His caution and the textual strategy it inspires recall
Calvin's denunciation of those who would take Paul's warnings
against the "dead and deadly letter" too literally and reject the reading
of Scripture in favor of "spiritual" revelations that have no apparent

connection with the written Gospels. Calvin warns that such Christians court disaster insofar as they may in fact be communing with demonic spirits: "Since Satan transforms himself into an angel of light, what authority can the Spirit have with us if he be not ascertained by an infallible mark?" The "image" that the Holy Spirit "has stamped on the Scriptures" guarantees the authenticity of any revelation (*Institutes* I.ix.2). At first glance, Hamlet appears to be following a rational Reformation strategy by producing the play "to catch the conscience of the King," to make this conscience visible and intelligible as an externally evident "mark" that could form the "grounds" to authorize the dubious Spirit's revelation.

Yet, as in Hamlet's earlier transcription of the "commandments," this Calvinist logic is undermined by Hamlet's penchant for allegory. Given that Hamlet expresses these doubts *after* he has laid out the plan for "The Mousetrap," we may wonder whether Hamlet's plotting is entirely inspired by "the healthy recognition of a very real threat," as Eleanor Prosser asserts (1967, 155). Hamlet explicitly identifies his weakness as melancholic; in doing so, he invokes the conventional Elizabethan belief that melancholy renders one particularly vulnerable to satanic temptation (Lyons 1971, 90). It is this melancholy that transforms the "questionable shape" (1.4.43) of the enigmatic apparition into the "pleasing shape" capable of enticing Hamlet into damnation. However, the fact that these doubts are posed as the motivating factor for yet another layer of artifice suggests that at the very moment Hamlet most seems to question the ethical status of the Ghost, he is most fully in the grips of a melancholia that feeds upon the enigmatic appearance of the spectre. If, as Benjamin proposes, melancholia is intimately tied to the allegorical imagination, we can more precisely define the temptation posed by the Ghost as a temptation into allegory, a temptation that Hamlet has succumbed to even more fully than he admits in this speech. The plotting of the play within the play bears all the hallmarks of an allegorical production, insofar as it is an attempt to endow the Ghost with an absolute, fixed signification determined by Hamlet himself through the use of a textual device, the "speech of some dozen or sixteen lines" (2.2.551) inserted in the player's script. "The Mousetrap" aims to determine the significance of the Ghost by recreating its primal scene, the murder by "leperous distillment" that occupies such a central place in the Ghost's injunction to revenge. As we have seen, this original moment is already loaded with allegorical overtones that infuse it with an air of inauthenticity. Hamlet adds an additional layer to the already incrusted enigma of the Ghost ostensibly in order to lay bare its actual referential status, to discover once and for all whether in truth it is a "spirit of health or goblin damned."

Hamlet's circuitous effort to make the Ghost into an object of knowledge, to "pluck out the heart" of its mystery, relies on yet another detour. Prior to the performance, he enlists Horatio in his project:

> Observe my uncle. If his occulted guilt
> Do not itself unkennel in one speech,
> It is a damnèd ghost that we have seen,
> And my imaginations are as foul as Vulcan's stithy
>
> (3.2.82–86)

Hamlet can determine the ethical substance of the Ghost only indirectly, through Claudius's reaction to the performance. He forgets his earlier certainty about Claudius's guilt when he insists that the King must become another object from which to extract an "occulted" secret—when the appropriate pressure is applied, "murder, though it hath no tongue, will speak / With most miraculous organ" (2.2.605–6). Moreover, Hamlet poses the test in absolutist terms; if Claudius fails to give the appropriate sign, both he and the Ghost are "damnèd," whereas, presumably, a guilty response clears both from all blame. Though "The Mousetrap" provokes the response Hamlet seeks—Claudius *does* "blench" at the reenactment of the ear poisoning, leading Hamlet to declare that he will "take the ghost's word for a thousand pound" (3.2.292–93)—it also thwarts his progress toward the goal of revenge. Giddy with the apparent success of his contrivance, Hamlet stumbles when he subsequently encounters the tableau of Claudius at prayer and misreads his outwardly pious posture as a genuine sign of repentance:

> Now might I do it pat, now 'a is a-praying,
> And now I'll do't. And so 'a goes to heaven,
> And so I am revenged. That would be scanned . . . Why, this is hire
> and salary, not revenge
>
> (3.3.73–79)[13]

Hamlet's failure at this moment is not the result of indecision as much as interpretive mania: he overestimates his own ability to "scan" accurately the images that confront him at the same time he underestimates the extent to which the conclusions that he draws are determined by his own subjective inclinations. He does not pause to consider the possibility of a discrepancy between Claudius's "words" and "thoughts" ("My words fly up, my thoughts remain below. / Words without thoughts never to heaven go" [3.3.97–98]).

It may seem that Hamlet loses his sense of purpose in the midst of all these intrigues, exceeding or simply forgetting the primary injunction of the Ghost. However, on a deeper level, he acts in accord with the allegorical framework of the Ghost's visitation, enthusiastically accepting its invitation into allegory. The essential dilemma of the Ghost's urgent order to revenge lies in the fact that it emerges from a enigmatic form guaranteed to draw Hamlet into an allegorical labyrinth that causes all direct action to "turn awry." On the surface, this Hamlet who deploys allegorical devices such as the falsified scriptural "commandments" or the staging of the play within the play in a calculating effort to gain knowledge or mastery, the Hamlet of the first four acts whose plots and counterplots form the framework of his notorious delay and indecision, seems to disappear in the final act, replaced by the newly resolute figure who affirms "a divinity that shapes our ends" (5.2.10). In the transformed Hamlet of act 5, critics often read either a sudden conversion to a Calvinist notion of "providence" or a turn to a pagan Stoic fatalism or some hybrid of these two doctrines.[14] Here, however, we will be concerned primarily with the fate of allegory in this final act, particularly as it emerges through Hamlet's transformed approach to textual production and the lingering traces of the meta-allegorical Ghost. Stephen Greenblatt notes that by act 5, the Ghost's presence in the play is barely detectable. The ghost of Hamlet's father dissipates, maintaining only a marginalized, fragmentary existence as a "marker of time" in the graveyard scene or as an incidental thing (the "signet" of Hamlet's sea narrative) (2001, 226). Greenblatt hypothesizes that the apparent effacement of the Ghost signals its successful interiorization by Hamlet. The Ghost maintains a form of presence "inside" Hamlet—by the end of the play, it seems "as if the spirit of Hamlet's father has not disappeared; it has been incorporated by his son" (229).

Yet, as we have seen, the Ghost profoundly disturbs the boundaries between interiority and exteriority from the beginning of the play. Can such a dislocating figure be safely consigned to an "inner space" that it has already ruptured in the opening scenes? Does Hamlet "incorporate" the Ghost or does the Ghost, as a metonymic figure for the larger phenomenon of allegory itself, incorporate Hamlet? Perhaps the condition of possibility for this newly resolute Hamlet is precisely the relinquishment of any claim to a circumscribed interiority, the very claim that he struggled to defend through the series of allegorical gestures that structure the first four acts. Paradoxically, the serenity of act 5 may not result from an abandonment of the allegorical, but rather from an absolute expansion of it. What Hamlet abandons in the celebrated turning point of act 5 is allegory as a restricted economy concerned with constructing fixed schemas that create the illusion of referentiality. This is the economy of allegory within which Hamlet circulates in the first four acts of the play. In contrast, the general economy of allegory to which Hamlet opens himself in act 5 no longer functions according to a referential schema that would oppose the interiority of the knowing subject to the external "world of things."

This shift becomes evident when we pay closer attention to Hamlet's final scene of "play-writing" midway through act 5, the very scene in which the dead father's "signet" makes a crucial cameo appearance. Hamlet begins the narration of his escape from what is quite literally the "dead and deadly letter," the document that announces his impending execution, by describing the state of inner conflict that overtakes him during the sea voyage to England:

> Sir, in my heart there was a kind of fighting
> That would not let me sleep. Methought I lay
> Worse than the mutines in the bilboes
>
> (5.2.4–6)

This struggle between violently opposed instincts induces a claustrophobic paralysis in Hamlet, as if he is now trapped within the very interior dimension that he had so elaborately constructed and maintained throughout the previous course of events. Hamlet only overcomes this paralysis by renouncing the compulsion to calculate that drives his earlier actions. In acting "rashly," he deserts his earlier attempts to master the world around him by imposing his own vision of order and coherence:

> Rashly
> (and praised be rashness for it) let us know,
> Our indiscretion sometime serves us well

> When our deep plots do pall, and that should learn us
> There's a divinity that shapes our ends
> Rough-hew them how we will
>
> (8–13)

Already, there is a marked contrast between this Hamlet and the earlier character who "plots" the play within the play in a bid to gain control over his desperate situation. Hamlet's decision to follow a course of "indiscretion" supersedes any concern with an inner state; the inwardness that has been such a source of concern throughout most of the play has now become prison from which he must escape by abandoning himself to a "rashness" with no determinable origin.

This divine "rashness" leads him through the dark, straight to the letter that announces his impending death. This revelation of what is quite literally the "dead and deadly letter" has a peculiar effect on Hamlet insofar as it pushes him into an act of writing that differs significantly from his previous textual productions:

> Being thus benetted round with villains,
> Or I could make a prologue to my brains,
> They had begun the play. I sat me down,
> Devised a new commission, wrote it fair.
> I once did hold it, as our statists do,
> A baseness to write fair, and labored much
> How to forget that learning, but, sir, now
> It did me yeoman's service
>
> (29–36)

Superficially, the counterfeit letter that Hamlet composes resembles his earlier "plots" insofar as it is another device of intrigue designed to shape a perilous situation to his advantage, this time by turning the tables on his treacherous companions. However, this particular instrument emerges from an interior that he no longer seems to possess or control ("Or I could make a prologue to my brains"), the product of a seemingly "forgotten" interior script that begins to exteriorize itself in the form of "play"-writing before he even begins to comprehend what is taking place. The theatrical language that Hamlet uses to describe his transcription of this fatal "new commission" underscores the difference between this "play"-writing and Hamlet's earlier productions. Though "The Mousetrap" is a calculated effort to establish the Ghost, Claudius, and Hamlet's mother as fixed points of reference that would provide suitable "grounds" to guarantee the stability of his subjective judgments, this "play" moves in precisely the opposite direction insofar as its composition undermines any notion of subjective stability or referential truth. In this moment of "rashness," the textual production is no longer an inherently self-reflexive, self-affirming activity; rather, writing becomes precisely the activity through which Hamlet abandons his former concerns with inner integrity.

It is as if, in this act of forgery, an automatic reaction to the document that prefigures his own death, Hamlet fully embraces his own guilty participation in a radically immanent world, the inexorable link that binds him most closely to the dead life of the Ghost. This possibility is heightened by the sudden, virtual reappearance of the Ghost itself, in the fragmentary "thingly" form of the dead father's signet, the authenticating "seal" for the deadly counterfeit:

> HORATIO: How was this sealed?
> HAMLET: Why, even in that was heaven ordinant.
> I had my father's signet in my purse,
> Which was the model of that Danish seal,
> Folded the writ up in the form of th'other,
> Subscribed it, gave't th'impression, placed it safely,
> The changeling never known. (48–53)

An instability suddenly appears here between the authentic and the counterfeit, the "model" and the copy—as if by chance, Hamlet produces an exact replica of the official signet that turns out to be more authentic than the seal it is used to dissimulate. In providing a final, validating touch for Hamlet's "rash" contrivance, the authentic seal, which itself is already the artificial emblem of authority, becomes indistinguishable from the inauthentic signet of the usurper Claudius.

The "father's signet" becomes the allegorical object *mise en abyme,* the annihilation of referentiality in the sheer multiplicity of prosthetic devices. If we consider this narrative in the larger context of the graveyard scene that immediately precedes it, in which the name of the father becomes a "marker in time" when the gravedigger reminds Hamlet of the coincidence between the date of his birth and old Hamlet's victory over old Fortinbras, then it appears that Hamlet's own singular identity is thrown into question in act 5 by being confronted with what Ned Lukacher describes as a "countersignature event," a "correlation of utterly random letters and dates and things" (1994,

151). Furthermore, the coincidental appearance of this fatal and falsi-
fying signet connects Hamlet's narration of this "breakthrough" scene
with the final catastrophe of the drama insofar as both the signet and
the deadly letter it seals prefigure what Benjamin describes as the
"drastic externality" of Hamlet's death: "Hamlet . . . wants to breathe
in the suffocating air of fate in one deep breath. He wants to die by
some accident, and as the fatal stage-properties gather around him, as
around their lord and master, the drama of fate flares up in the conclusion of this *Trauerspiel* . . ." (1998, 137). "Fate" (*Schicksal*), as
Benjamin defines it in an earlier essay, "Fate and Character," is "the
guilt context of the living" (1978, 308). In giving himself over to a fate
that remains beyond either calculation or control, Hamlet also acqui-
esces to his own implication in the guilt of a fallen world, without
attempting to mold this fallenness into a schema that would affirm his
ingenious self-aggrandizing mastery of this world. Instead, throughout
act 5, in the "Saturnian-melancholy emblem" that is the graveyard
scene and in the "accidental" collision of pseudo-sacramental objects
in the "sacrificial ritual" of the apocalyptic final duel,[15] Hamlet
immerses himself in an economy of allegory that is no longer subject
to the delusion of referential meaning and that no longer permits the
demarcation of interior soul from exterior materiality.

This immersion signals Hamlet's recognition of the fact that allegory actually "means precisely the non-existence of what it presents,"
that its figures only have significance "in the subjective view of melancholy" (Benjamin 1998, 233). In this regard, the resolute Hamlet of act
5 is already ghostly insofar as he claims only the liminal status of a life
delivered over to fate: "the interim's mine/and a man's life is no more
than to say 'one'" (5.2.73–74). Ensnared in the general economy of
allegory that frames his guilty existence, Hamlet persists in the "interim" between life and death, the interminable (almost Purgatorial)
empty time between certain damnation and unforeseeable redemption.
In this abandonment, Hamlet presents the spectacle of "melancholy
redeemed, by being confronted with itself" (Benjamin 1998, 158). In
his final section on allegory, Benjamin reveals that this "redemption"
demands the recognition that good cannot be essentially differentiated
from evil, that knowledge of evil is always "primary," whereas knowledge of good is merely illusory, and that the only hope of salvation lies
in the absolute collapse of the distinction between subjectivity and the

fallen world. Only through this impoverishment, this utter merging with the guilty world, can the melancholic subject be "incorporated into divine omnipotence . . . as hell" (234).

From Benjamin's perspective, Hamlet plays the Christian "martyr" in his final moments, achieving a paradoxical salvation only under the sign of an unmitigated immersion in evil. Melancholy only leads to salvation by means of a detour through total spiritual despair. In this regard, Hamlet's final abandonment recalls Luther's contention that God only appears beneath the "mask" of the devil; except there are few indications that Hamlet is still concerned with discerning the difference between the two. One sign of this peculiar melancholic martyrdom is Hamlet's refusal to dignify his own death in Christian terms. In his final lines, he fails to evoke any recognizably Christian conceptions of afterlife, neither a transcendent heaven nor a basely materialistic hell. Instead, Hamlet's concern is focused on ensuring the quality of his narrative or textual afterlife:

> O God Horatio, what a wounded name,
> Things standing thus unknown, shall live behind me!
> If thou didst ever hold me in thy heart,
> Absent thee from felicity awhile,
> And in this harsh world draw thy breath in pain,
> To tell my story.
>
> (5.2.345–49)

Though Hamlet may ultimately attain a passage to heaven through hell, in this appeal, the only kind of "transcendent" afterlife that he affirms is the partial, spectral transcendence of a vanished life transcribed into a "story." He looks forward to the kind of quasi-transcendental afterlife prefigured by his father's "steeled" Ghost, another spirit embedded in the opaque materiality of language. Hamlet envisions his "wounded name" surviving in another tale told "in pain," persisting in the disquiet of the deadly letter rather than the serenity of the living Spirit.

NOTES

I would like to thank Victoria Silver, Jane Newman, Claire McEachern, Ellen Burt, Brook Haley, Amanda Bradley, John Balkwill, and especially Julia Lupton for thoughtful suggestions and constructive criticism at various stages during the writing of this essay.

1. All citations are from Shakespeare, *Hamlet,* ed. Barnet (1998). An earlier form of the present essay was published in *Religion and the Arts* 7.1/2 (2003).

2. On the parallels between Hamlet's riddle and the actual Diet of Worms, see Waddington (1989, 28). On the disintegration of the King's Two Bodies into a "creaturely" political swarm, see Lupton (2001).

3. On the disputes over the status of the Eucharist between Luther and more radical reformers such as Zwingli, who held that a sacrament is merely a "sign," see Dickens (1989, 86). See also Waddington (1989, 28–29).

4. Greenblatt provides more extensive background on the theological context of early modern debates on the status of the Eucharist in an earlier essay, "The Mousetrap," in *Practicing New Historicism* (2000, 136–62).

5. On Tyndale's Bible, the first vernacular Bible in English, and his *Obedience of a Christian,* both produced somewhere between Wittenberg and Worms, see Dickens (1989, 93–99) and Greenblatt (1980, 84–109).

6. As the title of the chapter on Tyndale ("The Word of God in the Age of Mechanical Reproduction") suggests, Greenblatt invokes Benjamin's account of "aura" and its technological erasure. For relevant passages on "aura," see Benjamin (1968, 220–24) and (1968, 187–92) in *Illuminations.* In "Some Motifs," Benjamin offers this definition: "Experience of the aura thus rests on the transposition of a response common in human relationships to the relationship between the inanimate or natural object and man . . . To perceive the aura of an object we look at means to invest it with the ability to look at us in return" (188).

7. In *Unediting the Renaissance,* Marcus describes the possible resonance of the Wittenberg setting for audiences of *Doctor Faustus* in the same period as the first performances of Hamlet: "The fact that the play is cast in the ostensible Protestant setting of Wittenberg makes its potential for transgression against English orthodoxies of state much stronger than it would have been if the setting had been equivocally Catholic" (1996, 62). Yet Wittenberg also maintains a certain alien quality; its very difference from the situation of Reformed England allows such "transgressions" to continue to be performed on stage throughout the early seventeenth century. Marcus's observations on the theological and political overtones that might accompany the choice of Wittenberg as a tragic setting in Marlowe's era are also suggestive for the more subtle Wittenberg connection in *Hamlet,* which is roughly contemporaneous with the first performances of the *Faustus* B text. On the influence of the Geneva Bible and the political factors that prevented Wittenberg from

becoming a haven for the Marian exiles, see Dickens (1989, 341–44): "The exiles . . . produced the version on which Shakespeare and the great majority of our Elizabethans and Jacobeans were reared, and it takes its place among the factors which explain the Calvinist flavour of Elizabethan Anglicanism" (344).

8. Benjamin also emphasizes the "absorbing" quality of the early modern text, its crucial capacity to restructure perception: "In the context of allegory the image is only a signature of essence, not the essence itself in a mask. But there is nothing subordinate about written script; it is not cast away in reading, like dross. It is absorbed along with what is read. The printers, and indeed the writers of the baroque, paid the closest possible attention to the pattern of the words on the page" (1998, 215).

9. The most comprehensive argument that the host is an evil demon can be found in Prosser (1967). Battenhouse also argues that the Ghost is malevolent, although he places it within a classical, rather than Christian, frame of reference (1951). Matheson firmly identifies the Ghost as an essentially good Purgatorial Spirit (1995). Miola offers a fine account of the Ghost as a pastiche of the traditional Senecan "revenge ghost" whose "cry for revenge is resonant with overtones from Virgilian myth, Protestant and Catholic polemic, and folklore" (1992, 34).

10. On the significance of the ear for Shakespeare as an "instrument of deferral and delay," see Fineman (1991, 229–31). On the "ear" in Hamlet, Lukacher develops Fineman's thesis ("the ear becomes the figure for the suspensive 'languageness of language'") through a close reading of the "strange asymmetry" of the "countersignature" event in the Player's speech (1994, 128–35).

11. See Battenhouse (1951, 174–77) and Garber (1987, 149–53).

12. Ferguson also links Paul's discourse on the "letter" that kills to Hamlet's habit of "materializing the word" (1993, 292).

13. On the "prayer scene" in the context of debates between anti-theatrical nonconformists and proponents of a ritualistic state church in England, see Targoff (1977).

14. For a reading that insists on a Calvinistic turn in Hamlet's attitude in act 5, see Matheson (1995, 389–97). For a more balanced reading that concentrates on the subtle interplay between Calvinistic providentialism and Stoic fatalism, see Sinfield (1980, 89–97).

15. For a detailed analysis of the graveyard scene as an "autonomous" tableau of melancholic emblems, see Lyons (1971, 98–107). For an account of the duel scene as a parodic enactment of the Protestant caricature of the Catholic mass, see Kaula (1984, 254).

Works Cited

Battenhouse, Roy W. "The Ghost in 'Hamlet': A Catholic 'Linchpin.'" *Studies in Philology* 48.2 (1951): 161–92.

Benjamin, Walter. *The Origin of German Tragic Drama.* Trans. John Osborne. London: Verso, 1998.

_____. "Fate and Character." Trans. Edmund Jephcott. *Reflections.* Ed. Peter Demetz. 304–11. New York: Schocken Books, 1978.

_____. "The Work of Art in the Age of Mechanical Reproduction." *Illuminations.* Trans. Harry Zohn. 217–51. New York: Schocken Books, Random House, 1968.

_____. "Some Motifs in Baudelaire." *Illuminations.* Trans. Harry Zohn. 155–200. New York: Schocken Books, Random House, 1968.

Burton, Robert. *The Anatomy of Melancholy* [Abridged]. Ed. Joan K. Peters. New York: Frederick Ungar Publishing, 1979.

Calvin, John. *Institutes of the Christian Religion.* Trans. Henry Beveridge. Grand Rapids, Mich.: Eerdmans, 1989.

Dickens, A. G. *The English Reformation.* 2d ed. University Park, Pa.: Pennsylvania State University Press, 1989.

Ebeling, Gerhard. *Luther: An Introduction to His Thought.* Trans. R. A. Wilson. Philadelphia, Pa.: Fortress Press, 1970.

Eisenstein, Elizabeth L. *The Printing Revolution in Early Modern Europe.* Cambridge, England: Cambridge University Press, 1983.

Ferguson, Margaret. "Hamlet: Letters and Spirits." In *Shakespeare and the Question of Theory,* ed. Patricia Parker and Geoffrey Hartman. 292–309. New York: Routledge, 1993.

Fineman, Joel. "Shakespeare's Ear." *The Subjectivity Effect in Western Literary Tradition: Essays Toward the Release of Shakespeare's Will.* 222–31. Cambridge, Mass.: MIT Press, 1991.

Garber, Marjorie. *Shakespeare's Ghost Writers.* New York: Methuen, 1987.

Greenblatt, Stephen. *Hamlet in Purgatory.* Princeton, N.J.: Princeton University Press, 2001.

_____. *Renaissance Self-Fashioning: From More to Shakespeare.* Chicago, Ill.: University of Chicago Press, 1980.

Greenblatt, Stepehen, and Catherine Gallagher. *Practicing New Historicism.* Chicago, Ill.: University of Chicago Press, 2000.

Kaula, David. "Hamlet and the Image of Both Churches." *Studies in English Literature* 24 (1984): 241–55.

Lukacher, Ned. *Daemonic Figures: Shakespeare and the Question of Conscience.* Ithaca, N.Y.: Cornell University Press, 1994.

Luther, Martin. "Commentary of St. Paul's Epistle to the Galatians." In *Works* [American Edition], ed. Jaroslav Pelikan. Vol. 47. Philadelphia, Pa.: Fortress Press, 1955.

Lupton, Julia. "A Convocation of Politic Worms: Or, to Be or Not to Be in Civil Society." ms. May 2001.

Lyons, Bridget Gellert. *Voices of Melancholy: Studies in Literary Treatments of Melancholy in Renaissance England.* New York: Barnes and Noble, 1971.

Marcus, Leah. *Unediting the Renaissance: Shakespeare, Marlowe, Milton.* London: Routledge, 1996.

Matheson, Mark. "Hamlet and a 'Matter Tender and Dangerous.'" *Shakespeare Quarterly* 46 (1995): 383–97.

Miola, Robert S. *Shakespeare and Classical Tragedy.* Oxford, England: Clarendon Press, 1992.

Perkins, William. "A Dialogue of the State of a Christian Man, Gathered Here and There Out of the Sweet and Savoury Writings of Master Tyndale and Master Bradford." 1586. In *The Work of William Perkins,* ed. Ian Breward. 362–85. Abingdon, England: Sutton Courtnay Press, 1970.

Prosser, Eleanor. *Hamlet and Revenge.* Stanford, Calif.: Stanford University Press, 1967.

Shakespeare, William. *Hamlet.* Ed. Sylvan Barnet. New York: Signet Classic-Penguin, 1998.

Silver, Victoria. "Glossary of Lutheran Terms," ms. (n.d.).

Sinfield, Alan. "Hamlet's Special Providence." *Shakespeare Survey* 33 (1980): 89–97.

Targoff, Ramie. "The Performance of Prayer: Sincerity and Theatricality in Early Modern England." *Representations* 60 (1997): 49–69.

Waddington, Raymond. "Lutheran Hamlet." *English Language Notes* 25 (1989): 27–42.

Wills, David. *Prosthesis.* Stanford, Calif.: Stanford University Press, 1995.

11

The Accent and Gait of Christians: Hamlet's Puritan Style

by R. Chris Hassel Jr.

Vanderbilt University, Nashville, Tennessee

TO OUR FREQUENT DISCOMFORT and his own, Hamlet often preaches virtue and rails against vice. His most frequent targets are Ophelia, Gertrude, and Claudius, though neither Rosencrantz nor Guildenstern, Horatio nor the players are spared his moral diatribes. Hamlet even preaches to Polonius after he kills him. It may be only coincidental that Hamlet's dress—his "customary suits of solemn black"—suggests a Puritan's traditionally sober garb, or that the Puritans, also like Hamlet, carried "tables" or diaries to remind themselves of the dictates of conscience (1.2.78, 1.5.98, 107).[1] It is harder to dismiss as somehow "Puritan" Hamlet's analogous sense of calling, his being, as he says at the end of the scene with the Ghost, "born to set it right." The same might be said of his later self-designation as "patient merit," since "merit" is, according to Martin Van Beek, "a branded [Puritan] word insofar as it was applied to man's works" (1.5.189–90, 3.1.74).[2] Christopher Hill (1964, 249) describes the elect as setting themselves up as "an aristocracy of the spirit" against the "carnal aristocracy" that ruled the world. In his soliloquies as well as his Homilies, Hamlet also persistently exhibits this us-versus-them mentality as he laments both "all the uses of this world" and all the ills that "flesh is heir to" (1.2.134, 3.1.63). Encouraged by such parallels, this essay first explores the ways in which Hamlet's outspoken, even hyperbolic, righteousness toward himself and others echoes the unique diction, syntax, and imagery of the represented Puritan, if not always the real one. Then it suggests that Hamlet's concerns about idleness, his advice to the players, and even the complicated political and moral ground on which he so reluctantly stands may also be informed by Puritan forms and pressures of the late 1500s and early 1600s.

Historians have recently encouraged and complicated this endeavor by showing that actual Puritans were in many ways closer to the Protestant mainstream, and even that of the sixteenth-century continental humanist, than was thought to be the case twenty years ago. To be sure, Peter Lake (1988, 1995, 1996) and Patrick Collinson (1993) both reveal that the traditional us-versus-them mentality of the Puritans, as well as their sense of special election, has stood the test of this bracing revisionism.[3] However, Collinson (1996), Margo Todd (1993), and Ralph Houlbrooke (1996) have shown that the language of spiritual self-scrutiny and the assertions of moral scrupulousness once closely associated with the Puritans are in fact common to many Europeans of the time, Protestant and Catholic.[4] Marjorie McIntosh (1998) and Todd (1987) root even the general tendencies to control misbehavior in fields much broader in time and space than English Puritanism.[5] John Bossy has revealed the obverse of this coin by showing that the battle for the moral high ground, even on the issue of showing charity or civility toward one's disagreeing and often disagreeable Christian neighbors, was evenly spread across both Protestant and Catholic camps. Recusants and church papists, reformist and conservative Anglicans were apparently all concerned about the "censoriousness" and the "moral invidiousness" associated with their parties (1998, 75, 96).

Nowhere is the reappraisal toward consensus more widespread than in considerations of the "Puritan attitude" toward theater and the other verbal arts. Edward Muir and Collinson have argued that both mainstream English Protestants and continental Catholics turn out to be involved in a late sixteenth-century anti-mimetic trend that was once associated almost exclusively with the Puritans (Muir 1997, 165–81, 270–72; Collinson 1995, 45–46). In the other direction, Margot Heinemann (1980, 21, 30–31) and Collinson have also reminded us of Puritans like Milton who understood theoretically, if not always theatrically, the moral usefulness of theater, and of others who referred to details of performance in their polemical pamphlets.[6] Since Shakespeare and his contemporary dramatists leaned so heavily on the same Puritan stereotypes the historians are currently reappraising, our new critical stance must balance precariously between the usefulness and the limitations of the Puritan stereotype. Nowhere is this challenge greater than in the consideration of its resonance in a character and a play as complex and contradictory as *Hamlet*.[7]

I. HAMLET'S PURITAN ACCENT

Hamlet often expresses his moral indignation in the exaggerated imagery and diction of the represented Puritan, and sometimes the real one, too. His "nasty sty" sounds especially like the cage of "unclean birds" or the "locusts of the foul pit" Ananias uses to characterize his morally polluted city in *The Alchemist* (Jonson 1974). Hamlet also shares the imagery of the diseased state with *The Alchemist*'s Tribulation Wholesome. Both Hamlet and Ananias use the high-profile Puritan word "scruple," though Hamlet's "craven scruple" is characteristically more contradictory and perplexing than Ananias's usage. Hamlet also shares Zeal-of-the-Land Busy's chauvinistic idea in *Bartholomew Fair*, though of course it is not exclusively a Puritan idea, that "the disease of longing, it is a disease, a carnal disease, an appetite, incident to woman," when he says of Gertrude, "frailty, thy name is woman" (*Hamlet* 3.4.93–95, 1.5.188–89, 4.4.40, 1.2.146; *The Alchemist* 4.7.53, 5.5.13, 3.1.40–44, 4.7.75; *Bartholomew Fair* 1.6.45–46). Busy fears the devil's cozenage of this weaker vessel with the trinkets of the fair, Hamlet with the game of "hoodman-blind" that has lured Gertrude to Claudius, and to "Rebellious hell" (*Bartholomew Fair* 3.2.27–43; *Hamlet* 3.4.78, 83). What Van Beek describes as the popular Puritan metaphor of "the spot and corruption of sin" (1969, 51, 53, 57) is also prominent enough in *Hamlet* (esp. 3.4.148–50) for Francis Ferguson to center his fine interpretive essay on the play's image of the hidden impostume (1949). Hamlet's description of his mother's soul as an "ulcerous place / [Where] rank corruption, mining all within, / Infects unseen" is a particularly vivid example. According to Van Beek, "Face-painting" is another favorite Puritan phrase and target. Hamlet uses it once with Ophelia and again about all women (Van Beek, 57; and *Hamlet* 3.1.142–44; 5.1.181–82).[8]

Jonas Barish (1960), Eugene Waith (1963), and Alvin Kernan (1974) all help us hear how often the diction and imagery of Hamlet's hortatory voice are reinforced by a syntax and a sound also associated by the satirists with Puritan expressions of moral outrage. What Barish calls "devices of repetition" are particularly prominent in this style. Sometimes, as Waith says, they take the form of "repeated nouns with their increments of accumulated modifiers." "A disease, a carnal disease," or "an idol, a very idol, a fierce and rank idol" are good examples from the fictive Puritan Zeal-of-the-Land Busy. "A lustful love, a venereous love, a concupiscencious, bawdy, and bestial love," written by the actual Puritan moralist Philip Stubbes, is just as good. Hamlet's "O most pernicious woman! / O villain, villain, smiling, damned villain" (1.5.105–6) certainly rivals this rhetorical tic. Barish describes the "pyramids of verbs, adverbs or adjectives, with their appropriate modifiers" which intensify the moral outrage, as with Zeal's "troubled, very much troubled, exceedingly troubled." Anaphora and similar forms of cadenced parallelism, often embellished with alliteration, also intensify their expressions of rage, as with "the peeping of popery," "the page of pride," or "the bells of the beast." Waith also reminds us of the frequent linkage of exhortation and apostrophe.[9] Hamlet responds to what he perceives as the Player-Priam's showing-up of his own lassitude with a dressing-down of Claudius rivaling Zeal's own alliterative adjectives of outrage—"Bloody, bawdy villain." The pejorative string that follows, "Remorseless, treacherous, lecherous, kindless villain," echoes the style if not the superficiality of Ananias's "lewd, superstitious and idolatrous breeches" (*Hamlet* 2.2.565–66; *The Alchemist* 4.7.48). Barish and Kernan agree that the original model of such syntax is the Bible, its purpose in preaching and writing to assert authority. However, its caricature usually mocks the "sham biblicality" of "exhortation" when this style of "false biblical feathers" becomes "oratorical in the worst sense," "set[ting] up a trance-like rhythm" to "lull the listener into a narcotic doze."[10]

Hamlet's classic use of such incantatory devices as repetition, apostrophe, and anaphora comes in his vague but powerful expressions of moral outrage in Gertrude's bedroom:

> Such an act
> That blurs the grace and blush of modesty,
> Calls virtue hypocrite, takes off the rose
> From the fair forehead of an innocent love,
> And sets a blister there, makes marriage vows
> As false as dicers' oaths. O, such a deed
> As from the body of contraction plucks

The very soul, and sweet religion makes
A rhapsody of words!

(3.4.41–49)

Hamlet is characteristically excellent here with biblical cadences, especially the powerfully repeating verbs "blurs," "takes," "sets," "makes," "plucks," and "makes," all set within the anaphoric "such a" framework. Hamlet's "O shame, where is thy blush?" (3.4.83) even echoes the syntax of the famous biblical apostrophe "O death where is thy sting?" (1 Cor 15.55, King James version).

If the quantity of Hamlet's "exhortations, apostrophe, [and] verbal ornaments" rivals what Waith (1963, 12) describes as the Puritan model, their rhetorical intensity and originality often exceed it. The cadenced parallelism of "Eyes without feeling, feeling without sight, / Ears without hands or eyes, smelling sans all" is one good example. "Have you eyes?" "Ha! have you eyes?" "Sense sure you have" is another (3.4.79–80, 66, 68, 72). Rather than burlesque through diminishing, Shakespeare seems to have chosen to let Hamlet speak syntactic wonders to his mother. More like the parodied preachers than the biblical original, however, Hamlet's "incantational hum" disguises his lack of both specific evidence and a specific charge.[11] Indeed, for all his rhetorical brilliance, as William Holden says of the most hyperbolic preaching, so we might say fairly of Hamlet here, "ordinarily the zealot is verbose and noisy, condescendingly holy, and eternally in a pious fury" (1954, 117).

When Falstaff complains of Hal's incessant moral nagging, "O, thou hast damnable iteration, and art indeed able to corrupt a saint," he perversely connects himself to the Puritan tendency to call themselves "saints" and Hal to their often-parodied tendency to reiterate moral directions (*1 Henry IV* 1.2.85–86).[12] Though Falstaff's complaint about his young friend has some validity, such reiterated admonitions more often characterize Prince Hamlet's direction-giving than Prince Hal's. Hamlet says five times to Ophelia, "Get thee to a nunnery"; "Go thy ways to a nunnery"; "Get thee to a nunnery. Go, farewell"; "To a nunnery, go, and quickly too. Farewell"; "To a nunnery, go." With "Go not to my uncle's bed" and "Refrain tonight," Hamlet directs this "damnable iteration" to his mother rather than Ophelia. Busy similarly admonishes Winwife, "Walk in the middle way"; "Let not your eyes be drawn aside with vanity, nor your ears with noises"; "Look not toward them, hearken not," catching in the process much more obviously than

Hamlet just that biblical sound Barish and Kernan ascribe to Puritan admonition (*Hamlet* 3.1.121, 129–30, 137, 140, 149; *Bartholomew Fair* 3.4.160, 166). Of course, Hamlet has little in common intellectually or imaginatively with Ananias or Busy. But though they are far from twins, they are at least brethren in their Puritan idiom of moral disapproval and calling. As Lovewit says to Ananias, so we, too, might finally say to Hamlet as he grows more comfortable with his reforming role, "Good zeal, lie still / A little while" (*The Alchemist* 5.5.23–24).

Though Hamlet shares some of the pulpit rhetoric and much of the reforming zeal of the represented Puritan, this last example reminds us that he seldom speaks like their silliest stereotype. Such popularly satirized words as "verily," "heathen," "Canaan," "Christ-tide," "brethren," "the spirit," "zeal," "discipline," "perdition," "idol," and "vocation" are not Hamlet's words.[13] Also absent from Hamlet's usage are "saint" and "godly," derogatory references to Rome and the Papacy, or overly frequent biblical allusions, though Hamlet's naming of Polonius as Jephthah and Ophelia as his sacrificed daughter, like his allusions to Cain's jawbone and to the ranting Herod, may also color him a little by this last tradition.[14] *Hamlet* also lacks both idiom challenging controversial details of Anglican worship, words like altars, wafers, crucifixes, and genuflexion, and references to the Puritans' notorious psalm-singing, sermon-going, and Bible-reading, though Shakespeare does not elsewhere refrain from such satiric references, say with Falstaff.[15] On the other hand, Hamlet's frequent stock-in-trade words of moral certainty and moral outrage, words like "devil" (thrice) and "damned" (ten times), "sweet religion" and "heaven" (twenty times), "blush" and "shame," though not exclusively Puritan words, might still be associated by Shakespeare's contemporaries with popular representations of their extreme preaching and writing styles.[16] Stereotyping is efficient precisely because of such oversimplifications. However, the Puritan allusions and analogies in *Hamlet* allow Shakespeare to complicate rather than oversimplify the Prince and his problems. "How stand I then" in the Fortinbras soliloquy, followed by reflective references in the final scene to "my conscience," "perfect conscience," and "special providence" continue this pattern of visual, verbal, and conceptual markers of Hamlet's complicated relationship to the Puritan's characteristic moral assurance and fear, presumption and despair.[17]

II. Hamlet's Puritan Gait

Of course, Hamlet is never simplistically anything, and he is certainly never simplistically a Puritan. Apparently, even the Puritan was never simplistically a Puritan. Hamlet might share what Waith calls the Puritan's tendency to find "apocalyptic evil" among the targets of his self-righteousness, but his related "excessive zeal and hypocrisy," his "pious superiority and inhuman asceticism," unlike the represented (though not necessarily the real) Puritan, as often express self-doubt as self-assurance (Waith 1963, 7).[18] Even more complicated is the way Hamlet sometimes expresses his moral outrage in bawdy jokes, as when he calls Polonius a fishmonger, that is, Ophelia's pimp, when he jokes that Rosencrantz and Guildenstern hang about the secret parts of Fortune, and when he torments Ophelia about lying in maids' laps and between their legs (2.2.174, 225–32; 3.2.107–13).[19]

Hamlet also complains almost as loudly about tribulation as a represented Puritan such as Jonson's Rabbi Busy says he rejoices in it. In *Bartholomew Fair,* Busy, just placed in the stocks, proclaims himself "one that rejoiceth in his affliction," and "glad to be thus separated from the heathen of the land, and put apart for the holy cause" (4.6.75–79). In *The Alchemist,* Tribulation Wholesome is actually named after this stereotypical Puritan behavior. Hamlet, in stark contrast, habitually complains, paradoxically in terms sometimes reminiscent of Puritan diction, not only about what he considers wholesale personal mistreatment by his inferiors, "the spurns / That patient merit of the unworthy takes," but also, directly to "God, God," of "All the uses of this world," which he describes as "weary, stale, flat, and unprofitable." He often complains about human imperfection, that "dram of evil," "mole of nature," or "stamp of one defect," which someone more acceptant of tribulation might rather ascribe through the concept of original sin to God's mysterious will (3.1.70–74, 1.2.132–33, 1.4.36, 24, 31).[20] We see in such examples that Hamlet's Puritan resonances can reside as powerfully in difference as in similarity. The paradox is that we must catch the operative Puritan stereotype before we can see that Hamlet wears his rue, and his bawdy, with a difference.

I want to look closely at two more examples. Hamlet's Sidneyan defense of the truth of the stage introduces the Puritan, perhaps again more accurately the fundamentalist Protestant distrust of theatrical lying into his conversation with the players, just as his warning about extemporizing clowns suggests at least the establishment's analogous worries about the hyperbolic style and the potentially chaotic content of extemporaneous Puritan preaching. Hamlet's mixed assertions about busyness and idleness are also usefully referenced against the renowned (if also oversimplified) Puritan work ethic, especially some of its underlying psychological and political implications.

A. Hamlet and the Players

Which of Shakespeare's play-loving contemporaries would have failed to hear a kind of Puritan voice in the midst of Hamlet's admonitions to the players, especially when he exclaims, "O reform it altogether"? Like the extremist reformers of several parties, Hamlet even finds "indifferent" reform inadequate; he wants total reformation. On the other hand, and perhaps like the more moderate reformers, Hamlet would only outlaw those things that "would make the judicious grieve" (3.2.25, 34–36).[21] Indeed, at the same time that Hamlet is advocating total reform, Shakespeare is simultaneously defending the theater, not only against Puritan scrupulousness, but apparently also against an increasing anti-mimetic trend crossing all party lines in the late 1590s and early 1600s.[22] Both real and represented Puritans like Stephen Gosson and Rabbi Busy distrust theater because they believe that "disguise is sinful and imitation a form of lying." Hamlet disagrees.[23] It can "hold, as 'twere, the mirror up to nature," "show" "the very age and body of the time his form and pressure." Only if this is "overdone" will the precisian, the "judicious grieve" and "censure." Hamlet thus finds it completely congruous that "the accent of Christians" and "the gait of Christians" might be well performed. Hamlet's nervous "not to speak profanely," however, or Shakespeare's, also apologizes obliquely and tongue-in-cheek that the Puritan subset of these Christians is, sometimes through Hamlet himself, being represented in gait and speech, the walk and the talk as we might say today, in this very play (3.2.20–30).[24]

Most Puritans, many Protestants, and some Catholics would probably have been troubled by Hamlet's Sidneyan defense of the truth and virtue of the stage, even though in truth, it is a purist's and a puritanical defense.[25] Hamlet elsewhere shares aspects of their distrust, as, for example, when he apologizes to Rosencrantz and Guildenstern: "Let me comply with you in this garb, lest my extent to the players (which I tell you must show fairly outwards) should more appear like entertainment than yours" (2.2.372–75). Hamlet's somber dress and his tables of conscience are part of this outward show. So dressed, so somber, and so often morally outraged, Hamlet might thus seem to be pretending simply because he looks and sounds like the stereotype of the hypocritical Puritan. Worse, when he welcomes the players to Denmark in the "inky cloak," he will in his joy appear only to have pretended to be somber and melancholy earlier, as his mother seems already to have charged. In this lose-lose case, he must appear to be "entertaining," either playing false grief or playing false joy. The only way to avoid this appearance of hypocrisy is to dress himself falsely now, dress like the festive court, like Rosencrantz and Guildenstern. While speaking to the players, Hamlet has also associated his own acting with false stage gestures as well as illusory costuming and props. But if such gestures as "the windy suspiration of forced breath," "the fruitful river in the eye," "the dejected 'havior of the visage," indeed, "all forms, moods, shapes of grief" are "actions that a man might play," they are also the only way to "denote" "that within which passeth show," an inner truth that these outer forms, what Hamlet calls "the trappings and the suits of woe," can express only inadequately, and may also misrepresent (2.2.363–66; 1.2.74–86).[26] In similar terms, Thomas Nashe distrusts the Puritans' homiletic style as merely outward shows of piety and grief, "the writhing of the face, the heaving uppe of the eyes to heaven" (qtd. in Holden 1954, 55).[27] Hamlet's true woe seems both confined and defined, then, by the stereotype of Puritan hypocrisy and by their criticism of the most feigning stage. He looks suspiciously like the perpetually, ostentatiously grieved Puritan in his own shows of grief and moral outrage. He also looks like an actor.

Performative excesses like speaking too slow or too loud, sawing the air, tearing the "whirlwind of your passion" "to tatters" can be associated with the pulpit as well as the stage, Martin Marprelate as well as Herod, Termagant and the town crier (3.2.1–13).[28] Ironically, they can also describe Hamlet at his worst, preaching like a stage-Puritan to his mother and Ophelia. Hamlet's sincerity is also questionable when we see him overacting revenge after the appearance of the acting troupe in act 2, scene 2, or, for that matter, overplaying love and grief in competition with Laertes at Ophelia's grave. Gertrude complains twice that Hamlet's excessive volume might "split the ears."

Once she is amazed that he would "wag thy tongue / In noise so rude against me." Then she asks, "What act, / That roars so loud and thunders in the index?" She also accuses Hamlet of the very intemperance he warns the players against when she challenges "the heat and flame of thy distemper." Gertrude also calls his Homily to her an "ecstasy," and his affront to Laertes "mere madness." With all these invitations, it is unlikely that Shakespeare's contemporaries would have forgotten in this context that the extemporaneous Puritan preachers were sometimes called mad, even if almost no one actually believed that they were (3.4.40–41, 52–53, 124, 139, 5.1.271).[29]

Hill reminds us in *Society and Puritanism* (1964) that "the emphasis on preaching had been one of the essentials of Protestantism, and was strongly reinforced by marginal notes in The Geneva Bible." Paradoxically, the perceived political importance of the pulpit to Queen Elizabeth and her Protestant supporters led to some official discouragement of unlicensed and extemporaneous preaching. The presence and use of *Certain Sermons or Homilies Appointed to be read in Churches in the Time of Queen Elizabeth I* is only the most prominent illustration of this issue's importance in Shakespeare's time. Licenses for preaching under both James and Elizabeth explicitly required "sobriety and discretion in teaching the people" (Hill 1964, 2: esp. 31–38), though *ex tempore* preaching was never outlawed per se. The analogies to these forms and pressures in *Hamlet* are intriguing. Old Hamlet's ghost tries like Gertrude to silence Hamlet's extemporaneous preaching to his mother: "leave her to heaven." Hamlet, too, has earlier complained about extemporaneous excess when he preaches to the assembled acting company just before the Mousetrap play: "Let those that play your clowns speak no more than is set down for them." "That's villainous and shows a most pitiful ambition in the fool that uses it," especially if "some necessary question of the play be then to be considered" (1.5.87, 3.2.36–42).[30] But like the clowns he imagines inside the Globe Theatre, Hamlet cannot control his own extemporized Homilies to Gertrude or to Ophelia. The problem, in the play as in society, is that the actor's sense of "the question" might not coincide with the author's. For this among other reasons, Hamlet, like the zealous preachers who so often stand behind him in rhetoric and in attitude, is only momentarily silenced by the Ghost's kingly admonition that he keep to the approved script.

B. *Hamlet and Idleness*

When Hill calls the Puritans "the industrious sort of people," he asserts the basis of what we still call, with various mixtures of abhorrence and admiration, the Puritan work ethic. As Hill says, this legacy is a Puritan commonplace: "Most Europeans have for centuries embraced a religious code which condemned idleness as wicked. . . . The doctrine that labor was a duty to one's neighbor, to society, to the commonwealth, to mankind, came to be especially emphasized by the Puritan preachers." My mother, who was certainly a Protestant but only a kind of Puritan, never tired of telling me that "idle hands are the devil's business," and, bless her heart, she practiced what she preached for as long as she could. The famous "homily against idleness" in *Certaine Sermons* is a mainstream public assertion of this notorious aspect of Puritan "asceticism," the assurance that "whilst they are busily occupied in their labor, [people] be free from many occasions of sin." Even George Herbert's parson thought that idleness was "the great national sin," and Robert Burton and many others agreed (Hill 1964, 124, 128–29).[31]

Hamlet promises the Ghost a diligent obsession with his commandment of revenge:

> Remember thee?
> Yea, from the table of my memory
> I'll wipe away all trivial fond records,
> All saws of books, all forms, all pressures past,
> That youth and observation copied there,
> And thy commandment all alone shall live
> Within the book and volume of my brain,
> Unmixed with baser matter. . . .
> My tables—meet it is I set it down
> That one may smile, and smile, and be a villain.
> (1.5.95–108)

Unfortunately, the moral imperative Hamlet feels to act is contradicted by the moral danger he repeatedly discovers in this compelled busyness. Industriously erasing all learned wisdom from his literal (or metaphoric) tables of conscience and replacing it with the Ghost's perplexing imperative is a telling emblem of this danger. Falstaff might assert it no sin "to labor in one's vocation," even if that vocation is unlawful. To his credit, Hamlet is unsure enough to wonder almost immediately if enacting the Ghost's "commandment," "Revenge this foul and most unnatural murder," might prove a "cursed spite." Hamlet's apology to Horatio for the antic disposition he must assume to do the Ghost's work, "I must be idle," may even connect the moral complexity of this vocation with Hamlet's oddly Puritan nervousness about idleness (*Hamlet* 1.5.188–89, 25, 3.2.87; *I Henry IV* 1.2.98–99).

Verbal references to his revenge as labor suggest, in fact, that the Puritan work ethic variously informs Hamlet's delay. He calls himself a "rogue and peasant slave," for example, for not doing his work like "this player here." While Claudius tries to pray, Hamlet also rejects his best chance for revenge with imagery of a base labor that is "hire and salary, not revenge." He might even compare his hateful imperative to the laborer who would "fardels bear, / To grunt and sweat under a weary life." To be sure, Hamlet shows a distaste for all manual labor in the condescending tone of these references. But there is moral as well as social tension in these references. In contrast to the apparent clarity of the Homily against Idleness, "many occasions of sin" seem to lie for Hamlet not in idleness, but in carrying out the vocation to which he has been called. Hamlet's ironic benediction over the slain Polonius, "Thou findst to be too busy is some danger," suggests the same complexity (2.2.534, 3.3.79, 3.1.76–77, 3.4.34, 1.4.41). Because Hamlet's calling goes against the grain of his nature and his conscience, and because the call itself may come with "blasts from hell" rather than "airs from heaven," idleness may be his only salvation.

Of "all occasions" that "inform against me" (4.4.32), Fortinbras's busyness is arguably the most painful to Hamlet, and the most confusing. Hamlet claims that man, Fortinbras here, is made busy in the image and likeness of God, for God labored for six of the first seven days in creation. If busyness is godlike, then idleness is subhuman:

> What is a man,
> If his chief good and market of his time
> Be but to sleep and feed? A beast, no more.
> Sure he that made us with such large discourse,
> Looking before and after, gave us not
> That capability and godlike reason
> To fust in us unused
>
> (4.4.32–39)

Because reason is both godlike and God-given, not to mention uniquely human, its un-use is far worse than the "bestial oblivion" (1.2.50) of mere sleeping and feeding. Such "fust" abrogates human responsibility. But then Hamlet becomes confused, contradicting his earlier assertion and this one that man is superior to beasts in "discourse of reason" (1.2.150). "Thinking too precisely on the event" is "craven scruple" to Hamlet, a cowardly moralism (4.4.40; *Bartholomew Fair* 58).[32] Shakespeare elsewhere associates "precise" with the industriously moral Puritan in the line "Lord Angelo is precise."[33] Holden also reminds us that "precise" was associated with the Puritan "willingness to debate infinitely any smallest detail of doctrine or rite," a powerful coincidence, if that is what it is, given Hamlet's similar proclivity during his own moral self-scrutiny (1954, 41).[34] But such thinking does not qualify as working in Hamlet's confusion here, even though he says that the Creator made us thoughtfully as well as busily, with "large discourse," "looking before and after." As Hamlet says, "This thing's to do." This is not the first time Hamlet has complained in his paradoxical moral scrupulousness about the craven idleness of too much thought. In the "To be or not to be" soliloquy,

> the native hue of resolution
> Is sicklied o'er with the pale cast of thought
> And enterprises of great pith and moment
> . . . lose the name of action

(3.1.84–88)[35]

Though Collinson and Kaufman are both aware of a counter-movement in Jacobean Puritanism toward innerness, personal spirituality, some Puritans also associated such a contemplative bent as Hamlet's with idleness (Collinson 1987, 34–36; Kaufman 1996). As Hill says, "the worst that could be said of Little Gidding in 1641 was that 'men and women in health, of able and active bodies and parts,' had 'no particular callings,' or else abandoned them for a 'contemplative and idle life, as if diligence in our particular lawful callings were no part of our service to God'" (Hill 1964, 131).[36] Despite his birth and his intellect, Hamlet seems sometimes to buy into this universe of merely external industry. He thinks that he is letting down himself, his father, and his country in his delay, while he might be living up to his highest calling, precise moral thought. Paradoxically, Hamlet as an eager, impulsive laborer is most dangerous and least himself.

Even when Hamlet resolves to overcome his idleness, it is often in terms of speech acts, thoughts, and words, rather than actions. "Can say nothing" comes more naturally to his lips than "can do nothing." A typical resolve is the promise "From this time forth, / My thoughts be bloody or be nothing worth." A typical lament is that his enterprises "Lose the name of action." He calls himself an ass for unpacking his "heart with words" when he should be acting out his revenge. Once again, "prompted" itself, like "the motive and the cue for passion," and the actor who prompts this frustration, are all words from plays. The player works by cleaving "the general ear with horrid speech," as Hamlet will later "speak daggers, but use none" to his mother. The Ghost complains of this propensity to prefer words to deeds when he chides, "This visitation / Is but to whet thy almost blunted purpose," and Hamlet anticipates this criticism of his idleness:

> Do you not come your tardy son to chide,
> That lapsed in time and passion, lets go by
> Th'important acting of your dread command?
>
> (3.4.106–8)

Gertrude has earlier complained, "Come come, you answer with an idle tongue." Though we know that she means disrespectful, we cannot help but smile at this further ironic reference to Hamlet's truest and most persistent vocation, speaking daggers rather than using them. The Puritan work ethic stands both comically and seriously behind much of the criticism of this "lapsed" young man, whose tongue is seldom idle (2.2.554, 4.4.65–66, 3.1.88, 2.2.568, 571, 547, 3.2.381).[37]

As the chief worker in *Hamlet,* the Gravedigger also helps us connect Hamlet, idleness, and the Puritans. Hamlet is amused with the calloused sense of this worker, but he is also uncomfortable with his own privileged idleness. For Hamlet's is "The hand of little employment [that] hath the daintier sense." Hill frequently reminds us that this is a politically and morally subversive doctrine. If "God doth allow none to live idly," if the ministers often glorify "hard work, thrift, economy of time," if the Puritans "hated idleness like the devil," where does this leave not only the idle rich, but also the landed gentry, magistrates, even princes and kings, who only "labored in their minds," to reverse Philostrate's snobbery in *A Midsummer Night's Dream* (5.1.73)? The Puritan Richard Bernard asserted that to live idly is to live "contrary to nature, contrary to God's injunction that men should labor." "The calling of a gentleman" was therefore increasingly suspect as the Puritans rose to outspoken power. To Bernard, gentility is a profession "so abused to advance sin and Satan's kingdom as nothing more." Hill reminds us that in 1648, "idleness was made a punishable offense in Massachusetts" (1964, 140–41).[38] Though a severe work ethic is no more an exclusively Puritan preoccupation than moral scrupulousness, Jonson's Zeal-of-the-Land Busy is not idly named after the Puritan stereotype so widely available in Shakespeare's time and our own.

Could this social tension also lie behind the Gravedigger's attempt to identify his profession with gentility?: "There is no ancient gentlemen but gardners, ditchers, and grave-makers. They hold up Adam's profession." When the other demurs, "Was he a gentleman?" he hears that "A was the first that ever bore arms." The Gravedigger's irrefutable proof: "What, art a heathen? How dost thou understand the Scripture? The Scripture says Adam digged. Could he dig without arms?" (5.1.24–35). Here is the directly parodied Puritan idiom, working-class, biblical, homiletic, and wonderfully illogical, ahistorical, and literal-minded in its lecturing on what the scripture says. It is also revolutionary. When the Puritan Robert Cushman speaks in his *Discourse* of 1622 of the "idle drones [who] are intolerable in a settled commonwealth," he also points to Adam and his sons:

> Of what earth, I pray thee, art thou made? Of any better than the other of the sons of Adam? And canst thou see other of thy brethren toil their hearts out, and thou sit idle at home, or takest thy pleasure abroad? (qtd. in Hill 1964, 141)

Hamlet senses in the words of the Gravedigger this new age of reform and revolution, "so picked that the toe of the peasant comes so near the heel of the courtier that he gals his kibe" (5.1.128–32), and he is not entirely comfortable with such revolutionary currents. He is, however, part of them, a prince who shares with these predominantly lower class workers the frustration of what Hamilton has called the "disempowered male" with the corrupt establishment (Hamilton 1992, 74).

III. IDEALISM, HYPOCRISY, AND POLITICS

Collinson points to the "insinuation of the ancient heresy of perfectionism," Novationism, Catharism, Albigensianism, what you will, as one of the benchmarks of Puritanism. Their critics understood as well the irony of the commitment to a *sola fide* religion of these people "who never ceased to deplore their own sins," and lament the sinfulness of their society (Collinson 1987, 8). Hamlet, like some of these Puritans, finds it especially difficult to know or acknowledge himself as a part of the community of imperfection that so desperately needs grace and providential direction. Sometimes the resultant contradictions between Hamlet's mind and heart feel like moral and intellectual honesty; sometimes they surface as dishonesty or self-deception, as when he claims that he can kill Claudius in "perfect conscience"; disclaims all moral responsibility for the death of his two schoolfellows; argues to Laertes that it was not Hamlet but Hamlet's madness that killed Polonius; or tries to identify thought, conscience, and wisdom with cowardice (5.2.67, 58, 219–21, 4.4.40–43, 3.1.83). Hamlet's excuse that his murder of Polonius is the heavens' doing sounds especially like the iconoclastic Puritan whom John Cleveland describes as saying that he "intends no harm," while explaining "that the destruction of windows, altars, organs, railings, and treasure is the work of the Lord's anointed" (qtd. in Holden 1954, 68).[39]

After killing Polonius, Hamlet is honest enough to wonder aloud if in being God's "minister," he has also become his "scourge," but Hamlet's sense of calling to do God's will, God's work, is still more prominent than guilt in his words and thoughts. It is God who has "punished this with me, and me with this" (3.4.174–76).[40] Polonius is decentered and dehumanized by such self-justifying rationalizing; Hamlet in some ways absolves himself of moral responsibility. Holden tells us "the [stereotyped] Puritan with his talent for theological word-spinning could, in the midst of his sins, explain that what he was doing was not wrong, but was really in accord with good morals and sound religion." Kernan calls this the "verbal juggling some Puritans were adept at." How far is Hamlet's rationalization from what Holden calls the "labyrinthine explanation" of Ananias and Tribulation in Jonson's *The Alchemist,* "in the tradition of the theology of the stage Puritan," of the reasons why "casting is not counterfeiting, not illegal, and not a sin" (Holden 1954, 113, 134; Kernan 1974, 106)?[41]

Murder, too, is still murder, for all of Hamlet's self-justifying words. Even if we follow Van Beek's lead to the conclusion that the Puritans would have distinguished between the "gross" hypocrisy of a Claudius, which is contrived and purposeful, and the "formal" hypocrisy of a Hamlet, which is sometimes both unacknowledged and unknown, we are still left with Hamlet's hypocrisy (1969, 53). Hamlet's conscious and unconscious hypocrisy wears many cloaks, and some are woven in the style of Puritan representation. In such a complex world, his hand, head, and heart, like his soul and his tongue, cannot always agree. When they do, murder and treason are often the result of their integrity.

By reconfiguring such Anglican-Puritan tensions in a tragic context, Shakespeare raises the stakes of the controversy much higher than they seem in most of the contemporary masques and comedies.[42] Like Hamilton's description of the more revolutionary Puritans of the early and mid-seventeenth century, Hamlet resists the authority of a monarch's request for "outward conformity for the sake of union," and in so doing helps propel the state into both reform and chaos. He may, like the Puritans, finally strike his king down for the best and the worst of motives, but, also like them, the doing and the not doing would both produce dire consequences, "unacceptable hypocrisy" on the one hand, and outright revolution on the other (Hamilton 1992, 71–72).[43] When Hamlet finally admits frustrated ambition as one of his motives for killing Claudius, we see once more his complicated brush against what Hamilton calls "the conformist representation of the Puritan who, on a pretense of being busy about reform, seeks to realize his own ambitions" (1992, 97).[44] Hamlet, student of Wittenburg, one of the hotbeds of resistance theory, is dreadfully summoned to overthrow the established King of Denmark, his uncle, but "cursed" by the impossible complexity, personal and political, moral and religious, of this special calling.

In this odd and sometimes contradictory field of allusion and analogy, Hamlet thus becomes an unusually rich and sympathetic version of the often caricatured, oversimplified Puritan figure. His personal obsession with election and reprobation, his constant moral self-scrutiny, his self-righteous preaching to Gertrude, his disapproval of Claudius, Polonius, Ophelia, and most of Denmark seem less idiosyncratic in Hamlet, too—though no less self-absorbed and inconsiderate—if they are associated with the Puritan presence. In return, by being more noble in reason than the usual representation of the Puritan, more express and admirable in form and moving, apprehension and beauty, Hamlet's Puritan commands respect, even awe, for his prototypes, for all that we might resist his extremist edges and theirs. Much better than Busy or

Ananias, more like Angelo, perhaps, Hamlet also lives out the painful contradictions inherent in Puritan theory and practice, the impossible necessity to be perfect and to demand perfection in a world where only grace, faith, can save even the elect (Hassel "Solid Flesh" 1994).

NOTES

1. From *The Complete Pelican Shakespeare,* ed. Alfred Harbage (1969). Subsequent Shakespeare references cite this edition. Collinson, *English Puritanism* (1987, 36), speaking of "the absorption of the Puritan in the mystery of his own identity before God," also mentions the diaries, in which they "kept their heart and ways" "under constant review." See also Hill (1964, 243) and Lake, *Moderate Puritans and the Elizabethan Church* (1982, 116). *OED* (1 *Table* 2b) gives "table" for "diary," and *Bartholomew Fair* (4.3.42–32) has two Puritans, Grace and Winwife, call their diaries "tables."

2. In *An Inquiry into Puritan Vocabulary* (1969), Van Beek has formulated a Puritan idiom that contains only the "first appearance in decidedly Puritan writings of words of chiefly religious, partly also political, content," either "words occurring for the first time in Puritan writing," words "found in a novel sense," or words that "through their re-definition in Puritan writings . . . acquired a new connotation" (2). For "merit" and "calling," see 74–75, 78.

3. On "us-versus-them," see Lake, *Anglicans and Puritans* (1988, 3–6, 81–85, 121–23); Lake, "'A Charitable Christian Hatred'" (1996, 145–83); and Collinson, "Sects and the Evolution of Puritanism" (1993, 147–66); on the persistent sense of election and "sainthood," see Lake, "Calvinism and the English Church" (1995, 6, 184–88).

4. On the idea that expressions of righteous indignation and spiritual self-scrutiny were hardly exclusively Puritan phenomena, see Todd, "Puritan Self-Fashioning" (1993, 57–87); Houlbrooke, "The Puritan Death-Bed . . ." (1996, 122–44); and Collinson, "Elizabethan and Jacobean Puritanism as Forms of Popular Religious Culture" (1996, 42–46).

5. See McIntosh (1998) and "Work, Wealth and Welfare" in Todd's *Christian Humanism and the Puritan Social Order* (1987, 118–75). The *Journal of British Studies* has devoted an entire issue (July 1998) to the question of whether controlling misbehavior was exclusively or even primarily a Puritan obsession.

6. See also note 24.

7. Though she is, of course, not responsible for any of my historical or interpretive missteps, I would like to thank Margo Todd for some very useful suggestions on these matters of contemporary historiography.

8. Hamlet also shares diction and imagery with reformers from at least two court masques: Thomas Carew's Momus from *Coelum Britannicum,* and Jonson's Hercules from *Pleasure Reconciled to Virtue.*

9. Unless otherwise noted, the quotations from Jonson and Stubbes in this paragraph, and the comments about their syntax, come from Barish, *Ben Jonson and the Language of Prose Comedy* (1960, 197–203); Waith, *Bartholomew Fair* (1963, 12–13); and Kernan, *The Alchemist* (1974, 6). I have modernized the spelling here and elsewhere.

10. On the sham biblicality of this style, see Barish (1960, 198, 201) and Kernan (1974, 6).

11. Barish's phrase "incantational hum" (1960, 198) describes the traditionally hypnotic tone of the best of Puritan exhortation.

12. Van Beek reminds us that the Puritans often called themselves "saints" (1969, 35–36).

13. Early in the play, Horatio may alert us to such issues of controversial diction when he uses an outrageous circumlocution, "the day / Wherein our saviour's birth is consecrated," thus avoiding the controversial C-word, "Christmas," so abhorred by the Puritans.

14. Siegel notes that "From their close and continued reading of the Old Testament, Puritans, as caricatured in Thomas Middleton's *The Family of Love* and Jonson's *The Alchemist,* assumed Hebrew names and zealously studied Hebrew" (1962, 16). Cf. Van Beek (1969, 10), Holden (1954, 136), and Barish (1960, 199). *Hamlet* 2.2.393 ff.; 5.1.72–74; 3.1.13.

15. As in *1 Henry IV* 2.4.124–25; 1.2.142–46; 3.3.183; 4.2.24–25.

16. As in *Hamlet* 3.4.170, 163, 48, 83, 86.

17. See C. H. and Katherine George, *The Protestant Mind of the English Reformation* (1961, 95 ff.), on this commonly acknowledged tension. *Hamlet* 4.4.41; 5.2.58, 67. Van Beek (1969, 114) associates the phrase "special providence" with Shakespeare's famous neighbor, the Cambridge Puritan William Perkins.

18. Kaufman (1996) reminds us that moral self-scrutiny is common in the actual Puritan.

19. For "fishmonger" see Williams (1994, 1: 496).

20. See note 2 on the branded Puritan word "merit."

21. Collinson speaks of laments about "those that be too swift, and those that be to slow" (1987, 12–14). He includes Bishop Grindal's lament that the Reformation proceeded "but halfly forward and more than halfly backward" as part of a growing mood of "sour disillusionment" around the turn of the century among those "earnest for further reformation."

22. See Muir (1997, 165–81, 270–72) and Collinson (1995, 45–46).

23. See, for example, Heinemann (1980, 78, 31, 71). Touchstone also disagrees, but in a topsy-turvy way: "the greatest poetry is the most faining" (*As You Like It* 3.3.16–17).

24. See Hamilton (1992, 1–3) and Heinemann (1980, 39).

25. Hamlet's love of the stage is not so contradictory of the English Puritan as it might at first appear. As Heinemann says, "To see all Puritans as automatically hostile in principle to the theatre and the arts in general is . . . to misunderstand the depth and complexity of the intellectual and social movements that led to the upheavals of the 1640's" (1980, 21). Heinemann mentions Puritans such as Milton, Pembroke, one of Shakespeare's patrons, Leicester, and Walsingham, who were also sympathetic to the theater. Even Phillip Stubbes approved, like Hamlet, of edifying moral drama; Stephen Gosson (*The School of Abuse*) wrote plays; and both Heywood and Sidney, defenders of the theater, like Hamlet, were "authors known to have had some Puritan sympathies." The Marprelate pamphlets, too, "continually use theatrical jokes and allusions and obviously assume an audience which, like the writer, enjoys a play" (30–31). Collinson observes, however, in the 1590s and afterward an increasing opposition to all theater among many Christian communities, and a consequent increase in the segregation of the secular and the sacred in the plays themselves (1995, 46–47). See also White (1993), Diehl (1997), and Muir (1997, 165–81, 270–72) on varied Reformation attitudes toward theater.

26. When Waith tells us that "hypocrite" was "almost a cant term for Puritan" in the Renaissance, he does not mean, of course, that only Puritans were considered hypocrites (1963, 10). See also Kernan (1974, 6).

27. There are many references to illusory form in *Hamlet,* as in 1.1.43, 47–48; 1.5.72; 2.2.301–2, 304–5, 540–41, 535–36, 586; and esp. 3.1. 51, 53, 111–14, 129, 151, 153, 159–60, 162–64. In paradoxical parallel, the Puritans distrusted the mere form of church ceremonies, as when R. Bolton in 1612 says of church ceremonies, "all is form and outwardness" (qtd. in Van Beek 1969, 99). Van Beek adds that "formality" and "hollowness" were associated Puritan words (53, 101).

28. Todd shows how the "puritan firebrand" preacher William Gouge, "a vigorous opponent of the Blackfriars playhouse, to which his own parishioners . . . resorted, would nonetheless preach as a playwright" (1997, 40, 49). Collinson reminds us that William Prynne in *Histrio-Mastix* (1637) "deplored 'playerly gestures' in the pulpit as unseemly: 'He is the best Minister who is most unlike a Player, both in his gesture, habit, speech and elocution'" (1988, 114).

29. Holden (1954, 79 ff., 97–98) speaks of the "idiom of madness and possession usually directed against the nonconformists."

30. Hill tells us that James was almost as nervous as Elizabeth about the Puritans' "over-valuing of preaching," especially extemporaneous preaching, and adds that once in the decade before *Hamlet*, Elizabeth "forbade all preaching, particularly in London." See Hill (1964, 30–37, 44). Though Protestant consensus is his general theme in the essay "Calvinism and the English Church," Lake concedes that in the 1590s and early 1600s, there was still an observable Puritan overvaluing of sermons and an observable preference for public prayer and sacrament among the more conservative Protestants (1995, 187).

31. Hill says that in 1588–89, Robert Brown expressed the most radical version of this dis-ease, this sense of idleness as a betrayal of one's divine calling, when he said that "an idle person ceased to be a member of the church of God" (1964, 130). The Good Ship Enterprise and Capability Brown, not to mention Inspector Morse's unmentionable first name, are companions to Hamlet's frustration about idleness, however veiled they may be in the mists of economic, social, and religious history, not to mention anachronism.

32. For "scruple," see also *Bartholomew Fair* (58), Lake (1982, 10–15), Barish (1960, 201), and *OED* (2 *Scruple* 1).

33. For "precise," see *Measure for Measure* (1.2.71, 1.3.50) and note 342 in *A New Variorum* Measure for Measure, ed. Mark Eccles (1980).

34. See Hamilton (1992, 11–12), who calls "precise" "a word that was used to stigmatize a theological or ecclesiological position and one often applied to puritans."

35. Hassel discusses this paradox more fully in "'How Infinite in Faculties': Hamlet's Confusion of God and Man" (1994).

36. As Hill points out, the Homily concedes "divers sorts of labours, some of the mind and some of the body, and some of both" (250).

37. Since the Puritan obsession with idleness was related to their preoccupation with thrift, I wonder if Hamlet's macabre wisecrack, "Thrift, thrift Horatio," might be another Puritan flag, since the reference to the drunken, lecherous, treacherous Claudius as a thrifty parent coincides with what Hill describes as "a great increase in the Puritan literature advocating thrift in the years 1600–1604" (1964, 131).

38. To be fair, idleness was also an offense in More's *Utopia*. See Todd (1987, 124–27).

39. John Morrill is especially good on the complexity of the classic Puritan case of this providentialist self-understanding—Oliver Cromwell's. See his *Oliver Cromwell and the English Revolution* (1990, 141–42, 186–90, 199–202, 249–53).

40. Van Beek includes "minister" as a characteristic Puritan self-designation (1969, 48).

41. See also Kernan (1974, 6) and Holden (1954, 55, 117) on the association of Puritans and hypocrisy.

42. When he refers to the boys' companies, Hamlet may stir in even more of the controversy, for they produced many of the "anti-citizen and anti-Puritan" comedies. Middleton, for example, wrote most of his early satirical comedies against these dissenting groups, "particularly for the Children of Paul's" (Heinemann 1980, 63).

43. Shuger once calls Puritanism "an occluded expression of political frustration" (1990, 28).

44. Hamlet says that Claudius "Popped in between th'election and my hopes" (5.2.65).

WORKS CITED

Barish, Jonas. *Ben Jonson and the Language of Prose Comedy.* Cambridge, Mass.: Harvard University Press, 1960.

Bossy, John. *Peace in the Post-Reformation.* Cambridge, England: Cambridge University Press, 1998.

Collinson, Patrick. *Birthpangs of Protestant England.* London: Macmillan, 1988.

_____. "Elizabethan and Jacobean Puritanism as Forms of Popular Religious Culture." In *The Culture of English Puritanism, 1560–1700,* ed. Christopher Durston and Jacqueline Eales. London: Macmillan, 1996.

_____. *English Puritanism.* Rev. ed. London: The Historical Society, 1987.

_____. "The Protestant Culture and the Cultural Revolution." In *Reformation to Revolution,* ed. Margo Todd. London: Routledge, 1995.

_____. "Sects and the Evolution of Puritanism." In *Puritanism,* ed. Francis J. Bremer. Boston, Mass.: Massachusetts Historical Society, 1993.

Diehl, Huston. *Staging Reform, Reforming the Stage.* Ithaca, N.Y.: Cornell University Press, 1997.

Ferguson, Francis. *The Idea of a Theatre.* Princeton, N.J.: Princeton University Press, 1949.

George, C. H. and Katherine. *The Protestant Mind of the English Reformation.* Princeton, N.J.: Princeton University Press, 1961.

Hamilton, Donna. *Shakespeare and the Politics of Protestant England.* Lexington, Ky.: University Press of Kentucky, 1992.

Hassel, R. Chris Jr. "Hamlet's 'Too, Too Solid Flesh.'" *The Sixteenth Century Journal* 25 (1994): 609–22.

_____. "'How Infinite in Faculties': Hamlet's Confusion of God and Man." *Literature and Theology* 8 (1994): 127–39.

Heinemann, Margot. *Puritanism and Theatre.* Cambridge, England: Cambridge University Press, 1980.

Hill, Christopher. *Society and Puritanism in Pre-Revolutionary England.* New York: Schoken, 1964.

Holden, William. *Anti-Puritan Satire.* New Haven, Conn.: Yale University Press, 1954.

Houlbrooke, Ralph. "The Puritan Death-Bed. . . ." In *The Culture of English Puritanism, 1560–1700,* ed. Christopher Durston and Jacqueline Eales. London: Macmillan, 1996.

Kaufman, Ivor. *Prayer, Despair, and Drama: Elizabethan Introspection.* Urbana, Ill.: University of Illinois Press, 1996.

Kernan, Alvin, ed. *Ben Jonson's* The Alchemist. Alvin. New Haven, Conn.: Yale University Press, 1974.

Lake, Peter. *Anglicans and Puritans?* London: Unwin Hyman, 1988.

_____. "Calvinism and the English Church." In *Reformation to Revolution,* ed. Margo Todd. London: Routledge, 1995.

_____. "'A Charitable Christian Hatred': The Godly and their Enemies in the 1630's." In *The Culture of English Puritanism, 1560–1700,* ed. Christopher Durston and Jacqueline Eales. London: Macmillan, 1996.

_____. *Moderate Puritans and the Elizabethan Church.* Cambridge, England: Cambridge University Press, 1982.

McIntosh, Marjorie Kenniston. *Controlling Misbehaviour in England, 1370–1600.* Cambridge, England: Cambridge University Press, 1998.

Morrill, John. *Oliver Cromwell and the English Revolution.* London: Longman, 1990.

Muir, Edward. *Ritual in Early Modern Europe.* Cambridge, England: Cambridge University Press, 1997.

Shakespeare, William. *The Complete Pelican Shakespeare.* Ed. Alfred Harbage. Baltimore, Md.: Penguin, 1969.

_____. *A New Variorum* Measure for Measure. Ed. Marc Eccles. New York: Modern Language Association, 1980.

Shuger, Debora. *Habits of Thought in the English Renaissance.* Berkeley, Calif.: University of California Press, 1990.

Siegel, Paul. "Shylock the Puritan." *Columbia University Forum* 5.4 (1962): 14–19.

Todd, Margo. "A Captive's Story: Puritans, Pirates, and the Drama of Reconciliation." *The Seventeenth Century* 12.1 (1997): 37–56.

_____. *Christian Humanism and the Puritan Social Order.* Cambridge, England: Cambridge University Press, 1987.

_____. "Puritan Self-Fashioning." In *Puritanism,* ed. Francis J. Bremer. Boston, Mass.: Massachusetts Historical Society, 1993.

Van Beek, Martin. *An Inquiry into Puritan Vocabulary.* Groningen, Netherlands: Wolters-Noordhoff, 1969.

Waith, Eugene, ed. *Bartholomew Fair,* by Ben Jonson. New Haven, Conn.: Yale University Press, 1963.

White, Paul Whitfield. *Theatre and Reformation.* Cambridge, England: Cambridge University Press, 1993.

Williams, Gordon. *A Dictionary of Sexual Language and Imagery in Shakespearean and Stuart Literature.* London: Athlone, 1994.

12

Shakespeare on Monastic Life: Nuns and Friars in *Measure for Measure*

by *David Beauregard*
Our Lady of Grace Seminary, Boston

IN THE OPENING SCENE of *A Midsummer Night's Dream* (c. 1595), Shakespeare inserts some anachronistic lines, excised "on pious and/or anachronistic grounds" by every nineteenth-century production of the play except one (Griffiths 1996, 91). When Hermia refuses her father's command that she marry Demetrius, Theseus, the Duke of Athens, warns her:

> Therefore, fair Hermia, question your desires,
> Know of your youth, examine well your blood,
> Whether, if you yield not to your father's choice,
> You can endure the livery of a nun,
> For aye to be in shady cloister mewed,
> To live a barren sister all your life,
> Chanting faint hymns to the cold fruitless moon.
> Thrice blessèd they that master so their blood
> To undergo such maiden pilgrimage;
> But earthlier happy is the rose distilled
> Than that which, withering on the virgin thorn,
> Grows, lives, and dies in single blessedness
> $(1.1.67–78)$[1]

What is remarkable about this passage, aside from the fact that it was always cut in nineteenth-century productions, is its profoundly Catholic spirituality, its realistic distinction between married life as "earthlier happy" and monastic life as "blessed." Shakespeare's terminology suggests the distinction between the Aristotelian notion of happiness, which requires friendship and hence marriage, and the more complete but paradoxical New Testament notion of blessedness or beatitude (Mt 5:1–12), which is achieved through poverty, mourning, meekness, and the endurance of suffering. Renaissance philosophers and theologians were well aware of this distinction in relation to the summum bonum or highest good (Schmitt 1998, 318–19), but no sixteenth-century Reformed Protestant would have described monastic life as blessed, much less "thrice blessèd."

In the Shakespearean corpus as a whole, the treatment of Roman Catholic religious is exceptionally sympathetic.[2] Shakespeare treats Franciscans particularly well, especially in view of the fact that, aside from John Ford, other English Renaissance dramatists form an "antifraternal tradition," which depicts friars as "duplicitous, immoral, and satanic" (Voss 1993, 5). Such hostile characterization is not the case, however, with Friar Laurence in *Romeo and Juliet,* Friar Francis in *Much Ado About Nothing,* and Friar Peter in *Measure for Measure* (Bevington 1968, 202; Milward 1973, 73; Voss 9). Nor is it the case with Isabella and Francisca in *Measure for Measure.* What this suggests, as some recent lines of investigation contend, is that Shakespeare seems to have come, in cultural terms, from outside the "golden academic triangle" of Oxford, Cambridge, and London.[3] His favorable treatment of Franciscans is but one intimation of his cultural Catholicism, nurtured in the heavily Catholic counties of Warwickshire and Lancashire.

My intention in this essay is, therefore, to explore some important Roman Catholic theological dimensions of *Measure for Measure* having to do with monastic life, particularly its portrait of Franciscan religious, its representation of the sacrament of penance, and its concluding ambiguity regarding the Duke's offer of marriage to Isabella. Some recent accounts of the play, taking their bearings from Reformed theology or secular assumptions, have claimed that monastic life is satirized or demystified (Gless 1979, passim, Diehl 1998, 395). But such readings encounter three insuperable difficulties. First of all, they do not harmonize well with Shakespeare's generally favorable treatment of Franciscan nuns and friars, a favorable treatment poetically expressed in *Measure for Measure* when Isabella offers Angelo a bribe of heavenly "gifts":

> true prayers
> That shall be up at heaven and enter there
> Ere sunrise—prayers from preserved souls,
> From fasting maids whose minds are dedicate
> To nothing temporal.
>
> (2.2.157–61)

Second, Reformed readings do not account for Shakespeare's departure from the anti-Catholic conventions of English Protestant drama. As I shall argue, it is clear that Shakespeare works against those conventions by inverting their main features. The most striking indication of this is his portrayal of nuns and friars as Virtue figures over against a tradition that represented them as Vice figures. Third, such readings overlook the significance of Shakespeare's development of his sources. One would expect a Reformed Protestant or secular sensibility, whose intention was to demystify or satirize, to have taken advantage of the opportunity to allow Isabella to lose her virginity and finally accept an offer of marriage. This is precisely what her counterparts do in the sources for the play. But Shakespeare transforms his heroine into a nun, a prospective novice of the Poor Clares, who preserves her virginity and does not marry. It is difficult to see this as demystification or satire. In short, readings based on Reformed or secular assumptions do not enable us to explain the basic features and nuances of Shakespeare's development of his sources, nor do they account for his adversarial relation to the English Protestant dramatic tradition.

THE ANTIFRATERNAL TRADITION

First, then, in order to assess Shakespeare's portrait of Franciscan religious, it is necessary to investigate the relation of *Measure for Measure* to the antifraternal tradition. As the casual reader can see from the works of Boccaccio and Chaucer, the medieval tradition of antifraternal literature concerned itself with satirizing the moral failures of friars, particularly their sins of the flesh and their hypocrisy (Gless 1979, 61–69). With the advent of Reformed theology, however, the essential elements of the religious life itself came under literary attack, and such things as vows, the cloistered life, celibacy, and the priesthood were pilloried. In early Reformation drama, the conventional figure of the Vice was often portrayed as a Roman Catholic priest-player (White 1993, 171), and by virtue of their distinctive religious habits, the Franciscan friar and the cloistered nun became stage conventions (Pineas 1972, 23; Voss 1993, 5). In George Chapman's *May-Day* (1611) there is a telling reference to the convention:

> Out upon't, that disguise [of a "friar's weed"] is worn threadbare upon every stage, and so much villainy committed under that habit that 'tis grown as suspicious as the vilest.
>
> (qtd. in Miles 1976, 171)

Various other strategies were employed against stage nuns and friars— derogatory epithets, sarcastic asides, reversals of attitude, outright rejection of cloistered life, abusive flouting, physical punishment, and many others (Pineas 1972, 23–43).

Perhaps the most effective anti-Catholic strategy used in Reformation plays, then, was to identify the conventional figure of the Vice with Catholic figures (Pineas, 1972, 16). But Shakespeare's use of the Vice clearly does not follow Protestant lines. Rather than identify this stock figure with one of the Franciscan religious in *Measure for Measure,* which is what we would expect if the play is antifraternal satire, Shakespeare identifies the Vice with a secular figure. Thus, as the comic focal point of the sexual intemperance endemic in Vienna, Lucio is given the role of Vice. He is not explicitly tagged in the manner of the personifications of the old Morality plays, but rather he is represented in the newer realistic style in which the Vice becomes "a dramatic symbol for the attitude or force within the kingdom which the dramatist wishes to single out as a basic cause of contemporary evils" (Winston 1981, 233–41). Finally, at the end of the play, when by means of multiple marriages restitution has been made for various sexual irregularities, Lucio is fittingly punished as the play's scapegoat by being married to a prostitute. Significantly, none of the Franciscan monastic figures is punished for sins of the flesh or exposed as hypocritical.

But Lucio is not alone. There are other secular exemplifications of vice as well. The taxonomy of vice in the play can be found in the "Secunda Pars" of Aquinas's *Summa Theologica,* specifically under the virtue of temperance (1981, 2a2ae 146–58). Some suggestion of this taxonomy comes in the play's final scene, when Isabella speaks of Angelo's "intemperate concupiscible lust" (5.1.103), a precise Thomistic classification of lust as intemperance with respect to the concupiscible desire for sexual pleasure. On both the comic and serious level, this classification in its full form governs the play in some detail. As the action moves along, various instances of sexual irregularity are brought to our attention—Claudio has gotten Julietta pregnant, Angelo attempts to seduce Isabella, Lucio has impregnated and broken his promise to Kate Keepdown (3.2.194–96), and Angelo is found to be guilty of a "promise-breach" with Mariana. Thus Shakespeare depicts sexual intemperance in general (Lucio) and three of its various Thomistic species—fornication (Claudio), attempted seduction (Angelo), and sacrilege (Angelo; see Aquinas 1981, 2a2ae 154.1, 10). The representation is not rigidly schematic, as the compounded instance of Angelo indicates, but one can add prostitution (Mistress Overdone), drunkenness (Barnardine), and anger (Isabella's defiant reaction to Claudio) to the species of intemperance depicted (see Aquinas, 2a2ae 150, 158). Of course, the argument can be made that Shakespeare did not need the *Summa* in order to represent these commonplace species of sexual intemperance, but the precision of Isabella's phrase about "intemperate concupiscible lust" (5.1.103) and the tight cluster of virtues and vices described by Aquinas (2a2ae 146–58) and exhibited in the play (abstinence, fasting, sobriety, drunkenness, virginity, sexual intemperance, fornication, seduction, sacrilegious lust, clemency, severity, and anger) can hardly be coincidental (Beauregard 1995, 139–55).

It is important to note that all these sexual sins are transgressions by secular characters who inhabit the secular sectors of the city—the court, the stews, and the prison. By contrast, the four Franciscan religious pursue the contemplative life within the confines of the cloister, most pointedly in the case of Isabella, who embodies the virtue of virginal chastity. Aquinas's remarks are worth quoting:

> . . . if a man abstain from bodily pleasures, in order more freely to give himself to the contemplation of truth, this is in accordance with the rectitude of reason. Now holy virginity refrains from all venereal pleasure in order more freely to have leisure for Divine contemplation. . . .
>
> (2a2ae 152.2)

The traditional distinction between the active and the contemplative life is thus sharply reflected in the settings in monastery and convent, over against the court and prison. This distinction of course had little currency in Reformed circles.

Moreover, this distinction in the play's setting between the active and contemplative life is consistent with Shakespeare's treatment of the vow of chastity. For the Reformers, marriage was highly valued and consecrated virginity was considered impious, and it is therefore significant that a sense of the sacred permeates Shakespeare's conception of the vow of chastity. Shocked by his desire for Isabella, Angelo speaks of his "desire to raze the sanctuary" (2.2.178), clearly implying that Isabella's chastity is sacred. Contrariwise, what is striking is that all the transgressions of vows occur with the secular characters and not with the Franciscan religious. Claudio's "true contract" lacks the "denunciation of outward order," Angelo is guilty of "promise-breach," and Lucio has not kept his promise of marriage to Kate Keepdown (3.3.194–96). On the other hand, none of the Franciscan religious violates a vow of chastity, poverty, or obedience. Thus the critical claim that they are satirized and demystified is without substance, and critics are driven to vague charges of "hypocrisy," disparity between "behavior and perfection," or failure to live up to "ideals of purity and holiness" (Diehl 1998, 404–5). These general charges lack the precision of the Reformers' objections to the cloistered life: the charge that vows of chastity, poverty, and obedience were hypocritically presumptive, and the allegation that monastic life is a "flight from the world." Shakespeare's play in effect reverses these charges by showing us Isabella maintaining her chastity while both she and the Duke (with the help of the other friars) operate successfully in the world by bringing their virtue to bear on its problems.

To sum up thus far: Shakespeare reverses the main dramatic devices by which Reformed dramatists attacked Franciscan cloistered life, namely, by portraying them in the role of the Vice, by depicting their violation of vows (particularly chastity), and by showing them in flight from the world. With the monastic figures in *Measure for Measure,* however, there is no serious transgression of a vow, nor is there a flight from the world. Isabella (like her source figure) could easily have been made to sin against chastity and finally marry, and the drunken Barnardine could easily have been made a friar. Shakespeare declines to exploit these opportunities. Even further, as we shall see, he reverses other devices used against Catholic religious, whereby they were exposed as hypocrites, their deviousness and duplicity were made transparent, and their vows were repudiated in favor of marriage.

Nevertheless, Shakespeare's contemplative Franciscans have their faults. Awareness of the shortcomings of religious is, however, part of the pre-Reformation tradition of the English Morality play (Pineas 1962, 160), and Shakespeare, like Chaucer, is not given to a naive idealism about contemplative religious life, as is evident from Lucio's proverbial remark "Cucullus not facit monachum [a cowl does not make a monk]" (5.1.271). Accordingly, Shakespeare characterizes Francisca as excessively precise about her rule, a light satirical touch that constitutes an acknowledgement that religious have their shortcomings. Perhaps more seriously, Isabella is technically guilty of lying and false testimony (3.1.266; 5.1.106),[4] and Friar Peter pretends that the Duke is sick (5.1.157–58). But Shakespeare makes nothing of these dramatic deceptions, obviously because at their respective points in the action they are necessary to further the Duke's stratagem. If the matter must be considered from a moral standpoint, this insouciance about lying and deception would seem to best accord with the remarks of Aquinas:

> As regards the end in view, a lie may be contrary to charity, through being told with the purpose of injuring God, and this is always a mortal sin, for it is opposed to religion; or in order to injure one's neighbor, in his person, his possessions, or his good name, and this also is a mortal sin, since it is a mortal sin to injure one's neighbor. . . . But if the end intended be not contrary to charity, neither will the lie, considered under this aspect, be a mortal sin, as in the case of a jocose lie, where some pleasure is intended, or in an officious lie, where the good of one's neighbor is intended. (2a2ae 110.4)

It is clear that Shakespeare is aware of the transgressive character of the stratagem of the bed-trick, for the Duke says to Isabella "the doubleness of the benefit defends the deceit from reproof" (3.2.258–60), but it is equally clear that what is morally paramount is not the deceit but the consideration of the benefits to be achieved. That is, from a purely moral standpoint, the intention and the good to be achieved ameliorate the defective and transgressive nature of the act.

Similarly, just as the monastic figures are not free of faults, so the secular Vice figures are not without their virtues. Shakespeare does not have Lucio pursue vice with a rationalistic consistency, since this comic libertine displays compassion for Claudio, informs Isabella of her brother's plight, and helps her to argue her case more effectively. But again his benevolent actions are quite in accord with the dramatic tradition of the Vice who can "help as well as hinder" (Winston 1981, 236). In allowing the virtuous characters their faults and the Vice figures their virtues, Shakespeare's purpose, then, was not to construct perfect exemplars of Franciscan religious life, or pure examples of sexual evil, but to render images of virtue and vice with some plausibility and verisimilitude. He neither idealizes his religious figures nor demonizes his Vice figures.

NUNS

Granted that the main features of the antifraternal tradition are reversed by Shakespeare, it remains to see how these reversals play out in specific scenes dealing with nuns and friars. Much has been made of the play's fourth scene as an antimonastic satire (Gless 1979, 103). To be sure, with the arrival of Lucio at the convent, Francisca pays an overly precise attention to the rule and expresses a degree of timidity before a strange man. But her timidity throws into high relief Isabella's virginal poise and self-possession before Lucio's bold cynicism about virginity:

> LUCIO: Hail, virgin, if you be, as those cheek roses
> Proclaim you are no less. . . .
> ISABELLA: You do blaspheme the good in mocking me. (1.4.16–17, 38)

(Compare Aquinas's definition of blasphemy as "the disparagement of some surpassing goodness, especially that of God," 2a2ae 13.1.) By characterizing Lucio as profane and cynical—two scenes before he has been consorting with the prostitute Mistress Overdone—Shakespeare precludes any disrespect for Isabella and her entry into monastic life. So also he defuses Lucio's impertinent ridicule of the good, one of the conventional methods employed by the Vice (Pineas 1962, 162–63). Lucio's impertinence undercuts two other recent critical claims, in themselves too forced and recondite, that the scene is a parody of the Annunciation, with Lucio reminding us of the angel Gabriel, "my cousin Juliet" of Elizabeth, and Isabella of the Virgin Mary, and that it plays on the iconography of the saints' lives (Lupton 1996, 112–13). The parallels are too slight and unrealized to provide much parody, and Lucio's ridicule of the good simply serves to define his unsavory character. A more readily accessible and plausible source of typology exists in the dramatic tradition of the Vice, which would cast Lucio in the role of Lucifer, the tempter and the prince of lies (Winston 1981, 235). Lucio's name, his involvement in sexual vice, and his bold, cynical demeanor suggest this in much more forthright fashion.

Furthermore, there is much more to this convent scene than a simple touch of satire and profane mockery. This brief introductory vignette manifests the nascent virtue of Isabella, moved as she is by the desire for "a more strict restraint" and fewer privileges. In Aristotelian-Thomistic fashion, Shakespeare places Isabella between two extreme figures. She stands as something of a temperate mean between Francisca the timid rule-follower, who minces "may" and "may not" and recoils at the sound of a man's voice, and Lucio the sexual libertine, who is boldly contemptuous of virginity. If we were to apply the Thomistic taxonomy strictly, Isabella might be most accurately described as embodying the virtue of "honesty," one of the integral parts of the cardinal virtue of temperance. Its opposing extremes would be represented by Francisca as "shamefacedness" and Lucio as the vice of "intemperance." These three dispositions are discussed by Aquinas in sequence (2a2ae 142–45):

> Taken strictly virtue is a perfection. . . . Wherefore anything that is inconsistent with perfection, though it be good, falls short of the notion of virtue. Now shamefacedness is inconsistent with perfection, because it is the fear of something base, namely of that which is disgraceful. Hence Damascene says that shamefacedness is fear of a base action. . . . But one who is perfect as to a virtuous habit, does not apprehend that which would be disgraceful and base to do, as being possible and arduous, that is to say difficult for him to avoid; nor does he actually do anything base, so as to be in fear of disgrace. Therefore shamefacedness, properly speaking, is not a virtue, since it falls short of the perfection of virtue. (2a2ae 144.1)

As one of the integral parts of temperance, shamefacedness (*verecundia*) has none of the "spiritual beauty" characteristic of honesty (*honestum*), which springs from the honor attached to the excellence of virtue, "the disposition of the perfect to the best" (*dispositio perfecti ad optimum*):

> Now the disgraceful is opposed to the beautiful: and opposites are most manifestive of one another. Wherefore it seems honesty belongs especially to temperance, since the latter repels that which is most disgraceful and unbecoming to man, namely animal lusts. (2a2ae 145.4)

Fear of disgrace in failing to follow the rule seems to drive Francisca, whereas Isabella certainly seems her opposite in her more positive desire to pursue "the best." As the embodiment of virginity, she naturally describes her brother's fornication as "a vice that most I do abhor" (2.2.32), and so, when Claudio suggests she trade her virginity for his life (3.1.133–38 f.), her brief show of anger is more understandable. Obviously Shakespeare did not intend to illustrate Aquinas, but something close to this taxonomy seems to govern this scene.

Shakespeare quickly develops this embryonic scene by more precisely representing four virtues and vices allied to temperance, specifically severity and clemency, and virginity and lust (Aquinas, 152–54; 157.1–2). An essential distinction between Catholic virtue and Puritan vice becomes apparent, when in the second act Shakespeare stages two agonistic confrontations or "contentions" focused on these dispositions. The initial problem is the sexual transgression of Claudio in getting Julietta pregnant, and the question is whether to make an example of him. Shakespeare invites us to consider whether the proper response is severity or clemency. Angelo advocates severity for the sake of the common good of Vienna, whereas Isabella is moved to plead for clemency to preserve her brother's life. A clear parallelism begins to emerge as Angelo, in Puritan fashion, continues to insist on the severe penalty of death, whereas contrariwise Isabella in her Roman Catholic habit advocates a more moderate penalty ("O let him marry her"). Analogously, there is a contrast in penitential methods of controlling sexual transgressions. Angelo has previously subjected Claudio to a public shaming Puritan-style (1.2), and the Duke in Franciscan habit has privately heard Juliet's confession according to the Roman Catholic form of the sacrament of penance (2.3).

This contrast between Puritan severity and Catholic clemency continues to develop in subsequent scenes. Just as the first contention exhibits the severity of Angelo and the clemency of Isabella, the second contention underscores and develops another undeniable moral difference between these two main figures. In the guise of a novice of the Poor Clares, Isabella clearly embodies the virtue of virginity, one of the species of temperance. By contrast, Angelo, who like Isabella has been initially characterized as a severe ascetic, exhibits the opposing vice of lust. Significantly, he is not given a Franciscan habit but rather the sensibility (and in the BBC production the costume) of a Puritan. In the words of the Duke, he is "precise . . . [and] scarce confesses / That his blood flows or that his appetite is more to bread than stone" (1.3.50–53). To Lucio he is:

> . . . a man whose blood
> Is very snow broth; one who never feels
> The wanton stings and motions of the sense,
> But doth rebate and blunt his natural edge
> With profits of the mind, study, and fast.
> (1.4.57–61)

This description is sharply and explicitly critical, rather than lightly satirical en passant as with Francisca. Since Angelo denies the "motions of the sense," he is at first depicted in terms of the Aristotelian-Thomistic vice of insensibility, the extreme opposite to the intemperance we see in Lucio. In its Elizabethan Puritan form, outward austerity was allied with precision, hypocrisy, and zeal for laws against adultery, all qualities portrayed in Angelo (McGinn 1948, 131–35; Hamilton 1992, 111–12). Paradoxically, Angelo is at first harsh and condemnatory in his precision, and then he easily swings from the vice of insensibility to the other extreme of hypocritical and intemperate lust. His encounter with the beautiful Isabella is the catalyst that quickly turns his precision into intemperance. For all the initial severity and asceticism of Isabella and Angelo, therefore, a sharp distinction emerges between her Roman Catholic virtue and his Puritanical vice. Again reversing the conventions of the antifraternal tradition, Shakespeare takes up the charge of hypocrisy usually leveled by Reformed theologians against nuns and monks and their vows of chastity, and directs it against a Puritan sensibility. However, by discreetly not applying a religious label to Angelo, he indicates once more his interest in the exhibition of moral dispositions rather than the representation of theological polemics.

FRIARS

When we turn from Franciscan nuns to friars, similar configurations of virtue and vice become apparent. Our first encounter with friars comes in the third scene. Duke Vincentio is talking with Friar Thomas, and their conversation is carried on in a respectful tone. In explaining his intention of posing as a friar, the Duke shows Friar Thomas great trust and very respectfully addresses him as "holy Father," "holy sir," "pious sir," and "my father" (1.3.1, 7, 16, 39). This note of respect and trust toward friars continues in later scenes when the Duke confides in Friar Peter as his messenger (4.5) and appoints him to guide Mariana and Isabella in their suit against Angelo (4.6.9–15; 5.1.20). In the guise of friar, the Duke himself is called "holy" or "good" some ten times (see Spevack 1973 under "Father" and "friar"). Contrariwise, Lucio refers to friars merely as "Friar" (3.2.76, 82, 85, 97, 101). Only once does he refer to the Duke as "good Friar" (3.2.173). In the final scene, he severely berates him as "a meddling friar," "a saucy friar," "a very scurvy fellow," "a rascal," "Goodman Baldpate," "damnable fellow," "a bald-pated, lying rascal," and a "knave" (5.1.132, 140–41, 291, 312, 334–35, 347, 360, 361).

But, obviously, Duke Vincentio is not a true friar. He simply adopts the Franciscan habit as a disguise by which to observe "if power change purpose, what our seemers be" (1.3.54). He has been accurately described as a Counter-Vice or Anti-Vice, who uses his "craft against vice" (Winston 1981, 243). Thus, his disguise is employed as part of a political policy, which has as its end the discernment of character and the common good, rather than a fraudulent deception undertaken for evil purposes of seduction. The employment of disguise as a dramatic device again does not amount to a demystification or satire on monastic life. There is no suggestion of fraud here, no hidden villainies, no disparity between ideal and real practices as there are in Boccaccio and Chaucer.

Perhaps even more importantly, since there is no textual indication of a change in costume, the Duke remains dressed in his Franciscan robes after he has been unhooded by Lucio (5.1.363). The retention of his Franciscan habit lends to the proceedings a certain religious authority. Indeed, it is clear that Shakespeare intends Lucio's unhooding of the Duke as a reversal of the exposure of a friar. It also reverses the more general trope of Protestant apocalyptic exposure of Catholic corruption (Shell 1999, 23–32). Thus, Lucio's act of unhooding backfires, since it exposes the Duke in all his authority and undercuts the vituperative insolence of Lucio himself:

> LUCIO: Come, sir, come, sir, come, sir; foh, sir! Why you bald-pated, lying rascal, you must be hooded, must you? Show your knave's visage, with a pox to you! Show your sheep-biting face, and be hanged an hour! Will 't not off?
> [*He pulls off the friar's hood, and discovers the Duke. Angelo and Escalus rise.*]
> DUKE: Thou art the first knave that e'er mad'st a duke.
> First, Provost, let me bail these gentle three [Isabella, Mariana, and Friar Peter].
> [*To Lucio.*] Sneak not away, sir, for the Friar and you must have a word anon. Lay hold on him.
> LUCIO: This may prove worse than hanging. (5.1.363–68)

Here laughter is directed at the consequences of Lucio's anti-Franciscan action. The exposure of "Friar Lodowick" brings Lucio some deserved punishment. It is inaccurate and misleading, then, to maintain that in "using the clerical habit of the friar as a disguise that the Duke puts on and off and eventually discards, the play also demystifies monasticism, perhaps even reinforcing Protestant associations of friars with a fraudulent theatricality . . . and false disguise" (Diehl 1998, 395). The mere absence of the Duke's disguise in act 4, scene 5, takes place without comment, and there is no textual evidence that the Duke discards the habit in the final act. Neither scene carries any suggestion of demystification. If anything, friars and the Franciscan habit are associated with authority and truth, not with "fraudulent theatricality and false disguise."

Beyond the question of Duke Vincentio's disguise, there are the two important stratagems he undertakes: the bed-trick and the substitution of Ragozine's head for Claudio's. Only the first has received much critical attention. As a source for *Measure for Measure,* Shakespeare used George Whetstone's *An Heptameron of Civill Discourses* (1582), in which the story of Promos and Cassandra is immediately preceded by the tale of Friar Inganno (N1r–N2r). Whetstone's narrative strategy (by way of Giraldi Cinthio) proceeds in three steps. First, Friar Inganno (Friar Fraud) tells Dame Farina that St. Francis means to visit her at night as Friar Inganno. Next, the Friar's deceit is discovered when Dame Farina tells her parish priest. When Friar Inganno returns that night, he leaps into bed with an ugly maid named Leayda, who has been substituted for Dame Farina. At this point, the parish priest and others enter with candles and torches, and they begin singing "Salve, Saincte Francisce." Finally, they bind and strip Inganno, lay him in a bundle of nettles, scourge him, and cover him with honey so that he is tormented by hornets, wasps, and flies. The exposure of Franciscan vice ends in punishment and laughter.

With Shakespeare's *Measure for Measure,* this three-step process of stratagem, exposure, and punishment assumes a very different form. None of the Duke's three stratagems—his disguise as a friar, the bed-trick, and his substitution of Ragozine's head for Claudio's—is evil in its intention. In fact, all three stratagems are undertaken for good purposes, and with the help of Friar Peter they are turned to good account so that they succeed in preserving life and bringing about marital union for three couples. As we confront the various sexual problems created by the main figures—Claudio's getting Julietta pregnant, Angelo's attempted seduction of Isabella, Lucio's impregnation and broken promise to Kate Keepdown (3.2.194–96), and Angelo's "promise-breach" with Mariana—Shakespeare makes nuns and friars virtuous accomplices who aid the Duke in his project and help to bring everything to a just and proper conclusion. There is no punishment of any friar figure, as there is of the secular figures. In short, the antifraternal tradition in which friars are exposed as immoral schemers is again turned on its head.

IMAGES OF AURICULAR CONFESSION: JULIETTA, MARIANA, BARNARDINE

If Duke Vincentio's Franciscan disguise and stratagems are questionable as instances of "demystification" and satire, the same can be said for the Duke's priestly actions of giving pastoral counsel and hearing confession. The play presents the Duke counseling or confessing four characters, actions that are appropriate expressions of the play's concern with the virtue of clemency. Juliet is the first to confess to the Duke as Friar, and she is treated rather gently and sympathetically. Next, Claudio is counseled with the brilliant speech, "Be absolute for death" (3.1.5 f.), encouraging him to face his impending death. The speech seems well meant but somewhat severe. Although Claudio is initially persuaded, he relents and delivers an equally poignant speech, "Aye, but to die" (3.1.119 f.), which, significantly, the Duke listens to from a position of concealment. From this point on, the Duke begins to display greater compassion and clemency. Isabella is aided in her predicament. Mariana is told that she has not sinned and is helped to achieve her desire. Barnardine is in such a state that his execution is put off. And in the final scene, the Duke manifests a "tempered judgment." All of this seems in line with the general trajectory of the play as it moves from severity in the early scenes (with the Duke, Isabella, and Angelo) to a final clemency (with Isabella and the Duke).

But what of the representation of the sacrament of confession? The three confessional scenes, involving Julietta, Mariana, Barnardine, and Duke Vincentio in his friar's disguise (2.3; 4.1; 4.3), are obvious representations of Catholic sacramental practice. The primary indication of their Catholicity is of course the simple dramatic fact that they are conducted by a friar, not a Protestant pastor. One obvious difficulty, however, is that the Duke is not a true priest. Although this provides a perfect occasion for demystification of the priesthood and monastic life, the absence of any attempt at dramatic exposure of the "fraud," together with the favorable treatment of Franciscan religious and the regular reversal of anti-Catholic dramatic conventions, compels us to take the confession scenes as they are. Shakespeare makes nothing of this opportunity to demystify.

With respect to *Measure for Measure,* it is not difficult to determine which form of penance is represented, given the dramatic necessity of a selective representation (Beauregard 2000). During the English Reformation, the conception of penance was altered from its medieval scholastic form, in which it was a sacrament composed of three parts or movements: contrition, confession, and satisfaction. That form required the precise enumeration of sins in an "auricular confession" to a priest, who gave absolution and assigned penitential acts of satisfaction. In its secularized Protestant form, however, it became a purely interior form consisting of four parts or movements: contrition, confession, faith, and amendment of life (*Certaine Sermons,* 271). Confession was made to God, not to a priest. Auricular confession was merely allowed as a pastoral measure, and absolution was replaced by a declaration of forgiveness. Satisfaction or "doing penance" was dismissed as unnecessary and was generalized into "amendment of life." Thus, what was previously a sacrament with a social and external dimension requiring a precise examination of conscience with the aid of a priest became a completely privatized and interiorized exercise, which merely permitted and allowed for exteriorization in the form of auricular confession:

> I doe not say, but that if any doe finde themselues troubled in conscience, they may repayre to their learned Curate or Pastour, or to some other godly learned man, and shew the trouble and doubt of their conscience to them, that they may receiue at their hand the comfortable salue of GODS word: but it is against the true Christian libertie, that any man should bee bound to the numbring of his sinnes, as it hath beene vsed heretofore in the time of blindnesse and ignorance. (*Certaine Sermons,* 267)

The play presents a distinct contrast between two types of penitential action: one, the public punishment imposed on sinners by the Elizabethan bawdy courts; the other, the private confession of sins characteristic of Catholic pastoral practice. Properly speaking, the first type is a juridical action, and the second is a pastoral one. Shakespeare seems sensitive to the historical consequences of the suppression of auricular confession, namely that since sexual incontinence was no longer controlled through the private confessional it had to be through public punishment. Thus, Claudio's public shaming as he is led through the streets clearly suggests English Protestant social and civil practice, significantly ordered by the Puritanical Angelo. But it cannot be construed as the first part of a single penitential ritual that is later completed by Juliet's confession and reconciliation (Hayne 1993, 12). Rather, it provides a contrast with Catholic sacramental practice. With Juliet, there is clearly contrition and auricular confession to a Friar in Catholic fashion and in a pastoral rather than juridical context:

DUKE: Repent you, fair one, of the sin you carry?
JULIET: I do, and bear the shame most patiently.
DUKE: I'll teach you how you should arraign your conscience,
And try your penitence, if it be sound,
Or hollowly put on. . . .
JULIET: I do confess and repent it, Father.
DUKE: . . . But lest you do repent
As that the sin hath brought you to this shame,
Which sorrow is always toward ourselves, not heaven,
Showing we would not spare heaven as we love it,
But as we stand in fear—
JULIET: I do repent me as it is an evil,
And take the shame with joy.
DUKE: There rest. . . .
Grace go with you. *Benedicite!* (2.3.19–40)

Juliet makes an auricular confession to the Duke as Friar and "Father," complete with a suggestion of final absolution when the Duke bids her "Grace go with you. Benedicite." If the element of satisfaction is missing, still the representation is more in the Catholic than the Church of England form. Juliet is not simply showing "the trouble and doubt" of her conscience to her curate or pastor, or confessing to a layman. The Duke teaches her how to arraign her conscience and tests the authenticity of her sorrow, making sure she is not motivated by shame or fear, but by a real detestation of her sin. His role is that of authoritative teacher, director and priest, not that of confidante, advisor, and pastor.

Somewhat similar are the cases of Mariana and Barnardine. Although Mariana does not confess to the Duke, he pronounces a judgment in assuring her that the bed-trick is "no sin" (4.1.72). As for Barnardine, using a clearly Roman Catholic term, the Duke intends to "give him a present shrift" (4.2.207), a term that suggests Catholic practice and does not occur in the Homilies. But amusingly, Barnardine demands more time to prepare and refuses to "consent to die this day" (4.3.54–56). In short, in the Duke's activity as friar-confessor, we observe the truncated representation of Roman Catholic sacramental penance or auricular confession. It is sympathetically presented, whereas the public shaming of Claudio is not. As a minor parallel to this depiction of the sacramental function of the Friar-Duke, it is worth noting that the marriage of Angelo is carried out offstage by Friar Peter (5.1.377–79), manifesting, once again, the consistently Catholic mentality shaping the play.

CONCLUSION: MARRIAGE OR THE CONVENT?

The conclusion of *Measure for Measure* is notoriously ambiguous, and
so it has been construed in various ways. The final scene raises two
issues. Taken as a whole, it has been read as Isabella's release from
claustrophobic monastic confinement (Gless 1979, 213), as a Calvinistic
public rehearsal of shame (Diehl 1998, 409), and as an exercise in judicial recompense for sexual crimes (Friedman 1995, 456). Read with its
sources in mind and in concert with the play's representation of various
species of intemperance, the scene is most consistently read as a judicial
proceeding involving punishment and clemency. Several acts of pardon
and punishment occur. Having abandoned his initial policy of severity,
Duke Vincentio pardons Angelo, Barnardine, Claudio, and Lucio. He
also metes out a tempered punishment in the form of three rather sober
marriages. Angelo is sent offstage to marry Mariana, Claudio is to marry
Julietta, and Lucio is forced to marry the prostitute Kate Keepdown. The
overall tone is markedly less celebratory and more sober than in the
romantic comedies. In keeping with our account, this sobriety of tone
issues understandably from Shakespeare's concern with justice and
clemency, with his working toward the representation of a final "tempered judgment" in the person of the Duke.

The second issue has to do with Isabella's response to the Duke's
proffer of marriage. Again, several interpretations have been proposed.
One critic sees Isabella as accepting the Duke's offer (Gless 1979,
212). At the other extreme, another sees Isabella as shocked, as resistant to being "an object of exchange in an economy of male desire"
(Mullaney 1988, 110). A third critic reads the Duke's offer as an
attempt to recompense Isabella for the slanderous dishonor she has
received from participating in his scheme (Friedman 1995, 461). But
for these conjectures there is no evidence in the text. The ending is
conspicuously ambiguous.

Isabella's silence is remarkable in the light of other English
Renaissance plays dealing with a similar situation. In Greene's *Friar
Bacon and Friar Bungay* (1594), Margaret, after having taken her
vows, decides to leave the convent and marry Lord Lacy:

> The flesh is frail. My lord doth know it well,
> That when he comes with his enchanting face,
> Whatso'er betide, I cannot say him nay;

> Off goes the habit of a maiden's heart,
> And, seeing Fortune will, fair Framingham,
> And all the show of holy nuns, farewell.
> Lacey for me, if he will be my lord.
>
> (14.86–92)

Similarly, in *The Merry Devil of Edmonton* (1608), Millicent is a professed nun who decides to leave the cloistered life to marry her lover: "With pardon, sir, that name ["profest Nun"] is quite undone; / This true-loue knot cancelles both maid and Nun" (5.1.202–3). Finally, in Whetstone's *Heptameron of Civill Discourses* (1582), one of Shakespeare's sources, Lucia Bella, a prospective novice like Isabella, is explicitly won over to arguments in favor of marriage:

> Senior *Philoxenus*, by the vertue of this dayes exercise . . . so raysed the heartes of the companie, with the desire of Mariage, that *Lucia Bella*, who, in the beginning of Christmasse, was determyned to haue beene a *vestall* Nunne, now confessed that they were enemies to Nature, and not worthy the society of men, which scandylised, or scorned this sacred Institution. The rest of this honorable company, by plawsible speeches, confirmed *Lucia Bellas* opinion, or by silence shewed a willyng consent. (Z3r–Z3v)

It is clear that Shakespeare does not have Isabella explicitly confess that nuns are "enemies to Nature." Nor does he make of her silence a "willyng consent." Rather, since the Duke is made to repeat his offer of marriage twice, the text suggests a calculated ambiguity, if not a decided restraint.

> Give me your hand and say you will be mine.
> . . . Dear Isabel,
> I have a motion much imports your good,
> Whereto if you'll a willing ear incline,
> What's mine is yours, and what is yours is mine.—
> So, bring us to our palace, where we'll show
> What's yet behind, that's meet you all should know.
>
> [*Exeunt*] (5.1.503, 546–50)

Shakespeare does not have Isabella accept—or for that matter even respond to—the Duke's offer of marriage, the acceptance of which would be a full and clear capitulation to the Reformed distaste for vows of celibacy and the cloistered life. It is evident that Shakespeare's sources were disposed to allow Isabella (like her counterparts in Cinthio and Whetstone) to lose her virginity and finally accept an offer of marriage. The same pattern holds true for two of his fellow dramatists. If the intention here is satire or demystification or direct opposition inspired by Reformed theology, it is odd that Shakespeare leaves us wondering.

Moreover, the usual ending of Shakespearean comedy in marriage, realized only in the offing in this unromantic comedy, falls short with Isabella. By the end of the play, the Duke has clearly become open to the "dribbling dart of love," which early on he has gently scorned (1.3.2). Why, then, did Shakespeare not underline his point by having Isabella indicate in some fashion her willingness to abandon her religious vocation for marriage? If the patterns in his sources, in contemporary plays, and the usual trajectory of his romantic comedies disposed him in that direction, what prevented him from writing such a conclusion? The most plausible answer is that a calculated ambiguity would have done double service by not offending Catholics in the audience and by pleasing Protestants with an ending implying marriage. In either case, he would have pleased his heterogeneous audience.

*

The prospect of a Roman Catholic Shakespeare will seem understandably distressing to those for whom Catholicism is "sectarian." This fear of producing a partisan Shakespeare is largely unfounded. As I have suggested, the main focus of Shakespeare's plays is on moral psychology, not on theology. In the main, the plays represent the virtues, vices, and passions, not theological mysteries or doctrines. Moreover, by virtue of historical circumstance, Shakespeare is "universal" in that his Catholicism was largely suppressed and does not obtrude upon most of the plays. Nevertheless, it is ingenuous to suppose that the dogmatic oppositions between Catholic and Reformed had no impact on him, and that we can place him somewhere along a spectrum of gradations of anti-Calvinism. In their individualistic assumptions about the complexities of religious belief, critics who adopt such positions fail to comprehend the corporate nature of Elizabethan religion, wherein the churches defined the doctrines accepted by their individual members, and the interrelations between doctrines created a stable coherence. One would have paid the price of expulsion from the church community by expressing a laissez-faire attitude toward doctrine.

Behind the fear of a "sectarian" Shakespeare, one can detect the sensibility of Kant's "autonomous" individual—enlightened, skeptical, transcendent, isolate, free, and independent of any historical determination.[5] For such an individual religion is not only a sect apart from an undefined mainstream, but also a superstition rather than a confrontation with the realities of suffering, sin, and death. Thus, in the words of one critic, Shakespeare displays "an incomparable aloofness from all partisan religious issues" (Stevenson 1958, 80). Another characterizes him as "essentially secular, temporal, non-theological" and warns us against an "overly eager identification of Shakespeare's plays with Christian teachings in general and with the Catholic tradition in particular" (Frye 1963; 7, 293). Most recently, Shakespeare has become, if not a subversive interested in questions of power and containment, then a skeptical, nondogmatic Prince of Indeterminacy, a producer of "exploratory" plays, suffused with ambiguities, ambivalences, polar oppositions, dilemmas, and insoluble moral complexities. The problem is, of course, that these Enlightenment and Modern Skeptical models simply assume a privileged position, projecting onto Shakespeare their own sectarian doctrines and agenda. Hence, he is aloof, skeptical, indeterminate, and so on.

More seriously, such positions fail to address current research in a convincing way. With the recent surge of revisionist scholarship in English Reformation history, Renaissance philosophy, and Aristotelian virtue ethics,[6] there is a need to reposition Shakespeare in historical context. The one account of Shakespeare that remains unexplored is that he was a "church papist"; yet recent evidence increasingly indicates that he was precisely that.[7] And it can be argued that such a profile can incorporate and explain the subversive politics, the theological allusions, the moral complexities, and the strategic ambiguities all in more perfect alignment with biographical facts. We have seen the alternative—a bowdlerized Shakespeare, transcending theology and history, scandalizing nobody and "equally accessible to Christians and to the virtuous heathen" (Frye 1963, 272). But, as Gary Taylor has astutely pointed out, such a vacuous Shakespeare is a historical blank and an illusion, the child of skeptical scholarship (1994, 313). Such a sterilized figure, purged of any entanglement in history, does not allow us to explain the "single blessedness" passage in *A Midsummer Night's Dream*, the nuns and friars in *Measure for Measure,* or the Purgatorial background in *Hamlet,* not to mention other allusions in the plays to auricular confession, penitential satisfaction, merit, the Virgin Mary, intercessory prayer, prayers for the dead, and pilgrimage—all the theological doctrines and practices that were anathema to the Reformed churches in general and the Church of England in particular. It is impossible, moreover, to reconcile the Reformed theology of the *Homilies* and the *Thirty-Nine Articles* with Shakespeare's plays, and most especially with *Measure for Measure.* However, it is much easier, as I have argued, to reconcile Shakespeare with Roman Catholic theology. Imposing evidence of this is apparent in the favorable representation of Franciscan monastic life in *Measure for Measure.*

NOTES

1. All quotations of Shakespeare's plays are from *The Complete Works of Shakespeare,* ed. Bevington (1997).

2. Thus, Bevington points out that "Shakespeare's *King John* avoids all suggestion of moral laxity in the monasteries" (1968, 197). The treatment of cardinals and bishops is another matter, but they are criticized for their "moral crimes and political meddling, not for doctrine" (201). Bevington sees this as evidence of "mild anticlericalism," although by this reasoning Shakespeare's criticism of kings would make him antimonarchical as well. In any case, "mild anticlericalism" stemming from political meddling by the church hierarchy fits the profile of a moderate "church papist," as Milward suggests in the most comprehensive and judicious treatment of the subject (1973, 68–84).

3. For a summary of recent scholarship on the subject, see Beauregard, "New Light" (1997, 159–60). See especially Taylor (1994, 290–98) and Wilson (1997).

4. By refusing to exchange her chastity for her brother's life, Isabella has been accused of sin and a "lack of charity" (Gless 1979, 127–32; Velie 1972, 47; Hunter 1965, 217–18). This simplistic and absurd charge ignores the consequences of such a forced capitulation—the abuse, degradation, and violation that Isabella would undergo. Realistically, as the subsequent action explicitly indicates, such a "sacrifice" would in fact not save Claudio's life. Angelo orders Claudio killed anyway.

5. This mentality seems to be in recession and in the process of being replaced by a conception of the individual in relationship with nature and community. See Schneewind (1998), MacIntyre (1999), and Gablik (1992).

6. For recent studies in the English Reformation, see Todd (1995). For recent bibliography on Renaissance philosophy, see Schmitt (1988). For virtue ethics, see MacIntyre (1981) and Nussbaum (1994).

7. See note 2.

WORKS CITED

Abrams, William A., ed. *The Merry Devil of Edmonton (1608)*. Durham, N.C.: Duke University Press, 1942.

Aquinas, Saint Thomas. *Summa Theologica*. Trans. Fathers of the English Dominican Province. Westminster, Md.: Christian Classics, 1981.

Beauregard, David. "New Light on Shakespeare's Catholicism: Prospero's Epilogue in *The Tempest.*" *Renascence* 49 (1997): 159–74.

———. "Shakespeare Against the Homilies: The Theology of Penance in the Comedies." *The Ben Jonson Journal* 7 (2000): 27–53.

———. *Virtue's Own Feature: Shakespeare and the Virtue Ethics Tradition*. Newark, Del.: University of Delaware Press, 1995.

Bevington, David. *Tudor Drama and Politics: A Critical Approach to Topical Meaning*. Cambridge, Mass.: Harvard University Press, 1968.

Certaine Sermons or Homilies. Ed. Mary Ellen Rickey and Thomas Stroup. Gainesville, Fla.: Scholars' Facsmilies and Reprints, 1968.

Diehl, Huston. "'Infinite Space': Representation and Reformation in *Measure for Measure.*" *Shakespeare Quarterly* 49 (1998): 393–410.

Friedman, Michael D. "'O, let him marry her!': Matrimony and Recompense in *Measure for Measure.*" *Shakespeare Quarterly* 46 (1995): 454–64.

Frye, Roland Mushat. *Shakespeare and Christian Doctrine*. Princeton, N.J.: Princeton University Press, 1963.

Gablik, Suzi. *The Reenchantment of Art*. London: Thames and Hudson, 1992.

Gless, Darryl. *Measure for Measure: The Law and the Convent*. Princeton, N.J.: Princeton University Press, 1979.

Greene, Robert. *Friar Bacon and Friar Bungay*. Ed. J. A. Lavin. London: Ernest Benn Ltd., 1969.

Griffiths, Trevor, ed. *A Midsummer Night's Dream*. Shakespeare in Production Series. Ed. J. S. Bratton and Julie Hankey. Cambridge, England: Cambridge University Press, 1996.

Hamilton, Donna. *Shakespeare and the Politics of Protestant England Lexington*. Lexington, Ky.: University Press of Kentucky, 1992.

Hayne, Victoria. "Performing Social Practice: The Example of *Measure for Measure*." *Shakespeare Quarterly* 44 (1993): 1–29.

Hunter, R. G. *Shakespeare and the Comedies of Forgiveness*. New York: Columbia University Press, 1965.

Lupton, Julia Reinhard. *Afterlives of the Saints: Hagiography, Typology, and Renaissance Literature*. Stanford, Calif.: Stanford University Press, 1996.

MacIntyre, Alasdair. *Dependent Rational Animals*. Chicago, Ill.: Open Court, 1999.

_____. *After Virtue: A Study in Moral Theory*. Notre Dame, Ind.: Notre Dame University Press, 1981.

McGinn, Donald J. "The Precise Angelo." In *Joseph Quincy Adams Memorial Studies,* ed. James G. McManaway et al. Washington, D.C.: Folger Shakespeare Library, 1948.

Miles, Rosalind. *The Problem of "Measure for Measure": A Historical Investigation*. New York: Barnes and Noble, 1976.

Milward, Peter. *Shakespeare's Religious Background*. Chicago, Ill.: Loyola University Press, 1973.

Mullaney, Stephen. *The Place of the Stage: License, Play, and Power in Renaissance England*. Chicago, Ill.: University of Chicago Press, 1988.

Nussbaum, Martha. *Love's Philosophy: Essays on Philosophy and Literature*. Oxford, England: Oxford University Press, 1994.

Pineas, Rainer. "The English Morality Play as a Weapon of Religious Controversy." *Studies in English Literature* 2 (1962): 157–80.

_____. *Tudor and Early Stuart Anti-Catholic Drama. Bibliotheca Humanistica & Reformatorica*. Vol. 5. Nieuwkoop: B. De Graaf, 1972.

Schmitt, Charles B., et al., eds. *The Cambridge History of Renaissance Philosophy*. 303–86. Cambridge, England: Cambridge University Press, 1988.

Schneewind, J. B. *The Invention of Autonomy*. Cambridge, England: Cambridge University Press, 1998.

Shakespeare, William. *The Complete Works of Shakespeare*. Updated 4th ed. Ed. David Bevington. New York: Longman, 1997.

Shell, Alison. *Catholicism, Controversy and the English Literary Imagination, 1558–1660*. Cambridge, England: Cambridge University Press, 1999.

Spevack, Marvin. *The Harvard Concordance to Shakespeare*. Cambridge, Mass.: Belknap Press of Harvard University Press, 1973.

Stevenson, Robert. *Shakespeare's Religious Frontier*. The Hague: Martinus Nijhoff, 1958.

Taylor, Gary. "Forms of Opposition: Shakespeare and Middleton." *English Literary Renaissance* 24 (1994): 283–314.

Todd, Margo, ed. *Reformation to Revolution: Politics and Religion in Early Modern England*. London: Routledge, 1995.

Velie, Alan. *Shakespeare's Repentance Plays: The Search for an Adequate Form*. Cranbury, N.J.: Associated University Press, 1972.

Voss, Paul. "The Antifraternal Tradition in English Renaissance Drama." *Cithara* 33 (1993): 3–16.

Whetstone, George. *An Heptameron of Civill Discourses*. London: Richard Jones, 1582.

White, Paul Whitfield. *Theatre and Reformation: Protestantism, Patronage, and Playing in Tudor England*. Cambridge, England: Cambridge University Press, 1993.

Wilson, Richard. "Shakespeare and the Jesuits: New connections supporting the theory of the lost Catholic years in Lancashire." *Times Literary Supplement* (Dec. 19, 1997): 11–13.

Winston, Mathew. "'Craft Against Vice': Morality Play Elements in *Measure for Measure*." *Shakespeare Studies* 14 (1981): 229–48.

13

Helena and the Reformation Problem of Merit in *All's Well That Ends Well*

by *Maurice Hunt*

Baylor University, Waco, Texas

IN THE CHARACTER of Helena of *All's Well That Ends Well,* Shakespeare most fully represents the problematical complication of merit occasioned by the Reformation Protestant revaluation of the term in its debate with Catholicism. A preliminary examination of the topic in *Love's Labor's Lost* and *Othello* provides a context useful for the analysis of Helena's merit in *All's Well.* Early in act 4 of *Love's Labor's Lost,* the Princess of France jokes with a Forester. When at a deer hunt, he directs her to "[a] stand where [she] may make the fairest shoot," she purposely misunderstands him in order to coin a punning jest: "I thank my beauty, I am fair that shoot [release my arrow/shoot up (grow)], / And thereupon thou speak'st the fairest shoot [bowshot/blooming spray of a tree or flower (myself)]" (4.1.10–12).[1] When the anxious Forester replies, "Pardon me, madam, for I meant not so" (4.1.13), the Princess, playfully giving him some money for telling her a supposedly unpleasant truth, exclaims, "Fair payment for foul words is more than due" (4.1.19). "See, see, my beauty will be sav'd by merit," she concludes; "O heresy in fair, fit for these days! / A giving hand, though foul, shall have fair praise" (4.1.21–23). This jest registers Shakespeare's engagement early in his career with the Reformation debate over salvation by Protestant faith versus Catholic meritorious deeds.

In the above-quoted three-verse passage, the Princess jokes that her beauty—to use G. Blakemore Evans's phrasing—will be saved "(1) by its own deserts; (2) by my giving of gratuities" (Shakespeare, *The*

Riverside Shakespeare 1997, 224). In this latter instance, she jests that her beauty will be saved by her "meritorious" deed of giving the poor woodsman some money. She implies that she has had to preserve its existence by buying the Forester's report that it is a reality. Seriously reflected in this lighthearted case is a Reformation heresy of merit—that Catholics repaired and augmented the saving grace infused into them by performing meritorious works such as the giving of alms, purchasing of indulgences, saying of Ave Marias, and making of pilgrimages.[2] Thomistic doctrine had long maintained that

> a man who freely performed good works in a state of grace cooperated in the attainment of his salvation. . . . Secular living was in this way taken up into the religious life; good works became the sine qua non of saving faith. He who did his moral best within a state of grace received salvation as his just due. In the technical language of the [Catholic] theologian, faith formed by acts of charity (*fides caritate formata*) received eternal life as full or condign merit (*meritum de condigno*). (Ozment 1980, 233)

For Reformation Protestants, however, salvation was mainly a matter of faith in their divine election, which could not be altered by either the number or quality of meritorious deeds.

Admittedly, Reformation Protestants believed that the regular performance of good deeds was spiritually important. Martin Luther had distinguished between "two kinds of works: those done for others, which are the right kind . . . and those done for ourselves, which are of smaller value." "We wear and consume our bodies with watching, fasting and labor, but we neglect charity, which is the only lady and mistress of works," Luther concluded (qtd. in Christopher Hill 1975, 83). Christopher Hill asserts that "extern matters and ceremonial observations, nothing conducing to any spiritual purpose"—for example, the telling of beads, the lighting of candles—"were what the reformers had most of all in mind when they denounced 'works.' . . . Where good works in the wider sense were concerned—acts of mercy or charity— a protestant thought that *what* a man did was less important than the spirit in which he did it" (Hill, 83). The Elizabethan divine Richard Hooker stressed that both Protestants and Catholics believed that "through the merit of Christ we are delivered as from sin" (1954, 1:17–18). And they both believed that Christians, after baptism, partake of Christ's merit during that stage of the Pauline paradigm of sal-

vation known as justification, which concerns—in a Protestant definition—the "forgiveness of sins by Christ's satisfaction for them, and the
imputing of Christ's righteousness to [Christians] as a cloak or covering to hide [their] true filthiness and wickedness" (Lewalski 1979,
16–17).[3] For Protestants, the regular performance of deeds of holiness
and righteousness was also important during that stage of the Pauline
paradigm known as sanctification, which involves "the actual but grad-
ual repairing of the defaced image of God in the soul, whereby it
enjoys 'new life'" (Lewalski, 18). But because "the godly are still sinners, and their good works are always incomplete and redolent of the
vices of the flesh, there can be absolutely no question of human merit
attaching to any good works that they do; performance of the works of
righteousness (the Commandments) are evidences of election, and the
natural fruits of conversion and faith, but are not in any degree meritorious for salvation" (Lewalski, 18). The eminent Cambridge Protestant
William Perkins (1559–1602) in *The Whole Treatise of the Cases of
Conscience* (publ. 1606) concludes that his readers must "intreat the
Lord to pardon the wants of our workes [of sanctification]. . . . And the
reason is plaine; because in us there is no goodnesse, no holinesse, no
righteousnesse, nor any thing that may present us acceptable in his
sight" (1642, 43).

John Milton thus articulates an orthodox Protestant doctrine in book
3 of *Paradise Lost* when God tells his son:

> As in [Adam] perish all men, so in thee
> As from a second root shall be restor'd,
> As many as are restor'd, without thee none.
> His crime makes guiltie all his Sons, thy merit
> Imputed shall *absolve them who renounce*
> *Their own both righteous and unrighteous deeds,*
> And live in thee transplanted, and from thee
> Receive new life.[4]
>
>   (3.287–94, my italics)

Christ's imputed merit absolves the faithful Protestant who renounces
the personal worth of his or her righteous works performed as part of
the Pauline paradigm of salvation. This Christian knows that the worth
of these deeds derives wholly from Christ's imputed merit, which
becomes the Christian's as he or she lives "transplanted" in him.
Merritt Y. Hughes concludes that "[i]n the chapter on justification in

The Christian Doctrine (I.22; 40), Milton could condemn the doctrine of human merit as a factor in salvation . . . on the ground that saving faith and the meritorious works which it inspires are alike works of the [S]pirit, not our own" (1967–68, 7–8; also see Berthold 1975, 153–67). "*By* their doing though not *for* their doing" [my italics] the elect are saved, wrote Thomas Taylor (1576–1633) (1653, 166). Elizabethan and Jacobean Christians who expected salvation "for their doing"—because of the personal credit due their "meritorious" deeds—mistakenly believed that they could "earn" heaven.[5] After extensive examination of the works of Reformation English Protestant theologians or writers such as Perkins, Andrew Willet, Thomas Bell, Josias Nicholls, and Anthony Wotten, Dewey Wallace concludes that for Shakespeare's contemporaries, "justification was an imputed, not an inherent righteousness . . . faith involved some assurance of salvation . . . and salvation was by the free favor of God's grace, with no respect to human merit, the reliance on merit being seen as the very essence of popish falsehood" (1982, 63, 216). "[W]hat is the fault of the Church of Rome?" Hooker asked. "Not that she requireth works at their hands that will be saved: but that she attributeth unto works a power of satisfying God for sin; and a virtue to merit both grace here, and in heaven glory" (1954, 1:61). "We are accounted righteous before God," so begins Article XI of the 1563 Articles of the Church of England, "only for the merit of our Lord and Savior Jesus Christ by Faith, and not for our own works or deservings" (Bicknell 1947, 199).

Involved in the Princess of France's repartee in *Love's Labor's Lost* is an allusion to a notorious religious conversion that made the so-called heresy of merit painfully real for Protestant playgoers. Commentators on *Love's Labor's Lost* such as H. B. Charlton, Richard David, and Albert Tricomi have claimed that the phrase "fit for these days" in the Princess's exclamation, "See, see, my beauty will be sav'd by merit. / O heresy in fair, fit for these days!" invites the recollection of a recent royal heresy of merit (Charlton 1918, 266; Shakespeare, *Love's Labor's Lost* 1956, 63–64; Tricomi 1979, 31). Many critics, including those just cited, have noted striking similarities between Shakespeare's portrayal of the King of Navarre in this early comedy and the character of the French Huguenot King Henry of Navarre, who from 1589 to 1593 was a subject of enthusiasm in Elizabeth's court and the city of London (Hunt 1992, 174–79). In July 1593, Henry of

Navarre reconverted to Catholicism, a blow to English hopes for a Protestant stronghold in France against Spain. Thus the topical satire inherent in the Princess of France's banter amounts to a statement that, regarded from a Reformation Protestant viewpoint, salvation by merit (Catholic works) rather than Protestant faith seems in the present day especially heretical, chiefly because the present day has shown the world a French king's self-serving rejection of his Protestant vows and his return to Roman Catholicism.[6]

For Reformation Protestants, the heresy of merit applied not simply to the issue of salvation but to secular issues as well. (Convincing sixteenth-century illustrations of the transferability of theological conceptions of merit to secular kinds of service and reward appear in Langer 1988.) In Othello's case, merit pertains more to heroic than spiritual matters (Watson 1995; Hunt 1996, 352–57). Othello's grand martial deeds, recounted to Desdemona, win her love (1.3.128–70). Later, thinking he has lost the wife acquired by his meritorious feats, Othello laments the loss of the heroic occupation and the warrior identity that his deeds fashioned (3.3.347–57). Believing that his narrated deeds are not as compelling as he imagined and that they have betrayed him, Othello punishes himself by casting off the self that he assumes his accomplished merit created. The suddenness and magnitude of the collapse of Othello's identity resulting from this logic suggest a double meaning in many—if not all—of his earlier endorsements of his own merit. Othello has said,

> Nor from mine own weak merits will I draw
> The smallest fear or doubt of her revolt,
> For she had eyes and chose me
>
> (3.3.187–89)

Vainly believing his merits are strong and deserving, Othello employs the word "weak" in the phrase "weak merits" in the above-quoted pronouncement to project a presumably attractive modesty. Reconsidered in the light of his subsequent statement about the absolute loss of his heroic vocation, the word "weak" gains an embarrassing authenticity that belies its surface employment. Othello's merits in some sense must be weak if the self built on their foundation cracks and crumbles as easily as it does. And yet, Othello continues to insist publicly upon the strength of his merits until the moment of his death. The deed he recollects in his suicide speech in order to preserve a reduced but nevertheless heroic final image of himself concerns his meritorious service to Venice in striking down a malignant Turk (5.2.338–56). But in Gratiano's opinion (as well as in those of many playgoers and critics), Othello's stabbing himself prompts the judgment that "All that is spoke is marr'd" (5.2.357): the reprehensible deed negates the heroic self fashioned by the slaying of the Turk. This negation complements the "Nobody" that Othello in one sense becomes in Desdemona's using this word to name the person who has fatally strangled her (5.2.124). Othello may protest that his merits are strong, based as they are on this military prowess, and that they entitle him to Desdemona, but Iago's ease in getting the protagonist to become "nobody" indicates in *Othello* the categorical emptiness of a persona constructed from meritorious deeds. Othello apparently never realized the saving power inherent in faith.[7]

*

A potential heresy of merit informs Shakespeare's Jacobean comedy, *All's Well That Ends Well,* specifically his characterization of the poor physician's daughter Helena. As he does not do in *Love's Labor's Lost, The Merchant of Venice,* or *Othello,* Shakespeare at times suggests in *All's Well* that protestations of personal merit—and the deeds that sometimes accompany them—may not be heretical. In other words, he introduces into his play Catholic as well as Protestant contexts for positively appreciating merit. In doing so, he not only replicates the tensions and even impasses of a contemporary debate over the efficacy of personal merit, but he also makes the most secretive, enigmatical of his comic heroines appear even more so. Nevertheless, analysis of Helena's idea of merit, conducted within the matrices of an early modern English religious controversy, traces better than other topical studies have done the character development of this often perplexing young woman.

Helena deeply loves Bertram, the Count of Roussillon, but fears revealing her passion to him because of the likelihood of rejection based upon his aristocratic perception of the great difference in social rank between them. Helena lacks "desert," the blood-worth conferred by noble birth. "Nor would I have him," Helena tells the Countess of Roussillon, "till I do deserve him— / Yet never know how that desert should be" (1.3.199–200). Helena would like to be able to deserve an aristocratic pedigree, but she cannot imagine how blood-worth might be earned.[8] Nevertheless, she develops her scheme of curing the King of France's fistula and securing as payment his promise to wed her to the royal ward she chooses, Bertram in this case. Obviously, this plan represents an alternative to the insoluble problem of "earning" aristocratic identity. At the beginning of the play, Helena is an optimist. "Our remedies oft in ourselves do lie/Which we ascribe to heaven," she sanguinely pronounces to begin her soliloquy concluding act 1, scene 1.

> The fated sky
> Gives us free scope, only doth backward pull
> Our slow designs when we ourselves are dull
>   (1.1.218–21)

Editors typically read this utterance as testifying to Helena's belief that she can freely shape her future. And yet, the interplay between the words "fated" and "free scope" in the statement that "[t]he fated sky / Gives us free scope" creates a tension. Susan Snyder notes, concerning the word "fated," that in these verses David Bevington glosses it as meaning "invested with the power of destiny" (*Complete Works of Shakespeare* 1997, 89). Most Reformation English Protestants would have understood this gloss to mean "predestined." Article XVII of the 1563 Articles of the Church of England committed Reformation English Protestants to the doctrine of predestination, to the belief that God had determined the election of some souls to salvation and had precluded others from it. Predestined men and women lacked the "free scope" to alter their timeless predestination. Helena, however, is in this case thinking of her romantic fulfillment rather than her salvation, an earthly affair that she assumes she can freely shape to her advantage. "Who ever strove / To show her merit that did miss her love?" she rhetorically asks. "The King's disease—my project may deceive me, / But my intents are fixed and will not leave me" (1.1.228–31). By the word "merit," Helena refers to her own personal merit, as though in matters of the heart it will earn Bertram.

Both Protestant and Catholic ideas informing *All's Well* color Helena's romantic notion of her merit.[9] My introductory analysis of *Love's Labor's Lost* and *Othello* revealed that the Reformation heresy of merit had a secular as well as a theological relevance, and that the meaning of merit could be easily transposed from a religious context to a secular one and back again. In this bittersweet comedy, Shakespeare repeatedly projects what might be called a strongly Calvinist view of human nature: that born into Original Sin, humankind, lacking grace, amounts to little more than puffed-up dust. "I have been, madam, a wicked creature," the Clown Lavatch tells the Countess of Roussillon, "as you and all flesh and blood are, and indeed I do marry that I may repent" (1.3.35–37). Noting that this sentiment ought to apply to Bertram, David J. Palmer judges that "here the Calvinist doctrine of man's total depravity is glanced at" (1989, 97). He also concludes that "the Calvinist sense of man's ineradicable wickedness unless redeemed by grace" is echoed in First Lord's pronouncement, "Now, God delay our rebellion! As we are ourselves, what things we are!" and in Second Lord's reply, "Merely our own traitors" (4.3.19–21) (98; also see Tillyard 1968, 107–8). Made an outcast by his betrayal of his comrades, a contrite Paroles says, "Simply the thing I am / Shall make me live" (4.3.336–37). Time and again, Shakespeare, Calvinist-fashion, refers to presumptuously self-sufficient human beings as "things" of little worth unless they have the grace of God's election. Joking with Lafeu, the Clown claims that he serves in France a famous black prince—not the English Edward of this name celebrated by Chaucer—but "the prince of darkness, alias the devil" (4.5.43–44). "I am a woodland fellow, sir," the Clown darkly jests, "that always loved a great fire, and the master I speak of ever keeps a good fire. But sure he is the prince of the world, let his nobility remain in 's court. I am for the house with the narrow gate, which I take to be too little for pomp to enter. Some that humble themselves may, but the many will be too chill and tender, and they'll be for the flow'ry way that leads to the broad gate and the great fire" (4.5.48–56). The strait-is-the-gate standard of biblical morality introduced into the play by this plangent discourse reinforces the Calvinist elements elsewhere in it.[10]

The precision of Protestant allusions in *All's Well* can be gauged by this remark of the Clown's: "Though honesty be no puritan, yet it will do no hurt: it will wear the surplice of humility over the black gown of a big heart" (1.3.93–95). Jacobean ministers of the Church of England were required to wear a surplice, a loose-fitting white gown with wide sleeves. Puritanical churchmen sometimes rejected this garment because it reminded them of Roman Catholicism. Some preferred to wear only the black Geneva gown; others hypocritically wore the surplice over that gown. Given these and other Protestant elements in this comedy, playgoers and readers on a reacquaintance with *All's Well* are more inclined to translate the word "fated" in Helena's claim that the "fated sky" gives her "free scope" as "predestined"—"predestinarian."

Competing with this Protestant spirit is the Catholic dimension of this play; its events occur, after all, in France and Italy. Lafeu refers to the Reformation Protestant belief that miracles ceased with New Testament times, but he does so in a way that endorses the Catholic position in the contemporary debate on this subject.[11] "They say miracles are past," Lafeu asserts with regard to the King's unimaginable cure, "and we have our philosophical persons to make modern and familiar things supernatural and causeless. Hence is it that we make trifles of terrors, ensconcing ourselves into seeming knowledge when we should submit ourselves to an unknown fear" (2.3.1–6). By implying that miracles have not ceased, that in fact "modern" persons wrongly explain away present miraculous happenings, Lafeu represents a Counter-Reformation Catholic viewpoint. Moreover, Helena is Roman Catholic; otherwise she would not propose and undertake a penitential pilgrimage to the Spanish shrine of St. Jacques. Concerning Bertram, she says early in the play, "my idolatrous fancy / Must sanctify his relics" (1.1.99–100).[12] Her Catholicism renders problematical the status and value of merit in the play, simply because it suggests a certain efficacy in personal merit generally qualified or denied by Protestantism.[13] Playgoers hear this "Catholic" emphasis upon the efficacy of personal merit in her previously cited belief that those who strive to show their merit rarely—if ever—fail to attain their love (1.2.228–31).

Shakespeare subtly maintains this emphasis in Helena's subsequent reference to merit. When the King of France resists her invitation to try her father's medical prescriptions, she replies,

> Inspirèd merit so by breath is barred.
> It is not so with him that all things knows
> As 'tis with us that square our guess by shows.
> But most it is presumption in us when
> The help of heaven we count the act of men.
> Dear sir, to my endeavours give consent.
> Of heaven, not me, make an experiment.
>
> (2.1.146–52)

The merit that Helena refers to is apparently Gerard de Narbonne's—that of her famous French physician father, who created the remedies she wants to apply to the King's fistula. That merit, whether his at the time he concocted the marvelous prescriptions, or hers as his persuasive agent of the moment, is "inspired"—"breathed into" father and perhaps daughter by God. The root meaning of "inspired" is preferable in the above passage, for Helena is suggesting that heaven and not herself or her father should get credit for the King's projected cure. Here is an articulation of merit with which both early modern Protestants and Catholics apparently could agree. Richard Hooker did assert that both Protestants and Catholics believed that "through the merit of Christ we are delivered as from sin" (1:17–18). Helena's above-quoted opinion amounts to a secular version of this idea. Yet, Catholics subscribed to the doctrine that divine merit was infused into them—"inspired" into them—whereas Protestants thought it was "imputed" to them (see the conclusion of note 3). Milton could not be more orthodox in asserting that Christ's "merit / Imputed shall absolve" Christians renouncing both their righteous and unrighteous deeds (*Paradise Lost* in 1998, 3.290–92). By her adjective, "[i]nspirèd," Helena, in the final analysis, thus gives her formulation of merit a Catholic weighting, and so abolishes the potential for either doctrinal harmony or synthesis.

Once Helena's prescriptions have given him relief from the fistula, the King of France forgets Helena's eloquent claim that God acts through her and, apparently in gratitude, gives the poor physician's daughter all the credit. This royal opinion complements the innuendoes of courtiers who suggest that Helena's physical beauty and imagined sexual allure have regenerated the King (2.1.67–76, 93–96; 2.3.42–44; Wheeler 1981, 75–77; Parker 1992, 367–69). Referring to Helena's nonaristocratic status, the King pronounces, "From lowest place when virtuous things proceed, / The place is dignified by th' doer's deed" (2.3.126–27). In his mind, the virtuous cure has proceeded from the "lowest place," rather than from God on high. When Bertram, once chosen, tells the King and Helena that he cannot love her, the shocked monarch angrily exclaims,

> Here, take her hand,
> Proud, scornful boy, unworthy this good gift,
> That dost in vile misprision shackle up

> My love and her desert; that canst not dream
> We, poising us in her defective scale,
> Shall weigh thee to the beam; that wilt not know
> It is in us to plant thine honour where
> We please to have it grow.
>
> (2.3.151–58)

In the King's mind, Helena's cure stresses her "desert," her merit, rather than Christ's. Because he believes she has merit, he proposes to bestow "honour and wealth" upon her as a conventional dowry complementing her "dowry" of inherent virtue (2.3.144–45). In this way, he believes he will make a poor physician's daughter worthy of Count Roussillon. The unsatisfactory arbitrariness of such a conferral can be judged by Bertram's sarcastic rephrasing of it:

> Pardon, my gracious lord; for I submit
> My fancy to your eyes. When I consider
> What great creation and what dole of honour
> Flies were you bid it, I find that she which late
> Was in my nobler thoughts most base is now
> The praisèd of the King; who so ennobled
> Is as 'twere born so.
>
> (2.3.168–74)

Bertram denigrates his monarch's claims by suggesting that the King believes his royal word and a material dowry are enough to make someone honorable. David Berkeley and Donald Keesee note "the King does not [at this moment] in fact ennoble Helena. Even if he did," they remark, "his act might activate the proverb that 'The King cannot make a gentleman'" (1991, 255). What the French monarch finally promises Helena is "A counterpoise, if not to [Bertram's] estate / A balance more replete" (2.3.176–77). Both David Bevington and Stephen Greenblatt gloss the word "counterpoise" as "dowry," with the general sense being that it will approach or exceed Bertram's estate (Shakespeare, ed. Bevington 1997, 379; Shakespeare, ed. Greenblatt 1997, 2205). And yet, material wealth by itself makes a beneficiary neither honorable nor deserving. In summary, the King's "ennobling" of Helena remains as ambiguous as the source of her merit.

If God worked through Helena to cure the King of France, He used her love for Bertram to do so. Concerning Gerard de Narbonne's prescription for fistulas, Helena tells the Countess:

> My lord your son made me to think of this.
> Else Paris, and the medicine, and the King
> Had from the conversation of my thoughts
> Haply been absent then.
>
> (1.3.232–35)

This admission clearly tells playgoers that Helena's motives for curing the King were never disinterested, never performed solely for his benefit and the love of virtuous doing. These words tell us Helena, from the beginning, planned to use the cure in a barter to create a lottery by which she could pick Bertram for her husband and have the King enforce her choice. Such a scheme necessarily presumes her belief that the King (and Bertram) would want to recognize and reward *her* skills. Considered retrospectively, Helena's reference to the barring of "[i]spirèd merit" in connection with the resistance to her cure entails her silent wish that curing the King would reveal a merit within her that would make the King and then Bertram think she is worthy to be the Count's wife.[14] Thus Helena's allusion to her "[i]nspirèd merit," in addition to its heavenly overtones, carries a sense as personal as that in her earlier soliloquy:

> Who ever strove
> To show her merit that did miss her love?
> The King's disease—my project may deceive me,
> But my intents are fixed and will not leave me.
>
> (1.1.226–29)[15]

We may, then, retrospectively read merit in Helena's speech to the King of France in both Protestant and Catholic senses. Shakespeare, in a rarely quoted speech of act 1, implies that such an illogical coexistence represents a fictional possibility in this play.[16] Concerning the likelihood of husbands becoming cuckolds, the Clown Lavatch claims, "for young Chairbonne the puritan and old Poisson the papist, howsome'er their hearts are severed in religion, their heads are both one: they may jowl horns together like any deer i'th' herd" (1.3.52–55). The joke here concerns the supposed inevitability of male cuckoldry resulting from female adultery. This trivial, chauvinistic humor depends upon a principle important for my topic. Religious differences are overlooked, the Clown implies, when humankind must come to terms with the universality and strength of disturbing natural drives. In having to come to terms with an existential reality, Protestants and Catholics have the opportunity to recognize that "their heads are both one"—that on occasion they share the human condition. Later in *All's Well That Ends Well,* Shakespeare, in terms of this scenario, gave astute Protestant and Catholic playgoers and readers the opportunity to agree momentarily on an issue of religious difference—to heal momentarily the "severed heart." In *All's Well,* the natural drives of characters such as Helena and Bertram are especially strong and persistent. These sexual drives find their expression in the bed-trick of the play, which, as we shall see, provides grounds upon which Protestants and Catholics could have momentarily agreed about the value of Helena's merit.

In act 3, Helena begins redefining her idea of her merit. Bertram's ordering Helena home to Roussillon after his forced marriage to her and his secret flight to Italy and the wars being fought there shakes her confidence not only in her scheme for winning him, but also in her idea of her own worth. Her knowledge that Bertram would rather risk the penalties associated with disobeying the King of France undermines her belief that she was right to pursue him. Helena realizes that she could be considered the cause of either his premature death in the Italian wars or his lifelong exile from his inheritance and his grieving mother. Helena now considers her "ambitious love" (1.1.92, 3.4.5–7) a fault, one that has resulted in her being—to use the words of Bertram's letter to her—"'nothing in France'" (3.2.99).[17] "'Nothing in France until he has no wife,'" she exclaims, reading the awful words; "Thou shalt have none, Roussillon, none in France; / Then hast thou all again" (3.2.100–102). In a moment, Helena resolves to become the "nothing" of a poor, barefoot pilgrim to the famous Spanish Catholic shrine of St. Jacques le Grand in Compostela. Wherein resides the merit of this stripped Helena?

Her contradictory motives for her pilgrimage preclude an immediate, easy answer to this question. On the one hand, Helena seems literally to want to martyr herself. Concerning Bertram, she laments,

> I am the caitiff that do hold him to't,
> And though I kill him not I am the cause
> His death was so effected. Better 'twere
> I met the ravin lion when he roared
> With sharp constraint of hunger; better 'twere
> That all the miseries which nature owes
> Were mine at once.
>
> (3.2.114–20)

The self-sacrificial overtones of the couplet concluding her resolve to become a pilgrim are unmistakable: "He is too good and fair for death, and me, / Whom I myself embrace to set him free" (3.4.16–17). On the other hand, Helena, according to Catholic practices, implies that her pilgrimage constitutes a mortifying penitential series of deeds that atone for the supposed fault of desiring marriage to Bertram. "'Ambitious love hath so in me offended,'" she asserts, "'That barefoot plod I the cold ground upon, / With sainted vow my faults to have amended'" (3.4.5–7). These faults include the catalyst for winning Bertram: the claim to merit in the cure of the King that "earned" her Bertram. The amendment of faults through pilgrimage generally implies a purified worldly afterlife rather than martyrdom. In his word portrait of the devil's broad highway, the Clown claims that "[s]ome that humble themselves may" pass through "the narrow gate" to God's "house." Helena implies that she plans to atone for presumptuous claims of merit by performing a series of humbling penitential deeds in the context of pilgrimage to a famous shrine. One could say that, in her case, one kind of meritorious deed rectifies the bad consequences of an earlier act of merit—her "overweening" personal cure of the King.

Helena's redefined meritorious deeds include prayers on Bertram's behalf. In her letter to the Countess, Helena asks Bertram's mother to "'[b]less him at home in peace, whilst I from far / His name with zealous fervour sanctify'" (3.4.10–11). The Countess, reading the letter, elaborates this idea, strengthening the Roman Catholic characterization of Helena by investing her with the Marian role of Intercessor. "What angel shall / Bless this unworthy husband?" the Countess asks. "He cannot thrive"

> Unless [Helena's] prayers, whom heaven delights to hear
> And loves to grant, reprieve him from the wrath
> Of greatest justice.
>
> (3.4.25–29)

Mary the Intercessor for penitent Counter-Reformation Catholics invoking her aid converts God's wrath to mercy. Interestingly, the Countess, rather than thinking—as Helena does—that her adopted daughter lacks all worth, assumes that saintly merit resides within Bertram's wife.[18] In the older woman's view, Helena's meritorious prayers can make her son deserve God's compassion.

Playgoers and readers alike assume that Helena, walking to the Spanish shrine, performs these deeds en route and once there. That Helena does go to the shrine we know from First Lord's later report of her "death" there: "Her death itself, which could not be her office to say is come, was faithfully confirmed by the rector of the place" (4.3.57–59). The same lord also speaks of her letters sent to Bertram, wherein she describes her journey to the shrine and residence there, "which holy undertaking with most austere sanctimony she accomplished" (4.3.49–50).[19] We assume that Helena could have enlisted the help of St. Jacques's priest in the ruse of her "death" only through a face-to-face talk involving a lengthy explanation. But we must reconstruct this scenario after the fact, after hearing First Lord's words in act 4, scene 3. Shakespeare wrote no scenes showing Helena's penitential deeds on the way to Santiago de Compostela or once there. That she was there we know only from the report of a strange deception she perpetrates with the rector's aid.

In short, Shakespeare de-emphasizes Helena's merit. What we see instead in act 3 is Helena a pilgrim arrived in Florence, the Italian city easterly and southerly from Roussillon, far from the direct westerly and southerly route to the Spanish shrine. Shakespeare's playgoer or reader, encountering the play for the first time, at this moment has no idea whether she has been to Compostela, still plans to go there, or has no intention of going there (Sexton 1994, 279–81). Helena apparently resolves this ambiguity by telling Diana's mother, the Widow, that she is bound for "Saint Jacques le Grand" (3.5.34).[20] "You came, I think, from France?" (3.5.46), the Widow asks, having offered Helena lodging until she can join "the troops" of palmers that "come by" her house (3.5.40). The Widow of Florence thinks nothing odd about a French pilgrim traveling through Florence to get to a shrine in northern Spain. Moreover, G. Wilson Knight remarks that, although Helena "certainly knew that Bertram had gone to serve the Duke (3.1.54), we must not suppose that her finding him in Florence was part of a deliberate plan, since her letter to the Countess has already urged his immediate return to France (3.4.8)" (1958, 143). Helena's urging of the Countess makes sense only if she is truly penitent, travels first to Spain, persuades the priest of St. Jacques to write Bertram of her "death," and then begins a lonely, self-effacing wandering that leads to the Italian city associated with her husband (but in which—because of her letter—she cannot expect to find him). Rather than illustrating her deceptive nature, her going there shows (presumably without her knowing it) the working of the mysterious natural magnetism described in her earlier couplet, "The mightiest space in fortune nature brings / To join like likes and kiss like native things" (1.1.224–25).[21]

Certainly, the two months elapsed between Helena's vanishing and her appearance in Florence (4.3.47–48) permit the above-described chronology. In this interpretation, Helena's claim that she is bound to St. Jacques once she is in Florence could be an unpremeditated response to the Widow's remark, "God save you, pilgrim, whither are you bound?" (3.5.33). Still dressed in her pilgrim's garb, Helena self-protectively voices her first thought—the Spanish shrine to which she made her pilgrimage. Apparently, Helena never plans to return to Roussillon, imagining Bertram would leave there once she arrived, but to wander indefinitely as part of a pledge to never again separate him from his mother and his birthright.[22] This intention, if it is one, perhaps fulfills the desire for martyrdom that we heard in Helena's original formulation of her pilgrimage.

This hypothesized reconstruction is admittedly a bit fantastic. But it is the only one that makes sense of the staging and dialogue of acts 3 and 4 of *All's Well*. Shakespeare's dramaturgy renders ambiguous the nature of Helena's merit. Did she or did she not perform the Catholic good works of pilgrimage?[23] My reconstruction suggests that she probably did, but Shakespeare takes pains to make us uncertain. Where, then, does her merit more certainly reside? Strangely, Helena shows no surprise (or joy) when she learns from the Widow that Bertram is alive in Florence. Instead, learning that her husband woos the Widow's daughter Diana (an equally astonishing dramatic fact), Helena coolly proposes the bed-trick. After the failure of her marriage scheme, Helena's merit is a diminished thing. At least it is so in her opinion. In her talk with the Widow, she speaks of herself, the wife abandoned in France, in the third person so as not to reveal her identity. Helena says, concerning herself,

> In argument of praise, or to the worth
> Of the great Count himself, she is too mean
> To have her name repeated. All her deserving
> Is a reservèd honesty, and that
> I have not heard examined.
>
> (3.5.59–63)

Jonas Barish glosses her utterance "All her deserving / Is a reservèd honesty" as "Her only merit is a preserved chastity" (Shakespeare, ed. Barish 1964, 92), whereas Anne Barton and G. Blakemore Evans translate it: "Her sole merit is a carefully guarded chastity" (Shakespeare, ed. Evans et al. 1997, 559). In this common reading, they represent the majority of editors. No longer does Helena regard her merit as consisting of either an intellectual cleverness, a quality of perseverance, or capacities of eloquence and healing—any or all of which could be considered marks of divine election. Nor does she regard it as consisting of penitential deeds that she has performed. Instead, her desert—in her mind—now amounts only to her preserved virginity, a natural birthright that she cannot be said to have created or earned, although one might argue its preservation after girlhood to be a personal accomplishment to her credit. But even in this case, her achievement consists of a virtual negative (or non) deed. Helena has maintained her chastity by choosing not to become active, by remaining passive. Hers is a cloistered virtue, in the Miltonic sense. (In fact, the play suggests that a man has never tempted her sexually or propositioned her; thus she apparently has never had to act to protect her chastity by rebuffing salacious overtures, either by a verbal retort or by walking away from temptation.) Many of Shakespeare's Protestant playgoers might have judged that Helena's revaluation of her merit illustrates a humbling lesson concerning those who vainly or naively insist upon the importance of their personal merit. This audience most likely would have found the reduced Helena a more attractive comic heroine than the sanguine maiden speaking of her "[i]nspirèd merit" in act 1.

Helena has located her merit in her virginity. In the bed-trick, she "spends" this possession cleverly in order to fulfill Bertram's riddle and "earn" her husband. "When thou canst get the ring upon my finger, which never shall come off, and show me a child begotten of thy body that I am father to, then call me husband," Bertram has written, "[b]ut in such a 'then,' I write a 'never'" (3.2.57–60). By getting the Florentine Diana Capilet to talk Bertram out of his ancestral ring and then by substituting herself for the other virgin in the dark so that Bertram impregnates her, Helena accomplishes the terms of "a dreadful sentence" (3.2.61). If Helena's merit involves her virginity, and if she must lose that to satisfy the riddle and win her husband, then one could argue that in the process she loses her merit. Ascertaining the degree of truth in this syllogistic argument entails measuring the moral (or ethical) status of the bed-trick—the "goodness" of this deed.

Shakespeare's Protestant playgoers may have been as or more inclined than Catholics to have judged this deed good, part of a providential design in fact. More so than Roman Catholics of the time, Protestants, especially godly Protestants, were familiar with the finer details of the Old Testament (Bruce 1961, 84–85, 113–24; Daniell 1999, 165, 168–71).[24] In Genesis 29:15–30:14, they read that Jacob won Laban's younger daughter Rachel as a wife by serving her father for seven years. On the wedding night, however, Laban sent in to Jacob his elder daughter Leah instead of Rachel. In the dark, Jacob had sexual intercourse with one woman, thinking she was another. Laban's reason for the bed-trick involves the Hebraic custom of marrying the elder daughter before the younger (Genesis 29:26). But Leah's conception of Reuben, Simeon, Levi, and Judah is as necessary as that of the sons begotten by Jacob on Rachel (whom he later marries) and on the maids Bilhah and Zilpah to the fulfillment of the divine promise of twelve sons and twelve tribes. In this respect, the bed-trick involving Leah plays a blessed role in Judaic providence (Jagendorf 1984, 53–54). Helena tells the Widow of Florence,

> Doubt not but heaven
> Hath brought me up to be your daughter's dower,
> As it hath fated her to be my motive
> And helper to a husband
>
> (4.4.18–21)

Certain passages in the Old Testament substantiate Helena's confidence that heaven condones bed-tricks for elect individuals. In this context, one could claim that Helena spends the "merit" of her virginity to realize divine providence in several lives: her own, Diana's, the Widow's, and Bertram's.

Playgoers aware of the relevance of the story of Leah, Rachel, and Jacob for *All's Well That Ends Well* almost certainly would have also known the story of Judah and Tamar (Genesis 38:12–26). In fact, according to the 1559 *Book of Common Prayer,* Protestants heard "Genesis xxxviii . . . read aloud each year as the First Lesson of Morning Prayer on January 21" (Simonds 1983, 433). When Judah does not give his widowed daughter-in-law Tamar (the former wife of his firstborn Er) to his surviving son Shelah as promised, Tamar disguises herself as a prostitute and sits beside the road to Timnah, where Judah encounters her. Tamar exacts from Judah his signet ring, his bracelet, and his staff as pledges that he will give her later a kid as payment for sexual intercourse with her. Tamar conceives a child from this meeting. Later, the kid cannot be delivered because the prostitute cannot be found. Three months later still, friends tell Judah that his daughter-in-law is a whore because she is pregnant. Brought out to be burned, Tamar produces Judah's signet ring, bracelet, and staff as evidence that she was the disguised prostitute and that Judah is her child's father. "Then Judah acknowledged them and said, 'She is more in the right [more righteous] than I, since I did not give her to my son Shelah.' And he did not lie with her again" (Genesis 38:26).

Tamar's disguising herself as another woman so that a man ignorantly has sexual relations with her fulfills William Bowden's definition of the bed-trick in his exhaustive survey of this Renaissance dramatic convention (1969, 12). Her sly exacting of the man's signet ring and use of it later as proof of the woman's identity, hidden during an act of "immoral" sexual intercourse, begs comparison with the similar scenario of *All's Well* (Jagendorf 1984, 54–55, 56–58; Simonds 1983, 433–34, and 1989, 55–56). Most important, the "whorish" woman is deemed righteous in her deed. In fact, Tamar gives birth to twins, "[o]ne of [whom] is Pharez or Perez, direct ancestor of both David and Christ" (Simonds 1983, 434).[25] These details gain their significance for Shakespeare's play from their proximity to the biblical bed-trick involving Leah and Jacob. Both cases encourage biblically astute playgoers and readers to think of Helena's spending her merit in the bed-trick as a positive, redemptive deed. Biblical precedent for believing that natural drives can have providential results, that bed-tricks can fulfill avoided covenants, gave Shakespeare's Catholic and Protestant playgoers and readers a common ground on which they could agree that Helena's deed possesses merit, fulfilling the earlier suggestion that "young Chairbonne the puritan and old Poisson the papist" could occasionally become one (1.3.51).

That we are inclined to think of Helena as meritorious in the last acts of the play is also the result of Paroles's role in *All's Well*. Before his adoption of a humble persona, "[s]imply the thing [he is]" (4.3.336), Paroles functions in the play as a scapegoat for major characters; his pronounced vices by comparison make their comparable flaws seem less culpable. In Second Lord's judgment, Paroles is "a most notable coward, an infinite and endless liar, an hourly promise-breaker, the owner of no one good quality . . ." (3.6.9–11). These terms basically represent Helena's opinion of Bertram's fop (1.1.102–3). Lafeu verifies Paroles's role as community scapegoat when he says: "Methink'st thou art a general offence, and every man should beat thee. I think thou wast created for men to breathe themselves upon thee" (2.3.255–57). Shakespeare thus establishes Paroles in *All's Well* as a knave of little or no merit. Calling Paroles "[a] very tainted fellow, and full of wickedness," the Countess concludes, "My son corrupts a well-derivèd nature / With his inducement" (3.2.87–89). By this logic, Bertram's eventual understanding of Paroles's vices and his casting off the rogue play a part in the reclamation of his character.

Paroles performs a similar sacrophantic role for Helena with regard to merit. Shakespeare takes pains to portray Paroles's vain pride in his own merits. "France is a dog-hole," he tells the reluctantly wed Bertram, "and it no more merits / The tread of a man's foot" (2.3.274–75). In other words, Paroles implies that unheroic France does not deserve men of merit such as supposedly Bertram and himself. Concerning the drum lost in battle, Paroles exclaims, "But that the merit of service is seldom attributed to the true and exact performer, I would have that drum or another, or *hic iacet* ['die in the attempt']" (3.6.60–62). The reasoning behind this excuse for inaction assumes that Paroles enjoys a reputation for meritorious military service. So grand is this purported reputation that he would not risk it by recapturing the drum and not getting credit for the feat. These and other dramatic passages fix Paroles as a character of little desert who boasts of his merit. In this respect, he both resembles and does not resemble Helena. She never boasts of her merit, but she does initially seem to insist upon it. She has several virtues (while he has few), and she could be said to realize her "[i]nspirèd merit" in the King's cure (while he only brags of his desert). Paroles's exaggeration of a character complex within Helena both deflects criticism from her onto him and encourages playgoers to excuse her flaws, because they seem so much less than his.

Still, in the final analysis, Shakespeare qualifies Helena's meritorious spending of her virginity in the bed-trick. Regarded from another perspective, she conforms in this deed to the literary archetype of the

Clever Wench rather than to the blessed example of Leah or Tamar.[26]
When, at the play's end, Helena explains to Bertram that she has fulfilled his riddling terms and asks, "Will you be mine, now you are doubly won?" he enthusiastically replies, "If she, my liege, can make me
know this clearly, / I'll love her dearly, ever, ever dearly" (5.3.314–16).
Bertram conditionally converts his dislike for Helena into admiring
love, a dramatic fact that begs interpretation. Earlier Helena philoso-
phized, as noted, that "The mightiest space in fortune nature brings /
To join like likes and kiss like native things." Events in the play
demonstrate the likely reality of this magnetism, although, upon further consideration, providence rather than nature could be said to constitute the dynamic's energizer. Bertram does inexplicably draw
Helena to him across France, Spain, and Italy. The reality of this mag-
netic principle disturbingly suggests that Helena and Bertram are in
some powerful respects "likes." W. Speed Hill has judged that Bertram
"treasures the model of masculine love as simultaneously self-
assertive *and* self-fulfilling. . . . Exactly the same is true of Helena, and
in this respect the pair are ideally matched" (1975, 354–55). Moreover,
both characters possess a capacity for wiliness, for deception, even
prevarication. In a moment, Bertram, understanding that Helena has
fulfilled the conditions of his enigma, admires her tough resourcefulness and talent for deception, qualities that he has displayed in the
course of *All's Well* and that he presumably admires in himself.
Bertram's feelings for Helena revolve, and he conditionally promises
to love his like "dearly, ever, ever dearly."

To the degree that playgoers have not cared for these traits in Bertram,
their presence in Helena usually troubles them. Moreover, the manner by
which Helena "spends" her virginal merit complicates their misgivings
about the morality (or integrity) of her character, if for no other reason
than the failure of some playgoers to think of Leah or Tamar in connection with the bed-trick of *All's Well.* Yet, even for playgoers unaware
of—or dismissive of—the biblical precedents, Helena's carnal substitution of herself for Diana in the bed-trick could seem blameless: "the
Count he is my husband" (3.7.8), she assures Diana. The King of France
has legitimately married Helena and Bertram in a Christian ceremony
(2.3.179–81), even though the wedding remains unfeasted (2.3.181–83)
and, more important, unconsummated. Nevertheless, Helena ambiguously portrays the bed-trick to the Widow as

> ... wicked meaning in a lawful deed,
> And lawful meaning in a wicked act,
> Where both not sin, and yet a sinful fact.
>
> (3.7.45–47)

Helena's final utterance "and yet a sinful fact" undercuts her explanation of the legality of Diana's and especially her own participation in the bed-trick. By the words "a sinful fact," Helena means "a sinful deed." The deed does seem sinful, once one realizes that Bertram, believing that he copulates in the dark with Diana, must also believe that he is a sinner.[27] He knows he is Helena's husband by Christian sacrament and that he thus willingly commits adultery. That he does so in spirit rather than in actuality does not mitigate the destructive effects within him of the knowledge of evil. Helena's willingness to let him become a sinner in this sense casts doubt upon her claims of innocence with regard to the bed-trick. Like Isabella and Vincentio in *Measure for Measure,* she apparently rests content in creating the impression that two wrongs make a right in the matter of bed-tricks.

All these troublesome details seem designed to cause playgoers to question the means by which Helena's merit earns a husband. In retrospect, this questioning deepens once one realizes that something coldly calculating attaches itself to Helena's expense of her desert. A commercial quid pro quo value materializes in Helena's proposal to pay Diana—in the form of a dowry for a future husband—for her participation in the bed-trick. We detected this value earlier, during her dialogue about the use of virginity with the fop Paroles (1.1.112–67). When Paroles coarsely tells her that maids have no defense against men determined to "blow them up" (make them pregnant), Helena asks, "Is there no military policy how virgins might blow up men?" (1.1.123–24). Aroused by the obscene connotations of Helena's phrase "blow up men" (sexually excite their phalluses), Paroles wittily goes on to argue, libertine-fashion, that "[i]t is not politic in the commonwealth of nature to preserve virginity" (1.1.128–29). He commodifies virginity when he jokes, "Within ten year it will make itself two, which is a goodly increase, and the principal itself not much worse" (1.1.149–51). Perceived and judged retrospectively through the lens of this commercializing of virginity, Helena's bartering with Diana and her mother to accomplish the bed-trick suffers, partly because Paroles originally proposed this valuation. Paroles's argument apparently sways Helena. "How might one do, sir, to lose it to her own liking?" (1.1.152–53), she suddenly asks. By the word "liking," she means not simply "advantage" but "pleasure" as well. Sensing a conversion, Paroles jestingly continues in the commercial vein: "'Tis a commodity will lose the gloss with lying; the longer kept, the less worth. Off with't while 'tis vendible" (1.1.155–57). And when he finally asks, "Will you anything with it?" (1.1.165–66), the final word in Helena's four-word reply is a bit chilling: "Not my virginity yet—" (1.1.167).

Helena's "yet" speaks volumes (Godshalk 1974, 63). Even before she formulates her project to cure the King as a way of compelling marriage to Bertram, long before his riddling conditions and her scheme of the bed-trick, Helena commodifies the virginity that she might one day sell to buy herself a husband. David Scott Kastan concludes that in *All's Well*, "what should be freely given must be bought" (1985, 585). Since this commercialized virginity later becomes equated with her merit, one concludes that it participates in a materialistic value system rather than a spiritual one. In other words, her merit comes to have the stereotypical worth that early modern Protestants claimed Catholic indulgences had when they "bought" salvation for the purchaser. This awareness colors playgoers' admiration for the tenacious Helena and the stratagems by which she wins Bertram and "saves" him through the consummation of holy marriage. Reconsidered from another perspective, the bed-trick of *All's Well That Ends Well* gave Shakespeare's playgoers reason to maintain a religious severing of heart that plagued their own and their fathers' generations. That simply is to say that, more so than any other Shakespeare play, *All's Well* most fully represents his age's problemizing of merit. Shakespeare, in this dark Jacobean comedy, gave Protestants and recusants in his audience a basis upon which they could agree concerning Helena's expense of merit, yet he also appears to undermine the common ground. In this respect, he deviates from a dramatic method that implicitly worked to reconcile Catholics with Protestants in *Henry V* (Hunt 1998). With *Hamlet* (as described by Stephen Greenblatt) and with *All's Well*, Shakespeare seems to remain content, in matters of Catholic and Protestant doctrine—to use Greenblatt's words—with creating the final impression of "a deliberate forcing together of radically incompatible accounts" (2001, 240).[28]

Notes

An earlier form of this essay was published in *Religion and the Arts* 7.1/2 (2003).

1. All quotations of Shakespeare plays other than *All's Well That Ends Well* are taken from Shakespeare, *The Riverside Shakespeare*, ed. Evans et al. (1997); those of *All's Well* come from the Oxford Shakespeare text, ed. Snyder (1993). My only departure from the Oxford text is substitution of the name "Helena" for "Helen," which Snyder adopts throughout her edition. Her argument for this latter name is most fully provided in her article "Naming Names in *All's Well That Ends Well*," 271–72. I have revised Snyder's "Helen" to "Helena" simply because that is the heroine's familiar name throughout literary history.

2. Hooker, in a major 1586 sermon, characterizes this aspect of Catholic belief thus: "as the body may be more and more warm, so the soul more and more justified, according as grace shall be augmented; the augmentation whereof is merited by good works, as good works are made meritorious by it" (1954, 1:14–75, esp. 18–19).

3. Lewalski gives a short excellent account of the terms of the Pauline paradigm of salvation—election, calling, justification, adoption, sanctification, glorification (16–27). Reformation Protestants believed that the righteousness of Christ's merit was imputed to them, whereas Catholics thought that it was infused into them, making them capable of the meritorious works repairing and augmenting saving grace (Hooker 1954, 1:18–21).

4. From *The Riverside Milton* 424–25. Not surprisingly, Milton's Satan personifies blasphemy by sitting "High on a Throne of Royal State," "by merit rais'd / To that bad eminence" (*Paradise Lost* 2.1, 5–6).

5. In Luther's opinion, "good works, whether done within or outside the state of grace, never *contribute* to one's salvation" (my italics, Ozment 1980, 236). Berthold (1975) nicely demonstrates that in *Paradise Lost,* Satan's, Adam's, and Eve's concept of earned merit is a symptom—in fact, a consequence—of Original Sin.

6. This implicit satire in *Love's Labor's Lost* concerning salvation by merit is consistent with that entailed in Falstaff's characterization of the thief Gadshill: "O, if men were to be sav'd by merit, what hole in hell were hot enough for him?" (Shakespeare, *1 Henry IV* 1.2.107–8).

7. Shakespeare anticipates the implicit criticism of merit in Othello in *The Merchant of Venice.* In the earlier play, the inscription of the silver casket— "'Who chooseth me shall get as much as he deserves'" (2.9.36)—deceives the Prince of Arragon, who concludes,

> And well said too; for who shall go about
> To cozen fortune, and be honorable
> Without the stamp of merit? Let none presume
> To wear an undeserved dignity
>
> (2.9.37–40)

Assuming "desert" (merit) (2.9.51), Arragon finds, however, his reflection inside the chest in "the portrait of a blinking idiot" (2.9.54). "[U]se every man after his desert, and who shall scape whipping?" Hamlet will say (2.2.529–30). Significantly, Bassanio does not mention personal merit or assume desert of any kind when he hazards the fulfillment of marriage—companionate love and children—by choosing one of the three caskets. In the spirit of Reformation Protestantism, Bassanio places his "faith in a hidden treasure [that contained in the lead casket], and [so] merits [secular] salvation" (Stetner 1995). In *The Merchant,* the most authentic love—such as Portia's for Bassanio—is neither asked for nor given based on desert—either the lover's or beloved's (3.2.149–65). The foil to these preferred views is provided by Jessica, who says,

> It is very meet
> The Lord Bassanio live an upright life,
> For having such a blessing in his lady,
> He finds the joys of heaven here on earth,
> And if on earth he do not merit it,
> In reason he should never come to heaven!
>
> (3.5.73–78)

This is the same Jessica who, as Jewess, erroneously believes that her "meritorious" work of marrying the Christian Lorenzo ensures her salvation (3.5.19–20). I am indebted to my former Baylor graduate student Sam Joeckel for reminding me of Shakespeare's interrogation of merit in *The Merchant.*

8. Contemporary physiological and cultural reasons for fixing bloodworth in an inalterable hierarchy of value, from the blood of the peasant to that of the aristocrat, are described by Berkeley and Keesee (1991).

9. For the depth and breadth of the Protestantism of *All's Well,* see Palmer (1989).

10. But cf. Rossiter, who claims that the Clown's speech about the narrow and broad gates amounts to a "profane biblical allusion, delivered with a derisory parsonical smugness" (1961, 103). Other Calvinist elements in *All's Well* include the concept of irresistible grace—the idea that an elect Protestant cannot resist or refuse the grace God would confer on him or her. Commentators on the play such as Lewis (1990, 148–49) and Young (1992, 178) interpret Bertram's resistance to marrying Helena, and his final acceptance of it, in these theological terms.

11. For documentation of this Protestant belief see Thomas (1971, 80, 107–8, 124–25, 128, 203, 256, 479, 485, 490, 577–78, 643) and Hillerbrand (1996, 3:64–65). Samuel Harsnett's *A Declaration of Egregious Popish Impostures* (1603), a text informing Edgar's bogus miracle in act 4, scene 4, of Shakespeare's *King Lear,* amounts to a contemporary endorsement of the Protestant position concerning ceased miracles.

12. An exhaustive listing of the Roman Catholic elements of *All's Well* appears in Beauregard (1999, 221).

13. The commentator on the play who most closely approaches my topic in this essay is Beauregard. Arguing that Shakespeare "was well versed in theology and that a Roman Catholic—and not a Reformed—theology of grace informs the dialogue and action of *All's Well That Ends Well,*" Beauregard claims that "[b]asic to both halves of the play is the Catholic notion of merit, of reward given for virtuous behavior, which is dramatically rendered by the heroine's being twice rewarded for accomplishing two impossible tasks, first through divine grace and then through human effort" (1999, 220). I claim, however, that Shakespeare renders problematical the power of merit in *All's Well* by introducing both Protestant *and* Catholic contexts for understanding and evaluating merit, thus reprising a contemporary denominational debate over the efficacy and place of this essence. Beauregard basically perceives no conflict entailed in the representation of merit in the play, but instead argues for Shakespeare's sustained portrayal of Catholic conceptions of this quality. Richly textured and documented, Beauregard's essay should be read in conjunction with mine.

14. Cole judges that Helena regularly uses claims about heavenly sanction and providence to rationalize her own ambitious words and deeds (1981, 117–36). In his opinion, "the holy maid plays too nicely with her gospel" (122).

15. According to Bradbrook, a crux in the play involves "the social problem of high birth versus native merit" (1950, 290). In connection with this idea, she cites a series of Shakespeare sonnets, including Sonnet 26. Addressed to the Young Man, this poem's opening lines read: "Lord of my love, to whom in vassalage / Thy merit hath my duty strongly knit" (26.1–2). This phrasing and diction encourage the reader initially to think of Christ as well as the Young Man, thus ironically qualifying the notion that the Young Man possesses a native merit.

16. Greenblatt brilliantly demonstrates that a multitude of details in *Hamlet,* particularly those pertaining to the characterization of the Ghost, provoke virtually simultaneous Protestant and Catholic readings (2001, 235–49). For this commentator, Shakespeare gave fictive possibility to ongoing denominational controversies over doctrine in representations that caused playgoers to become more aware of their irreconcilability. The playwright's method thus

reinforced what Greenblatt calls "a fifty-year effect" involving the time at the very end of the sixteenth century and beginning of the seventeenth, a time "in the wake of the great, charismatic ideological struggle in which the revolutionary generation that made the decisive break with the [Catholic] past is all dying out and the survivors hear only hypocrisy in [Protestant] sermons and look back with longing at the [Catholic] world they have lost" (248).

17. For Helena's ambitious love, see Leech (1954, 19, 27). That Shakespeare may have regarded such ambitious love a fault, we have the testimony of Miranda in *The Tempest*. Prospero slows the breakneck pace of Miranda's passion for Ferdinand through his calculated devaluation of him. After reasoning that Ferdinand in Milan would appear a Caliban compared to most men there, Miranda says, "My affections / Are then most humble; I have no ambition / To see a goodlier man" (1.2.482–84).

18. The serious association of Helena with Mary the Intercessor in 3.4.25–29 was originally made by Robert Grams Hunter: "The Arden editor [G. K. Hunter] believes that 'a straightforward reference to the Virgin as intercessor is too Popish to be probable,' but a more 'Popish' activity than a barefoot pilgrimage to Santiago da Compostella is difficult to imagine, and yet Helena has just left on such an errand when these lines are spoken of her. Shakespeare evokes the Virgin here because Helena's function in the play is similar to that of the Mother of God in the 'Popish' scheme of things. Both serve as the means through which the grace of God can be communicated to man" (1965, 129–30). Also see McCandless (1994, 456). The most recent citing of the association of Helena with the Intercessor Mary is Beauregard's (1999, 221, 232–33). Dennis believes that, rather than Mary, Helena at this moment figuratively presents "the Divine Intercessor for all men, Christ" (1971, 82).

19. Shakespeare takes pains to confirm the details of Helena's and the rector's letters to Bertram. Second Lord asks, "Hath the Count all this intelligence?" and First Lord replies, "Ay, and the particular confirmations, point from point, to the full arming of the verity" (4.3.60–62).

20. Critics divide themselves into two camps over the question of the reality of Helena's pilgrimage to the Spanish shrine of St. Jacques in Compostela. Among those commentators believing that Helena planned from the beginning to hunt down Bertram in Italy may be listed Evans (1967, 151–57) and Levin (1980, 137–39). Those convinced, to some degree, of the sincerity of Helena's journey—the larger group—include Calderwood (1964, 282), Maxwell (1969, 191), Smallwood (1972, 53), and Gross (1983, 266).

21. I would argue that this phenomenon in *All's Well* is a providential rather than natural dynamic, in retrospect contributing to a heavenly design in Helena's and Bertram's lives.

22. In this reading, Helena's fabrication of her "death" with the rector's aid amounts to insurance that Bertram will return to Roussillon. In this sense, one could say it is more admirable than blameworthy. Admittedly, one could argue that Helena reports her "death" in order to get Bertram to value her in his imagination more highly once he believes she is lost forever. This is the dynamic of revaluation defined by Friar Francis in *Much Ado About Nothing* and proposed there as a way to get Claudio to convert his hatred for Hero into love for her (*Much Ado,* 4.1.200–236). Significantly, we never see evidence of such a revaluation in Bertram once he learns of the report of Helena's death. Her motive more likely resembles that described at the beginning of this note.

23. Answering this question is not at all difficult in Shakespeare's probable source of the *All's Well* story: that of Giletta of Narbonne as it appears in novel 38 of William Painter's *The Palace of Pleasure* (1575). "[L]oath [that] the Count for her sake should dwell in perpetual exile . . . [Giletta] determined to spend the rest of her time in pilgrimages and for preservation of her soul. . . . Wherefore, commending [the people] all unto God, she took her way with her maid and one of her kinsmen, in the habit of a pilgrim, well furnished with silver and precious jewels, telling no man whither she went, and never rested till she came to Florence" (Snyder in Shakespeare, *All's Well That Ends Well* 1998, 228). Giletta's "pilgrimage" is unambiguously a crass ploy to get her to Florence and Bertram as fast as possible; she never mentions any shrine in any country as her "penitential" goal.

24. Both Bruce and Daniell emphasize that the availability of the Great Bible (implicitly recognized by Mary Tudor) and the secretly imported Douai-Rheims Bible meant that an indeterminate but probably sizable number of English Catholics read the Bible in English during the sixteenth century.

25. Simonds claims the bed-trick "is a basic device in the cultural tradition of Western civilization to provide for the conception of a divine child who *must be born* into the world of man" (1983, 433). For a discussion of Shakespeare's more immediate sources for the bed-trick, see Briggs (1994).

26. For Helena as the Clever Wench, see Shakespeare, ed. Hunter (1959, xxxvi) and Neely (1985, 78).

27. In McCandless's rather extreme opinion, the bed-trick is "an act of prostitution, in which Helena services Bertram's lust and submits to humiliating 'use,' and a type of rape, in which Helena coerces Bertram into having sex with her against his will" (1994, 450). In this vein, also see Adelman (1992, 78).

28. See note 16 for speculation concerning a reason for this change in strategy.

WORKS CITED

Adelman, Janet. *Suffocating Mothers: Fantasies of Maternal Origin in Shakespeare's Plays,* Hamlet *to* The Tempest. London: Routledge, 1992.

Barton, Anne. Introduction to *All's Well That Ends Well.* In *The Riverside Shakespeare,* ed. G. Blakemore Evans et al. 533–37. Boston: Houghton Mifflin, 1997.

Beauregard, David N. "'Inspirèd Merit': Shakespeare's Theology of Grace in *All's Well That Ends Well.*" *Renascence* 51 (1999): 219–39.

Berkeley, David, and Donald Keesee. "Bertram's Blood-Consciousness in *All's Well That Ends Well.*" *Studies in English Literature* 31 (1991): 247–58.

Berthold, Dennis. "The Concept of Merit in *Paradise Lost.*" *Studies in English Literature* 15 (1975): 153–67.

Bicknell, E. J. *A Theological Introduction to the Thirty-Nine Articles of the Church of England.* London: Longmans, Green, 1947.

Bowden, William R. "The Bed Trick, 1603–1642: Its Mechanics, Ethics, and Effects." *Shakespeare Studies* 5 (1969): 12–23.

Bradbrook, M. C. "Virtue Is the True Nobility: A Study of the Structure of *All's Well That Ends Well.*" *The Review of English Studies* 1 (1950): 289–301.

Briggs, Julia. "Shakespeare's Bed-Tricks." *Essays in Criticism* 44 (1994): 293–314.

Bruce, F. F. *The English Bible: A History of Translations from the Earliest English Versions to the New English Bible.* New York: Oxford University Press, 1961.

Calderwood, James L. "Styles of Knowing in *All's Well.*" *Modern Language Quarterly* 25 (1964): 272–94.

Charlton, H. B. "The Date of *Love's Labour's Lost.*" *Modern Language Review* 13 (1918): 257–66, 387–400.

Cole, Howard C. *The "All's Well" Story from Boccaccio to Shakespeare.* Urbana, Ill.: University of Illinois Press, 1981.

Daniell, David. "Reading the Bible." In *A Companion to Shakespeare,* ed. David Scott Kastan. 158–71. Oxford, England: Blackwell, 1999.

Dennis, Carl. "*All's Well That Ends Well* and the Meaning of Agape." *Philological Quarterly* 50 (1971): 75–84.

Evans, Bertrand. *Shakespeare's Comedies*. Oxford, England: Oxford University Press, 1967.

Godshalk, William L. "*All's Well That Ends Well* and the Morality Play." *Shakespeare Quarterly* 25 (1974): 61–70.

Greenblatt, Stephen. *Hamlet in Purgatory*. Princeton, N.J.: Princeton University Press, 2001.

Gross, Gerald. "The Conclusion of *All's Well That Ends Well*." *Studies in English Literature* 23 (1983): 257–76.

Harsnett, Samuel. *A Declaration of Egregious Popish Impostures*. London, 1603.

Hill, Christopher. "Protestantism and the Rise of Capitalism." In *Change and Continuity in Seventeenth-Century England*. 81–103. Cambridge, England: Cambridge University Press, 1975.

Hill, W. Speed. "Marriage as Destiny: An Essay on *All's Well That Ends Well*." *English Literary Renaissance* 5 (1975): 344–59.

Hillerbrand, Hans J., ed. *The Oxford Encyclopedia of the Reformation*. Vol. 3. New York: Oxford University Press, 1996.

Hooker, Richard. *Of the Laws of Ecclesiastical Polity*. London: Dent, 1954.

Hughes, Merritt Y. "Merit in *Paradise Lost*." *The Huntington Library Quarterly* 31 (1967–68): 3–18.

Hunt, Maurice. "Predestination and the Heresy of Merit in *Othello*." *Comparative Drama* 30 (1996): 346–76.

———. "The Double Figure of Elizabeth in *Love's Labor's Lost*." *Essays in Literature* 19 (1992): 173–92.

———. "The Hybrid Reformations of Shakespeare's Second Henriad." *Comparative Drama* 32 (1998): 176–206.

Hunter, Robert Grams. *Shakespeare and the Comedy of Forgiveness*. New York: Columbia University Press, 1965.

Jagendorf, Zvi. "'In the Morning, Behold, It was Leah': Genesis and the Reversal of Sexual Knowledge." In *Biblical Patterns in Literature*, ed. David H. Hirsch and Nehama Aschkenasy. Brown Judaic Studies 77. 51–60. Chico, Calif.: Scholars Press, 1984.

Kastan, David Scott. "*All's Well That Ends Well* and the Limits of Comedy." *ELH* 52 (1985): 575–89.

Knight, G. Wilson. *The Sovereign Flower: Shakespeare as the Poet of Royalism.* New York: Macmillan, 1958.

Langer, Ullrich. "Merit in Courtly Literature: Castiglione, Rabelais, Marguerite de Navarre, and Le Caron." *Renaissance Quarterly* 41 (1988): 218–41.

Leech, Clifford. "The Theme of Ambition in *All's Well That Ends Well.*" *ELH* 21 (1954): 17–29.

Levin, Richard A. "*All's Well That Ends Well* and 'All Seems Well.'" *Shakespeare Studies* 13 (1980): 131–44.

Lewalski, Barbara K. *Protestant Poetics and the Seventeenth-Century Religious Lyric.* Princeton, N.J.: Princeton University Press, 1979.

Lewis, Cynthia. "'Derived Honesty and Achieved Goodness': Doctrines of Grace in *All's Well That Ends Well.*" *Renaissance and Reformation* 14.2 (1990): 147–70.

Maxwell, J. C. "Helena's Pilgrimage." *The Review of English Studies* 20 (1969): 189–92.

McCandless, David. "Helena's Bed-Trick: Gender and Performance in *All's Well That Ends Well.*" *Shakespeare Quarterly* 45 (1994): 449–68.

Milton, John. *The Riverside Milton.* Ed. Roy Flannagan. Boston, Mass.: Houghton Mifflin, 1998.

Neely, Carol Thomas. *Broken Nuptials in Shakespeare's Plays.* New Haven, Conn.: Yale University Press, 1985.

Ozment, Steven. *The Age of Reform 1250–1550: An Intellectual and Religious History of Late Medieval and Reformation Europe.* New Haven, Conn.: Yale University Press, 1980.

Palmer, David J. "Comedy and the Protestant Spirit in Shakespeare's *All's Well That Ends Well.*" *Bulletin of the John Rylands University Library of Manchester* 71 (1989): 97–107.

Parker, Patricia. "*All's Well That Ends Well: Increase and Multiply.*" In *Creative Imitation: New Essays on Renaissance Literature in Honor of Thomas N. Greene,* ed. David Quint et al. MRTS 95. 355–90. Binghamton, N.Y.: Medieval and Renaissance Texts and Studies, 1992.

Perkins, William. *The Whole Treatise of the Cases of Conscience.* London: J. Legatt, 1642.

Rossiter, A. P. *Angel with Horns and Other Shakespeare Lectures.* Ed. Graham Storey. New York: Theatre Arts Books, 1961.

Sexton, Joyce H. "'Rooted Love': Metaphors for Baptism in *All's Well That Ends Well.*" *Christianity and Literature* 43 (1994): 261–87.

Shakespeare, William. *All's Well That Ends Well.* Ed. Jonas A. Barish. Baltimore, Md.: Penguin, 1964.

———. *All's Well That Ends Well.* Ed. G. K. Hunter. The Arden Shakespeare. Cambridge, Mass.: Harvard University Press, 1959.

———. *All's Well That Ends Well.* Ed. Susan Snyder. The Oxford Shakespeare. 1993. Oxford, England: Oxford University Press, 1998.

———. *The Complete Works of Shakespeare.* Ed. David Bevington. New York: Longman, 1997.

———. *Love's Labor's Lost.* Ed. Richard David. The Arden Shakespeare. London: Methuen, 1956.

———. *The Norton Shakespeare.* Ed. Stephen Greenblatt. New York: Norton, 1997.

———. *The Riverside Shakespeare.* Ed. G. Blakemore Evans et al. Boston: Houghton Mifflin, 1997.

Simonds, Peggy Muñoz. "Overlooked Sources of the Bed Trick." *Shakespeare Quarterly* 34 (1983): 433–34.

———. "Sacred and Sexual Motifs in *All's Well That Ends Well.*" *Renaissance Quarterly* 42 (1989): 33–59.

Smallwood, R. L. "The Design of *All's Well That Ends Well.*" *Shakespeare Survey* 25 (1972): 45–61.

Snyder, Susan. "Naming Names in *All's Well That Ends Well.*" *Shakespeare Quarterly* 43 (1992): 265–79.

Stetner, Clifford. "The Protestant Reformation According to Launcelot Gobbo." Unpublished essay, 1995.

Taylor, Thomas. *Works.* London: J. Bartlet, 1653.

Thomas, Keith. *Religion and the Decline of Magic.* New York: Charles Scribner's Sons, 1971.

Tillyard, E. M. W. *Shakespeare's Problem Plays.* Toronto: University of Toronto Press, 1968.

Tricomi, Albert. "The Witty Idealization of the French Court in *Love's Labor's Lost.*" *Shakespeare Studies* 12 (1979): 25–33.

Wallace, Dewey D. *Puritans and Predestination: Grace in English Protestant Theology, 1525–1695.* Chapel Hill, N.C.: University of North Carolina Press, 1982.

Watson, Robert N. "Reforming the Morality Play: How *Othello* Demonizes Catholicism." Paper presented at the Shakespeare Association of America Annual Meeting, Chicago, Ill., March 23, 1995.

Wheeler, Richard P. *Shakespeare's Development and the Problem Comedies: Turn and Counter-Turn.* Berkeley, Calif.: University of California Press, 1981.

Young, Bruce W. "Ritual as an Instrument of Grace: Parental Blessings in *Richard III, All's Well That Ends Well,* and *The Winter's Tale.*" In *True Rites and Maimed Rites: Ritual and Anti-Ritual in Shakespeare and His Age.* Ed. Linda Woodbridge and Edward Berry. 169–200. Urbana, Ill.: University of Illinois Press, 1992.

14

Paris Is Worth a Mass:
All's Well That Ends Well
and the Wars of Religion

by *Lisa Hopkins*
Sheffield Hallam University, Sheffield, England

TWO OF THE THREE PLAYS that we now know as Shakespeare's problem plays are clearly focused on the present. *Measure for Measure,* with its portrayal of a shy, publicity-avoiding ruler who wishes to suppress brothels, is obviously a reflection on James VI and I; *Troilus and Cressida,* with its emphasis on the cult of chivalry, has been just as insistently read as a reflection on the Earl of Essex (Mallin 1995). By contrast, *All's Well That Ends Well* looks consistently to the past; but, I shall argue, it does so only in order to make a suggestion about the future. Indeed, its very title suggests a teleological and future-oriented perspective, and this proves to be abundantly borne out by the events of the play.

Despite its eschatologically oriented title, *All's Well That Ends Well* is a play whose focus initially appears to be firmly on what has already happened. There is, for instance, much talk of the dead in the opening scene of *All's Well,* with both Helena's and Bertram's late father discussed. There is the classical pull of the names of Diana and Helena, with the latter seeming particularly pointed both because it is an invention of Shakespeare's, since the equivalent character was called Gileta in the source, and also because it is made explicit in the Clown's song:

> "Was this fair face the cause," quoth she,
>   "Why the Grecians sackèd Troy?
> Fond done, done fond,
>   Was this King Priam's joy?"
>
> (1.3.68–72)

Moreover, the Clown here parodies not only the Troy story, but one of its most famous popularizers in England, Marlowe, whose *Dido, Queen of Carthage* had in effect brought a significant part of the *Aeneid* to the English stage; and Marlowe is remembered again in the play in the phrase "Bajazeth's mule" (at 4.1.41). Since Marlowe had died in 1593, reference to him seems deliberately intended to be antiquizing, as in *Hamlet* where *Dido, Queen of Carthage* is evoked as representing a long-lost dramaturgical style. Furthermore, these two ideas of the death of fathers and the recall of the past map onto one another, since so much of the impact of the Troy story in the Renaissance is precisely to do with a sense simultaneously of ancestry and loss.

There are also other gesturings to the past in *All's Well That Ends Well*. Some are classical, such as the clear parallel with *Venus and Adonis* (Simpson 1994, 179), but others seem to belong rather to the realm of fairytale, such as the fact of there being no heir to the kingdom. Most especially, there is a clear reference to the motif of the Fisher King, evoked by the nature of the King's wound: as Richard Levin points out, in the description of the fistula the language "is suggestive of some kind of lower body dysfunction; the circumlocution used to refer to the disease suggests that it is an embarrassment" (Levin 1997, 25–26). The specifically sexual nature of the King's dysfunction is also made clear elsewhere. It is hinted at in the opening negotiation between the King and Helena:

> KING: Upon thy certainty and confidence
> What darest thou venture?
> HELENA: Tax of impudence,
> A strumpet's boldness, a divulgèd shame;
> Traduced by odious ballads my maiden's name. (2.1.169–72)

What does his health have to do with her sexuality? Obviously, the two are linked on some deeper level, in a way more reminiscent of the leaps and hidden connections of myth than of logical thought. That more is at stake than meets the eye becomes even more obvious when the King abruptly ups the ante: "Sweet practiser, thy physic I will try, / That ministers thine own death if I die" (2.1.185–86). To this Helena docilely agrees, "Not helping, death's my fee" (2.1.189), and spiritual welfare is equally obviously at stake when the King makes his promise, "by my sceptre and my hopes of heaven" (2.1.192). This emphasis on the spiritual does not mean, though, that we lose sight of the sexual dimension, which is clearly present in the following exchange:

> KING: Thou knowest she has raised me from my sickly bed.
> BERTRAM: But follows it, my lord, to bring me down
> Must answer for your raising? (2.3.110–12)

Most particularly, the sexual dimension is apparent in Lafew's remark that

> I have seen a medicine
> That's able to breathe life into a stone,
> Quicken a rock, and make you dance canary
> With sprightly fire and motion; whose simple touch
> Is powerful to araise King Pippen, nay,
> To give great Charlemain a pen in's hand
> And write to her a love-line.
>
> (2.1.72–78)

Lafew's words offer a heady mingling of the sexual with the thaumaturgical, framed within the suggestively part-mythical, part-historical framework of Charlemagne and Pepin, both figures almost equally aligned with legend and with history. The mention of Charlemagne and Pepin, moreover, introduces a further motif, that of the play's Frenchness, and in particular its connections with French royalty—an idea also evoked in Lafew's insistence that "Why, your dolphin is not lustier" (2.3.25), with its clear allusion to the dauphin as well as to sexual prowess. I argue that this persistent emphasis on Frenchness, and above all on figures from France's past, proves crucial for *All's Well That Ends Well*'s blending of both the mechanisms and effects of fairytale, classical, and indeed Christian elements.

The reason why this blending of past and present in a French context lies at the heart of the play seems to me to be because the ideological heart of the play is in a recent past whose troubles, I argue, it thinks it can transcend by reference to a past still further back, in ways that will allow hope for the future. Thus, the King's greeting to Bertram, "Welcome to Paris" (1.2.22), not only inaugurates a complex series of allusions in which Bertram will actually *be* Paris, choosing between the resonantly named Diana and Helena, but also announces a geographical location. Moreover, though a classical model may be so strongly invoked, we are never allowed to forget the Frenchness of the setting either: the motif of a doctor's daughter and a sexually wounded king so closely recalls the marriage between Catherine de' Medici (whose name meant literally "of the doctors") and Henri II, unable to produce offspring for the first ten years of their marriage; and the sly link between the King's fistula and "The fundamental reason of this war," which "hath much blood let forth" (3.1.2–3), pokes fun at the French wars of religion and their complex interrelationships with questions of marriage and procreation. (The St. Bartholomew's Day Massacre directly followed the wedding of Henri of Navarre and Marguerite of France, daughter of Catherine de' Medici, and the entire question was made increasingly more urgent by the successive failures of Charles IX and Henri III, Catherine's sons, to beget legitimate heirs to the crown.)

As the pun implicit in "Paris" reminds us, however, an emphasis on France does not automatically disable the possibility of a classicizing perspective on events. The *Iliad* was part of the cultural background of the French as well as of the English: "[i]n the great festival held at Fontainebleau in 1564, there was a tourney in which the opposing sides fought in the dress of Greeks and Trojans" (Girouard 1983, 221), and Jean de Warrin's 1471 *History of England* shows Brutus camping on the Loire en route to England (Collins 1988, 103), whereas Shakespeare would have encountered in Geoffrey of Monmouth the claim that the city of Tours derived its name from Brutus's nephew Turnus (Monmouth 1966, 71). Most directly, the French claimed descent from Francus, son of Priam (James 1997, 15), which sparked something of a struggle for the position of true heir of Troy: "[w]hen Wace translated the legend into French and the history of Brittany, he prompted Layamon to wrest it back into the English language and culture, and the skirmishes among emergent nations increased the legend's currency and prestige" (James, 15). The differences between France and England, then, can be elided if both are viewed in terms of this common cultural heritage, just as the absence of an obvious same-religion heir to either crown provided a further link between the two countries; and indeed with *All's Well That Ends Well*, where there is no mention of who will be the King's heir.

For once, Shakespeare's representation of his setting should therefore be treated as reliable in *All's Well That Ends Well*: the ideological center of this play is in France and, above all, the France of the Wars of Religion, but also a France seen as fundamentally constituted by its profound awareness of its classical heritage. Shakespeare himself lodged with a family of Huguenot refugees, the Mountjoys, and would have been well aware of the religious turmoil across the Channel, while his allusion to Marlowe could also have brought memories of another of his great predecessor's plays, *The Massacre at Paris*. A dominant participant in these wars had been Queen Catherine de' Medici, and *All's Well That Ends Well* certainly seems to remember this, for there are many analogues in the play with the history of the Medicis: the King's sexual dysfunction, echoing that of Henri II, who eventually had to undergo an operation in order to enable him to father children (Lejeune 1989, 188), is the most obvious of these; but there are also the King's observations that

> We here receive it
> A certainty, vouched from our cousin Austria,
> With caution that the Florentine will move us
> For speedy aid.
>
> (1.2.4–7)

and his exhortation:

> Let higher Italy—
> Those bated that inherit but the fall
> Of the last monarchy—see that you come
> Not to woo honour, but to wed it.
>
> (2.1.12–15)

Both these reflect the geographical possessions and history of the Medici and their important historic alliances and intermarriages with the house of Austria, such as that between Francesco I de' Medici (1541–87) and Joanna of Austria, and Cosimo II de' Medici (1590–1620) and Maria Maddalena, sister of Ferdinand II. The explicit references to the King's cousinage with Florence are reinforced by the Duke's remark,

> Therefore we marvel much our cousin France
> Would in so just a business shut his bosom
> Against our borrowing prayers.
>
> (3.1.7–9)

This indicates an unusually precise geographical awareness for Shakespeare, and there even seems to be some attempt at suggesting local color in the Widow's comment, "That is Antonio, the Duke's eldest son; / That Escalus" (3.5.75–76). Moreover, Catherine de' Medici's mother had been called Madeleine, the name that is, uniquely in Shakespeare, conferred on Lafew's daughter.

As well as the comments about wars in Italy, however, *All's Well That Ends Well* also contains much evidence of the strife and paranoia produced by religious uncertainty in general, such as the following exchange:

> LAFEW: Your lord and master did well to make his recantation.
> PAROLLES: Recantation! My lord! My master!
> LAFEW: Ay. Is it not a language I speak?
> PAROLLES: A most harsh one, and not to be understood without bloody succeeding. (2.3.185–90)

Other elements of the play point more specifically to religious strife in general, and to religious strife in France in particular. The name Diana strongly suggests that of Diane de Poitiers, the mistress of Henri II, Catherine de' Medici's husband, and the allusion is sharply underlined by Bertram's otherwise inexplicable remark that "They told me that your name was Fontybell" (4.2.1) with its strong suggestion of Fontainebleau. This gathers further force if it is read together with Bertram's subsequent allusion to Diana as a goddess (IV.ii.3), and its evocation of the Diana iconography so often associated with Diane de Poitiers. Thus, in an atmosphere of the French rulers King Pippin and Charlemagne having their sexual potency restored, Diane/Diana and a Medici woman/daughter of a doctor are presented as the two possible partners of the same man. The French court and its religious troubles are also suggested by the name of Captain Dumaine, which echoes that of the Duc de Mayenne, younger brother of the Duc de Guise, and the fact that his brother has to be enquired after separately (4.3.274–75); in a time of religious and civil strife it cannot be taken for granted that brothers are similar, or will be following similar trajectories.

However, listing these parallels by no means exhausts the referential scope of *All's Well,* and some of the allusions deployed in the play are much less specific. There are many generally Christian trappings, and though some are suggestive of religious strife, others are much more neutral, and indeed are generally indicative of the commonalty of culture in Christendom rather than of any divisions within it, rather as the evocation of a classical background allows France and England to seem related. David Haley, for instance, argues that Bertram is "conceived . . . partly in the image of the biblical Ahab" and that more generally

> in *All's Well* Shakespeare has imitated the biblical parody frequent in the *Decameron*. Lavatch, the Clown, quotes Scripture more often than any Shakespearean character besides Falstaff, and Parolles, whose name may play upon the French for Holy Scripture (*la Parole de Dieu*), makes a self-revealing allusion to Balaam. Helena is at one point compared with the Lady Wisdom in Proverbs. (Haley 1995, 8, 10)

There is much evidence of popular piety and knowledge of scripture in the play, as when the Clown says, "I am no great Nabuchadnezzar, sir, I have not much skill in grass" (4.5.19–10), or when he says that his answer is as fit "as a pancake for Shrove Tuesday, a morris for Mayday, as the nail to his hole, the cuckold to his horn, as a scolding quean to a wrangling knave, as the nun's lip to the friar's mouth" (2.2.22–26). "Fitness," the keynote here, and the emphasis on food, ritual, and celebration all serve to stress what religious observance adds to life in the early modern period, rather than what religious strife takes from it.

Indeed an emphasis on a Christian perspective in *All's Well That Ends Well* allows even death to seem unthreatening in this play in which we hear so much of it. The language of the play often takes eschatological perspectives for granted—indeed Joyce H. Sexton asks, "If this, and all comedies, should end 'well,' can we expect a traditionally happy ending when 'ending well'—under an alternate definition of the term—necessitates death?" (Sexton 1994, 262). The Clown says the Countess is not well because, "One, that she's not in heaven, whither God send her quickly! The other, that she's in earth, from whence God send her quickly!" (2.4.10–12); and Parolles alleges of Dumaine that "Sir, for a cardecue he will see the fee-simple of his salvation, the inheritance of it, and cut th'entail from all remainders, and a perpetual succession for it perpetually" (4.3.270–73).

In fact, the spiritual viewpoint seems virtually reflex in this society. There are several instances of people referring to things spiritual when they are not explicitly relevant, as when the King warns Bertram, "As thou lovest her / Thy love's to me religious; else, does err" (2.3.181–82). Lafew, speaking of Parolles, says, "I have then sinned against his experience and transgressed against his valour, and my state

that way is dangerous, since I cannot yet find it in my heart to repent"
(2.5.9–11); and the following exchange ensues:

> BERTRAM: It may be you have mistaken him, my lord.
> LAFEW: And shall do ever, though I took him at's prayers. (2.5.40–42)

There is nothing in "mistaken" to suggest the idea of prayers; nevertheless, it is to them that Lafew's mind leaps.

Even war is looked at in spiritual terms. First Lord assures the Duke
of Florence,

> Holy seems the quarrel
> Upon your grace's part, black and fearful
> On the opposer.
>
> (3.1.4–6)

And the Countess is even able to elevate a spiritual perspective above
her maternal one:

> What angel shall
> Bless this unworthy husband? He cannot thrive,
> Unless her prayers, whom heaven delights to hear
> And loves to grant, reprieve him from the wrath
> Of greatest justice.
>
> (3.4.25–29)

Equally, Bertram co-opts the language of religion to woo when he
exhorts Diana, "Be not so holy-cruel. Love is holy" (4.2.32) and then
says glibly, "A heaven on earth I have won by wooing thee" (4.2.66).
Parolles, too, suborns religious discourses when he says of Bertram and
Diana, "indeed he was mad for her and talked of Satan and of Limbo
and of furies and I know not what" (5.3.259–60). Religion, it seems, is
woven into the fabric of these people's lives, thoughts, and language.

Most particularly, there are many Catholic trappings. These include
the importance of the pilgrimage motif, the emphasis on rings, and
Second Lord's remark that Parolles "hath confessed himself to
Morgan, whom he supposes to be a friar" (4.3.107–9). Indeed, as Joyce
H. Sexton argues,

> Overtly religious material is abundant in this play. Most of the charac-
> ters are pious . . . , and the dialogue contains much general theological
> comment on humankind's nature, earthly life, and eternal fate as well as
> an unusually large number of scriptural allusions . . . More obliquely,

passages of rhyming couplets appear intermittently, suggesting magic, incantation, or ritual. Further, many of the proper names Shakespeare chooses are connected with the religious history and culture of the Continent and its famous pilgrimages. (1994, 134)

Not only are pilgrimages mentioned, but they are discussed in some detail, as in the following exchange between Helena and the Widow:

> WIDOW: . . . Look, here comes a pilgrim. I know she will lie at my house; thither they send one another. I'll question her. God save you, pilgrim! Whither are bound?
> HELENA: To Saint Jaques le Grand.
> Whither do the palmers lodge, I do beseech you?
> WIDOW: At the Saint Francis here beside the port. (3.5.29–35)

Critics have been very scathing about the illogicality of Helena's alleged itinerary—from the South of France to Compostela via Florence—but the Widow is entirely unperturbed by it, asking merely, "You came, I think, from France?" (3.5.45) and continuing,

> Of enjoined penitents
> There's four or five, to great Saint Jaques bound,
> Already at my house.
>
> (3.5.93–95)

Maybe Shakespeare knows more, not less, than we give him credit for when he itemizes and names famous Catholic places of pilgrimage in Europe. Indeed, David N. Beauregard has argued that it is explicitly and clearly "a Roman Catholic—and not a Reformed—theology of grace [that] informs the dialogue and action of *All's Well That Ends Well*" (Beauregard 1999, 220).

As well as these signs of Catholicism, though, there is clear awareness of the Reformation. The King recalls religious controversy when he asks, "Is there no exorcist / Beguiles the truer office of mine eyes?" (5.3.303–4), since exorcism, as Shakespeare imaged in *King Lear,* was a hotly debated topic (Brownlow 1993). Indeed Cynthia Lewis has argued that the play as a whole repeatedly signals religious conflict: "*All's Well* alternates its own apparent judgments about election and free will. The play first promotes one seeming truth and then substitutes its antithesis. Never does the work satisfyingly arbitrate between the two "truths." Instead, *All's Well* constantly revises its own judgments and ever teases ours" (1997–98, 151). Religious controversy is flagged from the outset: the opening stage direction reads "*Enter young Bertram, Count of Rossillion, his mother the Countess, Helena, and Lord Lafew; all in black*" (1.i.s.d.), and at an early stage of the proceedings, Helena says, "I do affect a sorrow indeed, but I have it too" (1.1.52). Both of these clearly recall *Hamlet* and the religious controversy there encoded, especially in the context of mourning for fathers; moreover, as David Beauregard points out, Parolles's comment that "virginity murders itself, and should be buried in highways out of all sanctified limit" (1.1.140–42) "refers to the Roman Catholic refusal to allow suicides burial in consecrated ground, a refusal which was still customary but not yet specified in canon law within the Church of England" (Beauregard 1999, 221). Parolles's remark thus looks very like a pointed recollection of Ophelia in particular, as a virgin suspected of suicide, and of the attendant discussion between the gravediggers of the reasons for burying her in consecrated ground. And as many critics have observed, the Calvinist doctrine of double predestination is clearly glanced at in the King's instruction, "Thy frank election make; / Thou hast power to choose, and they none to forsake" (2.3.54–55). The controversy is all the more sharply relevant since the historical Roussillon itself was famous for Catharism, which seems perhaps to be recalled when the Clown refers to "The Black Prince, sir, alias the prince of darkness, alias the devil" (4.5.40–41) and says, "sure he is the prince of this world" (4.5.47), a phrase strongly associated with Catharism. Catharism is also recalled in the stress on the locality being emphasized by the name of Gerard de Narbon. (Narbonne lay in the heart of the Cathar territories.)

The splitting of Christendom effected by schism can only by healed (the healing here being imaged by the marriage) by reversion to a much older, quasi-magical mode of thought and worship that preceded the splitting of the faiths and the theological controversies that consequently ensued. This is a mode evoked by the classical names and mythic archetypes of *All's Well That Ends Well*. Within the comforting framework provided by this older world, the miraculous remains possible, as it seems no longer to be in the modern—as Lafew says, "They say miracles are past, and we have our philosophical persons to make modern and familiar, things supernatural and causeless. Hence is it that we make trifles of terrors, ensconcing ourselves into seeming knowledge when we should submit ourselves to an unknown fear" (2.3.1–5).

Most importantly, the "virgin birth" of Helena's child can be brought about and offer hope for the future.

The play does indeed offer such imagings of reconciliation rather than of strife between apparently conflicting religious positions. Lafew, for instance, says of the young men who show no enthusiasm for Helena's hand: "An they were sons of mine I'd have them all whipped, or I would send them to th'Turk to make eunuchs of" (2.3.86–88). Here the religious division with the Turk is both overlooked in Lafew's imagined making of a common cause with them, and at the same time provides an overarching cultural and material difference obscuring internecine ones (and glossing over the controversial historical alliance of France with Suleyman the Magnificent). Similarly, the Clown says, "young Charbon the puritan and old Poysam the papist, howsome'er their hearts are severed in religion, their heads are both one: they may jowl horns together like any deer i'th'herd" (1.3.51–55); again the potential of religious strife is subsumed in the culturally highly valorized discourse of the pastoral, which allows for language to operate symbolically rather than precisely. In the same vein, the Clown goes on, "Would God would serve the world so all the year! We'd find no fault with the tithe-woman if I were the parson" (1.3.82–83) and, "Though honesty be no puritan, yet it will do no hurt. It will wear the surplice of humility over the black gown of a big heart" (1.3.90–92). And Helena says,

> Thus, Indian-like,
> Religious in mine error, I adore
> The sun that looks upon his worshipper
> But knows of him no more.
> (1.3.199–202)

Here Indians are not despised, but identified with: doctrinal and even ethnic difference become subsumed in an overarching identity configured by love.

Most notably, the classical setting and imagery of the play sits easily alongside the Christian one, unusually so for the Renaissance world. There is no tension over the permissibility of suicide, for instance, or the nature of the afterlife. The Countess can refer in the same speech to "When I said 'a mother' / Methought you saw a serpent" (1.3.136–37), with its obvious connotations of Mother Eve and the Fall, and the classical "many-coloured Iris" (1.3.147), just as the King in the same speech can mention Plutus (5.3.101) and the saints (5.3.108). There is also Helena's easy blending of Christian and pagan persepctives in:

> There's something in't
> More than my father's skill, which was the greatest
> Of his profession, that his good receipt
> Shall for my legacy be sanctified
> By th'luckiest stars in heaven.
>
> (1.3.237–41)

"Sanctified" and "luckiest" might jostle uneasily against each other in other contexts, but here the one flows seamlessly into the other. Parolles speaks of Nessus and Hercules (4.3.244–47) and repeatedly of Mars (2.1.47, 2.3.281, 4.1.29–30), as does Bertram (3.3.9), Helena of Juno (3.4.13), Diana of Jove (5.3.286), the Clown of Cupid (3.2.14), and Lafew of Cressida (2.1.97–98), but these all rub shoulders easily with Christian perspectives, as in Helena's words:

> The greatest grace lending grace,
> Ere twice the horses of the sun shall bring
> Their fiery torcher his diurnal ring,
> Ere twice in murk and occidental damp
> Moist Hesperus hath quenched her sleepy lamp.
>
> (2.1.160–64)

Most interestingly in the context of these couplings, there are also many instances of pairings, such as the goddess Diana, who is evoked repeatedly (1.3.108, 1.3.207, 2.3.73), and the Diana of the play. Above all, there is, as Joyce H. Sexton argues, much use of typology. Typology as a technique depends on correspondences between the Old and New Testaments, and its reconciling and homologizing urge can in itself therefore be read as a seeing of each of the two confessions as a type of the other, and thus potentially reconcilable (Sexton 1994, 269). There may indeed have been trouble between the two in the past, as seen most recently and devastatingly in the French Wars of Religion, but it is not too late to hope for better in the future, because, after all, all's well that ends well.

WORKS CITED

Beauregard, David N. "'Inspirèd Merit": Shakespeare's Theology of Grace in *All's Well That Ends Well.*" *Renascence* 51.4 (1999): 219–39.

Brownlow, F. W. *Shakespeare, Harsnett, and the Devils of Denham.* Cranbury, N.J.: Associated University Presses, 1993.

Collins, Marie. *Caxton: The Description of Britain.* New York: Weidenfeld and Nicolson, 1988.

Girouard, Mark. *Robert Smythson and the Elizabethan Country House.* New Haven, Conn., and London: Yale University Press, 1983.

Haley, David. "Shakespeare's Bertram, Ahab, and Naboth's Vineyard." *English Language Notes* 32.4 (1995): 8–22.

James, Heather. *Shakespeare's Troy: Drama, Politics, and the Translation of Empire.* Cambridge, Mass.: Cambridge University Press, 1997.

Lejeune, Paule. *Les Reines de France.* Paris: Vernal/Philippe Lebaud, 1989.

Levin, Richard. "The Opening of *All's Well That Ends Well.*" *Connotations* 7.1 (1997–98): 18–32.

Lewis, Cynthia. "'Derived Honesty and Achieved Goodness': Doctrines of Grace in *All's Well That Ends Well.*" *Renaissance and Reformation* 14 (1990): 147–70.

Mallin, Eric S. *Inscribing the Time: Shakespeare and the End of Elizabethan England.* Berkeley, Calif.: University of California Press, 1995.

Monmouth, Geoffrey of. *The History of the Kings of Britain.* Trans. Lewis Thorpe. Harmondsworth, England: Penguin, 1966.

Sexton, Joyce H. "'Rooted Love': Metaphors for Baptism in *All's Well That Ends Well.*" *Christianity and Literature* 43.3/4 (1994): 261–87.

Shakespeare, William. *All's Well That Ends Well.* Ed. Barbara Everett. Harmondsworth, England: Penguin, 1970.

Simpson, Lynne. "The Failure to Mourn in *All's Well That Ends Well.*" *Shakespeare Studies* 22 (1994): 172–88.

15

Blasphemous Preacher: Iago and the Reformation

by Richard Mallette

Lake Forest College, Lake Forest, Illinois

"But words are words" (1.3.217): so says a bitter Brabanzio to the Senate after he has lost his daughter to the Moor. Exactly so, one might respond, but not merely in the cynical sense Brabanzio means—that words are ineffectual. "I never yet did hear," he continues, "That the bruised heart was pierced through the ear" (1.3.217–18).[1] But Brabanzio himself has just averred the opposite, by arguing that Othello has bewitched his daughter at least partly with words, with "spells and medicines bought of mountebanks" (1.3.61). Brabanzio rejects the efficacy of rhetoric by drawing on a scriptural trope popular in Reformation culture to describe the effects of preaching: the heart is pierced by the Word (Heb 4:12; Eph 6:17).[2] Contrary to Brabanzio's claim, Reformed preachers never tire of repeating that the heart is best pierced through the ear. "By the eare commeth knowledge," says Henry Smith, "and therefore it is likely that many would profite by Sermons, if they were taught how to heare" (1599, 295).[3] The celebrated Reformed preacher William Perkins claims that we have two kinds of ears, one corrupt and deaf, the other "a new eare pierced and bored by the hand of God, which causes a mans heart to hear the sound and operation of the Word" (1608–13, 1: 200). Perkins elsewhere adds that the redemptive stage after hearing the Word is "mollifying the heart, the which must be bruised in peeces" if the sinner is to be saved (1:79).[4] These well-known preachers might also have pointed out to Brabanzio, if only in the spirit of intertextuality, that "an euill eare lets all that is euill enter into the heart" (Smith, 307). Brabanziohas, after all, just witnessed ample evidence of the heart being penetrated through the ear—in Othello's narrative of his wooing of Desdemona, whose heart has been pierced by the Moor's glamorous words. For that matter, Othello's performance, which so moves the heart of the Senate as to rule in his favor, gives yet more evidence of the acuteness of rhetoric. The play throughout gives the lie to Brabanzio's dismissive tautology. Othello himself says, as Iago's words later work to the Moor's undoing, "It is not words that shakes me thus" (4.1.39–40).[5] But of course it is exactly words that shake him.

In denying the force of words, both Brabanzio and Othello call attention to their very power, a notable gesture in a play in which much seems to hinge on ocular proof. Brabanzio's conflation of scriptural and homiletic topoi underscores how this play uses contemporary religious rhetoric to dramatize the implications of his redundant apothegm. Words are words, but not all words have equal weight, as Brabanzio has just shown. Reformation culture knew almost by reflex that homiletic words have greater might, for preaching, Perkins nicely claims, "pierceth to the heart, and taketh holde of the affections" (1:360). *Othello* dramatizes how incisive homiletic words can be. This essay examines preaching in *Othello* and demonstrates how Iago's rhetorical effectiveness is grounded in his parodies of homiletic speech. The text provides him with a variety of preacherly skills, which he deploys and distorts for his own ends. These parodies also interlock with other contemporary religious preoccupations, such as controversies about free will and determinism, salvation and damnation, faith and doubt, comfort and despair. These discourses form a complex series of subtexts, which Iago's lines, miming the role of the diabolic preacher, surface and exploit. I shall show how the play is built upon some of the religious discourses that have become the focus of literary analysis in the current efflorescence of Reformation studies, and how a signal feature of Iago's rhetorical skill depends upon his engaging those discourses, particulary the art of preaching.

Early modern religious rhetoric enmeshes inextricably with other discourses, an embeddedness scholarship has only started to clarify. *Othello* has lately been interrogated under the auspices of various early modern preoccupations—of race, sexual difference, witchcraft, the body, marriage, and adultery, to name a few of the recent productive approaches to the play. Building on an earlier generation's recognition that the play is constructed on the conventions of the Morality play, more recent religious-minded critics have begun to demonstrate that it

also taps other Reformation issues, notably iconoclasm.[6] Where the
play intersects with religious discourses, especially at those pressure
points identified by poststructural analysis, we find words at their most
potent, piercing and bruising hearts. In tracking a variety of those
Reformation religious concerns, I argue that their characteristic belief
that language can save souls undergirds the play.

Iago's opening conversation with Roderigo hints at the variety of
contemporary religious problems that his performance will highlight
and exploit, especially his seemingly casual invocation of the foundational issue of the Reformation: "by the faith of man" (1.1.10). Insofar
as it carefully represents structural analogies between religious and
marital faith, *Othello* can be termed a play about faith, or the lack
thereof. It's not surprising, then, to find overlaps between the discourses of religion and love (for example, "Perdition catch my soul / But I
do love thee," says Othello [3.3.91–92]; "were't to renounce his baptism, / All seals and symbols of redeemed sin, / His soul is so enfet-
tered to her love," says Iago [2.3.317–19]). The play also centers on
free will, that supreme crux of the Reformation.[7] Is Othello's will free
or enslaved? Employing one of the chief tag phrases of the
Reformation, Iago says of Cassio, "he, sir, had th'election" (1.1.26).
Iago is not speaking theologically, of course, but his use of this charged
term, even metaphorically, draws attention to the discursive subtext. Is
any character among the elect, whatever that term may mean? Who, if
anyone, has free will?[8] Certainly, Iago claims we all do. His view that
"[o]ur bodies are our gardens, to the which our wills are gardeners"
(1.3.317–18) caricatures a voluntarist position associated with Richard
Hooker (Stempel 1969, 252–63; Whitaker 1953, 281–82). Othello
claims, on the other hand, at several moments of crisis, that he acts out
of marble compulsion, that he lacks free will, that his heart consists of
stone, that he slays his wife out of necessity. The falsity of such a determinism seems evident to many of us, but not necessarily to the
Calvinist psychology convinced that the unredeemed will can act only
to do evil. That the characters draw upon the fund of then-current religious discourses for self-justification is perhaps not a revelation. We
are accustomed to thinking of Shakespearean plays as secularizing religious themes and diction, often ironically. More unexpected is how the
play foregrounds those concerns in mapping the characters' moral and
emotional lives, and how the play's economies—racial, sexual, epistemological—are buttressed by those discourses.

Although I concentrate here on Reformed preaching and its attendant spiritual psychology, Homily is only one, of course, in a network of contemporary religious discourses. Iago makes this fact clear right from the start in his casual range of religious reference. During his opening conversation with Roderigo, for example, he claims, obscurely, that Cassio is "almost damned in a fair wife" (1.1.20); or, Iago says of hypocrites he admires, "these fellows have some soul" (54); "Heaven is my judge," he exclaims (59); "you have lost half your soul" (87); "you are one of those that will not serve God if the devil bid you" (110–11); the Venetian senators must turn to Othello "for their souls" (152). And these examples do not encompass the many biblical allusions that stud Iago's remarks here and throughout (Milward 1987, 61–111; Shaheen 1987, 125–43). In all these instances, he draws on the repository of contemporary religious language promiscuously, without seeming purpose. In doing so, he raises the polemical stakes, and he subliminally manipulates his listeners' awareness. He capitalizes on religious commonplace to gull his victims, and plays upon their (and the audience's) familiarity with contemporary religious concepts and what we now descriptively call buzzwords. In this agenda, he rapidly prospers, most markedly when his listeners, tenderly led by the nose, mime his way of speaking. Roderigo, for example, immediately follows Iago's discursive lead: "Do not believe" (131), he says to Brabanzio, negating the chief motto of Reformation solafideism. We are saved by faith. Do not believe, say the devil and his minions (Watson 1997, 238).

As Reformation preachers stressed endlessly, belief is best achieved through hearing the Word preached. Hence we find in early modern Protestant culture what has been aptly called a "cult of the ear" (Crockett 1995, 50–70; Wall 1979).[9] In the opening lines of the play, Iago calls attention to the power of hearing when he admonishes Roderigo, "'Sblood, but you'll not hear me!" (1.1.4). His blasphemous oath is a nice touch, because Iago functions as a blaspheming preacher. The Reformation diviner of scripture aimed to kindle in his hearers a passion for dogma; he wanted to pierce the heart and so inspire devotion. Iago later confides in soliloquy that his method will be "to abuse Othello's ears" (1.3.377). He might as well be following Henry Smith's maxim: "If the eare hearken to euill, then the heart must learne euill," for the devil "labours all he can to stay vs from hearing" the

Word preached (1599, 307). Iago's polemics is modeled on and distorts methods prescribed by sixteenth-century sermon theory. His warping of contemporary preaching makes him even more diabolical than hitherto recognized. He seizes on discourses that the Shakespearean audience was accustomed to regard as salvific, and he deforms them toward an evil end.

The emotional might of what the divines call "the Word preached" preoccupied Reformation writing. The English Reformers, above all others, proclaimed preaching as the means of illuminating the darkened mind, bruising the hardened heart, quelling doubt, and saving souls. They tirelessly quote Paul's prooftext: "How shal they heare without a preacher? And how shal they preache except they be sent? . . . For faith is by hearing, and hearing by the worde of God" (Rom 10.14–17). Calvin's many English followers as well as Protestant adherents across the spectrum affirm the value of preaching (Haller 1938; Davies 1970, 227–54; George and George 1961, 335–43; Collinson 1985). Richard Hooker calls sermons the "blessed ordinance of God" that serve "unto the sound and healthie as food, as physicke unto diseased mindes" (*Laws* 1977, 87).[10] Preaching becomes the source of life, and the preacher a physician. Richard Greenham states the matter baldly: "so it is that preaching brings hearing, hearing breedes beleeving, and by beleeving we are saued" (1615, 708). Such a formula of causation integrates preaching into every Reformed version of the *ordo salutis,* as Perkins's categorical pronouncement emphasizes:

> The preaching of the Gospell is the key of the kingdome of heauen: so that look how necessary it is for a man to haue his soule saued and to enter into Heauen, so behoouefull it is for him to heare Sermons: for that is the turning of the key whereby we enter into this kingdome. . . . He that is of God, heareth Gods word: and hee that heareth it not, is not of God. (1608–13, 3: 305)

Iago demands to be heard, but only to abuse his listeners' ears. He presents himself as a master homiletic performer. Since Stephen Greenblatt's analysis of the play as a tissue of performativity, many commentators have recognized Iago's actorly traits. Greenblatt notes that Iago's "successful improvisational career depends on role-playing" (1980, 235), a self-fashioning that necessitates his also casting those around him in roles. In improvising the godly preacher, he plays legerdemain with the basic sermon types identified by Reformation homiletic theory. His role depends on and demands the willing co-operation—through the medium of the ear—of his listeners, who themselves improvise familiar contemporary roles of those anxious to be among the elect. Iago's homiletic voice requires a listener, as well as his listener's cooperation, freely given. Greenblatt asks "why anyone would submit, even unconsciously, to Iago's narrative fashioning?" (237).[11] Like the anxious Protestant seeking assurance from the preacher, Iago's listener wants to know he is saved. This listener does not want, as Iago has said cryptically of Cassio, to be "almost damned in a fair wife." Iago refashions his listeners and inscribes them anew in a different narrative, modeled on the narratives of salvation and damnation, of faith and doubt that preoccupy early modern English culture. He entangles that narrative with other heightened discourses, such as marriage, adultery, and race (Pechter 1999, 25).

The ear, then, is the avenue of faith. When, in the Senate scene, Othello begins to justify his wooing of Desdemona, he appeals to this medium of truth: "So justly to your grave ears I'll present / How I did thrive in this fair lady's love" (1.3.124–25). Throughout this scene, he shows himself utterly confident of the power of hearing, and he presupposes that his auditors will recognize facts. In his long account of their courtship, he relies upon the ear as the source of truth and amorous faith. Brabanzio, he tells them, urged him to recount the story of his life with all its adventures. "These things to hear / Would Desdemona seriously incline" (144–45) and "with a greedy ear / Devour up my discourse" (148–49). Moved by the veracity of what he hears, the Duke acknowledges "this tale would win my daughter, too" (170). And so Brabanzio tries the same tactic. He asks them to "hear her speak" (174), hoping that Desdemona's words will affect the senators' ears as persuasively as Othello's have. And indeed hers do, but not as Brabanzio had hoped. Moreover, she soon uses their ears to have her way in one further respect, to accompany Othello to Cypress. "[L]end your prosperous ear" (244), she says to the Duke, and she is echoed by her husband, who urges them to "[l]et her have your voice" (259). "My life upon her faith" (293), says Othello to Iago, in a telling tropic convergence of religion and love. Meanwhile, this emphasis upon the superior power of the ear has not been lost on Iago, who says in soliloquy soon thereafter that he will "abuse Othello's ears" (377).

Critics have been so convinced that the ocular has pride of place that attention to the aural power in the play is recent. Karen Newman points out that the play and its commentary "have been dominated by a scopic economy which privileges sight, from the spectacular opposition of black and white to Othello's demands for ocular proof of Desdemona's infidelity." Newman claims that Desdemona is destroyed because her "non-specular, or non-phallic sexuality" proves frightening and dangerous. Newman therefore aligns Desdemona with the "oral/aural libidinal economy" of the play (1991, 86).[12] But Iago is the chief representative of the play's oral/aural economy, and his goal will be to draw others into that realm. He exploits the culturally privileged discourse of preaching, figured through the metonym of the ear, and implicates that discourse with the sexual economies of the play. We need to see, then, how preaching discourses overlap with erotic discourses, or how the analogies of marital and religious faith are structured. In both instances, hearts are pierced by words. Much later, for example, when Othello eavesdrops on Cassio talking with Iago about Bianca, the ear sustains as much damage as the eye. Othello hears as inaccurately as he sees, especially when Cassio laughs. Othello says, "Look how he laughs already" (4.1.108)—a tidy conflation of hearing and seeing. Hearing what he takes to be Cassio's derisive laughter irks him more than what he thinks he sees. And as Othello draws nearer, he overhears Cassio provide Iago with details that seem to refer to Desdemona. Both Cassio and Iago use the oath "Faith" several times in this scene, as though to signal that the issue here is how to instill and acquire faith—or its loss. Othello loses faith through both eye and ear. After Cassio has exited, Iago says to Othello, "Did you perceive how he laughed at his vice?" (164). "And did you see the handkerchief?" (166), Iago asks. Both ear and eye are the pathways to Othello's heart—for, as the Moor then says, "my heart is turned to stone" (175). Far from bruised and pierced, as the divines promise, Othello's heart now petrifies. To express that state he ironically employs one of Reformation culture's most popular figures to describe the process of acquiring faith. "And I wil giue them one heart, and I wil put a newe spirit within their bowels: and I wil take the stonie heart out of their bodies, and wil giue them an heart of flesh" (Ezek 11:19).[13] Othello's erotic career, however, inverts this process: he replaces his fleshly heart with stone.

Iago's verbal twisting manipulates Othello to this stony point, when eye and ear together work to his undoing. Iago's speech acts comprise an infernal parody of the Reformed Homily, for his rhetoric replicates a virtual typology of appointed kinds. A brief taxonomy will make plain how Iago draws upon the Homily and its idioms.

Reformation sermons come in five prescribed varieties, touching on three major topics: matters of doctrine, matters of morals, and matters of comfort. These topics reflect how radically the function of the sermon changed in the Reformation (Dyck 1983; Blench 1964, 228–30). The medieval Homily, which customarily taught by anecdote and exemplum, gave way to a sermon whose scope greatly expanded to include the newly configured doctrines of faith, good works, and grace—in fact, the entire Protestant *ordo salutis.* Furthermore, the sermon occupied a new prominence in the Reformed service and helped displace and dethrone the Roman Catholic emphasis on sacraments in the life of the faithful (Obermann 1961, 17). Greenham itemizes these changes in his summary of how the preacher is to "apply" Reformed theology in a Homily: "All application of doctrine must be referred to one of these heads: 1. To teach and establish true opinions; 2. Or to confute false opinion; 3. Or to correct evil manners; 4. Or to frame good manners; 5. Or to comfort the will" (1615, 772).[14] Each category speaks to matters either of faith ("opinions," that is, doctrine) or works ("manners," that is, morals), with the fifth category touching comfortably on both. Greenham's sketch of the complex interrelation of faith and works is duplicated with even greater compression when Richard Rogers says that the "Word is the first and principall" means to "strengthen the beleever and settle him in a good life" (1630, 283). The *Book of Homilies,* the official collection of sermons heard by every churchgoer in virtually every parish in the realm, encompasses the chief purposes of instruction in faith and admonition of behavior.[15] Like Reformation Homily generally, the *Homilies'* goals seek to induce faith, to promote sanctity, to assure and comfort.

As a means of showing how Iago's sermon parodies permeate his utterances, I list each sermon type and give instances of Iago's statements that parody the chief homiletic subgenres. These examples may be multiplied many times over; I choose only three salient illustrations in each category:

1. To teach doctrine:

"Our bodies are our gardens, to the which our wills are gardeners" (1.3.316)
"When devils will the blackest sins put on, / They do suggest at first with heavenly shows" (2.3.325–26)
"One may smell in such a will most rank, / Foul disproportions, thoughts unnatural!" (2.237–38)

2. To confute false doctrine:

"If she had been blessed, she never would have loved the Moor" (2.1.244)
"Reputation is an idle and most false imposition, oft got without merit and lost without deserving" (2.3.250)
"To be direct and honest is not safe" (3.3.383)

3. To correct evil manners:

"Beware, my lord, of jealousy" (3.3.169)
"Would that you would bear your fortune like a man . . . Good sir, be a man" (4.1.58)
"Do it not with poison" (4.1.197)

4. To frame good manners:

"I'll tell you what you should do . . . Confess yourself freely to her" (2.3.292)
"Look to your wife. Observe her well with Cassio. / Wear your eyes thus" (3.3.201–2)
"Strangle her in her bed" (4.1.197)

5. To comfort:

"Be assured of this" (1.2.11)
"[B]e you well assured" (4.1.30)
"I pray you, be content" (4.2.169)

Each of these statements carries the suasive force of Reformed sermon idiom. Like many of Iago's utterances, they are heavily didactic. They are intended to induce change of opinion or behavior in the listener, rather than, say, to testify to the speaker's own feeling or state. Most are exhortative, many are imperative. As Joseph A. Porter has noted in his linguistic analysis of Iago's speech acts, these imperatives "have the general illocutionary force of exhortation . . . [with] an undertone of directive" (1991, 77). Iago's employment of this mood lends great heft to his homiletic posturings throughout. He instructs his listener, often disguising his imperatives in the sheep's clothing of pastoral exhortation and solicitousness of his listener's well-being.

That solicitousness surfaces audibly when Iago comforts his listener. Iago's parodic role as the assurer and comforter begins in the first scene when he says to Roderigo, "Why, there's no remedy" (1.1.34). Playing on the conventional Reformed notion of the pastor as physician, Iago executes one of the preacher's chief duties, to provide a remedy for spiritual anxiety in the form of assurance and comfort. So in the next scene, his first conversation with Othello, Iago says to his general, "Be assured" (1.2.11). Two of Iago's favorite words compel special attention: "comfort" and "assure," both repeated throughout the play. The episode, and the play as a whole, represents a distorted version of early modern emotional therapy. The early scenes reproduce the age's chief medium of that curative process, Reformed spiritual counseling, which often consisted in the preacher's comforting and assuring the listener of the hope of salvation. Both words open parodically in *Othello* on vistas of the Reformed theology of grace. Calvinist commentators finely debated and shaded both beliefs: assurance that the promise of salvation applies to the elect individual, and comfort that the elect could not easily doubt or sin. But Calvinists were not alone; preoccupation with the assurance of salvation pervaded the spectrum of Reformation writers. Show diligence, says Hooker, to "this blessed assurance of faith unto the end" (*Tractates* 1977, 30). "Our dutie," says Perkins, "is, to labour to bee setled and assured in our conscience that God is our God: for first in this assurance is the foundation of all true comfort" (1608–13, 3: 520). The doctrines of assurance and comfort also comprise distinctive features of Reformed psychology.[16] Proceeding from the Lutheran conviction that the doctrine of *sola fide* is "comfortable" because it liberates fallen beings from either the ability or the need to contribute to their salvation by dint of good works originating in the sin-enslaved will, the Reformed doctrines of assurance and comfort gave the believer wellsprings of security and certainty. The redeemed were to be solaced that their salvation was sure, that their good works would follow inevitably from their election, that a sanctified life was indication of grace, a source of comfort, and assurance of salvation.

Iago carefully advertises himself from the outset as a preacherly figure, one of the godly, as they called themselves: "with the little godliness I have" (1.2.9) he says piously. And Othello responds as though assured of his own election: "my perfect soul / Shall manifest me rightly" (31–32), he says as he faces the prospect of being judged by the Senate. "My demerits"—he means his merits, which the godly claimed we of ourselves are altogether lacking—"May speak unbonneted" (23). He enjoys a "free condition" (26) and later speaks of his "redemption" (137) from slavery. These self-confident avowals, expressed in theological terminology, are Calvinist red flags. How is it possible for the godly to speak of their own merits or their perfect souls without lapsing into pride? Iago sounds like a preacher, and Othello sounds like a fully (even dangerously) assured member of the flock. Iago imitates the godly preacher providing comfort, Othello the sinner needing assurance—or (suspiciously) needing none. "Faith" (50), exclaims Iago (frequently), for one of his functions is to put his listeners in mind of the faith-assisting godly preacher.[17] One of his goals will be to deform the preacher's vocation by inducing in his hearers not faith, but doubt. The "assurance" Iago brings guarantees damnation.

So the situation between the two principals diabolically mimes the relationship of a godly divine to a member of his flock. From the perspective of the twentieth century, that relationship closely resembles the classic therapeutic bond. Indeed W. H. Auden notes, "Iago treats Othello as an analyst treats a patient, except that, of course, his intention is to kill, not to cure (1963, 266). The early modern affiliation between Reformed pastor and sinner clearly foretells the modern relationship of analyst and patient, an association carefully reproduced in Iago's treatment of Othello. But the therapy Iago practices will bring his listener neither comfort nor the assurance of salvation, but instead the assurance of torment, indeed torment itself.

The topos of "comfort" arises repeatedly and makes sense fully only with reference to Reformed spiritual psychology. The Venetians, for example, speak of it on Cyprus as they contemplate the Turkish threat. One Venetian notes of Cassio,

> though he speak of comfort
> Touching the Turkish loss, yet he looks sadly,
> And prays the Moor be safe, for they were parted
> With foul and violent tempest.
>
> (2.1.33–36)

Cassio himself comments that when Desdemona and Othello reunite, they will "bring all Cyprus comfort" (83). They refer to comfort as an emotional desideratum, as a means of talking about how the characters would like to feel. In theological parlance, comfort prognosticates future spiritual bliss. Hence at the end of the scene when Desdemona and Othello rejoin, they express their feelings in godly terms: "My soul hath her content so absolute," says Othello, "that not another comfort like to this / succeeds in unknown fate" (188–90). Desdemona echoes this sentiment, but insists that they will enjoy yet greater comfort: "The heavens forbid / But that our loves and comforts should increase" (190–91). They voice their ardor with words used elsewhere in Reformation culture to describe a particular kind of religious experience. A moment later, Othello tells her, "I dote / In mine own comforts" (203–4). In the light of subsequent calamities, we may well suppose him one of the unjustly comforted, deluded in his comfort or dangerously exulting in an unwarranted assurance of spiritual well-being. But of course the main point here (and throughout) is not theological. The play draws on the Reformed doctrine of comfort to show the fragility of his self-assured emotional state.[18] Iago's task will be to undermine that comfort, to provoke instead its opposite—despair—and to make Othello feel impending (emotional) damnation. Iago is, of course, present to witness the couple's paean to their "comfort." They have in effect provided him a discursive lead: he will burlesque the godly preacher by challenging Othello's easily iterated feeling of comfort.

But what of Desdemona, who also draws upon the same discursive lexicon to voice her emotions? When she attempts to assuage Cassio's despair, she invokes the same preacherly diction: "Be thou assured, good Cassio" (3.3.1); "be you well assured" (11); "Assure thee" (20), she says to him. Here Desdemona takes upon herself the office of the preacher. Her consoling words might at first seem to make her a healthy foil to Iago's falsity. But she has assumed the office, as it were, from Iago. Perhaps that's why her words seem so unconvincing and ineffective. She now unknowingly imitates Iago, the parodist par excellence. Hence the ineffectuality and pathos of her role-playing here and whenever she attempts to assure either Cassio or her husband. Her performance sounds feeble because she's miming another actor's performance; and she doesn't even know she's playing a role.[19] Critics have accused her of insincerity and worse, but she may more accurately be said to try too hard in a discursive domain Iago has laid prior claim to. Her failure comes from the poverty of her performance—a performance she cannot know she puts on. Thomas M. Greene has noted, "superior parody always engages its subtext in a dialectic of affectionate malice" (1982, 46). Part of Desdemona's ineffectuality originates in her weakness as a parodist of homiletic speech. She cannot realize she participates in this dialectic, so her engagement with it is neither affectionate nor malicious.

This ineffectuality further emerges when she presently takes up Cassio's cause with Othello. She fails at playing the advisor to her husband partly because she also employs the diction of Roman Catholicism to defend Cassio. "In faith, he's penitent," she says, trying to exonerate Cassio's "trespass" (64–65). "By'r Lady" (75), she exclaims, tapping a residual and officially outmoded Roman Catholic discourse. The effect of providing Desdemona with a papist ejaculation suggests, perhaps subliminally, not just the unproductive nature of her cause, but also the futile import of her rhetoric. It is inadvisable to aim at a rhetorical target with the armament of the cast-off, discredited religion. Desdemona has shown herself to be a bad actor, but not of course in the same moral sense that the term applies to Iago. At least in the early scenes, he plays the role of the comforting spiritual advisor quite well. Desdemona's improvisation miscarries because she plays her part at two removes from the original. She acts like a comforting counselor, a role that reflects well on her as a loving wife. But Iago has arrogated this function and cleverly made it his own. Desdemona's attempt to reclaim this role diminishes, entirely unwittingly, her own efficacy as an acting subject. She cannot assure or counsel, because these are Iago's functions and have been from the start. And yet, Desdemona does perceive that Iago is a bad pastor. When she talks to Iago and Emilia before Othello's arrival on Cyprus (2.1), a scene of which the function has caused some confusion to criticism, Desdemona rebukes Iago for his misogyny. She tells Emilia that Iago is "a most profane and liberal counsellor" (165). Here Desdemona detects the infernal parody Iago is enacting. Yet, she ironically mimics Iago in later scenes, when she tries to persuade Othello to exonerate Cassio. She then plays the pastor-physician and tries to counsel her husband. But she disadvantages herself by seeming to imitate the role of counselor Iago has already staked out and mastered.

Even in this conversation with Emilia and Desdemona, Iago mocks the preacher. He seems "to correct evil manners" and "to frame good manners," as when he tells them they are "Saints in your injuries; devils being offended" (2.1.114). He also praises, as Desdemona notes when she asks him, "What miserable praise has thou for her / That's foul and foolish?" (143). "Thou praisest the worst best," she says, seeing through him (146). In contrast to Desdemona, Iago seems to identify fully with his pastoral offices, and to control the dialectic of affectionate malice with his subtext. In the opening scenes, for example, Iago's tranquil voice seems entirely reasonable compared to Brabanzio's irrational cries of witchcraft. Iago's homiletic posturing in these early scenes underscores the wild implausibility of Brabanzio's charge that Othello has "practised on her with foul charms" (1.2.74). Among his accusations, Brabanzio associates Othello with damnation: "Damned as thou art" (64), he says to Othello—a condition he elides with Othello's race, his "sooty bosom" (71). Compared to him, Iago seems quite sensible and sane, at least in his utterances to others. When Brabanzio entreats the Senate to "find out practices of cunning hell" (102), one of the ways he discredits himself is that Iago has already sounded so levelheaded, indeed downright preacherly.

For example, at their first meeting, Iago says to Othello, "General, be advised" (1.2.56), spelling out one of the chief functions of the Reformed preacher. Iago gives ample advice to all. He can best master his listener by exercising a psychic power, which is figured in Reformed discursive terms. "Let thy soul be instructed. Mark me" (2.1.216), he says to Roderigo. "But, sir, be you ruled by me" (254), he repeats. His injunctions burlesque the preacher's task of advising his hearers. The typical homiletic voice employs a large number of linguistic performatives, which Iago mimes closely when he exhorts Roderigo to let his soul be instructed. As Cassio is soon to say in another context, "Iago hath direction what to do" (2.3.4). The characters quickly come to think that Iago has the moral and spiritual authority of the preacher. By arrogating to himself homiletic discourse, and then by adjusting it to his listeners' pathologies, Iago convinces them he has "direction what to do," which they freely choose to follow (often thinking they have no choice). Hence he can speak of Roderigo as a "sick fool" (2.3.44). When Cassio gets drunk on the watch that night, Iago tells Montano that he "would do much / to cure him [Cassio] of this evil" (2.3.127–28). He speaks of drink, but his diction reproduces the preacher-physician's. He confiscates the role of the ministering physician of the soul, wanting to "cure" Cassio of evil. And to usurp such a clerical posture allows him to pervert it, or to direct others to damn themselves. Iago cries to Cassio as the brawl breaks out, "God's will, lieutenant, hold, / You'll be ashamed forever" (145–46), as though he held preacherly possession of both God's will and the means of assisting salvation (both "1. To teach doctrine" and "3. To correct evil manners").

Iago's role as spiritual counselor enacts a common understanding in Reformed homiletics to express how preaching profits the hearer. It curbs fallen human nature. To be effective, preaching demands submission from its hearer. As Perkins puts it: "In the right hearing of the word, two things are required. The first, that we yeeld ourselues in subiection to the word we heare: The second that we fixe our hearts vpon it . . . Subiection to God must be yeelded in giuing subiection to his word: and our cleauing vnto God must be by fixing our hearts vpon his word" (1608–13, 1: 708).[20] The hearer masters his waywardness by subjecting himself to the preacher's advice. The Calvinist divine Edwin Sandys states the matter in another way: "To stand before the Preacher is to stand before God" (1585, sig. R1r).[21] Sandys intends this formulation to exalt the Word preached and God's power to give grace by means of the hearer's "subiection to his word." Iago demands exactly this kind of subjection to the guidance he offers. And so he further distorts the role of the preacher. To be ruled by the Word cannot be equated with being ruled by the preacher. Iago succeeds by convincing his listeners to follow his direction.

Hence he can pronounce upon the characters' spiritual states by seeming to reveal the mysteries of salvation and getting others to heed his revelations. "She's full of most blessed condition" (2.1.241), says Roderigo of Desdemona in a conversation with Iago replete with the discourse of Reformed Homily. What are the implications of such a remark in a play permeated by a religious lexicon? Surely the text does not speculate on the state of the characters' souls after the play has ended.[22] But the text does draw on the reigning discourses of salvation to dramatize the characters' emotional and moral states. And so Iago immediately responds, "If she had been blessed, she never would have loved the Moor" (244). This exchange is splendidly ironic. Both are using worldly evidence to deduce the state of someone else's soul—a task discouraged by many divines. But the divines do encourage the sinner to examine his own life for signs of election and reprobation. Perkins, for example, writes an entire treatise (*Whether a Man Be in the Estate of Damnation, or in the Estate of Grace*) designed to assist the faithful in learning whether they are among the elect or the reprobate, conditions God has mysteriously determined before the foundations of the world (1608–13, 1: 353–81). Iago doggedly taps the discourse of theological determinism—and helps others to think a determinism drives their lives. Moreover, he adapts this discourse to the characters' emotional conditions. Hence he tells Roderigo, "Very nature will instruct her . . . And compel her to some second choice" (228–29). He persuades people to act against their best interests by helping them conclude that a predetermined damnation awaits them, an end they in turn represent to themselves in theological terms. Iago wants the characters to believe that perdition has already caught their souls and that they lack agency. And, of course, with Othello he completely succeeds.

> 'Tis destiny unshunnable, like death.
> Even then this forked plague is fated to us
> When we do quicken,'
>
> (3.3.279–81)

says Othello after he has been persuaded of his wife's betrayal (Neely 1980).

The short interchange on salvation between Cassio and Iago in act 2 highlights how the play represents religious discourse.[23] Here the issue does not at first seem figurative or analogous, for they speak literally about Reformed views of salvation. Cassio advances the doctrinaire Calvinist notion that "there be souls must be saved, and there be souls must not be saved" (2.3.89–90). Although he speaks explicitly about theology, he speaks indirectly about the matter of the play. He expresses theologically the *emotional* determinism that Othello and other characters are in the process of succumbing to. They think of the world and themselves as being governed deterministically. And Iago exploits this belief. "It's true, good lieutenant," he replies to Cassio's soteriological truism. In the following lines, when Cassio says that "the lieutenant is to be saved before the ensign" (95–96), his theology becomes quite murky. He falls into a theological solecism: every believer knew that worldly distinctions of rank are meaningless in the eyes of God. So what is the interpretive point behind Cassio's remark?

In keeping with the play's method of representing emotional states in religious terms, Cassio's feeble theology surely exemplifies Othello's confusions, his moral and emotional turmoil.

This short exchange on salvation should be connected to Cassio's remarks after the brawl: "I ha' lost the immortal part of myself, and what remains is bestial" (247–48). He has changed his mind rather quickly about the state of his own salvation. Iago now ministers to him, worried that Cassio has sustained a "bodily wound" (250). But Iago's attentions reinforce Cassio's fear that he has been harmed more than merely bodily. Certainly, Cassio thinks his condition is self-induced: he has transformed himself into a "beast"—and he thinks all men do this (270–72). He generalizes about the human condition, which he depicts as fallen and hopeless. At this point, Iago becomes a full-fledged godly divine for Cassio. He begins to dispense wisdom freely. "You are too severe a moraller," Iago counsels (278). His advice seems intended, as the divines put it, to "frame good manners" ("mend it for your own good," he tells the dispirited lieutenant [281]). And Cassio responds accordingly: "You advise me well" (302), he says to Iago. Iago now plays the role of the spiritual advisor quite openly, as he admits in soliloquy: "this advice is free I give, and honest" (311). Not exactly "honest," however: he portrays himself explicitly as an infernal counselor:

> How am I then a villain,
> To counsel Cassio to this parallel [that is, suitable] course
> Directly to his own good? Divinity of hell"
>
> (322–24)

He makes advice a highway to destruction. He practices "divinity." And he paints himself candidly as a devil putting on "heavenly shows." Hence he can now turn his attention to Othello and devise how to "pour this pestilence into his ear" (330). This campaign fulfills the ultimate diabolic office, to infect the ear of the faithful. "We work," he presently tells Roderigo, "by wit and not by witchcraft" (345). His goal will be to induce despair, not comfort of salvation. As Cassio has just said, "I am desperate of my fortunes" (305–6).

Although the next scene—the temptation scene—most fully deploys Reformation discourses, earlier scenes have prepared for it well. For example, Othello has already demonstrated his vulnerability to "divinity of hell" by dangerously advertising his own assurance and comfort. The flimsiness of that facade is exposed by the ease with which he lapses into "doubt," that principal Reformation source of apprehension: "No, to be once in doubt / Is once to be resolved" (3.3.183–84); "Nor from my own weak merits will I draw / The smallest fear or doubt of her revolt" (191–92). Desdemona "chose me" (193), he says, obviously fearing he is not chosen. "I'll see before I doubt; when I doubt, prove" (194). He draws this diction from the reservoir of Reformation theology. Under the supervision of Iago's diabolic spiritual therapy, Othello swiftly reveals himself as a doubter and one who fears he is not among the (emotionally) elect. Greenblatt's observation that Iago "awakens the deep current of sexual anxiety in Othello" (250) has been echoed in a number of powerful analyses that account for Othello's response as a product of "sexual anxiety" (Snow 1980; Rose 1988, 131–39; Matz 1999). Iago also awakens an equally powerful spiritual anxiety in Othello, a fear of damnation arguably as deep in early modern culture as sexual anxiety. Where these two anxieties converge, Othello is caught. By this reckoning, he emerges as a prime candidate for preacherly ministration. As Iago begins his diabolic version of this counseling, Othello entreats him to "give thy worst of thoughts / The worst of words" (137–38). Iago complies. Othello asks him not to make his listener's "ear / A stranger to thy thoughts" (148–49). This infernal preacher has undertaken precisely this appeal to the ear. Othello fully participates in this alliance by ardently improvising his role as a fearful doubter needing comfort and assurance.

But when we look more closely at this scene, we find that Iago is not simply negating the techniques of the Reformed preacher ministering to an anxious listener. Recent scholarship has shown that the godly spiritual counselor was expected to induce in the hearer a preliminary "wretchedness." The full disclosure of the sinner's miserable estate was the indirect pathway to comfort, for, as Peter Kaufman has documented, "godly sorrow, with all its torments, and assurance of election were partners" (1996, 25).[24] The effective preacher produced in his listeners grief, alarm, and misery for their sins. Richard Greenham, for example, rose to fame for keeping his parishioners "in a bleeding plight" by encouraging self-accusation and wretchedness over their sinfulness (qtd. in Kaufman, 55). Greenham's *Sweet Comfort for an Afflicted Conscience* advises pastors to instill an acute sense of their listeners' own unworthiness. As Kaufman aptly puts it, "the elect had to discover how contemptible they were and experience 'grief and anguish' of mind. All this was 'a good token' because the pitched battle between spirit and flesh—and between faith and doubt—that followed signaled regeneration" (55–56). William Perkins claims that one of the goals of the preacher is to induce a hellish torment, a kind of "holy desperation" (1608–13, 1: 365).[25] Only this deep initial sense of desperation and wretchedness could eventually deliver a deep sense of divine mercy. Iago is shown to parody this feature of the godly Reformed preacher's duties. He cultivates in Othello an infernal version of the holy desperation that spiritual practitioners developed as a therapeutic tool. The pastor, says Greenham, "preacheth damnation vnto the obstinate, and such as remaine in their sinnes . . . By that meanes to beat them down, and bring them to a sight of their miserie" (1615, 347). Othello has shown himself from the start as one of the obstinate, one convinced that his merits can speak unbonneted, one exulting in his unhoused free condition and his perfect soul. As though to counteract his charge's dangerous spiritual self-satisfaction, Iago plays the role of the hammering Calvinist preacher-counselor, generating godly misery and despair.

Having awakened much-deserved wretchedness, the preacher was then expected to step in with assurance to the doubter that he is one of the elect, for, as Greenham puts it, "it is a greater thing in a Pastour to deale wisely and comfortably, with an afflicted conscience" (1615, 347). The preacher's method varied, but he was primarily to help the patient observe signs of faith and marks of God's having chosen the wretch for salvation. Iago's performance in this scene, then, parodies Reformed ministers not so much by distorting them (he actually mirrors their therapy—or elements of it—quite accurately) as by simply omitting what usually followed instigations of wretchedness and fulminations against sin, that is, assurance of salvation for the righteous. He deforms, then, the Reformation preacher's obligation to bring assurance that the hearer will be granted salvation. Instead, Iago brings Othello assurance of damnation. Iago begins by insinuating doubt and warns Othello of the danger of being "certain of his fate" (3.3.172). He sets himself up as a spiritual counselor, equipped to help his charges examine their souls (161). Iago mockingly points to those signs of salvation that the preacher is supposed to help the doubter find so as to dispel doubt. He urges his hearer to find "proof" (200) of Desdemona's love. In fact, he advises Othello to look for literal, visual evidence of favor. "Look to your wife. Observe her well with Cassio. / Wear your eyes thus" (201–2). Here the doubter is asked to find what every preacher knew was not reliable: proof of faith by means of the eye, ocular proof.[26] Even before Iago provides it, Othello in soliloquy shows that his advisor has succeeded in transforming him into a version of a reprobate, predetermined by God for inexorable damnation. ("'Tis destiny unshunnable, like death" [279]; "my relief / Must be to loathe her [271–72]; "[I'll] let her down the wind / To prey at fortune" [266–67]).

Moreover, Othello associates his damned condition with his race: "Haply for I am black" (267). The play's racial discourse here intersects with the religious. Recent attention to the racial dimensions of the play has highlighted how Othello internalizes the role of the "villainous Moor" of Elizabethan culture and of stage history.[27] He has cast himself in the part of the racially despised other his enemies have consigned him to. Brabanzio had said to Othello, "Damned as thou art" (1.2.64). Othello now can say to himself, "I am to blame" (286). He now convinces himself he is among the reprobate, a justly damned sinner. A few moments later, as he more fully casts himself in this role, he deploys racially charged language that interlocks with the discourse of reprobation: "Arise, black vengeance, from the hollow hell" (3.3.451). Although he does not yet know it, Othello has sunk deep in the process of damning himself, by his own choice (as the godly claimed all the reprobate do), a process that will not be completed until he learns the dreadful truth after Desdemona's murder. At that point he concludes the antivoluntarist project by consigning himself to perdition. "Who can control his fate?" (5.2.272), he asks as though acceding to the dictates of deterministic theology. And so just before his suicide he fully damns himself:

> Whip me, ye devils
> . . . Roast me in sulphur,
> Wash me in steep-down gulfs of liquid fire
> (5.2.284–87)[28]

Much earlier, he has spoken accusingly to Desdemona, whose remark rather distorts contemporary Protestant doctrine: "Faith, that's with watching" (3.3.289). Faith, for the Protestant, does *not* come with "watching." To say so would smack of Roman iconophilia. Faith comes through hearing. But "blame" might come through ocular proof. If the sinner comes to despair over his sins, it may be because his faith waivers, perhaps built on visual sensory evidence. Or, as Iago says in soliloquy,

> Trifles light as air
> are to the jealous confirmations strong
> As proofs of holy writ
>
> (3.3.326–28)

This assertion comes close to doctrine. To substitute the words "weak in faith" for "jealous" would spell out a textbook expression of the dangers of weak faith. This overlapping of formulations suggests one reason why ocular proof convinces Othello. The play uses the discourse of religion, in which faith provides both assurance and fearful anguish, to express the misery into which Othello's cognate career as faith-anxious lover has hurled him (Watson 1997, 235).

The famous passage is shot through with the discourse of the Reformation: "Give me the ocular proof," says Othello, on which he weighs the "worth of mine eternal soul" (3.3.365–66). He's constructed his love crisis as a crisis of faith and deformed it with a demand for visual evidence of his salvation.

> Make me to see't, or at the least so prove it
> That the probation bear no hinge nor loop
> To hang a doubt on
>
> (369–71)

The religious dimensions emerge explicitly: doubt and faith, on which the soul hangs. So, too, the peril of reprobation: "nothing canst thou to damnation add / Greater than that" (377–78). Hence he bids farewell to the "tranquil mind" "forever" (352–53)—as though he were damned—and attaches it to the "worth of mine eternal soul" (366) and to "damnation" (377). He has erected his plight with the materials of the Reformation: faith, doubt, salvation, damnation, free will, determinism. "Death and damnation!" (401), Othello cries. "I'll have some proof" (391), he says to Iago. At this point, the godly preacher would caution the doubter against the reliability of mundane proof, certainly proof derived by way of the eye. And the ungodly Iago does so exactly. "It is impossible you should see this" (407), Iago tells him, improvising the godly preacher quite precisely—with affectionate malice. So

Iago informs Othello that he cannot provide him with visual evidence. Instead he instructs him to rely on aural evidence, on the organ that the divines urged as superior to the visual. Iago therefore concocts the tale of what he "heard" Cassio say in his sleep: "I heard him say sweet Desdemona" (423). This in turn leads to the "other proofs" (435) of the handkerchief. Patricia Parker notes that the plot of jealousy in the play involves the substitution of "dilations" (3.3.128) for more direct forms of seeing (1985, 64). The ear, we might say, becomes a substitute for the eye. Iago cannot show Desdemona being "topped" (3.3.401), so he provides "dilation," the showing of what was secret. To do so, he engages the chief mechanism of preaching rhetoric, the ear, as his medium of deceitful suasion.

This medium guides Othello to a frozen determinism. He likens himself to the "Pontic Sea, / Whose icy current and compulsive course . . . keeps due on" to the "Hellespont" (457–59), a hell indeed to which he has just condemned himself. Iago has accomplished his goal by assuring Othello of his damnation. He helps Othello choose his own damnation. Iago has led Othello to discover his own (emotional) reprobation, and Othello demonstrates that he has no faith. From this point on, Iago has only to continue, with little effort, to improvise the clerical role. In a later scene, for example, he says to Othello, "Her honour is an essence that's not seen" (4.1.16). So much may be said of faith. Iago has become a sublimely diabolic copy of the godly preacher. He even provides Othello with comfort: "be you well assured" (30), he says as he urges him toward "faith" (32). All these subliminal assurances mimic the offices of the godly divine, whose function is to intervene, after the hearer has achieved a measure of holy despair, with the good news of salvation though faith. Iago's words do not involve, at this point, any more than an accurate reproducing of the preacher's diction. "Work on; my medicine works" (41), says Iago aside. In the subsequent ruse with Cassio and the handkerchief, Iago supplies more visual evidence, which further hardens the heart of the reprobate Othello: "My heart is turned to stone" (176), he says, as though proving his sense of his own reprobation.

When he next confronts Desdemona, he wants her to "damn thyself" and to "be double-damned" (4.2.37–39). It is not easy to interpret this interchange. Is Othello imposing on Desdemona his own feelings of reprobation? Or is he miming Iago, by playing the infernal spiritual advisor bent on helping his charge discover her own "estate"? In either event, Othello plays his role quite poorly. On the one hand, he merely foists on Desdemona his own fears of damnation. On the other, he doesn't see that he's badly imitating Iago, the great mime. Roderigo, however, who has functioned from the start as Othello's hoodwinked alter ego, verges on discovering Iago's ruse; hence the short interchange between him and Iago in the same scene, their final conversation. Roderigo nearly exposes Iago as a charlatan preacher. He accuses him of providing false "hope" and "comforts" (4.2.183, 193). Roderigo expresses his near-insight beautifully: "Faith, I have heard too much, for your words and performances are no kin together" (186–87). Faith, indeed. Roderigo sees that the "comforts" Iago has provided are spurious. He even uses Iago's preacherly diction against him: he threatens to seek out Desdemona and "repent my unlawful solicitation. If not, assure yourself I will seek satisfaction of you" (201–2).

The play's engagement with homiletic discourse virtually disappears after this point in act 4. Because Iago has accomplished his pastoral work, the need for Homily and spiritual counseling vanishes. What replaces it scholars long ago identified—the Roman Catholic mimicry of penance and works (Heilman 1956, 156–58; Vitkus 1997, 171–73). The play abandons homiletic discourse in the final scenes as though to signal that all is lost. Othello's deployment of the diction of the Roman priest substitutes for the Protestant clerical role that Iago has assumed throughout the play. This substitution functions as a last sign of Othello's emotional despair. When Othello invites Desdemona, on her deathbed, to "confess freely of thy sin" (5.2.58) and improvises the confessor priest, he is, in effect, aping Iago. But he does so in a particularly unnerving fashion. He plays Iago as a Roman priest. From a historical perspective, Iago's words have been completely successful. His charge now parodies Iago's parodic Reformed minister in Roman vestments, in the lineaments of the now much-despised religion of a benighted past. Iago can rightly say, after he has been exposed, "What you know, you know. / From this time forth I never will speak word" (5.2.309–10). Homiletic words need no longer be spoken. In fact, Othello has already deformed those words in the final ghastly scene. Now it is Othello's turn, as it was Desdemona's earlier, to imitate Iago the bogus godly preacher. Othello now acts at two removes from the original. Iago, for his part, need not speak, for Othello has appropriated, parodied, and denatured his words.

Or, as Graziano puts it after Othello's suicide, "All that is spoke is marred" (5.2.367). By contorting them into Roman Catholic configurations, Othello has marred Iago's (marred) homiletic words. To the godly Reformed ear, there sounded no greater maiming of language than that. The bruised heart has indeed been pierced through the ear.

NOTES

1. All parenthetical references to *Othello* are from Shakespeare, *Othello*, ed. Cohen (1997). No edition of the play identifies Brabanzio's allusions as I outline them here. Earlier textual variants and emendations, some substituting "pieced" for "pierced" or attempting a medical explanation, are listed in Shakespeare, *Othello*, ed. Furness (1965, 65–66). Modern editions have restored "pierced" but make no reference to the religious tropes Brabanzio employs.

2. Scriptural references throughout are to the Geneva Bible unless otherwise noted. "For the worde of God is liuelie, & mightie in operation, and sharper than anie two edged sworde, & entreth through, euen vnto the diuiding a sonder of the soule & the spirit, and of the ioynts, & the marow, and is a discerner of the thoghtes and intentes of the heart" (Heb 4:12). The gloss in the Geneva version reads: "an amplification taken from the nature of the word of God, the power of which is such that it entreth euen to the deepest and most inward and secret parts of the heart, wounding them deadly that that [*sic*] stubburne, & plainely quicking the beleevers." "And take the helmet of saluation, and the sworde of the Spirit, which is the worde of God" (Eph 6:17). For other scriptural passages that the Reformation deemed pertinent to preaching and hearing, see Isaiah 49:2 ("And he hathe made my mouthe like a sharpe sworde"); Zechariah 7:11 ("But they refused to hearken, & pulled away the shulder, and stopped their eares, that they shulde not heare"); Matthew 15:10 ("Then he called the multitude vnto him, and said to them, Heare and vnderstand"); Luke 11:28 ("blessed are they that heare the worde of God and keepe it"); Luke 8:18 ("Take hede therefore how ye heare"); Hebrews 4:2 ("For vnto vs was the Gospel preached as also vnto them, but the worde that they heard, profited not them, because it was not mixed with faith in those that heard it").

3. "The A.b.c. of a Christian is to learne the Art of *hearing*" (Smith 1599, 300).

4. Perkins glosses the first quotation with Psalms 40.6: "but my eares hast thou pierced." In the second quotation, Perkins is describing the means of "effectual calling." The first means is preaching ("sauing hearing of the word

of God"); the second is the bruised heart of repentance. The ear and the heart, in other words, are partners in advancing through the Reformed *ordo salutis*.

5. Stallybrass relates Othello's statement to the play's representations of the body: "there can be no simple opposition between language and the body because the body maps out the cultural terrain and is in turn mapped out by it" (1986, 138). Nowhere is this truer than in the metonym of the ear, and its relation to discourses of love and religion.

6. Chief among those who read the play as an heir of the Morality is Spivack, who discounts the "homiletic dimension of [Iago's] role, its didactic voice and naked moral display" as "relatively subdued and fragmentary" (1958, 430). In Iago's asides and soliloquies, Spivack does see, however, an indebtedness to the "homiletic dramaturgy of the moral play, where personified evil demonstrated its destructive operation and preached its own exposure" (436). Scragg evaluates other views on Iago's relation to both morality and mystery plays (1968). Diehl addresses the play's "problematic of sight" as "characteristic of early Protestant English culture" (1997, 127) and central to the play's epistemology. Diehl demonstrates how the ocular proof of the handkerchief raises vexed and unresolved issues of knowledge and faith that arise in Reformed discourse from the attack on images and their religious efficacy. Diehl is especially acute at showing how Reformed iconoclastic discourses, that is, fear of putting faith in a visible thing, bear on the role of the handkerchief and on Othello's knowledge of Desdemona's fidelity. Griffin examines how a Protestant audience might have seen the characters as embracing idolatry (1998, 81–86).

7. Hunter claims that the "*Othello* world is one from which God appears to have withdrawn, leaving its disposition to the freed wills of men. Or, to put it another way, in *Othello* the Pelagian possibility replaces the Augustinian possibility . . ." (1976, 128). Hunter (150–51) pursues the idea that human will, rather than providential guidance, directs the action. It leads him to focus tellingly on 3.4.144 ("We must think men are not gods," says Desdemona) and on the exchange about "lord" between Emilia and Desdemona at 4.2.104. Human love, says Hunter, fails the characters, and there is no divine love to replace it: "Othello has freely chosen to believe Iago, to kill Desdemona, and thus to transform himself into what he becomes" (157). The large critical body that once read *Othello* as a morality play also, implicitly or explicitly, reads it as a play about free will. These readings are listed by Hunt (1996, 375), who sees the play as "having incorporated two mutually exclusive theologies—a morality-play theology of free will, temptation, better and worser angels, and a seemingly voluntary fall from grace; and a predestinarian theology of non-election and gracelessness" (367). Watson treats the play as an allegory of "salvation by faith alone" (1997, 234).

8. The best summary I know of the Reformation controversy over the will is the exchange between Erasmus and Luther. "For although free choice is damaged by sin, it is nevertheless not extinguished by it" (1959, 51), says Erasmus; his position is outlined 89–91. Luther retorts, "there can be no such thing as free choice" (332); his position is outlined 319–27. For a sketch of Reformation positions on the will, see Mallette (1994, 338–40).

9. Renaissance Protestants are in general agreement that in matters of religious devotion, "the ear is to be trusted more than the eye" (Crockett 1995, 53); Crockett quotes Donne: "The organ that God hath given the natural man is the eye . . . The organ that God hath given the Christian is the ear; he hears God in his Word" (173). Gayle Greene (1981, 270–81) surveys the play's rhetoric, with no reference to the Reformation.

10. See also Hooker *Laws* (1977, 97–99, 106–8). Hooker's praise is qualified by his redefining of preaching to include the reading of scripture and, in the absence of preaching, of homily; in addition, he worries that the Reformed privileging of preaching in fact exalts the preacher over the Word.

11. MacDonald (1979), Pryse (1976), and Young (1990) have also examined the play's preoccupation with narrativity; Young is particularly attentive to how Iago, by means of soliloquy, aside, and confidence with the audience is made to enlist our sympathy and complicity.

12. In a note, Newman begins the point I develop in this paragraph: the "alternative libidinal economy" of Desdemona's ear/mouth suggests a "another trajectory of desire" between Iago and Othello, as heard in Iago's "repeated au/oral seduction" (1991, 164).

13. Wilcox believes that to overcome doubt with faith, God must "batter mens stonie and hard hearts" (1598, 116). As fitting perhaps as a gloss on Othello's line is another popular scriptural verse: "thei made their heart an adamant stone lest they shulde heare the Lawe and the wordes which the Lorde of hostes sent in his Spirit by the Ministerie of the former Prophetes" (Zech 7:11).

14. The five sermon genres identified in this essay are variously named by Reformation theorists. I have modified those named by Perkins (1608–13, 2:668–69), Hyperius (1577, fols. 17v–20v), and Hemminge (1574, fols. 17v–18v).

15. "If it shal require to teach any truth or reprove false doctrine, to rebuke any vice, to commend any vertue, to geve good counsail, to comfort, or to exhort, or to do any other thyng requisite for our salvacion, all those thinges . . . we maye learne plentifully of the Scripture" (Bond 1987, 62).

16. See Kendall (1979, 3–5, 25, 61–62, 67–76), Wallace (1982, 25–42), Tyacke (1987, 17–19, 249–52), Shuger (1990, 7–8, 78–83), Stachniewski (1991, 20–22, 32–34, 92–93).

17. Variants in Shakespeare (see ed., Cohen 1997, 2172–74) indicate how frequently they pertain to keywords from contemporary religious discourse. Act 3, scene 4, for example, has five variants of the word "faith."

18. Rose analyzes Othello's difficulty: "Othello's sexual tragedy therefore emerges not as insufficient repression, the criterion of the heroism of action, but as a misconstruction of his heroic quest" (1988, 143)—that is, a failure to recognize, as Reformation commentators on marriage had insisted, that marriage is a heroic endeavor, equal in its imperatives and importance to public action and other understandings of heroism.

19. Novy (1984, 84–87) points out that Desdemona plays both actor and audience at different times throughout, and that both roles lead to her destruction. Neely (1980) initiates recent reevaluations of Desdemona's motivations and disputes earlier attacks on Desdemona's character and motivations.

20. See also Perkins 3:430: hearers are "to heare [ministers] gladly, willingly, reuerently and obediently . . . Because they are sent from the high God."

21. He continues: "We must beseech God . . . to print into our hearts that which we heare with our eares."

22. Frye (1963, 22–31) sensibly cautions against critics' determining of the state of Shakespearean characters' souls; he is echoed by Vickers (1993, 378). But Hunt argues, "Shakespeare suggests that God may not have elected Desdemona for bliss" (1996, 359). Hunt resumes an inquiry of an earlier generation, summed up and challenged by West, who concludes "the realization of Othello's eternal destiny is simply no part of the play" (1964, 343).

23. The scene has been treated by three notable commentators: Frye (1963, 147–48), who sees the interchange on predestination as satirizing Cassio; Coursen (1976, 197–98), who sees the episode as prognosticating Othello's degradation; and Hunt (1996, 346–54), who sees the interchange as a seriocomic brooding over the doctrine of predestination and indicative of the play's dramatizing "the disasters that ensue partly from characters' mistaken assumption that their deeds either nobly define them, entitle them to the imagined prizes of life, or spiritually save them" (354).

24. Kaufman's chapter "Wretched" (41–102), expertly outlines the role of holy despair in godly spiritual counseling. Stachniewski (18–84, 86–87) documents how "Calvinism and puritanism were conducive to despair" (1991, 27).

25. Kaufman notes that Richard Hooker calls this condition "inward desolation" (1996, 68).

26. Diehl (130–55) analyzes the role of sight and visible signs in the play against the backdrop of Reformation iconoclasm: "Read in the context of the religious controversies of the Reformation, and in particular the radical reinterpretations of the validity of ocular proof in acts of faith, *Othello* may be said to rehearse the epistemological crisis created by the reformers when they

deny the magical efficacy of images and relics and yet assert the power of visible signs" (134).

27. See Barthelemy (1994), Neill (1989), Bristol (1990), Little (1993), Gillies (1994), Hendricks (1996), Adelman (1997), Vitkus (1997), Hall (1995), Pechter (1999, 33–37).

28. Snow performs a neo-Freudian analysis of the same issue: "when Othello refers to a reputation that has become 'black as mine own face' [3.3.387–88], we feel that he is being manipulated by a language calculated to make him despise himself" (1980, 401).

WORKS CITED

Adelman, Janet. "Iago's Alter Ego: Race as Projection in *Othello*." *Shakespeare Quarterly* 48 (1997): 125–44.

Auden, W. H. "The Joker in the Pack." In *The Dyer's Hand and Other Essays*. 246–72. New York: Random House, 1963.

Barthelemy, Anthony Gerard. "Ethiops Washed White: Moors of the Nonvillainous Type." In *Critical Essays on Shakespeare's "Othello,"* ed. Anthony Gerard Barthelemy. 91–103. Boston: G. K. Hall, 1994.

Berry, Lloyd E., ed. *The Geneva Bible: A Facsimile of the 1560 Edition*. Madison, Wisc.: University of Wisconsin Press, 1969.

Blench, J. W. *Preaching in England in the Late Fifteenth and Sixteenth Centuries*. Oxford, England: Blackwell, 1964.

Bond, Ronald B., ed. *Certaine sermons or homilies (1547): and, A homily against disobedience and wilful rebellion (1570): A Critical Edition*. Buffalo, N.Y., and Toronto: University of Toronto Press, 1987.

Bristol, Michael. "Charivari and the Comedy of Abjection in *Othello*." *Renaissance Drama*. New Series. 11 (1990): 3–21.

Collinson, Patrick. "The Elizabethan Church and the New Religion." In *The Reign of Elizabeth,* ed. Christopher Haigh. 182–93. Athens, Ga.: University of Georgia Press, 1985.

Coursen, Herbert R. Jr. *Christian Ritual and the World of Shakespeare's Tragedies*. Lewisburg, Pa.: Bucknell University Press, 1976.

Crockett, Bryan. *The Play of Paradox: Stage and Sermon in Renaissance England*. Philadelphia, Pa.: University of Pennsylvania Press, 1995.

Davies, Horton. *Worship and Theology in England from Cranmer to Hooker 1534–1603*. Princeton, N.J.: Princeton University Press, 1970.

Diehl, Huston. *Staging Reform, Reforming the Stage: Protestantism and Popular Theater in Early Modern England*. Ithaca, N.Y., and London: Cornell University Press, 1997.

Dyck, Joachim. "The First German Treatise on Homiletics: Erasmus Sarcer's *Pastorale* and Classical Rhetoric." In *Renaissance Eloquence: Studies in the Theory and Practice of Renaissance Rhetoric,* ed. James J. Murphy. 221–37. Berkeley and Los Angeles, Calif.: University of California Press, 1983.

Erasmus, Desiderius. *De libero arbitro.* Ed. and trans. E. Gordon Rupp. *Luther and Erasmus: Free Will and Salvation.* Vol 17. 35–97. Library of Christian Classics. Philadelphia, Pa.: Westminster, 1959.

Frye, Roland Mushat. *Shakespeare and Christian Doctrine.* Princeton, N.J.: Princeton University Press, 1963.

George, Charles H., and Katherine George. *The Protestant Mind of the English Reformation 1570–1640*. Princeton, N.J.: Princeton University Press, 1961.

Gillies, John. *Shakespeare and the Geography of Difference.* Cambridge, Mass.: Cambridge University Press, 1994.

Greenblatt, Stephen. *Renaissance Self-Fashioning: From More to Shakespeare.* Chicago, Ill., and London: University of Chicago Press, 1980.

Greene, Gayle. "'But Words Are Words': Shakespeare's Sense of Language in *Othello*." *Etudes Anglaises* 34 (1981): 270–81.

Greene, Thomas M. *The Light in Troy: Imitation and Discovery in Renaissance Poetry.* New Haven, Conn., and London: Yale University Press, 1982.

Greenham, Richard. *Workes.* London: 1615.

Griffin, Eric. "Unsaintly James: Or, *Othello* and the 'Spanish Spirits' of Shakespeare's Globe." *Representations* 62 (1998): 58–99.

Hall, Kim. *Things of Darkness: Economies of Race and Gender in Early Modern England*. Ithaca, N.Y., and London: Cornell University Press, 1995.

Haller, William. *The Rise of Puritanism.* New York: Columbia University Press, 1938.

Heilman, Robert B. *Magic in the Web: Action and Language in "Othello."* Lexington, Ky.: University of Kentucky Press, 1956.

Hemminge, Nicolas. *The Preacher.* Trans. John Horsfall. London, 1574.

Hendricks, Margo. "'The Moor of Venice': Or the Italian on the Renaissance Stage." In *Shakespearean Tragedy and Gender,* ed. Shirley Nelson Garner and Madelon Sprengnether. 193–209. Indianapolis and Bloomington, Ind.: Indiana University Press, 1996.

Hooker, Richard. *Of the Laws of Ecclesiastical Polity: Book V.* Ed. W. Speed Hill. *The Folger Library Edition of the Works of Richard Hooker.* Vol. 2. Cambridge, Mass.: Harvard University Press, 1977.

———. *Tractates and Sermons.* Ed. W. Speed Hill. *The Folger Library Edition of the Works of Richard Hooker.* Vol. 5. Cambridge, Mass.: Harvard University Press, 1977.

Hunt, Maurice. "Predestination and the Heresy of Merit in *Othello.*" *Comparative Drama* 30 (1996): 346–76.

Hunter, Robert. *Shakespeare and the Mystery of God's Judgments.* Athens, Ga.: University of Georgia Press, 1976.

Hyperius, Andreas [Gerardus]. *The Practis of Preaching.* Trans. John Ludham. London: Thomas East, 1577.

Kaufman, Peter. *Prayer, Despair, and Drama: Elizabethan Introspection.* Urbana and Chicago, Ill.: University of Illinois Press, 1996.

Kendall, R. T. *Calvin and English Calvinism to 1649.* Oxford, England: Oxford University Press, 1979.

Little, Arthur. "'An Essence That's Not Seen': The Primal Scene of Racism in *Othello.*" *Shakespeare Quarterly* 44 (1993): 304–24.

Luther, Martin. *De servo arbitro.* Ed. and trans. Philip S. Watson. In *Luther and Erasmus: Free Will and Salvation.* Vol 17. 101–334. Library of Christian Classics. Philadelphia, Pa.: Westminster, 1959.

MacDonald, Ross. "Othello, Thorello, and the Problem of the Foolish Hero." *Shakespeare Quarterly* 30 (1979): 51–67.

Mallette, Richard. "'From Gyves to Graces': *Hamlet* and Free Will." *JEGP* 93 (1994): 336–55.

Matz, Robert. "Slander, Renaissance Discourses of Sodomy, and *Othello.*" *ELH* 66 (1999): 261–76.

Milward, Peter, S.J. *Biblical Influences in Shakespeare's Great Tragedies.* Bloomington and Indianapolis, Ind.: Indiana University Press, 1987.

Neely, Carol. "Women and Men in *Othello:* 'What should such a fool do with so good a woman?'" In *The Woman's Part: Feminist Criticism of Shakespeare,* ed. Carolyn Lenz, Gayle Greene, and Carol Neely. 211–39. Urbana, Ill.: University of Illinois Press, 1980.

Neill, Michael. "Unproper Beds: Race, Adultery, and the Hideous in *Othello.*" *Shakespeare Quarterly* 40 (1989): 383–412.

Newman, Karen. *Fashioning Femininity and English Renaissance Drama.* Chicago, Ill., and London: University of Chicago Press, 1991.

Novy, Marianne. *Love's Argument: Gender Relations in Shakespeare.* Chapel Hill, N.C., and London: University of North Carolina Press, 1984.

Obermann, Heiko. "Preaching and the Word in the Reformation." *Theology Today* 18 (1961): 15–31.

Parker, Patricia. "Shakespeare and Rhetoric: 'dilation and 'delation' in *Othello.*" In *Shakespeare and the Question of Theory,* ed. Patricia Parker and Geoffrey Hartman. 54–74. New York and London: Methuen, 1985.

Pechter, Edward. *"Othello" and Interpretive Traditions.* Iowa City, Iowa: University of Iowa Press, 1999.

Perkins, William. *The Workes of That Famous and Worthy Minister of Christ in the University of Cambridge, Mr. William Perkins.* 3 vols. Cambridge, England: 1608–13.

Porter, Joseph A. "Complement Extern: Iago's Speech Acts." In *Othello: New Perspectives,* ed. Virginia Mason Vaughan and Kent Cartwright. 74–88. Rutherford, Madison, Teaneck, N.J.: Fairleigh Dickinson University Press, 1991.

Pryse, Marjorie. "Lust for Audience: An Interpretation of *Othello.*" *ELH* 43 (1976): 461–78.

Rogers, Richard. *Seven Treatises.* London: Thomas Man, 1630.

Rose, Mary Beth. *The Expense of Spirit: Love and Sexuality in English Renaissance Drama.* Ithaca, N.Y., and London: Cornell University Press, 1988.

Sandys, Edwin. *Sermons.* London: Henry Middleton, 1585.

Scragg, Leah. "Iago—Vice or Devil." *Shakespeare Survey* 21 (1968): 53–65.

Shaheen, Naseeb. *Biblical References in Shakespeare's Tragedies.* Newark, Del.: University of Delaware Press, 1987.

Shakespeare, William. *Othello.* Ed. Walter Cohen. 2091–2174. In *The Norton Shakespeare,* ed. Stephen Greenblatt. New York and London: W. W. Norton, 1997.

_____. *Othello: A New Variorum Edition of Shakespeare.* Ed. Horace Howard Furness. New York: American Scholar, 1965.

Shuger, Debra Kuller. *Habits of Thought in the English Renaissance: Religion, Politics, and the Dominant Culture.* Berkeley and Los Angeles, Calif.: University of California Press, 1990.

Smith, Henry. *The Sermons of Master Henry Smith.* London: Willow Orwin, 1599.

Snow, Edward W. "Sexual Anxiety and the Male Order of Things in *Othello.*" *English Literary Renaissance* 10 (1980): 384–412.

Spivack, Bernard. *Shakespeare and the Allegory of Evil: The History of a Metaphor in Relation to His Major Villains.* New York: Columbia University Press, 1958.

Stachniewski, John. *The Persecutory Imagination: English Puritanism and the Literature of Religious Despair.* Oxford, England: Clarendon, 1991.

Stallybrass, Peter. "Patriarchal Territories: The Body Enclosed." In *Rewriting the Renaissance: The Discourses of Sexual Difference in Early Modern Europe,* ed. Margaret W. Ferguson, Maureen Quilligan, and Nancy Vickers. 123–42. Chicago, Ill., and London: University of Chicago Press, 1986.

Stempel, Daniel. "The Silence of Iago." *PMLA* 84 (1969): 252–63.

Tyacke, Nicholas. *Anti-Calvinists: The Rise of English Arminianism c. 1590–1640.* Oxford, England: Clarendon, 1987.

Vickers, Brian. *Appropriating Shakespeare: Contemporary Critical Quarrels.* New Haven, Conn., and London: Yale University Press, 1993.

Vitkus, Daniel. "Turning Turk in *Othello*: The Conversion and Damnation of the Moor." *Shakespeare Quarterly* 48 (1997): 145–76.

Wall, John N. Jr. "Shakespeare's Aural Art: The Metaphor of the Ear in *Othello*." *Shakespeare Quarterly* 30 (1979): 358–66.

Wallace, Dewey. *Puritans and Predestination: Grace in English Protestant Theology, 1525–1695*. Chapel Hill, N.C., and London: University of North Carolina Press, 1982.

Watson, Robert. "*Othello* as Protestant Propaganda." In *Religion and Culture in Renaissance England*, ed. Claire McEachern and Debra Shuger. 234–57. Cambridge, England: Cambridge University Press, 1997.

West, Robert H. "The Christianness of *Othello*." *Shakespeare Quarterly* 15 (1964): 333–43.

Whitaker, Virgil. *Shakespeare's Use of Learning: An Inquiry into the Growth of His Mind*. San Marino, Calif.: The Huntington Library, 1953.

Wilcox, Thomas. *A Discourse Touching the Doctrine of Doubting*. Cambridge, England: 1598.

Young, David. *The Action to the Word: Style and Structure in Shakespearean Tragedy*. New Haven, Conn., and London: Yale University Press, 1990.

16

Love and Lies:
Marital Truth-Telling, Catholic
Casuistry, and *Othello*

by Paula McQuade
DePaul University, Chicago, Illinois

THAT *Othello* (1604) engages with the early seventeenth-century Protestant idealization of marriage as a spiritual and social partnership is scarcely news.[1] Stanley Cavell describes *Othello* as a play "in which not a marriage, but an idea of marriage, or let us say, an imagination of marriage is worked out" (1987, 131). Scholars often initially address this engagement by remarking upon the play's status as a domestic tragedy, but the classification is soon discarded. Underpinning this dismissal of *Othello*'s generic affiliations are two factors: domestic tragedy, with its focus upon marriage and family life, is widely perceived to be the poor relation of serious—that is, political—tragedy. "The critical category of domestic tragedy," writes Karen Newman, "[is] always implicitly or explicitly pejorative because of its focus on women, jealousy and a triangle . . ." (1991, 92). Of equal importance is the popular perception of domestic tragedy's religious didacticism. Although Catherine Belsey and Frances Dolan have demonstrated the sophistication and complexity of individual domestic tragedies such as *Arden of Faversham* (1592), many critics adhere to the argument articulated by Henry Hitch Adams more than seventy-five years ago: early modern domestic tragedies are moralistic exemplums depicting the costs and consequences of sexual transgression for an urban, largely Puritan audience; as such, they are related to early modern religious works and thus simplistic and moralistic (1943).[2]

Recent scholarship has challenged these assumptions by demonstrating both the sophistication of early modern English texts by or about women and domestic life, and the complexity of early modern religious thought. At the same time, scholars have increasingly questioned the designation of genre as a "merely literary" concern. In *Kinds of Literature* (1982), Alistair Fowler critiques the traditional conception of genre, whereby a work belongs to a genre because it possesses certain features, and subsequent works gain membership to the genre only when it can be demonstrated that they also possess these features. Instead, Fowler urges that we should consider literary genres, like Wittgenstein's language games, as a family, "whose sects and individual members are related in various ways, without necessarily having any single feature shared by all."[3] A text does not belong to a genre because it possesses certain features; instead, genre provides certain features—plot, characterization, or themes—which subsequent texts variously interpret.

The dynamism and intertextuality of this approach to genre, whereby texts respond both to inherited conditions and to one another, is appropriate for a study of a genre that flourishes within a discreet period of time and a defined locale—whether it be post-depression Hollywood comedies of remarriage or late sixteenth- and early seventeenth-century English domestic tragedies. Such an approach supports the claims of Douglas Brooks that contemporary criticism on the early modern theater ignores substantial evidence that suggests most early modern texts "were shaped" by "various networks of engagement" between playwrights, commercial theaters, publishers, and printers (2000, 2).[4] Because these "networks of engagement" include competition between theater companies, it seems appropriate to study *Othello* (performed by the King's Men in 1604) in relation to domestic tragedies performed by other companies in or around London during the same period.[5]

Othello is unique among early modern English domestic tragedies in its sustained investigation of conjugal honesty. Early modern English Protestant marriage manuals attempt to justify the emergent ideology of the companionate marriage by describing the pleasures of marital conversation; as we shall see, they identify wifely "honesty" as the signal characteristic of such conversation. Most early modern English domestic tragedies exploit popular misogyny by emphasizing the mendacity of the adulteress: in *Arden of Faversham,* for example, Alice Arden verbally manipulates cultural codes governing feminine behavior in order to satisfy her will. When her husband (correctly) accuses Alice of attempting to poison him, Alice shrewdly adopts the part of the neglected wife: "There's nothing that I do can please your taste," she complains, "You were best to say I would have poisoned you" (1.368–69). But *Othello* is unusual in that it depicts both the pleasures of honest spousal conversation and the destruction of this domestic happiness through a single act of verbal dishonesty: Desdemona's lie to Othello about the handkerchief. Traditionally, critics have generally considered this lie to be important for what it reveals about the character of Desdemona;[6] in this essay, I explore what it reveals concerning relations between theater, gender, and early modern (religious) culture.[7]

Through Desdemona's lie, *Othello* explores a contradiction at the heart of the Protestant ideal of the companionate marriage: it presumes that a husband and wife can be "friends" and thus speak truthfully, while at the same time it insists upon the social subordination of the wife. When Desdemona lies about the handkerchief, she simultaneously destroys the honest conversation constitutive of marriage and confirms Othello's perception of her infidelity. But this lie is produced within an exchange between Desdemona and Othello that connects violent and (apparently) unexplainable spousal jealousy with compelled female speech. *Othello* thus emphasizes the conflicting demands placed upon wifely honesty by a conjugal relationship that insists upon both the abstract possibility of honest communication between spouses and the reality of female inferiority.

Othello draws upon the methodology of Catholic casuistry to examine the unfulfilled promise of the companionate marriage. In early seventeenth-century England, one of the main cases used to justify the use of mental reservation by Catholic missionaries was a case concerning an adulterous woman who is questioned by her jealous husband concerning her fidelity.[8] Most Catholic casuists agreed that in this case, which I term "the case of the dishonest adulteress," the wife's linguistic dissimulation is lawful because she confronts a jealous husband who possesses no legal authority to decide her guilt or innocence. Shakespeare may have been familiar with the case of the dishonest adulteress, since it was well known among early modern English Catholic and Protestant casuists, but my argument does not assert Shakespeare's recusancy.[9] I do, however, argue that casuistic methods and procedures influence the representation of marital truth-telling in *Othello*.[10] Because casuistry examines how abstract principles apply in concrete circumstances, it is more realistic about the consequences of the marital hierarchy; it recognizes that the reality of a wife's social subordination may impede her ability to tell the truth. Casuistry thus provides *Othello* with a lens to explore early modern culture's complex, even contradictory, conceptions of love, marriage, and truth.

HONEST CONVERSATION AND THE COMPANIONATE MARRIAGE

Because of the importance accorded to marriage within contemporary Western culture, it is easy to overlook the extent to which the conjugal relationship was just beginning to be thought of as an important locus of affect in the early modern period. Medieval Catholic theologians generally conceived of marriage as an inferior state, available primarily to those men and women who were unable to remain celibate. When early Protestant reformers argued for the spiritual importance of marriage, they were forced to confront not only longstanding theological precepts, but also popular misogyny linking women with intellectual inferiority and moral laxity. Throughout the sixteenth and seventeenth centuries, Protestant theologians attempted to increase the importance accorded to marriage by describing it as a type of friendship.[11] In one of the most influential seventeenth-century marriage manuals, the Protestant minister Robert Cleaver argues that the classical understanding of friends as one soul in two bodies is perfected in the theological conception of husband and wife as one flesh: "If it be true," he writes, "as men do say, that friendship make one heart out of two, much more truly and effectually ought wedlock to do the same, which far surpasses all manner of both friendship and kindred" (1621, 108). In the oft-reprinted treatise, *Of Domestical Duties,* William Gouge argues that marriage can offer the unconditional love and support that classical authors insisted could only be found in masculine friendship. "That which Solomon said of a friend and a brother may fitly be applied in this case to a husband and a wife: a friend loveth at all times and a friend is born for adversity . . . of all friends none ought to be more careful, more faithful, than a man and wife" (1621, 246). By the middle of the seventeenth century, the Protestant campaign linking marriage and friendship had been so successful that the Protestant moral theologian Jeremy Taylor could confidently describe "marriage" as "the Queen of friendships, in which there is a communication of all that can be communicated by friendship" ("A Discourse" 1661, 3:41).

Protestant theologians argued that marriage surpassed masculine friendship because it allowed its participants to experience pleasures of both the mind and the body. Where medieval Catholic theologians denigrated sexuality as evidence of human sinfulness, seventeenth-century Protestant marriage manuals frankly admit sexual pleasure as one of the chief benefits of marriage, and describe sexual intercourse between husband and wife as "due benevolence."[12] Though this attention to physical pleasure is certainly remarkable, Protestant marriage manuals equally insist upon the pleasure of social intercourse between husband and wife. One Protestant author describes matrimony as "the felicity of man's life, the flower of friendship" (Tilney 1577, 10). Drawing upon the biblically derived metaphor of husband and wife as "one flesh," theologians describe marriage as a relationship in which the discreet boundaries of the self vanish; husband and wife, writes one seventeenth-century Protestant theologian, "should become such a union . . . that the flames of their dead bodies make one pyramid" (Taylor, "A Discourse" 1661, 3:41). Gouge writes "a wife is not only as a man's body, but as his person, his body and soul . . . she is as of himself, by reason of the bond of marriage, which makes one out of two. In which respect a wife is commonly called a man's second self" (1621, 77). Cleaver describes it thus: "therefore it is not said, marriage doth make one man, or one mind, or one body of two, but clearly one person" (1621, 108). What the marital bond offers, these theologians suggest, is the potential to experience union with another person, a union so complete that it is impossible to distinguish where one self begins and the other ends—what Julia Kristeva would subsequently describe as the "rapture of love" in which "the limits of one's own identity vanish"(1987, 2).[13] Whereas previous authors believed that this experience could be found only in mystical devotion or, alternatively, masculine friendship, seventeenth-century Protestant theologians locate it in the domestic and prosaic relationship of the marital bond. Charles Taylor has suggested that this effort to locate social and erotic energy within marriage is fundamental to the new "ethics of ordinary" life that emerged during the early seventeenth century and thus serves as a signal characteristic of modernity: implicit within the Protestant rejection of monasticism, writes Taylor, is an "affirmation that the fullness of Christian existence was to be found within the activities of this life, in one's calling and in marriage and the family. The entire modern development of the affirmation of everyday life was . . . foreshadowed and initiated . . . in the spirituality of the reformers" (1989, 218).

Protestant theologians recognize that this experience of "the rapture of love" is dependent upon language. As Jeremy Taylor puts it, "there is no love, no friendship, without the intercourse of conversation" ("A Discourse" 1661, 3:40). "If marriage is to be "a relation of love," the Protestant theologian Richard Baxter warns husbands, "your converse must be sweet" (1677, 40). To achieve this union of souls, husband and wife must converse with one another; they must reveal their hidden thoughts and desires without reservation. In *Matrimonial Honor,* Daniel Rogers reminds husband and wife that marital friendship depends upon communication: only "the mutual reflex and exchange of gracious and virtues in and from each other . . . can hold you in an invincible league of amity" (1642, 157). Robert Cleaver suggests that without such conversation, marriage devolves into emotional and spiritual bondage: "and thus there shall be in wedlock a certain sweet and pleasant conversation, without which it is no marriage, but a prison, a hatred, and perpetual torment of the mind" (1621, 84). Within the Protestant marriage manuals, spousal conversation serves as the cornerstone of the affective relation between the spouses; as surely as "due benevolence," it unites two discreet persons into one flesh.[14]

Although language enables husband and wife to experience this intimacy, it also has the potential to underscore their separation from one another. In *Tales of Love,* Kristeva suggests that the inherent instability of linguistic systems, together with the disruptive consequences of desire, makes the communication of love difficult. "Do we speak of the same thing when we speak of love?" Kristeva queries, " . . . and what thing? The ordeal of love puts the univocity of language and its referential and communicative function of language to the test" (1987, 2). At the same time that the slipperiness of signification makes it difficult to speak one's love, the act of speaking marks an irremediable breach between two selves, for if a person is to experience love, she must express her innermost feelings and desires to another human being, but the very act of communicating this love reveals her individuation.[15] Thus, if, as Protestant theologians suggest, conversation is the "glue" that bonds husband and wife into "one flesh," it is also a potential corrosive, able to dissolve the ideal union of one flesh into two distinct entities.

I have outlined two problems inherent in the early seventeenth-century marriage manuals' emphasis upon the pleasures of marital conversation: not only does the slipperiness of signification make communication of love difficult, but language itself reveals a person's individuation. To my knowledge, Protestant theologians do not address the latter problem, but they do discuss the first. Early modern marriage manuals remind husbands and wives that if they are to avoid misunderstanding, they must speak to one another with care and precision. In *Of Domestical Duties* (1622) William Gouge urges wives to "address their spouses respectfully as 'husband' and to avoid such demeaning endearments as 'sweet, sweeting, heart, sweetheart, love, joy, dear, duck, chick or pigsnie'" (qtd. in Stone 1979, 139). But perhaps the most significant way in which Protestant theologians attempt to guard against the disruptive potential of language is by insisting upon the importance of absolute honesty between husband and wife. Not only do Protestant marriage manuals contain frequent injunctions urging both husband and wife to avoid flattery, which theologians describe as a type of dissimulation inappropriate to the union of husband and wife, but theologians also make mutual truth-telling a defining characteristic of marriage: matrimony, writes Robert Cleaver, is "a lawful knot to the end that they may dwell together in friendship and honesty" (1621, 47). Implicit in such injunctions is the belief that absolute honesty is the precondition for emotional and physical intimacy, a belief manifest in Montaigne's analysis of friendship and still current among twentieth-century theorists.[16] To foster such intimacy, early modern Protestant theologians remind both husband and wife of their "mutual duty" to "admonish one another." Although they recognize that this may require the husband or wife to say something the other spouse does not wish to hear, marriage manuals insist that the telling of unpleasant truths is one of chief mutual duties of marriage and even describe it as a moral imperative. As Gouge remarks, "When either husband or wife is fallen into sin, a mutual duty it is for the other, to use what redress maybe of that sin: as if one of them were wounded, the other must take care for healing of that wound" (1621, 241).

Catholic Casuistry and the Case of the Dishonest Adulteress

Notably absent from the Protestant marriage manual's insistence upon marital truth-telling is any overt discussion of gender. Although the manuals suggest that the wife may occasionally need to "dissemble" her displeasure toward her spouse, they urge the husband to do likewise.[17] This absence of any gender differential in the injunctions concerning marital truth-telling originates in the premise of the married woman's spiritual equality. Because husband and wife are equally endowed with a conscience, they are equally responsible for telling the truth. But at the same time that a wife was her husband's spiritual equal, she was his social subordinate. Because marriage manuals primarily offer theoretical precepts, they fail to address the ways in which the practical circumstance of wifely subordination could impact the married woman's ability to tell the truth. Unlike the marriage manuals, however, casuistry examines how abstract precepts apply within concrete circumstances. Consequently, when Catholic casuists address cases concerning wifely honesty, they acknowledge that the practical circumstances of wifely subordination, as well as the importance accorded to a woman's honest reputation, affect a wife's ability to tell the truth.

The case of the dishonest adulteress originates in the sixteenth century. With few exceptions, Catholic casuists were less interested in resolving unique cases and establishing their reputation than in building upon the work of others; hence, although the case is frequently cited, it is referenced as originating with various theologians.[18] By the first decade of the seventeenth century, however, the case was well known and frequently discussed. As I will discuss in more detail subsequently, the prevalence of this case in early modern Catholic casuistry manuals suggests that despite the Council of Trent adding "mutual companionship" to the reasons for marriage in the Catholic Catechism of 1566, early modern Catholics remained less invested than Protestants in seeing marriage as a primarily affective—and hence, less overtly political—relationship (Leites 1986, 77–78).

Unlike Protestant casuists who rejected all forms of mental reservation as "heinous lies," most Catholic casuists agreed that in such a case, the wife might use mental reservation. Robert Parsons, a Jesuit missionary, relates the case thus:

> A wife being demanded by her husband, that is no competent judge, and compelled so to swear, whether she be an adulteress or no, may lawfully swear, if the sin be secret (say our doctors) that she is not, understanding *ut tibi revelem*—that I am bound to reveal to you—and thus avoid the danger that otherwise were likely to occur. (1607, 20)

Catholic casuists insist that the wife's linguistic deception is lawful in such a case because of what they saw as fundamental similarities between the position of the wife within marriage and that of a Jesuit missionary in late sixteenth- and early seventeenth-century England.[19] In their discussion of a case in which an English priest is interrogated concerning his identity by English authorities, Catholic casuists insist that the priest's linguistic manipulations are not intended to deceive his interrogators, but rather are employed as a form of self-preservation.[20] When they discuss the case of the adulterous wife, Catholic theologians suggest that just as the missionary priest deploys mental reservation only in self-defense, so the adulterous wife does not act with the intention to deceive another person, but to protect her own life. Parsons even describes the jealous husband as "proposing the present pain of death, except she answer directly thereunto" (1607, 290). By underscoring the physical danger to the wife, Catholic casuists implicitly acknowledge the physical disparity between the spouses. They suggest that in such cases, a wife's clever linguistic manipulation compensates for her lack of physical strength; although a wife may be unable to protect herself physically, she can defend herself using her "reason and wit"—which Parsons describes elsewhere as "the chief armor and weapon of mankind" (403).

Catholic casuists also suggest that the wife's linguistic manipulation is lawful because, like the missionary priest, she confronts an unjust authority who is not able to make unbiased determinations. A husband, Parsons specifies, does not possess lawful judicial authority over his wife; he is "no competent judge of her case." Although marriage grants the husband social and economic authority over his wife, it does not give him legal authority to determine her guilt or innocence. Moreover, a husband's emotional involvement in the case makes it impossible for him to act impartially. One of the primary reasons casuists argue that it is lawful for missionary priests to answer in any way they chose to their English interrogators is because English authorities are unable to make unbiased determinations. Similarly, they acknowledge that a husband often determines his wife to be an adulteress not on the basis of objective facts, but because of his own private suspicions or his jealousy. Casuists agree that a "jealous husband" is unable to act as a "competent judge" of his wife's case; hence, she may respond to his questions "as if no one were there."

Perhaps most interestingly, casuists suggest that the adulteress may manipulate language in order to preserve the public impression of her chastity, regardless of whether she has in reality remained faithful to her husband. Underpinning this conclusion is the recognition that in many cases, a woman's physical life depends upon her reputation or her fame—the popular perception of her "honesty." Navarre, a sixteenth-century Catholic casuist, points out that an adulterous woman who has born the children of a man other than her husband may be absolved for her sins; but if she confesses her sexual infidelity to her husband, "she may be in peril of her life and her loss of fame" (qtd. in Jeremy Taylor, "Ductor" 1661, 433).[21] Parsons puts it thus: if an adulterous woman were honestly to confess her dishonesty to her husband, "there goes her honor and her temporal life therein" (404). When they make such conclusions, casuists are adapting the importance traditionally accorded to the importance of a man's reputation and "good name" in late medieval and early modern Europe.[22] By the early seventeenth century, Catholic casuistry concerning the defense of one's honor and reputation was wide-ranging and unusually permissive; Pascal draws heavily upon such cases in his enumeration of the evils of Catholic casuistry in *The Provincial Letters* (1656–57).[23] But by extending this acknowledgement to the married woman's fame, Catholic casuists implicitly recognize honesty signifies differently for women than it does for men; whereas a reputation for dishonesty may sully a man's name, such a reputation may destroy a woman's life.

The case of the dishonest adulteress, then, foregrounds precisely what the Protestant emphasis upon marital truth-telling occludes: it reveals that relations between a husband and a wife are not equal and that the public perception of a woman's sexual honesty is the basis not only of her reputation, but also of her physical safety. Because a husband has social authority over his wife and possesses greater physical strength, and because husbands can and do act irrationally, the wife may need to protect herself through the manipulation of language. Put in slightly different terms, Catholic casuists recognize that gender differentially impacts a person's ability to tell the truth.

LOVE AND LIES IN *OTHELLO*

I turn now to an analysis of *Othello,* in which I argue that the exchange between Desdemona and Othello concerning the handkerchief is constructed to underscore the cultural pressures upon female honesty. Underpinning my analysis is the belief that it is impossible to separate questions concerning the representation of human agency within early modern tragedy from the analysis of a play's ideological structure. Anthony Giddens has argued "structure must not be conceptualized as simply placing constraints upon human agency, but as enabling . . . To enquire into the saturation of social practices is to seek to explain how it comes about that structure is constituted through action, and reciprocally how action is constituted structurally" (1993, 169). According to Giddens, one cannot examine character without analyzing the social processes and ideological forms that help produce it; at the same time, one should not focus upon structure without reflecting upon its implications for human agency. This approach, in which character and structure are dialectically intertwined, guides my reading of *Othello*: I am interested in analyzing how the play depicts the relation between Desdemona's decision, the pressures and dilemmas that she confronts, and early modern English (religious) culture.

The scene opens with an exchange between Desdemona and a clown. Although critics have traditionally dismissed the conversation, the Clown's repeated puns upon the equivocal meaning of the word "lies" foreground the instability of language and connect the play with early seventeenth-century casuistic debates over equivocation and mental reservation.[24] When the Clown leaves, Desdmona and Othello have the following exchange:

> OTHELLO: I have a salt and sorry rheum offends me; lend me thy handkerchief.
> DESDEMONA: Here my lord.
> OTHELLO: That which I gave you.
> DESDEMONA: I have it not about me.
> OTHELLO: Not?
> DESDEMONA: No, [faith], my lord.
> OTHELLO: That's a fault. (3.4.51–55)

Desdemona responds to Othello's initial request for the handkerchief with a technically true statement: "I have it not about me." Although

Protestant theologians would recognize such a response as equivocal, they would not necessarily deride it as immoral: Desdemona manipulates an idiomatic expression in an effort to conceal the handkerchief's loss. Most Protestant theologians recognized that such equivocal statements were morally licit in certain circumstances, although, as I suggested, they vigorously decried all forms of mental reservation, whereby a person withholds part of a statement in their mind in order to reverse the meaning of spoken words.

Othello responds to Desdemona's equivocal reply with an exotic narrative that associates the loss of the handkerchief with male inconstancy and sexual acquisitiveness; he claims that the Egyptian charmer warned his mother,

> if she lost it
> ... my father's eye
> should hold her loathed, and his spirits should hunt
> after new fancies

> (3.4.71–74)

As Carol Neely remarks, "both Othello's original description of the handkerchief and its part in the plot reveal that it is a symbol of women's civilizing power" (1994, 82). Desdemona replies by questioning the veracity of Othello's narrative:

DESDEMONA: [I' faith.] Is't true?
OTHELLO: Most veritable, therefore, look to't well.
DESDEMONA: Then would to [God] I had never seen it.
OTHELLO: Ha! Wherefore?
DESDEMONA: Why do you speak so startling and rash?
OTHELLO: Is it lost? Is't gone? Speak, is't out o' the way?
DESDEMONA: [Heaven] bless us!
OTHELLO: Say you?
DESDEMONA: It is not lost; but what and if it were?
OTHELLO: How?
DESDEMONA: I say, it is not lost.
OTHELLO: Fetch't. Let me see't.
DESDEMONA: Why so I can, [sir] but I will not now. This is a trick to put me from my suit.
Pray you let Cassio be received again.
OTHELLO: Fetch me the handkerchief, my mind misgives.
DESDEMONA: Come, come;
You'll never meet a more sufficient man.

OTHELLO: The handkerchief!
[DESDEMONA: I pray talk me of Cassio.
OTHELLO: The handkerchief!]
DESDEMONA: A man that hath all his time
Hath founded his good fortunes on your love,
Shar'd dangers with you—
OTHELLO: The handkerchief!
DESDEMONA: [I'faith], you are to blame.
OTHELLO: ['Zounds!]

Exit Othello. (3.4.75–97)[25]

Interestingly, the audience is never informed of the truthfulness of Othello's narrative. But because Desdemona readily accepts Othello's claims concerning its veracity, the narrative creates for her a complex moral dilemma: if she responds truthfully and confesses its loss, she risks losing Othello's love. But if she lies, she violates the honest communication that Protestant theologians insisted was constitutive of marriage and that, the play makes clear, cemented their union. Desdemona reveals the dilemma when she remarks that she wishes she had "never seen" the handkerchief; such remarks suggest that it is only by imagining a time when she did not possess the handkerchief that she believes she can escape the conflicting moral imperatives created by its loss.

Desdemona's case of conscience is further complicated by what moral theologians would designate as the "circumstance" of Othello's unprovoked anger. Earlier in the scene, Emilia insists that all husbands are jealous, but Desdemona asserts that Othello is incapable of such "baseness"; he is, she insists in a suggestive locution, "true of mind." Othello's erratic and verbally aggressive behavior in this scene contradicts this assessment; Desdemona herself foregrounds his transformation when she asks Othello, "Why do you speak so startling and rash?" As we have seen, Catholic moral theologians recognized that even an adulterous woman is not always bound to confess the truth to her irate husband; anger prevents the husband from acting as "a competent judge" and endangers the wife's life. But it is only when Othello draws upon his power as "supreme governor" within the household and commands Desdemona to answer his question— "Speak, is it out of the way?"—that Desdemona determines to lie; first, tentatively: "It is not lost, but what and if it were?" And later, more emphatically: "I say, it is not lost."

It would certainly be possible to follow Bradley (1957) at this junc-
ture and claim that such linguistic dissimulation provides crucial
insight into Desdemona's character, but its structural and thematic
position suggest otherwise. Articulated within a conversation that links
(apparently) unmotivated male jealousy and commanded female
speech, Desdemona's response reveals less about her personality than
the contradictory demands upon female honesty within a marriage
relationship that insists upon both the ideal of honest spousal conversation and the wife's social subordination.

WIFELY HONESTY

The remainder of *Othello* documents the tragic consequences of wifely dishonesty within a culture that sets up a hierarchical marriage relationship as privileged locus of affect, so that, as Cavell remarks, "a
ceremony of single intimacy is what we have to oppose to the threatened withdrawal of the world—of the realms of the natural, the social,
the political, the religious" (1987, 19). For Othello, Desdemona's "lie"
functions simultaneously as proof of her otherness and confirmation of
her sexual infidelity. As Neely has suggested, Desdemona's lie "signifies the loss of her maiden's power and innocence and confirms—
Othello believes—his notions about female depravity" (1994, 83).
Othello connects his love for Desdemona with his stable sense of self:
"Perdition catch my soul but I do love thee! And when I love thee not,
chaos is come again" (3.3.90–92). When Desdemona lies about the
handkerchief, she violates the honest communication constitutive of
married love and confirms her separation from Othello. That Othello
describes this differentiated self as "chaos" suggests the urgency of his
(impossible) desire to return to the utopian ideal of undifferentiated
selfhood proffered in the experience of "the rapture of love."

Peter Stallybrass has described the pervasive link in early modern
culture between female speech and sexuality, whereby "silence, the
closed mouth, is made a sign of chastity" (1988, 127). But this homology also has an ethical component: just as excessive speech signals
promiscuity, so dishonest speech constitutes infidelity. Early modern
marriage manuals suggest that two meanings were considered interchangeable; that is, they indicate that a woman's honest speech was

often taken to signify her sexual fidelity. Tilney suggests this linkage when he remarks: "to be brief, not only in chastity of body, but in honesty of behavior and talk, both the woman's honor and good name consist and is also maintained" (1577, 37).[26] Othello believes that Desdemona's verbal dishonesty constitutes proof of her erotic dishonesty, in large part because of Iago's skill in exploiting this cultural and linguistic homology. Much of Iago's considerable rhetorical energy in 3.3 is spent blurring the boundary between these two forms of honesty: he impugns at once Desdemona's sexual fidelity ("look to your wife/observe her with Cassio") and her capacity for honest communication ("She did deceive her father, marrying you"). In its place, Iago offers Othello his own reputation for honesty—a masculine honesty untainted by overt sexuality and variously associated with a lower-class frankness, avuncular commonsense, and a truthful appraisal of one's own motives.[27] The play thus resembles other early seventeenth-century domestic tragedies in depicting the competition between masculine friendship and the companionate marriage. As Lisa Jardine has remarked, "Once marriage is determined on the model of mutual affection and shared preference, it appears to come into direct conflict with the socially acceptable form of close partnership (friendship between adult men of good birth) quite as much as with traditional, parentally sponsored marriage alliance" (1996, 125).

As Othello prepares to murder Desdemona, he seems arguably as concerned with her dishonesty as with her infidelity; he repeatedly derides her as a "perjured woman." This obsession with Desdemona's truthfulness exists side by side with Othello's preoccupation with her sexual liaison with Cassio; at this point in the tragedy, Othello is unable to distinguish between them; one provides "proof" of the other. It is not surprising, then, that when Othello confesses to Emilia that he has murdered his wife, he justifies his act by insisting not upon her sexual infidelity, but upon her verbal dishonesty. When Emila hears the cries of the dying Desdemona, she asks her mistress, "O, who has done this deed?" Desdemona's reply, "Nobody, I myself. Farewell," stuns modern readers. But whether Desdemona blames herself or wants to protect her abusive husband, what is perhaps most remarkable is that Othello finds in this deathbed lie, together with Desdemona's earlier lie about the handkerchief, the ultimate justification for his actions. Paraphrasing the biblical punishment accorded to dishonesty, Othello exclaims, "She is like a liar gone to burning hell! T'was I that killed her" (5.2.128–29). For Othello, female mendacity signifies wifely infidelity. And for adultery, only one punishment is appropriate: death.

The irony of *Othello* is, of course, that the linkage proves false. Desdemona did lose her handkerchief—and lie about its whereabouts—but her chastity remained intact. The dramatic irony works to destroy the cultural linkage between a woman's verbal honesty and her sexual fidelity; at the same time, the tragedy reveals, like Catholic casuistry, the impossibility of absolute honesty—and correspondingly, marital friendship—within an ideology that insists upon wifely subordination.

Conclusion: Casuistry and Tragedy

Othello and Catholic casuistry, then, share a similar structure and concerns: both examine what happens to an abstract moral principle (here, the belief in marital honesty) when it is considered in the context of the concrete circumstances of the marital hierarchy. This structure makes casuistry and tragedy equally well suited to explore problems within prevailing cultural forms—in this case, the Protestant understanding of the companionate marriage. Literary scholars have long claimed this ability for drama; I claim it here for casuistry as well. In this sense, the play does less to evidence Shakespeare's religious convictions than to demonstrate the way in which the methods and procedures associated with early modern English Catholicism could be used to critique popular ideological forms in the early modern period.

At the same time, however, *Othello* moves beyond Catholic casuistry by insisting upon Desdemona's innocence. Catholic casuistry acknowledges that gender differentially impacts one's ability to tell the truth; because a reputation for "honesty" is crucially significant for a woman, a woman can employ mental reservation in order to preserve her fame, regardless of whether she has in actuality remained faithful to her husband. Like Catholic casuistry, *Othello* recognizes that marital hierarchy renders wifely honesty impossible; it also, however, analyzes the implications of this recognition within a culture that equates female honesty with sexual fidelity. By demonstrating the impossibility of wifely honesty within a marriage relationship that assumes that husband and wife can be "friends" and thus speak truthfully while insisting upon the husband's social superiority, and by showing how the cultural connection between a woman's verbal and sexual "honesty" can be manipulated so that a lying woman is (falsely) condemned as an adulteress, *Othello* offers a pointed examination of the contradictions at the heart of the companionate marriage.

NOTES

1. Greenblatt argues that *Othello* dramatizes a tension within the Protestant marriage manual's treatment of marital sexuality (1980, 222–25); Kirsch elaborates a similar argument from a more rigorously psychoanalytic perspective (1981, 10–40); Neely explores the play's treatment of marriage and gender (1994, 68–91); and Rose explores *Othello*'s engagement with the companionate marriage (1988).

2. See Belsey (1985, 129–49), Dolan (1994, 21–58).

3. Cavell, *Pursuits of Happiness* (1981, 28) also provides an illuminating discussion of genre.

4. See also Masten (1997), who similarly argues that we need to rethink our belief in the single "author" of Renaissance drama. In a related argument, McMillan and MacLean (1998) argue for the importance of theater companies in the development of early modern dramatic themes and genre.

5. The following list, while not comprehensive, suggests a sustained interest in domestic tragedy on the London stage during the late sixteenth and early seventeenth centuries: *Arden of Faversham* was published in 1592; *A Warning for Fair Women* was performed in 1589 by the Lord Chamberlain's men; *A Woman Killed with Kindness* was performed in 1603 by Worcester's men; *A Yorkshire Tragedy* was published in 1605 and performed by the Kings Men; and *The Miseries of Enforced Marriage* was performed by the Kings Men in 1606.

6. Bradley provides what is perhaps the most salient example of such character-criticism; according to Bradley, Desdemona "seems to know evil only by name and, her inclinations being good, she acts on inclination. This trait, with its results, may be seen if we compare her, at the crisis of her story, with Cordelia. In Desdemona's place, Cordelia, however frightened at Othello's anger about the lost handkerchief, would not have denied its loss" (1957, 161).

7. An important exception to the tendency to interpret Desdemona's lie about the handkerchief for what it reveals about her character is provided by Rose, who argues in *The Expense of Spirit* (1988) that Desdemona's lie has important implications for the play's treatment of the companionate marriage. But although Rose and I agree concerning the importance of the lie, we differ

in our interpretation of its significance. Rose argues that Desdemona's lie reveals the insurmountable dichotomy between public and private life, a gulf that she sees Desdemona as attempting to surmount in the "heroics of marriage" she undertakes when she marries Othello. In contrast, I am interested in the play's depiction of the moral requirement of marital honesty and its implications for our understanding of gender and early modern religious controversy; also, unlike Rose, I see the tragedy as advancing a critical (even antiheroic) view of the companionate marriage. This essay remains, however, indebted to Rose's discussion.

8. For more on the early seventeenth-century debate concerning equivocation and mental reservation, see McQuade (2001).

9. The first casuist to discuss the case of the dishonest adulteress in English was the Jesuit missionary Robert Parsons (1607). It is possible that Shakespeare was aware of Parsons's discussion of the case; the lawfulness of mental reservation was the subject of widespread public debate during this period due to its use by Henry Garnet, S.J., during his trial on charges for treason for his involvement in the Gunpowder Plot (November 5, 1605); Shakespeare's allusions in *Macbeth* to Garnet's trial are well documented. However, because most cases of conscience were discussed orally, the publication date of *Othello* is not crucial to my argument; Shakespeare could have heard the case discussed privately. Knowledge of the case among seventeenth-century Protestant casuists can be demonstrated: Jeremy Taylor addresses the case at length ("Ductor Dubitanium" 1661, 433). Finally, my argument does not presume Shakespeare's direct knowledge of the case, only with casuistic methods; my claim is that drama functions analogously to casuistry; it is possible that the casuists and Shakespeare independently advance similar arguments.

10. Although early Protestant reformers officially denigrated casuistry as part of a theology of works, case divinity survived—and indeed flourished—informally throughout the sixteenth century, as Protestant ministers increasingly adapted Catholic casuistry to serve their parishioners. For an example of mid-sixteenth-century Protestant casuistry, see *Practical Divinity,* ed. Parker (1998). By the end of the sixteenth century, Protestant divines were publishing their own collections of cases of conscience in which they acknowledge, with some reluctance, their debt to Catholic casuistry; see, for example, Perkins, *The Whole Treatise of Cases of Conscience* (1596). A posthumous collection, *The Whole Treatise* was a popular work; it went through ten editions in the seventeenth century. Because casuistry was practiced by both local Protestant ministers and university divines, it is likely that Shakespeare was familiar with casuistic methodology; it is also possible that he became familiar with Catholic case-divinity during his childhood, although this is difficult to prove. On the

importance and popularity of Catholic and Protestant casuistry in early modern England, see Jonsen and Toulmin (1988), also, Leites (1988). For casuistry's influence upon Renaissance drama, prose, and poetry, see Slights (1981)
and Gallagher (1991).

11. On the different conceptions of women and marriage within late
medieval Catholicism and early modern Protestantism, see Jordan (1990,
25–26, 214–20), Haller (1946), and Frye (1955). On marriage as a type of
friendship, see Leites (1986, 75–104).

12. Gouge explains "it is called benevolence because it must be performed
with good will and delight, willingly, readily and cheerfully; it is said to be
due because it is a debt which the wife owes to her husband and he to her"
(1621, 222). On the historical importance of the Protestant conception of marital sexuality, see Frye (1955, 148–59).

13. Kristeva is, of course, revisiting Freud. For Freud's view of love, see
"On the Universal Tendency" (1989) and "Observations on Transference
Love" (1989).

14. Kristeva remarks upon the centrality of conversation in the experience
of love: "in being able to receive the other's words, to assimilate, to reproduce
them, I become like him. One. A subject of enunciation. Through psychic
osmosis/identification. Through love" (1987, 26).

15. It is for this reason that Lacan claims that the acquisition of language
marks the birth of the self: to speak signifies both the loss of a pre-oedipal
unity and the advent of subjectivity. According to Lacan, it is the acknowledgment of this discrepancy, this lack, that constitutes the subject: "the cut in the
signifying chain [that] alone verifies the structure of the subject as discontinuity in the real" (qtd. in Fineman 1994, 114).

16. It is because friendship requires absolute honesty that Montaigne
argues that women are incapable of true friendship. "The normal capacity of
women is," writes Montaigne, "in fact, unequal to the demands of that communion and intercourse on which the sacred bond is fed; their souls do not
seem firm enough to bear the strain of so hard and lasting a tie" (1958, 95).
For a contemporary perspective on love and honesty, see hooks (2001).

17. In her analysis of marital dissembling in Milton's divorce tracts,
Zimmerman concludes that, "the critique of conjugal dissembling remains a
gender specific critique, a critique of man's dissembling, not the woman's"
(1999, 564). I found Zimmerman's article useful in thinking about the treatment of dissembling in Protestant marriage manuals. Unlike Milton's divorce
tracts, however, Protestant marriage manuals insist that both husband and
wife must occasionally "dissemble" their emotions. Tilney, for example,
advises the husband "to be sufferable in the importunities of the wife, sometimes dissembling . . ." (1577, 23–24). And Gouge advises the husband thus:

"and if he [the husband] shall have occasion to speak sharply and sometimes to reprove, he must be ware that he do not the same in the presence of others, but let him keep his words until a convenient time . . . and utter them in the spirit of meekness and perfect love" (1621, 80).

18. Parsons concludes his discussion of the case of the dishonest adulteress by quoting a number of casuists who agree with his analysis. "Navarre do[es] concur in this, [as does] Sylvester, Angelus De Clavasio . . . Tolet, Azor, and others" (1607, 436).

19. For more concerning the cultural connection linking Jesuit missionaries with women in early modern England, see Marotti (1999).

20. Parsons repeatedly describes mental reservation as a weapon that should be used primarily in self-defense. "Doubtful or amphibological speech," writes Parsons, "that hath a true meaning in the speaker's understanding and is used by him not to deceive or hurt, but to defend himself is no lie, nor falsehood at all, and consequently is lawful; it can not be reprehensible in just occasions to use the same" (1607, 403).

21. Taylor is, not surprisingly, horrified by Navarre's conclusion; he cites it as an example of Catholic moral laxity: "Navarre is the man whom I choose for all the rest . . . in the case of the adulteress, [Navarre writes] 'she hath sinned, but she may be absolved though she hold her peace, and be injurious to the supposed father, or wrong the heirs, that is, if she be in peril of her life or fears her loss of fame.' Against such prodigies of doctrine I intend this paragraph" (1661, 433).

22. On cases of conscience concerning reputation, see Jonsen and Toulmin (1988, 216–29).

23. Cases concerning the defense of honor are discussed primarily in letters seven and fourteen.

24. The example of punning upon the dual meanings of the word "lie" was common in Catholic discussion of equivocation; indeed, it was perhaps the most common example. Antiequivocation polemic frequently paints the equivocator as a "clown." James I describes the equivocator thus: "But what shall we say of these strange country clowns . . . the blow hot and cold out of one mouth?" (1994, 110).

25. All Shakespeare references are from Shakespeare, *The Riverside Shakespeare,* ed. Evans (1974), and are cited parenthetically within the text.

26. If we adopt Williams's distinctions, we can describe the second meaning of marital honesty—as signifying wifely chastity—as "residual"; the first as "emergent" (1977, 121–27). Williams's terminology is useful because it acknowledges the way in which both meanings exist simultaneously within a culture; at the same time it underscores how these meanings compete with one another for cultural prominence.

27. In "Honest in *Othello*," Empson briefly, but perceptively, remarks upon the structural significance of Desdemona's lie within Othello. He writes that "whereas it was Desdemona's simplicity that made her helpless . . . the fatal step was her lie about the handkerchief" (1965, 484).

WORKS CITED

Adams, Henry Hitch. *English Domestic, or Homiletic Tragedy.* New York: Benjamin Bloom, 1943.

Baxter, Richard. *A Christian Directory.* London: Robert White, 1677.

Belsey, Catherine. *The Subject of Tragedy.* London: Routledge, 1985.

Bradley, A. C. *Shakespearean Tragedy.* New York: Meridian Books, 1957.

Brooks, Douglas. *From Playhouse to Printing House: Drama and Authorship in Early Modern England.* Cambridge, England: Cambridge University Press, 2000.

Cavell, Stanley. *Disowning Knowledge in Six Plays of Shakespeare.* Cambridge, England: Cambridge University Press, 1987.

———. *Pursuits of Happiness: The Hollywood Comedy of Remarriage.* Cambridge, Mass.: Harvard University Press, 1981.

Cleaver, Robert. *A Godly Form of Household Government.* London: R. Field, 1621.

Dolan, Frances. *Dangerous Familiars.* Ithaca, N.Y.: Cornell University Press, 1994.

Empson, William. "Honest in *Othello*." In *Four Centuries of Shakespeare Criticism,* ed. Frank Kermode. New York, 1965.

Fineman, Joel. "The Sound of O in *Othello*: The Real of the Tragedy of Desire." In *Critical Essays on Shakespeare's* Othello, ed. Anthony Gerard Barthelemy. New York: G. K. Hall & Co., 1994.

Fowler, Alistair. *Kinds of Literature: An Introduction to the Theory of Genres and Modes.* Cambridge, Mass.: Harvard University Press, 1982.

Freud, Sigmund. "Observations on Transference Love." In *The Freud Reader,* ed. Peter Gay. New York: W. W. Norton, 1989.

———. "On the Universal Tendency to Debasement in the Sphere of Love." In *The Freud Reader,* ed. Peter Gay. New York: W. W. Norton, 1989.

Frye, Roland Mushat. "The Teachings of Classical Puritanism on Conjugal Love." *Studies in the Renaissance* (1955): 148–59.

Gallagher, Lowell. *Medusa's Gaze: Casuistry and Conscience in the Renaissance.* Stanford, Calif.: Stanford University Press, 1991.

Giddens, Anthony. *New Rules of Sociological Method: A Positive Critique of Interpretive Sociologies.* Stanford, Calif.: Stanford University Press, 1993.

Gouge, William. *Of Domestical Duties.* London: John Beale, 1622.

Greenblatt, Stephen. *Renaissance Self-Fashioning.* Chicago, Ill.: University of Chicago Press, 1980.

Haller, William. "Hail Wedded Love." *ELH* 13 (June 1946): 79–97.

hooks, bell. "Tender Hooks: bell hooks on the politics of love." Interview by Lisa Miya-Jervis. *Bitch: Feminist Response to Pop Culture.* Issue 13 (2001).

James I. "Triplici Nodo, Triplex Cuneus or An Apology for the Oath of Allegiance." In *King James VI and I: Political Writings,* ed. Johann P. Sommerville. Cambridge, Mass.: Cambridge University Press, 1994.

Jardine, Lisa. *Reading Shakespeare Historically.* London: Routledge, 1996.

Jonsen, Albert, and Stephen Toulmin. *The Abuse of Casuistry: A History of Moral Reasoning.* Berkeley, Calif.: University of California Press, 1988.

Jordan, Constance. *Renaissance Feminism.* Ithaca, N.Y.: Cornell University Press, 1990.

Kirsch, Arthur. *Shakespeare and the Experience of Love.* Cambridge, England: Cambridge University Press, 1981.

Kristeva, Julia. *Tales of Love.* New York: Columbia University Press, 1987.

Leites, Edmund, ed. *Conscience and Casuistry in Early Modern Europe.* Cambridge, England: Cambridge University Press, 1988.

_____. *The Puritan Conscience and Modern Sexuality.* New Haven, Conn.: Yale University Press, 1986.

Marotti, Arthur, ed. *Catholicism and Anti-Catholicism in Early Modern English Texts.* New York: St. Martin's Press, 1999.

Masten, Jeffrey. *Textual Intercourse: Collaboration, Authorship and Sexualities in Renaissance Drama.* Cambridge, England: Cambridge University Press, 1997.

McMillan, Scott, and Sally Beth MacLean. *The Queen's Men and Their Plays*. Cambridge, England: Cambridge University Press, 1998.

McQuade, Paula. "Truth and Consequences: Equivocation, Mental Reservation, and the Secret Catholic Subject in Early Modern England." *Ben Jonson Journal* 8 (2001): 277–90.

Montaigne, Michel. *Essays*. Trans. J. M. Cohen. London: Penguin, 1958.

Neely, Carol. "Women and Men in *Othello*." In *Critical Essays on Shakespeare's* Othello, ed. Anthony Gerard Barthelemy. New York: G. K. Hall & Co., 1994.

Newman, Karen. *Fashioning Femininity and English Renaissance Drama*. Chicago, Ill.: University of Chicago Press, 1991.

Parsons (Persons), Robert. *A Treatise Tending to Mitigation towards Catholic Subjects in England*. Saint-Omer: Printed by F. Bellet, 1607.

Parker, Kenneth, ed. *Practical Divinity: The Works and Life of Reverend Richard Greenham*. Brookfield, Vt.: Ashgate, 1998.

Pascal, Blaise. *The Provincial Letters*. Trans. A. J. Krailsheimer. London: Penguin, 1967.

Perkins, Williams. *The Whole Treatise of Cases of Conscience*. London: John Legat, 1596.

Rogers, Daniel. *Matrimonial Honour*. London: Thomas Harper, 1642.

Rose, Mary Beth. *The Expense of Spirit: Love and Sexuality in English Renaissance Drama*. Ithaca, N.Y.: Cornell University Press, 1988.

Shakespeare, William. *The Riverside Shakespeare*. Ed. G. Blakemore Evans. Boston: Houghton Mifflin, 1974.

Slights, Camille Wells. *The Casuistical Tradition*. Princeton, N.J.: Princeton University Press, 1981.

Stallybrass, Peter. "Patriarchal Territories: The Body Enclosed." In *Rewriting the Renaissance: The Discourses of Sexual Difference in Early Modern Europe,* ed. Margaret W. Ferguson et al. Chicago, Ill.: University of Chicago Press, 1988.

Stone, Laurence. *The Family, Sex, and Marriage in England 1500–1800*. New York: Harper Torchbooks, 1979.

Taylor, Charles. *Sources of the Self*. Cambridge, Mass.: Harvard University Press, 1989.

Taylor, Jeremy. "Ductor Dubitanium: Or, the Rule of Conscience." In *The Whole Works of the Right Reverend Jeremy Taylor.* 3 Vols. London: 1661.

_____. "A Discourse of the Nature, Offices, and Measures of Friendship." In *The Whole Works of Jeremy Taylor.* 3 Vols. London: 1661.

Tilney, Edmund. *A Brief and Pleasant Discourse of Duties in Marriage, Called the Flower of Friendship.* London, 1577.

White, Martin, ed. *Arden of Faversham.* New York: W. W. Norton, 1997.

Williams, Raymond. *Marxism and Literature.* Oxford, England: Oxford University Press, 1977.

Zimmerman, Shari. "Disaffection, Dissimulation, and the Uncertain Ground of Silent Dismission." *ELH* 66.3 (1999): 553–89.

NOTES ON CONTRIBUTORS

CLARE ASQUITH graduated MA with a congratulatory First in English from St. Anne's College, Oxford, in 1973. She has since worked in publishing and education and has lived and traveled widely with her family in Eastern Europe, where her husband was a diplomat. More recently, she has published articles on Shakespeare's poem "The Phoenix and the Turtle" in *The Shakespeare Newsletter* (Spring 2000) and *TLS* (April 13, 2000). She is currently preparing a book on Shakespeare and the Reformation, to be published by Scribners.

DAVID BEAUREGARD, O.M.V., is Dean of Studies at Our Lady of Grace Seminary, Boston. He is the author of *Virtue's Own Feature: Shakespeare and the Virtue Ethics Tradition* (1995), a study of Shakespeare's plays as representations of Aristotelian-Thomistic virtues and vices. He is currently working on a volume on Shakespeare's Catholic theology as it is manifested in several of the plays.

REGINA M. BUCCOLA is Assistant Professor of English at Roosevelt University. Her primary research interests are early modern British drama and twentieth-century British and American feminist drama. She has presented papers on these topics at the annual meetings of the Modern Language Association, the Renaissance Society of America, and the Group for Early Modern Cultural Studies, among others. Her publications include essays on American playwrights Megan Terry and Cherríe Moraga in *Tortilleras: Hispanic and Latina Lesbian Expression* and *Fake City Syndrome*, respectively, and poetry in *Aries, New Growth Arts Review, Reflections: A Poetry Quarterly,* and *Sparrowgrass Poetry Forum.*

RICHARD DUTTON is Professor of English at Ohio University State. He has published widely on early modern drama, especially on questions relating to censorship: his latest book on that theme is *Licensing, Censorship and Authorship in Early Modern England: Buggeswords*

(Palgrave, 2000). He has also edited a number of texts from the period, including *"Women Beware Women" and Other Plays by Thomas Middleton* (Oxford University Press, 1999) and *Jonson's* Epicene (Manchester University Press, 2003). He is currently editing, with Jean Howard, four Companions to Shakespeare's Works (Blackwell) and working on an edition of *Volpone* for the Cambridge *Ben Jonson.*

JOHN FREEMAN currently serves as acting Chair of the English Department at the University of Detroit Mercy. His scholarly interests include Renaissance literature, recusant Catholics, and the scientific modeling of texts. An article he wrote on *Tristram Shandy* and complexity theory will appear this summer in *Studies in the Novel.* His article on Thomas More's *Utopia* will be appearing in *ELH.* Currently, he is negotiating with the University of Florida Press for a book concerning intellectual property rights in More's *Utopia.*

KATHARINE GOODLAND is Assistant Professor of English at the College of Staten Island, City University of New York. Her article "'Us for to Wepe, No Man May Lett': The Ambivalent Voice of Female Grief in the Medieval English Lazarus Plays," is forthcoming in *Grief and Gendered,* edited by Jennifer Vaught and Lynne Bruckner (Palgrave Press). She is working on a book on grief and tragedy in early modern England.

GARY D. HAMILTON is Associate Professor of English at the University of Maryland. He is the author of several essays on political and theological dimensions of the writings of Milton and Marvell.

R. CHRIS HASSEL JR., Professor of English at Vanderbilt University, has spent much of his career studying Shakespeare and religion. His three books, *Renaissance Drama and the English Church Year; Faith and Folly in Shakespeare's Romantic Comedies;* and *Songs of Death: Performance, Interpretation, and the Text of* Richard III, all represent that interest from varied perspectives, as do a series of recent articles on Shakespeare, Reformation controversy, and religious iconography, among them: "Painted Women: Annunciation Motifs in *Hamlet*" (*Comparative Drama* 1998); "Intercession, Detraction and Just Judgment in *Othello*" (*Comparative Drama* 2001); and "'No boasting like a fool'? Herod and Macbeth" (*Studies in Philology* 2001). He is currently writing a Dictionary of Shakespeare and Religion (Athlone Shakespeare Dictionary series).

LISA HOPKINS is a Reader in English at Sheffield Hallam University and editor of *Early Modern Literary Studies*. Her publications include *Christopher Marlowe: A Literary Life* (Palgrave, 2000), *The Shakespearean Marriage: Merry Wives and Heavy Husbands* (Macmillan and St Martin's Press, 1998), and *John Ford's Political Theatre* (Manchester University Press and St Martin's Press, 1994). She has two books forthcoming: *Writing Renaissance Queens* (University of Delaware Press) and *The Female Hero in English Renaissance Tragedy* (Palgrave).

MAURICE HUNT is Professor of English and department Chair at Baylor University. He most recently published *Approaches to Teaching Shakespeare's Romeo and Juliet* (*MLA*, 2000). He has forthcoming articles on *The Winter's Tale* in *Studies on English Literature*, on *Cymbeline* in *Studies in Philology*, on *A Midsummer Night's Dream* in *Comparative Drama*, and on *Timon of Athens* in *English Studies*.

JOHN KLAUSE is Professor of English at Hofstra University. He is author of *The Unfortunate Fall: Theodicy and the Moral Imagination of Andrew Marvell*, and editor of the neo-Latin play *Andronicus Comnenus*. He has published on Marvell, John Donne, George Herbert, Shakespeare's sonnets, *Venus and Adonis*, and has published several essays (deriving from a continuing project) on the literary connections between Shakespeare and Robert Southwell.

RICHARD MALLETTE is Distinguished Service Professor of English at Lake Forest College. His most recent book is *Spenser and the Discourses of Reformation England* (Nebraska, 1997).

JEAN-CHRISTOPHE MAYER is Senior Research Fellow at the University of Montpellier, France. He has published articles in *Cahiers Elisabethains, Shakespeare Criticism,* and *Shakespeare Yearbook.* He has recently edited a collection of essays on Shakespeare's *Antony and Cleopatra* and is currently completing a book entitled *Shakespeare and the English Catholics.*

PAULA MCQUADE is Assistant Professor of English at DePaul University, Chicago. She has published articles exploring the intersection of gender and religion and early modern Catholicism in *Literature and History, Modern Philology,* and *The Ben Jonson Journal.* She is currently working on a book, *Casuistry and Tragedy,* which proposes and traces connections between Catholic and Protestant casuistry and representations of subjectivity on the early modern stage.

TIMOTHY ROSENDALE is Assistant Professor of English at Southern Methodist University in Dallas, Texas. His article "'Fiery Toungues': Language, Liturgy, and the Paradox of the English Reformation" recently appeared in *Renaissance Quarterly.* He is working on a book on liturgy, authority, and representation in early modern England.

JENNIFER RUST was the Murray Krieger Fellow in Literary Theory for 1999–2000 at the University of California, Irvine. Her current scholarly interests include political theology in early modern Europe and "theo-political economy" (discourses on idolatry and commodity fetishism in Reformation England). Most recently, she has been working on a new translation of Carl Schmitt's book on Shakespeare, *Hamlet oder Hekuba.*

DENNIS TAYLOR is editor of *Religion and the Arts,* and Professor of English at Boston College. His books include *Hardy's Poetry 1860–1928* (Macmillan, 1981, 1989), *Hardy's Metres and Victorian Prosody* (Oxford University Press, 1988), *Hardy's Literary Language and Victorian Philology* (Oxford University Press, 1993), and the Penguin edition of *Jude the Obscure* (1998). His current research is on Shakespeare and the Reformation.

INDEX

Adams, Henry Hitch, 415
Adelman, Janet, 248
Aeschylus, 69, 72
Aglionby, Edward, 255n3
Albright, Evelyn May, 116n4
Allegory, 4–5, 6, 9, 10–12, 94, 180–83
Allen, William, 227, 230, 236–38, 242, 247, 251
Antigone, 2, 5
Apelles. *See* Lucian
Aquinas, Thomas, 207–8, 314–15, 317, 319–20, 337
Arden, Edward, 229
Arden of Faversham, 415–17
Aretino, Pietro, 35
Arundell, Dorothy 205, 215n37
Auden, W. H., 392
Austen, Glyn, 27

Bacon, Francis, 110–11, 114
Bacon, Nicholas, 149–52
Baker, Oliver, 223
Baldwin, T. W., 26, 27–28, 30, 39, 39n1
Bale, John, 147
Bancroft, Richard, 146, 156n6, 215n43
Barish, Jonas, 138n5, 289–90, 292, 305nn10, 11, 352
Barnes, Paulinus, 232
Barroll, J. Leeds, 215n42
Barton, Anne, 352
Battenhouse, Roy, 234, 284n9

Baxter, Richard, 420
Beauregard, David N., 361n12–13, 362n18, 377–78
Beale, Robert, 109
Bede, 141–42
Bell, Thomas, 339
Bellarmine, Robert, 202
Belsey, Catherine, 415
Belson, Thomas, 83, 86, 91
Benjamin, Walter, 15, 266–67, 270, 275, 281–82, 283n6, 284n8
Berkeley, David S., 346, 360n8
Bernard, Richard, 300–301
Berthold, Dennis, 359n5
Bevington, David, 16, 55, 100n2, 312, 332n2, 342, 346
Birch, W. J., 234
Boccaccio, Giovanni, 313, 322
de Boisisse (ambassador), 114
Bolton, R., 306n27
Book of Common Prayer, 122–23, 127, 135–37, 168
Borromeo, Charles, 226
Bossy, John, 288
Bovet Richard, 175n16
Bowden, Wiliam, 354
Bradbrook, M. C., 361n15
Bradley, A. C., 428, 431n6
Bristow, Richard, 252, 254
Brooks, Douglas, 416
Brooks, Harold, 58, 61
Brown, John Russell, 185
Brown, Robert, 307n31
Brown, Theo, 237

Browning, Robert, 181
Brownlow, F. W., 215*n*37, 229, 377
Bruce, F. F., 363*n*24
Bucer, Martin, 51
Bullough, Geoffrey, 57
Burghley, William Cecil, Lord, 4, 80, 86, 94, 100, 108, 149–54, 217*n*53, 240, 246
Burton, Robert, 160, 265–66, 297
Butler, Martin, 138*n*5

Calvin, John, 86, 265, 275, 284*n*14, 343, 360*n*10, 386, 391
Camden, William, 27–28, 30, 107, 150
Campbell, L. B., 116*n*3
Campion, Edmund, 81, 100, 214*n*34, 231, 243, 246
Candido, Joseph, 26
Carew, Thomas, 305*n*8
Carey, John, 98
Carroll, William C., 175*nn* 11, 12
Carter, William, 101*n*15
Cartwright, Thomas, 82
Catholicism, 3, 6–7, 8–9, 10, 13, 18
Cavell, Stanley, 415, 428, 431*n*3
Cecil, Robert, 108, 111, 113–15, 151
Chambers, E. K., 223
Chapman, George, 314
Charles V, Holy Roman Emperor, 260
Charlton, H. B., 339
Chaucer, Geoffrey, 8, 20, 313, 317, 322
Cinthio, Giraldi, 324, 330
Clancy, Thomas H., 207
Clare, Janet, 155
Cleaver, Robert, 418, 420–21
Clegg, Cyndia Susan, 111
Cobham, William, 148
Cohen, Walter, 181, 211*n*2, 215*n*42

Cole, Howard C., 361*n*14
Colet, John, 96
Collinson, Patrick, 7, 103, 105, 146, 288, 299, 301, 304*nn*1, 3, 4, 305*n*21, 306*nn*25, 28
Constable, Henry, 99
Corpus Christi cycle plays, 48–49, 67, 69. *See also* Morality Plays
de Corro, Antonio, 86–87, 94
Corsini, Filippo, 113
Costello, William T., 245
Cottom, John, 231–32
Coursen, Herbert R., 408*n*23
Coverdale, Miles, 52
Cranmer, Thomas, 121
Crockett, Bryan, 385, 407*n*9
Cromwell, Oliver, 307*n*39
Crosse, Henry, 245
Cunningham, Henry, 27
Cushman, Robert, 301

Dacres, Ann, 205
Daniell, David, 363*n*24
Danson, Lawrence, 185–86, 215*n*42
David, Richard, 339
Davies, Richard, 143
Dennis, Carl, 362*n*18
Dickens, A. G., 283*n*3, 5, 7
Diehl, Huston, 125, 138*n*7, 312, 316, 323, 328, 406*n*6, 408*n*26
Diet of Worms, 247, 260–61
Dobbins, Austin C., 156*n*4
Dolan, Frances, 415
Donne, Henry, 88–89
Donne, John, 3, 5, 47, 82, 86, 88–89, 94, 98, 101*n*14, 407*n*9
Dowden, Edward, 16
Dronke, Peter, 49
Duffy, Eamon, 48, 50–51
Dutton, Richard, 116*n*4, 148
Dyos, Robert, 226

Ebeling, Gerhard, 264
Eisenstein, Elizabeth, 263
Elizabeth I, Queen of England, 5, 6,
  16, 34, 81, 83–84, 109–11, 126,
  141–42, 145, 149–50, 154, 166,
  172–73
Eliot, T. S., 299
Elyot, Thomas, 29, 34
Empson, William, 435*n*27
Erasmus, Desiderius, 5, 6, 20, 29,
  93, 96, 407*n*8
Essex, Robert Devereux, Earl of,
  5–6, 12, 16, 104, 106–16, 141,
  369
Euripides, 69
Evans, G. Blakemore, 336, 352

Famous Victories of Henry V, The,
  147, 153
Fawkes, Guy, 14
Fereguson, Francis, 289
Ferguson, Margaret, 284*n*12
Fineman, Joel, 284*n*10
Fiorentino, Giovanni, 182–83, 194,
  202, 211*n*7
Fitzherbert, Nicholas, 84
Florio, John, 90
Floyd, John, 236
Foakes, R. A., 26, 28
Ford, John, 312
Foxe, John, 143, 145–46, 148, 153;
  Book of Martyrs, 37, 38, 125,
  142, 147
Fowler, Alistair, 416
Franchot, Jenny, 14
Fraser, Russell, 226
Frayn, Michael, *Headlong,* 40*n*8
Freud, Sigmund, 433*n*13
Friedman, Michael D., 328
Frye, Northrop, 331
Frye, Roland, 408*nn*22, 23, 433*n*12

Garnet, Henry, 253, 432*n*9
Gascoigne, George, 26
Geary, Patrick, 237, 242, 244
Geoffrey of Monmouth, 372
George, C. H. and Katherine,
  305*n*17
Gerard, John, 222, 225, 241
Gesta Romanorum, 194, 211*n*3
Giddens, Anthony, 425
Giles, Paul, 14
Girouard, Mark, 372
Gless, Darryl, 312–13, 318, 328,
  332*n*4
Godshalk, William L., 358
Gosson, Stephen, 294, 306*n*25
Gouge, William, 306*n*28, 418, 421,
  433*n*12, 433*n*17
Gower, John, 26
Grammaticus, Saxo, 234
Grazia, Margareta De, 253
Greaves, Richard L., 46, 75*n*6
Greenblatt, Stephen, 3, 18, 45, 124,
  135, 138*n*6, 162, 185, 214*n*36,
  233, 235–36, 239, 247, 249, 254,
  261, 262, 267–68, 283*nn*4, 5, 6,
  346, 358, 361*n*16, 386–87, 431*n*1
Greene, Gayle, 407*n*9
Greene, Robert, 328
Greene, Thomas M., 128, 394
Greenham, Richard, 386, 389,
  399–400
Gregerson, Linda, 75*n*8
Griffiths, Trevor, 311
Grindal, Archbishop of Canterbury,
  86, 305*n*21
Gross, John, 181
Grubb, Shirley Carr, 58, 59, 69, 72
Gunpowder Plot, 1, 21, 432*n*9
Gurr, Andrew, 116*n*1

Haigh, Christopher, 223, 227
Haley, David, 375

Halio, Jay, 185
Hall, Edward, 143
Hamilton, Donna, 27, 40 *n*3, 116, 156*n*8, 301, 303, 307*n*34, 321
Hammer, Paul, 108–9, 156*n*10
Hammond, Antony, 72
Harpsfield, Nicholas, 142
Harrison, William, 246
Harsnett, Samuel, 361*n*11
Harvey, Gabriel, 90
Hatton, Christopher, 149
Hayne, Victoria, 326
Hayward, John, 104
Heffner, Ray, 116*n*4
Heilman, Robert, 404
Helgerson, Richard, 75*n*8
Heinemann, Margot, 288, 306*n*25, 308*n*42
Henri of Navarre (Henri IV, King of France) 2, 5, 40*n*4, 85, 86, 87, 88, 339–40, 372
Henry VIII, King of England, 9
Herbert, George, 204, 297
Herbert, William, 94
Herman, Peter C., 138*n*5
Herrick, Robert, 159
Hesketh, Thomas, 233
Heylyn, Peter, 129–30, 145–46
Heywood, Jasper, 88, 214*n*35
Hickman, Henry, 156*n*7
Hill, Christopher, 296–97, 299, 301, 307*nn*30, 31, 36, 337
Hill, W. Speed, 356
Hoby, Edward, 237
Hodgetts, William, 101*n*5
Hoghton, Alexander, 232–33
Hoghton, Thomas, 232
Holden, William, 299, 306*n*29, 308*n*41
Holleran, James V., 249

Holmer, Joan Ozark, 181, 194, 212*n*22
Homilies, 296–97, 326–27, 332, 389, 396
Honan, Park, 228–29
Honigmann, Ernst, 24, 232
Hooker, Richard, 337, 339, 345, 359*n*2, 384, 386, 391, 407*n*10, 408*n*25
hooks, bell, 433*n*16
Horne, Robert, 92
Houlbrooke, Ralph, 288, 304*n*4
Howard, Jean, 72, 138*n*5
Howard, Philip, Earl of Arundell, 205
Hughes, Merritt Y., 338
Hunt, Maurice, 406*n*7, 408*n*22–23
Hunt, Simon, 231
Hunter, G. K., 180
Hunter, R. G., 332*n*4, 362*n*18, 406*n*7
Huntington, Richard, 56

James I, King of England (James VI of Scotland), 10, 16, 20, 21, 105, 151, 160–62, 307*n*30, 369, 434*n*24
James, Heather, 372
Jardine, Lisa, 429
Jewel, John, 52, 81
Jocekel, Sam, 360*n*7
Jonssen, Albert, 434*n*22
Jonson, Ben, 161–62, 206, 289, 292–93, 299, 301–4, 305*nn*8, 14

Kant, Immanuel, 331
Kastan, David Scott, 358
Kaufman, Ivor, 299, 305*n*18
Kaufman, Peter, 399–400, 408*n*24–25
Kaula, David, 269, 284*n*15
Kay, Dennis, 54, 72

Keesee, Donald, 346, 360n8
Kempe, Margery, 48
Kernan, Alvin, 289–90, 292, 302, 305n10, 308n41
Kinney, Arthur, 36
Kirsch, Arthur, 431n1
Kitto, H. D. F., 234, 237
Knight, G. Wilson, 350
Knox, John, 156n6
Kristeva, Julia, 419–20, 433n13–14

Lacan, Jacques, 433n15
Lake, Peter, 288, 304n3, 307n30
Lang, Andrew, 160
Langdale, Alban, 217n53
Lauretus, Hieronymus, 35
Lee, Edward Dunn, 168
Leech, Clifford, 362n17
Leggatt, Alexander, 72, 76n16
Leicester, Earl of, 82, 149, 306n25
Leicester's Commonwealth, 82
Leites, Edmund, 422
Lepanto, Battle of, 37–38
Leslie, John, 149–52, 154
Levin, Richard, 370
Lewalski, Barbara, 138n5, 180–81, 338, 359n3
Lewis, Cynthia, 342, 360n10, 377
Lodge, Thomas, 99
Longland, John, 50–51
Lopez, Ruy, 185
Loraux, Nicole, 45
Low, Anthony, 234–36, 253
Lucian, 1, 28–30, 33, 34–36
Lukacher, Ned, 280, 284n10
Lupton, Julia, 283n2, 319
Luther, Martin, 261, 263–66, 282, 337, 359n5, 407n8
Lyly, John, 26
Lyons, Bridget Gellert, 284n15

Maclean, Sally Beth, 431n4
Macropedius, Georgius, 52
Malinowski, B., 46
Malone, Edmund, 225
Marcus, Leah, 283n7
Markham, Gervase, 52–53
Markidou, Vassiliki, 41n18
Marlowe, Christopher, 183, 185, 206, 212n19, 283n7, 370, 373
Marprelate, Martin, controversy, 146–47, 152, 168, 172, 295, 306n25
Marotti, Arthur, 434n19
Marshall, William, 35
Martin, Gregory, 101n15
Marx, Steven, 181, 211n6
Mary, Queen of Scots, 1, 4, 16, 54, 151
Massing, Jean Michel, 35–36
Masten, Jeffrey, 431n4
Mather, Anne E., 36
Matheson, Mark, 235, 284nn9, 14
McCandless, David, 363n27
McCoy, Richard C., 112
McGinn, Donald J., 321
McIntosh, Marjorie, 288, 304n5
McMillan, Scott, 431n4
Melanchthon, Philip, 29, 34, 35, 266
The Merry Devil of Edmonton, 329
Metcalf, Peter, 56
Meyrick, Gilly, 114
Middleton, Thomas, 305n14, 308n42
Milton, John, 288, 306n25, 338, 345, 352, 433n17
Milward, Peter, 4, 24, 24–25, 215nn42, 43, 312, 332n2, 385
Miola, Robert, 284n9
Moisan, Thomas, 214n35
Montagu, Anthony Browne, Lord, 216n53

Montaigne, 7, 8, 420, 433n16
Montrose, Louis, 124, 138n6
Morality Plays, 8, 63, 314, 317, 383, 406n6
More, Thomas, 5, 6, 29, 88, 93, 240, 307n38
Morrill, John, 307n39
Muir, Edward, 288
Mullaney, Stephen, 328
Munday, Anthony, 147

Nashe, Thomas, 212n19, 214n32, 295
Neely, Carole Thomas, 175n11, 363n26, 408n19, 426, 428, 431n1
Neill, Michael, 55, 56, 57, 75n4
Neville, Henry, 113
Newman, Karen, 388, 407n12, 415
Nicholls, Josias, 339
Northumberland, Henry, Earl of, 105
Novy, Marianne, 408n19

Obermann, Heiko, 389
O'Connor, Garry, 228, 231, 244
Oexle, Otto Gerhard, 244

Painter, William, 363n23
Palmer, David J., 343, 360n9
Parker, Kenneth, 432n10
Parker, Matthew, 51–52
Parker, Patricia, 403
Parks, Joan, 72
Parsons, Robert. See Persons, Robert
Pascal, Blaise, 424
Pechter, Edward, 387
Penry, John, 167–69, 172–73
Perkins, William, 265, 305n17, 338–39, 383, 386, 391, 396–97, 400, 405n4, 408n20–21, 432n10

Persons (Parsons), Robert, 6, 104, 107–12, 116, 143, 149, 155, 203, 207–8, 214n34, 215n47, 216n52, 217n53, 229–30, 237, 245–46, 251, 422–24, 432n9, 434n18, 434n20
Phelps, John, 214n32
Phillippy, Patricia, 76n12
Pigman, G. W., 51–52
Pineas, Rainer, 314, 317–18
Plautus, 26, 27, 37
Poole, Kristen, 146–47, 175n14, 176n20
Porter, Joseph A., 390
Pounde, Thomas, 217n53
Prosser, Eleanor, 234, 237, 275, 284n9
Prynne, William, 306n28
Purkiss, Diane, 166, 174n1

Rabelais, 7, 8
Rabkin, Norman, 138n10
Rackin, Phyllis, 58, 72, 138n10
Ralegh, Sir Walter, 84
Rand, Nicholas, 243–44
Recusants, 12
Rees, Joan, 176n18
Richmond, Hugh M., 76n15
Roberts, Jeanne Addison, 171, 175n17
Rogers, Daniel, 420
Rogers, Richard, 389
Rogers, Thomas, 239
Rose, Mary Beth, 408n18, 431n1, 431n7
Rossiter, A. P., 360n10

Saccio, Peter, 57
Sackville, Thomas, Lord Bathurst, 83
Sadler, Hamnet and Judith, 231

Sagar, Keith, 174n7

St. Bartholomew Day's Massacre, 150, 372

Sams, Eric, 225–27, 246

Sander, Nicholas, 81

Sandys, Edwin, 396

Santayana, George, 180

Saxl, Fritz, 34, 35

Schmitt, Charles B., 312

Schoenbaum, Samuel, 117n12, 224, 226–27

Scot, Reginald, 160

Scott, Walter, 160–61

Scragg, Leah, 406n6

Seaford, Richard, 59

Sehrt, Ernst Theodor, 216n50

Seneca, 69

Servetus, Michael, 94

Sexton, Joyce H., 350, 375–76, 380

Shaheen, Naseeb, 181, 385

Shakeshafte, William, 12–13, 232, 245

Shakespeare, Hamnet, 244

Shakespeare, John, 8, 12–13, 24, 162, 223–32, 234, 238, 243–44

Shakespeare, Susanna, 231

Shakespeare, William; *All's Well That Ends Well**, 16, 17–21, 22, 336–64, 369–80; *The Comedy of Errors**, 1, 4, 6, 16, 20–21, 22, 26–41; *Cymbeline,* 163–65; *Hamlet**, 3, 10, 12–16, 21, 222–55, 260–84, 287–308, 370; *Henry IV,* Part 1, 8, 129–30, 132–33, 142–56, 162, 359n6; *Henry IV,* Part 2, 131–32; *Henry V**, 5, 124, 127, 130–37, 143–44; *Henry VI,* Part 1, 56, 58; *King Lear,* 83; *Julius Caesar,* 182; *Love's Labor's Lost**, 4–5, 16, 18–19, 20, 80–101; *Macbeth,* 23, 432n9; *Measure for Measure**, 8, 16, 16–17, 311–33; *The Merchant of Venice**, 9, 10–12, 180–217, 360n7; *The Merry Wives of Windsor**, 9, 20, 159–76; *A Midsummer Night's Dream,* 17, 163–64, 167, 172; *Much Ado About Nothing,* 363n22; *Othello**, 9, 16, 21–24, 31, 37–38, 359n7, 382–409, 415–35; *Richard II**, 5, 6, 44–76, 103–18, 124, 126–30, 132–33; *Richard III** 3–4, 16, 20; *Romeo and Juliet,* 162; Sonnets, 19; *The Tempest,* 22, 162–63; *Troilus and Cressida,* 369; *Twelfth Night**, 8; *The Winter's Tale,* 17

Shapiro, James, 185–86

Shell, Alison, 245, 323

Shuger, Debora, 308n43

Sidney, Philip, 27–28, 30, 54, 136–37, 294, 306n25

Sidney, Robert, 109–10

Siegel, Paul N., 215n42, 305n14

Silver, Carole G., 174n2

Simonds, Peggy, 353–54, 363n25

Simpson, Lynne, 370

Sinfield, Alan, 284n14

Smith, Henry, 382, 385

Snow, Edward W., 409n28

Snyder, Susan, 342

Sohmer, Steve, 101n16

Southampton, Henry Wriothesley, Earl of, 5, 94, 115, 205, 210, 216n53

Southwell, Robert, 3, 11–12, 24, 97–99, 186–217, 230, 241, 247, 250–52, 254

Speed, John, 143

Spenser, Edmund, 9, 172

Spivack, Bernard, 406n6

Stachniewski, John, 408n24
Stallybrass, Peter, 406n5, 428
Stapleton, Thomas, 141–43, 152, 154
Stetner, Clifford, 360n7
Stevenson, Robert, 331
Stoppard, Tom, 253
Strachey, Lytton, 16
Strange, Ferdinand, Earl of Derby, 99
Strickland, Ronald, 54, 56
Stringer, Philip, 101n8
Stuart, Arabella, 151
Stubbes, Philip, 246, 290, 306n25
Sullivan, Ceri, 241, 252–54
Swann, Marjorie, 174n2
Swift, Jonathan, 209

Targoff, Ramie, 284n13
Taylor, Charles, 419–20
Taylor, Gary, 24, 104–5, 117n8, 143, 331
Taylor, Jeremy, 419–20, 432n9, 434n21
Taylor, Thomas, 339
Thomas, Keith, 10, 47
Thomson, Peter, 118n16
Throckmorton, Job, 168
Tillyard, E. M. W., 343
Tilney, Edmund, 419, 429, 433n17
Todd, Margo, 288, 304nn4, 5, 7, 306n28
Tofte, Robert, 99
Torok, Maria, 13, 250
Tresham, Thomas, 109
Tricomi, Albert, 339
Truax, Elizabeth, 40n7
Tyndale, William, 122, 253, 261–62

Updike, John, 234

Van Beek, Martin, 287, 289, 302, 304n2, 305nn12, 17, 306n27, 307n40
Velie, Alan, 332n4
Verstegan, Richard, 149–50, 152–54, 215n44
Vickers, Brian, 408n22
Vitkus, Daniel, 404
Voss, Paul, 312, 314

Waddington, Raymond, 265, 283nn2, 3
Waith, Eugene, 289–91, 293, 306n26
Wall, John N., 385
Wallace, Dewey, 339
Walsham, Alexandra, 223, 227–29, 240, 247, 250, 254
Walsingham, Francis, 149, 246, 306n25
Walton, Isaac, 89
Warner, Marine, 36–37
Warrin, Jean de, 372
Watson, Robert N., 340, 385, 402, 406n7
Webster, John, 161
Weimann, Robert, 125, 138n8
Wheeler, Richard P., 244
Whetstone, George, 324, 329–30
White, Paul Whitifield, 314
Whyte, Roland, 109–10
Wickham, Glynne, 69
Wilcox, Thomas, 407n13
Willett, Andrew, 339
Williams, Gordon, 305n19
Williams, Raymond, 434n26
Wills, David, 262–63
Wilson, Richard, 223, 232
Wilson, Thomas, 263